1996 BUYING GUIDE

The December 15, 1995, issue
of CONSUMER REPORTS
Volume 60, No. 13

 *This book is made with recycled paper.*

CONSUMER REPORTS (ISSN 0010-7174) is published 13 times a year by Consumers Union of U.S., Inc., 101 Truman Avenue, Yonkers, N.Y. 10703-1057. Second-class postage paid at Yonkers, N.Y., and at additional mailing offices. Canadian postage paid at Mississauga, Ontario, Canada. Canadian publications registration no. 2665247-98. Title CONSUMER REPORTS registered in U.S. Patent Office. CU is a member of the Consumers International. Mailing lists: CU occasionally exchanges its subscriber lists with those of selected publications and nonprofit organizations. If you wish your name deleted from such exchanges, send your address label with a request for deletion to CONSUMER REPORTS, P.O. Box 53029, Boulder, Colo. 80322-3029. Postmaster: Send address changes to the same address.

A note to readers

Since the first Buying Guide appeared in 1937, we've gathered each year, in one place, the best advice we can provide consumers.

This year, the pages of the Buying Guide are packed with information presented concisely and, we hope, in a way that's easy to use. Since we're in a race with an ever-changing marketplace, the Buying Guide issue can only be a year-end "final." We try to do that better and better each year. In this issue you'll find:

- Our latest buying advice on the major products.
- Our latest brand-name Ratings, as published in recent issues of CONSUMER REPORTS, with special updates on which models are availabile.
- Repair Histories to help you gauge a product's reliability.
- Product recalls to help you avoid unsafe products.
- An alphabetical listing of manufacturers' telephone numbers, most of them toll-free.
- A directory of the last time CONSUMER REPORTS published articles on var ious subjects and products, going back as far as eight years.

For many of our subscribers, this small book serves as a kind of big stick. Subscribers have told me that when they walk into a store with this book, they create a better balance between buyer and seller. They've got facts and down-to-earth advice to penetrate any blather and hype, and they have comparative data to help make the selection process less mysterious and more sensible.

And, equally important, the information in this volume comes from an organization that is beholden to no one but consumers, takes no outside advertising in its publications, and refuses all free samples and contributions from commercial interests. We buy our products in the marketplace, just as you do, test them impartially, and tell you plainly what we found.

With these thoughts, I wish you another year of sensible and satisfying shopping.

Rhoda H. Karpatkin
President

Contents

Illustrations by Beth McCash

About the Buying Guide

Each year, the Consumer Reports Buying Guide collects and updates buying advice on major consumer products. It combines in one handy volume the product-buying wisdom distilled from years of product testing with the latest brand-name Ratings. The Buying Guide is available on newsstands and in bookstores or by subscription as the 13th issue of CONSUMER REPORTS magazine.

The reports in the Buying Guide provide the basic buying information you need—the pros and cons of the choices, what you can expect to pay, and an explanation of features available.

The thumb index gives you fast access to types of products: autos, audio and video, appliances, health and recreation, yard, home office, and home care.

For easy reference to past issues of CONSUMER REPORTS, you'll find an eight-year index of the last full report at the back of this book. The original CONSUMER REPORTS publication date is also given at the top of each Ratings table. Back issues of CONSUMER REPORTS are available in most libraries. Some reports are also available by fax; see page 356.

The Buying Guide alerts you to brands that have shown themselves to be reliable—information available only from CONSUMER REPORTS. For the brand Repair Histories of products such as refrigerators, washing machines, CD players, dishwashers, microwave ovens, lawn mowers, and TV sets, see page 15. For model-by-model reliability information on cars, see the Frequency-of-Repair charts that start on page 284.

The Buying Guide also collects a years' worth of product recalls, based on notices issued by governmental agencies, as published in the monthly issues of CONSUMER REPORTS from November 1994 through October 1995. See page 320.

Using the Ratings

Once you've narrowed your choices, the Ratings in the Buying Guide can help point you to specific brands and models. If you have trouble finding a tested model, you can call the manufacturer. Phone numbers are listed by brand, starting on page 342.

When we rate a product, we include, as often as possible, models that we judge to be similar to the tested model in the Ratings Comments or Details. Just before the Buying Guide goes to press, we verify model availability for most products with manufacturers. Some tested models listed in the Ratings may no longer be available. Models that have been discontinued are marked [D] in the Ratings; some may actually still be available in some stores for part of 1996. In some cases, we've identified a "successor model" to the model tested. The successor, according to the manufacturer, should perform similarly to the model tested, but it may have different features. Such models are marked [S] in the Ratings. Keep in mind, however, that successor models have not been tested.

The general price ranges we give in the reports are based on real prices you'd pay in the stores. The prices in the Ratings are estimated average prices, based on national surveys done for the original report.

Our Ratings are based on laboratory tests, panel tests, reader surveys, and expert judgments of products bought at retail, usually without regard to price. If a product offers both high quality and relatively low price, we deem it **A Best Buy**. A product's Rating applies only to the model listed, not to other models sold under the same brand name, unless so noted.

About Consumer Reports & Consumers Union

CONSUMER REPORTS magazine is published monthly by Consumers Union, a nonprofit independent testing organization serving consumers. We are a comprehensive source for unbiased advice about products and services. Since 1936, our mission has been to test products, inform the public, and protect consumers.

We buy all the products we test.

We test products under controlled laboratory conditions. Most of our testing is done in 44 state-of-the-art labs at our National Testing and Research Center in Yonkers, N.Y., and at our test track in Connecticut.

We survey our millions of readers to bring you information on services and on the reliability of autos and major products.

We report on issues of consumer concern, bringing you information on matters that affect your health, money, and well-being.

We accept no ads from companies. Our income is derived from the sale of CONSUMER REPORTS and other services and from nonrestrictive, noncommercial contributions, grants, and fees. The ads in CONSUMER REPORTS and the Buying Guide are for our other services, which share the same aims. We don't permit use of reports or Ratings for any commercial purpose. If that happens, we take whatever steps are open to us. Reproduction of CONSUMER REPORTS is forbidden without prior written permission (and never for commercial purposes).

Subscriptions. CONSUMER REPORTS: U.S. rates: $24 for 1 year, $39 for 2 years, $54 for 3 years, $69 for 4 years, $84 for 5 years. Other countries: add $6 per year. (The Canadian rate is $35 if paying in Canadian dollars; Goods & Services Tax included GST #127047702.) For subscription service or to change an address, write to Subscription Director, CONSUMER REPORTS, P.O. Box 53029, Boulder, Colo. 80322-3029. Please attach or copy your address from the back cover of a monthly issue.

Contributions. Contributions to Consumers Union are tax-deductible. Contributors of $1000 or more (limit: $5000) can become Lifetime Members, receiving a lifetime subscription. Write to CU, Dept. MEM, 101 Truman Ave., Yonkers, N.Y. 10703-1057.

Readers' letters. We welcome reader comment. Write: CONSUMER REPORTS, P. O. Box 2015, Yonkers, N.Y. 10703-9015. We regret we are unable to respond to individual letters.

Back issues. Back issues of CONSUMER REPORTS up to 12 months old are available from Back Issue Dept., CONSUMER REPORTS, P.O. Box 53016, Boulder, Colo. 80322-3016: Single copies: $4; the Buying Guide: $10.

Bulk reprints. Selected reports are available. Write to CU, Reprints Dept., 101 Truman Ave., Yonkers, N. Y. 10703-1057.

Other Consumer Reports services

New Car Price Service. To help you negotiate a deal on a new car. See page 358. **Used Car Price Service.** Before you buy, sell, or trade in a used car, find out the current market value in your area. See page 357. **Consumer Reports Books.** More than 100 helpful books in print; see the back cover. **Facts By Fax.** Specially edited reports from CONSUMER REPORTS are available by fax or mail. See page 356. **Consumer Reports Travel Letter.** Monthly newsletter. $39/yr. Write Subscriptions, Box 51366, Boulder, Colo. 80321-1366. **Consumer Reports on Health.** Monthly newsletter. $24/yr. Write Subscriptions, Box 52148, Boulder, Colo. 80321-2148. **Zillions.** Bimonthly magazine for kids 8 years and up. $16/yr. (6 issues), $26/2 yrs. Write Subscriptions, Box 51777, Boulder, Colo. 80321-1777. **Electronic Publishing.** CONSUMER REPORTS is on America Online, CompuServe, Knight-Ridder, Nexis, Prodigy, and CD-ROM. Write CU Electronic Publishing, 101 Truman Ave., Yonkers, N.Y. 10703-1057. **Consumer Reports TV.** Informational videos. Write CRTV, 101 Truman Ave., Yonkers, N.Y. 10703-1057. **News Features.** Newspaper columns, TV news, and radio features. **Home Price Service.** Estimate home value for insurance, refinancing, buying, or selling. See page 360. **Consumer Reports Cars: The Essential Guide** (CD-ROM). See page 359.

RELIABILITY

Getting things fixed

Buying brands with a good track record betters your chances of trouble-free service. You'll find the latest brand Repair Histories for big-ticket items such as TV sets, washers, and lawn mowers beginning on page 15. While the data are historical and apply to brands, not specific models, they've been quite consistent over the years. You can improve your chances of getting a reliable product if you buy a brand that has been reliable in the past.

Even the best products, though, can experience problems. If a product breaks down during the warranty period the repair is usually covered. As a product nears the end of its warranty—manufacturer's warranty, service contract, or credit-card purchase protection—having even minor problems looked at can save you money in the long run. (For more information, see the report on extended-service contracts on page 14.) Once the warranty expires, you have three basic options: fix it yourself, have it fixed, or get rid of it.

With some products, the manufacturer may already have made the choice for you. The very designs and manufacturing methods that give us better, cheaper, and more durable goods may also make some goods difficult or impossible to repair.

These days, manufacturers prefer plastic for many uses because they can form it in a single molding operation, whereas metal often requires more steps on the assembly line and adds to costs. When metal is required, manufacturers may cut costs by crimping parts together instead of bolting them. The result: $9 mixers, $15 coffee makers, and other low-priced wares.

These products can be practically impossible to service. When they break, you have little choice but to get rid of them. Fortunately, many household products are still repairable—and worth repairing.

Option 1: Fix it yourself

Doing a repair yourself saves money and often leads to more satisfaction with the job, our readers told us in a survey we conducted a few years ago. People are most likely to fix products with mechanical innards: cars, clothes dryers, lawn mowers, vacuums, ranges, washing machines, and such. Many electronics manufacturers specifically advise against do-it-yourself repairs because of the product's complexity and potential shock hazard.

How-to advice. Major appliance manufacturers offer the most help to amateurs. General Electric, Whirlpool, Sears, and Frigidaire, for instance, provide technical assistance through a toll-free telephone number. GE and Whirlpool also publish manuals for amateurs. Other companies sell technical service manuals for their products, but they're not an easy read. Many books—from Time-Life, Reader's Digest, and other publishers—offer general fix-it-yourself advice.

Getting parts. Even the least handy person can fix a mixer with banged-up beaters, say—if the replacement parts are available. Here are some tips when you scout for parts:

- Make sure the model number is correct. Check the appliance itself, not just the owner's manual or the packaging.
- Contact the manufacturer directly for specialized parts. Telephoning is speedier and more effective than writing. Most companies have a toll-free telephone number or fax line. See page 342. Some companies will sell you the part directly; others will refer you to a parts distributor.
- Try local stores for common parts. Mass merchandisers like Kmart carry generic replacement parts such as carafes for coffee makers. Electronics specialty stores like Radio Shack are a good source for cordless-phone batteries. Parts stores and appliance dealers may also have parts on hand; check the Yellow Pages for names and locations.
- With some small appliances, a single part may cost almost as much as a new appliance. We paid $13 for a Black & Decker coffee carafe; the complete appliance sells for $15 at discount.

Option 2: Have it fixed

Repairs rank high on the list of transactions that make people anxious—and with good reason: Nearly one-quarter of the readers in our survey were dissatisfied to some degree with work done for them on major appliances and other big items. Problems cropped up 42 percent of the time on average. Repairs on small appliances were even less satisfactory. Readers complained most about repairs on expensive electronic products—computers, camcorders, VCRs, TV sets—complex products likely to be repaired in the shop. Mechanical goods such as major appliances, lawn mowers, and vacuum cleaners, had fewer problems.

The situation may be even worse than those statistics indicate. Some customers may have been "satisfied" with repairs that were unnecessary or overpriced. When our engineers "broke" vacuum cleaners, VCRs, and washing machines and sought repairs in three major cities, the charges for the same simple repair varied by as much as 350 percent. Fortunately, there are ways to minimize the risk.

Types of service. The three basic types include: factory service, in which the company has its own service center or service fleet; authorized service, privately run businesses accredited by companies to fix their brands (the store that sells the product sometimes acts as an authorized repairer); and independents, who set their own policy.

Manufacturers typically require factory or authorized service for warranty work. The owner's manual usually provides a toll-free number to call for the nearest factory-authorized service center or you can check our listing of phone numbers by brand on page 342.

Presumably manufacturers train factory and authorized technicians on the latest equipment to ensure a certain level of service quality. They can also hold authorized repairers to standards of performance by threatening to revoke their contractual agreement. Compared with factory service, which is available primarily for large appliances, authorized service has one disadvantage: Authorized repairers sometimes earn a commission for parts, an arrangement that can lead to unnecessary replacement. But shipping time and cost may make a factory center less appealing than a local authorized shop.

Independents can be a good choice for products whose warranty has expired. Check their reputation with friends, neighbors, and the Better Business Bureau.

Repairs at home. For emergency repairs such as loss of refrigeration, companies try to respond within 24 hours. The response time for other repairs may be one to three days. Companies may charge extra for weekend or evening service.

Before scheduling an appointment, ask whether there's a "trip" charge. The fee, typically $30 to $45, applies to work done out of warranty. It includes travel to and from your home and a minimum labor charge. Expect to pay it even if you don't go ahead with the work.

Find out whether you'll pay flat or hourly rates. If the charge is by the hour, how is it billed? Billing by the quarter hour is common. If you're having a large TV set fixed, ask if you have to pay a separate fee if the set must be hauled to the shop.

Arrange to be home during the service call. That way, a repairer may be less tempted to fix what doesn't need fixing. Try to get the repairer to commit to a time; the earlier in the day, the less likely that some other emergency will cause a delay.

Ask whether the repair carries a warranty. And ask to keep any replaced parts. That way, you'll know that a part you are billed for was actually replaced.

Repairs in the shop. If repairs are going to be made in-store, first get an estimate. A charge for the estimate may apply for work done out of warranty. Ask whether the service includes a standard cleaning or whether that costs extra. Ask how long the repair should take. One of our readers' biggest complaints about in-shop repairs was that they took more than two weeks. Also, find out the typical waiting time for parts. If the parts are on back order from the factory, be prepared to wait several weeks or more.

Be sure to get a claim check that shows the date your product went to the shop. It should describe the item by brand, model, and serial number and, if possible, have an authorized signature. Use a credit card to pay for repairs, so you can dispute, if needed.

If there's a problem. If you can't resolve a problem with an authorized repairer, write or call the manufacturer's main customer-relations office, usually in the owner's manual or see page 342. Keep notes of all phone calls and copies of all correspondence. With correspondence, include the model and serial number, a copy of the proof of purchase, and a copy of the written diagnosis. If you are still unhappy, complain to the Better Business Bureau in your area and notify local or state consumer agencies and the local newspaper.

If you can't resolve a problem with a major-appliance repair, you can contact the Major Appliance Consumer Action Panel, an independent complaint-mediation group, at 20 N. Wacker Dr., Chicago, Ill. 60606 (312 984-5858).

Option 3: Get rid of it

Sometimes the cost of repairs can be so high that fixing the product may not make sense. Repairers charge about $35 an hour on average, according to our information, and that figure is likely to have gone up. Replacement parts can be quite expensive, particularly if the product has been designed in preassembled units or modules. When you replace a module, you're buying parts you may not need along with those you do.

Other reasons a repair may not be a good investment: Replacement models have become a lot cheaper or are greatly improved; the product is near the end of its useful life (see table at right); the brand's reliability record is worse than that of most others so other repairs may be imminent.

Nowhere do products become obsolescent as quickly as in the electronics industry. Solid-state components have revolutionized just about every device we plug in or pop batteries into. They've led to products that are smaller, lighter, smarter, and—because they run cooler—more reliable. But such products are harder to service than old tube-based products. Diagnosing problems requires more expertise, because obvious signs of failure are rare.

Servicers are reluctant to repair parts individually. When an integrated circuit is faulty, they replace the entire circuit board. As a result, electronic failures are often costlier to fix than mechanical ones.

Readers in our survey said they didn't fix three-quarters of inexpensive products such as blenders, blow dryers, boom boxes, and telephones. Nor did they fix one in three larger, more expensive items—washing machines, TV sets, and vacuums.

Environmental issues. Safe disposal is complicated if a product contains substances harmful to the environment: chlorofluorocarbons from refrigerators; heavy metals like lead in circuit boards and cathode-ray tubes; cadmium in rechargeable batteries; mercury in old fluorescent lights, thermostats, and silent wall switches. If a landfill isn't properly maintained, those chemicals can leach and contaminate ground water supplies. And if trash is incinerated, mercury can escape into the air, and heavy metals can contaminate the ash.

Clearly, it's time for manufacturers to cut back on the harmful ingredients that go into durable goods. It's also time for government and industry to increase recycling of the useful ingredients. Eventually, the U.S. may need to address the disposal of durable goods on a national level, as Germany has. There, regulations require manufacturers to take back used refrigerators, television sets, computers, and other appliances to reclaim useful material. In

HOW LONG THINGS LAST

A product's useful life depends not only on its actual durability but also on such intangibles as your own desire for some attribute or convenience available only on a new model. These estimates are from manufacturers and trade associations.

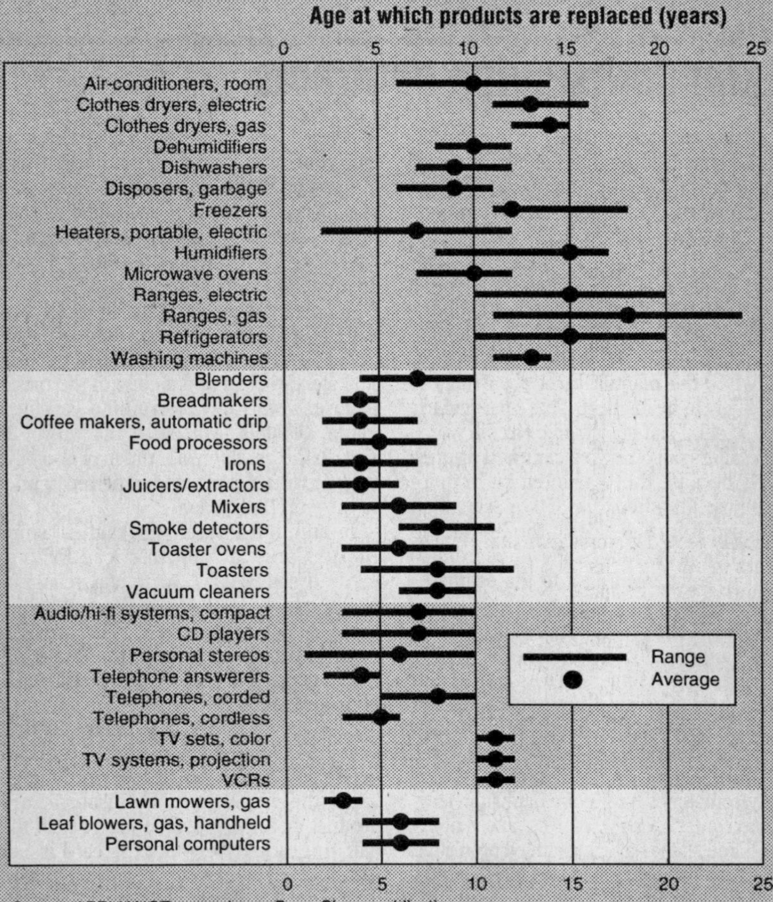

0 5 10 15 20 25

Air-conditioners, room
Clothes dryers, electric
Clothes dryers, gas
Dehumidifiers
Dishwashers
Disposers, garbage
Freezers
Heaters, portable, electric
Humidifiers
Microwave ovens
Ranges, electric
Ranges, gas
Refrigerators
Washing machines
Blenders
Breadmakers
Coffee makers, automatic drip
Food processors
Irons
Juicers/extractors
Mixers
Smoke detectors
Toaster ovens
Toasters
Vacuum cleaners
Audio/hi-fi systems, compact
CD players
Personal stereos
Telephone answerers
Telephones, corded
Telephones, cordless
TV sets, color
TV systems, projection
VCRs
Lawn mowers, gas
Leaf blowers, gas, handheld
Personal computers

Range
Average

0 5 10 15 20 25

Source: APPLIANCE magazine, a Dana Chase publication.

the meantime, America's consumers have few good choices for disposing of durable goods. One option is to extend the life of an old but functioning appliance by selling it or giving it away. Sometimes a shelter, school, or other nonprofit group can use the item. Or a repair shop may take it for parts.

Some utility companies take old refrigerators at no charge. Even if that's not the case where you live, it may be better for the environment to send an old, energy-guzzling refrigerator to the scrap heap than to keep using it. You may find groups that accept used goods through your town or state environmental agency or under "Recycling" in the Yellow Pages.

Extended-service contracts

With an extended warranty or service contract, you're betting that the appliance will break down after the manufacturer's warranty expires, but before the service contract does, and that the cost of repairs will exceed the cost of the contract. That's possible, but it's a long shot. Not only are products more reliable today, but they are often made in such a way that any defects tend to appear early on—within the first 90 days or so, when the manufacturer's warranty is still likely to be in effect. That's particularly true of solid-state electronic circuitry.

Retailers push service contracts aggressively because they can often make more money selling them, for $50 to $500, than they can from the sale of the product itself. Their profit ranges anywhere from 40 to 77 percent, according to the estimates we've seen.

Service contracts are a good deal for retailers specifically because they're such a bad deal for consumers. It's estimated that fewer than 20 percent of products covered by such contracts ever come in for repair.

Service contracts pose another risk: Over the past several years, a number of warranty companies have gone bankrupt, leaving customers with worthless pieces of paper. Some states have introduced protective legislation requiring that a service contract be backed by an insurance company.

If the idea of extra protection is appealing but you'd rather not pay for it, consider using your credit card. Items bought with American Express cards and some standard Visa and MasterCards (and all their "gold" cards) automatically double the manufacturer's warranty, increasing it a maximum of up to one year.

When a covered product breaks down, call the credit-card company for information about how to proceed. You'll need the original store receipt and a copy of the manufacturer's warranty at the time you file a claim. (Usually, you must file within 30 days of the breakdown.) You may also have to get a written estimate for the repair prior to the work being done.

In addition to their warranties, some MasterCards and all American Express cards toss in 90 days' worth of purchase insurance to replace or repair merchandise that is stolen or damaged. (Visa provides extra purchase insurance, too, but it excludes goods that are lost, and certain types of damage.)

Credit-card purchases receive further protection under the terms of the Fair Credit and Billing Act. It lets you "charge back" the purchase of an unsatisfactory product or service before you've paid the bill. You can request that the card issuer withhold payment to the retailer. The protection applies only to items priced at more than $50 and bought in your home state or within 100 miles of your mailing address. You must show a good-faith attempt to settle the problem with the store before asking to halt payment.

Our advice—as it has been for years—is to avoid extended-service contracts. You're better off taking the money a service contract would cost and setting it aside as a repair fund. If you feel you need some protection, buy with an appropriate credit card.

Repair Histories

Every year, CONSUMER REPORTS asks its subscribers to share their experiences with various products by answering questions on the Annual Questionnaire. One benefit is the automobile Frequency-of-Repair charts, beginning on page 284. Another result is what you'll find in this chapter—repair histories for various brands of major appliances, electronic items, and other products.

The graphs that follow represent the percentage of products in each brand that have ever been repaired, as reported to us by subscribers in the survey. It's important to keep two things in mind: Repair Histories apply only to brands, not to specific models of these products. And the Histories, being histories, can only suggest future trends—not predict them exactly. A company can at any time change its products' design or quality control so substantially as to affect their reliability. But our findings over the years have been consistent enough for us to be confident that these Repair Histories can improve your chances of getting a more trouble-free product.

Note, too, that the Repair Histories of different products are not directly comparable. Data for each graph have been adjusted differently—to compensate for differing age distributions, for instance—and the experiences summed up by different graphs may cover different years of purchase. The text associated with each graph explains exactly what type of product is covered and whether any special assumptions were made in the graph's preparation.

Use the following graphs in conjunction with the product reports elsewhere in the Buying Guide. Some of these brand Repair Histories have already appeared in the 1995 monthly issues of CONSUMER REPORTS; some are appearing here for the first time; others will be updated in the future issues of CONSUMER REPORTS.

VCRs

Based on more than 188,000 responses to our 1994 Annual Questionnaire. Readers were asked about any repairs to VCRs bought between 1989 and 1994. Data have been standardized to eliminate differences among brands due solely to age and usage. Differences of less than 3 points aren't meaningful.

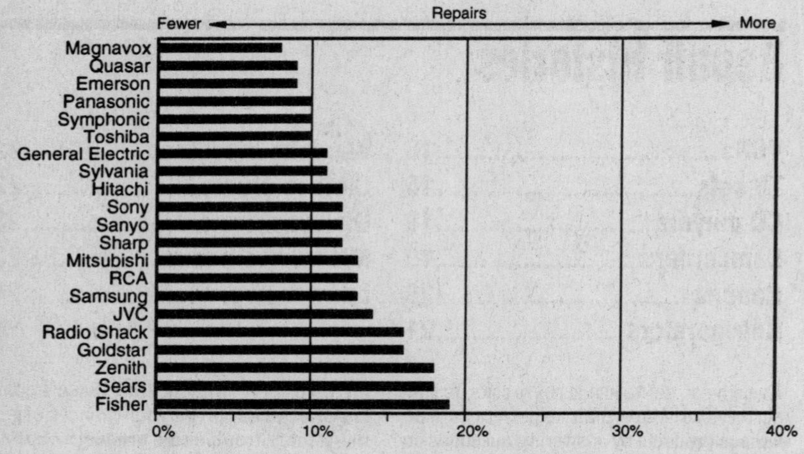

Television sets: 13-inch and 14-inch

Based on more than 30,000 responses to our 1994 Annual Questionnaire. Readers were asked about any repairs to a 13-inch or 14-inch color TV set with remote control bought new between 1989 and 1994. Data have been standardized to eliminate differences among brands due to age and usage. Differences of less than 3 points aren't meaningful.

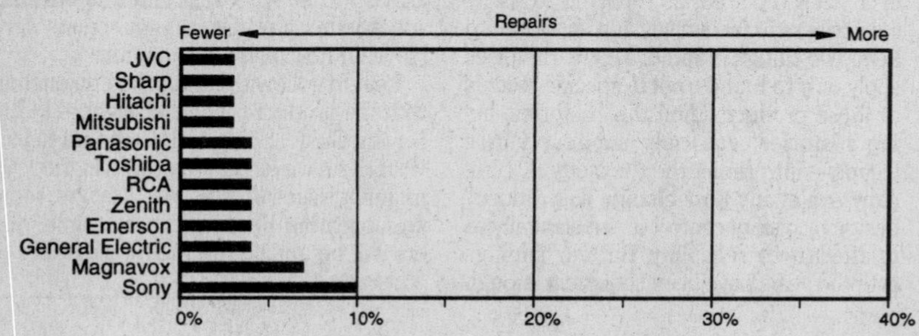

Television sets: 19-inch and 20-inch

Based on more than 75,000 responses to our 1994 Annual Questionnaire. Readers were asked about any repairs to a 19-inch or 20-inch color TV set with remote control bought new between 1989 and 1994. Data have been standardized to eliminate differences among brands due to age and usage. Differences of less than 3 points aren't meaningful.

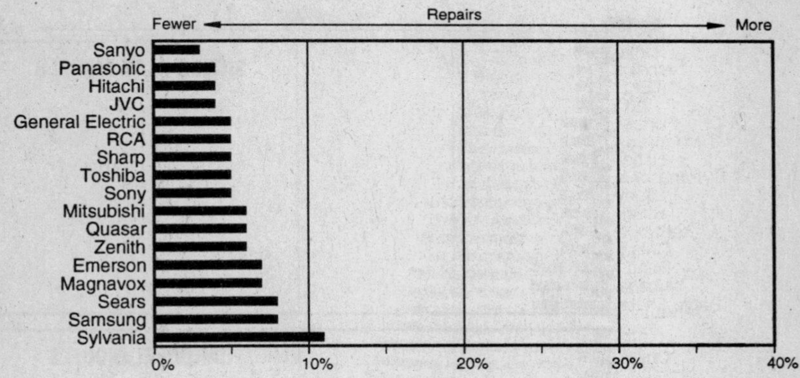

Television sets: 25-inch to 27-inch

Based on more than 82,000 responses to our 1994 Annual Questionnaire. Readers were asked about any repairs to a 25-inch to 27-inch stereo, color TV set with remote control bought new between 1989 and 1994. Data have been standardized to eliminate differences among brands due to age and usage. Differences of less than 3 points aren't meaningful.

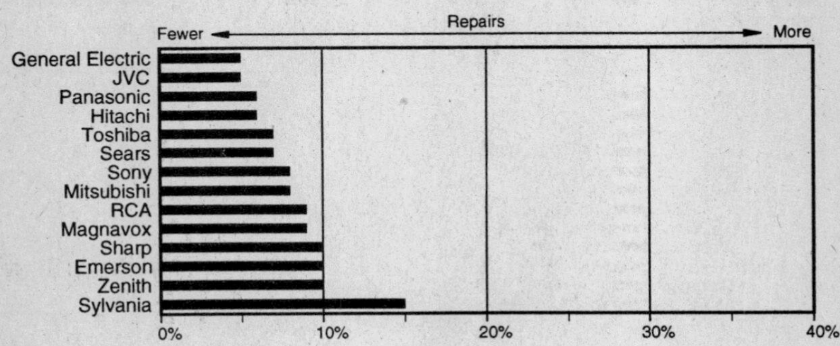

Compact-disc players

Based on nearly 89,000 responses to our 1994 Annual Questionnaire. Readers were asked about any repairs to a single-play or changer tabletop model bought new between 1991 and 1994. Data have been standardized to eliminate differences among brands due to age and usage. Differences of less than 3 points aren't meaningful.

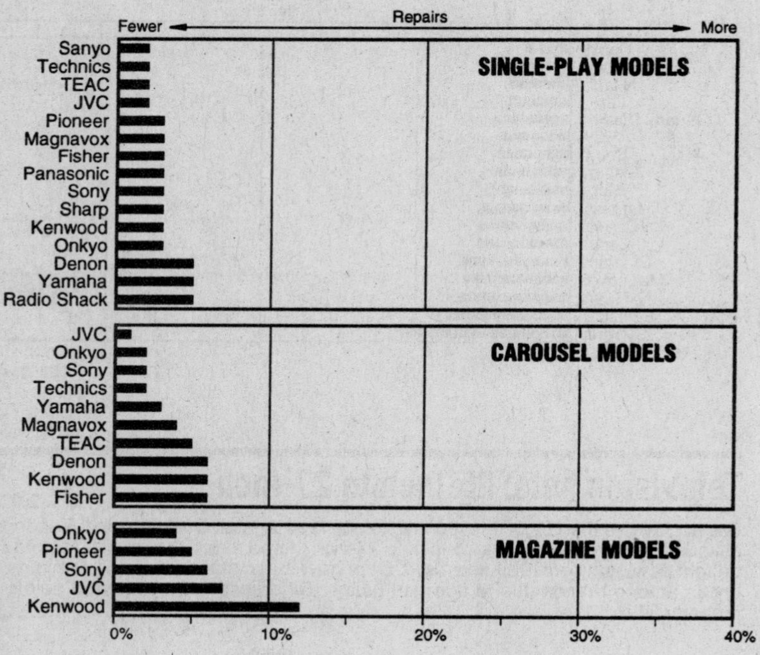

Full-sized VHS camcorders

Based on more than 18,000 responses to our 1994 Annual Questionnaire. Readers were asked about any repairs to a VHS camcorder bought new between 1989 and 1994. Data have been standardized to eliminate differences among brands due to age and usage. Differences of less then 3 points aren't meaningful. VHS repair rates cannot be compared directly with those of compact camcorders because the VHS models tended to be older and used less than the compacts.

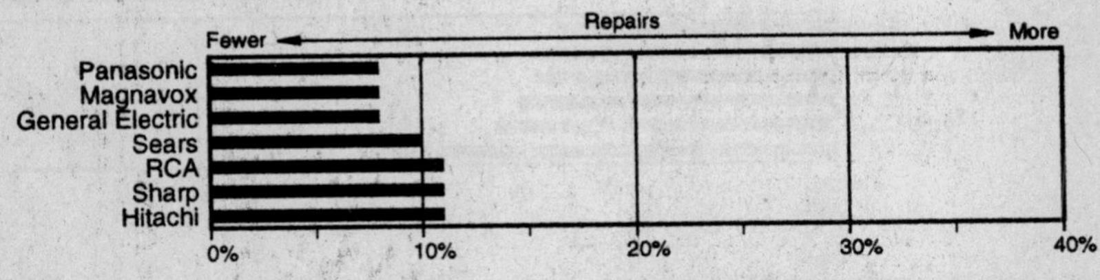

Compact camcorders

Based on almost 38,000 responses to our 1994 Annual Questionnaire. Readers were asked about any repairs to a compact (8mm, Hi8, or VHS-C) camcorder bought new between 1989 and 1994. Data have been standardized to eliminate differences among brands due to age and usage. Differences of less than 3 points aren't meaningful. Repair rates of compacts cannot be compared directly with those of full-sized VHS models.

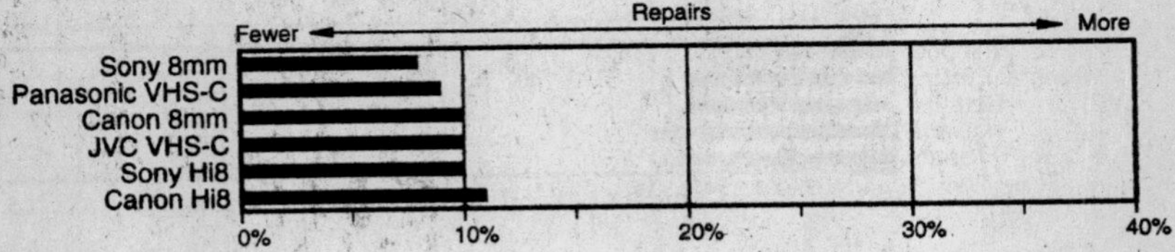

Gas ranges

Based on nearly 20,000 responses to our 1994 Annual Questionnaire. Readers were asked about any repairs to a freestanding, single-oven, self-cleaning gas range bought new between 1987 and 1994. Data have been standardized to eliminate differences among brands due to age. Differences of less than 3 points aren't meaningful.

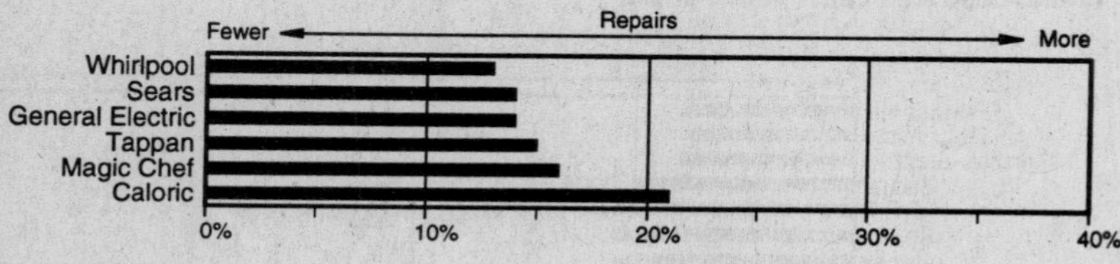

Electric ranges

Based on more than 37,000 responses to our 1994 Annual Questionnaire. Readers were asked about any repairs to a freestanding, single-oven, self-cleaning electric range with conventional heating coils bought new between 1986 and 1994. Data have been standardized to eliminate differences among brands due to age. Differences of less than 4 points aren't meaningful.

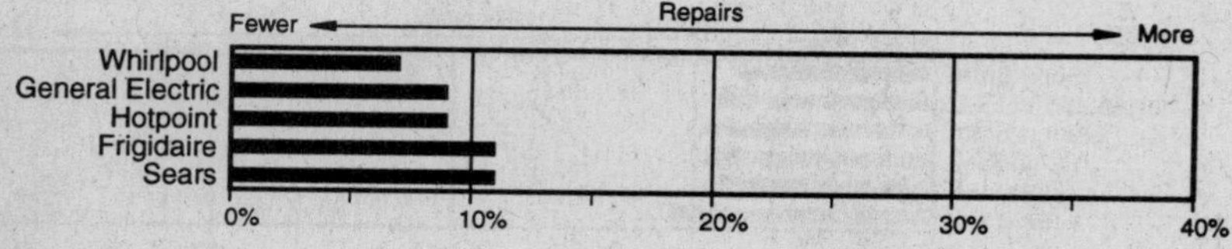

Side-by-side refrigerators

Based on almost 32,000 responses to our 1994 Annual Questionnaire. Readers were asked about any repairs to side-by-side, two-door, no-frost refrigerators bought new between 1988 and 1994. Data have been standardized to eliminate differences among brands due solely to age. Differences of less than 4 points aren't meaningful.

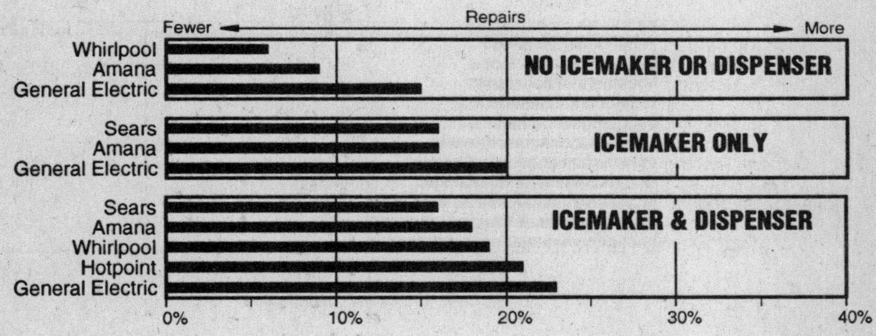

Top-freezer refrigerators

Based on almost 63,000 responses to our 1994 Annual Questionnaire. Readers were asked about any repairs to top-freezer, two-door, no-frost refrigerators bought new between 1988 and 1994. Data have been standardized to eliminate differences among brands due solely to age. Differences of less than 4 points aren't meaningful.

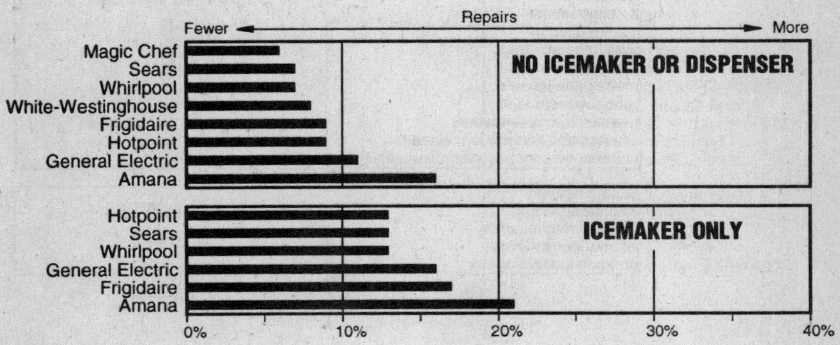

Washing machines

Based on more than 128,000 responses to our 1994 Annual Questionnaire. Readers were asked about any repairs to a full-sized washer bought new between 1988 and 1994. Data have been standardized to eliminate differences among brands due to age and usage. Differences of less than 3 points aren't meaningful.

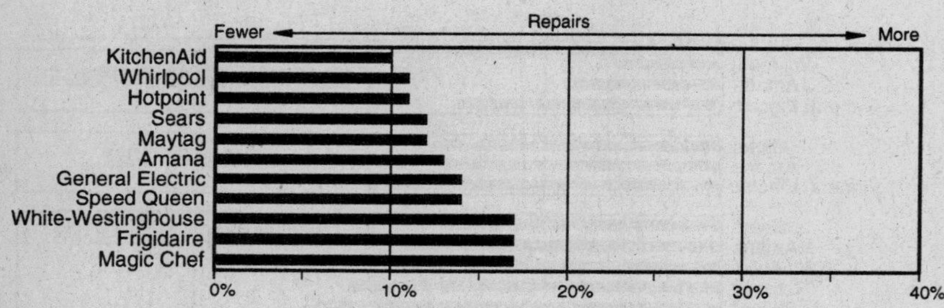

Clothes dryers

Based on more than 120,000 responses to our 1994 Annual Questionnaire. Readers were asked about any repairs to a full-sized electric or gas clothes dryer bought new between 1988 and 1994. Data have been standardized to eliminate differences among brands due to age and usage. Differences of less than 4 points aren't meaningful.

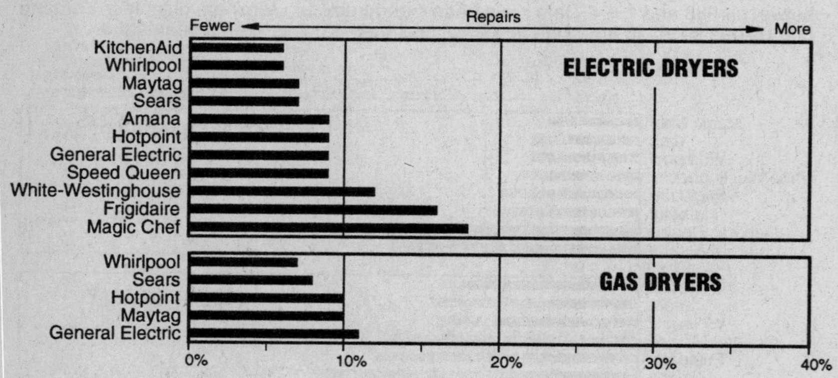

Dishwashers

Based on nearly 130,000 responses to our 1994 Annual Questionnaire. Readers were asked about any repairs to installed dishwashers bought new between 1988 and 1994. Data have been standardized to eliminate differences among brands due to age and usage. Differences of less than 4 points aren't meaningful.

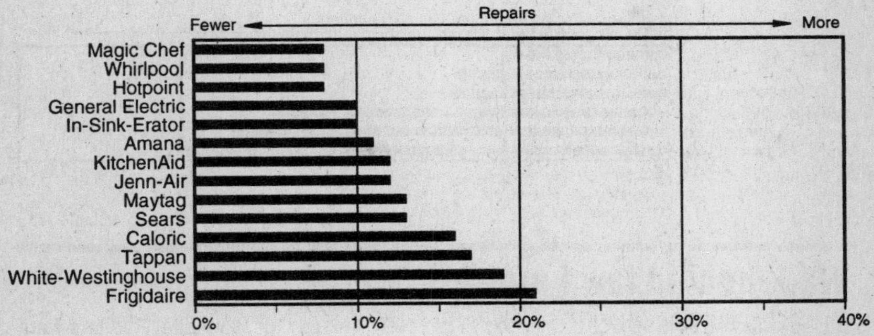

Microwave ovens

Based on more than 109,000 responses to our 1994 Annual Questionnaire. Readers were asked about any repairs to medium and large-sized microwave ovens bought new between 1988 and 1994. Data have been standardized to eliminate differences among brands due to age. Differences of less than 3 points aren't meaningful.

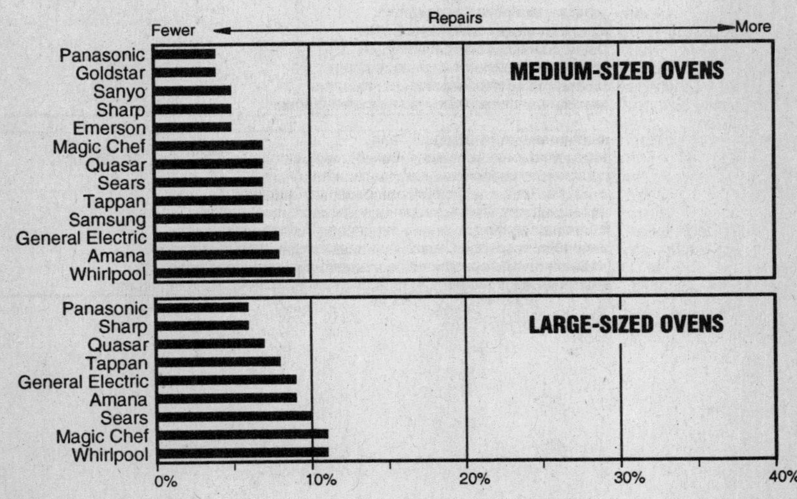

Lawn mowers and lawn tractors

Based on over 140,000 responses to our 1994 Annual Questionnaire. Readers were asked about any repairs to a manual, electric or gasoline walk-behind mower, a riding mower, or a lawn tractor bought new between 1988 and 1994. Data have been standardized to eliminate differences among brands due to age and usage. Differences of less than 4 points aren't meaningful.

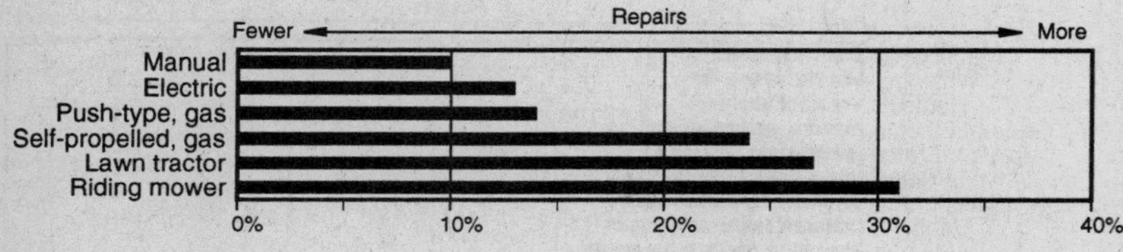

Walk-behind lawn mowers

Based on more than 71,000 responses to our 1994 Annual Questionnaire. Readers were asked about any repairs to any push or self-propelled gasoline mower with a cutting swath less than 25 inches that was bought new between 1988 and 1994. Data have been standardized to eliminate differences among brands due to age and usage. Differences of less than 4 points aren't meaningful.

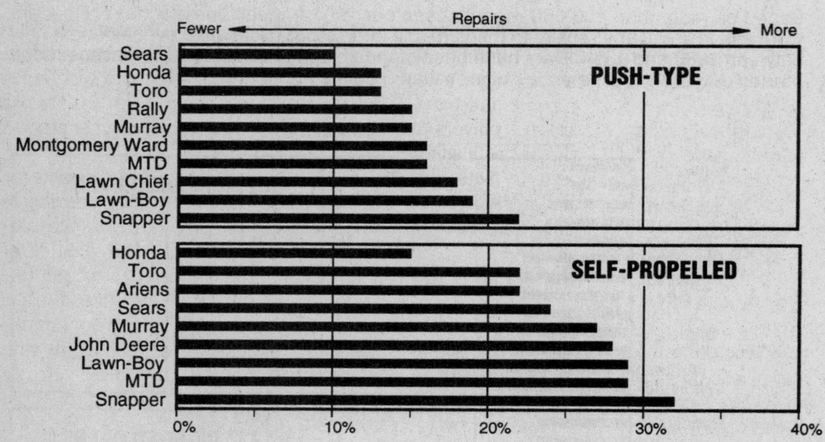

AUDIO & VIDEO GEAR

Two trends continue to drive home-entertainment products: digital technology and home theater. Digital technology is showing up on more and more components, from compact-disc players to digital tape decks to signal-processing circuitry in some receivers, TV sets, and personal stereos. Two new satellite systems rely on digital technology to produce high-quality sound and pictures.

Home theater is also having far-reaching effects, among them:

■ Most big-screen TV sets are stereo and can be connected to an external sound system. More and more sets come with an amplifier capable of driving external loudspeakers. Many big-screen sets can switch among several video sources. Sets with a 27-inch screen are among the big sellers, and large-screen sets are the fastest-growing part of the market.

True high-definition television (HDTV) is still some years away. Electronics companies and the Government have finally agreed on a format for HDTV, but no one expects it to be a popular consumer product anytime soon.

■ Most stereo receivers these days are audio/video receivers, capable of serving as the switching center for a home-theater system. Many mid-priced models come with special sound-effects features like Dolby Pro Logic. Pro Logic decodes and plays a special sound track through multiple speakers to add sounds such as ricochets or the swoosh of airplanes.

■ Speakers, once sold only in pairs, are available singly and in threes, the better to simulate a theater sound system.

■ Hi-fi sound has become a common feature in VCRs, the machines that started home theater.

■ Laser-disc players, once considered something of a technological dodo, have taken on new life, primarily because they deliver superb picture and sound quality.

■ Remote controls, formerly a mere accessory, are products in their own right.

Home-theater basics

At its fanciest, a home theater can cost more than a car. But a functional system can be inexpensive and simple: Upgrade your VCR to a hi-fi model for as little as $275, hook up the TV set to a pair of external speakers ($100 or so), or use a patch cord to connect the TV set's sound to the stereo receiver (about $5). Even if you start from scratch, you can assemble a whole system for well under $2000. Here's what you need to think about:

Decide on the heart of the system. Until recently, it had to be the stereo receiver. Now, many big-screen TV sets can drive external speakers and switch among several video sources. For a TV-based system, plan on spending at least $500 for a 27-inch set with decent speakers and switching features.

Using a receiver as the heart of the setup lets you build a more powerful and versatile system, because receivers typically have a more powerful amplifier and greater switching capabilities than even the best-equipped TV set. If you already have a TV set with an audio output, setting up a receiver-based system is less costly than a TV-based system. A receiver costs as little as $150. For an audio/video model that decodes Dolby Pro Logic sound, prices start at about $230.

Choose the sound-effects package. You typically make this choice when you buy a receiver, although some TV sets now come with sound-effects circuitry built in.

The most basic sound setup is two-channel stereo using one pair of speakers.

Dolby Pro Logic has displaced the earlier Dolby Surround. Both decipher encoded sound effects found on some movie soundtracks and a growing number of TV programs. You need an extra pair of loudspeakers—"surround" speakers—placed in the back of the room or on either side of the listeners. Pro Logic decodes more information; it enhances the separation between the front and rear channels; and it separates some sound, such as dialogue, for a fifth speaker. That center-channel speaker is positioned above or below the TV set so that the sound seems to come directly from the screen.

To drive the center channel, Pro Logic requires an additional amplifier. Most Pro Logic receivers have the amplifier built in; some low-end models come with the Pro Logic circuitry, but not the amp. Dolby 3 stereo, found on many Pro Logic receivers, lets you experience some of the surround-sound effect with only three speakers.

"Additional sound-processing" modes on many surround-sound receivers use digital signal-processing to add an echo to the sound signal on the way to the rear speakers. By selecting "stadium," "concert hall," or "night club" settings, you can simulate environments with various acoustic characteristics.

Plan on spending at least $230 for a receiver that decodes Dolby Pro Logic, plus an additional $150 or so for the center-channel and surround speaker.

Consider component compatibility. Speakers resist current in varying degrees, depending on their design—they are said to have an impedance of 8, 6, or 4 ohms. Other things being equal, a low-impedance speaker needs more electric current from the receiver than a high-impedance model does to produce a given level of sound. Multiple pairs of speakers complicate the picture. Two sets of speakers connected in parallel, as some receivers require, are a more difficult load than the same two sets of speakers connected in series, as other receivers require.

Although a speaker's impedance has nothing to do with its quality, you'll find increasing numbers of lower-impedance models as speakers go up in price. The mass-market brands such as Sony, Pioneer, and Radio Shack generally include a mix of speakers rated at 8 or 6 ohms. Many of the high-end "salon" speaker lines consist entirely of 4-ohm models.

Many leading manufacturers recommend against using their receivers with 4-ohm speakers. Since those speakers used to make up a substantial proportion of the market, it was quite easy to end up with incompatible speakers and receiver. In the last couple of years, however, more speakers are being designed at the higher impedance levels.

Set up the loudspeakers. The rule of thumb is for the main pair of speakers to form an equilateral triangle with the listener. Positioning additional speakers for home theater and surround sound is more complicated. The center channel speaker in a home-theater setup should be close to the TV set, so it can carry speech and other sounds closely associated with the picture; the rear speakers, which carry the surround effects, should be at least as far back from the television set as the viewer, and they should be mounted above or below ear level.

Some TV sets have built-in "psychoacoustic" effects, which let speakers located only a couple of feet apart simulate a more spacious acoustic environment.

Expect to pay about $200 to $400 for a main pair of speakers. The pair of rear, adjunct speakers in a surround-sound setup can be cheaper, since those off-screen sounds don't tax a speaker's capabilities.

Choose the playback devices. At a minimum, a home-theater setup needs a hi-fi VCR. Hi-fi models are available at discount for less than $300. Laser-disc players are generally $400 and up.

Consider the remote control. "Universal" remote controls, which operate more than one type and brand of component, often come with high-end TV sets and VCRs. You can buy them separately, too, for $10 and up. For more information on remote controls, see page 39.

The rest of the gear. Rounding out the list of home-entertainment possibilities are camcorders, analog or digital recording decks, headphones, and CD players.

Several new technologies have come onto the home-entertainment scene in the past couple of years. Digital audio, represented by Philips's Digital Compact Cassette and Sony's Minidisc, combines CD-quality sound with the ability to record as well as play. Interactive home multimedia devices such as those marketed by Philips and Panasonic give the family TV set computerlike capabilities. Digital audio recorders and interactive multimedia are still expensive, with uncertain futures, which makes investing riskier than for established technologies.

Cable and satellite dishes

Close to two-thirds of U.S. households subscribe to cable TV, but subscribers aren't all that happy. Complaints about high rates, missed service calls, and programming topped the list in a recent reader survey.

Cable. Consumers must deal with an

awkward interface embodied in the cable box. If you don't subscribe to scrambled premium channels, you may be able to hook up the set directly and avoid these headaches:

■ If you hook up a VCR to a TV set with a cable box, you may not be able to watch one channel while taping another unless you rent a second cable box for your VCR.

■ The cable box can make high-end features such as picture-in-picture and channel ID difficult or impossible to use.

■ A cable box often renders a TV set's remote control useless for changing channels. You'll pay perhaps a dollar or two in monthly fees to rent the cable company's remote. Another remedy: a "code entry" universal remote, which works most brands of cable boxes along with the TV set.

■ Cable can also introduce problems with the sound. For example, the company may not properly process the signal for programs that are broadcast in stereo. If your "stereo" sound is practically mono, you'll notice it most with surround sound and other ambience effects. Improper installation can create a buzz; so can the way many cable systems scramble their signals. Complaints to the cable company are the only way to solve such problems.

Small satellite dishes. RCA's 18-inch dish setup, called Digital Satellite System, or DSS, costs about $1000 installed, with programming billed monthly. The Primestar system, which uses a 36- to 39-inch dish, rents the equipment for about $8 per month, plus the monthly fee. The small dishes bring down signals from one or two satellites, which offer packages of up to 150 channels.

In our tests, we found the picture and sound quality of these systems to be excellent. But there were disadvantages:

■ You can't tape one channel and watch another.

■ To connect additional TV sets to a dish, you have to buy additional equipment for each set, or pay an extra programming fee, or both.

■ The satellites don't carry local stations. You have to use an antenna—or subscribe to cable as well—to get local fare.

Cable's near-monopoly is being threatened. It is facing competition from the new satellite delivery systems that use small roof-mounted dishes as well as from telephone companies attempting to start TV services.

Buying the gear

Our basic shopping advice: Shop around, and don't buy more than you need.

There are many places such gear is sold. Home electronics equipment is often sharply discounted, and the prices you pay depend in part on where you buy.

Local chains and stores. These include mom-and-pop operations, often with repair facilities, and audio/video salons equipped with special listening rooms. Expect personal service, but limited selection and small or no discounts.

Department stores. The few that carry electronics products tend to offer competitive prices during sales.

Electronics/appliance superstores. Stores like Circuit City and Best Buy offer a wide range of gear. Prices are generally good, and sales staff is plentiful, but the selling environment is often pressured.

Mass merchandisers. Stores like Walmart and Kmart tend to carry just a few brands, and those tend to be low-end "value" brands like Goldstar and Samsung. Don't expect knowledgeable clerks.

Warehouse clubs. Selection at places

like Sam's Club or the Price Club is likely to be skimpy, but prices are usually deeply discounted.

Mail order. Operations like Crutchfield and 47th St. Photo run ads in audio and video magazines and Sunday newspapers. Sometimes they publish catalogs as well. You can get good prices, but of course you can't hear or see what you're buying until it arrives on your doorstep.

Which brands to choose?

What do you get by buying a brand's more expensive models? Often, small but tangible improvements in performance, convenience, or versatility. Sometimes, however, you pay extra for a name and a look.

Mass-market brands such as RCA and Panasonic in video and Sony, Pioneer, Technics, and JVC in audio are widely available in stores and by mail, usually at substantial discount. Prestige brands such as Proton and ProScan video products are sold primarily through specialty audio and video dealers, with little discounting. Some companies—Sony, RCA, and Panasonic among them—manufacture separate lines of merchandise to reach both markets.

Our tests have shown no substantive performance advantage for the prestige brands over similarly featured mass-market brands. Indeed, prestige audio brands tend to give you fewer features for the money than mass-market brands. (That allows the control panels of many prestige products to be a model of simplicity.)

Reliability. Repairs of electronic equipment can be costly. You can improve your chances of avoiding a trouble-prone product by checking our advice on reliability in each report and in the Reliability chapter (see page 9). The Histories are based on reader experiences with actual products.

An extended-service contract is a bad investment. If solid-state electronic circuitry fails, it usually fails early, within the manufacturer's warranty period. Belts and other parts that wear out with heavy use usually aren't covered. Nor is accidental breakage. Stores make much of their profit from these contracts, so prepare yourself for a hard sell. If you feel you need some protection, make your purchase with one of the credit cards that doubles the manufacturer's warranty, increasing it to a maximum of up to one year. See page 14.

TV sets

▶ **Repair Histories on pages 16 and 17.**

As with most electronic gear, you get more TV set for your money these days. Large, square screens, stereo sound, and jacks to plug in other gear have become the norm. Most sets today provide good picture quality—fairly close to the best possible under current broadcast standards. Comb filters and dark screens, which allow a set to render greater detail and produce punchier pictures, are becoming commonplace on 27-inch and larger sets.

Even so, picture detail is still limited by the broadcast standard, which provides about 330 lines of horizontal resolution. Most good sets we've tested come close to that limit, although sets without a comb filter are apt to resolve just 270 lines. S-VHS and Hi8 gear and laser-disc players can produce up to 425 lines.

A significant improvement in picture quality probably won't come until high-definition television (HDTV) becomes available. Meanwhile, manufacturers have begun selling forerunners of tomorrow's HDTV sets, often recognizable by their wide screens and high price tags. While these models can offer better picture quality than traditional sets—achieved through a technology known as IDTV (improved-definition television)—don't confuse them with high-definition sets.

TV sound has also improved in the past decade, though sound quality is far more variable than picture quality. In general, sound gets better as sets get bigger. Medium-sized sets, even with stereo, deliver sound no better than a mediocre boom box. The "side firing" speakers on some TV sets offer a better illusion of stereo, as long you don't enclose the set in cabinetry. The best way to improve TV sound is to play it through good external speakers. Audio outputs for routing the sound through a hi-fi audio system are common on sets 20 inches or larger. Some high-end sets have an amplifier powerful enough to drive their own external speakers.

Sound enhancement systems abound. For instance, Toshiba's Digital Sound Processor feature aims to open the soundstage by delaying and then feeding back a part of the audio signal, almost like an echo. The Sound Retrieval System (SRS) on some Sony and RCA sets and Zenith's Spatial Equalization (SEq) manipulate right and left channels to enhance the stereo. We've found both systems quite effective. With any of these sound systems, the manipulated sound is most impressive in movies with exotic sound effects.

Larger TV sets may also come ready for Dolby Surround Sound or Dolby Pro Logic, with amplifiers built in to power from two to five external loudspeakers, which you purchase separately.

Three brands of TV sets—RCA, Magnavox, and Zenith—account for nearly half of all U.S. sales.

The choices

Mini sets. Color TV sets with screens of three inches or so are still in the fancy-gadget stage of evolution. On many models, the picture comes from a liquid-crystal display (LCD), rather than a regular picture tube. To look its best, the picture has to be viewed nearly head on. On some LCD sets, the picture is acceptable, but not as good as on tube sets. Bright outdoor lighting makes the picture all but vanish; even in shaded areas, the picture is only marginally acceptable. The 5- to 10-inch models use a conventional cathode-ray picture tube, which produces a picture with more natural-looking color. But the size of the tube makes these sets bulky. LCD sets are priced from $100 to $600; 5 to 10-inch conventional sets, $180 to $400.

Small sets. Sets with a 13-inch screen are regarded as "second" sets, so makers tend to make them plain. Expect monophonic sound, sparse features, and a price tag of $150 to $400.

Sets with a 19- or 20-inch screen are also seen as second sets. The 19-inch sets are made to be cheaper than 20-inch sets, with fewer features. Don't expect top-notch performance; they lack high-end picture refinements such as a comb filter or high-performance picture tube in most models. Some sets have mono sound. Models with stereo sound usually have extra inputs for plugging in a VCR and a laser-disc player. Their sound quality is equivalent to that of a mediocre boom box. Prices range from $200 to $500 with the 20-inch sets at the upper end.

Large sets. Sets with a 25- or 26-inch

screen tend to be economy models; those with 27-inch screens offer more features, including picture-in-picture, special sound systems, and universal remote controls. Sets of this size range in price from about $300 to more than $1500.

Manufacturers aim their 31-inch and larger sets at the home-theatre crowd. Those sets usually boast enhanced-sound systems and various high-end features, such as the ability to recall customized picture and sound settings. Prices range from less than $1000 to more than $2500. The largest TV sets weigh hundreds of pounds and are too wide and too high for conventional component shelving. You'll need a room big enough to comfortably view these sets without seeing the scan lines. (A rule of thumb: The closest viewing distance is four times the screen height.)

Rear-projection sets. These offer still more picture area—40 to 70 diagonal inches—but less clarity than a conventional tube. You'll need a viewing distance of at least 10 feet for a 50-inch set, more for larger ones. Brightness and, to some extent, color vary as you change your angle of view. Big-screen sets come with plenty of features, such as ambient sound and custom audio and video settings. Expect to pay from $1500 to more than $5500.

Features and conveniences

Some features are standard or nearly so:

Remote control. Just about all TV sets come with one. The simplest may only switch the set on and off, change channels, and adjust volume. More versatile units can shut off the set with a timer, block a channel from view, and control a VCR. On some sets, nearly all controls have been moved to the remote, no blessing if the remote is poorly designed or lost. One Magnavox feature helps you find the remote by making it beep when you hit the TV set's Power button. For more information about remote controls, see page 39.

Electronic channel scan. Direct tuning, which lets you hop from station to station, is standard. "Auto program" automatically tunes the TV just to channels active in your area. Most sets let you delete little-watched channels from the up/down channel scan.

Cable ready. These sets can receive cable TV signals (except for scrambled channels) without using a cable company's decoder box. High-end models offer two cable/antenna inputs, one for basic channels and the other for scrambled channels.

Alarm and sleep timer. This built-in clock can turn the set on or off at a predetermined time.

Closed captioning. Sets 13 inches and larger provide on-screen subtitles, which help the hearing-impaired as well as preschoolers learning to read and people learning English. Those subtitles also let you watch TV without disturbing others. Most prime-time and most of the top syndicated programs have closed captioning.

Features worth looking for:

Multichannel TV stereo. MTS is a built-in stereo decoder and amplifier that reproduces stereo broadcasts. Some low-priced sets from RCA and General Electric create a pseudostereo sound instead of the standard MTS variety.

Jacks or inputs. Audio and video jacks, mainly on sets 20 inches and larger, let you connect other gear. Some large sets have more than a dozen jacks. The preferred method of hooking up a hi-fi VCR, laser-disc player, camcorder, or sound system is to use video and audio inputs. You need an S-video input to display the highest-quality signals from S-VHS VCRs and Hi8 camcorders. Front jacks are convenient for video-game or camcorder hookups. Audio outputs let you run TV sound through external speakers or a hi-fi system.

Automatic volume control. This relatively new Magnavox feature, called Smart

Sound, keeps the TV volume from jumping when a commercial comes on or when you change channels.

Comb-filter circuitry. We highly recommend this feature. It increases resolution, cleans up image outlines, and eliminates most extraneous colors. Most 27-inch and larger sets have it.

Optional extra features include:

StarSight. This is a subscriber service that offers a versatile on-screen program guide. It aids VCR programming by allowing you to scroll through TV schedules hours or days ahead, but at about $5 per month, it's not cheap. It needs a decoder, either built into the set or bought separately (about $125).

Active-channel scan. This is automated channel-surfing. Press a button on the remote and the tuner runs through the viewable channels, pausing at each one for a few seconds.

Ambient-sound modes. They go by names like Sound Retrieval System (SRS) and Spatial Equalization (SEq). Basically, they're electronically enhanced stereo.

Channel block-out. You can render certain channels unviewable—usually, to limit a child's viewing.

Channel labeling (or captioning). This is helpful if you have lots of channels. It lets you program names like MTV, CNN, and ESPN to appear on screen with the channel number.

Commercial-skip timer. This lets you change channels long enough to miss the commercial and then automatically return to the original channel.

Dark screens. These enhance contrast, particularly noticeable when you watch TV in a brightly lit room. Their effect is muted in low-light viewing.

Dolby Surround Sound or Dolby Pro Logic. These features decipher the Dolby-encoded sound track of movie videos and a growing number of TV programs. They require two to five external speakers.

Flat screens. They're supposed to reduce distortion at the picture's edges, but we saw little effect in our tests.

Flesh-tone correction. It adjusts skin tones that are too green or red. It doesn't affect a set's basic performance.

Horizontal resolution. This is a measure of the detail a set can display on its screen. Beyond about 425 lines, big numbers are irrelevant.

Multilingual menus. On-screen menus are in English, Spanish, or French.

Picture-in-picture (PIP). This feature lets you see another channel or video source (a VCR or camcorder tape) as a small picture superimposed on the picture you're watching. Unless the set has two tuners, you must hook it up to a VCR or laser-disc player to use PIP. With a cable box you may need more complex connections, and possibly an extra box.

Programmable audio/video. This lets you customize picture and sound settings. On some sets, each input retains its own settings to compensate for signal differences from VCRs and camcorders.

Separate audio program (SAP). With certain broadcasts, it lets a viewer switch to another soundtrack—say, in Spanish.

Video noise-reduction filters. They smooth out "noisy" images. They don't affect a set's basic performance.

White-balance controls. These let you tint background whites toward red or blue but don't affect basic performance.

Reliability

Over the years, 13-, 14-, 19-, and 20-inch sets have proven more reliable than larger ones. Among 25- to 27-inch sets purchased new from 1989 to 1994, some of the more reliable brands were General Electric, JVC, Panasonic, Hitachi, Toshiba, and Sears. Some of the more reliable 19- and 20-inch brands include Sanyo, Panasonic, Hitachi, and JVC. Among 19- and 20-inch and 25- to 27-inch sets, Sylvania was the least reliable brand. Magnavox and Sony were less reliable than other brands of 13- and 14-inch sets in our survey. See the brand Repair Histories, pages 16 and 17.

Buying advice

For the best picture quality, look for a TV set with comb-filter circuitry. We also recommend multichannel stereo (MTS) and an ample supply of audio and video jacks. Beyond that, you can safely choose a model by its features, repair history, price, or the design of the remote control.

Don't put too much stock in comparisons of the picture you see on sets displayed in a store. You can't be sure that those TV sets are getting a uniform picture signal or that they have been uniformly adjusted.

VCRs

▶ **Repair Histories on page 16.**

The latest VCRs are smaller, cost less, and have more features than previous models. Remote control, on-screen programming, and cable compatibility are standard features. Models with hi-fi stereo capabilities, the VCR Plus programming system, and four video heads are becoming the norm; some sell for less than $350. If you don't need hi-fi sound, you can get a full-featured model for as little as $250.

These days, nearly all VCRs use the VHS format or its high-end variant, S-VHS. Of more than 40 brands, three—RCA, Magnavox, and Panasonic—account for about one-third of VHS VCRs sold in the U.S.

Newer formats such as 8mm and its high-end variant, Hi8, have come along to accommodate small-sized 8mm camcorders. Few VCRs are sold in those formats, since they can't use VHS cassettes.

Big changes loom on the VCR's horizon. Before long, digital VCRs may offer higher-quality pictures and sound. But recordable video discs, also in the offing, may erase any advantage offered by digital tape.

The choices

VCRs can cost less than $200 to more than $2000. Key features make the difference between one price level and another.

The basic VCR. While some very low-priced models are just playback machines (VCPs—videocassette players), the basic VCR is a two-head player with monophonic sound, priced at less than $200. Two play/record heads are all you need for everyday recording and playback.

An extra pair of heads offers some advantages: cleaner slow-motion and freeze-frames in the longer-play EP speed, and sometimes a slightly better picture during regular playback. Four-head models outsell two-head models and may soon be regarded as basic. Four-head models start at about $200.

Hi-fi models. Hi-fi VCRs record the audio tracks as diagonal stripes across the tape's width under the video track. The result is near-CD sound quality. Hi-fi VCRs use two extra heads for the audio and are sometimes called "six head" machines. Typical prices: $250 to $600.

S-VHS. You'll pay a premium of about $200 for this technical refinement of VHS. S-VHS gives a sharper picture than conventional VHS. S-VHS also stands up better if you're making multiple tape-to-tape generations. To take full advantage of the S-VHS format you need a high-resolution source of pictures (S-VHS or Hi8 camcorder) and a high-resolution TV set, equipped with an S-video jack.

S-VHS is partially compatible with regular VHS; an S-VHS machine can use regular VHS tapes, but a regular VHS machine can't play S-VHS tapes. Some VHS machines offer "Quasi-S-VHS" playback: They can play S-VHS cassettes, but they can't take advantage of the high resolution capabilities of the format.

S-VHS VCRs are generally priced from $550 to $2000 or more. An S-VHS cassette costs about $3 to $4 more than a regular VHS cassette.

Features and conveniences

Programming. On-screen programming is almost universal. A menu on the TV screen prompts you through a sequence of time and channel-selection steps. Voice-activated programming lets you program with oral commands. In our tests, the feature didn't always work well.

VCR Plus. This simplifies programming even further. It's sold as a separate product for $40, or as a built-in feature that adds about $20 to $80 to the list price of a VCR. You tap in a three- to seven-digit program code (found in the TV listings of many newspapers), and the device automatically orders the VCR into action at the right time. Most versions can program a cable box's multiple channels.

Auto channel set. This quickly eliminates vacant slots from the VCR tuner's channel lineup.

Auto speed-switching. The VCR automatically slows the recording speed from SP to EP if not enough tape is left to complete a recording.

HOW TO BUY VIDEOTAPE

In the real world of imperfect TV reception and VCR performance, differences between brands of videotape are likely to be all but unnoticeable. For many uses, the strategy of buying the cheapest tape may be perfectly fine.

Nearly all the videotapes we've tested, whether standard or "high grade," have performed well. Differences in tapes are likely to show up most when the signal quality is high quality, as from a camcorder. In addition, manufacturers recommend that high-grade tapes be used for videos you expect to keep for many years, but we know of no evidence that standard-grade tapes deteriorate more quickly than high-grade ones. Peace of mind alone, however, may justify spending the extra dollar or so when you tape important events.

Time-shifting vacationers may want to consider T160 and longer videotapes. Judging by our tests, superlong tapes aren't noticeably lower in quality than standard-length cassettes.

The best buying strategy: Stock up whenever tape is on sale. Prices range anywhere from about $2 to $14. You can also save by buying in quantity—four packs, five packs, and so on.

To protect videotapes you care about consider the following:

■ In the even of a catastrophe, make a duplicate and store it away from the original tape.

■ Enclose videotapes in plastic boxes in order to seal them from smoke, dust, and dirt.

■ Store tapes in moderate temperature and humidity. Never leave them in direct sunlight or in a hot vehicle.

■ Seldom-played tapes should be "exercised"—taken out for a spin at least once every year or two.

Auto clock set. This eliminates the flashing 12:00 by using information in the broadcast signal to set the VCR's clock.

Auto tracking. Now found on nearly all VCRs, this feature eliminates the need to adjust the tracking control for each tape viewed. It's useful when you play tapes recorded on other units.

Childproof lock. It disables the controls or locks the cassette door.

Front-mounted audio and video jacks. All VCRs let you plug in a camcorder of any format. Jacks on the front of the VCR are most convenient.

Go-to. This searches the tape by time to find the passage you want to watch. Some models can find stretches of blank tape to record on.

Index search. It's similar to Go-to, but more helpful. It places an electronic "bookmark" on the tape each time you begin to record. Then you can scan all the start points to locate a segment.

Power backup. The VCR retains clock and program settings during brief power outages.

Remote control. Even low-end models come with a remote. For more information about remotes, see page 39.

Skip search. You can fast-forward 30 seconds or a minute with each press of the button to skip commercials.

Tape indicators on console. A front display that shows when a tape is playing, recording, or rewinding is handy. Best are those that display minutes and hours instead of arbitrary units.

Those who intend to edit will need to pick and choose among additional features:

Audio dub. This lets you add music or narration to video images.

Flying erase head. This lets you string together edits seamlessly, with no glitch between segments.

Quick-start transport. This features cuts the time needed to shift from Stop to Play, or Play to Rewind or Fast Forward.

Title generator. Like those in still cameras, it lets you date or identify scenes.

Other editing features include an Edit switch that boosts the signal when you're copying a tape to improve the quality of second-generation signals. A Synchro-edit jack is helpful for coordinating a compatible camcorder or a second VCR used as a source. A Jog-shuttle control helps you locate a tape segment by running the tape backward or forward at continuously variable speeds.

Reliability

According to our 1994 Annual Questionnaire, one in eight of the machines our readers bought from 1989 to 1994 needed repair at least once. Magnavox, Quasar, and Emerson were among the least troublesome brands. Zenith, Sears, and Fisher VCRs have needed repairs more often than most other brands. See the brand Repair Histories on pages 16.

Buying advice

In our tests, we've found no clear correlation between price and picture quality. But spending more generally buys more features and convenience.

A two-head VCR or a basic four-head model is all you need for taping TV programs for viewing later or for watching rented movie videos.

To take advantage of movies with a stereo sound track or to hook the VCR into your stereo system as part of a home-theater setup, choose a hi-fi model. A hi-fi VCR is capable of producing superb sound, but only when it's piped through good external loudspeakers.

If you're interested in editing video tapes, check that the VCR and camcorder have compatible synchronization provisions. Unfortunately, the industry still hasn't standardized synchro-editing features.

TV/VCR combos

A TV/VCR combination is appealing because it's simple and neat. Most are less versatile and have fewer features than separate devices, but the combos seem to have found a niche as sets for the bedroom, kitchen, or playroom. The major brands include Emerson, Panasonic, Magnavox, Samsung, Zenith, Quasar, and Symphonic.

TV/VCRs are easy to set up and use, but they have limitations:

■ Most have only a single tuner, so you can't watch one program while taping another one.

■ Some lack such niceties as Fast-forward and Rewind controls on the console.

■ A combo is only as strong as its weaker part. If either the VCR or the TV breaks down, you lose the use of both while the combo is in the shop.

The choices

TV/VCRs typically have either a 13-inch or a 20-inch screen and generally lack picture enhancements like a comb filter or a high grade picture tube. Some ultra-miniature models with small LCD screens are also sold.

13-inch models. These are the most popular size. This size is typically a functional machine with Spartan features. Prices start at $300.

19- and 20-inch models. The 20-inch models tend to be a little more upscale. Some may have stereo sound and four-head VCRs. Prices start at $400.

Features and conveniences

All combos are likely to have cable-readiness; the ability to delete unwanted channels; a two-head VCR with on-screen menu programming; monophonic audio; and auto rewind at tape's end. All have a single remote that controls both components, but TV/VCR remotes are often cluttered and complicated. Other features:

Tuners. Most have only one—which means you can't watch something else while you're taping. Top-of-the-line models have two tuners.

Four-head VCR. This is a high-end feature for combos. Four heads are necessary for clean slow-motion and freeze-frame in the EP speed.

MTS stereo. Some high-end sets can handle stereo broadcasts.

Timed one-touch record. This is convenient for setting the VCR to start taping immediately.

Real-time tape counter. It gives elapsed time or time remaining on a selected portion of tape.

Memory backup. This saves clock settings during brief power outages.

Input jacks. Use them to pipe in external sources such as a camcorder. Most convenient are front-mounted jacks.

Reliability

We have no reliability data on TV/VCR combos, but our information on separate TV sets and VCRs suggests that the VCR portion of the combo may be more likely to break down.

Buying advice

A TV/VCR can be a good choice for a household's second or third set, or as an all-in-one unit for a college dorm room. Since picture quality is apt to be good enough for such use, you can generally choose a model by features. But steer clear of the lowest-end brands. The Symphonic and Zenith models we tested combined the worst TV set and VCR we'd seen in years.

Camcorders

▶ Repair Histories on page 19.

Compact camcorders—8mm and VHS-C—once commanded a premium. Now you can buy them for just a few hundred dollars. Each format also has a higher-resolution "high-band" cousin—Hi8 for 8mm, S-VHS-C for VHS-C—that commands a premium of several hundred dollars. What you get for the extra money are slightly sharper pictures that hold up well to copying.

Only a handful of manufacturers actually make camcorders, which they sell under various names. The biggest are Sony, Matsushita (Panasonic and Quasar), Hitachi, JVC, Thompson (RCA and GE), and Sharp. Sony is the major maker of 8mm camcorders, while Matsushita and JVC dominate the VHS world, including VHS-C.

The choices

8mm. Small, light, easy to tote, 8mm is the best-selling format. It enjoys two distinct advantages over VHS-C: longer playing time and better sound quality. Cassettes hold two hours of footage. In sound quality, 8mm models are the equal of hi-fi models in the other formats. For playback, you connect a cable from the camcorder to your TV or VCR. You can also connect the camcorder to your VCR to copy or edit your 8mm footage onto VHS tapes. A few 8mm VCRs are also available. Price: $450 to $1500.

VHS-C. JVC introduced this small, lightweight version of VHS—and kept the format alive when many had given it up for dead. Its one advantage over 8mm is that the cassettes are playable in any VHS VCR. To do so, you need an adapter—supplied with the camcorder or available in camcorder stores. Cassettes hold just 30 minutes of playing time at fast (highest quality) speed, 90 minutes at slow speed. Tapes that play one third longer are sold, but are not common. The quality of pictures shot at the slower, extended-play speed has steadily improved, and the images usually look decent now. Price: $500 to $1200.

Full-sized VHS. This oldest format still accounts for about 25 percent of sales. VHS models are heavy and bulky. The high-band S-VHS starts at about $1200.

Features and conveniences

The modern camcorder is an auto-everything device that's nearly as foolproof as an autofocus still camera. Features include a motorized zoom lens, automatic exposure and sound-level controls; a flying erase head that delivers clean scene changes even if you re-record something; auto-focus, which keeps the image sharp as the subject or the camera moves; and automatic white balance, which keeps colors normal under different lighting conditions.

Other standard features include date/time labeling, fade, a headphone jack (to monitor the audio portion), and jacks for playback or recording to another camcorder or VCR. Many also have a jack for an external microphone.

Other options:

Batteries. Most camcorders come with a rechargeable nickel-cadmium (nicad) battery that gives about an hour of taping on a full charge. Some come with a two-hour battery. Batteries of smaller capacity (to save weight) or larger capacity (for longer shooting) are available for most models. Consider buying a spare (about $60).

Unless they're fully discharged occasionally before recharging, nicad batteries temporarily lose some of their capacity. To get around that, most models now have a charger that lets you discharge the battery before recharging.

Color viewfinder. This feature, found on more and more models, lets you view scenes in color. One variant is a color LCD screen mounted on the back or side of the camera, as on some Sharp and Sony models; you hold the camera about a foot away from your eyes. Holding the camera steady in that position or seeing the screen clearly in bright sunlight can be very difficult. Indoors, on a tripod, is where these displays work the best.

Digital gain-up. This helps create passable pictures in dim light by slowing the shutter speed. The downside: Moving subjects or fast panning leaves a blur.

Digital zoom. Because digital zooming involves electronically enlarging the camcorder's pixels, image quality plummets as you go much beyond the basic zoom range provided by the lens.

Image stabilization. This increasingly common feature tries to iron the jitters out of handheld shots. Effectiveness varies considerably from brand to brand. The design that seems to work best uses optical stabilization. The alternative, electronic stabilizers, can slightly mar picture quality. At best, image stabilizers provide only a moderate improvement in image steadiness. A video tripod is still the best tool for steady shots.

Manual exposure control. Few models have this. Automatic exposure generally works well but doesn't offer the flexibility of a manual override, which is helpful in some lighting situations. The most useful type has a continuously adjustable control. Others have only one or two settings—for theater (or spotlight) and backlit subjects.

Remote control. More and more common, especially on 8mm models, a remote makes it easier to use the camcorder for playback and editing. It's also an alternative to a self-timer but may not work in sunlight.

Reset-to-auto switch. A single switch restores all settings to their normal automatic mode so you don't have to check each control.

Sound. The 8mm format is inherently superior to VHS and comparable to hi-fi VHS and hi-fi VHS-C. The built-in mike in most camcorders is suited for capturing speech, but you need an external mike to do justice to music.

Special picture effects. Picture fade can provide elegant transitions between scenes if it's not overused. Other effects, such as recording in sepia or adding old-time movie flicker, are less common—and less useful.

Title generator. In some models, a built-in character generator can superimpose printed titles and captions. In others, you can record and superimpose titles from artwork or signs. Most let you select a color for the title.

Wide-screen pictures. By blacking out the top and bottom of the picture, this feature lets you record images in a format similar to that of letterboxed movies.

Reliability

Most people don't use their camcorders a lot. Readers who own a camcorder bought new between 1989 and 1994 report using it an average of just 14 hours in the past year. Even so, nearly 1 in 8 of their camcorders has needed repair. And repair costs are considerable—about $125, on average. Among the most reliable VHS brands: Panasonic, Magnavox, and General Electric. There wasn't much difference among the compact brands we looked at. See the brand Repair Histories on page 19.

Buying advice

All models have the necessary equipment to make decent videos. Spending more buys extras that may make shooting more convenient or fun, but those fancy features have little effect on basic performance. Picture quality isn't likely to improve much until high-definition television reaches the market. High-band models generally provide a noticeably sharper picture.

Regardless of which format you choose, you'll need a tripod for professional results. For fast panning, a tripod-mounted compact is more manageable than a VHS model, because the compact's viewfinder is at the rear while the VHS's viewfinder is forward and on the side.

For our latest report on camcorders, see the December 1995 issue of CONSUMER REPORTS.

Remote controls

The remote control is now a standard accessory for virtually every type of home-entertainment gear. It has also become a product in its own right.

The choices

Dedicated remote. Typically found on CD players and the cheapest TV sets, VCRs, and receivers, it operates only the component it comes with.

Unified remote. This type also comes packaged with a component. A step up from a dedicated type, it can operate at least one other product of the same brand, though often in a limited way.

Universal remote. This type is often included with high-end TV sets, VCRs, and receivers, or sold as a stand-alone product. It operates gear from a variety of makers. Many work video gear only; some work everything. Universal remotes are priced from $10 to $60. A low-end, inexpensive model may be all you need.

Universal remotes often sell for less than a replacement from the manufacturer, making them a good choice for replacing a broken or lost one.

Most universal remotes are "code entry" models; only a few these days are "learning" models. Code-entry remotes come preprogrammed with an identifying code for scores of components. A directory of codes comes with the remote. You simply punch the appropriate code into the remote's keypad to activate the device.

Programming a learning remote is a bit more complicated. You align the remote with the one whose commands you want it to learn, then execute all its commands.

Learning remotes can mimic almost all the abilities of the original model, including the advanced commands for programming a VCR. Code-entry remotes may perform only the major functions.

A low-battery indicator is especially useful to safeguard the commands in a learning remote, which is tedious to reprogram if the battery dies.

Buying advice

Code-entry universal remotes may be all you need for everyday use. Learning remotes are more difficult to use and tricky to program, but they're more versatile.

Whatever you buy, make sure you can return it if it proves unsuitable. You may have to try more than remote to find the best match for your components.

Well-designed remote controls feel balanced and comfortable to hold and are easy to use with one hand. Look for buttons that are grouped by function and differentiated by size, shape, and color. Often-used buttons like Mute and Channel up/down should stand out the most. Especially handy are four-way rocker switches or north/south buttons that control volume and channels.

Receivers

▶ Ratings on page 53.

If any component exemplifies the growing influence of video and home theater, it's the receiver, the amplifier plus radio tuner at the heart of a component system. Besides its historical functions of amplifying sound and tuning the radio, the receiver can now integrate a TV set, a VCR, and, perhaps, a laser-disc player with the stereo audio system.

Three of every four receivers sold are designed to shuttle video as well as audio signals between components. Collectively, they are known as A/V (audio/video) receivers. More than half the A/V models offer surround sound, a heavily marketed feature for home theater.

Good performance as an amplifier and a switcher is a given. Models do differ in FM radio performance. But power and features are primarily what separate one class of receiver from another. Spending more on a receiver generally buys conveniences such as jacks to plug in ancillary equipment and numerous features—perhaps more than you need.

Receivers sell under more than 30 brand names. Five—Sony, Pioneer, Kenwood, Technics, and JVC—account for more than 60 percent of the market, however.

The choices

Basic audio-only receivers. They make up the low end of the market. For a conventional component-audio system, they can be more than adequate. A power output of 60 watts or so per channel is the norm. Expect to spend $175 to $250. Some audiophile brands offer the same no-frills basic models with more power, but for a lot more money.

A/V receivers. More than three-quarters of receivers sold fit this category. They have jacks for video gear, and they can drive extra "surround sound" speakers. Sophisticated Dolby Pro Logic has all but superseded lesser surround-sound technologies. Entry-level models with Pro Logic sell for about $250. Spending more—$400 to $500—will get you a receiver with more jacks, more power, and more features, such as digital signal-processing. Models priced from $500 to more than $2000 typically deliver lots of power and bristle with such esoterica as the ability to pipe different music or video material to different rooms.

THX receivers. These home-theatre sound systems use a patented circuitry to simulate the acoustics heard in theaters. A full-blown setup typically uses six power amplifiers to handle the five channels of sound, plus subwoofer, decoder, and controller components. An entry-level THX receiver costs $1000 to $2000; a complete setup, $10,000.

Features and conveniences

Audio/video switching. Any receiver can handle sound from a stereo TV set or a VCR. An A/V receiver does more: It is essentially a control center for selecting the component you want to hear or watch—either a video source (a TV set, VCR, or laser-disc player) or an audio source (a CD, cassette tape, or radio).

Elaborate controls. Mass-market receivers are notorious for their multitude of knobs, buttons, levers, and lights. Prestige brands, on the other hand, make a virtue of simplicity—no flashy display and limited switching and dubbing capability—even on high-priced models. Some models try to simplify their controls by using a

TV-based menu system à la those found on VCRs. Look for controls and displays that are logically arranged, clearly labeled, and readable from various angles.

Graphic equalizer. This tone control for contouring the sound shows up even on low-priced models. Equalizers with fewer than seven bands don't accomplish much more than regular bass and treble controls. Most high-end models offer an equalizer as part of digital signal-processing.

Some features—like a pulsing bar graph of the sound "profile," say—may be more hype than help.

Loudness switch. It boosts the bass when the volume is down, compensating for the human ear's insensitivity to bass at low volume. A variable control allows the most flexibility.

Mute switch. It turns sound off without changing the volume-control setting.

Multiroom option. This feature lets you control the unit from another room.

Multisource option. This lets you route sound form two sources to separate rooms. For example, you could send an FM broadcast to the main speakers and music from a CD to the home office.

Radio. Digital electronic tuning is standard. The display shows the station's precise frequency number: 101.9, say. Digital tuning minimizes noise and distortion. You may have to tune using an up/down Seek button that searches for the next listenable station. We prefer a numeric keypad that lets you enter a station's frequency.

Remote control. Nearly all receivers now have a remote—usually with rows and rows of undifferentiated tiny buttons, the way TV and VCR remotes used to be.

Sound system. Two-channel stereo is the most basic sound effect, well suited for

HOW MUCH POWER DO YOU NEED?

Even inexpensive receivers have plenty of power. But if you want an idea of how much power a system actually needs, here's how to figure it:

Determine the sound "liveness" of your listening room. A space with hard floors, scatter rugs, and plain wood furniture will be acoustically "live"; one with thick carpeting, heavy curtains, and upholstered furniture, relatively "dead." Locate the room size (in cubic feet) and type (live or dead) at right and note the multiplier. To determine the watts per channel needed, multiply that figure by the speaker's minimum power requirement, as stated by the manufacturer.

Let's say you have a 4000-cubic-foot room with average acoustics and speakers that require 12 watts of power. The multiplier from the chart, 1.5, times the watts needed, 12, equals 18. At minimum, you need an amplifier with 18 watts of power per channel to drive the speakers at moderately high volume. To be safe and to do justice to CDs or bass-heavy music, double or triple the figure.

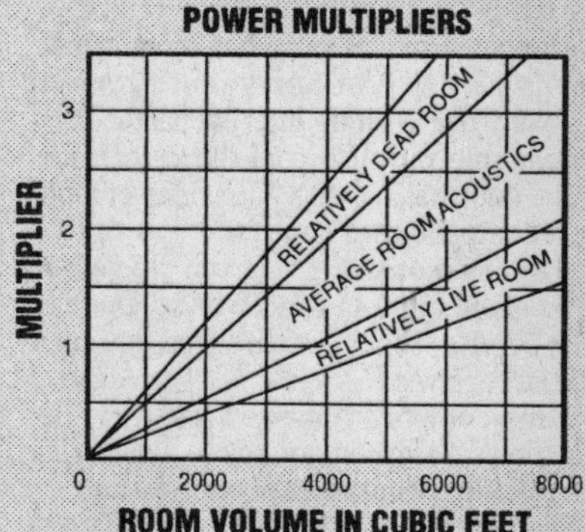

music. For movies and videos, Dolby Pro Logic provides greater realism through special circuitry that deciphers the sound effects encoded on many videos. Pro Logic uses two front main speakers, a pair of smaller surround speakers in the rear, and a center channel in the front to carry "center" sound from the direction of the TV screen. Look for a model that includes an amplifier for the center channel, and that provides the same wattage to the three front channels. Dolby 3 Stereo, a feature on many Pro Logic receivers, simulates four channels of sound using only three front speakers. Another sound effect common on middle-of-the-line receivers is a selectable ambience mode, which simulates the acoustics of a stadium or concert hall.

Speaker compatibility. Many speakers are rated at 4 ohms of impedance. But the labels on many receivers say they shouldn't be used with 4-ohm speakers. That's because the lower the speaker's impedance, the more current it will draw, and the hotter things get for the same power output.

If you want to abide by the labeling, you may have to forgo your first choice of receiver or speaker to get a proper match. If you ignore the 4-ohm restriction, monitor the temperature of the receiver. If its cabinet gets uncomfortably hot after a half-hour's play of bass-heavy music, you're probably overheating internal parts. Turn the volume down to cool things off. For more information, see "Consider component compatibility," page 26.

Switched outlet. It lets you plug other components into the receiver so you can shut off the whole system when you turn off the receiver.

Tone-control bypass. This lets you defeat tone settings temporarily so you can listen to a recording in its pristine form.

Wattage. How much you need depends on the size of the room, the speakers, and the type of music you play. Most modern receivers supply at least 50 watts per channel, which is plenty. Look for receivers in the 100-watt range only if you're driving extra speakers at loud volumes in large spaces or are using speakers that are particularly inefficient. The box on page 41 can help you calculate power requirements.

The tests

We base our evaluation primarily on a standard battery of laboratory tests, chiefly of the FM tuner. A first-rate tuner reproduces sound that's free of background noise and distortion. If a receiver is sensitive enough to pull in weak signals, it should resist interference from electrical sources, aircraft, and other radio signals.

We give a lot of weight to convenience—especially that of the control layout—and the presence of useful features.

Reliability

We do not collect data on receivers because they typically last for many years.

Buying advice

If you want to power a modest system purely for music listening or are content with stereo-only sound from your TV set or VCR, a low-end receiver, rated at 60 watts per channel, should be quite satisfactory. Such a receiver costs $150 or so.

Although some low-priced receivers can handle a TV/VCR/stereo setup, you'll probably have to buy a model higher in the line if you want the receiver to be the heart of even a modest home-theater system. Models in the $300-to-$450 range typically come with Dolby Pro Logic, enough jacks to for multiple components, and enough power to run more than one set of speakers.

Before buying any receiver, make sure it matches your other components and meets their power requirements. See "How much power do you need?" on page 41.

Loudspeakers

▶ Ratings on page 57.

Loudspeakers are the last place to economize in setting up a music system. But that doesn't mean you have to spend a fortune to get good sound. In our tests, we have found very good inexpensive speakers ($250 to $350 a pair) that are suitable as main speakers in a basic system or as front speakers in a home-theater setup.

Speakers differ most in their ability to handle bass. Differences in the audio spectrum among similarly scoring give each speaker its own distinctive sound, which you may or may not like. What you hear also depends a great deal on the size and furnishings of the room, the speakers' placement, and the type of music.

The nearly six million speakers sold each year comprise more than 300 speaker brands, many from small American companies. Bose and Radio Shack account for more than one-quarter of all sales.

The choices

Speakers are starting to diverge into "audio" models, sold in pairs, and "video" models, sometimes sold in groups of three or five. For home-theater applications, you'll also see magnetically shielded speakers sold singly for the center channel in a Dolby Pro Logic surround-sound setup. Most of the difference between audio and video speakers is packaging: You can put together a fine sound system for home theater using regular speakers.

Most speakers have a woofer for bass and a tweeter and sometimes a midrange driver for the rest of the music spectrum. As a practical matter, a speaker needs a big woofer to make big, loud bass. Manufacturers have tried, with mixed success, to design around that fact. Certain miniature speakers, for instance, can deliver good bass, though not very loudly.

Prices for speakers run from $30 or so a pair to more than $10,000. More money buys primarily a deeper reach into the bass.

Here are the main choices:

Small speakers. Miniature speakers, smaller than a shoebox, typically cost $100 and up per pair. Most are seriously deficient at reproducing bass.

Powered speakers are miniatures that have their own built-in amplifier. Some plug in; some run on batteries. They can turn a personal tape player or portable CD player into a small sound system. Powered speakers increasingly serve as an adjunct to a home computer, to help turn it into a "multimedia center."

Wireless speakers are powered speakers that come with a separate transmitter. Those with an infrared control must be in the same room with the transmitter. Those controlled by radio waves can be in another room. Powered speakers are priced from $30 to $400.

Bookshelf speakers. These are sized to fit sideways on a bookshelf. They're appropriate for undemanding listening in a medium-sized room or as the second pair of speakers in a surround-sound system. Prices for bookshelf speakers start at $80 per pair.

Main speakers. Medium-sized models can fill a medium-sized room with loud sound and a large room with fairly loud sound. In speakers this size, the woofer can push the large volumes of air needed to reproduce a full, rich, loud bass sound. Prices start at about $80 but figure on spending at least $300 for a decent pair.

Large speakers include conventional designs as well as esoteric audiophile equipment such as electrostatic speakers, in which tall, thin plastic diaphragms replace speaker cones. Not only do big speakers take up floor space, they often need to be several feet from the wall to produce their best sound. Big speakers cost anywhere from about $700 to thousands.

Some speakers save space by fitting into interior walls, a design that is becoming more and more popular.

Subwoofer and satellite systems. Three-piece subwoofer/satellite systems have grown increasingly popular. The satellites are small speakers that handle midrange and treble sounds. They can fit unobtrusively among furnishings. Since bass sounds are nondirectional, you can hide the large subwoofer section behind a sofa or TV set. Figure on spending anywhere from $250 to $800.

The tests

We set up lab instruments to measure speaker performance in an echo-free chamber and in a 14x23-foot carpeted, furnished room much like an ordinary living room.

For most speakers, we measure accuracy from a frequency of about 30 hertz in the bass to about 16,000 Hz in the treble and rate them on a 100-point scale. We don't rate ambience speakers below 100 Hz. Listeners will probably have trouble picking the more accurate of two models if the spread in our scores is eight points or less.

Tweaking a receiver's tone controls can improve a speaker's accuracy—dramatically, in some cases—and can compensate a bit for a room's acoustical drawbacks.

We also measure the minimum power the receiver must supply to a speaker to produce fairly loud sound in a medium-sized room.

Reliability

Speakers are likely to be problem-free.

Buying advice

Before you buy speakers, be sure you can return or exchange them if they don't sound as good in your home as they did in the showroom. Try to audition them in a good listening room at the store. Compare only two pairs of speakers at a time; each time, judge the pair you prefer against the next pair. Bring a recording whose music you know well—one that gives both the bass and treble ranges a good workout.

With speakers, especially low-priced ones, differences are most noticeable in the bass extension—in a speaker's ability to reproduce the lowest audible tones. Bass-handling at high volume, another aspect of low-frequency performance, is important if you favor fusion jazz, say, or contemporary dance music, with their typical driving bass sounds.

Once you have specific speakers in mind, be sure that your receiver can supply enough power to drive them, and that the speaker impedance isn't too low for the receiver's amplifier to handle (see "Set up the loudspeakers" on page 27 and "How much power do you need?" on page 41).

CD players

▶ **Ratings on page 59.** ▶ **Repair Histories on page 18.**

Virtually every CD player can reproduce superb hi-fi sound. You can take all the traditional indicators of sound quality for granted—wide dynamic range, accurate (flat) frequency response, and freedom from noise and distortion. The minor differences in sound-reproduction we've uncovered are apparent only to a trained listener or a laboratory instrument. Because the sound quality is uniformly excellent, we rate players according to their ability to cope with adverse conditions, like being bumped, or playing a damaged disc.

The world of CD players has more than 40 brand names. Five lead the pack: Pioneer, JVC, Sony, Technics, and Kenwood.

The choices

Full-sized players. These are available as single-disc models and multiple-disc changers. Prices start at about $125 for a low-end single-disc player and $150 for a multiple-disc changer. Changers can play hours of music nonstop. Three main types of changer are available:

Magazine type. This design uses a slide-in cartridge the size of a small, fat book. Magazines typically hold six discs—and they can double as convenient disc storage boxes.

Carousel type. This is the more popular design. It holds five or six discs around a platter. It's easier to load than a magazine, lets you change any of the discs that aren't playing without disturbing the one that is, and offers a wider selection of models. Carousels that use a slide-out drawer are a bit more versatile than those that load from the top. Unlike carousels with drawers, you can't sandwich a top-loading carousel into a stack of other stereo components.

CD jukebox. This design can store up to 100 discs. It varies in size and stacking compatibility with other stereo components. Prices reflect its newness to the market—$50 to $100.

Portable players. Some are part of an overgrown boom box; others are scarcely bigger than the disc itself and weigh less than a pound. Even smaller ones—Minidiscs—let you record and play (see page 49). Basic portables may have only rudimentary controls. More elaborate versions come with such features as a rechargeable battery pack, a built-in radio tuner, a cassette deck, and a panoply of controls similar to what you might find on a table model. Many boom-box systems have detachable speakers with a bass-boost feature. You can easily hook up a portable into a sound system or plug it into a car stereo through either a CD input jack or an adapter that fits into the cassette slot. Portable models sell from about $100 for a small, simple unit to more than $300 for a top-of-the line model.

Features and conveniences

The CD world is rife with jargon referring to technical specifications, particularly those connected with the conversion of digital information to analog sound waves: "oversampling," "MASH technology," "dual digital/analog converters," "bit stream" technology; triple laser beams, and so forth. None of it makes a difference you can consistently hear, our tests have shown.

The extras on a CD player don't always go hand-in-hand with price. Some less expensive models may be generously endowed. Features are most limited on portables.

Just about all home component models have a remote control and features that let you play, pause, stop, select a track, and program selected tracks to play in the order you choose. (Changers let you skip from one disc to another.) Also typical is a display that indicates which track is playing and the elapsed playing time. Other common options found even in basic models:

Calendar-type display. This shows a block of numbers representing the tracks on an active disc, and it highlights the track that's playing. Such a display is especially handy for making tapes, since it indicates you which tracks you've already programmed and those you haven't.

Fade out/fade in. This makes the music fade out slowly, then stop.

Headphone jack. This lets you listen without disturbing others.

Music sampling. This lets you play a few seconds from each track to help you figure which selection to listen to or tape.

Numeric keypad. This lets you program by punching in track numbers directly rather than fussing with Up/down buttons. It's more common on a remote control than on the console of a CD player.

On/off pause. It's handier than having to hit Play to resume playing.

Programming aids. Programming a CD player means telling the unit to play tracks in a particular order. Some players even remember your programs. This feature, called Favorite-track selection or Custom file, remembers programs you've encoded on the

MUSIC, LASER VIDEO & BEYOND

The technology of recording information for playback with lasers has moved from audio into the video, computer, and photography worlds. The rise of CDs reflects the move to convert electronic information to digital encoding, a trend called convergence.

Converting information to digital storage has many advantages: Large amounts of information can be stored in a small space at a low price; noise and interference can be virtually eliminated; duplicates are perfect copies of the original; and computers can manipulate digital information in ways that are difficult or impossible by any other means.

Laser-disc players reproduce exceptionally sharp television images. The typical laser-disc player is a "combi"—a combination device that can play LP-sized video discs as well as conventional audio compact discs. Pioneer is the market leader there.

A dozen or so CD formats and several types of players now exist. Besides standard audio-only CDs are these:

- CD-ROM (read-only memory). This format lets you retrieve data from the CD to use on a computer. Thousands of titles are available, including encyclopedias, games, and children's books.
- Compact videodiscs. These machines play movie-length programs from a conventional-sized compact disc. Two competing and incompatible formats, one backed by Sony and Philips, the other by Toshiba and Time-Warner, make future prospects uncertain.
- CD-I. Interactive discs that run on Philips and Magnavox CD-I players hooked to a TV set.
- CD-I video. A CD-I disc with a full-motion movie. Requires a special adapter to run on a CD-I player.
- Sega CD. Holds game software for Sega game systems.
- Photo CD. Stores about 100 high-quality photos from slides or prints that can "play" on most CD-ROM players.
- Recordable CD. Devices that can record as well as play images or sound or both, using a special compact disc. Prices are still steep, about $2000.
- 3DO. A promising new game format with improved graphics and sound. So far, few titles are available.
- CD+G. Contains still images to accompany music; not widely used.
- CD+MIDI. Plays on a specially equipped player and keyboard synthesizer; not widely used.
- CD-V. Holds up to 20 minutes of sound and 5 minutes of video for music videos; not widely used.

discs. Some models have a Delete-track function that skips over unwanted tracks.

Shuffle play. This mixes the playing order into a random sequence. Look for nonrepeat shuffle.

Special sound effects. Digital signal-processing circuitry creates such sound effects as the acoustics of a concert hall or stadium.

System jack. This lets you plug in a cable from a receiver of the same brand so the receiver's remote works the CD player.

Taping aids. These features, which work best with a same-brand tape deck, make taping easy. Auto-edit lets you punch in the recording time of one side of a tape so the CD player can suggest a track order that fits. With synchronized recording, you don't have to be present during the taping. You connect a cable from the player to a same-brand deck with Auto-reverse. When the deck is ready to record on the second side of the tape, it sends a signal to the CD player, and the taping resumes. Models with Music-peak finder can search for the loudest passage on a disc, letting you set the recorder to the proper sound level. Running total adds up track time as you program the disc so you can tell how many tracks will fit on a given tape. Digital output jacks let you connect a CD player directly to a digital tape or minidisc recorder.

The tests

Besides making the usual sound checks, we see how well the players can cope with bumps in playback and purposely damaged discs. We also measure how quickly the players can jump from track to track.

Reliability

Most CD players, particularly single-play models, hold up quite well. Only 5 percent or fewer of those bought new by our readers between 1991 and 1994 needed repair. By a slim margin, Sanyo, Technics, Teac, and JVC led the pack in reliability among single-play models. JVC, Onkyo, Sony, and Technics have been among the most reliable carousel changers. Magazine changers have been a little more troublesome than single-play models or carousel changers. Kenwood was the least reliable magazine changer. For more information, see the brand Repair Histories on page 18.

Buying advice

Superb sound from a CD player is a given. Differences boil down to how well the players handle physical abuse and what features they offer. If you need to save money in your system, do it here. By spending less, you give up niceties, not performance.

Changer models are priced a little higher than single-play units but offer the convenience of hours of uninterrupted play. We prefer the carousel design.

If uninterrupted play isn't crucial, consider a single-play model. You're likely to get more features for the money than you would with a changer.

For our latest report on portable CD players, see the December 1995 issue of CONSUMER REPORTS.

Cassette decks

▶ **Ratings on page 62.**

Though the conventional cassette deck has probably reached the peak of its audio capability, it's still the medium of choice for recording and playing music at home. Today's best decks satisfy all but the most critical ear, despite their inherent limitations—slow access to individual tracks, background hiss, and a limited ability to capture the whole audible spectrum. A deck that has Dolby S, the most advanced noise-reduction circuitry, sounds nearly as clean as a CD player. And conventional decks are still priced far less than the new, rival digital-tape technologies.

Although more than 30 brands are available, more than half of all U.S. sales go to Sony, Pioneer, JVC, and Technics.

The choices

Component tape decks are the most popular. Prices start at $100 or so and run to more than $1000. Expect to pay anywhere from $200 to $500 for a deck that performs well. More money buys more convenience features but may not improve the sound.

Portable decks include boom boxes and —typically for playback only—personal tape players. You can hook up most personal tape players to a stereo system. Their basic playing performance can be quite acceptable, although the small controls may not be convenient. Boom boxes sell for about $40 and up; personal tape players, $20 and up.

Component decks hold either one tape or two. Tape changers that hold five or six cassettes are still a novelty.

Single-deck machines. Many are designed for serious audio buffs. The tape drive in a single-tape deck is often a cut above the drive in a comparably priced dual-deck machine.

Dual-deck machines. This is the more common type. Also called "dubbing" decks, they lend themselves to copying tapes and playing cassettes in sequence. Dual decks come in two varieties: Single-record models allow play back from both cassette wells but can record from only one; dual-record decks allow playback and recording from both wells. With dual-deck models, you usually have to give up a little in audio performance. They tend to suffer slightly more from flutter (a wavery, watery sound defect), and their frequency response is slightly less accurate than that of single-decks.

Features and conveniences

Bias control. Modern tape coatings can deliver a wider dynamic range than standard ferric oxide (Type I) tape. By increasing the "bias" (an ultrasonic signal the deck uses to reduce distortion), all component decks can handle high-energy ferric (Type II) and metal (Type IV) tape. A deck with automatic Tape-type switches senses the type of tape loaded and switches bias accordingly. Some decks have a manual control you set by ear to fine-tune the bias setting. In some decks, an Auto-bias feature does it for you.

Noise-suppression circuits. Manufacturers use various techniques to mute tape hiss. Most decks rely heavily on electrical signal-processing to reduce noise. To use the circuits, a tape must be recorded and played back with the same circuitry. Standard on component decks are Dolby B and Dolby C; virtually all prerecorded cassettes use Dolby B. Better still, and available on some mid-priced models, is Dolby S, which records at near-digital quality.

Recording-level meters. These days, meters are lighted bar graphs rather than swinging needles. If you do a lot of recording, look for a deck with 12 or so segments on its recording-level meter. Numerous segments make it easy to establish the peak level of the music you are recording and to set the appropriate level. Two separate knobs, one for each channel, makes the level easier to adjust.

Dubbing. Dual decks dub, or copy, tapes at the press of a button. Many decks have an Edit dub feature that stops recording while you change tapes or fiddle with the playback deck. A High-speed dubbing feature cuts recording time in half, but it degrades the music somewhat.

Here are the features to look for:

Two-button recording and dubbing. A single Record button makes it too easy to start recording or dubbing accidentally.

Record-mute. This feature inserts a silence between selections when you record continuously, say from a CD or an LP. The silences act as signposts for the Music search and Scan features.

Auto-return or Memory rewind. Both let you cancel a recording and get the tape back to the starting point. Auto-return is easier to use.

Music search. This feature finds a particular selection by looking for the silences between selections. It's helpful for moving quickly from one selection to the next.

Tape counter. Look for one that shows elapsed time in minutes and seconds. A counter that shows how much time is left on the tape is even better.

Autoreverse. This reverses the tape automatically when it reaches the end so you can hear both sides without having to flip the tape. Many dual-deck models can play or record both sides of two tapes in

DIGITAL COMPETITORS TO CASSETTE DECKS

Several digital technologies compete for the space now occupied by conventional tape cassettes. All have great sound. Here's a rundown:

■ The digital compact cassette deck (DCC) offers more compatibility than other digital formats such as digital audio tape (DAT). DCC decks can play conventional cassettes and also record and play digitally. When recording on digital tape, DCC relies on a data-compression process that in essence records only what you hear, ignoring inaudible sounds. In our tests, DCC digital recordings sounded better than any conventional tape deck. DCC decks could create perfect copies of CDs, but copy-protection circuitry prevents digital copying of those copies. Philips, DCC's developer, is still promoting the product in European markets, but DCC sales in the U.S. have all but stalled.

■ The Minidisc, or MD, developed by Sony, is the first consumer-oriented compact-disc medium that can both record and play like a conventional cassette tape. MD uses data-compression technology similar to that used on DCC. Its 2½-inch discs play for up to 74 minutes. Sound is near CD in quality. Players provide nearly instant access to tracks, random play, and other features typical of CD players. The Minidisc also incorporates copy-protection circuitry. Portable, compact-sized, and console recorders sell for about $600 and up (for models that record).

■ Digital audio tape decks also offer CD-quality sound. Their cassettes are similar to miniature VCR cassettes. But since DAT decks can't play conventional cassettes, a DAT owner is faced with the prospect of building a new tape library from scratch. Like DCC and MD, DAT tape decks incorporate copy-protection circuits. Component-sized decks sell for about $600 to $800; portable models, about $600.

■ Recordable compact-disc players (CD-R) can produce discs playable on any standard CD player. Decks currently cost about $2000 but will probably drop in price over the next few years.

Promising as these new technologies seem, they won't send cassette tape the way of the LP record overnight. If you already have an extensive collection of tapes, stay with a conventional tape deck. If you choose the right deck, you won't sacrifice much in the way of performance.

HOW TO BUY CASSETTE TAPE

Audio cassettes haven't changed significantly in years. That's a good thing, because they're one of the biggest bargains in the world of electronics—inexpensive, yet high performing.

Tapes differ in playing time—C-60, C-90, and so forth. A C-90 tape plays 45 minutes per side. Tapes longer than C-90, such as C-120, haven't performed well in our tests.

Tapes differ in their type of coating and the strength of the signal—known as the bias—needed for a tape deck to control distortion.

Here are the three types:

Type I ("normal"). This is the oldest type of tape sold, the lowest quality and, about $1 to $3 per tape, the lowest priced. It's best suited for recording speech, undemanding music, or anything that will be played back under less than ideal conditions, such as in a small-speaker boom box.

Type II ("high bias"). This type minimizes tape hiss and handles high frequencies better than Type I. Use it to record FM broadcasts, to make tapes for the car from CDs, or to make tapes for a personal tape player. Expect to pay $2 to $5 per cassette.

Type IV ("metal"). This is the highest grade of cassette tape. Not all decks can take advantage of its capabilities when recording, but all decks should be able to play back this kind of recorded tape. Type IV is best suited for demanding applications, such as a live concert or music from a compact disc. Prices range from about $3 to as much as $7 per tape. For this type of tape, don't assume that the highest-priced brand is the best. In our tests, price did not correlate with quality.

sequence, a feature called Relay play or Relay record.

Quick reverse. This is similar to Autoreverse, but faster.

CD sync. This helps coordinate recording from a CD. It requires using the same-brand CD player and deck. Pushing a button cues up the deck and starts recording the instant the music begins.

Three heads. A deck with three heads doesn't record better than one with two heads, but it's more convenient. The third head lets you monitor a recording as you make it. On machines with bias adjustment, the third head also eases fine-tuning of the bias setting.

Parallel recording. On dual decks, this lets you record the same material onto two cassettes simultaneously.

Intro scan. You can find a desired selection on a tape by moving from song to song, playing the first few seconds of each.

The tests

We check decks for speed accuracy, as well as for flutter, which can make music sound wavery or watery. We measure frequency response—how smoothly and accurately a deck responds to sounds. We also measure dynamic range—the span between the loudest and the softest sound a unit records accurately.

Buying advice

If you frequently make tape-to-tape copies or like listening to long stretches of background music, choose a dual-deck model. Consider a single-deck model if you do a lot of serious recording at home.

The features you need depend on how you'll use the deck: If you intend to make a lot of tapes, look for a single deck with three heads, adjustable bias control, and Dolby B and C noise-suppression circuitry. You may want to pay extra for Dolby S circuitry as well.

If you want to tape CDs, look for Auto-edit or Sync-edit features.

For playing long periods of uninterrupted music, choose a dual deck with such features as Auto-reverse and Music search.

If you'll be making live recordings, look for a deck with a microphone jack—two jacks to record in stereo.

Mass-market brands like Sony and Technics can represent excellent value. A high-priced audiophile brand won't necessarily perform any better.

Boom boxes

▶ Ratings on page 64.

The boom box combines an AM/FM stereo radio, one or two cassette decks, and, quite often, a CD player in a single portable package.

Few boom boxes, particularly small ones, can reproduce the hi-fi sound of a decent component-based stereo system. But they can be just the thing for taking music to the beach, for use as a table radio, or for equipping a dorm room with an inexpensive source of music.

The Sony brand leads sales, sharing the market with some 30 brands.

The choices

The limiting factor in a box's sound quality is the size of the loudspeakers. Small boxes, which weigh 5 or 10 pounds, normally have small, nondetachable speakers that produce only so-so sound. Small boxes cost about $50 to $150.

Large boom boxes, which can weigh twice as much, often come with good-sized speakers that can be detached and spread apart for a better stereo effect. Their sound quality can be quite good, though not on a par with a decent component system. Most are priced between $150 and $250.

Features and conveniences

More money buys more features, but the extras don't necessarily contribute to sound quality.

Here's a rundown on what you'll find:

Batteries. All boom boxes use either house current or battery power. Boxes with a CD player typically take eight D cells. With alkaline batteries, you may get as many as 65 hours of radio listening, 45 hours of tape play, or 18 hours of CD play—or as little as half those times.

Clock. This built-in timer turns the unit off or on at a set time.

Extra bass. This bass-boosting switch or knob puts the boom in the box.

FM mono switch. This helpful feature lets you switch the radio to monophonic mode to improve the reception of a weak FM station.

Graphic equalizer. This fancy tone control lets you adjust bass, mid-range, and treble with slider switches for several bands of frequencies.

Inputs/outputs. Auxiliary inputs let you connect external sound sources, such as a tape deck or CD player, and use the boom box's amplifier and speakers. Some have a CD output, allowing you to pipe the box's CD player through a component stereo system.

Most models have a headphone jack so you can listen without disturbing others. Some have an input for an external microphone, so you can record live sounds onto the box's tape deck.

Surround sound. This top-of-the-line feature is supposed to make music seem more life-like. You need to hook up extra loudspeakers to take full advantage of it.

Tuning and presets. Boxes usually have a manual knob-and-pointer to tune the radio. A digital tuner that locks in a station and displays its frequency is better. Presets are instant-tuning buttons like a car radio's that you set for individual station frequencies.

CD features. Among helpful features for using the CD player is program memory. It lets you select the order of tracks you'll hear. A remote control lets you start, stop, and even scan the disc. Repeat disc lets you play a disc over and over.

Tape features. Boxes with dual cassettes let you listen to two tapes end-to-end, or copy one tape to another at faster-than-normal speed. If the box has Auto relay play, you can set it to start the second tape when the first one ends. Autoreverse plays the flip side of a tape when the first side is finished. Auto-stop automatically stops the tape drive when the cassette is finished. Full auto stop shuts off the drive in fast forward and rewind modes as well. Cue/review lets you listen while fast-forwarding or rewinding to find a particular point on the tape.

Synchro-start. When you want to tape off a CD, this lets you start the CD when you hit the deck's Record button.

The tests

We subject boom boxes to a series of laboratory tests similar to those we use for individual components such as CD players, receivers, speakers, and the like. We load the CD player with slightly defective discs so we can see how it copes with dirty or scratched discs. We also gauge how well it plays when it's jarred or knocked. With the tape deck, we check for flutter—a wavering of pitch—and background hiss. We see how well the FM tuner handles weak signals and how well it rejects interference from adjacent channels.

Buying advice

Sound quality and portability don't go hand-in-hand. Small, portable boxes lack the muscle to reproduce sound that is faithful to the original.

How to use the Ratings in the Buying Guide

- Read the brand-name recommendations for information on specific models.
- Note how the rated products are listed—in order of performance and convenience, price, or alphabetically.
- Look to the overall score to get the big picture in performance. Notes on features and performance for individual models are listed in the Comments or Details part of the Ratings.
- Note that models similar to the tested models, when they exist, are indicated in the Comments or Details. A model marked Ⓓ has been discontinued. A model marked Ⓢ is a successor to the tested model, according to the manufacturer, and is noted in Comments or Details. Features, though, may vary.
- Call the manufacturer if you have trouble finding a product. See page 342.
- To find our last full report on a subject, check the eight-year index, page 346.

RATINGS RECEIVERS

▶ **See report, page 40.** Last time rated in Consumer Reports: March 1995.

Brand-name recommendations: Among the basic receivers, the Yamaha RX-485, $285, had the best overall performance. Among low-priced Dolby Surround receivers, the top-rated Technics SA-GX470 (or its successor, SX-GX490), $270, was especially convenient to use.

For the typical receiver, expect: ■ Excellent amplifier performance, good to excellent FM tuner performance. ■ Enough power to produce loud, undistorted sound in a large room. Dolby Surround models have the amplifiers to drive additional speakers. ■ Digital FM and AM tuning, with 20 to 40 presets; buttons that let you scan for a station, step up or down a station at a time, or key in a station's frequency directly. ■ Dolby Surround-Sound, Dolby 3 stereo, and at least 1 other digital signal processing mode (in Dolby Surround models). ■ Inputs for turntable, CD player, and at least 1 more audio component. Dolby Surround models add video inputs and outputs. ■ Accommodation for 2 audio recording decks, 1 with monitoring. ■ At least 1 AC outlet, controlled by the receiver, that components can be plugged into. ■ A remote control that operates other same-brand components.

Notes on the table: Price is the estimated average, based on a national survey. **Overall score** is based primarily on tuner performance and convenience judgments. **FM tuner** judgments consider sensitivity, the ability to ignore interference from electrical appliances and aircraft transmissions, and selectivity, the ability to ignore other stations on the same frequency. **Amplifier power**, in watts per speaker channel, lists our measurements of the output of the main stereo channels at 8 and 6 ohms' impedance and the output of all channels at 8 ohms in the Dolby Surround mode. Models similar to those we tested are noted in Details; features may vary. **Model availability:** [D] means model is discontinued. [S] means model is replaced, according to the manufacturer; successor model is noted in Details. New model was not tested; it may or may not perform similarly. Features may vary.

Within type, listed in order of performance and convenience

E ⊜ VG ⊖ G ○ F ◒ P ●

Brand and model	Price	Overall score (P F G VG E)	FM tuner	Ease of use	Amplifier power: Main channels 8 ohms/6 ohms	Amplifier power: Dolby Surround
STEREO-ONLY MODELS						
Yamaha RX-485	$285		⊜	⊜	74/85	—
Sherwood RX-4030R, **A BEST BUY** [D]	150		⊜	⊖	73/84	—
Sony STR-D315, **A BEST BUY** [D]	185		⊜	○	110/126	—
Onkyo TX-V940	295		⊖	⊜	118/136	—
Kenwood KR-A5060 [D]	220		○	⊖	119/134	—

Ratings continued ▶

Ratings continued

Brand and model	Price	Overall score (P F G VG E)	FM tuner	Ease of use	Amplifier power: Main channels 8 ohms/6 ohms	Amplifier power: Dolby Surround
LOW-PRICED SURROUND-SOUND MODELS						
Technics SA-GX470 [S]	$270		⊜	⊜	112/128	55/62/20
Yamaha RX-V480 [S]	355		⊜	⊖	74/88	75/84/19
JVC RX-515VTN [S]	265		⊜	○	91/104	73/70/33
Sherwood RV-5030R, **A BEST BUY** [S]	245		⊜	⊖	89/102	69/81/27
Onkyo TX-SV414PRO	345		⊖	⊖	73/112	74/82/19
Sony STR-D615 [D]	275		⊖	○	110/125	67/73/14
Kenwood KR-V5560 [D]	280		○	⊖	81/94	86/84/23
Radio Shack Optimus STAV-3280 [D]	300		○	○	72/83	55/53/21
Pioneer VSX-453	280		○	○	109/122	70/69/21
MID-PRICED SURROUND-SOUND MODELS						
Onkyo TX-SV515PRO-II [D]	450		⊜	⊖	93/112	75/79/23
Sherwood RV-6030R, **A BEST BUY** [S]	330		⊜	⊖	113/133	74/81/24
Technics SA-GX770 [S]	450		⊖	⊜	139/157	126/126/66
JVC RX-715VTN [S]	345		⊜	○	132/154	84/89/31
Sony STR-D915 [D]	385		⊖	⊜	117/138	78/91/16
Philips FR951	405		⊜	○	117/137	114/61/8
Kenwood KR-V7060 [D]	375		○	⊖	111/131	111/131/39
Radio Shack Optimus STAV-3350	350		⊖	○	111/124	76/69/22
Pioneer VSX-D503S [D]	360		○	○	121/139	89/84/20

MODEL DETAILS

Want to know more about a rated model? They're listed here alphabetically.

JVC RX-515VTN [S] — Loudness switch; no key-in tuning. Remote speakers connected in series with main speakers when both pairs are used, which may reduce their accuracy. No 300-ohm FM antenna input, but can use adapter. **Successor:** RX-517VTN.

JVC RX-715VTN [S] — Loudness switch; no key-in tuning. Remote speakers connected in series with main speakers when both pairs are used, which may reduce their accuracy. Output for ext. subwoofer amplifier. No 300-ohm FM antenna input, but can use adapter. **Successor:** RX-717VTN.

Kenwood KR-A5060 [D] — Loudness switch. Can be used with 4-ohm speakers.

Kenwood KR-V5560 [D] — Loudness switch; tone bypass. Knob for source selector. No digital signal processing mode other than Dolby Surround. Can't use remote speakers in Dolby Surround mode.

Kenwood KR-V7060 [D] — Loudness switch; tone bypass; knob source selector. Can't use remote speakers in Dolby Surround mode. Can be used with 4-ohm speakers.

Onkyo TX-SV414PRO	Loudness switch; preset scan. No digital signal processing mode other than Dolby Surround. No Dolby 3 stereo. Can't use remote speakers in Dolby Surround mode. Output for ext. subwoofer amplifier.
Onkyo TX-SV515PRO-II Ⓓ	Loudness switch; preset scan. No Dolby 3 stereo. Can't use remote speakers in Dolby Surround mode. Multiroom option; remote speakers can be controlled from another room. Multisource option; allows 2 sources to be played and controlled from different rooms. Output for ext. subwoofer amplifier.
Onkyo TX-V940	Loudness switch. Can be used with 4-ohm speakers.
Philips FR951	Bass boost; tone bypass; front A/V selector; knob source selector. Remote speakers connected in series with main speakers when both pairs are used, which may reduce their accuracy. Multiroom option; remote speakers can be controlled from another room. No 300-ohm FM antenna input, but can use adapter. **Similar:** FR931.
Pioneer VSX-453	Bass boost. No digital signal processing mode other than Dolby Surround. Remote speakers connected in series with main speakers when both pairs are used, which may reduce their accuracy. Multiroom option; remote speakers can be controlled from another room. No 300-ohm FM antenna input, but can use adapter.
Pioneer VSX-D503S Ⓓ	Bass boost. Remote speakers connected in series with main speakers when both pairs are used, which may reduce their accuracy. Multiroom option; remote speakers can be controlled from another room. Can store several setups (source, mode, volume) in memory. Remote can be programmed to "learn" codes from other manufacturers' remotes. No 300-ohm FM antenna input, but can use adapter.
Radio Shack Optimus STAV-3280 Ⓓ	Bass boost; preset scan. Remote speakers connected in series with main speakers when both pairs are used, which may reduce their accuracy. No 300-ohm FM antenna input, but can use adapter.
Radio Shack Optimus STAV-3350	Bass boost; preset scan. Remote speakers connected in series with main speakers when both pairs are used, which may reduce their accuracy. Multiroom option; remote speakers can be controlled from another room. No 300-ohm FM antenna input, but can use adapter.
Sherwood RV-5030R, **A BEST BUY** Ⓢ	Loudness switch; preset scan; front A/V input; no key-in tuning. Remote speakers connected in series with main speakers when both pairs are used, which may reduce their accuracy. Multiroom option; remote speakers can be controlled from another room. **Successor:** RV-5050R.
Sherwood RV-6030R, **A BEST BUY** Ⓢ	Loudness switch; tone bypass; preset scan; front A/V input; no key-in tuning. Remote speakers connected in series with main speakers when both pairs are used, which may reduce their accuracy. Multiroom option; remote speakers can be controlled from another room. No 300-ohm FM antenna input, but can use adapter. **Successor:** RV-5050R.
Sherwood RX-4030R, **A BEST BUY** Ⓓ	Loudness switch; preset scan; no key-in tuning. Remote speakers connected in series with main speakers when both pairs are used, which may reduce their accuracy. Can be used with 4-ohm speakers.
Sony STR-D315, **A BEST BUY** Ⓓ	Bass boost switch. Remote speakers connected in series with main speakers when both pairs are used, which may reduce their accuracy. No connection for remote control of tape deck.

Ratings continued ▸

Ratings continued

Sony STR-D615 Ⓓ	Bass boost; no tape monitor. Remote speakers connected in series with main speakers when both pairs are used, which may reduce their accuracy. No connection for remote control of tape deck.
Sony STR-D915 Ⓓ	Bass boost; tone bypass; front A/V input. Remote speakers connected in series with main speakers when both pairs are used, which may reduce their accuracy. Can store several tone settings in memory. No connection for remote control of tape deck. No 300-ohm FM antenna input, but can use adapter. Can be used with 4-ohm speakers.
Technics SA-GX470 Ⓢ	No digital signal processing mode other than Dolby Surround. Can't use remote speakers in Dolby Surround mode. No 300-ohm FM antenna input, but can use adapter. **Successor:** SA-GX490.
Technics SA-GX770 Ⓢ	Loudness switch; front A/V input. No digital signal processing mode other than Dolby Surround. Can't use remote speakers in Dolby Surround mode. Output for ext. subwoofer amplifier. No 300-ohm FM antenna input, but can use adapter. Can be used with 4-ohm speakers. **Successor:** SA-GX790.
Yamaha RX-485	Variable loudness; tone bypass; no key-in tuning. Better than most at resisting interference from a station very close in frequency. No 300-ohm FM antenna input, but can use adapter. **Similar:** RX-385.
Yamaha RX-V480 Ⓢ	No key-in tuning. No Dolby 3 stereo. Better than most at resisting interference from a station very close in frequency. No connection for remote control of tape deck. No 300-ohm FM antenna input, but can use adapter. **Successor:** RX-V490.

HOW WE TEST AUDIO & VIDEO GEAR

All electronic products undergo a battery of tests, with measurements made by computers and lab instruments, as well as human eyes and ears.

The centerpiece of our video testing is picture-quality assessment. Over the course of several weeks, a trained panel of viewers compares picture quality of TV sets, VCR, or camcorders with the models tested side-by-side. The panel looks at still and moving images, judging picture clarity, color fidelity, and contrast.

Other tests, particularly those measuring sound quality, have been automated. A computer-directed system, running custom software written by our engineers, allows us to judge how well a product converts an input signal into an output signal and to evaluate the quality of the output. It lets engineers quickly choose a test, controls signals to and from the product being tested, and records and computes results.

Computer-assisted testing is used in measuring picture and sound performance in TV sets, VCRs, and stereo gear.

We also use a computer to measure speaker accuracy in an echo-free chamber. Each speaker is mounted on a computer-controlled platform near a laboratory microphone on a rotating arm. By rotating the speaker and microphone, engineers sample output from virtually every angle. As a reality check, we audition audio gear in our listening room, a 14x23-foot furnished space.

RATINGS MID-PRICED SPEAKERS

See report, page 43. Last time rated in Consumer Reports: March 1995.

Brand-name recommendations: Any of the top eight models in the Ratings would be a good choice for a top-quality sound system. See page 58 for lower-priced models that we recommend.

For the typical speaker in this class, expect: ■ Sound that's at least good, often superior. ■ Composite or laminate cabinet, either black or wood grain. ■ Removable grille. ■ Connectors that can take stripped wires or banana plugs.

Notes on the table: Price is the estimated average, based on a national survey. * means price paid. **Overall score** is based mainly on accuracy of the frequency response. A difference of 8 points or less is not significant. **Accuracy** shows how well the speaker reproduces sound with and without corrections. **Bass handling** gauges ability to reproduce lowest-frequency tones without distortion. The **best sound** is the tone-control adjustment, in decibels, that produced the highest accuracy. **Impedance,** in ohms, measures how much current demand a speaker puts on a receiver. Most speakers mate well with most receivers. **Min. power,** in watts, is our estimate of the receiver power needed to play music loudly and with a full range of frequencies in a medium-sized room. **Model availability:** Ⓓ means model is discontinued.

Within type, listed in order of frequency response and bass-handling ability

E VG G F P

Brand and model	Price	Overall score (P F G VG E)	Accuracy	Bass	Best sound	Impedance	Min. power
					BASS/TREBLE	MFR./CU	
Phase Technology 7T 37x10x12¼ in., 44 lb.	$600		91/91	E	0/0	8/6	25
RDL F-1 24¾x11x10½ in., 29 lb.	580		92/92	VG	0/0	8/7	41
Bose Acoustimass 5 Series II (satellite) 14x7½x19 in., 19 lb. 6½x3x5 in., 2 lb.	725		88/91	E	+2/+2	-/6	26
Signet SL-280 B/U 25x9¾x12 in., 34 lb.	700		90/91	G	0/+1	8/8	24
Yamaha NS-A325/YST-SW120 (satellite) 11¼x8½x15¾ in., 34 lb. 8x4¾x3¾ in., 3 lb.	500		90/91	VG	0/+1	6/7	27
Miller & Kreisel SX-7/VX-7 (satellite) 13¾x10x9¼ in., 22 lb. 7x4½x4¼ in., 6 lb.	745		89/89	G	0/+1	4/4	22
Boston Acoustics SubSat 7 (satellite) 15¾x9x19¾ in., 26 lb. 8½x5x4½ in., 5 lb.	750		86/86	VG	-1/0	8/4	51

Ratings continued

Ratings continued

Brand and model	Price	Overall score (P F G VG E)	Accuracy	Bass	Best sound (BASS/TREBLE)	Impedance (MFR./CU)	Min. power
Sony SS-TL4 [D] 40¼x9½x10½ in., 40 lb.	$435		83/90	○	+1/+5	8/6	29
Allison AL120 24½x11¼x10¾ in., 31 lb.	400		83/88	○	+2/+4	6/4	47
Cambridge Soundworks New Ensemble 11¾x21x4½ in., 16 lb. 8x5¼x4 in., 5 lb.	549		87/87	⊖	0/0	6/4	40
Polk Audio S10 30x12½x10¼ in., 29 lb.	600		80/89	⊖	-2/+3	8/4	21
Cerwin Vega DX-5 31¼x15x10¾ in., 41 lb.	500		81/83	⊜	-1/+1	8/7	6
NHT Super Zero/SW1P (satellite) 16x11¾x11¾ in., 23 lb. 6x5½x5 in., 6 lb.	650		83/90	⊖	+1/+5	8/7	39
DCM TF-400 Series Two 37¾x14¾x7 in., 36 lb.	500		79/85	○	-4/+2	6/4	23
Advent Heritage 37¾x10¾x13¾ in., 46 lb.	660		79/85	○	-4/+1	8/3	26
Infinity RS 525 32¼x9½x12¼ in., 35 lb.	575		76/86	○	-2/+4	6/4	21
Paradigm 7seMk3 33¾x8¼x14¼ in., 38 lb.	575		76/85	⊖	-2/+3	6/4	29
Altec Lansing 100 40½x10¼x10¾ in., 41 lb.	*500		74/81	⊖	-4/+3	8/3	27

SPEAKERS FOR BEST VALUE

Here, listed by type and price, are lower-priced models that rated well in 1994 and are still on the market. Surround rear and conventional speakers are sold in pairs, satellites as a three-piece system. Bass module speakers are sold singly. Prices are estimated national averages.

Brand and model	Type	Price
Sony SS-U-610	Conventional	$280
Infinity RS 325	Conventional	300
Cerwin-Vega L-7B	Conventional	345
Allison AL110	Conventional	360
Bose 301 Series III	Conventional	320
DCM CX-17	Conventional	365
Boston Acoustics HD5	Surround	$150
Bose 101 Music Monitor	Surround	200
Design Acoustics PS-CV/55	Surround/center*[1]	120
Bose Acoustimass 3 Series II	Satellite	400
Boston Acoustics SubSat6 Series II	Satellite	450
Design Acoustics PS-SW	Bass module	340

[1] *Or satellite when combined with Design Acoustics PS-SW.*

RATINGS CD PLAYERS

▶ **See report, page 44.** Last time rated in Consumer Reports: March 1995.

Brand-name recommendations: The four carousel models rated excellent deserve first consideration. All are priced around $250. If you have the money and the CD collection, either the 100-disc Sony CDP-CX151, $655, or JVC XL-MC100, $700, should serve. The Sony is easier to load and unload. The portable Sony D-131, $95, is better in many respects than the models that cost more; we rated it A Best Buy. Single-play models cost about $150. The Technics and Pioneer were best.

For the typical player, expect: ■ Excellent sound quality. ■ Remote control. ■ Play, Pause, Stop, Track-select, Program functions, and Repeat. ■ Audible fast-scanning. ■ Shuffle mode, for random play. ■ On changers, a carousel that holds 5 discs or a magazine that holds 6. ■ On carousel models, ability to change discs not currently playing. ■ 3- to 7-second interval before a disc starts playing; 8 to 14 seconds to change discs. **Choices you'll have to make:** ■ Portable or full-sized player. ■ Single-or multi-disc changer. Among multi-disc units: carousel, magazine, or 100-disc players.

Notes on the table: Price is the estimated average, based on a national survey. * means price paid. **Overall score** is based on performance, features, and convenience. Sound quality, excellent on all models, is not scored. **Error correction** shows how well a player compensates for dirty or scratched discs. **Bump resistance** is how well the player handles jarring or, for portables, being carried around. Models similar to those we tested are noted in Details; features may vary. **Model availability:** [D] means model is discontinued. [S] means model is replaced, according to the manufacturer; successor model is noted in Details. New model was not tested; it may or may not perform similarly. Features may vary.

Within type, listed mainly in order of performance

E VG G F P

Brand and model	Price	Overall score (P F G VG E)	Performance: Error correc.	Performance: Bump resist.	Ease of use	Taping ease
CAROUSEL CHANGERS						
Onkyo DX-C211 [S]	$270		E	F	G	F
Sony CDP-C445	230		G	G	E	E
Denon DCM-340	260		E	F	G	F
Technics SL-PD1000 [S]	260		VG	VG	VG	G
Philips CDC935 [S]	240		VG	E	VG	F
Kenwood DP-R6060 [S]	250		G	F	VG	VG
Marantz CC-45	*300		G	E	G	F
Yamaha CDC-645 [S]	270		G	F	VG	G

Ratings continued ▶

Ratings continued

Brand and model	Price	Overall score	Performance		Ease of use	Taping ease
		P F G VG E	ERROR CORREC.	BUMP RESIST.		
CAROUSEL CHANGERS *continued*						
Teac PD-D900 [D]	$155		○	○	◓	◒
Fisher DAC-2403 [S]	265		○	◓	○	◓
MAGAZINE CHANGERS						
JVC XL-M415TN [D]	230		◓	○	○	⊜
Optimus CD-7300 (Radio Shack)	250		○	○	◓	○
Pioneer PD-M703	240		○	◒	◓	○
SINGLE PLAY						
Technics SL-PG440 [S]	140		◓	○	◓	⊜
Pioneer PD-203 [D]	150		◓	○	◓	◓
JVC XL-V261TN	155		○	◓	◓	◓
Sony CDP-315	130		○	◒	◓	○
100 DISC CHANGERS						
Sony CDP-CX151	655		◓	◓	◓	◒
JVC XL-MC100	700		◓	◓	◓	◒
Pioneer PD-F100 [S]	560		○	○	○	◒
PORTABLES						
Panasonic SL-S180 [S]	130		◓	⊜	◒	◒
Sony D-131, **A BEST BUY** [S]	95		◓	○	◒	◒
Sony D-235CK	180		◓	◒	◒	◒
Panasonic SL-S351C [S]	180		○	◒	◒	◒

MODEL DETAILS

Want to know more about a rated model? They're listed here alphabetically.

Denon DCM-340	**Similar:** DCM-460.
Fisher DAC-2403 [S]	Music-sampling function. Also has single-play drawer. Inserts short silence between tracks, an aid to taping. Jukebox-type carousel holds 24 discs. **Successor:** DAC-2415.
JVC XL-M415TN [D]	Music-sampling function. No Scan function on remote. Also has single-play drawer. Can program by deleting tracks.
JVC XL-MC100	Music-sampling function. Headphone jack with vol. control. Can program by deleting tracks.
JVC XL-V261TN	Headphone jack with vol. control. Music-peak finder. **Similar:** XL-V161TN.

Kenwood DP-R6060 [S]	Headphone jack with vol. control. Inserts short silence between tracks, an aid to taping. **Successor:** DP-R6070.
Marantz CC-45	Music-sampling function. Music-peak finder. Inserts short silence between tracks, an aid to taping. Can fade in and out. **Similar:** CC-65.
Onkyo DX-C211 [S]	Carousel holds six discs. **Successor:** DX-C220.
Optimus CD-7300 (Radio Shack)	Music-sampling function. Headphone jack with vol. control. Can program by deleting tracks. Can fade in and out.
Panasonic SL-S180 [S]	Headphone jack with vol. control. **Successor:** SL-S190.
Panasonic SL-S351C [S]	Music-sampling function. Headphone jack with vol. control. **Successor:** SL-S291C.
Philips CDC935 [S]	Music-sampling function. Headphone jack with vol. control. No Scan function on remote. Inserts short silence between tracks, an aid to taping. Pressing Pause twice resets track to beginning. **Successor:** CDC936.
Pioneer PD-203 [D]	Music-sampling function. Headphone jack with vol. control. Music-peak finder.
Pioneer PD-F100 [S]	Inserts short silence between tracks, an aid to taping. **Successor:** PD-F904.
Pioneer PD-M703	Music-sampling function. Headphone jack with vol. control. No Scan function on remote. Can program by deleting tracks. **Similar:** PO-M603.
Sony CDP-315	Music-sampling function. Headphone jack with vol. control. Music-peak finder. Can fade in and out. **Similar:** CDP-215.
Sony CDP-C445	Music-sampling function. Headphone jack with vol. control. Music-peak finder. Can program by deleting tracks. Can fade in and out. **Similar:** CDP-C545.
Sony CDP-CX151	Music-sampling function. Can program by deleting tracks. **Similar:** CDP-CX100.
Sony D-131, **A BEST BUY** [S]	Music-sampling function. Headphone jack with vol. control. **Successor:** D-141.
Sony D-235CK	Headphone jack with vol. control. **Similar:** D-231.
Teac PD-D900 [D]	Music-sampling function. Headphone jack with vol. control.
Technics SL-PD1000 [S]	Music-sampling function. Inserts short silence between tracks, an aid to taping. Can program by deleting tracks. Memory buffer, shortens silence between discs. **Successor:** SL-PD1010.
Technics SL-PG440 [S]	Headphone jack with vol. control. Music-peak finder. Inserts short silence between tracks, an aid to taping. Can fade in and out. **Successor:** SL-PG450.
Yamaha CDC-645 [S]	Music-sampling function. Headphone jack with vol. control. Also has single-play drawer. **Successor:** CDC-655.

RATINGS CASSETTE DECKS

▶ **See report, page 47.** Last time rated in Consumer Reports: March 1995.

Brand-name recommendations: Your best choice among dual-deck models is the Sony TC-WR645S deck. At $255, we judged it A Best Buy since it performed as well as the top-rated single deck. If you want the additional features of a dual-record deck, consider the Technics RS-TR979, $300. For serious recording at home, look first at a single-deck machine such as the Sony TC-K615S, $305, or the JVC TD-V661, $310. The Aiwa AD-F850, $280, is also a worthy performer.

For the typical deck in this class, expect: ■ Dolby B and C noise-reduction circuitry. ■ Ability to recognize and record on all types of tape. ■ Light-touch keys. ■ Digital display that includes counter(s) of time or digit type and recording level meters. ■ Digit or time counter or both. ■ Cable-link remote. ■ CD sync. ■ Record-mute. ■ Music search. ■ Manual or auto bias control. ■ FM multiplex noise filter. **For dual decks, expect:** ■ Autoreverse on both decks. ■ Relay playback. ■ Dubbing at normal and double speed. ■ Dual-record capability. **For single decks, expect:** ■ Tape monitor to check recording level. ■ Manual tape bias adjustment. **A choice you'll have to make:** ■ Single or dual deck.

Notes on the table: Price is the estimated average, based on a national survey. * means price paid. **Flutter** is how free the decks were from a wavery sound of tape-speed irregularities. **Overall accuracy** shows how accurately a deck reproduced the frequency content and level of a signal when recording and playing, and (in parentheses) dubbing. **Model availability:** D means model is discontinued. S means model is replaced, according to the manufacturer; successor model is noted in Details. New model was not tested; it may or may not perform similarly. Features may vary.

Listed in order of performance and convenience

E ⊜ VG ⊖ G ○ F ◒ P ●

Brand and model	Price	Overall score (P F G VG E)	Flutter	Overall accuracy	Ease of use	Controls
DUAL DECKS						
Sony TC-WR645S 1 S **A BEST BUY**	$255		⊖	⊜ (⊜)	⊜	⊖
Technics RS-TR979 D	*300		⊖	⊜ (⊖)	⊜	○
Onkyo TA-RW414 S	290		⊖	⊜ (⊜)	◒	◒
Pioneer CT-W703RS S	255		○	○ (○)	○	○
Aiwa AD-WX727 1	230		⊖	⊜ (⊖)	○	○
Kenwood KX-W8060 S	290		⊖	○ (●)	⊜	⊜
Teac W-800R D	260		○	⊖ (○)	○	⊖
Optimus SCT-55 1 D	250		○	⊖ (⊖)	◒	○
Yamaha KX-W382 1	285		○	○ (⊖)	●	●

Brand and model	Price	Overall score (P F G VG E)	Flutter	Overall accuracy	Ease of use	Controls
DUAL DECKS *continued*						
Sherwood DD-6030C [D]	$270		○	○ (○)	○	○
SINGLE DECKS						
Sony TC-K615S	365		⊖	⊜	⊖	⊜
JVC TD-V661	310		⊜	⊜	○	⊜
Aiwa AD-F850	280		⊖	⊜	○	⊖
Yamaha KX-580	350		○	⊜	◒	◒
Teac V-1010 [D]	300		⊖	⊖	◒	⊖
Denon DRM-740	360		⊜	⊜	◒	◒
Marantz SD-63	*330		⊖	⊜	◒	○

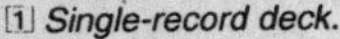
[1] *Single-record deck.*

MODEL DETAILS

Want to know more about a rated model? They're listed here alphabetically.

Aiwa AD-F850	Tape monitor lets you check recording quality.
Aiwa AD-WX727	No bias control. Can pause to change source tape when dubbing. One button starts dubbing. Can skip blank portions during playback. Intro scan.
Denon DRM-740	Tape monitor lets you check recording quality.
JVC TD-V661	Backlight helps you see tape position. Tape monitor lets you check recording quality. Headphone vol. control.
Kenwood KX-W8060 [S]	Has track repeat. One-button record. One button starts dubbing. Can skip blank portions during playback. Intro scan. **Successor:** KX-W8070S.
Marantz SD-63	Tape monitor lets you check recording quality.
Onkyo TA-RW414 [S]	No bias control. Can pause to change source tape when dubbing. One button starts dubbing. **Successor:** TA-RW414.
Optimus SCT-55 [D]	No bias control. Can pause to change source tape when dubbing. One button starts dubbing. Can skip blank portions during playback.
Pioneer CT-W703RS [S]	One button starts dubbing. Separate control for microphone recording-level. Can skip blank portions during playback. Has mono microphone input. **Successor:** CT-W704RS.
Sherwood DD-6030C [D]	No bias control. Can pause to change source tape when dubbing. One button starts dubbing or relay or parallel recording. Has mono microphone input.
Sony TC-K615S	Opt. remote. Tape monitor lets you check recording quality.
Sony TC-WR645S, **A BEST BUY** [S]	Has track repeat. Opt. remote. Can pause to change source tape when dubbing. **Successor:** TC-WR665S.
Teac V-1010 [D]	No music search. Tape monitor lets you check recording quality. Headphone vol. control. Motor runs continuously while power is on.

Ratings continued ▶

Ratings continued

Teac W-800R Ⓓ	No bias control. Can pause to change source tape when dubbing. One button starts dubbing or relay or parallel recording. Can skip blank portions during playback. Intro scan. Has mono microphone input.
Technics RS-TR979 Ⓓ	Can pause to change source tape when dubbing.
Yamaha KX-580	Has track and segment repeat. Intro scan. Headphone vol. control.
Yamaha KX-W382	No bias control. Opt. remote. Can pause to change source tape when dubbing. One button starts dubbing. Both decks share function keys, confusing.

RATINGS BOOM BOXES

▶ **See report, page 51.** Last time rated in Consumer Reports: December 1994.

Brand-name recommendations: The best of the big boxes were the Aiwa CA-DW550, $230, and the Panasonic RX-DT610, $210. Both have been replaced by successor models—the Aiwa CA-DW600 and the Panasonic RX-DT650. Several other boom boxes were nearly as good. Look for the features you want and a price you can handle. The best of the small boxes was the Panasonic RX-DS15, and its successor RX-DT30, $125.

For the typical boom box, expect: ■ AM/FM stereo radio. ■ Programmable CD player. ■ 2 cassette decks. ■ At least 2 speaker drivers. ■ Ability to record from radio or CD player. ■ AC power cord. ■ Ability to operate on batteries, generally 8 D cells. ■ Built-in telescoping antenna that pivots. ■ No remote control. ■ No tuner presets.

Notes on the table: Price is the estimated average, based on a national survey. * indicates catalog price. **Weight** is in lbs. and includes batteries. **Sound quality** rates the accuracy of speaker, amplifier, and tone control, and includes test results plus listening judgments by engineers. **FM performance** depends on 3 factors: selectivity, capture ratio (the ability to reject the weaker of 2 stations at the same frequency), and sensitivity. **Model availability:** Ⓓ means model is discontinued. Ⓢ means model is replaced, according to the manufacturer; successor model is noted in Details. New model was not tested; it may or may not perform similarly. Features may vary.

Within types, listed in order of performance and convenience

Better ⟷ Worse: ⊜ ⊖ ○ ◒ ●

Brand and model	Price	Weight	Overall score (P F G VG E)	Sound quality	Ease of use	FM PERFORMANCE	FM SENSITIVITY
LARGE BOOM BOXES							
Aiwa CA-DW550 Ⓢ	$230	19½		⊜	⊜	⊜	⊖
Sharp GX-CD610 Ⓓ	190	17½		⊜	⊜	⊖	⊖
Panasonic RX-DT610 Ⓢ	210	19		⊜	⊜	○	⊜

Brand and model	Price	Weight	Overall score (P F G VG E)	Sound quality	Ease of use	FM PERFORMANCE	FM SENSITIVITY
JVC PC-X130 [D]	$255	19½		⊜	⊜	○	○
Panasonic RX-DT670 [S]	255	22		⊜	⊜	○	⊜
JVC PC-X110	215	18½		⊖	⊜	⊖	⊖
RCA RP-7958 [D]	190	19½		⊜	⊖	⊖	⊖
Magnavox AZ9435 [S]	160	16½		⊜	⊖	⊜	⊜
Fisher PH-D360 [S]	205	20½		⊜	⊖	○	○
Sony CFD-560	190	18½		⊖	⊖	⊜	⊜
Sanyo MCD-S860 [S]	150	15½		⊜	⊖	◒	○
SMALL BOOM BOXES							
Panasonic RX-DS15 [S]	125	10½		◒	⊜	⊜	⊜
JVC RC-Q50 [D]	165	10		◒	⊜	⊖	⊖
Aiwa CSD-EX30u [D]	125	8½		◒	⊜	⊖	⊜
Sony CFD-110	150	12		◒	○	⊖	⊖
RCA RP-7964 [D]	125	12½		◒	⊜	⊖	⊖
Sanyo MCD-Z43 [S]	140	11½		○	○	⊜	⊖
Fisher PHDS220 [S]	135	12½		◒	○	⊖	○
Sharp WQ-CH600 [S]	165	16½		◒	⊖	⊜	⊖
Sony CFD-12 [S]	110	11		◒	○	◒	◒
Radio Shack CD-3309 [D]	*150	12½		◒	⊖	◒	○
Koss HG900 [S]	110	14½		◒	◒	○	◒

MODEL DETAILS

Want to know more about a rated model? They're listed here alphabetically.

Aiwa CA-DW550 [S]	Built-in digital clock; auxiliary input jacks; input for ext. microphone; full auto-stop. Remote lacks vol. control. Tuner presets. **Successor:** CA-DW600.
Aiwa CSD-EX30u [D]	1 tape deck.
Fisher PHD360 [S]	CD display shows only track number; 1 deck has autoreverse; input for ext. microphone. **Successor:** PHO560.
Fisher PHDS220 [S]	Worse than average at playing bad discs. **Successor:** PHDS55.
JVC PC-X110	Lacks in-use light; has built-in clock/timer; remote; full auto-stop. Tuner presets.
JVC PC-X130 [D]	Built-in clock/timer; remote; full auto-stop. Tuner presets.
JVC RC-Q50 [D]	Built-in clock/timer; remote; full auto-stop; uses 6 D batteries. Tuner presets. 1 tape deck.
Koss HG900 [S]	CD lacks Scan. **Successor:** HG910.

Ratings continued ▶

Ratings continued

Magnavox AZ9435 [S]	Input for ext. microphone; opt. "power stick" (rechargeable batteries); full auto-stop. **Successor:** AZ904017.
Panasonic RX-DS15 [S]	Deck has Cue/review; full auto-stop. 1 tape deck. **Successor:** RX-DT30.
Panasonic RX-DT610 [S]	Lacks in-use light; has CD output jacks; decks have Cue/review; full auto-stop; uses 10 D batteries. Tuner presets. **Successor:** RX-DT650.
Panasonic RX-DT670 [S]	Decks have Cue/review; full auto-stop; uses 10 D batteries. Tuner presets. **Successor:** RX-DT690.
Radio Shack CD-3309 [D]	—
RCA RP-7958 [D]	CD output jacks; 1 deck has autoreverse; input for ext. microphone; remote.
RCA RP-7964 [D]	CD output jacks; deck has autoreverse; input for ext. microphone. 1 tape deck.
Sanyo MCD-S860 [S]	Lacks FM stereo light; CD display shows only track number; one deck has autoreverse; input for ext. microphone. **Successor:** MCDS980.
Sanyo MCD-Z43 [S]	Lacks in-use light, FM stereo light, FM mono switch, and relay play; CD display shows only track number; 1 deck has autoreverse. Remote lacks vol. control. Worse than average at playing bad discs. **Successor:** MCD-Z57.
Sharp GX-CD610 [D]	Tuner presets.
Sharp WQ-CH600 [S]	Much worse than average at playing bad discs. **Successor:** WQ-CH900.
Sony CFD-110	Lacks FM stereo light and relay play; has input for ext. microphone; uses 6 D batteries.
Sony CFD-12 [S]	Lacks FM mono switch and FM stereo light; has input for ext. microphone. Worse than average tape flutter. 1 tape deck. **Successor:** CFD-17.
Sony CFD-560	Lacks FM mono switch; has input for ext. microphone; remote.

How to use the Buying Guide

- Read the article for general guidance about types, features, and how to buy. There you'll find the market overview, the choices you'll face, and key advice.
- Read the brand-name recommendations for information on specific models.
- Note how the rated products are listed—in order of performance and convenience, price, or alphabetically.
- Look to the overall score to get the big picture in performance. Notes on features and performance for individual models are listed in the Comments or Details part of the Ratings.
- Note that models similar to the tested models, when they exist, are indicated in the Comments or Details. A model marked [D] has been discontinued. A model marked [S] is a successor to the tested model, according to the manufacturer, and is noted in Comments or Details. Features, though, may vary.
- Call the manufacturer if you have trouble finding a product. Manufacturers' phone numbers are listed alphabetically by brand name starting on page 342.
- To find our last full report on a subject, check the eight-year index for the original publication date. You'll find the index in the reference section, page 346.

MAJOR APPLIANCES

You can thank Federal regulation for the current trend toward energy-efficient appliances. Since 1990, refrigerators—traditionally among the most energy-hungry of home appliances—have become about 30 percent more efficient. Washers, dryers, and dishwashers have slowly followed suit, as Federal standards have continued to stiffen. You can estimate energy consumption for yourself by checking the bright-yellow energy-guide label found on many appliances. It provides an estimate of typical yearly energy costs and compares the efficiency of the labeled model with others like it.

The brand names are familiar—the same, perhaps, that your parents owned years ago. Most of the top 25 appliance brands are built by just five companies: General Electric, Whirlpool, Maytag, Amana, and Frigidaire. The GE brands include Hotpoint and RCA, as well as GE. Whirlpool sells Whirlpool, KitchenAid, and Roper. Maytag sells Jenn-Aire, Magic Chef, and Admiral products, as well as Maytag. Amana sells Amana, Speed Queen, and Caloric brands. Frigidaire uses its name and that of White-Westinghouse, Gibson, Kelvinator, and Tappan. And most microwave ovens, no matter what name they carry, are built by Japanese or Korean companies.

Except for microwave ovens, which retailers often sell alongside TV sets, most of these products are sold in appliance, department, and consumer electronics stores. Many stores purport to be discounters. Some are and some aren't, so shop around.

Price depends on where you live. Where competition among merchandisers is keen, prices tend to be lower. Appliances are not discounted as sharply as audio and video equipment, but special sales are common. Discontinued models, which may differ only slightly from their newer replacements, may be the biggest bargain.

The more you pay, the more features you get, as a rule. But some features represent a manufacturer's attempt to get the consumer's attention, or to structure a product line along a range of popular prices. Electronic controls on major appliances can add precision and versatility not possible with dials and switches. But for appliances that work in cycles, dials can often be easier to understand.

What's more, electronic controls and fancy features often go hand in hand with repair headaches. Features like ice-makers and water dispensers in refrigerators can make an appliance less reliable, as our brand Repair Histories show.

Microwave ovens

▶ Ratings on page 92. ▶ Repair Histories on page 23.

Despite years of trying, manufacturers still haven't come up with a microwave oven whose cooking ability can compete with that of a traditional range or cooktop. A microwave oven doesn't brown well, despite various browning inventions. Nor does it bake well: A microwaved potato just isn't the same as a potato baked the traditional way.

Those shortcomings haven't seriously hampered the usefulness of a microwave oven, however. The number of foods designed specifically for microwave cooking is larger than ever. And microwave ovens still provide the fastest, most convenient way to cook vegetables, reheat leftovers or tea, defrost frozen foods, and pop popcorn.

Sharp dominates the microwave-oven market. Other prominent brands include General Electric, Panasonic, and Tappan. People buy microwave ovens most often at discount stores like Walmart and Kmart, followed by appliance/TV stores and Sears.

The choices

Size and power. The labeled size refers to the cooking cavity. The Association of Home Appliance Manufacturers defines the sizes as follows: subcompact, 0.59 cubic foot or less; compact, 0.60 to 0.79 cubic foot; mid-sized, 0.8 to 1.09 cubic feet; family-sized, 1.1 to 1.39 cubic feet; and large-sized, 1.4 or more cubic feet. How that space translates into three dimensions depends on the cabinet's design, which can be more or less efficient of space.

Most ovens sit on a countertop. Small models can be mounted under cabinets. Some medium-sized models are specifically designed to be mounted over the range under specially sized cabinets.

Size aside, the main difference between large and small ovens is the power produced by the magnetron, which generates the high-energy microwaves that do the cooking. Family-sized models generally generate 900 to 1000 watts; mid-sized models, 800 to 900 watts; compact ovens, 600 to 700 watts. The more powerful the oven, the more quickly it heats food—a difference especially noticeable when you cook large quantities.

Full-sized ovens are the preferred size among today's consumers because they can hold lots of food. But they also take up lots of space—they're typically 22 to 24 inches wide and 15 to 19 inches deep. Price: \$200 to \$350. Mid-sized ovens are much less bulky, and they sacrifice little in capacity, power, and versatility. It's the size we recommend. Price: $150 to $250.

The smallest ovens, somewhat larger than a toaster oven, may be too small for some frozen dinners or containers. But for basic chores like popping corn and warming beverages and leftovers, a small oven may be fine. Price: $100 to $150.

Combination ovens. To remedy the microwave oven's cooking deficiencies, some manufacturers combine microwaving with convection cooking. In convection cooking, an electric element heats the air while a fan circulates it, crisping the outside of the food. The microwave/convection oven works as fast as an ordinary microwave oven in the microwave-only mode; in the dual mode, it works slower to allow browning. Price: $470 to $600.

Features and conveniences

Electronic controls. Nearly all models have electronic controls rather than a mechanical timer. That's important, a mechanical timer is sloppy enough to miss the mark by 20 or 30 seconds, and seconds count in microwave cooking. Most touchpads are easy to read and use. On the best models, numbers and letters are printed clearly and the control pad is well labeled and laid out so that related buttons are near each other.

Along with electronic controls come automated features, and programming them can be vexing. The easiest to use are models whose prompts take you through each command step by step and scroll the instructions across the display. To program a cooking routine typically requires entering numerical codes for foods. Ovens that have the codes printed on their face are particularly convenient. Some models allow you to enter cooking instructions for your own recipes into the computer's memory or summon preprogrammed instructions for a variety of foods at the touch of a button.

One-button cooking. With this convenient design, you press just one touchpad to start cooking. This activates predetermined time and power-level settings. Most ovens have a Popcorn button and one-minute timed touchpads for quick cooking. Some ovens have as many as 12 action touchpads devoted to special foods. Often you must estimate quantity or weight for those shortcuts to work.

Multistage cooking programs. These programs instruct the oven to cook at one power level for a while, then switch to another—helpful for going directly from Defrost to Timed Cook or for recipes that call for a few minutes at high power and a few more at a reduced setting. Basic models typically allow two programs; fancy models offer several.

Power levels. Most ovens have anywhere from 6 to 10. Our tests show that five well-spaced settings are plenty. Models with a high-power default automatically cook at full power unless you program them otherwise.

Turntable. Most models have a turntable. It improves cooking uniformity, but it also reduces an oven's usable space.

Moisture sensor. In our tests, ovens with a moisture sensor reheated foods almost flawlessly. The sensor is also helpful for tasks like cooking vegetables.

Automatic defrosting. Any microwave oven can thaw food if you set a low power, break up the food as it defrosts and turn the pieces occasionally. Most models save you some of those steps with automatic defrosting. With most ovens, the feature works by lowering the power level during thawing for a time period programmed according to the weight of the food. Many ovens signal when it's time to turn the food or remove defrosted sections. They may also go into a "standing" mode periodically to equalize temperature. A couple of models use sensors, measuring the food's weight or the moisture from the food. The moisture sensor worked well. Models that thaw best, without cooking parts of the food or leaving icy spots, may not be the fastest, since uniform thawing takes time.

Delay start. This allows the oven to start automatically at a specified future time, a procedure suitable only for foods that don't need refrigeration.

Child lock-out. Nearly standard on mid- and full-sized models, this feature uses a simple numerical sequence to disable the power. Models with a lock-out display remind you to unlock the oven.

Conveniences. A push-to-open button near the other controls is typical and handy to use. Check window visability. Look for an interior light bright enough to illuminate the food during cooking. A bulb that goes on when the door opens and that you can change yourself without a service call is worthwhile. A lip on the turntable helps contain spills. And a clearly written, organized instruction book simplifies operation.

The tests

Our evaluation includes a judgment of heating speed based on heating measured amounts of water over specific time periods. Also, a battery of cooking tests gauges evenness of heating, a major concern in microwave cooking. We defrost ground beef, reheat leftovers, melt cheese-topped slices of bread, and pop popcorn. We also measure capacity and review conveniences.

Reliability

Mid-sized microwave ovens have been slightly more reliable than full-sized models, our surveys show. Panasonic and Sharp are among the full-sized ovens with the best repair records for models bought between 1988 and 1994. Panasonic and Goldstar were among the most reliable mid-sized ovens. See the brand Repair Histories on page 23.

Buying advice

Mid-sized microwave ovens give the best value. Many are priced just a little higher than small ovens but cook faster and offer more features. Given their limited capacity and power, small ovens are worthwhile only if space is truly at a premium. Large models are for cooking family-sized portions.

Look for one-touch special cooking touchpads to minimize pushing buttons. We also recommend a moisture sensor for the best reheating performance. A display that provides instructions as you use the oven beats having to refer to the instruction book.

Ranges, cooktops & ovens

▶ Ratings on pages 89 and 96. ▶ Repair Histories on page 20.

Today's "cooking center" may consist of a single basic range or a cooktop and wall oven. Your choice should depend largely on budget, personal preference, and cooking style, as well as on the kitchen layout, energy source, and desired conveniences.

General Electric, Whirlpool, and Sears, with its Kenmore brand, account for more than half the electric ranges sold. GE also sells the most gas ranges, with Sears, Tappan, and Magic Chef close behind. The big names in cooktops and wall ovens include GE, Jenn-Air, Maytag, Magic Chef, Sears, and Whirlpool.

Configurations

Cabinetry and floor plan will probably dictate the width and position of the range.

Freestanding ranges. These are the most popular and offer the widest selection. They can be used in the middle of a counter or at the end. Width ranges from 20 to 40 inches, but most are 30 inches wide. Price: $200 to $1500.

Built-in ranges. They come in two types: slide-ins, which fit into a space between cabinets, and drop-ins, which fit into cabinets connected below the oven. Drop-ins lack a storage drawer. Both types look built-in. Price: $450 to $1600.

Dual-oven ranges. This arrangement combines two ovens, as the name implies. The second oven—sometimes a microwave—is usually stacked above the other. Price: about $1000.

A **cooktop plus wall oven.** This pairing allows the most flexibility. Most cooktops are of porcelain—coated steel or ceramic glass, 30-inches wide, with four burners; some are 36-inches wide, with space for an extra burner. The burners may be gas or electric. Some cooktops are modular, with pop-in grills, rotisseries, and other options.

Wall ovens come in 24-, 27-, and 30-inch widths (but some 30-inch ovens require a 33-inch cabinet). You can install one oven at eye level, nest the oven under a cooktop, or stack two ovens. Together, a cooktop and wall oven typically cost more than an all-in-one range. Price: $150 to $800 for the cooktop, $375 to $2000 for the wall oven.

Element and burner types

Gas burners. Gas cooktops can be glass, porcelain-coated steel, or stainless steel. Burners that are sealed, with no space for spills to seep below the cooktop, are easier to clean up. Gas burners—even so-called high-speed burners—tend to heat more slowly than electric elements.

Electric elements. Electric cooktops have two important advantages: fast heating and the ability to maintain low heat levels. Electric cooktops offer more choices than do gas cooktops:

Coil elements are still the most common and least expensive type. Range cooktops with coil elements usually have a porcelain surface. Coils are fairly forgiving of warped and dented pots, and if they break, they're easy and cheaper to replace. Cleanup isn't the easiest, although spills often burn off the coils and require no special care.

Elements in a smoothtop lie beneath a black or grayish-white ceramic glass, often of a brand called Ceran. The patterned surface on some smoothtops, particularly in grayish-white, shows smudges and fingerprints less than a shiny black surface. Spills are easy to clean, but sugary foods, which can pit the glass, should be wiped up promptly. Manufacturers recommend a special cleaner.

Under the glass are radiant, halogen, or induction elements or burners. Radiant burners are essentially very thin coils; halogen burners are tungsten-halogen bulbs. Indicator lights on both types of cooktop signal when the surface is hot, even if the elements are off. A temperature limiter guards against overheating.

For efficient heating, radiant and halogen burners require flat-bottomed pots with about the same diameter as the heating element. Halogen burners cook faster than radiant burners with the same wattage, but radiant burners come in higher wattages.

Induction burners use "magnetic induction" from a high-frequency electrical coil to heat the pot without heating the glass surface. Removing the pot from the surface turns off the heat. Heat goes on and off instantaneously, much as with a gas flame. Pots must be iron or steel (magnetic metal) but needn't have a flat bottom. Induction burners are more expensive than other burner types.

Features and conveniences

Oven cleaning. Most ovens are still lined with plain porcelain enamel, which must be cleaned with an oven cleaner. For $100 to $150 extra, you can opt for a self-cleaning oven. It uses a high-heat cycle (usually two to four hours at temperatures as high as 1000°F) to turn accumulated spills and splatters into ash. When the cycle is complete, you wipe away the residue with a damp sponge.

Another option is a "continuous clean" oven, whose special textured surface camouflages dirt and dissipates grime.

Cooktop cleanup. Sealed burners on gas cooktops make cleaning easier. They add about $50 to $100 to the price of a gas range. Among electric cooktops, smoothtops are easiest to clean but require special cleaners and some care.

Look for the various features that ease cleaning: seamless corners and edges (especially where the cooktop joins the backguard); a glass backguard instead of a painted one (and glass won't scratch as easily); a raised edge around the cooktop to contain spills; and no chrome edges. On a conventional electric range with coil elements or regular gas range with burners, look for deep wells to contain spills and minimal clutter in the area under the cooktop. And make sure you can prop up or remove the cooktop for the inevitable cleaning. Porcelain drip bowls are easier to clean than chrome ones.

Oven capacity. Models with similar exterior dimensions often differ in capacity because of shelf supports and other protrusions. In general, though, ovens in electric ranges are larger than those in gas ovens. Some ovens don't let you cook

GAS, ELECTRIC, OR BOTH?

This decision often depends on whether a gas hookup is available. If both are available, you might consider "dual-fuel cooking." Some cooks choose gas for the cooktop and electricity for the wall oven or even combine gas and electricity in the same cooktop.

The advantages of gas cooking:

- Generally cheaper to use than electric.
- Instant temperature response.
- Clear view of heat setting.
- Can adjust flame to size of pot.
- Can be used with warped or dented pans or with pans whose size doesn't match the burner's.
- Stays usable during power outage.

But:

- Can be hard to clean because of irregular surfaces and tendency of spills to burn.
- Some models aren't good at holding low temperatures.
- At the highest setting, generally slower to heat than electric units.
- Gas ovens have a smaller usable capacity than electric ovens.
- More likely to need repair than an electric unit. See "Reliability" at right and page 20.

The advantages of electric cooking:

- Less expensive to buy.
- If a smoothtop, very easy to clean
- Electric ovens have a larger capacity than gas ovens.
- Generally heats food more quickly.
- Excellent at maintaining low temperatures.

But:

- Coils can be harder to clean than smoothtops.
- For efficient heating, pots and pans should be flat-bottomed and the same size as the burner, particularly for smoothtops.
- Fairly slow to respond to changes in the heat setting.

casseroles on two racks at the same time. Ovens that double as convection ovens typically lose some space to the fan.

Oven controls. Dials and knobs are generally less expensive than electronic controls. They also tend to be more reliable and simpler for setting the oven temperature. They use analog clocks as timers for starting and stopping the oven.

But electronic controls—digital timers with touchpads and light-emitting diode (LED) displays—are more precise. The least complicated designs have prompts and a telephone-style keypad for entering time directly. A design with a smooth surface is easier to clean.

Cooktop controls. Dials are still the norm. Freestanding electric ranges have the controls laid out on the backguard; gas ranges in front of the cooktop. On electric ranges, controls may be divided up left and right, with the oven controls in between, giving you a quick sense of which control works which element.

Controls that are separated into right and left pairs and in double rows, rather than lined up are easier to track with front and back elements. Controls clustered in the center of the backguard are visible even when tall pots sit on back elements. On gas ranges, the oven controls are on the backguard, where their visibility usually isn't blocked by large pots.

Downdraft vents. These vents eliminate the need for a range hood by venting from underneath the unit. They're frequently installed in the counter of an island or peninsula.

The tests

We judge speed of heating—the time it takes to heat measured quantities of water. To test simmering prowess, we melt baking chocolate in a saucepan, keep heat low for 10 minutes, and then check for scorching. We judge evenness of heating in each model's oven and broiler by baking cakes and broiling burgers.

We evaluate the oven's self-cleaning feature by baking on and then removing a our own special blend of gunk. We assess cooktop space (clearance for a wide skillet, for example), cleanability, and features. We also consider oven and storage-drawer capacity, as well as safety considerations such as hot spots during self-cleaning.

Reliability

Over the years, electric ranges have proven more reliable than gas ranges, according to our reader surveys. Models of either type with conventional dial controls have been more reliable than those with electronic controls.

Our 1994 survey found few, if any, differences in reliability among electric ranges with heating coils purchased between 1986 and 1994 of the following leading brands: Whirlpool, Hotpoint, General Electric, Frigidaire, and Sears Kenmore.

Among gas ranges bought between 1987 and 1994, Caloric had the worst record of the six brands included in our survey. For details, see the brand Repair Histories on page 20.

Buying advice

The least expensive and most common range is a freestanding electric model. A typical 30-inch electric model with four coil elements, conventional dial controls, and a self-cleaning oven sells for about $450 to $550; a comparable gas range is priced higher, from $650 to $700. Sealed burners (on gas) or a smoothtop (on electric) also add to the price of a range. On both electric and gas types, electronic controls raise the price, too.

You'll pay a stiff premium for the more stylish specialized and modular units—built-ins, cooktop and wall ovens, cooktop and dual or combination ovens.

Refrigerators

▶ Repair Histories on page 21.

Because of U.S. Department of Energy regulations, today's refrigerators use two-thirds or less of the electricity of models made 10 years ago. And more changes are on the way: By the end of 1995, new insulation materials and new refrigerants will completely replace chloroflurocarbons (CFCs), which contain ozone-destroying chlorine. The new CFC-free models are likely to use even less energy than last year's models.

Efficiencies notwithstanding, a refrigerator still uses a lot of electricity over its typical 15-year life. Even today's models are likely to cost as much to operate over their lifetime as they cost to buy. Operating costs depend largely on size and type. But design matters, too. Our tests regularly show differences in the amount of electricity used by refrigerators with similar configurations.

General Electric, Sears Kenmore, and Amana are the big names in sales of top-freezer models. Those plus the Whirlpool name account for nearly three-quarters of the sales of side-by-side models.

The choices

Top-freezer models. These are the most common type—generally the least expensive to buy and run. They offer the widest choice of sizes, styles, and features. Width ranges from about 24 to 36 inches.

The eye-level freezer offers easy access to its contents. Fairly wide shelves in the refrigerator compartment make it easy to reach things at the back, but you have to bend or crouch to reach the bottom shelves. Nominal capacity ranges from about 10 to almost 26 cubic feet, but usable capacity is about 25 percent less than its claimed capacity. Overall, top-freezer models comes closest to delivering promised capacity—16½ usable cubic feet for models that claim 22. Expect icemakers to take up about a cubic foot of freezer space. Icemakers with ice and water dispensers use up about 1.8 cubic foot of space. Typical 20- to 22-cubic-foot units sell for $500 to $1500.

Side-by-side models. These tend to be larger (about 19 to 30 cubic feet of nominal capacity, 30 to 36 inches in width) and cost the most to buy and run. Advantages that may justify the expenditure: You can store food at eye level in both freezer and refrigerator. The tall, thin shape of the compartments makes it easy to find stray items (but hard to get at items in the back). Doors are narrower than those of a top-freezer model and require less clearance to open. The freezer is larger than in comparable top- or bottom-freezer models. Side-by-side models come in a fairly wide selection of capacities, styles, and features. Ice and water dispensers are most common on this configuration. Selling price: $800 to $2200.

Bottom-freezer models. These form a tiny part of the market and may be hard to find. Fairly wide, eye-level shelves in the refrigerator provide easy access to your most frequently used items. The freezer is low, but often has a pull-out basket. Bottom-freezer models are more expensive than top-freezer units, and in-door ice and water dispensers are unavailable. Nominal capacity: 20 to 22 cubic feet; width, about 33 inches. Price: about $1000.

Built-in models. Built-ins, sized from 10 to 33 cubic feet, are designed to fit flush with surrounding kitchen cabinets. They're only 24 inches deep—a half-foot shallower than conventional models. They're also higher and wider than typical refrigerators. You can face them with custom door panels to match the cabinetry. Built-ins are expensive: $3000 to $5500. Installation can also be a major expense.

Built-in-style models. These come with door panels to match cabinetry like built-ins but aren't as shallow or wide as built-ins. Typical capacity is 20 or 21 cubic feet. Price: $1800 or more.

Compact models. No more than six cubic feet in nominal capacity, this type is handy for a college dorm, office, or small apartment. They don't defrost automatically. Freezers, typically within the refrigerator compartment, get no colder than 15° or 20°F and can keep ice cream for only a few hours before it turns soupy. If you adjust the control to make the freezer colder, items in the refrigerator compartment freeze, too. This size generally isn't energy-efficient.

In this segment of the market, you'll find familiar appliance names such as General Electric and Whirlpool, and also names known better in electronics, such as Sanyo and Goldstar. Price: $150 to $350.

Features and conveniences

Temperature controls. Typically, they're dials in the refrigerator compartment. With some designs, you may have to move food to adjust the controls. The most convenient controls are those near the front. Some models have additional controls—a louver or valve for vegetable crispers or meat-keepers, say. The effectiveness of those controls has varied greatly in our tests.

Electronic touchpad controls, available on high-end models, are usually easy to use. They indicate when a door is ajar, when the unit is too warm, and when the coils need cleaning. In addition, such controls can flag problems needing repairs.

Shelves and bins. Shelves in the refrigerator compartment can usually be rearranged; so can some freezer shelves and door shelves. Tempered-glass shelves are increasingly common, especially on high-end models. They're preferable to

MAKING THE MOST OF YOUR REFRIGERATOR

■ A full refrigerator operates more efficiently than an empty one.

■ Test the magnetic seals by darkening the kitchen, putting a lit flashlight in the refrigerator, and looking for light leaks all around the perimeter.

■ Clean the coils. Condenser coils need cleaning at least once a year, a task easiest to do with a special brush or a vacuum. When they collect dust, they become less effective at dissipating heat and may reduce efficiency. Some models locate the coil at the rear of the refrigerator; the coil gathers less dust in that location, but is hard to get at. Other models have the coil in front, behind the grill at the bottom.

■ On models equipped with a switchable moisture-control heater, turn it to the Off or Energy-saver setting during the heating season and On only when the door starts to sweat. If you have air-conditioning, you may be able to leave the heater off all year.

■ Check the temperature settings. Use a thermometer to make sure the freezer isn't much colder then 0°F.

■ Watch what you keep on top. Blocking air circulation around the refrigerator makes it work harder to keep its cool.

wire shelves because they confine spills to one level and are easier to clean, but they show dirt more readily and may scratch. Shelves that slide out help you find stray items. Removable bins are handy for ice cubes.

Top-of-the-line refrigerators may have such niceties as a utility shelf fitted with storage and serving containers you can pop right into a microwave oven; adjustable, extra-deep door shelves for gallon-sized food or beverage containers; movable retainers on door shelves to keep tall bottles from toppling; and a temperature-controlled beverage chiller on the door.

No-frost operation. This is practically a given these days, except on smaller models. Most self-defrosting models defrost once a day, after their compressor has run for a certain number of hours. There are a few models with state-of-the-art defrost systems that adapt to changing conditions to modify the frost cycle as needed.

Icemakers. Icemakers can keep you in ice cubes—about four to six pounds per day. Icemakers shut off when their bin is full or when you raise and lock a wire arm. But an icemaker is a mixed blessing. Besides taking up space in the freezer, it can nearly double the chances that the refrigerator will need repairs.

Installation involves connecting it to the home's cold-water line, a job do-it-yourselfers should be able to handle if a cold-water line is nearby.

Ice and water dispensers. Through-the-door ice dispensers can conveniently drop a few cubes into a glass or fill an ice bucket. We prefer the dual push-in cradle dispensers, modeled after those in soda fountains. Cold-water reservoirs typically hold about 1½ quarts.

Icemakers, ice dispensers, and water dispensers jack up a refrigerator's price by $100 to $250. The plumbing connections for icemakers and dispensers also are available in kit form, for as little as $55 to $100.

You should use such features regularly to keep them working and to keep the ice and water tasting fresh.

Door opening. Top- and bottom-freezer models have reversible doors, which can hinge either on the right or left, depending on the kitchen workspace. The narrow doors on side-by-side models are ideal for an area where space is tight.

Reliability

Refrigerators with icemakers—top-freezer or side-by-side models—were much more likely to need repairs than those without, according to data supplied by CONSUMER REPORTS readers.

Among top-freezer models without icemakers or water dispensers bought new between 1988 and 1994, Magic Chef, Kenmore (Sears), and Whirlpool were among the more reliable brands. Among side-by-side refrigerators bought during the same period, General Electric's relatively poor record was probably due to faulty compressors in refrigerators purchased in the late-1980s. See the brand Repair Histories on page 21.

Buying advice

Decide on the type, then decide on capacity. Too large a model may be needlessly expensive, besides wasting space and energy. Look at what you currently have and use that to gauge the capacity you'll need.

Kitchen space is another consideration. Check how much clearance the doors need. Some doors demand an extra foot on the side so you can slide out bins and shelves. Side-by-side models require the least amount of clearance for the doors.

In the store, try out a model's controls, and check the sliding bins, shelf placement, and compartment doors. Such seemingly minor items can cause major dissatisfaction in daily use.

Dishwashers

▶ Ratings on page 99. ▶ Repair Histories on page 23.

Most dishwashers use relatively little hot water—less than you'd probably use if you washed dishes under a running faucet. Models built since mid-1994 are especially frugal since they must meet tough new U.S. Department of Energy standards.

The top-selling U.S. brands—Sears Kenmore, General Electric, Whirlpool, and Maytag—account for nearly three-fourths of the dishwashers sold. You'll also find European-made models such as Bosch, Miele, Asko, and GE's Monogram.

The choices

Dishwashers are priced from $250 to $700, but most people buy in the $300-to-$500 price range. For more money, you get electronic controls, specialized cycles, a self-cleaning filter, and better sound insulation. Top-of-the-line machines boast "fuzzy logic," a technology that adjusts cycle times and temperature according to the dishes.

Nearly all dishwashers these days are built-in, under-cabinet models. Sales of portable models with faucet hookup have been declining steadily.

Built-in models. This type attaches permanently to a hot-water pipe, a drain, and electrical lines. It generally fits into a 24-inch-wide space under the countertop, between two base cabinets. Compact models fit in an 18-inch space.

Portable models. A portable has a finished exterior, casters, a plug-in cord, and a hose assembly you attach to the sink faucet. Most portables can convert to an under-cabinet installation.

Features and conveniences

Controls. Manual controls consist of simple push buttons and a dial, which let you reset cycles quickly. Electronic models are a lot fancier. They couple touchpads with displays that show the time for various dishwasher operations or flash warnings about clogged drains, blocked wash-arms, and so on. Some electronic as well as manual models have a hidden touchpad that locks the controls to keep children from playing with them. Needless to say, machines with manual controls cost less than those with electronic controls.

Cycles. A cycle is a combination of washes and rinses. The Normal or Regular cycle generally comprises two washes and two or three rinses. A Heavy cycle can entail longer wash cycles, a second wash, hotter water, or all of those. A Light cycle usually includes one wash. Those three basic cycles are really all you need. Dishwashers clean best on their heaviest cycle, but a light cycle may be sufficient for lightly soiled dishes.

Extra cycles. Many models have a Rinse-and-hold cycle that rinses dishes until you have enough for a full load. Additional cycles—Pot Scrubber, Soak-and-Scrub, and China-and-Crystal—are mainly an excuse for a higher price tag. Regardless of what the names imply, a machine cannot scrub the way muscle and old-fashioned abrasive cleaners do. Nor can a dishwasher baby your heirloom crystal or good china. The machine jostles dishes, and harsh detergents can etch them. Gold trim is especially vulnerable.

Noise. Quiet operation is a major selling point, but claims and labels are little help when it comes to selecting a less raucous machine. European-made models were the quietest in our latest test. The "whisper clean" Tappan and the "Quiet II" Frigidaire we tested were among the noisier models in our tests. To lower the noise level, manufacturers use insulating material, special water pumps, and redesigned washer arms. European-made models use laminated stainless steel tubs.

Saving water and energy. Most of the energy a dishwasher uses is in the form of hot water from your water heater. Electricity to run the pump, motor, and heating element is, by comparison, smaller but still significant use. A booster heater system in the tested models further heats the water if necessary, thus letting you keep your water heater at a lower, more economical setting.

A Delay-start setting lets you program the dishwasher to start later, a useful feature if you have off-peak energy rates. All dishwashers let you choose between a heated dry cycle and the more energy-efficient no-heat dry. A few models also use a blower to aid drying, though some do very well without one.

Filter. Our tests have shown that machines with filters clean much better than those without them. Self-cleaning filters require no attention, unlike filters that require manual cleaning.

Soft-food disposer. Models with this feature grind and dispose of soft food.

Rinse-aid dispenser. This releases a conditioning agent in the final rinse to help prevent water spots and speed up drying. Some models indicate when the dispenser is empty. For models without dispensers, you can use rinse-aids sold in tiny baskets that you hook onto the top rack.

Racks. Most racks hold cups and glasses on top and plates on the bottom. Some models have racks with folding shelves to let you add extra cups and glasses. Some have small spring-loaded arms to secure lightweight items. Others let you adjust the upper rack for tall glasses. Flatware baskets are typically in the main dish rack, occasionally on the door. Some have covered compartments to secure small items.

The tests

We judge performance by how well a dishwasher cleans place settings soiled with some of the most challenging foods: chili, spaghetti, mashed potatoes, fried egg yolk, peanut butter, raspberry jam, cheese spread, cornflakes and milk, oatmeal, stewed tomatoes, and coffee. Then we let the soiled dishes stand in the machines overnight. We repeat the test a number of times with each machine, with 120°F water.

Reliability

Magic Chef, Whirlpool, and Hotpoint have been some of the most reliable dishwasher brands, according to our readers' experiences with dishwashers bought new from 1988 to 1994. White-Westinghouse and Frigidaire were among the least reliable. See the brand Repair Histories on page 23.

Buying advice

We usually find substantial performance differences in our tests among various models of dishwashers—more than with other major appliances. In our last test, cleaning performance corresponded fairly closely with price, as did quietness of operation. Still, you can find solid performers for less than $500. Avoid budget models—we've found that they're not likely to clean nearly as well.

When shopping, inspect the dishwasher's racks with your dishes in mind—take two or three of your dinner plates to the store. Some models, allow more space for tall, upright objects, others, more space for small ones. Construction material is important, too. A porcelain-coated steel tub resists stains better than a plastic tub, but steel is vulnerable to chipping. The most durable tub material is stainless steel, but it can dent.

Washing machines

▶ Ratings on page 83. ▶ Repair Histories on page 22.

The conventional top-loading design has been refined to the point where just about any machine can wash clothes satisfactorily. Design tweaks made to meet the mid-1994 Federal energy standards haven't hurt performance. But future standards are likely to renew interest in front-loaders, which uses less water, electricity, and detergent.

Cosmetically, new washers are distinguished by monochromatic colors and control-panel styling. Functionally, current attractions include quieter operation, electronic touchpad controls, and larger capacity. European models incorporate such features as a Delay-Start cycle, which lets you take advantage of off-peak electricity rates, and a built-in water heater that lets you turn down the temperature on the household hot-water heater (although doing so lengthens wash time).

Just four brands—Sears Kenmore, Whirlpool, Maytag, and General Electric—account for the majority of the washers sold in the U.S.

The choices

Washers range in price from about $250 to more than $900. Often, models within a brand line contain identical basic components. But the higher-priced models typically have more cycle-and-speed combinations, sound damping materials, and a wider selection of water temperatures and fill levels.

Top-load or front-load. Top-loaders are the bigger sellers in this country; they're roomy and relatively inexpensive. Front-loaders use water much more efficiently (typically, about 16 to 25 gallons versus 39 to 45 gallons in a regular wash cycle), but they're more expensive, and they don't hold as big a load. Selection is currently limited to a Whirlpool and a Frigidaire model plus a few imported brands.

Size and capacity. Most washers are about 27 inches wide. Tub capacities usually vary between "large" and "extra large." But there's no standard definition of capacity and the labeled sizes mean little: Our tests show that capacity labeled "extra large" can vary by as much as 50 percent.

Manufacturers also make a few compact, stackable washer/dryer models. Such duos can't hold as much as a full-sized machine, and they're likely to be more expensive. There are also a few "portable" rolling models you hook up to a sink.

Multiple speeds. Most washers come with two or more wash/spin speed combinations. The slower combination handles delicate items more gently. Although some machines offer several speed combinations, just two—a normal-speed agitation with normal spin and slow agitation/slow spin—suffice for most clothes.

Features and conveniences

Some frills add to a model's price but not its performance:

Extra cycles. Regular, Permanent press, and Delicate are all you usually need. The cycle you choose may also determine the speed and water temperature, though on many models those choices are up to you. More expensive machines offer a Soak/prewash for badly soiled laundry or an extra rinse cycle at the end. Manually resetting the dial gives the same result.

Temperature settings. You generally need only three wash temperatures: hot, warm, and cold, followed by a cold rinse. Warm water doesn't rinse any better than cold water, and it wastes energy.

Water levels. The most economical way to wash is with a full load. When that's not practical, it's helpful to be able to lower the fill level to save water, detergent, and energy. On most large-tub models, the minimum fill requires roughly half as much water as the maximum. A selection of three fill levels is usually enough.

Controls. Washing-machine controls, whether knobs and buttons or electronic touchpads, should be straightforward since you'll have to use them every time you do laundry. Large, clearly marked, easy-to-turn knobs are preferable. Electronic controls add to the machine's price and are likely to cost more to repair.

Noise. Models vary greatly in the amount of noise they generate. Claims for quietness did not correlate with the results of our latest test.

Finish. Porcelain and paint have been the standard choices of finish for the washer's top and lid. Of the two, we prefer porcelain, which, though prone to chip, is better able to withstand the inevitable scraping and scratching.

But more and more washing machines are switching over to plastic-based finishes with trademarked names like Dura-Finish and Enduraguard. The new coatings are supposed to be tougher than paint but softer than porcelain.

Tubs. Manufacturers are using more plastic inside the machines, too. The new plastic tubs should work as well as the porcelain-coated steel type. The plastic tub in some washing machines is backed with a 25-year warranty.

Lid/door opening. Top-loaders have lids that open up toward the back or to the right or left. We prefer a lid hinged at the rear, with instructions printed on the underside. The direction isn't reversible so make sure it's suitable for your particular installation. Doors to front-loader washers open down (creating a handy shelf but making you stretch to reach into the tub) or to the side.

Special features. Some machines have dispensers that release bleach and fabric softener at the appropriate time. Others come with a little basket that fits inside the main tub for very small loads. A new suds-return feature on a few Maytag models saves water by pumping the used wash water into an external tub for use with the next load.

Reliability

Based on our readers' experience with washing machines bought new between 1988 and 1994, KitchenAid, Whirlpool, Hotpoint, Kenmore (Sears), and Maytag top-loaders have been among the most reliable brands; among the least reliable, White-Westinghouse, Frigidaire, and Magic Chef. For more information, see the brand Repair Histories on page 22.

The tests

To test washing ability, we wash uniformly soiled cloths, comparing color and shade before and after. We measure water and energy usage, tub capacity, noise, water extraction, and the ability to cope with unbalanced loads.

Buying advice

A top-loading washer is still the more practical choice overall, even if it isn't the most economical type. Look for a brand with a solid repair history.

Top-of-the-line washers with fancy electronics and specialized settings don't provide good value. Nor does a machine loaded with unnecessary features. A three-cycle, two-speed model with a choice of three water levels should be ample for most chores. Look for controls that are clearly labeled, logically arranged, and easy to push and turn.

Clothes dryers

▶ Ratings on page 86. ▶ Repair Histories on page 22.

Virtually any modern dryer will dry clothes adequately. Differences among dryers are largely a matter of convenience and capacity. Highly automated models sell for hundreds of dollars more than the simple ones.

Like washing machines, dryers must meet Government energy standards that took effect in mid-1994. To do so, all dryers must have at least one automatic-drying cycle. (The cheapest dryers used to offer only timed drying.)

The biggest-selling brands are Sears Kenmore, Whirlpool, General Electric, and Maytag.

The choices

Prices of dryers vary from about $200 to more than $600. At the high end of that range, you're likely to get electronic touchpad controls, a large drum capacity, more automatic settings, and a moisture sensor to control drying time.

The main decisions you'll have to make:

Gas or electric. If you have gas service, you're better off with a gas model. Gas dryers tend to cost about $50 more than comparable electric models, but if your utility rates for a therm of gas are less than 25 times those for a kilowatt-hour of electricity—as they almost always are—running a gas dryer is cheaper. Gas dryers, however, are slightly more trouble-prone. See page 82.

Size and capacity. Full-sized models are 27 to 29 inches wide and have a drum capacity of 5.3 to 7 cubic feet. Some brands offer only one size of drum for all dryers in their line; other brands offer a larger drum in their more expensive, top-of-the-line machines. The larger the drum, the more easily a dryer handles bulky items such as a comforter, and the less likely big loads are to come out wrinkled.

Manufacturers also make compact models (mostly electrics) with capacities of about 3½ cubic feet—roughly half that of full-sized models. Often, a compacts can be stacked atop a companion washer. And it can plug into a regular outlet instead of a heavy-duty, 240-volt line. But drying takes much longer with a compact. Compacts generally sell for about $300.

Features and conveniences

Here are the differences that separate top-of-the-line models from their bare-bones brandmates:

Cycles. Bottom-of-the-line dryers offer just one automatic-drying cycle. More expensive models typically offer two or three—Regular, Permanent Press, and Knit/delicate, for instance—plus unheated settings. A more-dry-to-less-dry range on the automatic settings lets you fine-tune to suit the load.

Auto-dry systems. Most dryers use a thermostat to check dampness indirectly. As clothes dry, air leaving the drum gets progressively hotter. When the temperature rises enough, the sensor signals the thermostat to cycle off, and the timer advances until the heat goes on again. The process is repeated until the heating part of the cycle has ended.

New top-of-the-line models and some mid-priced models use moisture sensors that touch the clothes to gauge dryness. Those sensors are usually more accurate than thermostats, but they're not infallible.

Two-way tumbling. Models with this feature tumble in one direction for about five minutes, then reverse direction for about half a minute. Frigidaire says that two-way tumbling cuts drying time by a third and reduces wrinkling.

Controls. Top-of-the-line dryers come with electronic controls. Such controls may prove slightly more convenient, but only after you've mastered them. Our tests show that electronic controls tend to work better than dial controls. Some electronic controls allow you to create custom programming and save it in "memory." Regular dial controls generally work well as long as the designers don't try to squeeze too many choices onto too few controls.

Antiwrinkling. Most dryers let you extend the period of cool tumbling for anywhere from 15 minutes to a couple of hours after the end of the automatic drying cycle. This useful feature, sometimes called "Wrinkle Guard" or "Press Guard," helps prevent wrinkling if you can't empty the dryer right away.

Less useful is what's called "Wrinkle Remove" (or a similarly named feature), which promises to save you some ironing. It puts clean, wrinkled clothes through a short spell of tumbling at low or no heat followed by a cool-down. But any dryer that has a temperature selector can do that. Just set the selector to low or no heat and the tumble time to, say, 20 minutes.

Finish. The cabinet top and drum on most dryers are finished with a coat of baked enamel. More expensive models have a porcelain top, which resists scratching better.

End-of-cycle signal. Most models have a buzzer or other warning that sounds the end of the drying cycle. You can disarm the signal or adjust loudness in some models. Some dryers also warn you when it's time to clean the lint filter.

Door opening. A large opening makes loading and unloading easier. Some doors open down, some to the right, and a few are reversible. A door that opens down creates a useful shelf but makes you stretch to reach into the drum.

Other features. A drum light is useful for hunting down errant socks, even in a laundry room with good lighting. Some dryers come with a special rack for drying items like sneakers without tumbling.

Reliability

Data from our reader surveys show that Magic Chef and Frigidaire electric dryers purchased between 1988 and 1994 have been significantly more trouble-prone than other brands of electric or gas dryers. For gas dryers, Whirlpool and Kenmore (Sears) have been among the more reliable brands. See the brand Repair Histories on page 22.

Buying advice

If you have gas service, opt for a gas dryer. Although gas dryers are priced about $50 more than electrics, they are cheaper to run. The energy you save during the first year of ownership should offset the price difference.

Choosing a dryer by price is fairly safe, since nearly all the models we've tested in the past five years dried ordinary loads well. Even basic models now offer an auto-dry cycle. A moisture sensor can further reduce wasteful overdrying, but that feature comes only in mid- and high-priced models.

Whichever dryer you choose, clean the lint filter regularly—ideally, after every load. Lint that builds up in the exhaust duct can cause a fire.

RATINGS WASHING MACHINES

See report, page 79. Last time rated in Consumer Reports: February 1995.

Brand-name recommendations: Four top-loaders—the Sears 25841 and 25821, the Amana LW8203W2, and the Frigidaire FWS445RBO—led the field. Both of the Sears models have been replaced by the 25882 and 25822, respectively. Among front-loaders, the high-priced Asko 10504 was by far the better of the two we tested. (It has been discontinued and replaced by the 10505.) The front-loading White-Westinghouse LT350RX performed only about as well, overall, as the lower-rated top-loaders. Although it has been discontinued, it may still be available in some stores.

For the typical mid-priced washer, expect: ■ 3 wash/spin speed combinations set automatically by choosing Regular, Permanent Press, or Delicate cycle. ■ Variable water-level controls. ■ Dispenser for bleach and fabric softener, but not for detergent. ■ Push buttons and dial controls. ■ Self-cleaning lint filter. ■ Porcelain-coated steel tub, painted cabinet top and lid. ■ Ability to wash at least 8 lbs. of laundry. ■ Some difficulty handling unbalanced loads. ■ 38- to 50-min. cycles. ■ Very good washing performance. ■ Lid opens and lies flat. ■ Water use 39 to 47 gal. for top loader; 16 to 25 gal. for front loaders.

Notes on the table: Price is the estimated average, based on a national survey. * means price paid. **Overall score** summarizes performance for washing ability, gentleness, capacity, efficiency, convenience, and features. **Gentleness** shows how carefully each model treated a load of laundry. **Capacity** ranges from the Asko's 7 lbs. to 14 lbs. for the largest. **Water efficiency** is for max. load and 8-lb. load. **Cost efficiency** rates overall costs per lb.—for electricity to heat the water and run the washer and for detergent—for max. load and 8-lb. load. **Controls** reflect our assessment of their logic, legibility, and ease of use. Models similar to those we tested are noted in Details; features may vary. **Model availability:** Ⓓ means model is discontinued; Ⓢ means model is replaced, according to the manufacturer; successor model is noted in Details. New model was not tested; it may or may not perform similarly. Features may vary.

Better ⟷ Worse: ⊜ ⊖ ○ ◒ ●

Listed in order of washing performance and efficiency

Brand and model	Price	Overall score (P F G VG E)	Cycle used	Gentleness	Capacity	Efficiency WATER	Efficiency COST	Controls
TOP-LOADERS								
Sears 25841 Ⓢ	*$580		Heavy	○	⊜	⊖/○	○/◒	⊖
Amana LW8203W2	405		Reg.	○	⊜	⊖/○	○/◒	⊖
Sears 25821 Ⓢ	*460		Heavy	○	⊜	⊖/○	○/◒	⊖
Frigidaire FWS445RB0	395		Reg.	⊖	⊖	⊖/○	○/◒	⊖
Whirlpool LSC8244B Ⓢ	425		Heavy	○	⊖	⊖/○	○/◒	○
Sears 25732	*430		Heavy	○	⊖	⊖/○	○/◒	⊖

Ratings continued ▶

Ratings continued

Brand and model	Price	Overall score (P F G VG E)	Cycle used	Gentleness	Capacity	Efficiency WATER	Efficiency COST	Controls
TOP-LOADERS *continued*								
Whirlpool LSP9245B [S]	$435		Heavy	○	⊖	⊖/○	○/◒	○
Whirlpool LSR7233B [S]	405		Reg.	○	⊖	⊖/○	○/◒	○
Speed Queen AWM472W2	395		Reg.	⊖	⊖	⊖/○	○/◒	⊖
KitchenAid KAWE565BWH	425		Reg.	⊖	⊖	⊖/○	○/◒	○
Magic Chef W205KV [D]	365		Reg.	⊖	⊖	⊖/○	○/◒	○
Admiral LATA200AAW [S]	360		Reg.	⊖	⊖	⊖/○	○/◒	○
Roper RAX7245B	390		Heavy	○	⊖	⊖/○	○/◒	○
Maytag LAT9704AAE [S]	530		Reg.	⊖	◒	○/◒	◒/◒	○
Maytag LAT9604AAE [D]	525		Reg.	⊖	◒	○/◒	◒/◒	○
General Electric WWA8950S [D]	425		Reg.	⊖	◒	◒/◒	◒/●	⊖
General Electric WWA8600S [D]	410		Reg.	⊖	◒	◒/◒	●/●	⊖
Hotpoint WLW3600S [D]	360		Reg.	⊖	◒	◒/◒	●/●	⊖
FRONT-LOADERS								
Asko 10504 [S]	*1042		Reg.	⊜	●	⊜/⊜	⊜/⊜	○
White-Westinghouse LT350RX [D]	605		Reg.	⊖	◒	⊖/⊖	⊜/⊜	◒

MODEL DETAILS

Want to know more about a rated model? They're listed here alphabetically.

Admiral LATA200AAW [S]
Infinitely variable water levels. No fabric-softener dispenser. Plastic inner tub. **Successor:** LATA200AAE.

Amana LW8203W2
Infinitely variable water levels. 2 wash/spin combinations. Quiet. Spin extracts less water than on others. Stainless steel tub. **Similar:** LW8203L2, LW4203W2, LW4203L2.

Asko 10504 [S]
Automatic water level, detergent dispenser. On light. Washing performance not as good as most. Difficult to service. Rinses better than others without extra rinse. Spins clothes drier than others. Quiet. Handles unbalanced loads much better than others. Requires 208/240V. Stainless steel tub. **Successor:** 10505.

Frigidaire FWS445RB0
Infinitely variable water levels. Spin extracts less water than on others. Plastic inner tub. **Similar:** FWS445RBT, F21C445RB, WW5445RB.

General Electric WWA8600S [D]
2 selectable wash/spin combinations. Washing performance not as good as most. Difficult to service. Good bleach dispenser. Extra rinse can't be turned off in Heavy cycle. Noisy. Porcelain top and lid.

General Electric WWA8950S Ⓓ	Infinitely variable water levels. No fabric-softener dispenser. Optional extra-rinse setting. Separate inner agitator for gentle loads. Selectable wash/spin speeds. Washing performance not as good as most. Difficult to service. Good bleach dispenser. Noisy. Spin extracts less water than on others. Porcelain top and lid.
Hotpoint WLW3600S Ⓓ	No fabric-softener dispenser. 2 selectable wash/spin combinations. Washing performance not as good as most. Difficult to service. Good bleach dispenser. Extra rinse can't be turned off in heavy cycle. Noisy. Porcelain top and lid.
KitchenAid KAWE565BWH	Porcelain top and lid. No fabric-softener or bleach-dispenser. 2 wash/spin combinations. Quiet. Easy-to-read controls. **Similar:** KAWE570B, KAWE577B, KAWE578B.
Magic Chef W205KV Ⓓ	Plastic inner tub. Infinitely variable water levels. No fabric-softener dispenser.
Maytag LAT9604AAE Ⓓ	Porcelain top and lid. On light. No bleach dispenser. 2 wash/spin combinations. Quiet. Cycle dial harder than others to turn. Spin extracts less water than on others.
Maytag LAT9704AAE Ⓢ	Porcelain top and lid. Infinitely variable water levels. On light. 2 wash/spin combinations. Good bleach dispenser. Quiet. Cycle dial harder than others to turn. Spin extracts less water than others. **Successor:** LAT9605
Roper RAX7245B	Bleach dispenser worse than others.
Sears 25732	Open lid doesn't lie flat. Bleach dispenser worse than others. Easy-to-read controls.
Sears 25821 Ⓢ	Open lid doesn't lie flat. Can blend hot & cold to preset temperature. 4 selectable wash/spin combinations. Bleach dispenser worse than others. Easy-to-read controls. **Successor:** 25822.
Sears 25841 Ⓢ	Infinitely variable water levels. Open lid doesn't lie flat. Can blend hot & cold to preset temperature. 4 selectable wash/spin combinations. Bleach dispenser worse than others. Easy-to-read controls. Porcelain top and lid. **Successor:** 25882.
Speed Queen AWM472W2	Infinitely variable water levels. No fabric-softener dispenser. 2 wash/spin combinations. Quiet. Spin extracts less water than others.
Whirlpool LSC8244B Ⓢ	Infinitely variable water levels. Optional extra-rinse setting. Bleach dispenser worse than others. **Successor:** LSC8244D.
Whirlpool LSP9245B Ⓢ	End-of-cycle signal. Optional extra-rinse setting. 4 selectable wash/spin combinations. Easy-to-read controls. Bleach dispenser worse than others. **Successor:** LSP9245D.
Whirlpool LSR7233B Ⓢ	Easy-to-read controls. Bleach dispenser worse than others. **Successor:** LSR7233D.
White-Westinghouse LT350RX Ⓓ	Infinitely variable water levels. End-of-cycle signal. Tub light. No fabric-softener or bleach dispenser. Washing performance not as good as most. Difficult to service. Rinses better than others without extra rinse. Coins left in clothes can get caught in machine; may require service. Cycle dial hard to turn. Spin extracts less water than others. Handles unbalanced loads much better than others.

RATINGS CLOTHES DRYERS

▶ **See report, page 81.** Last time rated in Consumer Reports: May 1995.

Brand-name recommendations: Machines with a moisture sensor generally performed better in our tests than those that use a thermostat. But any machine in the Ratings will do a good job of drying ordinary loads. Good choices among the electrics include the top-rated electric, the Sears 65831, $420 (and its successor, 65882), and either of the KitchenAid models, which sell for about $425. Among gas dryers, the top three models are good performers. The Whirlpool LGR6848AWO (and its successor, LGR7848D) is the only gas dryer we tested with a moisture sensor.

For the typical mid-priced dryer, expect: ■ A thermostat for dryness control. ■ 2 or 3 automatic drying cycles with a separate temp. control, at least 1 extended cool-down tumble, a timed dry cycle of at least 60 min., and the ability to dry without heat for at least 40 min. ■ Door that opens down. ■ Lint filter removable from inside the drum. ■ Mechanical rotary or push-button controls. ■ Venting from the rear only. ■ End-of-cycle signal that cannot be adjusted or turned off.

Notes on the table: Price is the estimated average, based on a national survey. * means price paid. **Overall score** summarizes performance in our tests of drying capacity, noise, ease of use, and features. **Drum capacity** ranges from about 5½ to 7 cu. ft. **Model availability:** D means model is discontinued. S means model is replaced, according to the manufacturer; successor model is noted in Details. New model was not tested; it may or may not perform similarly.

Within type, listed in order of performance and convenience

E = ⊜ (Excellent), VG = ⊖ (Very good), G = ○ (Good), F = ◒ (Fair), P = ● (Poor)

Brand and model	Price	Overall score (P F G VG E)	Drum cap.	Automatic dryness: Mixed load	Automatic dryness: Delicates	Noise	Ease of use
ELECTRIC DRYERS							
Sears 65831 S	$420		⊜	⊖	○	⊖	⊖
KitchenAid KEYE770BWHO	425		⊜	⊖	○	○	⊖
Magic Chef YE208K S	*389		⊜	○	⊖	⊖	⊖
KitchenAid KEYE670BWHO	420		⊜	⊖	○	○	○
Sears 65821 S	360		⊜	○	○	○	⊖
Admiral LDEA400ACE S	290		⊜	○	⊖	⊖	○
Whirlpool LER6848AWO S	335		⊜	⊖	○	○	○
Maytag LDE9304ACE D	445		⊖	⊖	○	⊖	○
Speed Queen AEM697W2 D	320		⊖	○	⊖	⊖	○
Maytag LDE7304ACE D	420		⊖	○	○	⊖	○
Amana LE8407W2	350		⊖	○	⊖	⊖	○
General Electric DDE8500SAMWW D	365		⊖	○	○	○	⊖

Brand and model	Price	Overall score (P F G VG E)	Drum cap.	Automatic dryness: Mixed load	Automatic dryness: Delicates	Noise	Ease of use
General Electric DDE9605SAMWW [D]	$400		⊖	○	○	○	○
Whirlpool LER7646AWO [D]	325		⊖	⊖	○	○	○
Hotpoint DLB3800SBLWH [D]	290		○	○	○	○	⊖
Frigidaire FDE546RBSO [D]	285		○	○	○	⊖	⊖
Roper REX5636AWO [D]	300		⊖	○	○	○	◒
Whirlpool LER5638AWO [S]	360		⊜	○	○	○	◒
White-Westinghouse WDE546RBWO	275		○	○	○	⊖	○
GAS DRYERS							
Whirlpool LGR6848AWO [S]	370		⊜	⊖	○	○	○
Amana LG8409W2	395		⊖	○	⊖	⊖	○
Maytag LDG7304AAE	450		⊖	○	○	○	○
General Electric DDG8580SAMWW [D]	410		⊖	○	○	○	⊖
Hotpoint DLL3880SBLWH [D]	330		○	○	○	○	⊖
Frigidaire FDG546RBSO [D]	330		○	○	○	⊖	⊖
White-Westinghouse DG546RBWO [D]	310		○	○	○	⊖	○

MODEL DETAILS

Want to know more about a rated model? They're listed here alphabetically.

Admiral LDEA400ACE [S]	Drum light. On/off switch part of cycle selector. **Successor:** LDEA400ACE.
Amana LE8407W2	Filter can be viewed and cleaned without removal. Drum light. End-of-cycle signal very long, but can be adjusted or turned off. Cycle control turns in one direction. No-heat cycle limited to 15-20 min. On/off switch part of cycle selector. Lint filter secured to dryer.
Amana LG8409W2	Gas. Filter can be viewed and cleaned without removal. Drum light. End-of-cycle signal very long, but can be adjusted or turned off. Cycle control turns in one direction. No-heat cycle limited to 15-20 min. On/off switch part of cycle selector. Lint filter secured to dryer.
Frigidaire FDE546RBSO [D]	Filter can be viewed and cleaned without removal. Drum light.
Frigidaire FDG546RBSO [D]	Gas. Filter can be viewed and cleaned without removal. Drum light.
General Electric DDE8500SAMWW [D]	Filter can be viewed and cleaned without removal. Drum light. End-of-cycle signal very long, but can be adjusted or turned off. Opt. extended tumble.
General Electric DDE9605SAMWW [D]	Moisture sensor. Filter can be viewed/cleaned without removal. Drum light. End-of-cycle signal very long, but can be adjusted or turned off. Controls inconvenient to use. Opt. extended tumble.
General Electric DDG8580SAMWW [D]	Gas. Filter can be viewed and cleaned without removal. End-of-cycle signal very long, but can be adjusted or turned off. Opt. extended tumble.

Ratings continued ▶

Ratings continued

Model	Comments
Hotpoint DLB3800SBLWH [D]	Filter can be viewed and cleaned without removal. Drum light. End-of-cycle signal very long, but can be adjusted or turned off. Optional extended tumble. Porcelain-coated drum.
Hotpoint DLL3880SBLWH [D]	Gas. Filter can be viewed and cleaned without removal. Drum light. End-of-cycle signal very long, but can be adjusted or turned off. Opt. extended tumble. Porcelain-coated drum.
KitchenAid KEYE670BWHO	Moisture sensor. End-of-cycle signal too short. No-heat cycle limited to 15-20 min. Porcelain-coated top.
KitchenAid KEYE770BWHO	Moisture sensor. Drying rack. Drum light. End-of-cycle signal too short, but can be adjusted or turned off. No-heat cycle limited to 15-20 min. Porcelain-coated top.
Magic Chef YE208K [S]	Drying rack. Drum light. End-of-cycle signal can be adjusted or turned off. Opt. extended-tumble. On/off switch part of cycle selector. **Successor:** YE228LV.
Maytag LDE7304ACE [D]	End-of-cycle signal too short. Porcelain-coated top.
Maytag LDE9304ACE [D]	Moisture sensor. Drum light. End-of-cycle signal too short. Dryness monitor indicates dryness level of load. Didn't handle small mixed loads as well as large ones. Porcelain-coated top.
Maytag LDG7304AAE	Gas. End-of-cycle signal too short. Porcelain-coated top.
Roper REX5636AWO [D]	End-of-cycle signal too short. No-heat cycle limited to 15-20 min. No extended tumble. Single control model; cycle selector determines fabric temp.
Sears 65821 [S]	End-of-cycle signal can be adjusted or turned off. Lint filter can be removed from top of cabinet. Extended tumble period at end of all cycles. No-heat cycle 30 min. long. **Successor:** 65862.
Sears 65831 [S]	Better than others at permanent press auto drying. Moisture sensor. End-of-cycle signal can be adjusted or turned off. Extended tumble period at end of all auto cycles. No-heat cycle 30 min. long. **Successor:** 65882.
Speed Queen AEM697W2 [D]	Filter can be viewed and cleaned without removal. Drum light. End-of-cycle signal very long, but can be adjusted or turned off. Cycle control turns in one direction. No-heat cycle limited to 15-20 min. On/off switch part of cycle selector. Lint filter secured to dryer. Variable temp. control.
Whirlpool LER5638AWO [S]	No end-of-cycle signal. No-heat cycle limited to 15-20 min. No extended tumble. Single control model; cycle selector determines temp. **Successor:** LER6638D.
Whirlpool LER6848AWO [S]	Gas. Moisture sensor. End-of-cycle signal too short. Lint filter can be removed from top of cabinet. Extended tumble period at end of all auto cycles. No-heat cycle 30 min. long. **Successor:** LER7848D.
Whirlpool LER7646AWO [D]	End-of-cycle signal too short. Didn't handle small mixed loads as well as large ones. Lint filter can be removed from top of cabinet. Extended tumble period at end of all auto cycles. No-heat cycle 30 min. long.
Whirlpool LGR6848AWO [S]	Moisture sensor. End-of-cycle signal too short. Lint filter can be removed from top of cabinet. Extended tumble period at end of all auto cycles. No-heat cycle 30 min. long. **Successor:** LGR7848D.
White-Westinghouse DG546RBWO [D]	Gas. Filter can be viewed and cleaned without removal.
White-Westinghouse WDE546RBWO	Filter can be viewed and cleaned without removal.

RATINGS COOKTOPS

See report, page 70. Last time rated in Consumer Reports: July 1994.

Brand-name recommendations: Except for a couple of low-rated gas models, very good performance was the norm. The least expensive type is coil; the top four models in that group deserve first consideration. Smoothtops—radiant/halogen and induction—are more expensive. The Maytag CSE9000ACE, $440, costs much less than the top-rated Thermador CH30W, $850, and was nearly as good. Among gas models, the KitchenAid KGCT305A, $540, was only slightly better than the much less expensive Magic Chef 8241RV, $290.

For the typical cooktop, expect: ■ 30 in. x 21 in. deep. ■ 4 burners. ■ Dial controls (except electronic for induction models) that are continuously variable. ■ Easy-to-use controls. ■ For gas cooktops: Sealed burners, spark igniter, convertibility to liquid propane, glass or porcelain surface. ■ For coil cooktops: Wide availability, removable elements with drip bowls, porcelain surface. ■ For radiant/halogen smoothtops: On light, light to show burner is too hot to touch. ■ For induction smoothtops: Lock feature, auto shutoff when pot is removed, auto shutoff if unit overheats.

Notes on the table: Model numbers are for the color tested, usually white. **Price** is the estimated average, based on a national survey. **Overall score** is based on performance, convenience, and features. **Cleaning** reflects how easy it was to get baked-on grime off cooktop surfaces. **Spills** reflect how easy it was to clean up liquid sloshed around the burner. **Model availability:** [D] means model is discontinued. [S] means model is replaced, according to the manufacturer; successor model is noted in Details. New model was not tested; it may or may not perform similarly. Features may vary.

Within type, listed in order of performance

E ⊜ VG ⊖ G ○ F ◒ P ●

Brand and model	Price	Overall score (P F G VG E)	Heat HIGH	Heat LOW	Cleaning	Spills	Controls
ELECTRIC MODELS							
COIL ELEMENTS							
KitchenAid KECS100S	$265		E	E	VG	VG	VG
Frigidaire FEC3X5XA [S]	220		VG	E	G	VG	VG
General Electric JP325R [S]	230		VG	E	VG	VG	G
Whirlpool RC8400XA [S]	220		E	E	G	G	G
Tappan 13-3028 [S]	185		VG	E	G	VG	G
Magic Chef 8610PV	195		VG	E	G	G	G
RADIANT/HALOGEN SMOOTHTOP							
Thermador CH30W	850		G	E	E	E	G
Maytag CSE9000ACE	440		VG	E	E	E	VG

Ratings continued ▶

Ratings continued

Brand and model	Price	Overall score (P F G VG E)	Heat HIGH	Heat LOW	Cleaning	Spills	Controls
RADIANT/HALOGEN SMOOTHTOP *continued*							
Amana AK2H30W1 [S]	$655		⊖	⊜	⊜	⊜	○
Amana AK2T30W [S]	480		⊖	⊜	⊜	⊜	○
KitchenAid KECC500W [S]	520		○	⊜	⊜	⊜	○
Whirlpool RC8600XXQ-1 [S]	500		⊖	⊜	⊜	⊜	○
INDUCTION SMOOTHTOP							
General Electric JP3930R1WG	825		○	⊜	⊜	⊜	⊖
GAS MODELS							
KitchenAid KGCT305A [S]	540		◒	○	◒	◒	⊜
Magic Chef 8241RV	290		○	⊜	◒	⊖	⊖
Maytag CSG7000BAE [S]	385		◒	⊜	○	⊖	⊖
Thermador GG30WC-02 [S]	680		○	⊜	●	○	○
General Electric JGP331EP2WG [S]	475		○	○	○	◒	○
Modern Maid PGT130UWW	485		●	⊜	◒	◒	○
Whirlpool SC8630EXQ-5 [S]	275		○	●	○	⊖	○

MODEL DETAILS

Want to know more about a rated model? They're listed here alphabetically.

Amana AK2T30W [S]	**Successor:** AK2T30W1.
Amana AK2H30W1 [S]	**Successor:** AK2H30W3.
Frigidaire FEC3X5XA [S]	Front surface cooler than most. Opening around control stem sealed. Control markings especially clear. Knobs comfortable. Hinged, for easy cleaning. **Successor:** JGPEVP331EV.
General Electric JGP331EP2WG [S]	Gas. Comfortable knobs. **Successor:** JEP336WEV.
General Electric JP325R [S]	Opening around control stem sealed. Hinged, for easy cleaning. Comfortable knobs. Burner assembly looser than others. **Successor:** JP326WV.
General Electric JP3930R1WG	Front surface cooler than most. Each burner has an On light. Spills can leak inside unit and cabinet.
KitchenAid KECC500W [S]	Hot light for each burner. Comfortable knobs. Burner design aids in centering pot. Paint on metal rim came off easily on first sample tested; second sample OK. **Successor:** KECC501B.
KitchenAid KECS100S	Opening around control stem sealed. Easy to match control with burner. Hinged, for easy cleaning.

KitchenAid KGCT305A [S]	Gas. Front surface cooler than most. Burners reignite when blown out. Control markings especially clear. Burner selection especially easy. Comfortable knobs. **Successor:** KGCT3058.
Magic Chef 8241RV	Gas. Porcelain surface. Control markings especially clear. High-power burners look the same as low-power. Front surface hotter than most.
Magic Chef 8610PV	Front surface cooler than most. Opening around control stem sealed. Control markings especially clear.
Maytag CSE9000ACE	Opening around control stem sealed. Control markings better than others. Front surface hotter than most.
Maytag CSG7000BAE [S]	Gas. Control markings especially clear. No shielding around control stem. Burner grates pop out of position more easily than others. **Successor:** CSG7000BAE.
Modern Maid PGT130UWW	Gas. Front surface cooler than most. Burners reignite when blown out. Control selection very easy. Burner grates pop out of position more easily than most.
Tappan 13-3028 [S]	Opening around control stem sealed. Hinged, for easy cleaning. **Successor:** TEC3X3XCW/D/C.
Thermador CH30W	One dual burner. Front surfaces cooler than most. Opening around control stem sealed. On light and Hot light for each burner.
Thermador GG30WC-02 [S]	Gas. **Successor:** GGN30W.
Whirlpool RC8400XA [S]	Opening around control stem sealed. Control markings especially clear. **Successor:** RC8400XB.
Whirlpool RC8600XXQ-1 [S]	Spills can leak inside cabinet. Front surface hotter than most. Two samples in black were defective. **Successor:** RC8600XB.
Whirlpool SC8630EXQ-5 [S]	Gas. Porcelain surface. Comfortable knobs. Opening around control stem is unshielded. Burner grates tip and pop out of position more easily than most. Not convertible to liquid propane. **Successor:** SC8630EB.

How to use the Ratings in the Buying Guide

- Read the brand-name recommendations for information on specific models.
- Note how the rated products are listed—in order of performance and convenience, price, or alphabetically.
- Look to the overall score to get the big picture in performance. Notes on features and performance for individual models are listed in the Comments or Details part of the Ratings.
- Note that models similar to the tested models, when they exist, are indicated in the Comments or Details. A model marked [D] has been discontinued. A model marked [S] is a successor to the tested model, according to the manufacturer, and is noted in Comments or Details. Features, though, may vary.
- Call the manufacturer if you have trouble finding a product. See page 342.
- To find our last full report on a subject, check the eight-year index, page 346.

RATINGS MICROWAVE OVENS

▶ **See report, page 68.** Last time rated in Consumer Reports: August 1995.

Brand-name recommendations: The Panasonic NN7703 topped the Ratings for large ovens but it may not be available. The new Panasonics will have a telephone-style touchpad. The next four models—the General Electrics, Sharp, and Samsung—performed nearly as well. The Samsung MW6430W is A Best Buy at $135. Some GE ovens have been discontinued; replacements differ in color or labeling. Among mid-sized ovens, consider the Sharp R-3A66 or Admiral KSA-8551A—both Best Buys at $140.

For these microwave ovens, expect: ■ 5 to 10 power levels. ■ Electronic controls with numbered touchpads. ■ Programming of timed settings up to almost 100 min. ■ A touchpad for tapping in min. at full power. ■ Several instant-on settings. ■ Automatic, adjustable reheat and defrost settings. ■ Automatic popcorn settings. ■ Helpful prompts displayed during programs. ■ Delay-start timer. ■ Turntable that must be in place when oven is on. ■ Push-panel door latch. ■ Child lock-out feature. ■ Room for 8x8-in. dish, 5-qt. casserole, 10¼-in. plate, or a large chicken. ■ 1200 to 1680 watts of power.

Notes on the table: Price is the estimated average, based on a national survey. * means price paid. **Rated power,** in watts, as claimed by the manufacturer and verified in our tests. **Inside fit** assesses how well the oven can hold dishes of various shapes and sizes. **Space efficiency** is based on the ratio of useful capacity to overall size. Models similar to those we tested are noted in Details; features may vary. **Model availability:** [D] means model is discontinued. [S] means model is replaced, according to the manufacturer; successor model is noted in Details. New model was not tested; it may or may not perform similarly. Features may vary.

Within sizes, listed in order of performance and convenience

E VG G F P

Brand and model	Price	Overall score (P F G VG E)	Rated power	Inside fit	Space efficiency	Cooking uniformity	Auto-defrost	Ease of use
LARGE MODELS								
Panasonic NN7703 [D]	*$290		900	E	G	G	E	VG
General Electric JE1550GN [S]	270		1000	E	VG	G	G	E
Sharp R-5H06	245		1000	E	VG	F	VG	E
General Electric JE1530GN [D]	240		900	E	VG	G	VG	G
Samsung MW6930	*185		1000	VG	VG	G	G	E
Sanyo EM-V830 [D]	190		1000	VG	G	VG	G	VG
Panasonic 6813A [D]	215		1000	VG	VG	F	G	VG
General Electric JE1250GN [D]	250		1000	VG	G	F	G	E
Samsung MW6430W, **A BEST BUY**	135		900	VG	VG	G	G	E

Brand and model	Price	Overall score (P F G VG E)	Rated power	Inside fit	Space efficiency	Cooking uniformity	Auto-defrost	Ease of use
Sharp R-4X06	*$269		1000	⊖	○	◒	◒	⊜
Sharp R-4A56	160		900	⊖	⊖	◒	◒	⊜
Goldstar MA-1164M [D]	140		850	○	⊖	◒	○	⊜
Whirlpool MT9160XBQ	230		900	⊜	⊖	●	⊖	○
Kenmore (Sears) 89682	250		900	⊜	○	◒	⊖	◒
Kenmore (Sears) 89481	200		900	⊖	○	◒	○	○
Whirlpool MT6120XBQ	200		900	⊖	○	●	◒	○
Quasar MQS1540E [D]	210		900	⊜	○	○	[1]	●
Amana RSBG669T	220		1000	○	◒	◒	○	◒
MID-SIZED MODELS								
Sharp R-3A66, **A BEST BUY**	140		850	○	○	⊖	⊖	⊜
Sharp R-3A05	170		1050	○	○	⊖	○	⊖
Sharp R-3H95 [D]	190		850	○	○	⊖	⊖	⊜
Admiral (M. Ward) KSA-8551A, **A BEST BUY**	*140		850	○	○	⊖	⊖	⊖
General Electric JE950GN [D]	*219		1000	○	○	◒	○	⊜
Panasonic NN5803A [D]	180		800	○	○	○	⊜	⊖
Amana MW96T	155		800	○	○	○	○	⊜
Goldstar MA-891S	145		850	◒	○	○	⊖	⊖
General Electric JE940WN [D]	200		800	○	○	◒	○	⊖
Samsung MW5430W	120		800	○	○	◒	◒	⊜
Sanyo EM-704T [D]	140		800	○	○	⊖	○	○
Kenmore (Sears) 89381	180		800	○	○	○	⊖	○
Welbilt MR95TW	120		850	◒	○	○	⊖	○
Whirlpool MT2081XBQ	140		800	◒	○	◒	⊖	○
Tappan TMS084T1W [S]	130		800	◒	○	◒	⊖	○
Emerson MT3091 [D]	120		830	◒	○	○	⊖	◒
Magic Chef DM85K	*129		900	○ [2]	◒ [2]	◒	○	◒

[1] *No auto-defrost setting.*

[2] *With turntable stationary, ⊜ for inside fit; ◒ for space efficiency.*

Ratings continued ▶

Ratings continued

MODEL DETAILS

Want to know more about a rated model? They're listed here alphabetically.

Admiral (M. Ward) KSA-8551A, **A BEST BUY**	Minutes-at-full-power touchpad also extends heating time (by a min. per tap) at lower power settings.
Amana MW96T	Minutes-at-full-power touchpad also extends heating time (by a min. per tap) at lower power settings. **Similar:** ME96T.
Amana RSBG669T	No minutes-at-full-power touchpad. No instant-on touchpads. Less-gentle heating than most at low power settings. Interior light bulb can be replaced by user. (Others require a service call.) Door handle judged less convenient than push-panel on other models. **Similar:** RSW669T, RSL669T.
Emerson MT3091 D	Count-up touchpads in units of 10 min., 1 min., 10 sec. No true auto-reheat; just minutes-at-full-power setting. No instant-on touchpads. No child-lockout feature. Display characters hard to read. No light goes on when door is opened.
General Electric JE1250GN D	Moisture sensor worked well in auto-reheat. 30-sec.-at-full-power touchpad also extends heating time (by half a min. per tap) at lower power settings.
General Electric JE1530GN D	No auto reheat settings. Interior light bulb can be replaced by user. (Others require a service call.)
General Electric JE1550GN S	Moisture sensor worked well in auto-reheat. 30-sec.-at-full-power touchpad also extends heating time (by half a min. per tap) at lower power settings. Interior light bulb can be replaced by user. (Others require a service call.) **Successor:** JE1550GV.
General Electric JE940WN D	30-sec.-at-full-power touchpad also extends heating time (by half a min. per tap) at lower power settings.
General Electric JE950GN D	Moisture sensor worked well in auto-reheat. 0-sec.-at-full-power touchpad also extends heating time (by half a min. per tap) at lower power settings.
Goldstar MA-1164M D	No minutes-at-full-power touchpad. No light goes on when door is opened.
Goldstar MA-891S	Moisture sensor worked well in auto-reheat. Also uses sensor for auto-defrost. No minutes-at-full-power touchpad.
Kenmore (Sears) 89381	No instant-on touchpads. Less-gentle heating than most at low power settings. **Similar:** 89380.
Kenmore (Sears) 89481	No instant-on touchpads. Less-gentle heating than most at low power settings. **Similar:** 89480.
Kenmore (Sears) 89682	Moisture sensor worked well in auto-reheat. No instant-on touchpads. Less-gentle heating than most at low power settings.
Magic Chef DM85K	No minutes-at-full-power touchpad. No instant-on touchpads. Less-gentle heating than most at low power settings. No child-lockout feature. Plastic turntable may discolor and must be shielded from packaged popcorn. Can operate without turntable, which increases usable capacity.
Panasonic 6813A D	Moisture sensor worked well in auto-reheat. Count-up touchpads in units of 10 min., 1 min., 10 sec., 1 sec. No instant-on touchpads.
Panasonic NN5803A D	Moisture sensor worked well in auto-reheat. Count-up touchpads in units of 10 min., 1 min., 10 sec., 1 sec. No instant-on touchpads.

Panasonic NN7703 [D]	Count-up touchpads in units of 10 min., 1 min., 10 sec., 1 sec. No instant-on touchpads.
Quasar MQS1540E [D]	Display characters hard to read; can't be seen at all in dim light. No auto reheat settings. No min.-at-full-power touchpad. No instant-on touchpads. Display lacks prompts. No child-lockout feature. Display characters hard to read; can't be seen in dim light.
Samsung MW6430W, **A BEST BUY**	Minutes-at-full-power touchpad also extends heating time (by a min. per tap) at lower power settings.
Samsung MW5430W	Minutes-at-full-power touchpad also extends heating time (by a min. per tap) at lower power settings.
Samsung MW6930	Minutes-at-full-power touchpad also extends heating time (by a min. per tap) at lower power settings.
Sanyo EM-704T [D]	No instant-on touchpads. Less-gentle heating than most at low power settings.
Sanyo EM-V830 [D]	No instant-on touchpads. Less-gentle heating than most at low power settings.
Sharp R-3A05	Minutes-at-full-power touchpad also extends heating time (by a min. per tap) at lower power settings.
Sharp R-3A66, **A BEST BUY**	Minutes-at-full-power touchpad also extends heating time (by a min. per tap) at lower power settings.
Sharp R-3H95 [D]	Moisture sensor worked well in auto-reheat. Minutes-at-full-power touchpad also extends heating time (by a min. per tap) at lower power settings.
Sharp R-4A56	Minutes-at-full-power button also extends heating time (by a min. per tap) at lower power settings. **Similar:** R-4A57.
Sharp R-4X06	Moisture sensor worked well in auto-reheat. Minutes-at-full-power touchpad also extends heating time (by a min. per tap) at lower power settings.
Sharp R-5H06	Moisture sensor worked well in auto-reheat. Minutes-at-full-power touchpad also extends heating time (by a min. per tap) at lower power settings. **Similar:** R-5H16.
Tappan TMS084T1W [S]	No auto reheat settings. No minutes-at-full-power touchpad. No light goes on when door is opened. **Successor:** TMS083U1W.
Welbilt MR95TW	No instant-on touchpads. No minutes-at-full-power touchpad. No kitchen timer. Power level not displayed and cannot be recalled with oven in use. No light goes on when door is opened.
Whirlpool MT9160XBQ	Minutes-at-full-power touchpad also extends heating time (by a min. per tap) at lower power settings.
Whirlpool MT6120XBQ	Minutes-at-full-power touchpad also extends heating time (by a min. per tap) at lower power settings.
Whirlpool MT2081XBQ	Auto-reheat setting can't be adjusted. No minutes-at-full-power touchpad. No light goes on when door is opened.

RATINGS ELECTRIC RANGES

▶ **See report, page 70.** Last time rated in Consumer Reports: July 1995.

Brand-name recommendations: All these models are fine performers, varying only slightly in their basic capabilities. Among the conventional ranges, the Hotpoint RB757GT, $410, stands out for its low price. As with the conventional ranges, performance differences among smoothtop models are modest; spending more buys small conveniences or different colors.

For the typical range in this class, expect: ■ A self-cleaning oven that bakes well and broils at a variable temp. ■ An oven window, 2 flat racks, a broiler pan, and a light that goes on when oven door is opened. ■ Four burners—two 8 to 9 inches in diameter, two 6 to 7 inches—controlled by dials. ■ An oven-temp. control that can be calibrated, and that beeps when desired temp. is reached. ■ Controls you can reach even with an 8-qt. pot on rear burner. ■ Anti-tip device to help prevent accidents when oven door is open. ■ Storage drawer. ■ Operation on 120/240 or 120/208 volts. **For the typical conventional range, expect:** ■ Removable coil elements. ■ Dial controls. ■ A cooktop that can be propped up for cleaning. ■ A raised edge around cooktop to contain spills. ■ 1-piece chrome drip bowls. **For the typical smoothtop range, expect:** ■ 4 radiant burners under a ceramic cooktop. ■ Keypad to control oven temp. ■ A digital clock/oven timer. ■ A cooktop that requires a special cleaner. ■ A "hot" light on the cooktop that stays on as long as the burner remains hot.

Notes on the table: Price is the estimated average, based on a national survey. * means price paid. **Cooktop speed** is based on performance of the highest-wattage burners in heating water. Models similar to those we tested are noted in Details; features may vary. **Model availability:** Ⓓ means model is discontinued.

Within type, listed in order of cooktop speed, oven size, and ease of use

Better ⟵⟶ Worse: ⊜ ⊖ ○ ◒ ●

Brand and model	Price	Overall score (P F G VG E)	Cooktop: SPEED	Cooktop: CLEANING	Oven: SIZE	Oven: WINDOW VIEW	Ease of use
CONVENTIONAL (COIL-ELEMENT) MODELS							
Hotpoint RB757GT	$410		⊖	○	○	⊖	⊖
Designer Series (M.Ward) 484440	429		⊜	○	⊖	●	⊖
Kenmore (Sears) 93541	500		⊜	○	○	⊖	○
General Electric JBP46GS Ⓓ	565		⊖	○	○	○	⊖
Tappan 31-2862-00 Ⓓ	455		⊜	○	⊖	●	○
Frigidaire FEF350CAS	475		⊜	○	⊖	●	⊖
White-Westinghouse WEF350CAS Ⓓ	520		⊜	○	⊖	●	○
General Electric JBP21GS Ⓓ	440		⊖	○	○	—	○
Magic Chef 3842VRV	475		⊜	○	⊖	●	○
Whirlpool RF365PXYQ Ⓓ	460		⊜	○	○	●	○

Brand and model	Price	Overall score	Cooktop		Oven		Ease of use
		P F G VG E	SPEED	CLEANING	SIZE	WINDOW VIEW	
SMOOTHTOP MODELS							
KitchenAid KERC500Y	$875		⊖	⊖	○	⊖	⊜
Magic Chef 3868XVW	625		⊖	⊜	⊖	⊖	⊖
General Electric JBP79WS [D]	815		⊖	⊜	○	○	⊖
Maytag CRE9600BCE	710		⊖	⊜	⊖	⊖	○
Whirlpool RF396PXYQ [D]	760		⊖	⊜	⊖	●	○
Amana ART663WW [D]	720		⊖	⊖	○	◒	○
Kenmore (Sears) 95845	*800		⊖	⊖	○	●	○
Frigidaire FEF367CAS	720		⊖	⊜	⊖	●	○
Tappan 31-4972	590		⊖	⊖	⊖	●	○

MODEL DETAILS

Want to know more about a rated model? They're listed here alphabetically.

Amana ART663WW [D]	**Pluses:** Door locks automatically in self-cleaning. Control-panel light. Burners in more than 2 sizes. **Minuses:** "Hot" light doubles as "on" light. Grease on rack in broiling tests.
Designer Series (M.Ward) 484440	**Pluses:** Door locks automatically in self-cleaning. 11-qt. pot on rear burner doesn't block controls. **Minuses:** Got very hot in self-cleaning. No beep when oven temp. reached. Storage drawer smaller than others. **Similar:** 484411, 484479.
Frigidaire FEF350CAS	**Pluses:** Door locks automatically in self-cleaning. **Minuses:** Got very hot in self-cleaning. 8-qt. covered pot on rear burner blocked some controls. Storage drawer smaller than others. **Similar:** FEF350BAD, -BAW, & -CCT.
Frigidaire FEF367CAS	**Pluses:** Door locks automatically in self-cleaning. Burners in more than 2 sizes. **Minuses:** Got very hot in self-cleaning. No beep when oven temp. is reached. 8-qt. covered pot on rear burner blocked some controls. Burners show fingerprints. Storage drawer smaller than others. **Similar:** FEF367CAT.
General Electric JBP21GS [D]	**Pluses:** Digital clock/timer. Self-cleaning instructions on oven. **Minuses:** No variable broiling temp. No oven window. Broil-pan insert hard to clean.
General Electric JBP46GS [D]	**Pluses:** Digital clock/timer. Porcelain drip bowls. Self-cleaning instructions on oven. **Minuses:** No variable broiling temp. Broil-pan insert hard to clean.
General Electric JBP79WS [D]	**Pluses:** Control-panel light. Self-cleaning instructions on oven. Burners in more than 2 sizes. High and low broil-temp. settings. **Minuses:** Broil-pan insert hard to clean.
Hotpoint RB757GT	**Pluses:** Digital clock/timer. Porcelain drip bowls. Self-cleaning instructions on oven. **Minuses:** No variable broiling temp. **Similar:** RB755GT, RB756GT.
Kenmore (Sears) 93541	**Pluses:** Digital clock/timer. Porcelain drip bowls. **Minuses:** No variable broiling temp. Manual oven light. **Similar:** 93545, 93548.
Kenmore (Sears) 95845	**Pluses:** Burners in more than 2 sizes. High and low broil-temp. settings. **Minuses:** Manual oven light. **Similar:** 95846, 95849.

Ratings continued ▶

Ratings continued

KitchenAid KERC500Y	**Pluses:** Door locks automatically in self-cleaning. Markers help to center cookware. Direct-entry keypad. Self-cleaning instructions on oven. Burners in more than 2 sizes. **Minuses:** Broil-pan insert hard to clean. Storage drawer hard to open and close. **Similar:** KERC500YAL, KERC500YBL.
Magic Chef 3842VRV	**Minuses:** No beep when oven temp. reached. No self-clean lock indicator. 8-qt. covered pot on rear burner blocked some controls. Grease on rack in broiling tests. Oven-temp. calibration cannot be adjusted by user. Manual oven light. **Similar:** 3842SRA, -SRW, -XRA, & -XRW.
Magic Chef 3868XVW	**Pluses:** Self-cleaning instructions on oven. High and low broil-temp. settings. **Minuses:** Single beep at end of timer countdown. Grease on rack in broiling tests. Manual oven light. **Similar:** 3868XVA, -VVV, & -VVD; 3888VVA, -VVV, & -XVB.
Maytag CRE9600BCE	**Pluses:** High and low broil-temp. settings. **Minuses:** Single beep at end of timer countdown. Grease on rack in broiling tests. **Similar:** CRE9600BCL, & -BCW; CRE9800BCB & -BCE.
Tappan 31-2862-00 D	**Pluses:** Door locks automatically in self-cleaning. 11-qt. pot on rear burner doesn't block controls. **Minuses:** Got very hot in self-cleaning. No beep when oven temp. reached. Oven-temp. calibration cannot be adjusted by user. Storage drawer smaller than others.
Tappan 31-4972	**Pluses:** Door locks automatically in self-cleaning. **Minuses:** Got very hot in self-cleaning. No beep when oven temp. reached. Burners show fingerprints. Storage drawer smaller than others.
Whirlpool RF365PXYQ D	**Pluses:** Porcelain drip bowls. Self-cleaning instructions on oven. **Minuses:** No beep when oven temp. reached. Broil-pan insert hard to clean. No self-clean lock indicator. Manual oven light.
Whirlpool RF396PXYQ D	**Pluses:** Control-panel light. Burners in more than 2 sizes. **Minuses:** Single beep at end of timer countdown. Broil-pan insert hard to clean. Failed pot-fit test; front burner too close to rear burner.
White-Westinghouse WEF350CAS D	**Pluses:** Door locks automatically in self-cleaning. 11-qt. pot on rear burner doesn't block controls. **Minuses:** Got very hot in self-cleaning. No beep when oven temp. reached. Oven-temp. calibration cannot be adjusted by user. Storage drawer smaller than others.

RATINGS DISHWASHERS

▶ **See report, page 77.** Last time rated in Consumer Reports: October 1995.

Brand-name recommendations: The three Best Buy models offer the best combination of performance, energy-efficiency, and price. The top-rated Kenmore ($565) and Whirlpool DU980QPDQ ($470) are slightly more convenient to use but are priced higher.

For a typical dishwasher in this class, expect: ■ Heavy, Normal, and Light wash cycles (at least) plus Rinse-and-Hold cycle. ■ Self-cleaning filter. ■ Plastic tub and door liner. ■ Dial, display, or lights to show progress through a cycle. ■ Flatware basket in lower rack. ■ Rinse-conditioner dispenser with refill indicator. ■ Telescoping spray tower or fixed tower in center of lower basket.

Notes on the table: Price is the estimated average, based on a national survey. * means price paid. The **washing** score is for the Normal cycle. **Energy** costs are annual and take into account the energy used to heat the water, the use of electricity for the wash motor, the internal heating of wash water, and heated drying. **Water use** is for the normal cycle. Models similar to those we tested are noted in Details; features may vary. **Model availability:** D means model is discontinued. S means model is replaced, according to the manufacturer; successor model is noted in Details. New model was not tested; it may or may not perform similarly. Features may vary.

Within type, listed in order of performance (mainly washing ability)

E ⊜ VG ⊖ G ○ F ◒ P ●

Brand and model	Price	Overall score (P F G VG E)	Washing	Noise	Energy cost (ELEC./GAS)	Water use
BUILT-IN MODELS						
Kenmore Ultra Wash III (Sears) 16941	$565	▬	⊜	○	$61/38 yr.	7.5
Whirlpool Quiet Partner DU980QPDQ	470	▬	⊜	⊖	66/42	7.5
Kenmore Ultra Wash III (Sears) 16779, **A BEST BUY**	400	▬	⊜	○	66/43	7.5
General Electric Profile GSD4930XWWA	560	▬	⊜	○	66/36	10.0
KitchenAid Superba Whisper Quiet KUDA23SBWHO	840	▬	⊖	⊖	56/32	7.5
Kenmore Ultra Wash III (Sears) 16649, **A BEST BUY**	369	▬	⊜	○	69/47	7.5
Whirlpool QuietWash Plus DU920QWDQ, **A BEST BUY**	390	▬	⊜	○	66/42	7.5
Maytag Quiet-Plus DWU9921AAE S	550	▬	⊜	⊖	66/35	9.5
KitchenAid Whisper Quiet KUDP230BO	510	▬	⊖	⊖	58/35	7.5
Maytag IntelliSense-Plus DWU9961AAE	755	▬	⊜	⊖	76/41	11.5
Maytag JetClean Quiet Plus DWU9200AAX S	460	▬	⊜	⊖	65/35	9.5

Ratings continued ▶

Ratings continued

Brand and model	Price	Overall score (P F G VG E)	Washing	Noise	Energy cost (ELEC./GAS)	Water use
BUILT-IN MODELS *continued*						
Magic Chef DU5JV	$330		⊖	⊖	$60/30 yr.	9.5
Maytag Quiet DWU7400AAE [S]	400		⊜	○	66/35	9.5
Jenn-Air DW960W	470		⊖	⊖	57/30	9.0
General Electric Potscrubber GSD1230T [S]	400		⊜	○	71/42	9.0
KitchenAid KUDB230BO	380		⊖	◒	59/35	7.5
White-Westinghouse WDB632RBS0	350*		○	◒	56/32	7.5
Caloric CDU600C [D]	375*		⊖	○	70/40	9.5
General Electric Profile GSD1930T [S]	450		⊖	○	69/41	9.0
Hotpoint HDA430V [S]	290		⊖	◒	70/40	9.5
Tappan Whisper Clean TDB668RBS0 [S]	379*		○	○	71/45	8.0
Frigidaire FDB878RBS0 [S]	280		○	○	73/45	9.0
Frigidaire FDB663RBS0	320		○	◒	70/45	8.0
Kenmore (Sears) 16541 [S]	319		⊖	◒	70/40	9.5
PORTABLE/CONVERTIBLE MODELS						
Kenmore Ultra Wash III (Sears) 17659	450		⊜	○	63/39	7.5
Whirlpool DP920QWDP	450		⊜	○	58/34	7.5
Maytag Jet Clean DWC7400AAW	480		⊜	○	62/31	10.0
General Electric Potscrubber GSC1200TWH [S]	435		⊜	◒	71/42	9.5

MODEL DETAILS

Want to know more about a rated model? They're listed here alphabetically.

Caloric CDU600C [D] — Delay start with all cycles. Upper rack has fold-down trays. Detergent dumped when cycle reset. Parts on interior stained in testing. **Similar:** CDU510CWW, CDU510CBB.

Frigidaire FDB663RBS0 — Delay start with Power Scrub and Normal cycle. Cannot fit tall glasses. Parts of interior discolored in testing.

Frigidaire FDB878RBS0 [S] — Delay start with all cycles. Child-proof controls. Cannot fit tall glasses. Upper rack has fold-down tray. Parts of interior discolored in testing. Did not restart after electrical interruption. **Successor:** FDB878GCS0.

General Electric Potscrubber GSC1200TWH [S] — Delay start with all cycles. Push buttons and dial controls. 2 flatware baskets. Wood-veneer top. Detergent is dumped when cycle is reset. **Successor:** GSC1200XWH.

General Electric Profile GSD4930XWW	Smart model: Senses soil level and adjusts wash cycle. Electronic controls. Digital display shows time left. Has systems monitor. Child-proof controls. Delay start with all cycles. Smooth control panel. Push buttons with indicator lights/display. Has adjustable utility shelf in upper rack. 2 flatware baskets. Did not restart after electrical interruption. **Similar:** GSD4920XBB, GSD4910XAA.
General Electric Potscrubber GSD1230T [S]	Delay start with all cycles. Upper rack has fold-down trays. 2 flatware baskets. Detergent dumped when cycle reset. Parts on interior stained in testing. **Successor:** GSD123OXWW.
General Electric Profile GSD1930T [S]	Delay start with all cycles. China/Crystal cycle with reduced-force spray. 2 flatware baskets. Utility shelf in upper rack. Detergent dumped when cycle reset. Parts on interior stained in testing. **Successor:** GSD1930XWW.
Hotpoint HDA430V [S]	Rinse-aid dispenser lacks indicator. Detergent dumped when cycle reset. **Successor:** HDA430XWW.
Jenn-Air DW960W	Smooth electronic control panel and time display. Delay start with all cycles. Parts on interior stained in testing.
Kenmore (Sears) 16541 [S]	Rinse-aid dispenser lacks indicator. Detergent dumped when cycle reset. Parts on interior stained in testing. **Successor:** 16551.
Kenmore Ultra Wash III (Sears) 16649, **A BEST BUY**	Center spray arm limits height in both racks. Cannot fit tall glasses. Extra utility basket, and utensil basket on upper rack. Upper rack has fold-down trays. Detergent dumped when cycle reset. Parts on interior stained in testing. **Similar:** 16949; 15849; 16849; 15749; 16749; 15649; 17659.
Kenmore Ultra Wash III (Sears) 16779, **A BEST BUY**	Delay start with Pots/Pans and Normal cycle. Center spray arm limits height in both racks, but upper rack adjusts to compensate. Extra utility basket and utensil basket on upper rack. Upper rack has fold-down trays. Detergent dumped when cycle reset. Parts on interior stained in testing. **Similar:** 16949; 15849; 16849; 15749; 16749; 15649; 17659.
Kenmore Ultra Wash III (Sears) 16941	Smooth electronic control panel with systems monitor that displays malfunctions, cycle status, time left. Delay start with all cycles. Child-proof controls. Center spray arm limits height in both racks, but upper rack adjusts to compensate. Extra utility basket and utensil basket on upper rack. Upper rack has fold-down trays. Parts on interior stained in testing. Did not restart after electrical interruption. **Similar:** 16949; 15849; 16849; 15749; 16749; 15649; 17659.
Kenmore Ultra Wash III (Sears) 17659	No delay start. Push buttons and dial controls. Center spray arm limits height in both racks, but upper rack adjusts to compensate. Upper rack has fold-down tray. Formica top. Detergent is dumped when cycle is reset.
KitchenAid Superba Whisper Quiet KUDA23SBWHO	Smooth electronic control panel with systems monitor that displays malfunctions, cycle status, time left. Delay start with all cycles. Center spray arm in protective cage limits height in both racks, but upper-rack adjusts to compensate. Rinse-aid dispenser lacks indicator. Hidden heating element; safer. Door gasket stained in testing. Porcelain-coated tub liner. **Similar:** KUDA235B.
KitchenAid Superba Whisper Quiet KUDB230BO	Center spray arm limits height in both racks. Cannot fit tall glasses. Rinse-aid dispenser lacks indicator. Door gasket stained in testing. Porcelain-coated tub liner.
KitchenAid Whisper Quiet KUDP230BO	Delay start with all cycles. Pushbuttons only with indicator. Center spray arm limits height in both racks, but upper rack adjusts to compensate. Rinse-aid dispenser lacks indicator. Door gasket stained in testing. Porcelain-coated tub liner.

Ratings continued ▶

Ratings continued

Magic Chef DU5JV	Rinse-aid dispenser lacks indicator. Parts on interior stained in testing. **Similar:** DU5J.
Maytag IntelliSense-Plus DWU9961AAE	Smart model: Senses soil level and adjusts wash cycle. Electronic controls. Digital display shows time left. Has systems monitor. Child-proof controls. Delay start with all cycles. Smooth control panel. Push buttons with indicator lights/display. Upper rack has fold-down tray. Lower rack has fold down section. Interior discolored less than others. **Similar:** DWU9961AAX.
Maytag Jet Clean DWC7400AAW	No delay start. Push buttons and dial controls. Wood-veneer top. Interior discolored less than others.
Maytag Quiet DWU7400AAE [S]	**Successor:** DWU7400BAE.
Maytag JetClean Quiet Plus DWU9200AAX [S]	Delay start only with Pots/Pans cycle. Upper and lower racks have fold-down trays. **Successor:** DWU9200BAR.
Maytag Quiet-Plus DWU9921AAE [S]	Smooth electronic control panel with systems monitor that displays malfunctions, cycle status, time left. Delay start with all cycles. Upper and lower racks have fold-down trays. **Successor:** DWU9921BAE.
Tappan Whisper Clean TDB668RBS0 [S]	Delay start with all but Light cycle. Cannot fit tall glasses. Extra utility basket. Upper rack has fold-down tray. Rinse-aid dispenser lacks indicator. Parts of interior discolored in testing. **Successor:** TDB668RBR0.
Whirlpool Quiet Partner DU980QPDQ	Child-proof controls. Delay start with all cycles. Smooth control panel. Push buttons with indicator lights/display. Center spray arm limits height in both racks, but upper rack adjusts to compensate. Upper rack has fold-down tray. Flatware/utensil baskets on door. **Similar:** DU980QPDB.
Whirlpool Quiet Wash Plus DU920QWDQ, **A BEST BUY**	Child-proof controls. No delay start. Smooth control panel. Push buttons with indicator lights/display. Center spray arm limits height in both racks, but upper rack adjusts to compensate. Flatware basket on door. **Similar:** DU920QWDB, DU940QWDQ, DU940QWDB, DU940QWDZ.
Whirlpool DP920QWDB	Child-proof controls. No delay start. Smooth control panel. Push buttons with indicator lights/display. Center spray arm limits height in both racks, but upper rack adjusts to compensate. Flatware basket on door. Formica top.
White-Westinghouse WDB632RBS0	Cannot fit tall glasses. Rinse-aid dispenser lacks indicator. Parts of interior discolored in testing. **Similar:** WDB632RBR0, WDB662RBR0,WBD664RBR0.

SMALL APPLIANCES

Breadmakers

A breadmaker is a food mixer and oven all in one package that is, yes, somewhat bigger than a bread box. You pour measured ingredients or a packaged bread mix into the pan, press some buttons, and walk away. A small propeller-shaped paddle kneads the dough, stops to let it rise, and sometimes repeats the cycle. Then the oven bakes the bread.

A few years ago, there were nine main breadmaker brands; today there are about 20. Welbilt is the biggest brand, but its share of the market has been declining as new brands such as Toastmaster, West Bend, and Black & Decker have made significant gains. With competition up, prices are going down; you can buy a basic breadmaker for about $100; a full-featured model, for about $350.

The choices

Size. The newest breadmakers make larger loaves. The 1-pound size has given way to the 1½- and 2-pound size. The 1½-pound size, which takes about three cups of flour, yields 10 to 13 slices (compared with 20 slices in store-bought bread).

Loaf shape. New models come closer to producing a conventionally-shaped loaf that's more or less square.

Features and conveniences

Loading and cleanup. The machines generally have a nonstick bread pan with the paddle attached to the bottom. That design lets you load the pan outside the machine and simplifies cleanup.

Controls. All models have a digital display indicating the stage of preparation and time left. Setting controls is usually easy; you push a few touchpad buttons and a Start button.

Special cycles. Most breadmakers have a rapid cycle that cuts an hour or so off the kneading and rising time. However, bread made that way is generally not as high or fluffy as the standard-cycle bread. A Dough cycle shuts off the machine before the oven heats up so you can remove the dough to shape it and bake it in a conventional oven. Programmed cycles adjust the time, temperature, or handling for light or whole-grain breads. One of our tested models let you create custom cycles.

Delay-start timer. Most breadmakers let you add the ingredients and select a time (up to 13 hours ahead) for the bread to be ready. A timer is useful if you like to wake up to fresh bread in the morning.

Mix-in signal. A buzzer lets you know when to add raisins for raisin bread, caraway seeds for rye, and so forth. If you add them at the start, some machines pulverize them by the end of the mixing.

Viewing window. Most breadmakers have a small window on top to let you view the action.

Buying advice

All breadmakers make good or very good bread with correctly measured, fresh ingredients. But a model with well-designed controls and simple loading and cleanup is easier to live with. You'll generally find the best prices at stores like Sears or Walmart and at warehouse clubs.

For the latest report, see the December 1995 issue of CONSUMER REPORTS.

Coffee makers

▶ Ratings on page 115.

Coffee lovers, spoiled by the fine brew they get in gourmet coffee shops, are taking more care to make a better cup of coffee at home. While there are various ways to make coffee, most people use the drip-style coffee maker.

In addition to Mr. Coffee, which leads sales, big brands in automatic-drip sales include Black & Decker and Hamilton Beach. Braun and Krups, small, brands whose automatic-drip models are popular among CONSUMER REPORTS readers, lead the espresso/cappucino market. Melitta dominates sales of manual drip coffee makers.

The choices

Electric automatic-drip. These popular machines usually consist of a water reservoir, a basket to hold the filter and coffee grounds, a carafe to hold and serve the coffee, and a hot plate to keep the carafe's contents warm. Electric elements heat the water and hot plate. To brew a pot of coffee, you pour a measured amount of cold tap water into the reservoir and flip a switch. Prices range from $15 to $150.

Percolators. They brew coffee by circulating water continually through the coffee grounds. Electrics start at about $60; nonelectrics, much less.

Manual types. The simplest manual drip brewers consist of a plastic cone to hold the filter and coffee grounds. You place the cone over a cup and pour boiling water over the coffee grounds. Another type of manual brewer, the French press, consists of a glass cylinder and a plunger that is fitted with a fine metal screen at the end. You put coffee grounds in the cylinder, pour hot water over them, and let the brew steep a few minutes. You then push the grounds to the bottom with the plunger. Typically, the brew contains more sediment than drip coffee does, and cleanup can be messy. But you save on filters—there aren't any. Prices: $10 to $60.

Espresso/cappucino machines. The better ones use a pump to force almost-boiling water under high pressure through finely ground, tightly packed coffee for about 20 to 30 seconds to produce one or two cups at a time. Other types use steam pressure to force water through the grounds, making a poorer quality coffee. Many come with attachments for making steamed milk, which, when combined with a shot of espresso, makes cappuccino or caffe latté. Prices run anywhere from about $40 to $200.

Features and conveniences

Size and capacity. Automatic-drip machines range from single-cup models to full-sized units that brew 12 cups at a time. Ten-cup machines are the biggest sellers. Actual capacity, however, depends on one's definition of a cup. With five-ounce cups, we found, actual capacity could be two cups less than stated.

Reservoir. A reservoir with a large, unobstructed opening is easy to fill. A reservoir marked with cup measurements makes measuring water almost foolproof.

Basket. The basket that holds the filter and coffee grounds should be easy to remove and insert. One that swings out is handier than one that slides out or sits directly on the carafe.

Filters. Many units use a basket-style paper filter; others, a cone-style. Filters are typically paper, but reusable metal or plastic ones are available.

TIPS FOR MAKING THE FRESHEST BREW

Grinding whole beans just before brewing makes a fresher-tasting pot of coffee. Buy coffee beans in a store with lots of turnover, or by mail order.

Even if you don't go to such trouble, storing coffee in a sealed, dry, airtight container will keep it fresher.

If you'll finish the coffee within a week, keep it in the refrigerator. If you use it more slowly, put it in the freezer. (You can grind frozen coffee without defrosting it.) Don't store opened coffee at room temperature.

Drip stop. This lets you siphon off a cup before the coffee is completely ready without having coffee dribble onto the warming plate.

Controls. Avoid models whose controls are crowded or poorly labeled. Since it's easy to forget that the coffee maker is on, a prominent On light is important. Auto shut-off turns off the machine after a certain amount of time, generally two hours. Programmable models let you load the machine the night before and set it to start brewing the following morning.

Some models have a brew-strength control, but a simpler, less wasteful way to make a mild brew is to use less grounds. More useful is a "small cup" switch that alters the brewing process when you make only a few cups of coffee. It worked well on our tested models and eliminates the need to add a little more coffee per cup when brewing just a few cups.

The tests

To judge drip coffee makers, an expert taster sips coffee freshly brewed by the machines. We use the same brand of coffee and the same amount of grounds for each cup. We also judge features and convenience.

Buying advice

An auto-drip coffee maker should turn out consistently good brew. Nearly all do. Good models are also convenient to use.

If kitchen-counter space is tight, or if you usually want only a cup or two at a time, consider a manual coffee maker or a four-cup electric machine. A junior electric is no better or cheaper than a full-sized model, just smaller. A manual setup is the simplest but less convenient.

Toasters

▶ Ratings on page 117.

Of all the toast-making appliances, a toaster still makes the best toast. It has been making fine toast for some time, in fact, with the same basic components—a spring-loaded carriage, hot wires, and a rotary knob or sliding switch to regulate the toast color.

In recent years, several design changes have boosted sales of toasters. Many models now have a plastic housing that stays cool to the touch. On some, the parallel slots have given way to a single long slot wide enough to accept thick slices.

Eight of 10 toasters sold are made by three companies: Toastmaster, Hamilton Beach/Proctor-Silex, and Black & Decker.

The choices

The biggest difference among models is capacity. Two-slice models have the familiar two side-by-side slots or a single long slot. Most four-slice toasters still have four individual slots.

Most toasters sit on the counter, but at least one model mounts under a cabinet.

Prices range from about $25 to $50 for two-slice models and $50 to $120 for four-slice models.

Features and conveniences

Wide slots. The opening should be at least 1⅛ inches wide to accept English muffins or bagels. Even better are 1⅜-inch-wide slots. Some models that advertise "wide slots" have openings no wider than the standard three-quarters of an inch.

Controls. Although you'll see an occasional electronic touchpad, most models have mechanical controls. A Keep-warm setting keeps the toast lowered after it's finished so it can bask in the toaster's residual heat. A more sophisticated version is the Warm-up setting, which cycles the power on and off for up to four minutes.

Crumb cleanup. A removable crumb tray is the easiest way to clean out a toaster's crumbs. More common is a hinged tray through which you shake out crumbs. The least convenient are models that need shaking upside down.

Housing. A toaster with an all-plastic exterior doesn't get as hot as a metal one.

Self-centering. This keeps the slice from leaning sideways in the slot, supposedly to ensure even toasting. In our tests, it didn't seem to make much difference.

The tests

We look for toasters that brown toast predictably and uniformly. We toast one slice at a time, in full batches, and in consecutive batches. We also note conveniences and features.

Buying advice

If you eat a lot of toast, buy a toaster, not a toaster oven. In general, we've found, two-slice models work better than four-slicers. If your taste runs to bagels or thick hand-cut slices from crusty loaves, look for a toaster with slots at least 1⅛ inches wide. If you want a four-slicer, make sure it comes with separate controls for each pair of slots.

Portable & stand mixers

▶ Ratings on page 119. ▶ Guide to food-fixers on page 109.

Regular stand mixers can handle heavy-duty chores such as kneading bread and cookie doughs, as well as light chores such as whipping cream and mixing cake batter. Even so, their portable cousins, which tackle only light and moderate tasks, have far outdistanced them in sales because of convenience, price, and size. Models that work both as a heavy-duty portable and light-duty stand mixer give you the worst of both worlds; they're too wimpy for big mixing jobs and too big to store in a drawer.

Black & Decker, Hamilton Beach/Proctor-Silex, and Sunbeam, the biggest brands of portables, are sold mainly through mass merchants like Walmart and Bradlees. KitchenAid and Sunbeam dominate sales of stand mixers, which are usually found in catalogs, department stores, and specialty stores.

The choices

Portables. Also known as hand mixers, these are either corded or battery-powered. Battery-powered portables can mash potatoes, mix cake batter, and perform other light and moderate chores. But between tasks, they must stay on a charging base plugged into an outlet. Corded mixers generally do those tasks much better than cordless mixers, and they can fit into a drawer. A corded mixer sells for about $15 to $60. Cordless mixers range from $30 to $60. Portable models typically offer three to five speeds.

Stand mixers. Stand mixers come in heavy- and light-duty versions. The strongest heavy-duty mixers can mix and knead at least six cups of flour, enough for two loaves of bread, while others can take only 3½ cups of flour to make one loaf. Light-duty mixers are essentially hand mixers resting on a stand. Prices: $40 to $300 for heavy-duty models.

Features and conveniences

Weight. Most portables weigh between 1¾ and 2¼ pounds. With time-consuming tasks, the heavier models may begin to feel leaden. Stand mixers are much heavier, but that should matter only if you have to lift it onto the counter each time you use it.

Speeds. Though many models offer lots of speeds or a continuously variable speed, three well-spaced settings—slow, intermediate, and fast—are all you need. The slower the speed, in fact, the less spattering. Some stand mixers have a Pulse control, which keeps the machine on for as long as you push the button.

Beaters. Though the shape of the beaters doesn't matter for most chores, a wire whisk or beaters with no center post usually work best for whipping air into foods like whipped cream. These beaters are also easiest to clean. Two beaters are better than one; cordless models with a single beater don't mix food nearly as well. Some portables and most stand mixers also come with a dough hook.

Handle. The design of the handle is important for portables. A comfortable grip makes the mixer easier to hold.

Controls. Most are switches or buttons, but top-of-the-line models have touchpads and digital displays. Controls positioned toward the front of the handle allow you to adjust the speed with the same hand you use to hold the mixer.

Stability. With its beaters in place, a hand mixer should be balanced enough to stand solidly on its heel. Models with a narrow heel rest are usually unstable. More and more stand mixers offer a Head lock, which lets you lock the beaters in the raised position (so they won't crash into the bowl when they're laden with dough) or in the Down position (to hold the beaters in a stiff dough).

The tests

To test stand mixers, we whip heavy cream, mash potatoes, knead bread dough, and mix cookie dough. We also cycle each mixer on at medium speed for two minutes, then off for four minutes, with the beaters immersed in a goo with the consistency of cake batter, for a total of 65 hours "on" time.

Buying advice

If you bake a lot, consider a stand mixer. Although some portable mixers can manage dough, it takes a firm grip to keep the dough hooks from recoiling. For kneading bread dough and mixing cookie batter, heavy-duty models do the best job. Light-duty stand mixers perform like portable mixers but are less useful because they don't store easily.

For occasional use and less taxing chores, a conventional plug-in portable model is best. Cordless mixers are relatively expensive, and many routine tasks leave them wheezing.

Blenders

▶ **Guide to food-fixers at right.**

Today's standard blenders are much like their Depression-era prototypes, but innovative designs are reshaping the product. Some models are capable of crushing ice. Touchpad controls simplify cleanup considerably and handheld models allow more mobility.

The biggest brands in blenders are KitchenAid, Sunbeam/Oster, Waring, Hamilton Beach, and Proctor-Silex.

The choices

Handheld models. Handheld blenders work like a simplified portable mixer. To blend, you simply plunge the blade into a container of ingredients.

Most models have one or two speeds that you control with a switch or dial. Handheld models weigh only a couple of pounds, so they're easy to maneuver and store. They're ideal for mixing liquids and making soup. Some handhelds also come with attachments for chopping nuts and grinding cheese. Prices range from about $20 to $45.

Standard models. The standard blender—a jar with a rotating blade at the base—is more powerful than the handheld variety, letting you blend larger quantities. Standard models generally come with more speeds than you'll need. Prices range from about $20 to $125.

Features and conveniences

Controls. One or two speeds, typical of a handheld model, are enough for mixing liquids. Especially handy is a continuously variable speed. On standard models, six speeds are enough for most chores, though the range of speeds is more important than the number. A Pulse control keeps the blades whirring only as long as you depress it.

Containers. Markings that aid measuring are an obvious convenience. A wide-mouth container eases the loading of food, as does a large, removable insert in the lid. A wide-mouth container also eases cleaning. Handheld blenders usually come with plastic containers; standard models use plastic or glass. Plastic is lighter and more durable, but it may get scratched and cloudy over time. Blend-and-store containers make leftovers easy to store and minimize cleanup. Containers of standard blenders typically hold more than twice as much as containers of handheld models.

Cleanup. With handheld models, simply hold the blades under hot running water. Standard models with few controls, well-spaced buttons, or flat touchpad controls are easiest to clean. Containers are almost always dishwasher-safe, but plastic may not hold up as well as glass in the dishwasher. Blades shouldn't be hard to clean, but they may rust if left to soak in water overnight.

Buying advice

Differences in performance tend to be slight, so choose by type and price. Handheld models are best for foamy drinks and diet preparations. They let you mix and serve in the same container, and they made the best milk shakes and whipped cream in our tests.

Standard blenders are most effective for tasks like puréeing vegetables. They also do a nice job with mixing icy drinks and grating Parmesan cheese.

Buying the right food-fixer

Use the chart below to pick the machine that's best suited for the food-fixing task at hand.

	Standard blender	Handheld blender	Portable mixer	Stand mixer	Food processor	Food chopper
Puréeing vegetables	✔					✔
Mixing frozen drinks	✔					
Mixing frozen shakes	✔	✔				
Whipping cream			✔	✔		
Mashing potatoes			✔	✔		
Mixing cake batter			✔	✔		
Mixing pie crust				✔	✔	
Mixing cookie dough				✔	✔	
Crumbling crackers					✔	
Shredding and slicing vegetables					✔	
Chopping vegetables					✔	✔
Grating Parmesan	✔				✔	✔

Food processors

▶ Ratings on page 113. ▶ Guide to food-fixers on page 109.

Food processors can't turn a cook into a chef, but they can make chopping vegetables for a soup or stew much easier. They can make quick work of salad fixings like onions, mushrooms, and cucumbers. And they're also handy for crumbling graham crackers for a pie crust or for mixing pastry dough.

For kitchen tasks that need a lighter touch, however, other appliances are better. An electric mixer makes the best mashed potatoes or whipped cream. And nothing tops a standard countertop blender for liquefying foods, puréeing baby food, and concocting exotic drinks. (See the guide to food-fixers on page 109.)

Although the Cuisinarts Company, which pioneered the product two decades ago, no longer exists, Conair has taken over the name. Today, Hamiliton Beach/Proctor-Silex, Cuisinart, and Sunbeam/Oster are the leading brands.

The choices

Standard processors. Two sizes are available—compact and full-sized. Compact models need a bit less kitchen space, and they're easier to lift and clean. Full-sized processors are useful for ambitious menus or large meals. Size definitions are not standardized: One company's "compact" may have a larger processing bowl than another's "full sized." Models we consider full-sized have a bowl that holds at least 5½ cups of food. Compacts hold 2½ to 4¼ cups. Even by that measure of capacity, some compacts are taller than full-sized models. Prices: full-sized, $45 to $300; compact, $35 to $215.

Mini food-choppers/food processors. This appliance chops, grinds, and purées in small quantities—half a cup or so at a time. Unlike a food processor, it cannot slice or shred. Price: $15 to $35.

Salad gun. This is essentially a feed tube with a motorized cone that holds a blade. It can slice and shred but is much less effective and versatile than a regular food processor. Price: $20 to $45.

Multipurpose fixer. This megamachine may combine a food processor, blender, salad maker, stand mixer, juice extractor, or food mill; the mix varies with make and model. You attach the appropriate accessory to a motorized base. In our tests, no one model performed all its tasks well. Price: $250 to $300.

Features and conveniences

Chute. With most food processors, the sliced or shredded food drops into a bowl, which you must empty when it's full. Other machines use a separate chute to divert the flow of food, or a device that slings food out of the bowl, through an opening in the lid, into another container.

Bowl. All standard food processors have a transparent plastic work bowl, usually with a handle. A bowl can hold more dry food than liquid. Filled to capacity with a thin liquid, the bowl usually overflows during processing.

Blades and disks. An S-shaped metal chopping blade and a slicing/shredding disk are standard. Some models have separate slicing and shredding disks. Additional attachments, either standard or optional, may include thin and thick slicing/shredding disks, a cheese-grating disk, and a disk for cutting french fries. Attachments such as a plastic whipping accessory for cream and a plastic blade for mixing dough are less useful.

Feed tube and pusher. With most processors, you slice or shred food by inserting it into a feed tube on the bowl's lid, using a plastic pusher if need be. Some feed tubes are wide enough to swallow a medium-sized tomato. Some incorporate a slender inner tube for holding narrow foods like carrots upright.

Controls. Besides an On/off switch, most standard processors have a Pulse provision, which keeps the machine running as long as you push a switch. Some processors have touchpad controls instead of switches. Other models go on and off whenever you move the lid into and out of a latch on the housing. We found controls on the handle inconvenient. One speed is all you need.

Cleanup and storage. Machines with smooth lines and no food-trapping gaps are the easiest to clean. Tough to clean: large, convoluted feed tubes. Most components are dishwasher-safe. Place them on the top rack, away from the heating element. And don't let blades soak in water overnight—they might rust.

Buying advice

If you need to chop, purée, mix, or slice on a grand scale, consider a full-sized processor. A compact model should suit someone who doesn't make food for a crowd. Don't count on a compact to save much space, however. While it takes slightly less counter space than a full-sized model, a compact may actually be taller.

You needn't pay top dollar. Expensive processors in our tests were powerful, quiet, and well appointed, but some less expensive models in our tests worked well and were more convenient.

Steam irons

▸ **Ratings on page 120.**

Any steam iron is likely to smooth out wrinkles nicely, according to our tests, but some do it more easily than others. Features like a nonstick soleplate, fast heat, retractable cord, and auto shutoff add to an iron's convenience—and its price.

Black & Decker, which makes more irons than all other companies combined, divides the ironing public into two categories: "batch ironers," who take on a basket of wrinkled clothes at a time, and "ad-hoc ironers," who iron garment by garment as necessary. It targets the first type with a heavy-duty model, and the second with a model that is supposed to heat up quickly and store easily.

Besides Black & Decker, important brand names among irons include Hamilton Beach/Proctor-Silex and Sunbeam/Oster. Most irons sell for $20 to $40, though models at the pricey end—represented by the Rowenta and Tefal brands—may reach $130.

The choices

Standard irons. Most can use tap water. Vents in the soleplate—the flat, working surface of the iron—discharge steam. You set the iron to the right temperature for the fabric you're ironing and push a button to activate the steam level. These irons also let you turn off the steam for delicate items.

Cordless irons. These otherwise standard irons are pricey—and we don't think they're worth the extra expense. Though there's no cord to get in the way as you work, you must constantly return the iron to its base to reheat it. One cordless model we tested can also be used with a cord.

Travel irons. These compact and light

irons are easy to carry. But they don't get as hot or steam as much as standard irons, and their small soleplate prolongs the job. Travel-irons typically come with a pouch and a provision for overseas voltage.

Steamers. These are designed to smooth wrinkles from clothes on hangers. They don't have controls; they're on when plugged in, off when unplugged.

Features and conveniences

Automatic shutoff. Many irons turn themselves off if you don't move them for a while. Most close down after about half a minute lying flat and from 8 to 15 minutes standing upright. An indicator light usually flashes or shines until the iron is reactivated. Some irons beep when they shut off.

Controls. Whether it's on the front of the iron handle or underneath it, the list of fabric settings should be easy to read. And controls should be easy to set. On some irons, a Burst-of-Steam button adds extra steam to penetrate wrinkles on hard-to-iron fabric. A Spray button helps you iron challenging fabrics like linen, set creases, and do spot-dampening.

Soleplate. A soleplate with a nonstick coating won't necessarily glide more smoothly than others, but it's generally easier to keep clean. Some soleplates have grooves that are supposed to let you iron more easily around buttons.

Cords. Rear-mounted cords that don't hit your wrist or drag on the fabric are the least annoying. Some can pivot left or right for convenience. Extra long cords of about 12 feet eliminate the need for extension cords. A provision for wrapping the cord around the base is a nice touch. The retractable cord on some Panasonic models is even better.

Water tank. An iron usually performs best when its water tank is full—and the best water tanks let you see the water level. Removable tanks are the easiest to fill.

Heel rest. The heel of an iron should hold the iron upright securely.

The tests

We check the range of temperature settings and the time each iron takes to heat up and cool down. Using appropriate settings, we iron wrinkled linen, cotton, permanent-press, rayon, acrylic, and acetate fabrics. We judge the effectiveness of features, and we evaluate how easy it is to set the controls, fill the water tank, and clean the soleplate.

Buying advice

Some simple steam irons work well, but features like Burst-of-Steam and Spray make the job easier. Extra features almost always increase the price.

Choose an iron that feels comfortable in your hand, with a cord that won't get in your way. The controls should be easy to read and set, and you should be able to see the water level in the tank easily.

RATINGS FOOD PROCESSORS

▶ **See report, page 110.** Last time rated in Consumer Reports: August 1992.

Brand-name recommendations: The top-rated model, the Braun UK11, $104, boasts generous capacity (11½ cups); except for being noisy, it got high marks in most tasks. The Panasonic MK-5070, $115, was nearly as good and much quieter.

For the typical food processor, expect: ■ Transparent plastic bowl with a handle. ■ S-shaped metal chopping blade. ■ Slicing/shredding disk. ■ Feed tube with pusher to insert food. ■ Safety interlock that prevents operation unless lid and bowl are latched. ■ On/off switch and Pulse. ■ Single speed. ■ Blades to rust if left soaking. ■ Good or better performance at whipping cream, puréeing carrots, grinding peanuts and beef cubes, chopping carrots and prosciutto, slicing mushrooms, shredding zucchini and cabbage. **A choice you'll have to make:** ■ Full-sized or compact.

Notes on the table: Closely ranked models generally differed little in quality. **Price** is the estimated average, based on a national survey. * means approx. retail price. **Size** measures max. capacity in cups of dry food and S-shaped chopping blade in place. **Power** measures performance with heavy-duty tasks. **Blending** is tested with soup; **grinding** with graham crackers; **slicing** with carrots. **Model availability:** [D] means model is discontinued.

Within types, listed in order of performance

Better ⊜ ⊖ ○ ◒ ● Worse

Brand and model	Price	Size	Power	Ease of use	Blend	Grind	Slice
FULL-SIZED MODELS							
Braun Multipractic UK11	$104	11½	○	⊜	○	○	◒
Panasonic Kitchen Wizard MK-5070	115*	8¼	○	⊖	○	⊜	⊖
Cuisinart DLC-7 FPC [D]	300	12¼	⊜	◒	●	◒	⊖
Cuisinart Custom 11 DLC-8M [D]	188	10	⊖	◒	◒	○	⊜
Regal La Machine II K588GY [D]	65	9½	○	⊜	●	○	⊖
Waring Professional PFP15	240	7¾	⊖	◒	○	○	○
Braun Multipractic MC100	60	6½	◒	⊖	◒	◒	○
Braun Multipractic MC200	80	6½	◒	○	◒	○	⊖
Regal La Machine I K813GY	37	6½	◒	○	●	◒	○
Sunbeam Oskar 3000 14201 [D]	90	5½	◒	◒	⊜	⊖	⊜
COMPACT MODELS							
Cuisinart Little Pro Plus	94	4¼	—	⊜	○	⊜	⊜
Black & Decker Handy Shortcut HMP30 [D]	30	2¼	—	⊖	○	⊜	⊜
Sunbeam Oskar 14181 [D]	35	2¾	—	●	⊜	⊜	⊖

Ratings continued ▶

Ratings continued

MODEL DETAILS

Want to know more about a rated model? They're listed here alphabetically.

Model	Details
Black & Decker Handy Shortcut HMP30 [D]	Controls well marked, easy to use. All blades can be stored in bowl. Very narrow feed tube.
Braun Multipractic MC100	Blade stops instantly when switched off. Cord storage. Blade inserts pose slightly greater danger of cutting fingers. Hole on blade hub can admit foods, which can create a mess.
Braun Multipractic MC200	Blade stops instantly when switched off. Cord storage. Blade inserts pose slightly greater danger of cutting fingers. Hole on blade hub can admit foods, which can create a mess.
Braun Multipractic UK11	Has reversible thin/thick disks for slicing or shredding, disk for grating cheese, and disk for french fries. No leaks with 4 cups of liquid. Blade stops instantly when switched off. Cord storage.
Cuisinart Custom 11 DLC-8M [D]	Controls well marked, easy to use. Good-sized feed tube but hard to use and clean. All blades can be stored in bowl. Liquids leaked.
Cuisinart DLC-7 FPC [D]	Controls well marked, easy to use. Good-sized feed tube but hard to use and clean. All blades can be stored in bowl.
Cuisinart Little Pro Plus	Controls well marked, easy to use. Slicing/shredding disk easy and safe to mount and remove. Comes with regular lid and chute for slicing or shredding. All blades can be stored in bowl.
Panasonic Kitchen Wizard MK-5070	Controls well marked, easy to use. No leaks even with 3⅓ cups of liquid. Blade inserts pose slightly greater danger of cutting fingers.
Regal La Machine I K813GY	Blade stops instantly when switched off. All blades can be stored in bowl. Liquids leaked. Blade inserts pose slightly greater danger of cutting fingers.
Regal La Machine II K588GY [D]	Slicing/shredding disk easy and safe to mount and remove. Blade stops instantly when switched off. All blades can be stored in bowl. Cord storage.
Sunbeam Oskar 14181 [D]	Hard-to-use chute instead of feed tube. Liquids leaked.
Sunbeam Oskar 3000 14201 [D]	Coarse shredding disk worked well. Cord storage. Poorly located On/off/pulse switch. Liquids leaked.
Waring Professional PFP15	Liquids leaked.

RATINGS DRIP COFFEE MAKERS

▶ **See report, page 104.** Last time rated in Consumer Reports: October 1994.

Brand-name recommendations: All the machines can make very good coffee. Differences are in their convenience and features. Mr. Coffee models top the list of basic machines. The two highest-rated programmable machines—the Krups 136, $100, and the Braun KF187, $109—offer an unequaled array of features.

For the typical coffee maker, expect: ■ Very good brewing performance. ■ A full carafe of brew in 8½ to 15 min. ■ A glass 10- or 12-cup carafe (actual capacity may be 2 cups less.) ■ Drip-stop, which lets you pour before brewing has stopped and minimizes drips. ■ A plastic housing. ■ A swing-out holder for basket or cone-shaped filter. ■ A warming plate with a nonstick coating. ■ For programmable models, a digital clock, auto shut-off, and brewing that can be set up in advance.

Notes on the table: Price is the estimated average, based on a national survey. * means price paid. **Model availability:** Ⓓ means model is discontinued.

Within types, listed in order of convenience and features

E ⊜ VG ⊖ G ○ F ◒ P ●

Brand and model	Price	Overall score (P F G VG E)	Ease of use	Comments
BASIC MODELS				
Mr. Coffee Accel PR12A	$27		⊜	Filter basket has drip-stop on removable insert. Auto shut-off.
Mr. Coffee Accel PR16	25		⊜	Filter basket has drip-stop on removable insert.
Braun FlavorSelect KF140	60		⊖	Carafe has rim guard. Brew relatively hot.
Krups ProCafe Plus 201	50		⊖	Carafe dribbled a lot when filling reservoir. Brew relatively hot.
Mr. Coffee BL110	22		⊖	Pull-out filter basket. Brew relatively hot.
Proctor-Silex Morning Maker 42401	35		⊖	Auto shut-off. Carafe dribbled a lot when filling reservoir. Warming plate uncoated.
Proctor-Silex Morning Maker 42301	20		⊖	Warming plate uncoated.
Braun Aromaster KF400	35		○	Carafe dribbled a lot when filling reservoir.
Krups Brewmaster Plus 140	40		⊖	No drip-stop. Carafe has very comfortable handle, dribbled a lot when filling reservoir. Filter basket must be removed to pour coffee.

Ratings continued ▶

Ratings continued

Brand and model	Price	Overall score (P F G VG E)	Ease of use	Comments
BASIC MODELS *continued*				
Black & Decker DCM901 [D]	$22		○	Uncomfortable handle. Pull-out filter basket. Brew relatively hot.
Bunn NHB	40		○	Porcelain-coated warming plate. Pull-out filter basket. Very comfortable handle. No drip-stop. Brew relatively hot.
Melitta Aroma Brew ACM-10S	*30		○	Uncomfortable handle. No On light. Brew relatively cool.
Black & Decker DCM900WH [D]	20		◒	Pull-out filter basket. Uncomfortable handle. Reservoir hard to fill. No On light, drip-stop. Brew relatively hot.
West Bend Quik Drip 56660	35		◒	Pull-out filter basket. Uncomfortable handle. Brew relatively hot.
Betty Crocker BC-1732 [D]	19		◒	Reservoir hard to fill. Carafe dribbled a lot when filling reservoir. Warming plate uncoated. Brew relatively cool.
PROGRAMMABLE MODELS				
Krups Coffee Time Plus 136	100		⊖	Carafe dribbled a lot. Filter basket has removable inserts with drip-stop. Brew relatively hot.
Braun FlavorSelect KF187	109		⊖	Metal filter. Carafe has rim guard. Beeps when coffee ready. Warming-plate temp. adjustable. Brew relatively hot.
Mr. Coffee Accel PRX20	50		⊖	Metal filter. Filter basket has removable insert. Brew relatively hot.
Betty Crocker BC-1740	35		⊖	Carafe dribbled a lot when filling reservoir. Has drip-stop on removable insert. Brew relatively hot.
Proctor-Silex A8737G or A8737T	40		⊖	Metal filter. Easy to program. Dim On light. Brew relatively hot.
Black & Decker Spacemaker SDC3AG [D]	50		⊖	Under-cabinet installation option. Reservoir can be filled at sink. Keep-warm coutdown timer. Uncomfortable handle. Carafe lacks markings on both sides. Pull-out filter basket. No drip-stop.
Black & Decker DCM903	32		○	Easy to program. Uncomfortable carafe handle. Pull-out filter basket.
Panasonic Premiere Brew NC-F12MP	140		○	Comes with water filter. Lid falls off during pouring. Beeps when coffee is ready. Brew relatively hot.
West Bend Quik Drip 56650	35		◒	Keep-warm countdown timer. Pull-out filter basket. Uncomfortable carafe handle. Reservoir hard to fill.
Regal Kitchen Pro K7631BK [D]	80		◒	Plastic mesh filter. Keep-warm countdown timer. Uncomfortable carafe handle. Clock-timer hard to operate. Filter basket falls over. Brew relatively hot.
Farberware L4260	50		◒	Plastic mesh filter. Reservoir awkward to fill. Carafe dribbled a lot when filling reservoir.

RATINGS TOASTERS

▶ **See report, page 106.** Last time rated in Consumer Reports: August 1994.

Brand-name recommendations: For the most part, relatively small differences separate the better models. The best single-slot toasters were the Oster 3826 and Sunbeam 3824, priced at $35. Nearly as good but cheaper were the single-slot Maxim ET-9, $25, and the Betty Crocker BC-1613, $19, a two-slot model. We judged each A Best Buy. The best of the four-slicers was the Black & Decker T440, $55.

For a typical toaster, expect: ■ White plastic housing. ■ Hinged tray that opens for crumb disposal. ■ Manual push-down/automatic pop-up carriage. ■ Rotary color control to set darkness. ■ 2- to 3-ft. power cord.

Notes on the table: Price is the estimated average, based on a national survey. * means price paid. **Slot width** shows how well a model handles thick items like bagels and muffins. **Cool touch** shows which models protected users from high exterior temperatures. **Model availability:** Ⓓ means model is discontinued.

Within type, listed in order of toasting performance and ease of use

E, VG, G, F, P

Brand and model	Price	Overall score (P F G VG E)	Slot WIDTH/NO.	Cool touch	Ease of use	Comments
TWO-SLICE MODELS						
Oster 3826	$35		VG/1	E	E	Centers bread. Hard to retrieve English muffins.
Sunbeam 3824	35		VG/1	E	E	Centers bread. Hard to retrieve English muffins.
Krups 118	43		VG/1	E	E	Centers bread. Warm-up setting. Removable tray. 4-ft. cord (with storage provision).
Maxim ET-9, **A BEST BUY**	25		VG/1	E	E	Centers bread. Stores cord.
Cuisinart CPT-2	92		G/1	E	VG	Electronic controls, programmable settings. Centers bread. Warm-up, Keep-warm settings. No tray. Hard to retrieve English muffins. Ready bell.
Betty Crocker BC-1613, **A BEST BUY**	19		VG/2	E	E	Centers bread. Slide-lever color control. Thin bread slipped through carriage.
Rowenta TP-200 Ⓓ	40		VG/1	E	E	Centers bread. Removable tray. Keep-warm setting.
Toastmaster 740	25		VG/1	E	G	Centers bread. Color control hard to adjust. Fuse shuts off power if carriage jams; technician must replace.

Ratings continued ▶

Ratings continued

Brand and model	Price	Overall score P F G VG E	Slot WIDTH/NO.	Cool touch	Ease of use	Comments
TWO-SLICE MODELS *continued*						
Salton TO-6	*$28		⊖/1	⊜	◒	Centers bread. Color control not clearly marked and hard to adjust. No tray.
Proctor-Silex T4300	26		○/2	⊜	⊖	Centers bread. Hard to retrieve English muffins. Color control hard to adjust.
Black & Decker T215	23		◒/2	⊜	⊖	Slide-lever color control (not clearly marked). Thin bread slipped through carriage.
Proctor-Silex T620B	13		◒/2	◒	◒	Slide-lever color control.
Sunbeam 3817	*18		◒/2	◒	○	Hard to retrieve English muffins.
Proctor-Silex T4400	20		○/2	◒	⊖	Centers bread. Hard to retrieve English muffins.
Farberware T2920	21		◒/2	◒	◒	Color control not clearly marked. Hard to retrieve English muffins.
Sunbeam 3816	80		◒/2	○	○	Slide-lever color control. Self-lowering carriage (but didn't work on several samples). Hard to retrieve English muffins.
FOUR-SLICE MODELS						
Black & Decker T440	*55		◒/4	⊜	⊜	Slide-lever color control.
Proctor-Silex 24400	33		○/4	⊜	⊖	Centers bread. Hard to retrieve English muffins.
Toastmaster D777	34		◒/4	⊖	⊜	Slide-lever color control.
Toastmaster 786	*70		◒/4	⊖	◒	Mounts under cabinet. Single color control for all 4 slots. Ready bell. Power-on light.

RATINGS STAND MIXERS

▶ **See report, page 107.** Last time rated in Consumer Reports: November 1994.

Brand-name recommendations: If you need a stand mixer, choose the heavy-duty KitchenAid K45SS, $195, or the KitchenAid KSM90, $215. If you don't make much bread or cookie dough, consider the Sunbeam 01401/2355, $95, or Oster 5600-20A/2381, $110.

For the typical stand mixer, expect: ■ Excellent performance at whipping cream. ■ At least 1 beater and dough hook. ■ 3 or more speeds. ■ Tilting head that locks in Down position. ■ For heavy-duty mixers: A 4-qt. bowl; wire whisk; ability to knead enough bread dough for 2 loaves; stationary bowl, moves as bowl spins. ■ For medium-duty mixers: A 4-qt. bowl plus a smaller bowl; bowl that rotates as beaters spin; 2 beaters that aren't interchangeable; ability to knead enough bread dough for 1 loaf; continuously variable speeds, and large, easy-to-use speed dial with mixing guide. ■ For light-duty mixers: Body detaches and can be used like a hand mixer.

Notes on the table: Price is the estimated average, based on a national survey. For **mixing**, we used cookie dough; for **mashing**, potatoes; for **kneading**, bread dough. **Model availability:** Ⓓ means model is discontinued.

Within type, listed in order of performance and convenience

E ⊜ VG ⊖ G ○ F ◒ P ●

Brand and model	Price	Overall score (P F G VG E)	Performance: MIX	MASH	KNEAD	Comments
HEAVY-DUTY MIXERS						
KitchenAid K45SS	$195		◉	◓	◉	Little clearance to add ingredients.
KitchenAid KSM90	215		◉	◓	◉	Little clearance to add ingredients. Handle on bowl.
KitchenAid K5SS	260		◉	◓	◉	Little clearance to add ingredients. Handle on bowl. 5-qt. bowl.
Kenwood KM-210 (Rival Select)	202		◉	◓	◉	Noisy. Beater hard to replace. Little clearance to add ingredients. Pulse, cont. variable speeds. 5-qt. bowl.
Kenwood KM220 (Rival Select)	254		◉	◓	◉	Noisy. Beater hard to replace. Little clearance to add ingredients. Cont. variable speeds. 5-qt. bowl.
MEDIUM-DUTY MIXERS						
Sunbeam 01401/2355	95		◓	◉	○	Glass bowls.
Oster 5600-20A/2381	110		○	◉	○	Stainless-steel bowls.
Sunbeam 2358	125		○	◉	◒	Quiet. Beaters hard to remove. Detachable body. Stainless-steel bowls.

Ratings continued ▶

Ratings continued

Brand and model	Price	Overall score (P F G VG E)	Performance: MIX	MASH	KNEAD	Comments
MEDIUM-DUTY MIXERS *continued*						
Sunbeam 2360	$114		○	●	◒	Beaters hard to remove. Detachable body. Glass-bowls.
LIGHT-DUTY MIXERS						
Krups 747	100		●	◒	○	Good at whipping cream. Hard to set up. Beater-socket area hard to clean. Pulse setting, plastic bowl.
Hamilton Beach 64500	30		●	◒	—	Fair at whipping cream. Noisy. Power-burst. Glass bowl.
Waring HM201 Ⓓ	25		●	◒	—	Poor at whipping cream. Noisy. Inconvenient speed controls. Small glass bowl. Whisk.

RATINGS STEAM IRONS

▶ **See report, page 111.** Last time rated in Consumer Reports: January 1995.

Brand-name recommendations: The top five are excellent steamers and have spray and automatic shutoff. Of those, the Sunbeam 3956 is a A Best Buy at $38; it lacks a burst-of-steam feature, however. If you simply want a good steamer and don't care about features like auto shutoff and burst-of-steam, check out the Norelco 513. It's only $30.

For the typical iron, expect: ■ Spray, auto shutoff, nonstick soleplate, and variable steam. ■ Temp. control under handle. ■ Cord (7 to 8 ft.) that pivots down in use, wraps for storage. ■ 1 or 2 clear-tube water gauges. ■ Indicator lights on handle, where they're easy to see. ■ Notched, or grooved, or tapered soleplate for buttons. ■ Water gauge that's reasonably easy to see through. ■ Easy to fill.

Notes on the table: Price is the estimated average, based on a national survey. * means approx. retail price. **Overall score.** Where scores are the same, irons are listed in order of increasing price. **Steam rate.** Stronger ones smooth wrinkles better. **Setting ease.** Fabric guide should list major fabrics, be easy to read. Thermostat should be clearly marked; the most convenient are on front of handle. Models similar to those we tested are noted in Comments; features may vary. **Model availability:** Ⓓ means model is discontinued. Ⓢ means model is replaced, according to the manufacturer; successor model is noted in Comments. New model was not tested; it may or may not perform similarly. Features may vary.

Listed in order of performance and convenience

Better ⟵⟶ Worse: ⊜ ⊖ ○ ◒ ●

Brand and model	Price	Overall score (P F G VG E)	Steam rate	Setting ease	Comments
Philips Azur 80 [S] [1]	$70		⊜	◒	No perm.-press on fabric guide. Less stable than most. Has burst-of-steam. Self-cleans. **Successor:** Norelco Ultima 65.
Sunbeam 3956, **A BEST BUY**	38		⊜	○	Indicator light less easy to see. Very good spray. Self-cleans. **Similar:** 4000, 3957, 3953, 3930.
Oster 3993	*60		⊜	○	Indicator light less easy to see. Lacks non-stick soleplate. Very good spray. Self-cleans. **Similar:** 3994, 4001, 3996.
Tefal 1980 [D]	*80		⊜	○	Cord clip. Soleplate ridges collect dirt. Has burst of steam. Best steamer in 10-min. test. Designed for tap water only; requires special filter.
Rowenta DE-534 [D]	73		⊜	●	Has burst of steam. Spray worked sporadically when used continuously. Designed for tap water, except in areas with very hard water. Lacks nonstick soleplate. Fabric guide must be attached to heel rest.
Salton SR375	42		○	◒	No perm.-press on fabric guide. Unmarked burst, spray controls. Far-reaching spray. Has burst-of-steam. 12-ft. cord.
Singer 867	30		○	○	Poorly marked steam control. Less stable than most. Self-cleans. Has burst-of-steam.
Black & Decker F650S	60		○	⊖	Cord hits wrist. Self-cleans. Has burst-of-steam. 12-ft. cord.
Tefal 1620	70		⊖	○	Spray trigger easy to accidentally activate. Soleplate ridges collect dirt. Self-cleans. Varies steam. Has burst-of-steam. Tap water only.
Panasonic NI-480E [D]	*50		○	○	Removable water tank. Cord retracts. Lacks variable steam. Lacks auto shutoff.
Black & Decker F895S	58		○	○	Indicator light hard to see. Inconvenient On switch. Cord hits wrist. Self-cleans. Has burst-of-steam. 12-ft. cord.
Braun PV73S	63		⊖	◒	Poorly marked steam, spray controls. No perm.-press on fabric guide. Far-reaching spray. Has burst-of-steam. Lacks auto shutoff. 12-ft. cord. Soleplate resisted scratching better than most.
Norelco 513	30		⊖	○	Self-cleans. Lacks auto shutoff.
Black & Decker F605S	38		○	⊖	—
Sunbeam 3955	34		○	○	No indicator light. Very good spray. Self-cleans. Lacks auto shutoff.

[1] *Also available for $60 (as #882666) in Best Products Co. catalog (800 950-2378).*

Ratings continued ▶

Ratings continued

Brand and model	Price	Overall score P F G VG E	Steam rate	Setting ease	Comments
Rowenta CS-03 (corded/cordless) [D]	*$110		◒ [2]	○	Reheat in base when used cordless. Removable water tank. Has burst-of-steam. Lacks auto shut-off. Designed for tap water, except in areas with very hard water.
Panasonic NI-1000 (cordless)	120		●	⊜	Reheat in base. Electronic touchpad temp. control.
Black & Decker F497L [D]	40		⊜	⊜	No indicator light. Cord hits wrist. Lacks nonstick soleplate. 12-ft. cord.
Proctor-Silex 14400 [S]	30		◒	⊜	Uncomfortable steam/spray controls. Has burst-of-steam. **Successor:** 18440.
Sunbeam 3999	33		○	○	No indicator light. Very good spray. Lacks variable steam, auto shutoff. 12-ft. cord.
Proctor-Silex 17115	20		○	⊜	No indicator light. Cord is hard to rotate. Lacks variable steam, auto shutoff, nonstick soleplate.
Proctor-Silex 17220	20		○	⊜	Cord is hard to rotate. Lacks variable steam, nonstick soleplate, spray.
Black & Decker F392	30		○	⊜	No indicator light. Cord hits wrist. Lacks variable steam, auto shutoff, nonstick soleplate.

[2] *Steam rate is with cord attached; rate without cord is ⊜.*

How to use the Buying Guide

- Read the article for general guidance about types, features, and how to buy. There you'll find the market overview, the choices you'll face, and key advice.
- Read the brand-name recommendations for information on specific models.
- Note how the rated products are listed—in order of performance and convenience, price, or alphabetically.
- Look to the overall score to get the big picture in performance. Notes on features and performance for individual models are listed in the Comments or Details part of the Ratings.
- Note that models similar to the tested models, when they exist, are indicated in the Comments or Details. A model marked [D] has been discontinued. A model marked [S] is a successor to the tested model, according to the manufacturer, and is noted in Comments or Details. Features, though, may vary.
- Call the manufacturer if you have trouble finding a product. Manufacturers' phone numbers are listed alphabetically by brand name starting on page 342.
- To find our last full report on a subject, check the eight-year index for the original publication date. You'll find the index in the reference section, page 346.

HOME MAINTENANCE & SAFETY

Vacuum cleaners

▶ Ratings on page 148.

Upright vacuum cleaners used to be the cleaning machine of choice for homes with lots of carpeting. Canister vacuums were best for hard floors, stairs, upholstered furniture, and specialized chores. The two are becoming more alike—and more versatile. Most uprights now have a flexible hose and tools for cleaning upholstery and bare floors, and many canisters have a power nozzle for deep-cleaning carpets.

Lightweight electric brooms, stick vacs, compact canisters, and handheld vacuums come in handy for small cleaning jobs. Stick vacs fit in a tiny broom closet. Handhelds can often be wall-mounted for easy access.

Four brands account for two-thirds of all upright vacuums sold: Hoover, Eureka, Royal, and Sears Kenmore. Sears dominates the canister market. Black & Decker and Royal Dirt Devil account for three-fourths of all handheld vacs.

The choices

Uprights. Uprights outsell canisters by more than five to one. Most are easier to handle than a canister vacuum, require less storage space, and cost less. Uprights, which have a vertical bag, come in two basic designs: those with a soft bag, and those with a bag enclosed in a stiff housing. Pushing the machine around is usually easy, since most weigh only 13 to 18 pounds. Some of the heavier models propel themselves with motorized rear wheels.

Uprights have a rotating beater brush, which beats the dust and dirt out of pile carpet. They're less effective on hard surfaces; they generally have limited suction, and their brushes may disperse debris rather than vacuum it up. Most come with a long hose and an assortment of attachments for vacuuming stairs, under furniture, upholstery, and such. Price: about $70 to $1000.

Canisters. In the past, their superior suction made canister vacuums ideal for vacuuming bare floors. But lacking a power nozzle, they weren't effective on carpeting. Most full-sized canister vacs now include a power nozzle that helps to deep-clean carpets.

Full-sized canister vacuums weigh more than uprights (most weigh more than 20 pounds). The canister's hose and numerous detachable wands can be cumbersome to store. The bag is often smaller than an upright's, but it's easier to change. Prices range from about $75 to $1100, but most sell for less than $300.

Compact canister vacs are easier to carry and store. However, their performance in deep-cleaning tests was disappointing.

Electric brooms. These are lightweight versions of an upright. Pricier electric brooms with a built-in power nozzle are usually strong enough to remove only crumbs from the surface of a carpet, not ground-in grit. Nevertheless, their light weight (usually six pounds or so) and small head make them very portable and easy to maneuver—ideal for quick cleanup in small areas. Some electric brooms have a removable plastic dirt holder; others require disposable bags. All have limited capacity. Prices are usually less than $50.

Handheld vacuums. Cordless models can do their job anywhere, but even when they're fully charged, they can work for only about 10 minutes. Wet/dry models can deal with the odd dust bunny or a spilled bowl of cereal and milk. Plug-in hand vacuums can't roam as freely as cordless units, although models with a long power cord—as long as 25 feet—are almost as convenient. Plug-in models generally provide more suction than rechargeables. Some have built-in revolving brushes, useful for deep-cleaning sand from a car's carpeting. Car vacs, a variation of plug-in handhelds, have a 15- or 20-foot cord that plugs into the car's cigarette lighter. They can run for extended periods without draining the car battery much. Prices of cordless and plug-in vacuums overlap: about $10 to $50.

Features and conveniences

Amps and horsepower. Vacuums are labeled with claims of amperage, peak hp, and "cleaning effectiveness per amp," but we've found no correlation between claims and performance.

Controls. An On/off switch that's high on an upright's handle is easy to use. On/off switches on most canisters are designed to be triggered by a foot. Most canisters have a separate foot switch to turn off the power nozzle. That's helpful when an object like a scatter rug gets stuck and you need to free it quickly to avoid overheating the power-nozzle motor. (On some models, an automatic shutoff prevents overheating.)

Power nozzle. Look for a model that allows raising or lowering the motorized beater brush with a dial, sliding lever, or pedal. Some models claim to adjust height automatically, but they usually aren't as effective as those you adjust. With some uprights, you can switch off the beater brush to prevent scattering dirt on hard floors.

In a hand vac, a revolving brush improves carpet cleaning, but it also competes with suction, flinging coarser soil about instead of sucking it in. A few battery-powered models come with such a brush.

Hoses. The most convenient ones swivel. Nonswiveling hoses can kink annoyingly as you vacuum.

Pushing and carrying. Big wheels or rollers make uprights easier to push than canisters, especially when the beater brush is set to the proper height. Self-propelled models require very little effort.

You can carry most uprights with one hand. With a canister, you maneuver only the nozzle assembly. The stubby tank follows on wheels—a setup that makes the unit more agile than an upright—but you have to give the hose a determined yank from time to time. Tug and twist the hose too much and it's likely to tangle. Hoisting the tank and hose assembly of a canister requires two hands.

Stair climbing. The longer the hose, the better the reach. Uprights usually have too large a "footprint" to fit securely on a stair; canisters tend to be more cooperative. Some vacuum cleaners come with a small motorized brush for vacuuming carpet on stairs. The less dead space between the powered brush and the outer edge of its housing, the closer you can get to the back of the stair and to baseboards.

Suction adjustment. When you vacuum loose or billowy objects, excessive suction can cause the vacuum to inhale the fabric. Most canisters and some uprights let you reduce suction by uncovering a hole or valve near the handle. Models with more than one speed let you vary suction.

Vacuum bags. Most full-sized cleaners collect dirt in a disposable paper bag. Some models signal when the bag is full or airflow is blocked. Soft-body uprights have the largest bags (about a four-quart capacity), but bigger isn't necessarily better: Clogged pores in the bags decrease suction, so bags often have to be changed before they're full.

Installing a bag is easiest if its cardboard collar drops into a slot. It's not as easy where you slide the bag's sleeve over a tube and secure it with a spring band. Removing the bag without dumping the contents is a challenge.

The plastic dust collectors on most electric brooms and hand vacs are easy enough to remove and empty. Small vacuums with replaceable bags generally install the same way as bags for full-sized vacuum cleaners.

Cord storage. Canisters usually have a button or pedal, that rewinds the long power cord for you. Uprights generally have two hooks around which you wind the cord. If one or both hooks swivel, you can release the cord quickly. Some machines have an awkward cord-storage arrangement, and some have no cord storage at all.

Noise. No vacuum cleaner can be called quiet, but the canister models we tested were slightly less noisy than the uprights. Among uprights, hard-body models were less noisy than soft-bodies. Electric brooms and handheld vacs tend to be higher pitched than their full-sized cousins, and just as annoying.

Dust control. Despite what ads may say, even the best vacuum won't capture all dust and debris. Uprights with the fan in front of the vacuum bag tend to capture the most. Canisters generally emit the most dust in their exhaust. As a rule, machines that use paper dust bags are better than bagless dust collectors or elaborate water-filtration systems at trapping fine dust.

Microfiltration dust bags that supposedly minimize dirt dispersion are an option on some vacuums. Our tests show that most are no more effective than standard, cheaper bags. The best way to control dust and allergens is to limit carpeting in your house.

The tests

To find the best deep cleaners, we embed silica and talcum powder into medium-pile nylon carpet and pass each vacuum back and forth over the carpet eight times. We then weigh and measure the debris inside each machine's dust collector. To judge suction, we measure airflow with a new bag and gradually feed each machine wood flour, a fine powder that easily clogs vacuum bags. To measure emissions—how much dust spews back into the air—we vacuum fine sawdust from carpeting and then use precise instruments to detect dust in the air.

Buying advice

Uprights that come with a hose and attachments are the most practical choice for most households. As a rule, they're easy to move and convenient to store: Their tools usually travel on board. Uprights are also cheaper than canisters. Canisters are often better suited for bare floors than for rugs or deep-pile carpeting.

Electric brooms can be handy for quick touch-ups, but not much more. Their light weight and compact size also makes them useful for people with limited mobility or hand strength.

Hand vacs are versatile picker-uppers when they're stored accessibly. The plug-in variety lacks the mobility but is more powerful than a rechargeable.

If an electric outlet is close to your car, a plug-in hand vac or a regular full-sized vacuum with attachments is the most effective vacuum. Those designed specifically for cars generally aren't very powerful.

Water treatment

Public concern over the quality of drinking water often centers on how the water looks, smells, or tastes. But such aesthetic problems are usually caused by calcium, sulfur, chlorine, or iron, which are harmless. Of more concern are pollutants such as lead, radon, and nitrate, which pose a health hazard.

Before buying any equipment or taking the expensive route of buying bottled water, find out what's in your water.

You can ask the water company for a copy of its latest water analysis. Or, if you draw water from a private well, call the local public health department to find out about any groundwater problems. If testing is warranted, see "Where to get water tested," page 129.

Water-treatment devices range from simple filtering carafes and faucet attachments to whole-house systems. They're sold in places as diverse as drug stores and TV home-shopping networks. As a rule, hardware stores, home centers, department stores, and mass merchandisers sell the more modest devices for as little as $20. Sophisticated systems, which can cost more than $1000, are sold by water treatment dealers and direct-marketing companies. Major brands include Ametek, Amway, Brita, Culligan, Glacier Pure, Instapure (Teledyne/WaterPik), Mr. Coffee, NSA, Omni, Pollenex, Rainsoft, and Sears.

Problem pollutants

Lead. Chronic lead exposure, even at low levels, could cause permanent learning disabilities and hyperactivity. It's particularly dangerous for pregnant women and children. In adults, chronic exposure is linked to high blood pressure and anemia.

Lead gets into water primarily through corrosion of household plumbing and the service line (the pipe connecting the home plumbing with the water main). Installation of lead service lines has been banned for nearly a decade, but many homes more than 30 years old still have them. They may also have copper pipes with lead solder (also banned). Lead in water can also come from brass in faucets and well pumps.

Since 1991, the U.S. Environmental Protection Agency (EPA) has required water companies to run spot tests for lead contamination. If more than 10 percent of the households checked have lead levels above 15 parts per billion (ppb), the company will have to take action, either by treating the water or by replacing lead service lines. The deadline for companies serving more than 50,000 people is January 1997; smaller systems have until 1999.

In 1992, CONSUMER REPORTS undertook its own testing of water in the homes of 2643 readers in eight cities. We found worrisome results in some cities, including Chicago, New York, and Boston. We recently retested 1280 homes in those cities and in Portland and St. Paul, where the EPA had found fairly high lead levels.

The water supply in Chicago had improved considerably. New York showed modest improvement. Although Boston has been treating the water in its reservoir for years, results still show room for improvement; in fact, the city plans to add a buffering agent closer to customers' taps. Lead concentrations remained too high in St. Paul even after running the water. In Portland, first-draw water (which has stood in the pipes for hours) had moderate levels of lead; purged-line water (drawn after running for a while) had almost no lead.

To minimize your exposure to lead from pipes, use only cold water for cooking and drinking; hot water dissolves more lead. Running the water for a minute or so to flush the pipes may help, but it's not a sure cure. If you have more than 5 ppb of lead in your water even after letting it run, you need to take action.

Radon. This probably poses a greater health risk than any other waterborne pollutant. According to the EPA, radon, a naturally occurring radioactive gas, may cause more than 10,000 lung-cancer deaths each year. Most of the radon seeps into homes from the ground. But some well water contains dissolved radon, which escapes into the air from showers and washers.

Waterborne radon is usually confined to private wells or small community water systems that use wells. Before testing water for radon, test the air inside your house for radon (see page 140). If the level is high and you use well water, have the water tested. If the level of radon in the air is low, don't worry about the water.

Although experts disagree as to the level of radon you should do something about, one EPA official we spoke with says you should take action if the level in the water is 10,000 picocuries per liter or higher. Radon is easily dispersed in outdoor air, so aerating the water before it enters the house is usually the simplest solution. Ventilating the bathroom, laundry room, or kitchen may also help.

Nitrate. High nitrate levels in water pose a risk mainly to infants. Bacteria in immature digestive tracts convert nitrate into nitrite; that combines with hemoglobin in the blood to form methemoglobin, which cannot transport oxygen. The resulting ailment, methemoglobinemia, is rare but can result in brain damage or death. Some adults, including pregnant women, may also be susceptible.

Chemical fertilizers and animal wastes are prime sources of nitrate contamination, so homes in agricultural areas with private wells should have their water tested regularly. Some state health departments test wells for free. High nitrate levels may also signal the presence of other contaminants.

Treatment methods

The chart on page 128 shows which technologies work best for which sub-

Water problems and solutions

Action is recommended if your drinking water contains more than the maximum contaminant level.

	Maximum contaminant level [1]	Carbon filter	Reverse osmosis [2]	Distiller	Water softener	Activated alumina cartridge	Aerator
AESTHETIC PROBLEMS							
Dissolved iron	—				✔		
Rust stains	—			✔			
Calcium	—				✔		
Magnesium	—				✔		
Chlorine	—	✔		✔			✔
Salty taste	—		✔	✔			
'Skunky' taste	—	✔					
Total dissolved solids (TDS)	500 ppm		✔	✔			
HEALTH HAZARDS—Organic							
Benzene	5 ppb	✔					✔
Carbon tetrachloride	5 ppb	✔					✔
Lindane	0.2 ppb	✔		✔			
Methoxychlor	40 ppb	✔		✔			
Trichloroethylene	5 ppb	✔					✔
Trihalomethanes (THM)	100 ppb	✔					
HEALTH HAZARDS—Inorganic							
Arsenic	50 ppb		✔	✔			
Barium	2 ppm		✔	✔	✔		
Cadmium	5 ppb		✔	✔	✔		
Chromium	100 ppb		✔	✔			
Fluoride	2.2 ppm		✔	✔		✔	
Lead	15 ppb [3]	[4]	✔	✔		✔	
Mercury	2 ppb	✔	✔	✔			
Nitrate	10 ppm		✔	✔			
Selenium	10 ppb		✔	✔		✔	
HEALTH HAZARDS—Radiological							
Dissolved radon	10,000 pc/l	✔					✔

[1] *ppm = parts per million; ppb = parts per billion; pc/l = picocuries per liter.*
[2] *Most will also remove organic substances.*
[3] *Action level.*
[4] *Some will remove lead.*

stances. Some products, called single-stage filters, use one of the methods explained below; others, called multistage filters, combine two or more. Note: None are suitable for treating bacteriologically contaminated water, which requires sterilization with ultra-violet rays, ozone, or chlorine.

Carbon filtration. This is the most popular method of water treatment. Carbon filters overcome a variety of problems. They remove residual chlorine, improving the water's taste. They can also remove organic compounds such as pesticides, solvents, and chloroform. Some carbon filters are effective for lead; some aren't. The whole-house variety is especially useful for removing radon.

Where lead contamination is known to be a problem, a larger filter is better. Small pour-through filters and fist-sized units that thread onto the faucet can improve the taste of water, but they're only moderately effective against hazardous chemicals. There, a high-volume under-sink or countertop filter is the best choice. Replaceable filter cartridges made either with a "carbon block" or granulated carbon are better than those made with powdered carbon.

Reverse-osmosis (RO). This method excels at removing inorganic contaminants, such as dissolved salts, ferrous iron, chloride, fluoride, nitrate, and heavy metals such as lead. RO works slowly, producing only a few gallons of fresh water per day, and is wasteful, for every gallon of water purified, several gallons are wasted.

Most RO systems use a carbon filter. They have a second filter, a cellophane-like semipermeable membrane, that's easily clogged by minerals in hard water. (To extend its life, install a separate sediment prefilter upstream of the carbon filter. A 5- to 10-micron mesh is fine enough.) The membrane needs replacement every few years; carbon filters, more often.

Distillation. Distillation improves the taste of brackish water, and they demineralize water polluted with heavy metals. But it's ineffective against volatile organics like chloroform and benzene, which vaporize in the distiller and wind up in the condensed water. The process is slow—it takes a couple of hours to produce a quart of water—and uses a lot of electricity. Since it collects and concentrates minerals, scale can build up quickly and must be cleaned out.

Water softeners. Water softeners remove hard water minerals, stain-producing iron and, in some cases, lead. They don't remove radon, nitrate, or pesticides.

Systems vary in size but all consist of a large tank near the main supply of water to a house. As a result, softeners are effective against lead only if contamination occurs in service lines outside the house.

Activated alumina. If lead is your only

WHERE TO GET YOUR WATER TESTED

Companies that sell water-treatment equipment often offer a free or low-cost water analysis. Don't depend on that kind of test: The results may be biased. Instead, ask your water company, health department, or cooperative extension agency for a referral. You can also check the Yellow Pages under "Laboratories—Testing," or contact a mail-order laboratory.

To get water tested for lead by mail, contact any of the following: Clean Water Lead Test Inc., Ashville, N.C., 704 251-6800 ($17); Environmental Law Foundation, Oakland, Calif., 510 208-4555. ($16.50); SAVE, New York, N.Y., 718 626-3936 ($20).

Avoid do-it-yourself home testing kits. Those we've looked at in recent years haven't produced consistent results.

problem, activated alumina cartridges, which come in faucet-mounted filters, and in-line units, are an effective treatment.

Aeration. Aerators are effective at removing chlorine, radon, benzene, carbon tetrachloride, and trihalomethenes.

Treatment products

Reverse-osmosis devices are installed in the water line under the sink by a professional. They have their own spigot and storage tank. If your household needs maximum lead removal, consider one of these. Their large storage tank holds a supply of treated water ample enough for most uses. Operation cost is fairly low. However, if you should empty the tank, you'll have to wait two or three hours for it to process another gallon. Price: $300 to $700.

Distillers, which aren't plumbed-in, sit on the counter and are plugged into an electric outlet. They're a good choice if you need highly effective lead removal and don't consume a lot of water. Although cheaper to buy than a reverse-osmosis system, they're much more expensive to operate. Price: $150 to $350.

Undersink filters are plumbed-in and have their own spigot. This type is best suited for a household that uses a lot of water. It produces purified water on demand, at a rate of about one-third gallon a minute. They're less expensive and easier to install than reverse-osmosis devices. An undersink filter can be installed by a do-it-yourselfer whose counter has an opening for the unit's spigot or who is willing to drill an opening. Price: $70 to $200.

Countertop filters sit next to the sink and attach to the existing faucet with flexible tubing. Like an undersink filter, a countertop model provides filtered water on demand, but it requires no major changes in plumbing. This type of unit takes up counter space, and its connector tubes can get in the way when you're using the sink. Price: $50 to $300.

A faucet-mounted filter is similar to a countertop unit, but it has no tubing at all, is smaller, and sits atop the faucet. It gives purified water on demand without taking up counter space or requiring much installation. But you may not like the way it looks perched on your faucet, and it may get in your way. Price: $15 to $80.

Carafes filters are stand-alone units that require no connection to the plumbing. They sit on a counter; you simply pour water through them. Water poured into the top compartment trickles through the filter and collects in the pitcher below. A carafe is best used to process only small amounts of water, perhaps a gallon or two a day. Price: $20 to $40. Filters: about $5 each.

Buying advice

The chart on page 128 summarizes the best methods for the most common water problems. Before doing business with a water-treatment company you don't know, call the Better Business Bureau or a local consumer-protection agency to find out whether any complaints against the company are unresolved.

Low-flow toilets

▶ **Ratings on page 144.**

An aging commode uses 3.5 to 5 gallons of water per flush. New models are limited to 1.6 gallons by Federal guidelines.

Plumbing-supply stores, kitchen and bath installers, and home centers commonly sell toilets. Kohler, American Standard, and

Eljier dominate the market. Artesian/ Crane, Mansfield, Universal-Rundle, Briggs, and Gerber are other widely available brands. Prices range from as little as $90 to more than $1000.

The choices

Gravity-flush. Most toilets still rely on gravity to flush. Price: $90 to $600.

Pressure-assisted. These toilets rely on stored pressure from the household's water supply to boost the force of the flush. They're more efficient flushers than gravity models, but they're relatively noisy and expensive. Price: $200 to $700.

Older toilet designs have two pieces, the tank and the bowl. Modern, one-piece designs command a premium—about $200 more than two-piece models. There's a broad choice of colors and bowl shapes, as well as special features. Some toilets, for instance, are higher than normal for easy use by the elderly or disabled.

The tests

We check water consumption to see whether the toilets meet the Federal standard of 1.6 gallons per flush. We also evaluate how long each toilet takes to flush and refill, and how noisy it is. We test to see how readily a toilet flushes away solids into the drain line—the most important test of a toilet—and how effectively it moves waste through a drain line that's in good functioning order. Since soiling and odor are frequent complaints with low-flush toilets, we check the potential for those problems and evaluate how well the toilets wash down the bowls during a flush. To evaluate the thoroughness of each flush, we dye the toilet's water and observe how much dye remains after a flush.

Buying advice

Unless you have exorbitant water bills or high sewer fees, replacing old toilets in good working order makes little financial sense. Even an inexpensive low-flush toilet may take 10 years to pay for itself. (And in localities that bill a flat rate for usage minimums, a low-flush toilet probably won't cut water bills at all.) Some new low-flush toilets may not work as well as the older toilets. If you're remodeling a bathroom or replacing a toilet that isn't working well, you'll have to buy a low-flow model. We recommend choosing a pressure-assisted model for best performance.

Paints, stains & finishes

Paint is the material of choice when you're redoing the walls of a room. It provides a fairly tough film of resins and pigments that covers small blemishes and shields the surface from wear and tear. It can be applied over primer, old paint or in the case of stains, over bare wood. And it comes in almost every conceivable color. Computers in stores have made color matching so sophisticated that a dealer can mix paint to match a thin stripe in a necktie or scarf, generally with remarkable accuracy.

Stain soaks into the wood instead of covering it, thereby accentuating the natural wood grain. You can use stain instead of paint on wood trim—moldings, baseboards, doors, and window frames—of a room or on the outside of a house if the wood hasn't been painted previously (or if the old paint has been removed).

Color choices for stains are limited. The most popular exterior colors are browns, reds, grays, and whites. Wood colors are traditionally used inside.

Interior transparent stains and clear finishes reveal wood in its entirety. Surface finishes, like varnish form a hard, durable coat. They're either water- or solvent-based.

For help in choosing the right finish, see the charts opposite and on page 134.

Oil versus water

The makeup of paints and stains is similar. Both contain binder, solvent, and pigment. The binder forms the film, holds the pigment, and gives adhesion. Pigment provides hiding and color. Paint contains more pigment than most stains; as the transparency of stain increases, the amount of pigment decreases. The solvent—water and alcohols in latexes, and petroleum spirits in alkyds (oil-based paints and stains)—helps determine how easily the paint goes on and its adhesion and coverage.

Latex formulas dominate the paint market. Modern latexes can do just about everything oil-based products can. They adhere well and provide a durable surface. (About the only area where an oil-based product has an edge is an exceptionally damp bathroom or basement.) Many current formulations, often called "low odor" paints, contain fewer air pollutants than alkyd products. Latexes also tend to remain more flexible than do alkyds, and less prone to crack. Latexes go on easily and dry quickly. You can apply them to a damp surface. And if you clean up promptly, you can use soap and water.

But there's a tradeoff for those conveniences. Latex paint is somewhat more prone to damage from water and marring than alkyds. Latex, especially glossy latex, may remain tacky long after drying, causing books to stick to shelving and windows to sills—a problem known as "blocking." And you have to be careful about storage—freezing can ruin latex.

Because of the water-resistant skin of hardened resin that an alkyd forms, oil-based paints and stains are tough and water resistant. Alkyds make sense for the kitchen and bathroom and for surfaces such as bookshelves.

Their petroleum-based chemistry, however, makes them messy to use. They may be hard to apply, and the surface they go on must be completely dry. Cleanup of spills and brushes requires mineral spirits. Alkyds smell like solvent while they're drying—and each coat may take a day to dry.

The stain market is pretty evenly divided between latex and alkyd products. The characteristics of latex and alkyd paints apply to stains of the same family, too.

Glidden, Sears, Sherwin-Williams, Dutch Boy, and Benjamin Moore are the biggest-selling brands of paint in the U.S. Olympic, Thompson's, and Behr are the leading brands of stain.

The choices in paints

Interior paints. Interior paints come in a variety of gloss levels: flat, eggshell, satin, semigloss and gloss. Generally, the higher the shine, the more durable the paint. Unfortunately, there are no standard definitions for glossiness. One maker's "eggshell" may shine like another's "satin."

On the inside of the house, flat paint is traditionally used on ceilings; flat, satin, or eggshell, on walls in the living room, dining room, and bedrooms. Glossier paints are used for trim work and in rooms that take a lot of abuse, such as bathrooms and kitchens. Higher gloss levels stand up better to scrubbing, so you can repeatedly wash away fingerprints around door knobs and spatters around sinks without washing away paint. But they also call attention to cracks or flaws in the wall surface.

Today, higher gloss levels are often used on walls—partly for fashion and partly for practicality. Some paint companies offer what they claim are specially formulated paints for children's bedrooms and playrooms. In fact, these paints are just specially packaged glossy paints. They don't wear any better than ordinary glossy paints.

Glossy latexes don't dry as quickly as flat finishes. Avoid closing windows fully or replacing books on shelves for at least 24 hours, or until the tackiness is gone.

Exterior paints. Exterior paints also come in a variety of sheens. A higher gloss generally weathers better and lasts longer than a flat paint.

Exterior paints are formulated to withstand strong sunlight and the weather. Most also combat mildew. A white paint that "chalks" continually sloughs off chalky powder along with dirt, so the finish appears fresh and white longer. Formulations may vary by region. "Southern" formulations, for instance, usually contain more antimildew ingredients and chalk more.

Specialty paints. Rust-protecting paints contain rust-inhibiting compounds. But if the surface is prepped correctly—by grinding or sanding off all rust until the metal shines, then priming the surface with a metal primer—you can use almost any paint for the top coat. Brushed-on coats are thicker and sturdier and cover better than aerosol sprays. Several coats are better than one heavy one.

Don't count on a basement-waterproofing paint to halt outright seepage. Even the best we've tested allow a small amount of water to seep through. The most water-resistant are two-component epoxies—expensive, strong-smelling coatings that

Matching interior surface to finish

	Latex, acrylic	Latex	Alkyd	Urethane/ Varnish	Stain	Floor paint	Aluminum paint
WOOD							
Floors				✔	✔	✔	
Paneling	✔	✔	✔	✔	✔		
Stair risers	✔	✔	✔	✔	✔		
Stair treads				✔	✔	✔	
Trim/furniture	✔	✔	✔	✔	✔		
MASONRY							
Concrete walls	✔					✔	
Kitchen/bath walls	✔		✔				
New masonry	✔						
Old masonry	✔						✔
Plaster	✔	✔	✔				
Wall board	✔	✔	✔				
METAL							
Aluminum windows	✔	✔	✔				✔
Steel windows	✔	✔	✔				✔
Radiators/pipes	✔	✔	✔				✔

Note: Unless surface has been previously finished, primer or sealer may be required. Consult manufacturer's instructions.

harden through a chemical reaction between a resin and catalyst. The epoxy must be mixed in precise amounts and applied to a sound surface. Next best: oil-based paint formulated for masonry.

The choices in stains

Exterior stains. Exterior stains resemble thinned paint. They come in latex and alkyd formulations, as well as in transparent, semitransparent, and opaque (solid-color) varieties.

Interior stains. Interior stain is essentially a varnish containing a colored dye. Many cabinet-quality stains are water-based. You brush them on, wipe off the excess, then seal the wood with varnish or polyurethane. Wiping off the stain takes

Matching exterior surface to finish

	Latex, acrylic	Alkyd	Wood stain	Trim paint	Porch paint	Urethane	Aluminum paint	Water-repellant/ preservative
WOOD								
Clapboard	✔	✔						
Natural siding/ trim			✔	✔				
Shutters/ trim	✔	✔	✔	✔				✔
Window frames	✔	✔	✔	✔				✔
Porch floor/ deck					✔			✔
Shingle roof			✔					✔
MASONRY								
Brick	✔							✔
Cement/ cinder block	✔							✔
Porches/ floors	✔				✔			
Stucco	✔							
METAL								
Aluminum windows	✔	✔		✔			✔	
Steel windows	✔	✔		✔			✔	
Metal siding	✔	✔		✔			✔	
Copper surfaces						✔		
Galvanized surfaces	✔			✔			✔	
Iron surfaces	✔	✔		✔			✔	

Source: Adapted from U.S. General Services Administration

a bit of finesse. Wipe too soon, and you may remove most of the color; wait too long, and the finish may be too dark.

The choices in clear finishes

Varnish. This is a combination of resins and, sometimes, oils that coat the surface of the wood. It's much like paint, but minus the hiding pigment. On interior wood trim, varnish protects the wood from wear and tear without changing its color.

Polyurethane. Urethane-oil-based varnish is widely used on floors, but water-based varnishes, which clean up with soap and water, are also available. Both types come in several gloss levels.

Penetrating oils. Products like tung oil or Danish oil soak into the wood's pores to provide a natural-looking, low-luster finish.

Lacquers. These are resins dissolved in strong solvents. As the solvents evaporate, the lacquer dries to a thin, tough film.

It's best to apply any clear finish in several thin coats, lightly rubbing down the surface with fine sandpaper between coats. Trying to do the job with one or two heavy coats may result in sagging, wrinkling, missed spots, or uneven gloss.

Environmental concerns

The solvents in paints and other finishes include hydrocarbons and other volatile organic compounds (VOCs). As the finish dries and those solvents evaporate, they can react with other pollutants in the air to produce ozone, a major ingredient of smog. When applied indoors, they may cause dizziness or headaches.

Oil-based products contain a high percentage of VOCs. Because of VOC regulations, the sale of solvent-based paint has been restricted in some states. As a result, manufacturers have reformulated or stopped making oil-based paint.

Lead, once widely used in paint pigments and drying agents, was banned from house paints in the 1970s. But it continues to pose dangers. Old paint on walls and woodwork may contain lead, so be careful when removing it.

Buying advice

Choose a finish that's compatible with the surface you want to cover, and make sure the surface is clean and smooth. Our advice: When painting over latex paint, stay with a latex product; when painting over oil, you can switch to latex permanently or continue using an oil-based product. (You can safely use latex paint over an oil-based primer, however.)

Prices for indoor and outdoor paints range from less than $10 to more than $35 a gallon. Custom colors usually cost more than standard colors. Latexes tend to be cheaper than alkyds, and flat-finish paints cheaper than glossy ones. Stains are priced similarly to paints.

We recommend products from the high end of the brand lines. In our tests over the years, bargain-priced paints have fallen down in qualities such as hiding power, washability, and adhesion, which lead to long-term dissatisfaction.

Claims of one-coat coverage—a big selling point—assume that the paint is spread thickly, covering only about 450 square feet per gallon. Usually, you have to use a brush rather than a roller to achieve that degree of thickness. We've found that with normal rolling, a gallon covers up to 650 square feet; and at that spreading rate, coverage usually suffers.

Shades of brown, blue, barn red, and dark green generally cover best. Pale colors, especially yellows, will probably need more than one coat. However, hiding is secondary to protection for exterior paint, where you need a sufficient film to resist the elements. Some finishes—especially reds and yellows—are apt to fade when exposed to sunlight.

Fire extinguishers

▶ Ratings on page 152.

Most homes have smoke detectors, but few have fire extinguishers. Where there's smoke, there's fire, so the detector and extinguisher are logical companions.

Two brands—Walter Kidde and First Alert—dominate the selection in home centers, discount stores, and hardware stores. Prices range from $7 or so for small models to $100 for large ones.

The choices

Fire extinguishers spray water, carbon dioxide gas, or dry chemicals. Halon-gas extinguishers have all but disappeared because halon vapor damages the earth's ozone layer. The most common fire-fighting material is a dry-chemical mix.

Fire extinguishers are grouped by the type of fire they're meant to fight and the size of fire they can fight, according to Underwriters Laboratories, an independent testing organization.

Fire type. Letter codes define the types. "A" fires involve combustibles like paper, wood, cloth, and upholstery, and they can be put out with water. "B" fires involve flammable liquids—cooking grease, paint solvents, gasoline. "C" fires involve electrical equipment like a TV set or a fuse box.

Multipurpose units with A, B, and C designations are the best choice for rooms that have a wood-burning stove or fireplace. Models labeled B:C are particularly useful in kitchens, because the sodium bicarbonate powder typically used in these models helps to smother grease fires.

Fire size. Numbers preceding the A:B:Cs denote the size of the fire an extinguisher can fight. You'll see labels that read 2-A:10-B:C or 5-B:C (no size is assigned to "C" fires, the electrical variety). Other things being equal, an extinguisher rated at 10-B, will put out twice as much flaming liquid as a 5-B unit. Those numbers also relate to how long each extinguisher can spray. Usually, the higher the number, the longer the spray time. A longer spray time buys you critical extra seconds to fight a fire—time you may need if, like most people, you fumble with the extinguisher and misdirect some of the spray. But the higher the number, the bigger the unit: Large models are clumsy to store and heavy to use.

Features and conveniences

Weight. The multipurpose units we tested range in weight from 4 to 37 pounds, B:C tested models, 1 to 33 pounds. Try lifting a model before you buy.

Pressure indicators. Extinguishers with a dial-type gauge show at a glance whether the unit has sufficient pressure. Some models use a pressure-check pin instead of a dial. You push down on the pin; if it pops back, the pressure is fine.

Mountings. A simple hooklike hanging bracket is easier to use in a hurry than a marine bracket. With a marine bracket, you must unsnap the ring that holds the unit to the hanging bracket. The ring, however, prevents an extinguisher from being knocked off the wall accidentally.

Recharging. Once an extinguisher is discharged, even partially, it must either be recharged or replaced. Most extinguishers can be recharged after a fire or a drop in pressure (look under "Fire Extinguishers" in the Yellow Pages). Recharging is less wasteful than disposal, but it may cost as much as a buying a new one and provide less fire-fighting capacity.

Models that aren't rechargeable should

be replaced after about 12 years—sooner if the manufacturer recommends or if the pressure has ebbed.

The tests

We judge an extinguisher mostly on ease of use. We evaluate the security of its bracket and the effort needed to remove the extinguisher. We pull the safety catch or pin, and squeeze the handle or press the push button. We measure the unit's spray time. Durability testing tells us how well the tank and valve mechanism are apt to survive a fall or prolonged exposure to high temperatures.

Buying advice

Every home should have at least one extinguisher on every level. An A:B:C extinguisher is the most versatile, capable of handling fires of all common burning materials. In the store, first handle a large model rated at 3-A:40-B:C to see if you can manage its weight and size. If the larger one is too cumbersome, choose a medium-sized extinguisher (rated at 2-A:10-B:C).

Small, supplemental extinguishers provide coverage for individual rooms. A small B:C extinguisher is inexpensive and worth adding to your basic kitchen equipment. Its sodium bicarbonate spray will be more effective than the spray from a multipurpose extinguisher.

It's a good idea to become familiar with using a fire extinguisher before an emergency occurs. It may be worthwhile to buy some inexpensive disposable models to practice with.

Smoke detectors

▶ Ratings on page 142.

Having a working smoke detector in your home cuts the risk of dying in a fire by half, according to some studies. "Working" is the operative word: Most homes have smoke detectors, but perhaps one-third aren't working because of missing or dead batteries.

One company, BRK Electronics, makes most of the smoke detectors you'll come across in discount and hardware stores and home centers. BRK's First Alert and Family Guard detectors account for three out of every four units sold. Brands sold through electrical suppliers include names like BRK, Firex, Fyrnetics, Dicon, and Visual Alert.

The choices

Most smoke detectors use a 9-volt battery; some are also AC-powered. If the battery isn't in place, current detectors won't close—or they signal visually. That precaution is in addition to the audible signal that sounds when the battery is weak.

AC-powered models are wired directly into the household current, usually by an electrician. Most AC-powered models have a back-up battery so they'll work during a power outage. Two or more detectors can be interconnected so all sound when one senses smoke. State and local building codes often require these dual-powered units for newly built or renovated homes.

Detectors vary in how they work:

Ionization. This is by far the most widely sold and easiest type to find. Ionization detectors use radioactive material (an amount so small it poses no significant hazard) to make the air in the detector chamber conduct electricity. Smoke interferes with that electric current and triggers the alarm. Ionization detectors are the most effective way to sense blazes that give off little smoke. Battery-powered models sell from $7 to $25.

Photoelectric. These smoke detectors shine a small beam of light past a sensor. Smoke disperses the light, tripping the alarm. Photoelectric models are best at sensing a smoldering, smoky fire—the kind that might start in upholstery, say.

Photoelectric detectors can be hard to find. For store locations, we suggest you call the manufacturers: BRK (800 323-9005) or Dicon (800 387-4219). Battery-powered models sell for $25 to $30.

Combination. Some models use both ionization and photoelectric sensors. These models may be AC-powered, run on a battery, or offer both options. Price: $30 to $35. Again, you may have to phone First Alert to find out where they're sold.

For the hearing-impaired. Smoke detectors for the hearing-impaired rouse sleepers with a flashing strobe. Most are AC-powered ionization units. Prices start at about $100.

Features and conveniences

Alarm testing. Most smoke detectors have a small LED (light-emitting diode) that flashes every minute or so to indicate a state of readiness. All detectors have a button that lets you test the unit's circuitry, battery, and horn. When a detector is mounted on the ceiling it can be hard to reach for regular testing. Flat buttons are easier to press with a broom handle than rounded ones. Some models respond to a flashlight beam. Units with automatic testing sound the alarm briefly every week at the same time.

Alarm loudness. An industry standard specifies a minimum loudness of 85 decibels. Many alarms are far more raucous, a consideration if you're hard of hearing.

Hush button. Detectors will sound as long as there's smoke, even if the cause is burnt toast. Most are hard to silence once they go off. As a result, many people resort to detaching the battery and forget to reconnect it. A Hush button solves the problem. It deactivates the alarm for 10 or 15 minutes—long enough for innocuous smoke to dissipate.

Weak-battery warning. All models chirp or beep periodically to indicate a weak battery. The warning continues for at least 30 days or until the battery is replaced.

Missing-battery indicator. Almost all smoke detectors signal the absence of a battery, as the safety standard requires.

Auxiliary light. When some models sound the alarm, they also turn on built-in reflector lights to help guide you through the smoke. But the lights are usually too small and weak to be of much use in a smoky fire. Instead, consider keeping a large halogen-bulb flashlight handy.

The tests

We mount the detectors on the ceiling of a room-sized test chamber and high on its walls (the recommended installation sites) and pit them against several types of fires: a smoky paper blaze (which goes rapidly from hot smoke to leaping flames); a smoldering fire (whose smoke begins slowly and builds gradually); and a flaming fire (which is largely smoke-free). We measure each model's response time and also consider conveniences.

Buying advice

You should have at least one smoke detector on every level of your house and, ideally, you should have at least one of each type of detector—ionization and photoelectric—for the earliest possible warning of different types of fires.

Make sure smoke detectors currently installed are in working order. To be on the safe side, any detector more than 10 years old should be replaced.

Carbon-monoxide detectors

About 200 people die accidentally each year from carbon monoxide (CO), a colorless, odorless gas, and another 5000 require treatment in hospital emergency rooms. But the real toll is probably higher, since the symptoms of CO—dizziness, nausea, vomiting, and fatigue—can easily be mistaken for the flu.

An inefficient or faulty furnace, space heater, water heater, or wood stove is usually the culprit, especially in a tightly weather-sealed house. Proper maintenance of such equipment is the best way to reduce the risk of CO poisoning, but a CO detector that monitors the air is a crucial backup.

Most CO detectors are bought in hardware stores and home centers. First Alert dominates the market, but many other brands are available.

The choices

CO detectors look like smoke detectors and shriek the same way when the alarm goes off. Prices range from $40 to $100.

Plug-in or hard-wired. Both run on household current. Most plug-ins have a 6-foot power cord. They work by heating a metal-oxide sensor that reacts with CO. Some plug-ins have battery backup.

Battery powered. This type has a translucent disk that darkens upon prolonged exposure to CO, a change that is detected by an infrared sensor. In our tests, this type tended to take hours rather than minutes to recover after the air was cleared. Its sensor also tends to accumulate CO over time; thus predisposing the alarm to react to a prolonged spell of urban air pollution.

Sensor-card. A sensor "spot" on the card is supposed to change color in the presence of CO. Since you have to look at the card to know if there's danger, a card is not suitable as a sole source of CO detection.

Features and conveniences

CO detectors usually have a light that shows that power is on, and most have a test button so you can check the alarm.

Alarm loudness. A horn sounds an 85-decibel alarm in response to hazardous levels of CO. The alarm should stop automatically when fresh air clears out the CO.

Hush/reset button. This silences the alarm and allows the sensor to take another reading. The noise resumes after a few minutes if CO levels remain high.

Older battery-operated models without a reset button require that you pull the battery/sensor pack to silence the alarm. That's inconvenient, and it renders the unit ineffective. Models produced after October 1995 have a reset button that allows five minutes of silence followed by another alarm if CO is still present.

Low-level warning. A warning light is designed to signal low levels of CO, but most weren't reliable in our tests. One plug-in unit has an LED display that gives the current CO level, helpful when CO levels are too low to trigger the alarm.

Buying advice

If your home has any fuel-burning appliance or fireplace, you should have at least one CO detector installed in a hallway or bedroom. We recommend the plug-in or hard-wired type.

In our most recent test, we judged the *Nighthawk 2000* A Best Buy at $40. But any of the following are also a good choice: *Enzone Air-Zone II*, $59; *Pama GHD-2010*, $60; *S-Tech COAH-2*, $60; *American Sensors CO-200*, $42; *Radio Shack 49-463*, $80.

Radon detectors

Radon is responsible for 5,000 to 20,000 lung-cancer deaths each year, according to the U.S. Environmental Protection Agency (EPA). Radon is easy to detect and to get rid of, but most people don't bother to test their homes for radon until it's time to sell the property.

Radon detection kits are widely available at hardware stores, home centers, and other retail outlets. Key, First Alert, and Air Check are the most widely distributed brands.

The choices

There are two main types of test kits that let you measure the radon yourself. Kits cost from $10 to $30, including lab analysis and a written report.

Short-term kits. This type uses a charcoal-containing canister, envelope, or tray to track radon levels for up to seven days.

Long-term. A small piece of plastic picks up an imprint from the radon gas to give an average reading of exposure for 90 days or more.

Both kits work in much the same way. You place the open kit in the lowest occupied living area. If you have and use a finished basement playroom, that's the place. If you visit your basement only a few times a week to load and unload the washer, test the first-floor living space instead. After the specified period of time, you seal the kit and promptly send it to a laboratory for analysis.

Buying advice

If you are considering buying a house, use a short-term test kit for quick feedback (usually within two weeks). Any of the following short-term models worked fine and were accurate within the EPA's recommended range: the *Air Check Radon Test Kit* (mostly mail-order), $10; *Key-Rad-Kit Radon Home Testing Kit*, $17; *First Alert Radon Gas Detector RD1*, $18; *RTCA Professional Radon Test*, $25; *Home Diagnostics Radon 7-Day Test 102*, $28; or *Teledyne Isotopes*, $30.

Otherwise, use a long-term kit that will smooth out any short-term fluctuations—brought about by temperature, barometic pressure, even wind—that might lead you to misgauge a problem. We recommend two models: the *Key-Trac-Kit*, $19, or the *Rad Trak Alpha-Track Radon Gas Detector*, $25.

If levels are above 4 picocuries, you'll need to take action. The radon-remediation industry is well regulated now, so finding competent help should be easy. According to the EPA, nearly all radon problems can be completely resolved for less than $2500—often, for much less.

Garage-door openers

▶ Ratings on page 155.

An automatic garage-door opener lets you open and close the door at the touch of a button while you sit in the car. Once the door is shut, it's locked.

Operating safety has long been a concern with this procedure. All openers made within the past 13 years have a safety mechanism that automatically reverses the door within two seconds of contacting anything in its path. Models made within the past two years have additional safeguards. The most popular design uses an electric eye, mounted on the garage door's jamb, to detect anything in the door's path and trigger the auto-reverse before it hits. Some models have a sensor that attaches to the bottom or edge of the door .

Major brands are Sears, Genie, Stanley, and Challenger. Most openers are install-it-yourself units sold in hardware stores or home centers; others are sold by dealers or installers.

The choices

Openers come with a power unit that raises and lowers the door, a remote control, a wall switch, and a manual release cord. The power unit, mounted near the ceiling, uses a chain or worm gear to drive the trolley along a rail between the power head and the front of the garage. As the trolley moves, so does the door. Besides a wall switch, the opener comes with a remote control to operate the opener from the house or the car. A manual-release cord lets you disengage the opener. Most models work with most doors—single- or double-width, one-piece or sectional, and doors without tracks. Price: about $120 to $250.

Installation. Do-it-yourselfers need respectable mechanical skills and six to eight hours' time. Openers weigh about 30 pounds—light enough for one person to set up, but easier with two.

With openers sold at stores, you must assemble sections of rail, connect the rail to the power head, mount the works on the ceiling, and connect the opener to the garage door. You must also install the electric eye, if so equipped, and adjust the door's travel and force.

Most openers sold by garage-door specialists come with fully assembled rails, so they take less time to put together. Directions may be sketchy or hard to follow and some hardware may be missing.

Hiring someone to handle installation will cost about $70 to $100. Dealer-installers tend to carry premium-priced models.

Horsepower. The motors that drive the openers come in three sizes: ¼, ⅓, and ½ hp. The ¼ hp is adequate for a single door. In general, the brawnier motors don't necessarily work any faster or compensate more effectively for an unbalanced door than lower horsepower models.

Features and conveniences

Remote control. Most openers come with a battery-powered digital remote that operates from up to several hundred feet away. A second one costs $20 to $35. Compact remotes fit in a pocket; others clip on the car's sun visor.

To set the code that operates the remote, you generally flip small On-off switches in the remote and duplicate those settings on the switches in the power head. Most systems provide at least 10 switches—enough for more than 1000 different code settings—which should deter any intruder. More elaborate remotes can learn a setting electronically, and remember up to five different settings keyed in from different remotes. Another type dispenses with switch-setting; it has built-in factory settings you activate by pressing two buttons. Basic models worked just as well as the fancier models in our tests.

Manual release. A manual disconnect is a standard feature, and the only way to open the door in a power failure. A tug on the rope disengages the trolley from the door. Look for a model that lets you release the rope to work the door. Some make you keep the rope under constant tension when pulling the door, a nuisance, especially if the trolley stops in midcourse.

Lights. Every opener's power head has a provision for a light bulb. The bulb goes on when the door opens or closes and stays on for several minutes, ample time to see your way into the house. On many models, the light flashes when the electric eye reverses the door.

Some garage-door openers have extras: A small auxiliary light built into the wall switch to guide you in the dark, and a "vacation" switch to render the opener deaf to all radio signals. But an accessible conventional light switch is a better solution to the dark, and simply unplugging the opener is an easy way to disable the opener while you're away.

Outside operation. Optional accessories enable you to open the door when you don't have access to the remote. The one that provides the best security is a battery-powered, wireless keypad, about $40, that mounts on an outside wall. The keypad must be the same brand as the opener. Other options include a key switch or a key disconnect, typically a $20 option. Both are essentially cylinder locks, which aren't very secure.

The tests

We use a 16-foot-wide sectional door fitted in a garage-sized frame to test ease of assembly, installation, and adjustment. We also evaluate speed of operation, safety features, and a unit's ability to cope with unbalanced doors.

Buying advice

Good performance and a competent safety system are the norm with garage-door openers these days. All the models we tested worked competently and their safety systems functioned properly.

As a result, you can let price and features be your guide. Most models cost less than $200. If you buy from a garage-door installer, expect to pay a premium.

RATINGS SMOKE DETECTORS

▶ **See report, page 137.** Last time rated in Consumer Reports: May 1994.

Brand-name recommendations: We recommend both an ionization-type and a photoelectric-type detector for an early warning of any fire. All photoelectric detectors we tested proved competent. The three top-rated ionization detectors merit first consideration. Of the three, the Firex and a successor for the First Alert are available.

For the typical smoke detector, expect: ■ Unit to carry Underwriters Laboratory (UL) certification. ■ For battery-powered models, a 9-volt battery, replaceable by user. For photoelectric models: ■ Best response to smoldering, smoky fires. ■ Limited availability. ■ Fewer false alarms triggered by cooking. For ionization models: ■ Best response to flaming fires with little smoke. ■ Wide availability.

Notes on the table: Price is the estimated average, based on a national survey (batteries not included). * means price paid. **Power** source is either a 9-volt battery (Bat.), household current (AC), or household current with battery backup (AC/Bat.). **Response** to fires is indicated for smoky fires, which smolder, and for flaming fires, which create little smoke. **Model availability:** Ⓓ means model is discontinued. Ⓢ means model is replaced, according to the manufacturer; successor model is noted in Comments. New model was not tested; it may or may not perform similarly. Features may vary.

E VG G F P

Listed in order of overall quality

Brand and model	Price	Power	Overall score (P F G VG E)	Response: SMOKY	Response: FLAMING	Comments
PHOTOELECTRIC MODELS						
First Alert Double System SA301	$25	Bat.		E	G	Hard to test if ceiling-mounted.
Dicon Photoelectric 440	24	Bat.		E	F	—
First Alert Photoelectronic SA203	20	Bat.		E	F	Hard to test if ceiling-mounted.
IONIZATION MODELS						
Firex 0465/C	12	Bat.		G	E	Smaller than most. Loud alarm.
First Alert Hall/Stairway SA150LT [S]	20	Bat.		G	E	Can test with flashlight. Sounded cooking false alarm. **Successor:** SA150LTD.
Safe House 49-458 (Radio Shack) [D]	13	Bat.		G	E	Hush button. Sounded cooking false alarm.
Dicon Micro 300	11	Bat.		G	E	—
First Alert Kitchen SA88	15	Bat.		F	E	Hush button. Can test with flashlight.
Code One 2000 D	13	Bat.		F	E	Self-tests weekly. Smaller than most. Loud alarm. Renamed Code One D.
Family Gard FG1000C [D]	14	Bat.		F	E	—
BRK 83R [1]	14	Bat.		F	E	Loud alarm. Sounded cooking false alarm.
Safety's Sake Petey-the-Puppy [2]	18	Bat.		F	E	Loud alarm. No monitor light. Designed for children.
Family Gard FG888D	7	Bat.		F	E	—
Dicon 370LB [D]	24	AC/Bat.		F	VG	Hush button.
Lifesaver 0918	16*	Bat.		F	VG	Hush button. Hard to test if ceiling-mounted. Sounded cooking false alarm.
Lifesaver 1275	21*	AC/Bat.		F	VG	Hush button. Hard to test if ceiling-mounted.
BRK 1839N12R [D]	28*	AC		F	E	Loud alarm. Sounded cooking false alarm. No backup battery.

[1] *Not available in stores; call 800 323-9005.*

[2] *May be ordered directly from mfr. (800 877-1250); price includes shipping.*

Ratings continued ▶

Ratings continued

Brand and model	Price	Power	Overall score	Response		Comments
			P F G VG E	SMOKY	FLAMING	
IONIZATION MODELS *continued*						
Firex 0440/FX 1218	$18	AC/Bat.		◒	⊖	Hard to test if ceiling-mounted.
Code One 2000 0192/E	16	Bat.		◒	○	Loud alarm. Renamed Code One 0192/E.
Kidde KSA-700	18*	Bat.		◒	○	Loud alarm.
Generation 2 1001	23*	AC		◒	○	Sounded cooking false alarm, hard to shut off. Mounts in ceiling light fixture.

[1] *Not available in stores; call 800 323-9005.*
[2] *May be ordered directly from mfr. (800 877-1250); price includes shipping.*

RATINGS LOW-FLOW TOILETS

▶ **See report, page 130.** Last time rated in Consumer Reports: February 1995.

Brand-name recommendations: The top-rated Gerber Ultra Flush 21-302 is A Best Buy at $210 despite a few minor flaws. The next highest-rated toilet, the Kohler Trocadero Power Lite K-3437, performs similarly (if more quietly) but costs an exorbitant $815. The Ultra Flush and Trocadero Power Lite, which pressurize the flush water, both clean their bowl as effectively as most gravity-flush toilets. If your budget is limited, consider a high-rated gravity-flush model such as the Universal Rundle Atlas 4079 ($195). Its higher-than-normal seat is a boon for elderly or handicapped people, but a drawback for young children.

For the typical toilet, expect: ■ A flush of about 1.6 gal. ■ A rim about 14 to 15 in. above the floor. ■ Flush and refill to take about 1 min. ■ 2-piece design, with an elongated bowl. ■ Availability in a range of colors. **A choice you'll have to make:** ■ Gravity flush or pressure flush.

Notes on the table: Price is an estimated average, based on a national survey, for a white toilet. Expect to pay more for other colors. * means price paid. **Overall score** is based on liquid and solid waste removal and wash-down. **Waste removal** is how readily the toilet flushes away solids. **Dilution** measures performance at flushing liquid and fine, dispersed solids. **Soiling, odor** reflects the potential for those problems. **Wash-down** judges the toilet's ability to self-clean as it flushes. **Drain carry** reflects the toilet's capacity to push waste through the drain line. Models similar to those we tested are noted in or Details; features may vary.

Listed primarily in order of waste removal and wash-down

Better ⟵⟶ Worse: ⊜ ⊖ ○ ◒ ●

Brand and model	Price	Overall score (P F G VG E)	Waste-removal	Dilution	Wash-down	Soiling, odor	Drain carry
Gerber Ultra Flush 21-302, **A BEST BUY**	$210		⊜	⊜	⊖	⊖	⊖
Kohler Trocadero Power Lite K-3437	815		⊜	⊜	⊖	⊖	○
Kohler San Raphael Lite K-3394	570		⊜	⊜	●	⊖	○
American Standard Cadet El Pa 2168.128	390		⊜	⊜	○	⊖	○
Eljer Berkeley 081-1595	485		⊜	⊖	⊖	◒	○
Kohler Wellworth Lite PC K3458	265		⊖	⊜	⊜	○	◒
Universal Rundle Atlas 4079	195		⊖	⊖	⊖	◒	○
American Standard Fontaine El Pa 2042.417	700		⊜	⊜	●	○	○
Universal Rundle Amega 4063-L	*308		⊜	⊜	●	⊖	⊖
American Standard Cadet El Pa 2292.203	300		⊜	⊜	●	○	○
Gerber Space Saver 23-712	115		○	⊜	⊜	●	○
American Standard Hydra	130		○	⊜	⊖	●	○
Kohler San Martine Lite K-3435-X	575		⊖	⊖	●	◒	○
Briggs Abingdon 4775	75		⊖	●	○	○	◒
American Standard Cadet II El 2174.139	130		◒	⊜	⊜	●	⊖
Mansfield Elderly 137-160	155		○	○	⊖	◒	○
Universal Rundle Atlas 4099	*149		◒	⊜	○	◒	○
Toto Kiki CST 703	*107		◒	⊜	○	◒	⊖
W.C. Inc. Savex 6040-42	*65		◒	⊜	○	○	○
Eljer Triangle Ultra 091-4100	180		●	⊖	⊖	⊜	○
Universal Rundle Nostalgia 4065	235		◒	⊜	○	○	○
Mansfield Alto 135-160	95		◒	◒	⊖	◒	○
Mansfield Quantum 150-1	220		○	⊖	◒	○	◒
Peerless Pottery Hydro Miser 5660	90		◒	◒	⊜	◒	○
Kohler Wellworth Lite K- 3420	140		●	⊜	⊖	◒	○

Ratings continued ▶

Ratings continued

Brand and model	Price	Overall score (P F G VG E)	Waste-removal	Dilution	Wash-down	Soiling, odor	Drain carry
American Standard Hamilton El 2092.017	$370		◒	○	⊜	◒	◒
Briggs Ultra Conserver 4725	105		●	⊜	⊜	●	○
Eljer Patriot 091-1175	255		●	⊜	⊜	◒	○
Eljer Patriot 091-1125	105		●	⊜	⊜	◒	○
The following models were downrated due to excessive water consumption.							
Crane CraneMiser 4607	125		○	⊜	○	○	⊜
Crane Avon Lite 4618	100		◒	⊜	○	○	⊜
Crane Summerset Plus Lite 4617	260		◒	○	○	◒	⊜

MODEL DETAILS

Want to know more about a rated model? They're listed here alphabetically.

American Standard Cadet El Pa 2168.128	Pressure flush. Seat close to water; possible splashing problem. Higher than most (useful for elderly and disabled people). Poor rim wash-down. Flush button, on top of tank. Noisy. **Similar:** 2168.100.
American Standard Cadet El Pa 2292.203	Pressure flush. Poor rim wash-down. Seat close to water; possible splashing problem. Flush button, on top of tank. Noisy. **Similar:** 2292.100.
American Standard Cadet II El 2174.139	Instructions for adjusting flush volume. Smaller water surface.
American Standard Fontaine El Pa 2042.417	Pressure flush. Poor rim wash-down. Flush button, on top of tank. 1-piece.
American Standard Hamilton El 2092.017	Dirt, hard water could clog rim outlets. Seat included. Instructions for adjusting flush volume. 1-piece. Smaller water surface.
American Standard Hydra	Instructions for adjusting flush volume. Round bowl. Smaller water surface. **Similar:** 2116.016.
Briggs Abingdon 4775	Round bowl.
Briggs Ultra Conserver 4725	—
Crane Avon Lite 4618	Used more than 2 gals. as received, adjusted before testing to use less. Round bowl.
Crane CraneMiser 4607	Used more than 2 gals as received; adjusted before testing to use less.
Crane Summerset Plus Lite 4617	Used more than 2 gals. as received; adjusted before testing to use less.
Eljer Berkeley 081-1595	Seat included. 1-piece.
Eljer Patriot 091-1125	Instructions for adjusting flush volume.
Eljer Patriot 091-1175	Higher than most; useful for elderly and disabled persons. Instructions for adjusting flush volume.

Eljer Triangle Ultra 091-4100	Seat close to water; possible splashing problem. Poor rim wash-down. Instructions for adjusting flush volume. Round bowl.
Gerber Space Saver 23-712	White only. Smaller water surface. **Similar:** 21-712.
Gerber Ultra Flush 21-302, **A BEST BUY**	Pressure flush. Seat close to water; possible splashing problem. Dirt, hard water could clog rim outlets. Flush button, on top of tank. Round bowl.
Kohler San Martine Lite K-3435-X	Poor rim wash-down. Dirt, hard water could clog rim outlets. Optional: battery-powered activation of flush, when seat lid closes. Seat included. 1-piece.
Kohler San Raphael Lite K-3394	Pressure flush. Poor rim wash-down. Dirt, hard water could clog rim outlets. Seat included. 1-piece.
Kohler Trocadero Power Lite K-3437	Pressure flush. Miniflush. Dirt, hard water could clog rim outlets. Electric water pump; installation may require electrician. Seat included. Round bowl. 1-piece. White only.
Kohler Wellworth Lite K- 3420	Dirt, hard water could clog rim outlets.
Kohler Wellworth Lite PC K3458	Pressure flush. Dirt, hard water could clog rim outlets. Noisy.
Mansfield Alto 135-160	—
Mansfield Elderly 137-160	Higher than most (useful for elderly and disabled people).
Mansfield Quantum 150-1	Pressure flush. Poor rim wash-down. Flush button, on top of tank. Noisy.
Peerless Pottery Hydro Miser 5660	—
Toto Kiki CST 703	Dirt, hard water could clog rim outlets. Round bowl.
Universal Rundle Amega 4063-L	Pressure flush. Poor rim wash-down. Flush button, on top of tank. Noisy. **Similar:** 4063.
Universal Rundle Atlas 4079	Higher than most (useful for elderly and disabled people). Instructions for adjusting flush volume. **Similar:** 4078, 4073, 4072.
Universal Rundle Atlas 4099	Instructions for adjusting flush volume. Smaller water surface.
Universal Rundle Nostalgia 4065	Poor rim wash-down. Instructions for adjusting flush volume. Round bowl.
W.C. Inc. Savex 6040-42	Round bowl. Smaller water surface.

RATINGS VACUUM CLEANERS

▶ **See report, page 123.** Last time rated in Consumer Reports: January 1995.

Brand-name recommendations: Four of the uprights are closely ranked at the top of the Ratings. The least expensive of them is the Eureka Bravo! The Boss ($95). The Eureka Powerline Plus ($150) offers a little more suction than the Bravo! and also adds a headlamp for working under furniture. Both machines are much lighter than average and are superb carpet cleaners, as is the Hoover Power Drive Supreme ($300). The Kirby G4 is also a top performer, but at $1350 too expensive to recommend. Among canisters, the Eureka World Vac ($190) was as competent as the top-rated uprights on carpeting and excelled at bare-floor cleaning. The Hoover Futura S3567 ($205) is also attractively priced and is only slightly inferior to the Eureka in performance and noisiness.

For the typical vacuum cleaner, expect: ■ The ability to clean bare surfaces and to deep-clean carpet of various heights. ■ Easy conversion from carpet cleaning to suction-only cleaning. ■ Power switch that's convenient to operate by hand or foot. ■ Headlamp on power nozzle/power head. **A choice you'll have to make:** ■ Upright or canister. **For the typical upright, expect:** ■ Hard-body design. ■ Very good or excellent at controlling debris exhaust. ■ Fair or poor clearance under furniture. ■ A built-in power head. ■ Easier storage than the typical canister vacuum. ■ Greater maneuverability than the typical canister model. ■ A 3- to 7-ft. hose. ■ Cord storage on 2 hooks, 1 of which is quick-release. **For the typical canister, expect:** ■ Fair or poor at controlling debris exhaust. ■ Good or better clearance under furniture. ■ A detachable power nozzle and nonpowered floor brush. ■ More maneuverability on stairs than the typical upright vacuum. ■ Less trouble changing the bag or cleaning up spills inside the housing than with the typical upright vacuum. ■ A 4- to 9-ft. hose. ■ A suction-control adjustment. ■ A cord that stores inside the canister and rewinds automatically.

Notes on the table: Price is the estimated average, based on a national survey. * means price paid. **Manufacturer's rating** gives electrical current draw, in amperes. Models with superior **air flow** should excel at cleaning bare surfaces, including floors. Models similar to those we tested are noted in Details; features may vary. **Model availability:** [D] means model is discontinued. [S] means model is replaced, according to the manufacturer; successor model is noted in Details. New model was not tested; it may or may not perform similarly. Features may vary.

Listed in order of performance and convenience

Key: E = excellent, VG = very good, G = good, F = fair, P = poor

Brand and model	Price	Mfr.'s rating (AMP)	Overall score (P F G VG E)	Performance: CARPET	Performance: AIR FLOW	Convenience: NOISE	Convenience: DIRT CAPACITY/DISPOSAL
UPRIGHT VACUUMS							
Hoover Power Drive Supreme U6323-930	$300	7.8		E	G	F	VG/G
Kirby G4	1350	7		VG	E	F	E/P
Eureka Bravo! The Boss 9334DT	95	9		E	G	F	E/P

Brand and model	Price	Mfr.'s rating (AMP)	Overall score (P F G VG E)	Performance: CARPET	Performance: AIR FLOW	Performance: NOISE	Convenience: DIRT CAPACITY/ DISPOSAL
UPRIGHT VACUUMS *continued*							
Eureka Powerline Plus 9741AT	$150	12		⊜	⊖	◒	⊜/◒
Sharp Twin Energy EC-12TXT6 D	230	10		⊖	○	⊖	○/○
Kenmore (Sears) Whispertone 35612 D	200	12		○	⊜	○	⊖/⊖
Royal Dirt Devil Lite Plus 085300	85	7		⊖	○	●	⊖/●
Hoover Elite Supreme U5043-930 S	130	7.2		⊜	●	◒	◒/○
Hoover Dimension Supreme U5221-930	195	7.3		⊖	◒	◒	○/○
Panasonic MC-6955 D	195	11		○	○	○	○/○
Hoover Encore Supreme U4261-930	80	7		⊖	○	◒	○/●
Eureka Excalibur 6410 Type AT S	195	12		○	○	○	⊖/○
Fantom F1061 00 S	*400	11		○	○	○	○/○
Royal Dirt Devil Classic 086600	100	9.5		⊖	○	◒	◒/○
Kenmore (Sears) Power Center 34190 D	100	9		⊖	◒	●	○/●
White-Westinghouse Designer Limited WWU5000	120	9		⊖	◒	●	○/○
Electrolux Epic Series 3500 SR	600	10		⊖	◒	◒	◒/⊜
Panasonic Quickdraw MC-5190-1	120	7.2		◒	○	⊖	⊖/○
Kenmore (Sears) Proformance 34495 D	80	9.5		⊖	●	●	◒/○
Royal Dirt Devil Deluxe 8201 D	140	11		◒	○	◒	○/⊖
Regina Plus HO6505	120	10		◒	◒	◒	◒/⊖
Singer SB 1275	70	7.5		○	●	◒	◒/◒
Singer HB 14100	*210	10		⊖	●	◒	●/○
CANISTER VACUUMS							
Eureka World Vac 6865A	190	12		⊜	⊖	○	○/⊖
Hoover PowerMAX Supreme S3611	300	9.8		⊖	○	○	○/⊖
Oreck Super Celoc XL1500	500	9.5		○	⊖	◒	⊖/⊖
Hoover Futura S3567	205	9.8		⊖	○	○	○/⊖
Electrolux Epic Series 6500 SR	780	11		⊖	◒ 1	○	●/⊜
Kenmore (Sears) Whispertone 24412 S	400	12		◒	⊖	○	⊖/⊖

1 *Motor shut off prematurely in test with wood flour. May perform better with coarser material.*

Ratings continued ▶

Ratings continued

Brand and model	Price	Mfr.'s rating	Overall score	Performance			Convenience
		(AMP)	P F G VG E	CARPET	AIR FLOW	NOISE	DIRT CAPACITY/ DISPOSAL
CANISTER VACUUMS *continued*							
Rexair Rainbow Performance Edition SE [D]	$1600	11.5		⊖	⊖	○	◒/◒
White-Westinghouse V.I.P. WWP9500	120	11.5		⊖	○	○	◒/⊖
Kenmore (Sears) 24211 [D]	250	11		◒	⊖	◒	⊖/⊖
Royal Deluxe Power Team M4600	725	12		○	○	◒	◒/⊖
Hoover Encore Supreme S3395-040	160	8.6		○	◒	◒	○/⊖

MODEL DETAILS

Want to know more about a rated model? They're listed here alphabetically.

Electrolux Epic Series 3500 SR	Good clearance under furniture. Debris-exhaust level judged fair. Long hose, cord. Full-bag indicator. Suction control. Tools not on board. Stairs brush. Extra tools. No carpet-height adjustment. Prone to tip over when hose is extended. Motor shuts off if overheated or jammed. Power-head brush can be turned off.
Electrolux Epic Series 6500 SR	Debris-exhaust level judged good or very good. Long hose. Short cord. Full-bag indicator. Can be used as blower. Stairs brush. Mfr. claims automatic carpet-height adjustment. Motor shuts off when bag is full. Motor shuts off if overheated or jammed. Power-nozzle brush can be turned off.
Eureka Bravo! The Boss 9334DT	Short hose. Belt-trouble indicator. Lacks headlamp. Soft body. Awkward or no cord storage and release.
Eureka Excalibur 6410 Type AT [S]	Long cord. Full-bag indicator. Suction control. On/off switch difficult to reach. Prone to tip over when hose is extended. Power-head brush can be turned off. **Successor:** 6425.
Eureka Powerline Plus 9741AT	Long cord. Belt-trouble indicator. Too bulky to use on stairs. **Simiar:** 9751AT.
Eureka World Vac 6865A	Full-bag indicator. Swivel joint on canister. Lacks bumper guard. Cleans closer to edges than most. Mfr. claims automatic carpet-height adjustment. Motor shuts off if overheated or jammed.
Fantom F1061 00 [S]	Long cord. Full-bag indicator. Suction control. Cleans closer to edges than most. Prone to tip over when hose is extended. Debris-exhaust level judged excellent only with opt. $100 HEPA filter. **Successor:** F11063.
Hoover Dimension Supreme U5221-930	Long cord.
Hoover Elite Supreme U5043-930 [S]	On/off switch difficult to reach. **Successor:** U5071-930.

Model	Comments
Hoover Encore Supreme S3395-040	Full-bag indicator. Short cord. Lacks bumper guard, headlamp. Cleans closer to edges than most. Awkward or no cord storage and release. Mfr. claims automatic carpet-height adjustment.
Hoover Encore Supreme U4261-930	Lacks headlamp. Soft body. On/off switch difficult to reach.
Hoover Futura S3567	Full-bag indicator. Swivel joint on canister. Cleans closer to edges than most. Mfr. claims automatic carpet-height adjustment. **Similar:** S3569.
Hoover Power Drive Supreme U6323-930	Long cord. Full-bag, belt-trouble indicators. Cleans closer to edges than most. Self-propelled. **Similar:** U6317-930, U6329-930.
Hoover PowerMAX Supreme S3611	Multispeed motor. Belt-trouble, full-bag indicators. Swivel joint on canister. Cleans closer to edges than most. Mfr. claims automatic carpet-height adjustment. Motor shuts off if overheated or jammed. Power-nozzle brush can be turned off. **Similar:** S3603.
Kenmore (Sears) Power Center 34190 D	Short cord. Soft body. Cleans closer to edges than most. Prone to tip over when hose is extended.
Kenmore (Sears) 24211 D	Full-bag indicator. Swivel joint on canister. Motor shuts off if overheated or jammed.
Kenmore (Sears) Proformance 34495 D	Short cord. Cleans closer to edges than most.
Kenmore (Sears) Whispertone 24412 S	Debris-exhaust level judged good or very good. Full-bag indicator. Swivel joint on canister. Cleans closer to edges than most. Motor shuts off if overheated or jammed. Power-nozzle brush can be turned off. **Successor:** 25312.
Kenmore (Sears) Whispertone 35612 D	Long cord. Suction control. Cleans closer to edges than most. Prone to tip over when hose is extended. Motor shuts off if overheated or jammed. Power-head brush can be turned off.
Kirby G4	Suction control. Long hose, cord. Belt-trouble indicator. Can be used as blower. Tools not on board. Soft body. Manual carpet-height adjustment especially easy to use. Self-propelled.
Oreck Super Celoc XL1500	Debris-exhaust level judged good or very good. Long hose. Full-bag indicator. Can be used as blower. Lacks headlamp. Mfr. claims automatic carpet-height adjustment. Prolonged use with blocked hose damaged vacuum. Power-nozzle brush can be turned off.
Panasonic MC-6955 D	Long cord. Cleans closer to edges than most. Mfr. claims automatic carpet-height adjustment. Dust sensor.
Panasonic Quickdraw MC-5190-1	Short hose. Lacks headlamp. Mfr. claims automatic carpet-height adjustment. Prone to tip over when hose is extended.
Regina Plus HO6505	Debris-exhaust level judged fair. Awkward or no cord storage and release. Prone to tip over when hose is extended.
Rexair Rainbow Performance Edition SE D	Lacks On/off control on power nozzle, bumper guard, headlamp. Picks up wet spills. Extra tools. No carpet-height adjustment. Motor shuts off if overheated or jammed. Power-nozzle brush can be turned off.
Royal Deluxe Power Team M4600	Debris-exhaust level judged good or very good. Long hose, cord. Multispeed motor. Can be used as blower. Cleans closer to edges than most. Awkward or no cord storage and release. Motor shuts off if overheated or jammed. Power-nozzle brush can be turned off.

Ratings continued ▶

Ratings continued

Royal Dirt Devil Classic 086600	Prone to tip over when hose is extended.
Royal Dirt Devil Deluxe 8201 Ⓓ	Debris-exhaust level judged fair. Long cord. Short hose. Prone to tip over when hose is extended.
Royal Dirt Devil Lite Plus 085300	Lacks headlamp. Soft body. No carpet-height adjustment.
Sharp Twin Energy EC-12TXT6 Ⓓ	Long cord. Short hose. Full-bag indicator. Multispeed motor. Mfr. claims automatic carpet-height adjustment. Prone to tip over when hose is extended.
Singer HB 14100	Debris-exhaust level judged fair. Long cord. Full-bag indicator.
Singer SB 1275	Debris-exhaust level judged fair. Short hose. Soft body. On/off switch difficult to reach.
White-Westinghouse Designer Limited WWU5000	Suction control. Too bulky to use on stairs.
White-Westinghouse V.I.P. WWP9500	Long hose. Belt-trouble, full-bag indicators. Lacks bumper guard, headlamp, floor brush. Awkward or no cord storage and release. Mfr. claims automatic carpet-height adjustment. Motor shuts off if overheated or jammed.

RATINGS FIRE EXTINGUISHERS

▶ **See report, page 136.** Last time rated in Consumer Reports: May 1994.

Brand-name recommendations: For a full-floor model, consider the Buckeye 5HI SA-40 ABC, $45, and the Ansul Sentry SY-0516, $40, both 3-A:40-B:C models that weigh less than 10 pounds and have a wide spray pattern. Additional coverage for individual rooms is available from supplemental models. A multipurpose extinguisher such as the Kidde FA110G, $14, a 1-A:10-B:C model would be a good choice for a den. Consider the Kidde FA5G, $11, a 5-B:C model, and the Kidde KK2, $12, a 2-B:C model, for the kitchen.

For the typical fire extinguisher, expect: ■ Easy activation by handle, after removing a safety pin. ■ A marine-bracket mounting. ■ Fire-engine-red finish. ■ 9 to 24 sec.'s spray of dry chemical, depending mostly on the extinguisher's size. For full-floor models: ■ A rating of at least 2-A:10-B:C, indicating sufficient capacity and versatility to be the sole extinguisher on 1 level of a home. ■ A dial gauge to check pressure conveniently. ■ The capability to be recharged. ■ A hose to help direct the spray. For supplemental models: ■ A spray nozzle that provides less control than a hose. ■ Small and medium models that spray more slowly and are more susceptible to impact and high-temp. damage. ■ The inability to be recharged. **A choice you'll have to make:** ■ Size (full-floor extinguishers, large or medium supplemental extinguishers).

Notes on the table: Within groups (full-floor and supplemental), extinguishers are separated by Underwriters Laboratories designations of capability and capacity. **Price** is an estimated average, based on a national survey. * means price paid. **Abuse** is based on tests of resistance to physical damage on impact and to high temperature. **Model availability:** Ⓓ means model is discontinued.

Within type, listed in order of ease of use and durability

Better ⊜ ⊖ ○ ◒ ● Worse

Brand and model	Price	Overall score (P F G VG E)	Ease of use	Abuse	Spray time	Comments
FULL-FLOOR MULTIPURPOSE MODELS						
UL SIZE 3-A:40-B:C						
Buckeye 5HI SA-40 ABC	$45		⊜	⊜	⊜	Spray wider than most.
Ansul Sentry SY-0516	40		⊜	⊜	⊖	Optional marine bracket. Spray wider, faster than most.
General TCP-5LH	38		⊜	⊜	⊖	Needs forceful squeeze to spray. Spray narrower, faster than most.
American LaFrance 5MB-6H	38		⊜	⊜	○	Optional marine bracket. Spray faster than most. Now called Full Security 5MB-6D.
Kidde FA340HD	30		○	⊜	⊜	Needs forceful squeeze to spray. Spray wider than most.
UL SIZE 2-A:10-B:C						
Ansul Sentry SY-0515 [1]	39		⊜	⊜	⊜	Optional marine bracket.
First Alert FE2A10 [1]	30		⊜	⊜	⊜	Pressure gauge. Wall hook.
American LaFrance 5MB-7H	37		⊜	⊜	⊖	Optional marine bracket. Now called Full Security 5MB-7D.
Buckeye M-5 ABC-II-100	55		⊜	⊖	○	Pressure gauge.
SUPPLEMENTAL MODELS						
LARGE MULTIPURPOSE (UL SIZE 1-A:10-B:C)						
Ansul Sentry SY-0216	28		⊜	⊜	◒	Optional marine bracket.
Kidde FA110G	14		⊖	⊖	○	Needs forceful squeeze to spray. Spray narrower than most. More susceptible than others to impact damage.
Fyr Fyter D1A10 [D]	20		⊖	○	○	No pressure gauge. More susceptible than others to impact damage. Safety catch is not a pin, but bracket prevents accidental discharge.
American LaFrance P250 MA-1	23		⊖	⊜	◒	Optional marine bracket. Needs forceful squeeze to spray. Now called Full Security P250MD-1.
First Alert FE1A10	15		⊖	○	◒	No pressure gauge. Spray narrower, faster than most. More susceptible than others to impact damage.

[1] *These two models are similar.*

Ratings continued ▶

Ratings continued

Brand and model	Price	Overall score (P F G VG E)	Ease of use	Abuse	Spray time	Comments
SUPPLEMENTAL MODELS *continued*						
LARGE, FOR FLAMMABLE LIQUID AND ELECTRICAL FIRES (UL SIZE 10-B:C)						
Ansul Sentry SY-0236	$31		⊜	⊜	○	Optional marine bracket. Rechargeable.
General CP-2 1/2J	23		⊜	⊜	◒	Rechargeable. Spray narrower than most.
General CP-5J	41		⊜	⊜	◒	Rechargeable. Spray narrower, faster, than most.
American LaFrance 275RA-1	27		⊜	⊜	◒	Rechargeable. Spray narrower than most. Now called Full Security 275MD-1.
Buckeye 2.5 STD-100	35		⊜	○	◒	Rechargeable. High temp. damaged some samples.
Kidde FA10G	12		⊖	○	○	Spray wider than most. High temp. damaged some samples. More susceptible than others to impact damage.
First Alert FE10	14		⊖	○	◒	No pressure gauge. Spray narrower than most. More susceptible than others to impact damage.
Fyr Fyter D250	23*		○	○	○	No pressure gauge. Optional marine bracket. High temp. damaged some samples. More susceptible than others to impact damage. Safety catch is not a pin.
MEDIUM, FOR FLAMMABLE LIQUID AND ELECTRICAL FIRES (UL SIZE 5-B:C)						
Kidde FA5G	11		⊖	○	○	Needs forceful squeeze to spray. Spray wider than most.
Fyr Fyter 210D [D]	14		○	○	◒	No pressure gauge. Push-button operation. Safety catch is not a pin.
SMALL, FOR FLAMMABLE LIQUID AND ELECTRICAL FIRES (UL SIZE 2-B:C)						
Kidde KK2	12		◒	○	◒	No pressure gauge. Push-button operation. Spray narrower than most. Safety catch is not a pin. Wall hook.
Kidde PKG 200	13		◒	○	◒	Not damaged by high temp. Safety catch is not a pin. No bracket.
Fyr Fyter PKP 100 [D]	23 [2]		◒	○	◒	No pressure gauge. Push-button operation. Spray narrower than most. Safety catch is not a pin. No bracket.

[2] *Price is per extinguisher in package of two.*

RATINGS GARAGE-DOOR OPENERS

▶ **See report, page 140.** Last time rated in Consumer Reports: January 1994.

Brand-name recommendations: Every opener worked competently and safely in our tests. Price, not performance, separates these products. If you hire someone to handle the installation, plan to spend an additional $70 to $100 or so. And if you buy an opener from a garage-door installer, you'll pay a premium. The openers sold by installers are at the bottom of the Ratings because of price, not quality.

For the typical garage-door opener, expect: ■ Chain-and-cable drive. ■ Main automatic-reversal safety system controlled by an electric eye, with a secondary safety system that will reverse the door's direction within 2 sec. after contact with a person or an object. ■ Design that will open a hinged, sectional door up to 16-ft. wide; most also work with 1-piece tracked and trackless doors. ■ At least 1 digital remote control with an ample range, and a wall-mounted push-button control. ■ Built-in light that stays on at least 4 min. after door closes. ■ Lock-off feature for manual operation of door. ■ Light flashes when electric eye triggers auto-reversal. **A choice you'll have to make:** ■ Whether you want a way to open the garage door from the outside without the remote control using a key switch, touch pad, or key-disconnect feature.

Notes on the table: A ⋆ preceding the model name denotes an opener sold only by professional garage-door installers. **Price** is the estimated average, based on a national survey. **Speed.** All models opened or closed a door in 10 to 14 sec. **Reverse force** reflects the average max. force exerted before the opener reversed direction. **Assembly** shows how easy we found the openers to assemble. **Model availability:** [D] means model is discontinued. [S] means model is replaced, according to the manufacturer; successor model is noted in Comments. New model was not tested; it may or may not perform similarly. Features may vary.

Models listed in order of increasing price

Better ⟵⟶ Worse: ⊜ ⊖ ○ ◒ ●

Brand and model	Price	Speed	Reverse force	Assembly	Comments
Stanley ST200 Standard	$129	○	○	○	Trolley easy to disengage. Lock-off was very easy to disengage. Trolley very easy to re-engage with door closed.
Sears Craftsman 53325	140	⊖	◒	○	Very easy to set code. Limited code-changing options. Remote can operate products connected to in-house receivers.
Chamberlain 2100 Standard Duty	142	⊖	○	◒	Very easy to set code. Limited code-changing options.
Stanley ST400 Deluxe	143	○	⊜	○	Trolley easy to disengage and very easy to re-engage with door closed. Lock-off was very easy to disengage.
Genie G8000	158	⊖	⊖	◒	Trolley easy to disengage. Lock-off was very easy to disengage. Needs more than 2-in. clearance between door and ceiling. Worm-gear drive.

Ratings continued ▶

Ratings continued

Brand and model	Price	Speed	Reverse force	Assembly	Comments
Sears Craftsman 53425	$160	⊖	○	○	Very easy to set code. Limited code-changing options. Remote can operate products connected to in-house receivers.
Chamberlain 5100 Premium Heavy Duty	169	⊖	○	◒	Very easy to set code. Limited code-changing options. Remote can operate products connected to in-house receivers.
Stanley SL700 Light Maker	169	○	⊖	○	Trolley easy to disengage. Lock-off was very easy to disengage. Trolley very easy to re-engage with door closed.
Master Mechanic Premium	188	⊖	○	◒	Very easy to set code. Limited code-changing options. Includes 2 remotes. Remote can operate products connected to in-house receivers.
Genie GXL9500	199	⊖	⊜	◒	Trolley easy to disengage. Lock-off was very easy to disengage. Includes 2 remotes. Remote can operate products connected to in-house receivers. Needs more than 2-in. clearance between door and ceiling. Worm-gear drive.
Sears Craftsman 53525	200	⊖	◒	○	Very easy to set code. Limited code-changing options. Includes 2 remotes. Remote can operate products connected to in-house receivers.
***Lift-Master** 1260 Premium	231	⊖	◒	⊖	Very easy to set code. Limited code-changing options. Lacks hanging hardware. Chain drive.
***Challenger** 9500	235	⊖	○	⊖	Easy to change codes. Trolley very easy to re-engage with door closed. No lock-off when disengaging trolley. Lacks hanging hardware. Chain drive.
***Genie** Pro 98-S Premium	257	⊖	⊜	⊖	Easy to change codes. Trolley easy to disengage. Lock-off was very easy to disengage. Lacks hanging hardware. Needs more than 2-in. clearance between door and ceiling. Worm-gear drive.
***Stanley** GT400	261	○	⊖	○	Trolley easy to disengage. Lock-off was very easy to disengage. Heaviest tested (51 lb.). Needs more than 2-in. clearance between door and ceiling. Chain drive.
***Overhead** 656 Heavy Duty [D]	285	⊖	⊖	⊖	Very easy to set code. Trolley easy to disengage. Lock-off was very easy to disengage. Trolley hard to re-engage with door closed. Lacks hanging hardware. Includes 2 remotes. Remote can operate products connected to in-house receivers. Chain drive.
***Raynor** R-260 [S]	304	⊜	⊜	⊜	Easy to change codes. Lacks hanging hardware. Chain drive. **Successor:** R-270.

HEATING & COOLING

Fans

In many climates, a fan may be all you need to moderate summer's heat. Fans represent a simple approach to keeping cool. Fan makers adapt the basic pieces—blades powered by a motor—to create window, floor, ceiling, and whole-house fans.

Portable fans

Portable fans ventilate a room either by pulling in fresh air from outside or by merely creating a breeze. With their 9- to 20-inch blades, portable fans are small enough to move around. They range in price from less than $20 for a basic blower to $150 for a "high velocity" model with a powerful motor. In general, larger fans move more air with less noise than do small fans. Brands include Galaxy, Patton, Windmere, and Lakewood. Kmart, Sears, and Home Depot have their own brands.

The choices

Window fans are designed to go in or near a window. Some screw to the window casing, allowing you to close the window with the fan in place. **Box fans** (with a square housing) are often suitable for window use, but check the instructions. Some pose an electrical hazard if they get wet.

Floor fans come with a pedestal or stand. They mainly recirculate room air rather than bring in fresh air. Some floor models can be adapted for use in a window by rotating their legs or stands.

Table fans recirculate air like floor fans.

Features and conveniences

Child safeguards. Look for grilles and housings with small, rigid openings that keep out fingers. Some models have a child-resistant On/off switch that you must depress and turn at the same time.

Speed control. Three fan speeds are typical. The highest setting moves the most air, but it can be noisy. So-called high-velocity fans can be uncomfortable for someone sitting directly in the air stream.

Oscillation. Common to table fans, this control moves the fan from side to side to recirculate room air. Look for an oscillation range of 90 degrees.

Airflow angle. Nearly all circulating fans have a tilt adjustment to direct air upward or downward.

Thermostat. This device turns off the fan when the set temperature is reached.

Buying advice

First decide on the type of fan. Buy as large a fan as will reasonably fit to get the best performance. For circulating air in one room, consider a large table or floor fan.

Ceiling fans

▶ **Ratings on page 170.**

Ceiling fans efficiently and unobtrusively move lots of air. They deliver a downdraft a foot or two wider than the blade's swath. The air column reaches the floor, spreads out toward the walls, and turns upward to be recirculated. In general, large fans distribute air more uniformly and widely than do small ones.

These nostalgic appliances have evolved from a utilitarian object into an interior-design statement so don't be surprised to see prices ranging from $20 to more than $1000, although most are priced at $50 to $200. Models priced at $200 and up generally offer superior quality and durability. Their heavy-duty castings, sealed bearings, and weighted and well-balanced blades contribute to smooth, quiet operation.

Major brands include Hunter, Fasco, Liberty, Casablanca, and Lasko.

The choices

Most ceiling fans come with four or five blades in diameters that range from 29 to 62 inches. A blade sweep of about 42 to 52 inches is most common.

Ceiling fans require an eight-foot ceiling to keep the blades a safe seven feet from the floor. Models that mount flush against the ceiling provide more head room than those that hang. But fans suspended from a downrod can pull air down more effectively than flush-mounted fans.

Features and conveniences

Lights. Some ceiling fans come with attached light fixtures. Others can be fitted with lights sold separately. A light fixture reduces head room.

Controls. Typically via a pull-chain with two or three speeds. A switch reverses the blades (and the direction of the air flow). A wall-mounted control or a remote control is a necessity for a fan on a cathedral ceiling. Some models come with a remote control. Remotes that operate most fans are also available separately.

Speeds. Two or three are normal, and

all you need. Available but not common is a variable-speed control.

The tests

A fan's air-moving ability and air distribution are most important. We measure noise and efficiency—how much air the fan moves.

Buying advice

Expect to spend $150 or so for a model with good construction and durable parts.

Whole-house fans

A whole-house fan mounted in the attic can make the entire house feel cool in a hurry. And in many parts of the country, drawing in the cool night air may be all you need to survive summer's heat. If the outside temperature drops from, say, 85°F to 75° in two hours, the inside temperature may take another four hours to drop that much. A whole-house fan cuts that time considerably. And it can ventilate an entire house on the electricity an air-conditioner would use to cool a single room.

On the downside, a whole-house fan requires substantial space and effort to install. It usually means cutting and framing a hole in the ceiling and fitting it with a louver, usually a job for a professional.

Whole-house fans sell for about $150 to $300. Installation can double that.

The choices

Shutters. "Automatic" shutters are simple and cheap. They are moved by the fan's suction or blowing action. Shutters that open and close mechanically or electrically cost more but don't restrict air flow as much.

Size. Blades range from 24 to 36 inches. As a rule, the larger the blades, the more air they move (expressed in cubic feet per minute, or cfm).

To calculate the size fan you need, figure out the cubic feet of the space to be ventilated. Include halls and stairways, but not closets, pantries, store rooms, or the attic. If your summers are sweltering, choose a fan that can completely change the house air every two minutes at maximum speed. For a house with 12,000 cubic feet of living space, you would need a fan that can move 6000 cfm. Where the heat is less intense, a lower capacity should suffice.

Manufacturers sometimes rate their fans for unrestricted "free-air delivery." More useful is a rating that gives air delivery when working against a standard resistance (usually, 0.1 inch of water). If that number isn't available, use 80 to 85 percent of the free-air delivery as a guide.

Buying advice

Consider a whole-house fan where nighttime and daytime temperatures differ greatly for much of the summer, and where the humidity isn't constantly high.

Room air-conditioners

▶ **Ratings on page 165.**

A room air-conditioner that runs much of the year can use hundreds of dollars' worth of electricity. Choosing an efficient air-conditioner can reduce that cost dramatically. A model's "Energy Efficiency Rating"—EER—is marked on its yellow Energy

WHAT SIZE?

Don't ask a salesperson how much cooling capacity you need from a room air-conditioner. You may be steered toward the model the store wants to sell, not the one that best meets your needs. This table, developed by a manufacturer, gives a capacity based on the size of the room.

Room area in square feet	Capacity in Btu per hour
100 to 150	5,000
150 to 250	6,000
250 to 300	7,000
300 to 350	8,000
350 to 400	9,000
400 to 450	10,000
450 to 550	12,000
550 to 700	14,000
700 to 1000	18,000

- If the room is heavily shaded, reduce the capacity by 10 percent.
- If the room is very sunny, increase the capacity by 10 percent.
- If more than two people normally occupy the room, add 600 Btu for each additional person.
- If you're using the air-conditioner in a kitchen, increase the capacity by 4000 Btu to compensate for heat from cooking and appliances.

Source: Carrier Corp.

For a more precise cooling-capacity estimate, CU can provide a detailed worksheet, adapted from one published by the Association of Home Appliance Manufacturers. The worksheet is free. To order, send a stamped, self-addressed envelope to Consumers Union, Dept. DY, 101 Truman Ave., Yonkers, N.Y. 10703.

Guide label. The higher a product's rating, the lower the energy cost for a given amount of cooling.

Choosing the right-sized model also helps reduce costs. An undersized unit lacks the muscle to cool a big room, while an oversized one will cycle off before it extracts enough humidity from the air.

Even though there are more than two dozen brands of air-conditioners, many come from the same makers. Fedders, for instance, makes Emerson Quiet Kool and Airtemp models. Frigidaire makes Gibson and White-Westinghouse. Matsushita Electric makes Panasonic and Quasar.

Sears Kenmore is the leading brand. Kenmore, Fedders, General Electric, and Whirlpool account for more than half of all sales in the U.S.

The choices

All air-conditioners contain pretty much the same components. The part facing outdoors contains a compressor and condenser; the part facing indoors, a fan and and an evaporator. A model's cooling capacity and energy efficiency are the main things that distinguish one air-conditioner from another.

Cooling capacity. An air-conditioner's cooling capacity is measured in British thermal units per hour (Btu/hr). How much you need depends mainly on the size of the room, the number of windows, and the local climate. The smallest models, suitable for a small bedroom, are generally rated at 5000 Btu/hr. Medium-sized models are about 8000 Btu/hr. Large models, those rated at 11,000 to 14,000 Btu/hr, can cool about 500 square feet—a large room, or areas that run together, such as a living room/dining room. Models larger than that usually require a 220-volt line.

Small units (less than 8000 Btu/hr) are generally priced from $200 to $500; midsized models (8000 to 10,000 Btu/hr), from

$400 to $700; large units (greater than 10,000 Btu/hr), from $500 to $850.

Energy efficiency

Federal law requires appliance manufacturers to label air-conditioners with an Energy Efficiency Rating as a guide to energy consumption. The EER is figured by dividing the Btu of cooling per hour by the watts of power used. Other factors being equal, the higher the EER, the lower the energy consumption. Manufacturers are likely to call all models "high efficiency," even those that barely meet the Government minimum.

Features and conveniences

Energy-saving options. A 24-hour timer turns an air-conditioner on before you get home—no need for it to run all day. An Energy-saver setting, included on many models, cycles the fan on and off with the compressor instead of letting the fan run continuously. But without the fan running, temperature control can suffer, something that some models compensate for.

Controls. Look for a thermostat with clear markings. A few models have an electronic thermostat with a light-emitting diode (LED) readout of the room temperature and a signal light showing that the power is on.

'Power thrust.' Also called "Super Thrust" and the like, this is a fan control that sends the air farther into the room. It's useful if you must mount the unit at the narrow end of a long room.

Louvers. Many room models can't direct the air effectively. Directional control is especially important if the unit is in a corner or if you want spot-cooling. Models that let you close some louvers can redirect air more forcefully through the open ones. A Vent setting blows some room air outdoors. Some models also draw in fresh air, although not effectively.

'Low profile.' These L-shaped units stow most of their machinery outside and below the window, so they obstruct the view less.

Installation. Most room air-conditioners are designed to fit in a double-hung window. A more limited selection of models are sized for casement windows. Alternatively, some models are made for through-the-wall installation so they don't block a window.

A slide-out chassis greatly simplifies installation: You secure the empty cabinet in the window, then slide the machine's innards in or out.

Air-conditioners are heavy and should be installed by at least two people; low-profile models that must be lifted over the sill can be especially unwieldy.

The tests

We test air-conditioners by mounting them in a room within an environmental chamber, simulating an "inside" and an "outside." The air-conditioner's task is to maintain a temperature of about 75°F "inside" when the "outside" temperature is 95°. We keep outdoor humidity at 70 percent and measure each machine's ability to dehumidify and to keep variations within 5 percent. Sensors mounted in front of the air-conditioner determine how uniformly each model distributes cool air.

Buying advice

Just about any air-conditioner should perform well under normal circumstances if it's the right size for the job. Besides checking price tags and energy-guide labels, see whether the controls are clear, logically arranged, and easy to operate. A model with adjustable air louvers offers more flexibility in air distribution than does a model with fixed louvers. Find out how easily the air filter can be removed for cleaning and replacement.

Dehumidifiers

▶ Ratings on page 172.

In basements, where air can become oppressively humid, a dehumidifier can be a big help. It can dry out the chronically damp air that makes pipes sweat and tools rust and makes a room smell musty.

Despite the 40 or so brands of dehumidifier on the market, there are only eight manufacturers. Whirlpool makes the two leading brands—Sears Kenmore and Whirlpool.

The choices

Dehumidifiers are all similar in exterior dimensions, but they vary in the amount of water they can remove from the air in a day—25, 40, 50, or 60 pints per day.

Most cost between $150 and $250, although some go as high as $600. The larger a dehumidifier's capacity, as a rule, the less time it must run—something you'll appreciate if you have to listen to the unit buzz and whine as it works. And while a larger dehumidifier can always be throttled back, a small one can't always be turned up enough to bring humidity down to a tolerable level.

Features and conveniences

Controls. Most dehumidifiers include an adjustable humidistat that lets you set the humidity level. Humidistats aren't always precise, but they allow some control.

A signal light to show when the tank is full is helpful. Most come with one. An automatic shutoff to keep the tank from overflowing is standard. A few models also shut off while you empty the tank, which avoids a puddle accumulating beside the unit.

Tank design. Most tanks have to be emptied every couple of days under normal conditions, daily if the air is particularly muggy. Tanks that are easy to empty have a narrow opening and a handle for easy carrying. Unfortunately, a design that makes a tank easy to empty also makes it difficult to clean. Their narrow opening makes it hard to reach all the inside surfaces.

More convenient than any tank is a direct line to a drain. Most models let you thread a hose from the tank to a nearby floor drain. Some models don't even need a hose; you park the unit over the drain and remove the water tank, and the condensate drips directly into the drain.

The tests

We evaluate ease of operation, cleaning, emptying, and mobility. To see how well dehumidifiers can remove moisture, we run the models in various temperature and humidity conditions.

Buying advice

We think a large-capacity unit—one rated at least 50 pints a day—is the size to choose. A more modest unit may not be able to dry out the air satisfactorily all the time and may even be more expensive to own in the long run.

A low-capacity dehumidifier, though less expensive to buy than a large-capacity unit, may work less efficiently—and so be more costly to operate. The $50 to $100 you typically save by buying a small-capacity dehumidifier can easily evaporate if the cheaper unit uses significantly more electricity to do the job, as some small-capacity machines do.

Whatever type you choose, note that the tank needs to be cleaned at least once a year to keep molds and bacteria from growing.

Humidifiers

▶ Ratings on page 168.

When dry winter air saps moisture from your home, a humidifier can help. It reduces static electricity and protects wood furniture. Moister air can make you feel warmer and helps protect your respiratory system against viruses and air pollutants.

Duracraft is the leading brand. It, along with Holmes Air and Sunbeam, account for more than half of all humidifiers sold. Other big names include Emerson and Toastmaster.

The choices

Types. Humidifiers work in various ways, but by far the most common is evaporative. Typically, capillary action draws water into a wick filter. A fan pulls air through the filter, allowing water to evaporate and sending it into the room. Such models use little energy, run on tap water, and are easy to clean. They're unlikely to spread bacteria and white dust. But they can be somewhat noisy, and they remove heat from the room.

Impeller models use fan blades to sling droplets of water into the air. They use little energy, need less-frequent refills than other types, and have a tank (but not impeller) that's very easy to clean. They're very inexpensive to buy. On the downside: They can splatter, and spew microorganisms along with water. They require soft water, distilled water, or a demineralization cartridge. (With distilled water, one year's running cost can exceed the purchase price.) Also, the sloshing noises from the fan/impeller assembly can be annoying.

Models that use steam mist boil the water to release steam. Boiling kills microorganisms, so filters aren't needed. They can use tap water, and they have no moving parts. Such models emit little or no white dust, but they use a lot of energy. Their heating element may need extra cleaning to remove accumulation of hard-water minerals. If a tank top is off, the water and mist can scald. This type of humidifier may emit bits of dead microorganisms, triggering allergic reactions.

Warm-mist humidifiers work similarly to steam-mist units, except a fan mixes cool air with the steam. They require no filters, and they emit little or no white dust. There is less risk of scalding, since the mist is relatively cool. The disadvantages are similar to those of the steam-mist type.

Size. Tabletop models are the smallest and best-selling kind. They're designed to humidify one room, or two at most. They sell for about $20 to $150.

Furniture-sized consoles are typically the evaporative type. The smallest can humidify several rooms or an entire house. Prices range from about $100 to $300.

A central unit can be installed in a forced-air heating system. Cost: about $125 to $250, before installation. Installation involves minor plumbing to provide water and electrical wiring. It offers the considerable advantage of humidifying the whole house and automatic refilling.

Features and conveniences

Controls. Tabletop models often lack a humidistat, which is essential for regulating humidity. Humidistats aren't always precise, but some control is better than none. Also sometimes missing is an On/off switch. A switch that's separate from the humidistat and fan control saves resetting each time you turn on the unit. Fans can usually run at Low or High; on High, some units are as noisy as a room air-conditioner.

Indicator lights. They warn when to fill the tank or when to clean the filter.

Auto-shutoff. This feature turns off the humidifiers when the tank runs dry.

Tank design. A wide opening eases refilling (usually required daily), and it lets you get your hand inside to clean (generally required weekly). A full tank can be heavy, so carrying handles are important. Wheeled units can roll to the sink. A hose that connects to a faucet speeds filling.

Cost of operation and maintenance. Most tabletop models use about $5 worth of electricity a year, while consoles use $11 to $14 a year (at the 1995 national average rate of 8.7 cents per kilowatt-hour). Humidifiers that boil their water use about twice as much electricity as consoles.

Warm-mist and steam-mist models have essentially no maintenance costs. Yearly costs for table-top evaporative units are about $10 to $20. For impeller models, assuming they require distilled water or demineralization cartridges, costs are $20 to $40, and for consoles, $20 to $50.

The tests

We evaluate ease of cleaning and access to the interior. To see how long the humidifiers can run on a tank of water, we run them at high speed until they run dry—which, in our most recent tests, took from nine hours to 2½ days. To see how they cope with neglect, we run them with hard tap water for 1000 hours.

Buying advice

Match the size of the humidifier to your needs. Most tabletop humidifiers have ample capacity for one or two rooms; small console models are fine for a large apartment or a moderate-sized house. The largest console is suitable for most houses

Models that are easy to clean—those that are easy to disassemble and have a tank with a large opening and few nooks and crannies—are easier to live with.

THE CHOICES IN AIR CLEANERS

The most effective way to control indoor pollution is to eliminate indoor pollution sources and open the windows. If the trouble is pollen, an air-conditioner set to recirculate indoor air should work. Try an air cleaner only if those measures fail. If the problem is cigarette smoke, odors, or gases, most air cleaners won't help.

The best room models in our tests have been electrostatic precipitators and those using a high-efficiency-particulate-arresting (HEPA) filter. In general, tabletop units haven't been nearly as good; the best were ionizers with what are called electret filters.

We've found electrostatic precipitators designed to fit in the ductwork for central heating or air-conditioning to be nearly as effective as the best room models. A disposable electret filter was only a notch less effective. A do-it-yourself self-charging electrostatic in-duct filter performed about on a par with a small tabletop air cleaner, at best.

Avoid ozone generators; the models we've tested can generate unhealthy levels of ozone.

Energy and maintenance costs vary widely among models, and in some cases can exceed the purchase price within a year or two. Energy costs range from about $20 to $60. HEPA replacement filters cost $30 to $120 a year; other types of filters, $20 to $80.

RATINGS SMALL & MID-SIZED ROOM AIR-CONDITIONERS

▶ **See report, page 159.** Last time rated in Consumer Reports: June 1995.

Brand-name recommendations: These air-conditioners range in cooling capacity from 5000 to 8600 BTU per hour, which should be sufficient for a guest room, a den, or a moderately large living room in most parts of the country. All were good to very good overall, but five deserve first consideration: the Panasonic CW-606TU, $380, in the 5000- to 5800-Btu group; the Whirlpool ACQ062XD0, $370, and the Fedders A3Q06F2B, $360, in the 6000- to 6700-Btu group; the Panasonic CW-806TU, $440, and the Friedrich SS08J10, $685, in the 7800- to 8600-Btu group.

For the typical air-conditioner, expect: ■ 3 cooling speeds and 2 fan-only speeds. ■ Adjustable louvers, vent for exhausting room air, and slide-out air filter. ■ Installation only in double-hung window. ■ Expandable side panels, plus sash lock. ■ Power cord at least 5 ft. long. ■ Need for grounded 15-amp, 120-volt circuit protected by time-delay fuse.

Notes on the table: Price is the estimated average, based on a national survey. * means price paid. **Overall score.** Comfort tests, noise tests, and efficiency received the greatest emphasis. **EER.** The energy-efficiency rating, a standard measure of efficiency. **Comfort** score shows how well the units cool without wide variations in temp. and humidity. Models similar to those we tested are noted in Details; features may vary. **Model availability:** Ⓓ means model is discontinued.

Within type, listed in order of performance and convenience

E = Excellent, VG = Very good, G = Good, F = Fair, P = Poor

Brand and model	Price	Overall score (P F G VG E)	EER	Comfort	Directional control: LEFT	Directional control: RIGHT	Noise indoors: ON LOW	Ease of use
5000-5800 BTU/HR.								
Panasonic CW-606TU	$380		10.0	VG	G	F	E	VG
Sharp AF-505M6	*300		9.7	E	—	—	VG	G
Kenmore (Sears) 75055	300		10.0	E	VG	P	E	G
Carrier UCA051B	300		10.0	VG	E	G	E	G
Fedders Portable Series A3Q05F2A	250		9.5	VG	E	P	VG	F
Gibson Extra Value Series GAC056T7A1 Ⓓ	*339		9.2	E	VG	P	E	G
Friedrich QStar SQ05H10D	380		10.0	G	G	G	VG	VG
Whirlpool DesignerStyle ACQ052XD0	320		9.5	E	E	P	G	G
Amana Quiet Zone 5QZ21TB	360		9.7	VG	VG	E	VG	G

Ratings continued ▶

Ratings continued

Brand and model	Price	Overall score (P F G VG E)	EER	Comfort	Directional control LEFT	Directional control RIGHT	Noise indoors ON LOW	Ease of use
6000-6900 BTU/HR.								
Whirlpool DesignerStyle ACQ062XD0	$370		9.5	⊜	⊜	●	○	○
Fedders Portable Series A3Q06F2B	360		10.0	⊖	⊜	●	⊖	◒
Amana Quiet Zone 7QZ21TB	400		10.0	⊖	⊖	⊜	⊖	○
White-Westinghouse Mobilaire WAB067T7B1 D	400		10.0	○	○	⊜	⊖	○
Friedrich QStar SQ06H10D	420		10.3	○	○	○	⊜	⊖
Carrier VisionAire LCA061P	350		9.1	○	⊖	●	⊖	⊖
General Electric Value Line ACV06LAD1 D	310		8.6	⊜	—	—	⊖	○
7800-8600 BTU/HR.								
Panasonic CW-806TU	440		10.0	⊜	○	◒	⊜	⊖
Friedrich Quietmaster Electronic SS08J10	685		10.8	⊜	⊖	○	⊖	⊖
Sharp AF-802M6 D	*430		10.0	⊜	⊖	⊜	⊖	○
Kenmore (Sears) 75089 D	450		9.7	⊜	●	◒	⊖	○
Whirlpool DesignerStyle ACQ082XD0	440		9.6	⊜	⊖	●	⊖	⊖
Carrier Siesta Series TCA081P	480		10.0	⊖	○	⊜	○	⊖
Fedders Portable Series A3Q08F2B	430		9.5	⊖	⊜	●	⊖	◒
General Electric Value Line ASV08ABS1 D	385		9.0	⊜	—	—	⊖	○
Carrier Siesta Series TCA081D	400		9.2	⊖	○	⊜	○	⊖
Gibson Extra Value Series GAC086W7A1	365		9.5	⊖	⊖	●	○	○
White-Westinghouse Continental WAC083T7A2 D	360		9.2	⊖	⊖	●	○	○
Amana Cool Zone 9P2MY	400		9.0	⊖	⊖	⊜	○	○

MODEL DETAILS

Want to know more about a rated model? They're listed here alphabetically.

Amana Cool Zone 9P2MY	Exterior support bracket. No slide-out filter or up/down louver control.
Amana Quiet Zone 5QZ21TB	Exterior support bracket. No slide-out filter or up/down louver control.
Amana Quiet Zone 7QZ21TB	Exterior support bracket. No slide-out filter or up/down louver control.
Carrier Siesta Series TCA081D	Handles to ease carrying. Has exterior support bracket. No vent. Only 2 fan speeds on Cool.
Carrier Siesta Series TCA081P	Handles to ease carrying. Exterior support bracket. Only 1 fan-only setting.
Carrier UCA051B	Through-the-wall installation instructions provided. Harder to install. Slide-out chassis. No upper sash lock. Only 2 fan speeds on Cool. No vent. Filter pulls out from bottom; may hit sill.
Carrier VisionAire LCA061P	Handles to ease carrying. Exterior support bracket. No vent. Only 1 fan-only setting. Low-profile design.
Fedders Portable Series A3Q05F2A	No upper sash lock. Exterior support bracket. No slide-out filter or up/down louver control. **Similar:** Emerson Quiet Kool 5GC53.
Fedders Portable Series A3Q06F2B	No upper sash lock. Exterior support bracket. No slide-out filter or up/down louver control. **Similar:** Emerson Quiet Kool 6GC53.
Fedders Portable Series A3Q08F2B	No upper sash lock. Exterior support bracket. No slide-out filter. No up/down louver control. **Similar:** Emerson Quiet Kool 8GC73.
Friedrich QStar SQ05H10D	Slide-out chassis. Through-the-wall installation instructions provided. No upper sash lock. Thermostat not marked with numbers.
Friedrich QStar SQ06H10D	Slide-out chassis. Through-the-wall installation instructions provided. No upper sash lock. Thermostat not marked with numbers.
Friedrich Quietmaster Electronic SS08J10	Slide-out chassis. No expandable side panels. Exterior support bracket. Through-the-wall installation instructions provided. Harder to install. No upper sash lock. 4 fan speeds, auto fan-speed control, timer, electronic controls. No slide-out filter.
General Electric Value Line ACV06LAD1 [D]	No vent. Only 2 fan speeds on Cool. Handles to ease carrying. No left/right or up/down louver control.
General Electric Value Line ASV08ABS1 [D]	Through-the-wall installation instructions provided. Only 2 fan speeds on Cool. Filter pulls out from bottom; may hit window sill. Slide-out chassis. No left/right louver control.
Gibson Extra Value Series GAC056T7A1 [D]	—
Gibson Extra Value Series GAC086W7A1	—
Kenmore (Sears) 75055	No fan-only setting. Thermostat not marked with numbers.
Kenmore (Sears) 75089 [D]	No fan-only setting. Thermostat not marked with numbers. Louvers can be partially closed to increase air velocity.

Ratings continued ▶

Ratings continued

Panasonic CW-606TU	Harder to install. Slide-out chassis. No upper sash lock. Only 2 fan speeds on Cool. Installation kit available for casement or sliding windows. **Similar:** GE AMH06LAM1, Quasar HQ2062KH.
Panasonic CW-806TU	Harder to install. Slide-out chassis. No upper sash lock. Only 2 fan speeds on Cool. Panasonic and Quasar offer installation kit available for casement or sliding windows. **Similar:** GE AMH08FA, Quasar NQ2082KH.
Sharp AF-505M6	No vent or upper sash lock. Only 1 fan-only setting. No left/right louver control.
Sharp AF-802M6 Ⓓ	Shorter power cord than most. No upper sash lock. Slide-out chassis. Only 1 fan-only setting. No slide-out filter.
Whirlpool DesignerStyle ACQ052XD0	Only 1 fan-only setting. Thermostat not marked with numbers. No up/down louver control.
Whirlpool DesignerStyle ACQ062XD0	Only 1 fan-only setting. Thermostat not marked with numbers. No up/down louver control.
Whirlpool DesignerStyle ACQ082XD0	Slide-out chassis. Through-the-wall installation instructions provided. Shorter power cord than most. Only 1 fan-only setting. Thermostat not marked with numbers.
White-Westinghouse Continental WAC083T7A2 Ⓓ	—
White-Westinghouse Mobilaire WAB067T7B1 Ⓓ	Thermostat not marked with numbers. Handles to ease carrying. Low-profile design.

RATINGS HUMIDIFIERS

See report, page 163. Last time rated in Consumer Reports: October 1994.

Brand-name recommendations: Among tabletop units, the best in our tests was a warm-mist model, the Duracraft DH-904, about $64. Also worth considering were three evaporative models: the Duracraft DH-831, the Toastmaster 3408, and the Emerson HD850. All should cost much less to run than a warm-mist model. Among the console models, the Toastmaster 3435 and Emerson HD14W1 (and successor, HD15W0) are nearly equal in overall performance.

For the typical tabletop model, expect: ■ A portable tank with handles or side grips for convenience. ■ Sufficient capacity to humidify a medium- to large-sized room. **For the typical console model, expect:** ■ A humidistat to control relative humidity. ■ Sufficient capacity to humidify an average-sized house. ■ Casters or wheels. ■ A switch that shuts the unit off when the water tank is empty.

Notes on the table: Models are evaporative type unless otherwise noted. **Price** is an estimate of the average retail from the mfrs. * means price paid. **Operating cost** is based on 1000 hrs. of use per year, at the highest output setting and includes energy cost (based on the national average electricity rate of 8.4¢). **Humidistat** scores reflect how precisely this control kept relative humidity steady. **Model availability:** Ⓓ means model is discontinued. Ⓢ means model is replaced, according to the manufacturer, successor model is noted in Comments. New model was not tested; it may or may not perform similarly. Features may vary.

Within type, listed in order of performance and convenience

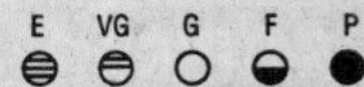

Brand and model	Price	Overall score (P F G VG E)	Operating cost	Humidistat	Comments
CONSOLE MODELS					
Toastmaster 3435	$135		$33	VG	—
Emerson HD14W1 [S]	145		40	G	Variable fan speed or mist setting. Hose to fill tank. **Successor:** HD15W0.
Bemis 4973	140		60	E	Variable fan speed or mist setting. Hose to fill tank.
Kenmore (Sears) 32-14412 [S]	115		43	F	Variable fan speed or mist setting. **Successor:** 14452.
Bionaire W-6S [S]	168		31	F	Indicates if filter needs cleaning. Tank cap hard to use. **Successor:** W-6.
TABLETOP MODELS					
Duracraft DH-904	64		28	E	Warm mist type.
Duracraft DH-831	74		17	F	—
Toastmaster 3408	53		14	—	Tank is hard to fill or clean.
Emerson MoistAir HD850	59		11	F	No handle.
Kaz 3300	29		10	—	Only 1 fan speed or mist setting.
Duracraft DH-805	64		18	F	—
Holmes Air HM-2000 [D]	43		13	—	—
Bionaire CM-3 [D]	105		32	F	Tank cap hard to use. Hard to clean. Warm mist type.
Holmes Air HM-5150	55		27	—	Steam mist type.
Holmes Air HM-460 or 460B	60		19	—	Variable fan speed or mist setting. Tank cap hard to use. Splatters mist or water when running. Ultrasonic type.
DeVilbiss/Hankscraft 5920D/1100 [D]	*37		12	—	Filter hard to install or remove.
Holmes Air HM-5100A [S]	38		26	—	Tank is hard to fill or clean. Only 1 fan speed or mist setting. Steam mist type. **Successor:** 5110A.
Bemis 7260	45		26	—	Filter hard to install or remove.
The following were downrated due to the high cost of using distilled water or a demineralization cartridge.					
Kaz 2000	27		35	—	Splatters mist or water. Only 1 fan speed or mist setting. Impeller type.
Holmes Air HV-8005	27		42	—	Splatters mist or water. Impeller type.
Sunbeam 658-8 [D]	*23		32	—	Splatters mist or water. Only 1 fan speed or mist setting. Impeller type.
DeVilbiss/Hankscraft 0240D/1250 [D]	*25		25	—	Tank cap hard to use. Splatters mist or water. Impeller type.

RATINGS CEILING FANS

See report, page 158. Last time rated in Consumer Reports: June 1993.

Brand-name recommendations: Among the large fans, the ultramodern and pricey Beverly Hills Stratos topped the Ratings, with high marks for air-moving ability and air distribution. We consider two models Best Buys: The Harbor Breeze Wellington and the J.C. Penney 854-8968-03 (and its successor, 8322547), both about $100. The Casablanca Lady Delta, $220, was the top-rated small fan. It moved as much air as the best large fans but was a bit raucous and ran fast at high speed. But see lower right for information about the recall of Casablanca fans.

For the typical ceiling fan, expect: ■ 4 to 6 blades. ■ 3 speeds. ■ Very good air distribution. ■ Pull-chain speed control (a few have wall-mounted control or a remote). ■ Do-it-yourself assembly. ■ Blades operate in reverse direction. ■ To provide 7-ft. clearance between blades and floor.

Notes on the table: Bracketed models were judged about equal in quality and are listed in order of increasing price. **Price** is the approx. retail price. * means price paid. **Air moving** indicates the amount of air pushed toward the floor on High. **Air-flow range** is the range of air movement between High and Low. **Noise** is judged at high speed. **Model availability:** [D] means model is discontinued. [S] means model is replaced, according to the manufacturer; successor model is noted in Comments. New model was not tested; it may or may not perform similarly. Features may vary.

Within type, listed in order of performance

Better ⊜ ⊖ ○ ◒ ● Worse

Brand and model	Price	Air moving	Air-flow range	Noise	Comments
LARGE MODELS, 52-INCH					
Beverly Hills Stratos 4605	$274	⊜	⊖	⊖	Very efficient. Inconvenient to reverse fan direction.
Casablanca Panama Gallery Edition 12002R/12002T	900	⊜	⊜	○	Not efficient. Comes with light fixture kit.
Harbor Breeze Wellington 37771, **A BEST BUY** [1]	97	⊖	◒	⊖	Very efficient. Comes with light.
J.C. Penney 854-8968-03, **A BEST BUY** [S]	*100	⊜	○	⊖	Comes with light fixture kit. **Successor:** 8322547.
Hunter Studio Series Remote 25730	184	⊖	○	⊜	—
Emerson Northwind Designer CF755BK	134	⊖	○	⊜	—
Hunter Orion ORN-03 25827	249	⊖	○	⊖	Comes with light fixture kit.
Fasco American Spirit Collection RM995BR [D]	460	⊜	⊜	⊖	Not efficient.

Brand and model	Price	Air moving	Air-flow range	Noise	Comments
LARGE MODELS, 52-INCH *continued*					
Encon Spectrum 5S-52WPB [S]	$65	⊖	○	⊖	Motor made noise. Comes with light fixture kit. **Successor:** 5AR52PBC.
Kmart Atlantic Air 61-86-35	*60	⊖	○	⊜	Motor made noise. Comes with light fixture kit.
Hunter Low Profile 22426	105	○	◒	⊖	—
Encon Contempra 5CP52PBP [S]	60	◒	●	⊜	Not efficient. Blades were warped on 2 samples. Motor vibrated or wobbled and made noise. Comes with light fixture kit. **Successor:** 5RC52WPC.
SMALL MODELS, 42- TO 44-INCH					
Casablanca Lady Delta 16222D [S]	220	⊜	⊖	○	**Successor:** 2722T.
Emerson Legend CF3342PB [D]	344	⊜	⊖	○	Motor made noise.
Hunter Coastal Breeze CTL-0123500	67	○	◒	⊖	Very efficient. Motor made noise.
Kmart Atlantic Air 61-93-50	39	◒	●	⊜	Comes with light fixture kit.
Fasco Gulf Stream 975-42BR [D]	69	◒	●	⊖	—
Beverly Hills Designer Colors 2003	90	○	◒	⊖	Motor made noise.
Encon Premier Deluxe PF-42ABA [D]	45	◒	●	⊖	Blades were warped on 2 samples. Motor vibrated or wobbled. Comes with light fixture kit.

[1] *Sold at Lowe's, a home-center chain in the South and Midwest.*

Note recall of Casablanca ceiling fans (all models) sold from 1981 to 1993.

Problem: Fans could fall from ceiling mount. **Fans affected:** 3.3 million fans sold 1/81-1/93. Fans are identifiable by words "Casablanca" on metal nameplate on fan exterior. Recalled models also have serial no. on nameplate whose second letter is either A, B, C, O, P, R, S, T, U, V, W, X, or Y. Recall doesn't involve Pasadena brand fans, which are made by Casablanca.

What to do: Call 800 390-3131 for repair kit and instructions. (Because fans made before 3/91 were marketed by another company, free installation may not be available; phone to find out whether your model qualifies.)

RATINGS DEHUMIDIFIERS

▶ **See report, page 162.** Last time rated in Consumer Reports: June 1995.

Brand-name recommendations: All the dehumidifiers we tested will do at least an adequate job of drying humid air in your home. Two 50-pint-per-day machines stand out: the Whirlpool AD0502XA0, $245, and the Kenmore 22-5350, $240 (now replaced by 5550). Those models were highly efficient, even under severe conditions. Their main drawback is a tank that's not as easy to empty as some.

For the typical dehumidifier, expect: ■ An adjustable humidistat. ■ A removable water tank with a hose coupling for disposal to a drain. ■ A signal light to show when the tank is full and an automatic shutoff to prevent an overflow. ■ Casters or wheels. ■ A current draw between 5 and 9 amps. ■ No problem handling electrical "brownouts." ■ A weight of 50 to 60 lbs. empty. ■ A 6-ft. power cord.

Notes on the table: Price is the estimated average, based on a national survey. * means price paid. **Performance** reflects how close the unit's daily moisture removal comes to its Association of Home Appliance Manufacturers rating, in 2 conditions: cool (70°F/70 percent relative humidity, as in a cool basement) and warm (80°/60 percent relative humidity). **Efficiency.** How well the model used energy to remove water. **Humidistat.** How steadily the dehumidifier could hold the air at a certain humidity. **Model availability:** D means model is discontinued. S means model is replaced, according to the manufacturer; successor model is noted in Details. New model was not tested; it may or may not perform similarly. Features may vary.

Within type, listed in order of performance and efficiency

E VG G F P

Brand and model	Price	Overall score (P F G VG E)	Performance (COOL/WARM)	Efficiency	Humidistat	Noise	Ease of use
LARGE CAPACITY (50 PINTS PER DAY RATING)							
Whirlpool AD0502XA0	$245		E/E	E	E	F	F
Kenmore (Sears) 22-5350 S	240		E/E	E	VG	G	G
Emerson Quiet Kool DG60G [1]	285		F/G	E	G	F	G
Because the following large-capacity models appear identical in basic construction, their performance scores have been averaged.							
Aqua-Dri 50EB2	590		VG/VG	VG	P	P	G

[1] *Rated at 60 pints per day.*

Brand and model	Price	Overall score	Performance	Efficiency	Humidistat	Noise	Ease of use
		P F G VG E	COOL/WARM				
LARGE CAPACITY (50 PINTS PER DAY RATING) *continued*							
Frigidaire MDD50TF1 **Gibson** MDD50TG1 **Signature** 2000 93301 (Montgomery Ward) **White-Westinghouse** WED50P3 [S]	$235-270		⊖/⊖	⊖	●	●	⊖
MEDIUM CAPACITY (40 PINTS PER DAY RATING)							
Whirlpool AD0402XA1	215		⊜/⊜	⊜	⊖	○	◒
General Electric AHD40SSS1 [D]	230*		⊜/⊜	⊜	⊜	◒	⊖
Kenmore (Sears) 22-53401 [S]	200		⊜/⊜	⊜	⊖	○	○
SMALL CAPACITY (25 PINTS PER DAY RATING)							
General Electric AHD25SSS1 [D]	205		○/⊖	⊖	●	○	○
Kenmore (Sears) 22-59254 [S]	170		⊜/⊖	◒	○	○	◒
Whirlpool AD0252XA1	185		⊜/◒	◒	◒	○	◒

MODEL DETAILS

Want to know more about a rated model? They're listed here alphabetically.

Aqua-Dri 50EB2	Tank easy to remove, replace but difficult to carry without spilling. Disassembly for cleaning requires tools.
Emerson Quiet Kool DG60G	Can be emptied directly into drain without tank. Tank easy to carry, empty without spilling. Unit stays on when tank removed; may cause minor spill. Disassembly for cleaning requires tools.
Frigidaire MDD50TF1	2 fan speeds. Tank difficult to clean but easy to remove, replace, carry, empty without spilling. Disassembly for cleaning requires tools.
General Electric AHD25SSS1 [D]	Removes moisture very well under hot, humid conditions. Tank easy to remove, replace. Only 2 front wheels; unit must be tilted to maneuver.
General Electric AHD40SSS1 [D]	Can be emptied directly into drain without tank. Tank easy to remove, replace. Unit stays on when tank removed; may cause minor spill. Only 2 front wheels; unit must be tilted to maneuver.
Gibson MDD50TG1	Basic construction identical to Frigidaire MDD50TF1. See above.
Kenmore (Sears) 22-5350 [S]	Removes moisture very well under hot, humid conditions. 2 fan speeds. Tank difficult to carry without spilling. Has fragrance dispenser. **Successor:** 5550.

Ratings continued ▶

Ratings continued

Kenmore (Sears) 22-53401 [S]	2 fan speeds. Tank difficult to carry without spilling. Has fragrance dispenser. **Successor:** 5541.
Kenmore (Sears) 22-59254 [S]	Tank difficult to carry without spilling. Unit stays on when tank removed; may cause minor spill. **Successor:** 5525.
Signature 2000 93301 (Montgomery Ward)	Basic construction identical to Frigidaire MDD50TF1. See page 173.
Whirlpool AD0252XA1	Unit stays on when tank removed; may cause minor spill. Only 2 front wheels; unit must be tilted to maneuver. Tank difficult to carry without spills.
Whirlpool AD0402XA1	Tank difficult to carry without spilling. Unit stays on when tank removed; could cause minor spill. Only 2 front wheels; unit must be tilted to maneuver.
Whirlpool AD0502XA0	Removes moisture very well under hot, humid conditions. Tank difficult to carry without spilling. Unit stays on when tank removed; may cause minor spill. Only 2 front wheels; unit must be tilted to maneuver.
White-Westinghouse WED50P3 [S]	Basic construction identical to Frigidaire MDD50TF1. See page 173. **Successor:** White-Westinghouse MDD50WW.

DISPOSING OF A DEHUMIDIFIER

By law, an old dehumidifier or refrigerator with environmentally damaging R-12 or R-500 refrigerant cannot be discarded unless the chemical has been properly removed. The refrigerant a model uses is listed on its nameplate, along with such things as the serial number and power requirements. Models made after January 1, 1996 must use another refrigerant, most likely R-22. Telephone your municipality for directions on disposal. In some cases, you may have to pay for the dehumidifier to be drained.

WORKING AT HOME

Computers

Rising power and falling prices have produced a computer that, for less than $2000 can do all the usual computer tasks—as well as show moving pictures and produce high-fidelity sound. The most popular and powerful medium in which these multimedia machines run software is called CD-ROM, and computer stores are brimming with encyclopedias, games, "edutainment," and other interactive CD-ROM topics.

Change happens so quickly in the computer industry that many prospective buyers hesitate for fear that equipment will soon be replaced by cheaper, faster gear. We expect competition among manufacturers and retailers to remain fierce for the near future, with the choices in continual flux. You may find good deals on machines that are only slightly out-of-date.

The personal computer market is divided into two main camps—IBM-compatible and, since the introduction of Macintosh "clones" that run the operating system Mac-OS, Apple Macintosh-compatible. Apple still holds the lion's share of the Macintosh-compatible market. While differences between the IBM and Mac systems have shrunk with the introduction of Windows 95, a Macintosh-compatible is still easier to set up, use, and upgrade. Apple's newer *Power Macintoshes* offer speed and price similar to those of IBM-compatibles. Some Macs now come with a built-in processor that runs IBM-compatible software, such as Microsoft Windows. Others, with the help of special software, can run software written for Windows.

Most personal computers sold today are IBM-compatibles, and most available software is designed to run on this type of machine. Besides IBM, major IBM-compatible brands include AST, Compaq, Dell, Gateway 2000, and Packard Bell.

IBM-compatibles are far easier to use than they used to be, since they now come with Windows 95, a user interface that lets you work visually and carry out commands with the click of a button.

The choices

Desktop computers. There are three types: the traditional full-sized personal computer; the all-in-one computer with the built-in monitor, which has the smallest footprint; and the minitower, whose case stands upright on the floor, allowing it to take the least amount of desk space. You can buy one with plenty of speed and capacity—along with a printer and some software—for the price of a notebook computer alone.

Notebook and smaller computers. Notebook computers are the leading kind of portable computer because they're small enough to transport easily, yet powerful enough to handle the same chores as a desktop machine. Smaller machines, known as subnotebooks and palmtops, can't do as much. Pint-sized keyboards aren't meant for touch-typing. Postcard-sized displays aren't well-suited for complex tables of data. The smallest computers also lack the capacity to handle some popular software.

Features and conveniences

Computers consist of various components whose power and capacity determine the capabilities of the machine.

Processor. This is the computer's brain. It determines how fast the computer runs and, to some extent, how much it costs. Motorola 680x0s and the new PowerPC processors control Macintoshes; Intel processors—chiefly the 80486 and the Pentium—dominate IBM-compatible machines. The chips come in various model designations, priced according to performance. The speed of the processor's internal clock is expressed in megahertz (MHz), usually between 25 and 150. Combine those elements and you get the "models" shown in ads, such as 486DX2-66, which denotes an 80486DX2, 66-MHz chip.

A fast processor speeds up such tasks as searching through a document or performing complex calculations, but it won't speed up other components such as a hard drive or modem. Intel's Pentiums achieve the blazing speeds it advertises only with special software. Without it, the 60-MHz version of the Pentium is no faster than some of the speedier 486 processors. The Pentium is just hitting its stride, but PowerPC processors (available in computers from Apple, Motorola, and IBM) may provide competition at the high end.

Memory. Random access memory (RAM) determines how much data the computer can process at once. It is measured in megabytes (MB), each equal to about a million typewritten characters. A program will run slowly, or not at all, if the computer has insufficient memory. To run Windows applications at their best, an IBM-compatible machine needs at least 8 MB of RAM. Memory costs about $40 per megabyte. You can save money by using inexpensive software that simulates extra memory.

Hard drive. This is the computer's storage compartment. Storage space is measured in megabytes; common sizes range from about 200 to 1200 MB. Prices run about 30 to 50 cents per megabyte and are continually dropping. The two most popular drive types, roughly equal in speed for home uses, are Small Computer System Interface (SCSI) and the slightly cheaper Integrated Drive Electronics (IDE).

Conventional wisdom says to buy the largest hard drive you can afford. Plan on at least 500 MB for a Windows 95-based computer or a Macintosh. If you're upgrading a computer, file-compression software can be a cheap alternative to a new hard drive.

Video. The screen on notebook models is built in. Desktop monitors come in various sizes, based on the diagonal measurement of the tube; 14, 15, and 17 inches are the most common. Some monitors of the same nominal size may, in effect, be larger, with a housing that shows more of the tube. "Dot pitch" describes the spacing between the display's color phosphors, which should be .28 or smaller. "Noninterlaced" monitors cause less eye strain than those that are "interlaced."

A monitor connects to a plug-in video card, which limits the monitor's speed and maximum resolution (number of rows and columns of dots on the screen). A "bus" ties the monitor and video card to the rest of the machine.

Notebook displays commonly are either monochrome, dual-scan passive color, or active matrix color, which is brighter, sharper, and more costly than passive color.

Multimedia. This requires a CD-ROM drive (a compact-disc player adapted for computers), a plug-in sound card (if the computer doesn't have sound built in, as all Macs and most newer IBM-compatibles do), and speakers—components available built in or sold either separately or together as a "multimedia upgrade kit" for $300 to $400. Installing these components can be tricky on IBM-compatibles but will become easier under Windows 95. Buy a computer with the multimedia items already installed or, if you're upgrading, have a dealer install the upgrade kit. On a Mac, a CD-ROM drive merely plugs into the SCSI port, and it's ready to go.

The CD-ROM drive should be quad-

WHERE TO BUY A COMPUTER

Computer stores. These include local shops and superstores like CompUSA and Computer City. Both store types are likely to have knowledgeable salespeople. A local shop specializes in personal service; a superstore has the widest selection. With either, it's easy to have a computer repaired or customized.

Consumer electronics stores. These have fewer models to choose from than a computer store, and salespeople are less likely to be knowledgeable. An on-site repair shop is a plus here.

Office-supply and department stores. These carry just a few brands. Salespeople can range from knowledgeable to clueless. Don't count on being able to customize the computer.

Warehouse clubs. Don't expect great selection or service at places like Sam's Club or the Price Club. Models aren't always the most up-to-date.

Mail order. Whether you buy from a dealer or directly from the manufacturer, mail-order buying often saves money and makes customizing easy. But if the manufacturer includes a poor-quality monitor, you won't know until the carton arrives at your door. Another risk is that small mail-order manufacturers may go out of business.

Regardless of where you buy, check the dealer's return policy and use a gold credit card for the protection it offers.

speed ("4X") drive; the sound card, "16 bit" (a measure of how it moves data); and the loudspeakers, self-powered and magnetically shielded (to prevent interference with the monitor).

Fax/modem. With the rapid growth of the Internet and on-line services such as America Online, eWorld, CompuServe, Prodigy, and Microsoft Network, many computers come with a fax/modem that combines fax capability with the device computers use to communicate over the telephone. Typically an internal card, a fax/modem is a cost-effective replacement for most fax uses. But it's no fax machine; you can send only what is already inside the computer (you'll need a computer scanner to convert paper documents into computer faxes), and you can receive faxes only when the computer is turned on. Some older fax cards can send, but can't receive.

Whether it's part of a fax card or a separate component, a modem gives you access to on-line services and can exchange files with another computer. An internal plug-in modem saves space on the desk, but installation can be tricky. An external modem connects to a "serial" port in the back of the computer. Speeds range from 2400 to 28,800 baud, a measure of how quickly the modem sends and receives information; higher speed modems also work at the lower speeds. Look for at least a 14,400 baud modem. It should cost less than $100—little more than slower ones.

Buying advice

Whether to buy an IBM-compatible or Macintosh-compatible is mostly a matter of personal preference. Whichever you buy, get one that's upgradeable and can accept a faster replacement processor—for IBM-compatibles, a faster Pentium or PowerPC, and for Macintosh-compatibles, a faster PowerPC.

If you have the room and don't need to move the computer very often, get a desktop model. But if work space is limited or you need a computer while traveling, choose a notebook machine.

Consider a model's energy efficiency. You can identify models that comply with the U.S. Environmental Protection Agency's Energy-Star Program by the Energy-Star logo. They save energy by powering down the monitor and other components after a certain amount of time.

Computer printers

▶ **Ratings on page 189.**

Thanks to fast-changing technology, you can expect higher-quality computer printers for home-use at more affordable prices than existed just a few years ago. Now, printers that print in crisp, clear type are the norm, and printers that can print color are increasingly common.

Home models sell for anywhere from $200 to $600. Brands you'll find include Hewlett-Packard, Canon, Epson, Panasonic, Apple, and Okidata.

Printers have to be compatible with the computer type: IBM-compatible or Macintosh-compatible. Since more IBM-compatibles are sold than Macs, you'll find a greater variety of those printers.

The choices

Ink-jet printers. This type squirts ink onto the page line by line. Black-and-white models have just one cartridge. Color models may have as many as four. Models with separate black-and-white cartridges (called "CMYK," for cyan, magenta, yellow and black, the colors of the ink) print true blacks unlike one-cartridge models (CMY), which print a composite mixed black. Most ink-jets print acceptable color and black-and-white graphics and photographs on copier paper, even better quality on recommended paper.

The drawbacks of this type: Ink-jets are slow, producing about 2 to 3 text pages per minute. They use water-soluble ink that smears when using a highlighter pen. Most manufacturers do not recommend printing labels. Even though ink-jets will accept plain copier paper, they may require specially coated paper for the best results with color output.

Monochrome printers typically carry price tags from $200 to $250. Color ink-jets are priced higher—about $350 to $550. Paper and printing costs: 3 to 7 cents per page.

Page printers. Other technologies compose and print whole pages at a time, producing images with either a scanning laser or an array of LEDs (light-emitting diodes). Using technology like that in photocopiers, they quickly reproduce an almost limitless variety of type forms and sizes, as well as complex graphics. The output is clean and crisp and won't smudge—quality significantly above what ink-jets produce. Page printers produce each page of text in about half the time of most ink-jet printers. They can also print labels.

Prices range from $400 to $700. To print PostScript documents such as those created by page-layout programs, you'll need more than a basic model. Prices for color printers remain high—$5000 and up. Paper and printing costs: 3 to 4 cents a page.

Portable printers. Most of these use ink-jet technology, which requires little electrical energy. They're lightweight and portable enough to fit inside a briefcase. Results, we've found in our tests, are fair; far below what a good tabletop ink-jet model can produce. Portables are very slow—less than 1 to 2 pages per minute. Prices start at $250 or so. Paper and printing costs: 6 to 31 cents a page.

Features and conveniences

Resolution. Resolution—the fineness of a machine's output—isn't an infallible guide to print quality. Some printers with 300 dots per inch (dpi) resolution printed better in our tests than those with 600 dpi—a resolution that's becoming the norm.

Printing speed. The pages-per-minute figures used in ads may be based on performance at the fastest possible print setting, which may produce poor results.

Paper feed. Printers typically handle single sheets of letter-sized paper. Page and ink-jet printers use an automatic-feeder tray. Paper trays hold from 70 to 250 sheets. Some models offer optional higher-capacity trays. Most models have envelope feeders.

Size. Most have a footprint on the desktop larger than letter-sized paper. The most space-efficient are upright models that stack paper vertically. Height may be a consideration for a printer on a shelf.

The tests

We test printers by judging samples of identical text, graphics (pie and bar charts), and photographs produced in the printer's best print mode. A panel of staff members grades the samples. In addition, we measure the time each machine takes to print a page of double-spaced black text with standard margins.

Buying advice

For printing high-quality text, a monochrome page printer is more economical and much faster than most ink-jets. They're priced from $400 to $600. Spend more only if you need near-flawless text.

Before you buy, check prices in computer magazines and the business section of your newspaper. They're falling fast.

Telephones

Few products have changed as much as the telephone. It has assumed whimsical shapes, lost its cord, and mated with other devices—answerers, fax machines, clock radios. And it has bloomed with features, from the size of the memory to the ability to show you who's calling before you pick up.

Phone companies continue to add new ancillary services, such as calling back your most recent caller or automatically redialing a busy number until it's available.

Another innovation is the prepaid calling card. Some of those cards offer lower rates than traditional calling cards and substantial savings over coin-phone rates.

As telecommunications undergo deregulation, phone service will continue to change rapidly. Long-distance and local carriers have begun competing. As cable-TV companies enter the market, too, the distinction between phone service and cable TV is expected to fade.

Corded telephones

▶ **Ratings on page 193.**

Phones are sold under a multitude of brand names. AT&T dominates the corded- and cordless-phone business.

The choices

A conventional, corded phone has basically two pieces: a handset and a base that plugs into a telephone jack. Dual-handset phones are also available; they come with two cordless handsets or one corded and the other cordless.

Console models. These are the updated version of the traditional Bell desk phone, although most no longer sound the traditional Bell ring. Console models range in price from $50 to more than $200.

Trim-style models. These are space-savers; the push buttons are on the handset itself, and the base is about half as wide as a console's. They range in price from about $20 to $75.

Features and conveniences

The features that make a phone cost more include a speakerphone, two-line capability, caller ID, and LCD displays.

Speakerphone. This feature lets you have a conversation without the handset. Sound quality isn't as good as with the handset.

Two-line capability. With this, you get the ability to handle a second phone line—and to "conference" two callers in a three-way conversation with you.

Caller ID compatibility. This can be built into a phone or bought as a standalone device. With it, subscribers to the phone company's service can see the phone number and, in some locations, the name of the person calling.

LCD display. This shows information such as the number dialed, time of day, and perhaps the time you'd spent talking.

Speed-dial memory. Most phones with memory can store from three to 15 numbers of up to 16 digits or more, generally sufficient for international dialing. The redial feature recalls the last number dialed. A few models can redial a busy number several times automatically. One-touch speed-dialing stores a number that you can then call by touching a single key. A Save feature lets you store a phone number you've just dialed in an available memory slot.

Ring sound. Few models actually ring a bell. Most sound a chirp; some warble.

Volume controls. One control raises or lowers the volume at the handset; another, the phone's ringer. Speakerphones also have a volume control for the speaker in the base. Mute disconnects the microphone so a caller can't hear sounds from your end. Hold cuts the mike and earpiece.

Easy-to-see keys. Keys that are lighted let you dial in the dark. Big keys make dialing easy for kids or for those with poor eyesight or poor coordination.

Pulse/tone dialing. Most phones have a switch that lets you go back and forth between pulse and tone dialing. That lets you use computer or voice-mail systems even if you don't have tone service.

Flash. This feature lets you take advantage of call-waiting. It briefly disconnects a call, which signals the phone company that you can take another call on the same phone.

The tests

We test phones in various ways to simulate actual use. We note each model's ability to render speech, based on such factors as its fidelity over the range of crucial audio frequencies and loudness. We measure how accurately you can hear and be heard. We subject the phones to a variety of abuses that include 15,000-volt electrostatic discharges, 800-volt line surges, and falls from a height of several feet onto a hard floor. We also judge convenience of use and features.

Reliability

In a recent survey of CONSUMER REPORTS subscribers, about a third said they had replaced a broken phone within the past three years. A fifth of the broken phones were no more than a year old. Our latest test of corded phones supports that: Almost three phones in four failed one or more of our durability tests—an extraordinarily high failure rate.

Buying advice

Sound quality may vary from model to model, though that will make a difference only under extreme circumstances, such as a phone located in a very noisy environment. That's something you'll know only after you take the phone home. And some features are likely to be better designed than others.

A reasonable buying strategy: Buy by features and price at a store with return privileges and, considering the fragility of phones, use a credit card that doubles the manufacturer's warranty. Expect to pay somewhat more for two-line models and speakerphones.

Cordless telephones

With a cordless phone, the base stays plugged into your phone line; the detachable handset communicates via radio waves with the base. Thus, you can wander around with the phone, as far as a hundred feet from the base for nondigital models and several hundred feet for digital models.

Cordless-phone technology continues to improve, but it isn't perfect. These phones often suffer from static. They may pick up signals from other cordless phones or from other devices or simply quit when approaching the limit of their range. Your callers may complain that your voice may is not as clear as with a regular phone. And if you forget to replace the handset in its charger, the batteries may give out quite unexpectedly.

Models we've tested recently demonstrate better sound quality and less background noise than older cordless models. All now use a digital "combination code" to prevent "call stealing." "Compander" circuitry is built into most models to suppress background noise. Voice scrambling, available only on a few brands, makes eavesdropping less likely.

The choices

10-channel models. Ten channels assure you "space" to talk if others in the area are using cordless phones, too. Should interference occur, most let you change channels while you continue to talk. Some models automatically select a clear channel when you first pick up the phone. These typically cost between $50 and $150.

Some models have a speakerphone in the base, which permits hands-free operation. On some, the base and handset can work as an intercom system; other models offer two phone lines. Some models have two keypads, one on the handset and one on the base; others offer additional charging cradles or handsets.

Two-channel models. These low-priced phones, about $50 to $80, are disappearing as the prices of 10-channel models come down. Their main shortcoming is vulnerability to interference from nearby cordless phones that are operating on the same radio channel.

900-Megahertz models. These utilize a different transmission frequency than other cordless models, one that provides a much wider operating distance and better ability to transmit around obstructions. Digital versions are static-free and virtually impossible to eavesdrop on without exotic equipment.

They're still quite expensive—$300 to $600—but prices are dropping.

Combination phone-answerers. These units marry a cordless phone with an answering machine. The combination takes up less space than separate products and is usually less expensive than buying separate components.

Features and conveniences

Batteries. All models use replaceable batteries. A typical 46/49 MH phone's battery that's fully charged will last about eight hours in continuous use; a 900 MHz phone's battery, about half as long. Many will last two to three weeks on "standby."

Two-way paging. Pushing a button on the base sounds a paging signal on the handset, or vice versa. The signal can also lead you to a misplaced handset.

Ringer in base. When you're near the base, this alerts you to an incoming call, no matter where the handset may be.

Out-of-range tone. It warns you that the handset is too far from the base.

Power-off switch. Located on the handset, it can lengthen battery time.

Speed-call memory. This stores frequently called numbers and lets you dial them by pressing one or two buttons. Many phones can store more than 10 phone numbers of up to 16 digits each.

Volume control. This raises or lowers the volume of the handset's speaker. Mute/hold lets you talk to someone nearby without letting the person on the other end of the phone hear.

Voice scrambling. This feature reduces the possibility of eavesdropping by inverting audio frequencies.

Low-battery indicator. It lets you know when to recharge the battery.

Rubber antenna. Rubber is more forgiving than rigid metal. The flexibility of a rubber antenna eliminates accidental bending and breaking.

Buying advice

Look for a cordless model with a lightweight, comfortable handset and at least 10 channels. For added range and privacy, you may want to spend the additional $200 or so for a 900-MHz model, though you may sacrifice some features.

It's not a good idea to rely on a cordless phone to replace the regular phone in your household. Cordless phones won't work during a power failure unless you have the rare model that features a battery back-up in the base.

Cellular telephones

Over the past years, cellular phones have graduated from toys to practical consumer appliances. A survey of CONSUMER REPORTS readers shows that emergency use and staying in touch with family were the most common reasons for buying a cellular phone. Business use was the next most common reason.

The appeal of cellular phones has grown as their operating range expanded, the result of billions of dollars invested by the companies that operate local cellular systems. The way phones and phone service are sold has also attracted more users. In most areas, the hardware is sold very cheaply—sometimes even given away—if you sign up for service. Such "bundling" pays off for the companies because of monthly service fees and per-call charges, which exceed regular phone rates.

The phones themselves have been changing. Permanently installed mobile phones and bulky, heavy, "transportable" phones have given way to handheld portable models petite enough to fit in a pocket. Mobile and transportable models still have an edge over portables, with more power and somewhat better connections.

Motorola is the leading brand, accounting for about one-fifth of the cellular phones sold. Other major brands include Audiovox, Mitsubishi, NEC, Nokia, NovAtel, Panasonic, and Uniden.

The choices

Mobile phones. This type, the original cellular phone, is permanently installed in a vehicle, usually by a professional. It transmits three watts and requires an external antenna. Price: anywhere from $100 to $300, without a service contract.

Transportable phones. This is basically a mobile phone you can remove from the car. It draws power from a rechargeable battery pack or a car's cigarette-lighter plug. Though technically portable, such a phone can weigh more than you might care to tote—five pounds or so. Price: from $30 to $100, without a service contract.

Portable and microportable phones. This lightweight, handheld model is the best-selling type. A battery-operated, portable model looks like the handset of a cordless phone. Its power is limited—usually a mere 0.6 watts—so coverage may be worse than with mobile or portable units in areas where cellular service is poor. A kit that boosts power to three watts is available for some models. Price: $50 to $300, without a service contract.

Features and conveniences

Here are some common features offered by cellular phones:

Memory and speed dialing. Most models can store at least 30 numbers. You can usually speed-dial a number by pressing two or three buttons.

Call timer. Cellular calls are expensive, so keeping track of air-time is important. Besides displaying elapsed time, some models have a second timer to tally all your calls over a given period. You can also set most phones to beep at fixed intervals for time keeping.

Low-battery indicator. Cellular-phone

SELECTING CELLULAR SERVICE

Most carriers offer plans tailored to common calling patterns, with a fixed fee for a monthly time allotment, something the sales brochures persist in describing as "free." If you exceed the allotment, you pay a certain amount for each extra minute used during "peak" hours (usually daytime weekdays) and a lower amount for "off-peak" use.

If you're not sure which plan is best for you, or if you plan to use the phone only for emergencies, start with the plan with the lowest monthly fee. There should be no problem switching to a higher-volume plan before the contract is up. If you call mostly at night, look for the lowest "off-peak" rates. The fine print can sometimes hide major differences between carriers, such as the number of "peak" hours in a day.

If you are concerned about call security, look for a carrier that has taken measures to thwart eavesdroppers and phone-number thieves. A phone and carrier that operate digitally provide the best security, but digital service is still not available widely.

Some carriers make you dial extra numbers to reach a long-distance company other than the one with which they're affiliated; others let you select your own company when you sign up.

batteries, typically nickel-cadmium, sustain conversation for at least an hour and standby status for a minimum of eight hours. An indicator warns visually or audibly that the battery is running low. If you're home, recharge the battery; on the road, insert a fresh battery.

Own-number display. Every cellular carrier assigns its own phone number. Should you forget the number you're using, the phone's display can summon it up.

Roaming features. In cellular parlance, "roaming" is the term for leaving the area covered by your carrier. Calls made outside your area are charged at a higher rate. Most models can be assigned more than one phone number, allowing you to register with more than one carrier to reduce roaming charges. All models can be programmed to halt roaming temporarily so you don't inadvertently run up extra charges.

Built-in help. With many phones, hitting a key or two displays instructions for features you don't use often.

Extra features and conveniences include:

Automatic number selection. If you have numbers for more than one carrier, this feature switches them automatically.

Fast recharge. This cuts recharging time from more than eight hours to one or two. If your phone doesn't come with this, you can probably buy a separate product that does the same thing.

Answering features. These ease phone use while driving. Any-key answer lets you pick up incoming calls by pressing any key—not a specific key, as with many models. Automatic-answer picks up for you after a couple of rings.

One-touch dial. The dial has keys with preset numbers to shorten dialing time.

Speakerphone. This feature lets you talk with both hands on the wheel.

Voice activation. Mostly on mobile phones, this lets you verbally send and receive calls and access memory.

Buying advice

In cities or in areas with flat terrain, most models should be adequate. Suburban and rural areas, where cellular coverage may be spotty, make tougher demands.

If you make most calls from a vehicle, a permanently installed mobile phone makes the most sense; it has more power and is usually less expensive than a portable.

If you use a portable phone in a car, a cigarette-lighter adapter to power the phone from the car battery will be extremely useful. Other car-related accessories let you boost transmitting power or use an external antenna.

Because cellular phones are often bundled with a service commitment, identical models may differ in price by hundreds of dollars. Shop for a carrier and a contract as if they were part of the cost of the phone. Typically, you'll spend more for a year's service than you will for the phone itself.

Expect monthly bills to run about $56, which is the average according to an industry trade group.

Telephone answerers

Answering machines keep getting smaller, better, and easier to use. Playing back messages can be as simple as pressing a single button. Voice-actuated circuits reduce annoying empty messages by hanging up automatically if no one speaks.

AT&T accounts for about a third of all answering machines sold in the U.S. Other major brands include General Electric, Panasonic, and Phonemate.

The choices

A phone answerer can be a separate machine you attach to a phone, or it can come integrated with a corded or cordless phone, or even fax machines and computers. An answerer with a built-in phone saves space and may be less expensive than a separate phone and answerer. The trouble with integrated units is that if any part fails, everything must go to the repair shop. Integrated phone/answering machines are typically priced between $75 and $300; answer-only units, between $50 and $160.

Answerers, with or without phones, use various recording designs:

Single or dual cassette. Declining in popularity, these use a tape cassette for both the outgoing and incoming messages or one cassette for each. Single-cassette machines, the cheapest type, can be compact, but messages are often limited to a minute or two apiece, and callers must wait for the tape to shuttle forward before they can leave a message. On a dual-cassette machine, callers can leave a message without delay, and the outgoing message can be longer than on a single-cassette machine.

Digital/microcassette or all-digital. These types are currently the most popular. Memory chips like those found in computers are used to store the greeting; on hybrid models, a cassette records the message. All-digital machines do away completely with the cassette, storing both greeting and messages on memory chips. Digital models are supposedly less likely to break down than cassette models, since moving parts are replaced with circuits. They let you skip through messages more quickly and delete messages with the press of a button. Memory chips limit recording time, and they're more expensive than tape. They can also lose messages if they are without power. Prices of these machines have fallen—in some cases, below $100. In past tests, voice quality on machines with chips was clear, but less natural than taped messages. These answerers tend to be smaller than the other types.

Features and conveniences

Higher-priced machines offer additional features, including:

Audible message indicator. Machines with this feature beep when a message has been received so you know without looking that there's a new message.

Greeting bypass. Callers who don't want to hear your outgoing message can bypass it by pressing a touch-tone key, usually the asterisk.

Room monitor. This lets you call in and listen to the room sound—useful for checking on children.

Announce-only. This lets you post a greeting without recording incoming calls.

Multi-outgoing greetings. This lets you use two greetings and switch between them, useful for a home-based business.

Selective save and delete. Some digital answering machines can store or delete messages in a random fashion without losing space for new incoming messages.

Voice prompt. This instructs you on how to program for time, date, remote operation, and other functions.

Message transfer. This automatically dials a preprogrammed telephone number when a message comes in.

Two-way record. Records both you and the caller at the press of a button.

Time and date. The machine notes the time and date of each incoming message and announces them when you play back the message.

Voice mailboxes. Some digital answerers provide "mailboxes" for people who share an answering machine. Callers are instructed on how to leave a message for the specific person they want to reach.

Two-line capability. This lets the machine take messages for two phone numbers on separate lines.

Certain features have become standard:

Call counters. Some machines use a light to signal that at least one message is waiting. Better are units that blink the light to tell you how many messages there are. The best displays provide a digital readout of the number of calls. Most counters ignore hang-ups occurring before the beep.

Call screening. This lets you listen to a message as it comes in, so you can avoid nuisance calls and not miss important ones. If you decide to take a call, a machine with Auto-disconnect automatically stops recording as soon as you pick up any phone in the house; a machine with Auto-reset stops recording and resets itself.

Number of rings. You can set the number of rings the machine will wait before it answers the call—no need to race to the phone to beat the machine's pickup. When you're out, you can set it to answer after fewer rings.

Pause and Skip. These help control playback of recorded messages. Pause temporarily stops a message so you can jot down a name or number. Skip speeds things up by moving the tape back or forward one message.

One-touch. This rewinds, plays messages, and sets the machine for new calls.

Power backup. Most answerers keep their memory at least for a short time in the event of power failure, but some reset the call counter to zero. The best designs have a battery backup that holds the settings for hours, which is critical for an all-digital machine. A battery-strength indicator warns you when to replace the battery.

Remote access. Almost all machines let you use a touch-tone phone to hear messages when you're away from home. Some prompt you with vocal messages, similar to voice mail. Some models have a programmed security code; others let you set the code yourself. Three-digit codes offer the most security.

Remote activation. If you've left the unit off, this allows you to turn it on from another phone.

Toll-saver. This lets you avoid a charge for calling your machine long-distance to check for possible messages. You set the machine to answer the first call after four or five rings and later calls after only one or two. You save money because if the machine hasn't picked up by ring number three, you know there are no messages.

Buying advice

If your needs are simple and you don't want a new telephone—or if you're away from home for extended periods and need maximum space for messages on a machine—look for a plain answerer with dual tape cassettes or for a digital/microcassette machine. You'll find the best prices for models with taped message-taking. A digital machine is priced a bit higher but given their few moving parts, they should be less likely to need repairs, a big problem with answerers.

You'll find similar choices among answering machines with built-in telephones. Choices on those machines range from plain-vanilla telephones to cordless models with lots of features.

An alternative to a phone-answering machine is a service offered by many local phone companies. When you're out or if your line is busy, the phone company receives and stores messages; you retrieve the messages with a touch-tone phone. The advantages are obvious—there's no machine to break down, an increased capacity for receiving messages, and the ability to take messages while the phone is in use. The drawbacks, however, are serious: There's no provision to screen incoming calls nor is there any visible indicator to tell you whether you have messages. And there's no absolute guarantee of privacy. If there's a network failure, you can loose messages. Charges for this service can run $5 to $10 per month.

Home fax machines

With little fanfare, the facsimile machine has claimed considerable turf in the nation's offices and on the telephone network. The American home is likely to be next. Although the fax machine has found its way into only 6 percent of U.S. households, more people are using home faxes to order things like newsletters, maps, reprints or take-out food and catalog purchases. Others use home faxes to telecommute.

Four brands dominate sales: Sharp, Panasonic, Canon, Hewlett-Packard, Brother, and Muratec/Murata..

The choices

Fax machines come as stand-alone units or, the latest trend, as multifunction machines that include a telephone answering machine, a computer printer, a scanner, a modem, and a copier. Prices for stand-alone fax machines currently range from $200 to $900 and continue to fall.

Fax machines use one of two technologies to print:

Thermal printing. This is the most common and least expensive type. Home machines typically print incoming documents on long rolls of chemically treated stock, using tiny heating elements to form the letters. That system helps keep both size and cost down, but the copies tend to fade after a while, and copies made at the end of a roll are likely to curl.

The cheapest of this type lack a document feeder and automatic paper cutter. Not having a feeder means each page sent must be inserted manually by someone standing over the machine; no cutter means someone has to cut scrolls of output into page-sized sheets. Price: $200 to $400.

Ink printing. Ink-cartridge and ink-jet fax machines use a high-speed lead to print on plain paper. Ink faxes include basic and LED fax machines. Price: $500 to $1000.

Features and conveniences

Sending modes. These determine the resolution of a faxed document and the speed at which it can be sent. In Standard mode, faxes break an inch of the page into 100 scan lines, each some 1700 dots across. Sending in Standard mode takes about a minute per page. Faxes can also be sent in Fine mode (twice the scan lines, double the time) for small print that might otherwise be unreadable. Some models offer Superfine, with still higher resolution, but they work only if the same brand of fax is at the other end. Many offer a Halftone mode, for photos and artwork, rendering grays in 16 to as many as 64 steps from black to white. Sending in Halftone, however, can take several minutes per page.

One-touch dialing. A fax machine's built-in memory typically sports at least a few buttons to program frequently dialed numbers. More numbers are usually programmable for speed-dialing.

Auto retry. Typically, a fax machine will persistently redial a busy number for a few minutes until it connects.

Delayed sending. This allows you to time a document for transmission to take advantage of cheaper phone rates.

Remote start. If you answer an extension phone that shares the fax's line and find the call is an incoming fax, this feature lets you start your fax receiving by pressing a short code from the extension.

Paper. Most machines use a glossy, slippery thermal paper, which is notorious for curling and being hard to handle. Some models take a grade of thermal paper more like standard paper. Thermal paper comes in rolls of 49, 64, 98, and 328 feet. Rolls 98 feet or longer are more convenient than the 49-foot roll, which runs out quickly. Plain-paper fax machines are the standard in commercial use but cost twice as much as machines that use thermal paper.

Anticurl system. This feature flattens thermal fax paper.

Paper cutter. The cheapest machines use paper on a roll that must be cut apart. Paper-cutter models are well worth their slightly higher cost.

Document feeder. A feeder tray lets you feed 5, 10, or 20 pages at a time rather than insert the pages one by one.

Memory, broadcasting. If a fax runs out of paper when receiving, some models can capture a few pages of text in memory for later printing. Typically, those models can also use their memory to "broadcast" a document you want distributed to a routing list of phone numbers.

Activity reports. Most faxes print a listing of documents recently sent or received, along with phone numbers, times, and dates, and can confirm transmission.

Buying advice

Judging by our tests, sending and printing clear text isn't a problem for modern light-duty fax machines. Features, however, can make or break a machine.

Thermal units are still the most practical and the most reasonably priced. Two musts: a document feeder, to send long faxes, and an automatic paper cutter, for multipage documents.

Look for a unit that easily shares the phone line with a regular phone—it can save installing a phone line just for the fax. An answerer/fax interface that works smoothly and capably is also worthwhile.

RATINGS COMPUTER PRINTERS

▶ **See report, page 178.** Last time rated in Consumer Reports: September 1995.

Brand-name recommendations: If you use a printer infrequently, for text that needn't be of the highest quality, choose a good black-and-white ink-jet printer such as the Epson Stylus 400 (now replaced by Stylus Color IIs), $200, or the Apple StyleWriter II (now replaced by StyleWriter 1200), $270. If color and graphics matter to you, our first choice would be the Canon BJC-4000, but it has been discontinued. Our second choice is the Epson Stylus Color (now replaced by II), $520. For printing text, we judged the Brother HL-630, $400, and the Panasonic KX-P4400, $450, Best Buys, but they're both discontinued. Instead, consider the more expensive Okidata OL410e, $570. The expensive printers that top the Ratings are worth considering only if you demand text that's near-flawless.

For a typical model, expect: ■ Much faster printing of text than of graphics and photos. ■ Ability to print envelopes, labels, and transparencies. ■ A density control to lighten printing, cut ink/toner use. ■ For IBM-compatible models: ability to run with either Microsoft Windows or DOS. ■ Quiet operation. ■ Paper tray that typically holds 100 sheets. ■ Minimal power consumption (3 to 15 watts) when idling. ■ Extra cost for printer cable. **For a typical portable, expect:** ■ Light weight (less than 5 lbs.) and footprint about half the size of many desktop models. ■ Option for battery-powered operation. ■ No paper tray.

Notes on the table: ▪ means color capability. **Price** is estimated average, based on a national survey. * means price paid. **Type.** Laser and LED printers compose and print one page at a time, using toner. Ink-jet and thermal printers print line by line, with ink. **IBM/Mac.** Indicates computer compatibility. A price, if shown, is the extra cost of the Mac upgrade. **Score** is based mainly on text quality and speed, with graphics and photo quality also considered. **Print quality** (black-and-white). Reflects a staff panel's judgment of samples with identical text and graphics (pie and bar charts) produced in the best print mode. Printing was judged on plain copier paper, and on any special paper recommended by the mfr. (second score). **Speed.** How quickly each printer turned out a page of double-spaced black text with standard margins in the best print mode. **Model availability:** Ⓓ means model is discontinued. Ⓢ means model is replaced, according to the manufacturer; successor model is noted in Details. New model was not tested; it may or may not perform similarly. Features may vary.

Listed primarily in order of quality and speed of text printing

Better ⊜ ⊖ ○ ◒ ● Worse

Brand and model	Price	Type	IBM/Mac	Score (P F G VG E)	Print quality (B&W) TEXT	Print quality (B&W) GRAPHICS	Speed B&W TEXT
DESKTOP MODELS							
Brother HL-660	$700	Laser	✓ / $613		⊜	⊖	⊜
NEC Silentwriter SuperScript 660i Ⓓ	690	Laser	✓ / —		⊜	○	⊜
Okidata OL410e	570	LED	✓ / —		⊜	⊜	○
Epson ActionLaser 1400	600	Laser	✓ / —		⊜	○	○

Ratings continued ▶

Ratings continued

Brand and model	Price	Type	IBM/Mac	Score (P F G VG E)	Print quality (B&W) TEXT	Print quality (B&W) GRAPHICS	Speed B&W TEXT
DESKTOP MODELS *continued*							
Hewlett Packard LaserJet 4L [D]	$500	Laser	✓ / —		⊜	○	○
Texas Instr. microLaser 600	829*	Laser	✓ / ✓		⊜	○	⊖
Brother HL-630, **A BEST BUY** [D]	400	Laser	✓ / $80		⊖	○	⊜
Canon LBP-430 [D]	565	Laser	✓ / —		⊜	◒	○
Lexmark WinWriter 400 [D]	725	LED	✓ / —		⊜	○	⊖
Panasonic KX-P4400, **A BEST BUY** [D]	450	LED	✓ / —		⊖	⊜	○
▪ **Epson** Stylus Color [S]	520	Inkjet	✓ / ✓		◒/⊜	⊖	◒
Apple Personal LaserWriter 300	600	Laser	— / ✓		⊖	⊖	○
▪ **Canon** BJC-4000, **A BEST BUY** [D]	350	Inkjet	✓ / —		○/⊖	⊖	○
▪ **Hewlett Packard** DeskJet 560c [S]	475	Inkjet	✓ / ✓		○/○	⊖	○
▪ **Hewlett Packard** DeskJet 540 [S]	270	Inkjet	✓ / ✓		○/○	○	○
Apple StyleWriter II [S]	270	Inkjet	— / ✓		⊖	◒	◒
Epson Stylus 400 [S]	200	Inkjet	✓ / —		○	⊖	◒
Canon BJ-200e [D]	220	Inkjet	✓ / —		○	⊜	○
▪ **Apple** Color StyleWriter 2400	450	Inkjet	— / ✓		○/◒	⊜	○
Lexmark WinWriter 100 [D]	250*	Inkjet	✓ / —		◒	◒	○
▪ **Radio Shack** JP 1000	399	Inkjet	✓ / —		◒	⊖	◒
▪ **Texas Instr.** microMarc Color [D]	380*	Inkjet	✓ / —		◒	●	⊖
PORTABLE MODELS (WEIGHT)							
▪ **Citizen** PN60 Pocket Printer (1.7 lb.)	300	Thermal	✓ / $39		◒	—	●
Apple Portable StyleWriter (4.4 lb.) [S]	400	Inkjet	— / ✓		◒	—	●
Canon BJ-10sx (4.4 lb.) [S]	250	Inkjet	✓ / —		●	◒	◒

MODEL DETAILS

Want to know more about a rated model? They're listed here alphabetically.

Apple Color StyleWriter 2400	Color. Printed test graphics slower than most. Printer status displayed on computer screen. Has energy-saving mode. Resolution: 360x360.
Apple Personal LaserWriter 300	Printed test graphics slower than most. Printer status displayed on computer screen. Has energy-saving mode. Resolution: 300x300.
Apple Portable StyleWriter [S]	Cannot print graphics or photos. Printer status displayed on computer screen. Label printing not recommended by mfr. Resolution: 360x360. **Successor:** Color StyleWriter 2200.

Apple StyleWriter II [S]	Printed test graphics slower than most. Printer status displayed on computer screen. Resolution: 360x360. **Successor:** StyleWriter 1200.
Brother HL-630, **A BEST BUY** [D]	Printed test graphics faster than most. Printer status displayed on computer screen. Has printer console program for DOS. Has energy-saving mode. Serial interface standard or optional. Resolution: 300X300.
Brother HL-660	Printed test graphics faster than most. Printer status displayed on computer screen. Has printer console program for DOS. Option for PostScript capability. Has energy-saving mode. Resolution: 600x600.
Canon BJ-10sx [S]	Battery pack costs extra. Label printing not recommended by mfr. Resolution: 360x360. **Successor:** BJ-30.
Canon BJ-200e [D]	Label printing not recommended by mfr. Resolution: 360x360.
Canon BJC-4000, **A BEST BUY** [D]	Color. Printed test graphics slower than most. Has resolution enhancement, technology claimed to improve print quality. Label printing not recommended by mfr. Resolution: 720x360.
Canon LBP-430 [D]	Has printer console program for DOS. Has resolution enhancement, technology claimed to improve print quality. Has energy-saving mode. Toner cartridges can be recycled by mfr. Resolution: 300x300.
Citizen PN60 Pocket Printer	Color capability, $7.50 extra. Cannot print graphics or photos. Serial interface standard or optional. Battery pack costs extra. Cost per page: 31¢. Resolution: 360x360.
Epson ActionLaser 1400	Printed test graphics faster than most. Printer status displayed on computer screen. Has printer console program for DOS. Option for PostScript capability. Has energy-saving mode. Resolution: 600x600.
Epson Stylus 400 [S]	Has energy-saving mode. Label printing not recommended by mfr. Resolution: 360x360. **Successor:** Stylus Color IIs.
Epson Stylus Color [S]	Color. Printed test graphics faster than most. Has resolution enhancement, technology claimed to improve print quality. Has energy-saving mode. Requires more hard-disk space than other models. Serial interface standard or optional. Label printing not recommended by mfr. Resolution: 720x720. **Successor:** Stylus Color II.
Hewlett Packard DeskJet 540 [S]	Color capability, $40 extra. Mac Version: DeskWriter 540. Printer status displayed on computer screen. Has printer console program for DOS. Has resolution enhancement, technology claimed to improve print quality. Has energy-saving mode. Label printing not recommended by mfr. Resolution: 600x300. **Successor:** DeskJet/DeskWriter 600.
Hewlett Packard DeskJet 560c [S]	Color. Mac Version: DeskWriter 560c. Printed test graphics slower than most. Printer status displayed on computer screen. Optional font cartridge. Has resolution enhancement, technology claimed to improve print quality. Has energy-saving mode. Requires more hard-disk space than other models. Label printing not recommended by mfr. Resolution: 600x300. **Successor:** DeskJet 660c, DeskWriter 660c (Mac version).
Hewlett Packard LaserJet 4L [D]	Printer status displayed on computer screen. Has printer console program for DOS. Has resolution enhancement, technology claimed to improve print quality. Has energy-saving mode. Toner cartridges can be recycled by mfr. Resolution: 300x300.

Ratings continued ▶

Ratings continued

Lexmark WinWriter 100 Ⓓ	Printer status displayed on computer screen. Must use Microsoft Windows to print. Has resolution enhancement, technology claimed to improve print quality. Has energy-saving mode. Resolution: 600x300.
Lexmark WinWriter 400 Ⓓ	Printed test graphics faster than most. Printer status displayed on computer screen. Must use Microsoft Windows to print. Has resolution enhancement, technology claimed to improve print quality. Has energy-saving mode. Requires more hard-disk space than other models. Toner cartridges can be recycled by mfr. Resolution: 300x300.
NEC Silentwriter SuperScript 660i Ⓓ	Printed test graphics faster than most. Printer status displayed on computer screen. Has printer console program for DOS. Option for PostScript capability. Has resolution enhancement, technology claimed to improve print quality. Has energy-saving mode. Requires more hard-disk space than other models. Resolution: 600x600.
Okidata OL410e	LCD on front panel indicates printer status. Optional font cartridge. Has resolution enhancement, technology claimed to improve print quality. Has energy-saving mode. Serial interface standard or optional. Resolution: 600x600.
Panasonic KX-P4400, **A BEST BUY** Ⓓ	LCD on front panel indicates printer status. Option for PostScript capability. Cannot print envelopes. Has energy-saving mode. Resolution: 300x300.
Radio Shack JP 1000	Color capability, $70 extra. Optional font cartridge. Serial interface standard or optional. Label printing not recommended by mfr. Resolution: 300x300.
Texas Instruments microLaser 600	Has printer console program for DOS. Serial interface standard or optional. PostScript capability standard. Resolution: 600x600.
Texas Instruments microMarc Color Ⓓ	Color. Printed test graphics faster than most. Label printing not recommended by mfr. Resolution: 300x300.

How to use the Buying Guide

- Read the article for general guidance about types, features, and how to buy. There you'll find the market overview, the choices you'll face, and key advice.
- Read the brand-name recommendations for information on specific models.
- Note how the rated products are listed—in order of performance and convenience, price, or alphabetically.
- Look to the overall score to get the big picture in performance. Notes on features and performance for individual models are listed in the Comments or Details part of the Ratings.
- Note that models similar to the tested models, when they exist, are indicated in the Comments or Details. A model marked Ⓓ has been discontinued. A model marked Ⓢ is a successor to the tested model, according to the manufacturer, and is noted in Comments or Details. Features, though, may vary.
- Call the manufacturer if you have trouble finding a product. Manufacturers' phone numbers are listed alphabetically by brand name starting on page 342.
- To find our last full report on a subject, check the eight-year index for the original publication date. You'll find the index in the reference section, page 346.

RATINGS CORDED TELEPHONES

▶ **See report, page 180.** Last time rated in Consumer Reports: November 1995.

Brand-name recommendations: The top three basic phones are worth considering—the Radio Shack ET-206 ($50), AT&T Trimline 230 ($24) and GE 2-9267 ($32). Two of those earned Best Buys status: The AT&T 230, a trim-style phone, features a lighted keypad and generous speed-dial capacity. The GE 2-9267, a big-button console, was a pleasure to use but limits speed-dial numbers to eight. Both models delivered a notch less voice quality and loudness than the top-rated Radio Shack. Our pick of the full-featured phones is the AT&T 822 ($70), a two-line speakerphone that was the only one of its type to survive our durability testing.

For most of these telephones, expect: ■ Mute or Hold, Flash, and Last-number-redial. ■ Switchable Pulse and Tone settings. ■ Speed-dial capability with memory for at least 10 phone numbers. ■ Electronic ringer with Loudness and Off settings. ■ Ability to be mounted on wall.

Notes on the table: Price is the estimated average, based on a national survey. An * means price paid. **Overall score.** Performance in our drop, static, and surge tests carried the most weight, followed by features and voice quality. **Model availability:** Ⓢ means model is replaced, according to the manufacturer; successor model is noted in Details. New model was not tested; it may or may not perform similarly. Features may vary.

Within type, listed mainly in order of durability

Better ⊜ ⊖ ○ ◒ ● Worse

Brand and model	Price	Type	Overall score (P F G VG E)	Ease of use	Voice: Quality	Voice: Loudness	Ringer loudness
BASIC PHONES							
Radio Shack ET-206	$50	Big button		⊜	⊜	◒	⊖
AT&T Trimline Memory 230, **A BEST BUY**	24	Trim style		⊖	○	⊖	⊖
General Electric 2-9267, **A BEST BUY**	32	Big button		⊖	○	○	⊜
AT&T Big Button	38	Big button		○	○	○	⊜
Southwestern Bell FC2544	17	Trim style		○	○	◒	⊖
Unisonic 6772	18	Trim, Big button		○	○	⊜	○
General Electric 2-9290	33	Trim style		○	○	⊖	○
BellSouth 483EV	25	Trim style		○	○	⊜	○
Radio Shack ET-273	20	Trim style		●	○	○	⊖
Radio Shack ET-145	100	Console		◒	○	○	◒
Sony IT-B3	29	Console		◒	◒	⊖	○
Conairphone SW3100WCS	*20	Big button		◒	○	⊖	⊜

Ratings continued ▶

Ratings continued

Brand and model	Price	Type	Overall score (P F G VG E)	Ease of use	Voice: Quality	Voice: Loudness	Ringer loudness
BASIC PHONES *continued*							
AT&T Traditional 100	$29	Console		●	○	⊖	○
Conairphone SW204 [S]	13	Trim style		●	○	◒	○
TWO LINE AND SPEAKERPHONES							
AT&T 822	70	Two-line, Speaker		⊜	⊜	⊖	◒/◒
General Electric 2-9390	99	Speakerphone		⊜	⊖	⊖	◒
AT&T 812	55	Two-line		⊜	⊜	⊖	◒/◒
Panasonic KX-T3175-B	95	Two-line, Speaker		⊜	○	○	○/⊖
Panasonic KX-T2315	46	Speakerphone		⊜	○	○	◒
Conairphone XS1200 [S]	*64	Two-line		⊖	○	⊖	○[1]
Sony IT-D250	81	Two-line, Speaker		⊜	○	○	○/⊜
General Electric 2-9435	60	Two-line, Speaker		⊜	○	○	◒/◒
Southwestern Bell FT360B	63	Two-line, Speaker		⊖	○	⊖	⊖/⊖
AT&T Speakerphone 870	130	Speakerphone		⊖	○	⊜	⊜
BellSouth 350	*50	Speakerphone		⊖	◒	⊖	◒
Spectra-phone FP-13M	*30	Speakerphone		◒	◒	○	◒

[1] *Two-line phone, but only one ringer.*

MODEL DETAILS

Want to know more about a rated model? They're listed here alphabetically.

AT&T 812	Failed surge and static tests. Memory can store mixed dialing sequences of pulse and tones. Listening-vol. control amplifies weak voices across wider range. Feature keys: Has Save (just-dialed number to memory), Flash, Pause, Mute, Hold, Listening vol. control.
AT&T 822	Memory can store mixed dialing sequences of pulse and tones. Listening-vol. control amplifies weak voices across wider range. Auto-redial repeatedly redials busy numbers. Feature keys: Has Save (just-dialed number to memory), Flash, Pause, Mute, Hold, Listening vol. control.
AT&T Big Button	No Flash key (can use switch hook with Call Waiting). Feature keys: Has Save (just-dialed number to memory), Listening vol. control.
AT&T Speakerphone 870	Failed drop and static tests. Listening-vol. control amplifies weak voices across wider range. Needs AC for speakerphone and display. Feature keys: Has Save (just-dialed number to memory), Flash, Mute, Hold, Listening vol. control.
AT&T Traditional 100	Failed surge tests. No speed-dial capability. No Flash key (can use switch hook with Call Waiting). Feature keys: Has Mute.

AT&T Trimline Memory 230, **A BEST BUY**	Memory can store mixed dialing sequences of pulse and tones. Keypad is backlit. No Flash key (can use switch hook with Call Waiting). Feature keys: Has Save (just-dialed number to memory), Mute, Listening vol. control.
BellSouth 350	Failed all survival tests. Memory can store mixed dialing sequences of pulse and tones. Needs batteries for speakerphone and display. Feature keys: Has Flash, Pause, Hold.
BellSouth 483EV	Failed surge and static tests. Keypad is backlit. Lacks ringer vol. adjustment. Feature keys: Has Save (just-dialed number to memory), Flash, Pause, Listening vol. control.
Conairphone SW204	Failed drop and surge tests. No speed-dial capability. Keypad is backlit. Lacks ringer vol. adjustment. No Flash key (can use switch hook with Call Waiting). Feature keys: Has Mute.
Conairphone SW3100WCS [S]	Failed surge and static tests. No speed-dial capability. Feature keys: Has Flash, Pause. **Successor:** SW3100CS.
Conairphone XS1200 [S]	Failed drop tests. Memory can store mixed dialing sequences of pulse and tones. Keypad is backlit. Feature keys: Has Save (just-dialed number to memory), Flash, Pause, Hold. **Successor:** XS1202.
General Electric 2-9267, **A BEST BUY**	Memory can store mixed dialing sequences of pulse and tones. Feature keys: Has Save (just-dialed number to memory), Flash, Listening vol. control.
General Electric 2-9290	Failed static tests. Feature keys: Has Flash, Pause.
General Electric 2-9390	Failed surge tests. Memory can store mixed dialing sequences of pulse and tones. Needs AC to use speakerphone and display. Caller ID display. Feature keys: Has Save (just-dialed number to memory), Flash, Pause, Mute, Hold.
General Electric 2-9435	Failed surge and static tests. Memory can store mixed dialing sequences of pulse and tones. Auto-redial repeatedly redials busy numbers. Feature keys: Has Save (just-dialed number to memory), Flash, Pause, Mute, Hold.
Panasonic KX-T2315	Failed static tests. Memory can store mixed dialing sequences of pulse and tones. Needs batteries for speakerphone and display. Feature keys: Has Flash, Pause, Mute, Hold.
Panasonic KX-T3175-B	Failed static tests. Memory can store mixed dialing sequences of pulse and tones. Auto-redial repeatedly redials busy numbers. Needs batteries for speakerphone and display. Feature keys: Has Flash, Pause, Mute, Hold, Listening vol. control.
Radio Shack ET-145	Failed surge tests. Listening-vol. control amplifies weak voices across wider range. Needs batteries or AC to use phone. No Flash key (can use switch hook with Call Waiting). Feature keys: Has Pause, Listening vol. control.
Radio Shack ET-206	Memory can store mixed dialing sequences of pulse and tones. Listening-vol. control amplifies weak voices across wider range. Feature keys: Has Flash, Pause, Hold, Listening vol. control.
Radio Shack ET-273	No speed-dial capability. Lacks ringer vol. adjustment. Feature keys: Has Flash.
Sony IT-B3	Failed surge and static tests. Memory can store mixed dialing sequences of pulse and tones. No Flash key (can use switch hook with Call Waiting). Feature keys: Has Pause.

Ratings continued ▶

Ratings continued

Sony IT-D250	Failed surge and static tests. Memory can store mixed dialing sequences of pulse and tones. Auto-redial repeatedly redials busy numbers. Needs batteries for speakerphone and display. Feature keys: Has Save (just-dialed number to memory), Flash, Pause, Mute, Hold.
Southwestern Bell FT360B	Failed surge and static tests. Memory can store mixed dialing sequences of pulse and tones. Feature keys: Has Save (just-dialed number to memory), Flash, Pause, Hold.
Southwestern Bell FC2544	Memory can store mixed dialing sequences of pulse and tones. Keypad is backlit. Lacks ringer vol. adjustment. Feature keys: Has Flash, Mute, Listening vol. control.
Spectra-phone FP-13M	Failed all survival tests. Lacks ringer vol. adjustment. Feature keys: Has Save (just-dialed number to memory), Pause.
Unisonic 6772	Failed surge tests. Memory can store mixed dialing sequences of pulse and tones. Keypad is backlit. Lacks ringer vol. adjustment. Feature keys: Has Save (just-dialed number to memory), Flash, Pause.

UPSCALE PHONE FEATURES: ARE THEY WORTH THE PRICE?

The presence of certain features—speakerphone, two-line capability, caller ID compatibility, and LCD displays—automatically steps up the price of a phone. Whether or not they're worth the price depends on how important they are to you.

Here's what they do:

Speakerphone. This feature frees you from the handset so you can, say, fix dinner while you have a conversation on the phone. Sound quality is still not as good as with the handset, and varies greatly from one model to another.

Two-line capability. With this extra, you get the ability to handle a second phone line so a spouse, teen-ager, or the modem can have a separate line. It also enables you to "conference" two callers in a three-way conversation with you.

Caller ID compatibility. This allows you to see the phone number of several of your last callers (the number varies) and, in some locations, the name of the person calling.

LCD display. This shows handy information such as the number just dialed, the time of day, and perhaps the time you've spent talking.

YARD & GARDEN

The environmental impact of lawn and garden power tools has become a major issue. Mowing a lawn for a half hour with a typical mower can contribute as much smog as driving a car 172 miles, according to the California Air Resources Board. California and the U.S. Environmental Protection Agency are working on emissions restrictions for the small engines used on lawn mowers, trimmers, and other lawn tools. Because of another kind of pollution—noise—many municipalities have placed restrictions on the use of leaf blowers.

The design of the engine is a major pollution factor. An overhead-valve design burns fuel more efficiently than the more common side-valve type. Four-stroke engines run more cleanly than two-stroke.

You can minimize emissions from mowing and other lawn-care jobs by regularly tuning up your equipment. Another way is to buy a spillproof nozzle for the fuel container (spills from lawn and garden equipment cause significant emissions).

Nonpowered—and nonpolluting—alternatives are worth considering for small lawn-care jobs. You can cut a small lawn with a manual reel mower, trim around the edges with a pair of shears, and gather leaves with a rake. Of course, those options require physical effort. To many, that's another benefit of the "green" choice.

Power tools require safety precautions. In general, don't operate a power tool when children or pets are close. Wear protective clothing, including eye and ear protection. Don't use electric tools in wet conditions.

Gasoline-powered tools deserve special caution. Fill the fuel tank carefully, after the engine has cooled. Don't handle the blade of a machine unless the engine is stopped and the ignition is disabled.

Lawn mowers

▶ Repair Histories on page 24.

Each type of mower—manual reel, electric, gasoline-powered, or tractor—has its own advantages and disadvantages; each differs in noise, ease of use, maintenance, and performance in tall grass and weeds.

Safety

As a safety precaution, all walk-behind power mowers have a "deadman" control that stops the blade when you let go of the handle. That and other safety features seem to have made mowing safer. Injuries due to walk-behind mowers have dropped to about half what they were just 10 years ago. Still, thousands of people head to hospital emergency rooms every year because of an injury caused by a lawn mower or tractor.

When you mow, keep safety in mind:

- Mow only when and where it's safe. Don't mow when the grass is wet; your foot could slip under the mower. Push a mower across a slope, not up and down. If you have a riding mower or tractor, travel up and down, not across. If the slope is more than about 15 degrees, don't mow at all; on slopes that steep, a push-mower can get away from you, and a ride-on mower can tip over.
- Wear sturdy shoes and close-fitting clothes. Consider wearing ear protection for a noisy mower.
- Before mowing, pick up toys, hoses, rocks, and twigs. Make sure no people or pets are nearby; a mower can hurl objects.
- Keep hands and feet away from moving parts.
- Don't defeat safety devices.
- Don't let children use or ride a mower.

Reliability

The more complex the mower, the greater the probability it will need repair, according to our readers' experience. One exception: Hondas. Their repair rates for push-type and self-propelled models were equally low. Overall, readers report that about 16 percent of push-type mowers bought since 1988 needed repairs. About 25 percent of self-propelled models needed repair during the same time period. See the brand Repair Histories on page 24.

Buying advice

Let the size, terrain, and landscaping of the lawn determine the type of mower you buy. A hilly half-acre calls for a different kind of mower than a half-acre. A lawn dotted with landscaping needs a mower that cuts close to walls, edging, or railroad ties.

The best time to shop for a mower is after the Fourth of July. No matter when you buy, expect to pay more at a hardware store or specialty mower shop than at a home center, discount store, or catalog retail outlet. But small stores may offer better service and a higher-quality line of mowers.

Manual reel mowers

▶ Ratings on page 214.

Concern about air and noise pollution, along with nostalgia for the good old days, has renewed interest in old-fashioned, you-push-'em reel mowers. While the reel mower has been brought up to date with lightweight alloys and plastic parts, the way it works hasn't changed since the days of the 60-pound cast-iron clunkers. A series of blades linked to the wheels slice the grass. Reel mowers are best suited to small, flat lawns. They're priced from $65 to $100 (a few $200 models are available).

One company—American Lawn Mower Company/Great States Corp.—makes most of the reel mowers. Sales of reel mowers have doubled over the past 10 years, and the selection has expanded.

Reel mowers are quiet, inexpensive, and relatively safe to operate. They require no maintenance aside from occasional sharpening or blade adjustment. However, they don't mow as well as might be expected. Typically, most can't be set to cut higher than 1½ inches, and those we tested had a hard time plowing through thick, high grass. Mowing around obstacles is limited to no closer than three inches. Their cutting swath ranges from 14 to 18 inches (most rotaries cut 20 to 22 inches).

Features and conveniences

Grass-catcher. It's available for most models as a $15 to $50 option, but we don't recommend it. The catchers hold very little grass. They require brisk mowing to get the clippings into the bag.

Handle. The most convenient have a rest position high enough so you don't have to stoop. Padding on the handle is worthwhile.

Cutting height. Look for a machine that adjusts easily and without tools to as high as 2 or 2½ inches, which allows for a healthier lawn than does a closer cropping.

The tests

CU tests manual mowers on grass that's been precut to about three inches—about as tall as you should let the grass grow if you're using one of these mowers. We assess each model's cutting evenness, ease of pushing, ease of making U-turns, and operating convenience—a catchall category that includes ease of adjusting cutting height and bedknife position, and the height of the handle at rest.

Buying advice

Consider a reel mower only if you have a small, level lawn that's relatively free of weeds and obstacles.

Electric mowers

▶ **Ratings on page 205.**

Electric versions of the rotary power mower use a motor to spin the blades while you push (there aren't any self-propelled electrics). The motors are less powerful than the engines on gasoline-powered mowers, but some electrics are actually better at cutting tall grass than some gas models. Black & Decker, Sears, and MTD sell most of the electric mowers on the market; Black & Decker, Ryobi, and Husquarna make battery-powered models.

Advantages. Electric mowers are quiet and require little maintenance. They tackle tall and thick grass or weeds as well as most gasoline-powered mowers do. Many models mulch.

The choices

Corded. These are by far the most common type of electric mower. They run on standard house current, typically through a 100-foot extension cord (about $15). Such models are suitable for lawns of about one-quarter-acre—typically, what can be reached by the 100-foot cord. (Ganging more cords may reduce power to the motor; it's certainly makes the cord harder to handle.) The cord can be a nuisance. Prices range between $150 and $250.

Cordless. Battery models can cut about one quarter of an acre on one charge; recharging takes up to 24 hours. The battery makes these models heavy and thus hard to push. Prices: about $275 to $400.

Features and conveniences

Motor size. Motors range from 6.5 to 12 amps. More amps doesn't always correlate with improved cutting ability.

Cord handling. A sliding clip lets the cord flip from side to side, always remaining on the side of the mower facing the electric outlet, no matter which way you're walking. That arrangement is better than a handle that you flip over every time you reverse direction.

Grass-catcher. Look for a catcher with a large handle for easy handling. We didn't like those with a zipper or a spring-loaded door that makes attaching and removing the catcher hard.

Handle. Look for a comfortable handle. A few models let you adjust the height of the handle.

Battery-capacity indicator. This keeps track of the charge for battery models.

The tests

CU tests electric mowers on grass that's been precut to about four inches. We assess each model's cutting evenness, vacuuming, and catcher capacity; for mulching models dispersal of clippings. Our handling judgment includes ease of pushing, making U-turns, side-to-side jockeying, and cord handling. We assess convenience factors such as handle comfort and the ease of using the grass-catcher.

Buying advice

Electric mowers are an attractive alternative to gas mowers, suitable for lawns about one-fourth acre in size. Many can handle thick grass and high weeds. Most are very easy to push. Those with the wheels set in can mow close to objects, though such objects can complicate cord-handling. Battery-powered models avoid the cord problems but are expensive and awkward to use.

Gasoline-powered mowers

▸ Ratings on page 210. ▸ Repair Histories on page 24.

Walk-behind gasoline-powered mowers are best suited for mowing lawns of up to one-half acre and for trimming larger lawns. The engine is typically a one-cylinder, four-stroke design that spins a 20- to 22-inch blade; power ranges from 3.5 to 5.5 hp. (A few models use a two-stroke engine, which requires a gasoline/oil fuel mixture and emits more pollutants.)

Gasoline-powered mowers are free to roam as long as there's fuel in the tank. Many can gobble up tall and thick grass or weeds. Handling for most ranges from easy to very easy. Most models can mulch—chop grass up extra fine so clippings can decompose naturally in the lawn. But gasoline-powered mowers are noisy, and they require regular maintenance and blade sharpening.

Sears and Murray sell about half the gas-powered mowers, mostly low-priced models. Other brands—Toro, Lawn-Boy, Snapper, Ariens, Honda, John Deere—concentrate on the higher end of the market.

The choices

Push-type. This type uses the engine only to spin the cutting blade, and you to supply the forward motion. It's the most widely sold type of mower in the U.S.

Some cost as little as $100, but can go as high as $650.

Self-propelled. For $175 to $800 more than push-type mowers, self-propelled models move themselves forward. If your lawn is a half-acre or larger, or if it's hilly, this is the type preferred.

The engine powers either the front or rear wheels. Rear-drive models are better at climbing hills but can be a bit harder to maneuver through U-turns. According to our reader surveys, self-propelled mowers are less reliable than push types.

Features and conveniences

Deadman control. Higher-priced models are often available with a convenient deadman control that stops the blade but not the engine when you release the handle. Called a blade-brake/clutch, it lets you stop mowing—say, to empty the grass-catcher—without shutting off the mower.

Grass-catcher. One mounted in the rear rather than the side makes for easier maneuvering. Models with rear-mounted catchers also tend to mow better when using the catcher. (Many mowers with a side-mounted-catcher mow better when discharging than when bagging.) Make sure the catcher comes off, empties, and goes back on easily. Some mowers make you line up tabs or hold open a strong, spring-loaded flap.

Mulching conversion. The easiest method involves inserting a plug in the discharge chute. Avoid models that make you change the blade or use tools to mulch.

Electric starter. This makes starting a bit easier than tugging on a rope but comes at a price.

Engine choke. Look for it on the engine. A choke is easier to operate than a primer bulb.

Mowing-height adjustment. A single control for adjusting all four wheels is easier than separate controls at each wheel—and much easier than removing and reattaching bolt-on wheels.

Variable or multiple drive speeds. On a self-propelled model, these let you adjust the speed to the terrain. A clutch that lets you "feather" the mower into gear rather than start it abruptly makes maneuvering easier.

The tests

We test gas mowers on grass that's been precut to four inches. Except for cord-handling, the tests are the same as those for electrics. For self-propelled models, we test speed-gear shifting and clutching.

Buying advice

Our tests show that with a cheap mower you give up a degree of cutting performance, considerable capacity in the grass-catcher, a more convenient deadman control, and a choke. You have to decide whether those factors are worth several hundred dollars extra.

Riding mowers & tractors

Riding lawn mowers and small tractors are best suited for lawns and properties about one-half acre and larger. They have wider cutting swaths than walk-behind mowers, so they can get the job done faster. And, since you ride them, the job takes less effort.

Prices range from $900 to $4000 for a riding mower or a lawn tractor; $2000 to $5000 for a garden tractor.

The choices

All of these big mowers have an electric-start engine. Most models can cut grass in any of the three cutting modes: bagging, side-discharging, and mulching.

Riding mowers. These have an 8- to 10-hp engine in the rear. Besides cutting grass with their 30-inch blade, they can use a large grass-catcher and perhaps a utility cart.

Lawn tractors. These small versions of a farm tractor have a 12- to 14-hp engine in front. They cut grass with a 38- to 45-inch deck that houses two or three blades, and they collect clippings in a large grass-catcher. They can take several accessories, including a snow blade or blower, leaf vacuum, and utility cart.

Garden tractors. These are large versions of lawn tractors. The front-mounted engine produces between 16 and 20 hp. The cutting deck is similar to the lawn tractor's but up to 60-inches wide. A garden tractor is more versatile than its cousin because the garden tractor can take a wider variety of pull-along and powered accessories for lawn-care and gardening jobs.

Features and conveniences

Safety. Look for a deadman control that stops the engine and blade when you dismount and, when you're riding without mowing, stops the engine alone.

Transmission. A variable-speed or multispeed transmission lets you mow slowly or briskly. Look for positive gear-shift detents, which make shifting easier.

Buying advice

There's little reason to buy a riding mower when you can get a more versatile lawn tractor for about the same price. A hydrostatic (variable speed) transmission is better for maneuvering in tight spaces. For safety's sake, avoid models without a seat-linked cutoff switch.

String trimmers

String trimmers put the finishing touches on a mowed lawn. They do the same kind of work once tackled with clippers and shears, minus the bending and blisters. A trimmer cuts tall grass and weeds by spinning a plastic line fast enough to slice through leaf and stem but with too little inertia to hurt a properly shod foot. Still, a lashing from a trimmer's whirling line can draw blood from bare skin and fling dirt and debris with considerable force, good reason to wear long pants, sturdy shoes, and goggles.

The Homelite brand dominates trimmer sales. Other big names are Weed Eater, Ryobi, Echo, Stihl, McCulloch, and Toro.

The choices

Gasoline-powered models are particularly noisy. In fact, gas trimmers typically generate about 100 decibels of noise, loud enough to warrant use of hearing protection.

Electric-powered. One-handled models are for light trimming. Cutting swath: 8 to 10 inches. Weight: about three pounds. Some two-handled electric models can cut as well as gasoline-powered models. The typical model has a motor mounted over the cutting head; better balanced models have the motor mounted above the main handle. Cutting swath: 10 to 17 inches. Weight: less than 10 pounds. Price: about $25 to $75.

Cordless. The battery-powered electric models we've tested have run for about 20 minutes on a charge—typically, with much less power than plug-in models. Cutting swath: 6 to 10 inches. Weight: 3 to 5 pounds. Price: $35 to more than $110.

Gasoline-powered. Most have a two-stroke engine located at the top of the shaft, but Ryobi makes several models with a cleaner-burning four-stroke engine. Cutting swath: 15 to 18 inches. Weight: 9 to 15 pounds. Price: $80 to more than $225.

Wheeled. These gasoline-powered machines tackle areas of wood or plantings that are too large or rough for a power mower or that would require the prolonged use of an ordinary trimmer. Cutting swath: 17 to 18 inches. Price: $400 and up.

Features and conveniences

String advancement. Most models use the bump-feed system: You tap or bump the trimmer head on the ground, and the line advances. A metal cutter on the head shears off any excess line. Automatic or push-button line-advance is even more convenient than bump-feed.

Starting. Electrics usually have a rocker switch; gas-powered models, a rope starter. A few offer push-button electric start.

Attachments. On some models, a metal blade can replace the string for cutting woody stems up to an inch thick. *Ryobi* models with the "TrimmerPlus System" accept a power blower, vacuum, edger, cultivator, pruner, and snow thrower.

Engine/motor location. One of the best indicators of good balance is an engine or motor mounted high on the shaft, above the handle. With large gasoline-powered trimmers, which weigh nine pounds or more, good balance is critical.

Shoulder strap. For heavy models, this is a way to improve balance during horizontal trimming and to take some of the load off your arms.

Pivoting trimmer head. For edging, you typically have to orient the trimmer's head so the line spins vertically. A pivoting head makes the chore easier by letting you grip both handles in their regular position.

Translucent fuel tank. This makes the fuel level easy to check.

Buying advice

Match the trimmer to the task: If your property is large, or if you must tackle heavy or woody undergrowth, consider a gasoline-powered trimmer. If overgrown weeds or the tether of an extension cord doesn't present a problem, a two-handled electric model may make the most sense. For touching up a small, well-tended plot, either a one-handled electric or cordless trimmer should do the job nicely.

Power blowers

▶ Ratings on page 207.

These noisy machines blow away leaves and grass clippings from the lawn and vacuum debris from decks, walks, and the driveway. For people with a large lawn or plenty of trees, they can make cleanup jobs much easier than doing them with a rake. Despite their usefulness, some communities have placed restrictions on when they can be operated because of the racket they make. The noisiest generate enough din to make ear protection desirable.

Four brands—Sears Craftsman, Weed Eater, Toro, and Black & Decker—dominate U.S. sales of power blowers.

The choices

Blowers use an electric motor or gasoline engine and a fan to push or pull air through a set of tubes. Vacuuming models also shred debris so more can fit into their collection container.

Handheld electric. Quieter than gasoline models, but in many cases just as powerful. Price: about $50 to $75.

Handheld gasoline-powered. Most have a two-stroke engine, which uses a gasoline-oil fuel mixture that produces more pollution than a four-stroke engine. Price: $110 to $200.

Backpack gasoline-powered. Easier to carry (even at 20 pounds) than handheld models, but sometimes noisier and not necessarily more powerful. They don't vacuum. For big lawns, they are much less tiring than a handheld blower. Price: $175 to more than $450.

Other types. Electrics that blow but don't vacuum cost about $30. Cordless electrics ($70 or so) have only enough power to clean smooth surfaces like a deck or driveway. The top of some shop vacuums can be lifted off, fitted with tubes from a conversion kit (about $130), and used as a (somewhat anemic) blower. You can also clear leaves from the lawn with a push-type chipper-shredder, a lawn mower or, of course, a rake.

Features and conveniences

Power. Manufacturers boast various engine sizes, horsepower, motor amperage, and nozzle air speed. Our tests show that bigger or more isn't necessarily related to a blower's effectiveness.

Blower nozzle. The blowers that were best at lawn cleaning in our tests had a round-end nozzle. Models with a rectangular-end nozzle were not quite as effective.

Second handle. Makes it easier to maneuver the blower.

Starter-cord location. If it's near the center of the engine housing, pulling it is less likely to make the blower twist.

Switch location. Whether it's the engine-kill switch on a gas model or the On/off switch on an electric, the best place for the switch is where you can reach it with the hand that holds the main handle.

Lower-speed settings. For the times you want less force, such as when cleaning a gravel driveway or a mulched flower bed.

The tests

We test power blowers on a suburban estate with plenty of trees, shrubs, and scraggly, tall grass. We measure a blower's effectiveness by observing how well it blows leaves into elongated rows. Lawn-cleaning ability is determined by a blower's ability to completely rid a lawn of a heavy accumulation of leaves. We also assess vacuuming, handling, convenience, and noise.

Buying advice

If you have a smallish lawn with few trees, an inexpensive electric blower ($30 to $40) that doesn't vacuum may be all you need. For bigger jobs that can be reached by an extension cord, consider the somewhat more expensive) electric blowers/vacuums ($65 to $75).

Gas handheld models no longer have any power advantage over the better electric models and are noisier to boot, but they're not limited by an electric cord. A backpack gas blower is much less fatiguing to use than any handheld model. But it's expensive and also noisy. For big jobs, an alternative might be renting a backpack or hiring a professional lawn service.

RATINGS ELECTRIC MOWERS

▶ **See report, page 199.** Last time rated in Consumer Reports: June 1995.

Brand-name recommendations: The top-rated Cub Cadet 387, $245, the MTD 184-387-000 (now discontinued), $180, and the Craftsman 37025, $250, produced a smooth, even cut and can mulch clippings, bag them, or send them out the side. Any of the three cordless models we tested is worth considering. The Husqvarna 43RC, $340, handled best.

For most electric mowers, expect: ■ Discharge chute included, side-mounted catcher extra. ■ Ability to mow in at least 2 of 3 modes; no tools needed to change modes. ■ The need to use a heavy-duty extension cord that plugs into a standard 15-amp circuit. ■ Deadman control doubling as On/off switch and operated on only one side of the handle. ■ Easy pushing. ■ Sliding clip for flipping cord. ■ Handle that folds for storage but has no height adjustment.

Notes on the table: Price is the estimated average, based on a national survey. For side-bagging mowers, a catcher generally costs $30 to $55 extra. For rear-baggers, a discharge chute is usually extra (the catcher is included). Where applicable, the Comments also give the price of a mulching kit. **Score** is based mainly on mowing performance but includes handling and convenience as well. **Even** is mower's ability to produce a smooth, carpetlike cut. **Vacuum** is the mower's ability, when bagging, to clean up clippings. **Spread** is how well clippings were dispersed during discharging or mulching. **Tall grass** indicates performance on 8- to 12-in.-high grass. **Model availability:** D means model is discontinued.

Within type, listed in order of performance and convenience

E ⊜ VG ⊖ G ○ F ◒ P ●

Brand and model	Price	Score (P F G VG E)	Bagging EVEN/VAC.	Spread SIDE/MULCH	Tall grass	Comments
CORDED						
Cub Cadet 387 [1]	$245		⊖/⊖	⊜/○	◒	Handle has height adjustment. Hard to attach catcher, adjust cutting height. Clippings may leak through catcher seal. Mulching kit included.
MTD 184-387-000 [1] [D]	180		⊖/⊖	⊜/○	◒	Handle has height adjustment. Hard to attach catcher; adjust cutting height. Clippings may leak through catcher seal. Mulching kit, $30.
Craftsman (Sears) 37025 [1] [2]	250		⊖/⊖	⊜/○	◒	Comfortable handle with height adjustment. Hard to attach catcher, adjust cutting height. Clippings may leak through catcher seal. Inconvenient cord attachment. Mulching kit included.

[1] *Rear-bagger; catcher included; discharge chute extra.*

[2] *Discharge chute not available from Sears. MTD chute 190-104-000 works as well as on MTD.*

Ratings continued ▶

Ratings continued

Brand and model	Price	Score (P F G VG E)	Bagging EVEN/VAC.	Spread SIDE/MULCH	Tall grass	Comments
CORDED *continued*						
Black & Decker MM450 D	$200		○/⊖	◓/⊖	⊜	Comfortable handle. Easy to: jockey side-to-side, adjust cutting height. Mulching kit included.
Yard-Man 187-107-401 D	200		○/○	○/⊖	⊜	Comfortable handle. Hard to adjust cutting height. Mulching kit included.
Craftsman (Sears) 37028 D	250		○/○	○/⊖	⊜	Comfortable handle. Hard to adjust cutting height. Mulching kit included.
Black & Decker M200	150		○/⊖	◓/—	⊖	Easy to push, U-turn, jockey side-to-side. Hard to adjust cutting height. Reversing direction makes vacuuming worse, requires jockeying into position; handle's locking lever flimsy and hard to move.
Lawn Chief EA919	180		◓/○	●/—	○	Comfortable handle. Easy to attach catcher. Reversing direction requires jockeying into position. Hard to jockey side-to-side.
Wheeler WS0119	170		◓/○	●/—	○	Comfortable handle. Easy to attach catcher. Reversing direction makes vacuuming worse, requires jockeying into position. Hard to jockey side-to-side, adjust cutting height.
MTD 184-427-000 D	144		◓/○	⊖/—	⊖	Cutting evenness improved in discharge mode. Reversing direction makes vacuuming and discharge dispersal worse, requires jockeying into position. Hard to U-turn, jockey side-to-side.
CORDLESS						
Husqvarna 43RC 3	340		○/—	—/⊖	◒	Comfortable handle. Easy to adjust cutting height. Deadman allows use with either hand. Quiet. 24-volt lead-acid battery. Blade has hinged tips.
Ryobi BMM2400 3	360		○/—	—/⊖	◒	Comfortable handle. Easy to adjust cutting height. Deadman allows use with either hand. Handle has height adjustment. Quiet. 24-volt lead-acid battery. Hard to push, U-turn, jockey side-to-side. Also sold as Craftsman 37027, $375.
Black & Decker CMM650 D	380		○/○	◓/○	⊖	Comfortable handle. Easy to adjust cutting height. 12-volt lead-acid battery. Hard to U-turn, jockey side-to-side. Flimsy charger plug. Mulching kit included.

3 *Mulching only.*

RATINGS POWER BLOWERS

▶ **See report, page 203.** Last time rated in Consumer Reports: September 1995.

Brand-name recommendations: If an extension cord is practical, we suggest an electric blower rather than a gasoline-powered model. The four highest-rated electric blowers out-performed the handheld gasoline-powered models. A gas-powered blower frees you from the limitations of the extension cord. The electric Black & Decker BV 1000, $75, was the only model to earn top scores in both blower power and vacuum speed. The gasoline-powered Craftsman 79799, $125, was judged A Best Buy. It had plenty of blowing power and vacuuming speed, and easily converted between the two modes. But it's one of the loudest models tested.

For the typical power blower, expect: ■ Gas models to be much louder than electrics. ■ Blower tube with round or rectangular nozzle on electrics; rectangular nozzle on gas-powered models. ■ Ignition-cutoff switch or On/off switch that's hard to reach with the hand holding the main handle. ■ Off-center starter cord, if gas-powered. ■ If gas-powered, a 2-stroke engine. ■ Blowing/vacuuming changeover using a screwdriver.

Notes on the table: Price is the estimated average, based on a national survey. **Score** is based mainly on performance as a blower, and includes vacuuming performance, noise, and convenience. **Noise** was measured at the operator's ear. We recommend hearing protection with any model rated ● or ◒. **Blowing power** shows how forcefully the blowers could gather and pile up leaves. **Cleaning** scores how effectively the blowers could leave a lawn free of debris. **Vacuuming speed** timed vacuuming and shredding a measured pile of leaves. **Model availability:** Ⓓ means model is discontinued.

Ratings key: E = Excellent, VG = Very good, G = Good, F = Fair, P = Poor

Within types, listed in order of overall score

Brand and model	Price	Score (P F G VG E)	Noise	Blowing: Power	Blowing: Cleaning	Vacuuming speed
HANDHELD ELECTRIC MODELS						
Black & Decker BV 1000	$75		G	E	VG	E
McCulloch Air Stream II	75		G	E	E	VG
Weed Eater 2580 Ⓓ	65		G	E	E	G
Stihl BE 55	64		G	VG	G	VG
Craftsman (Sears) 79838 Ⓓ	65		F	E	E	VG
Toro 850 Super Blower Vac Ⓓ	67		G	VG	E	G
Weed Eater 2560 Ⓓ	55		VG	VG	G	F
Toro 700 Rake-O-Vac Ⓓ	60		VG	G	VG	P
McCulloch Air Stream I	68		G	G	VG	G
Ryobi 180r	62		VG	F	G	G

Ratings continued ▶

Ratings continued

Brand and model	Price	Score (P F G VG E)	Noise	Blowing: POWER	Blowing: CLEANING	Vacuuming speed
HANDHELD GASOLINE-POWERED MODELS						
Stihl BG 72	$188		◒	⊖	○	⊖
Craftsman (Sears) 79799, **A BEST BUY** Ⓓ	125		●	⊜	○	⊖
Echo PB 1000	150		◒	⊖	○	○
John Deere 2BV	185		◒	⊖	○	○
Echo ES1000 Shred 'n' Vac	200		◒	⊖	○	⊖
Husqvarna 132HBV	148		●	⊜	○	⊖
Weed Eater GBI 22V	117		◒	⊖	○	○
Homelite HB180VGK	148		○	⊖	○	○
Ryobi 310 BVr	112		◒	○	○	⊖
McCulloch Super Air Stream IV Ⓓ	128		◒	○	◒	○
BACKPACK GASOLINE-POWERED MODELS						
Echo PB4600	400		●	⊜	⊜	—
Husqvarna 140B	390		●	⊜	⊜	—
Tanaka TBL 4600	440		●	⊜	⊜	—
Homelite BP 250	155		◒	⊖	○	—

MODEL DETAILS

Want to know more about a rated model? They're listed here alphabetically.

Black & Decker BV 1000	Comes with second, smaller blower nozzle for better cleaning. Comfortable handle. 2 speed settings. 2-handed use needed.
Craftsman (Sears) 79799, **A BEST BUY** Ⓓ	Pulling starter cord doesn't make unit twist. Collection bag easy to remove. Awkward choke control.
Craftsman (Sears) 79838 Ⓓ	2 speed settings. Side-to-side motion difficult when blowing. Collection bag difficult to empty. Comes with second, rectangular blower nozzle, better at leaf-gathering.
Echo ES1000 Shred 'n' Vac	On/Off switch easily reached by hand holding main handle. Comfortable handle. 2 speed settings. Side-to-side motion difficult when blowing. Small auxiliary handle vibrates excessively. Collection bag drags on ground. Hard to convert between blowing and vacuuming.
Echo PB 1000	Engine-kill switch easily reached by hand holding main handle. Comfortable handle. 2 speed settings. Collection bag easy to remove. Side-to-side motion difficult when blowing. Auxiliary handle vibrates excessively. Hard to convert between blowing and vacuuming. Vac. attachment, $45.
Echo PB4600	Comfortable handle on blower tube. Convenient controls. Comfortable throttle control. Convenient carrying handle.

Homelite BP 250	Comfortable handle on blower tube. Convenient controls. Convenient carrying handle. Pulling starter cord doesn't make unit twist.
Homelite HB180VGK	Pulling starter cord doesn't make unit twist. Starter cord easy to pull. 6 throttle settings. Small auxiliary handle vibrates excessively. Collection-bag exhaust tube bumps user. Engine exhaust blows at user through vacuum bag. Vacuum tubes fell off unless taped together.
Husqvarna 132HBV	Pulling starter cord doesn't make unit twist. Collection bag easy to remove. Auxiliary handle vibrates painfully. Awkward choke control.
Husqvarna 140B	Comfortable throttle control. Large, easily reached fuel tank. Hard to put on.
John Deere 2BV	Engine-kill switch easily reached by hand holding main handle. Comfortable handle. 2 speed settings. Collection bag easy to remove. Side-to-side motion difficult when blowing. Auxiliary handle vibrates excessively. Hard to convert between blowing and vacuuming. Vac. attachment, $44.
McCulloch Air Stream I	2-handed use required, but awkward.
McCulloch Air Stream II	2 speed settings. 2-handed use needed but awkward.
McCulloch Super Air Stream IV [D]	Engine-kill switch easily reached by hand holding main handle. Auxiliary handle vibrates excessively. 2 speed settings. Collection-bag exhaust tube bumps user. Awkward choke control. Hard to convert between blowing and vacuuming.
Ryobi 180r	Comfortable handle. Requires stooping when vacuuming. Vacuumed material sticks to inside of collection bag. 2 speed settings. Not very effective at reducing volume of vacuumed material.
Ryobi 310 BVr	Pulling starter cord doesn't make unit twist. Engine-kill switch easily reached by hand holding main handle. Throttle-trigger guard interferes with operation. No throttle presets. Awkward choke control. Vacuumed material sticks to inside of collection bag.
Stihl BE 55	On/Off switch easily reached by hand holding main handle. Comfortable handle. 2 preset speed settings. 2-handed use needed. Not very effective at reducing volume of vacuumed material. Vac. attachment, $25.
Stihl BG 72	Engine-kill switch easily reached by hand holding main handle. Comfortable throttle control. Hard to convert between blowing and vacuuming. Not very effective at reducing volume of vacuumed material.
Tanaka TBL 4600	Some controls hard to reach. On-off switch illogical.
Toro 700 Rake-O-Vac [D]	On/Off switch easily reached by hand holding main handle. Comfortable handle. 4 speed.
Toro 850 Super Blower Vac [D]	Comfortable handle. 2 speed settings. 2 handed use required, but awkward.
Weed Eater 2560 [D]	On/Off switch easily reached by hand holding main handle. Collection bag easy to remove. 2 speed settings. 2-handed use required. Requires stooping when vacuuming. Not very effective at reducing volume of vacuumed material.
Weed Eater 2580 [D]	Comes with second, circular blower nozzle for better cleaning. 2 speed settings. Collection bag easy to remove. Especially effective at reducing volume of vacuumed material. Requires stooping when vacuuming. 2-handed use needed.
Weed Eater GBI 22V	Pulling starter cord doesn't make unit twist. Collection bag easy to remove. Requires stooping when vacuuming. Auxiliary handle vibrates excessively. Awkward choke control.

RATINGS GASOLINE LAWN MOWERS

See report, page 200. Last time rated in Consumer Reports: June 1995.

Brand-name recommendations: Unfortunately, the Yard-Man 106C, $190, unsurpassed in all three cutting modes has been discontinued. Almost as good was the Cub Cadet, $250, and the much cheaper MTD Yard Machine, $140. The MTD Yard Machine is about as inexpensive as it gets for a mower this good. The Murray Mark IV 2nOne, $175 including a mulching kit, was the top rear-bagger. It combined competent bagging and mulching with the best tall-grass cutting of any of the push-type mowers. Any of the self-propelled mowers would make a good choice. The John Deere, $660, and the Kubota, $760, came closest to matching the top-rated Snapper, which is no longer available.

For push-type gas mowers, expect: ■ Deadman that stops engine and blade. ■ 4-stroke, side-valve 3½- to 4½-hp Briggs & Stratton or Tecumseh engine with primer bulb for starting. ■ Throttle control on handle. ■ Ability to mow in 3 modes (blade change needed for mulching). ■ Handle whose height isn't adjustable. ■ For side-baggers, width of more than 35 in. with catcher. ■ For side-baggers, discharge chute included; catcher extra. For rear-baggers, catcher included; chute extra. ■ Cutting swath of 20 to 22 in. **For expensive self-propelled gas mowers, expect:** ■ Deadman that stops blade alone. ■ 4-stroke, side-valve 4½- to 5½-hp engine with choke for starting. ■ Rear-mounted catcher included; discharge chute extra. ■ Cutting swath of 21 in.

Notes on the table: Price is the estimated average, based on a national survey. * means price paid. A catcher generally costs $30 to $55 extra. For rear-baggers, a chute is usually extra (the catcher is included). The Details note where any of the normally extra-cost choices are included. Where applicable, the Details give the price of a mulching kit. **Score** is based mainly on mowing performance but includes handling and convenience as well. **Evenness** is mower's ability to produce a smooth, carpetlike cut. **Vacuum** is the mower's ability, when bagging, to clean up clippings. **Spread** is how well clippings were dispersed during discharging or hidden during mulching. **Tall** grass indicates performance on 8- to 12-in.-high grass. Models similar to those we tested are noted in Details; features may vary. **Model availability:** [D] means model is discontinued. [S] means model is replaced, according to the manufacturer; successor model is noted in Details. New model was not tested; it may or may not perform similarly. Features may vary.

Within type, listed in order of performance and convenience

E VG G F P

Brand and model	Price	Score (P F G VG E)	Bagging	Discharging	Mulching
			EVEN/VAC.	EVEN/SPREAD/TALL	SPREAD
PUSH-TYPE (SIDE-BAG)					
Yard-Man 106C 115-106C401 [D]	$190		VG/VG	VG/VG/VG	VG
Cub Cadet 072R	250		VG/VG	VG/VG/VG	G
MTD Yard Machine 072A 115-072A000	140		VG/VG	VG/VG/VG	G
White SD074 115-074A190 [D]	220		G/G	VG/VG/VG	G

Brand and model	Price	Score (P F G VG E)	Bagging EVEN/VAC.	Discharging EVEN/SPREAD/TALL	Mulching SPREAD
PUSH-TYPE (SIDE-BAG) *continued*					
White SD050 115-050A190 D	$170		○/○	⊖/⊖/⊖	○
Lawn-Boy Silver Series 10202	270		○/○	○/⊖/○	○
Craftsman (Sears) 38274	220		⊖/⊖	○/◒/○	⊜
Lawn Chief 60 D	190		○/○	○/◒/◒	○
Lawn-Boy Silver Series 10201	270		○/○	○/⊖/○	○
MTD Yard Machine 081B 115-081B000	140		○/⊖	○/○/●	⊖
Rally 1B101	130		○/◒	○/○/●	—
Poulan Pro PP722SKA	210		○/○	○/⊖/⊖	○
Signature 2000 37086 1	140		○/⊖	○/○/●	⊖
Lawn Chief 63 D	200		○/○	○/◒/●	○
Murray 20221X92 2	100		○/○	⊖/●/●	—
MTD Yard Machine 031A 115-031A000	130		○/●	○/◒/◒	—
Dynamark 20211X18	100		○/○	⊖/●/●	—
Vulcan 90-9520	*99		○/◒	○/●/○	—
Craftsman (Sears) 38271	180		○/○	○/◒/●	⊖
Atlas A2031 D	*150		○/○	◒/●/●	—
Rally 3P209	150		○/◒	○/○/⊖	○
Garden Pride 30-9522	*189		○/○	○/◒/◒	○
Murray Convertible Mulcher 22276	190		⊖/○	○/●/●	⊖
Dynamark 22255X18	*139		⊖/○	○/●/●	⊖
Murray 22265	120		⊖/○	○/●/●	⊖
Wheeler WB20 D	*140		○/○	◒/●/●	—
PUSH-TYPE (REAR-BAG)					
Murray Mark IV 2nOne 21678X92 2	*175		⊖/○	○/◒/⊜	⊖
Poulan Pro PP835SKA	250		○/○	○/○/○	○
Dynamark 21665X18	169		⊖/○	⊖/◒/○	○
Murray 21665	160		⊖/○	⊖/●/○	⊖
Rally 2P379	*205		○/◒	○/○/○	○
MTD Yard Machine 410A 410A000	190		○/○	○/○/◒	○
Craftsman (Sears) 38277	240		○/⊖	○/●/○	⊖
Lawn Chief 81 D	250		○/○	○/○/●	○

1 *Sold only at Montgomery Ward.*
2 *Sold only at Walmart.*

Ratings continued ▶

Ratings continued

Brand and model	Price	Score	Bagging	Discharging	Mulching
		P F G VG E	EVEN/VAC.	EVEN/SPREAD/TALL	SPREAD
SELF-PROPELLED					
Snapper XP21500 ⓓ	$585		⊜/⊜	⊜/⊖/⊜	⊜
John Deere 14SB BM18271	660		⊜/⊜	⊖/○/⊜	⊖
Kubota W5021SC	760		⊖/⊖	⊖/⊖/⊜	⊖
Ariens LM216SP 911052 ⓢ	670		⊖/⊖	⊖/⊖/○	⊖
Honda Harmony HRM215SXA	630		⊖/⊖	○/○/◒	⊖
Toro 20465	640		⊖/⊖	⊖/◒/◒	⊖

MODEL DETAILS

Want to know more about a rated model? They're listed here alphabetically.

Ariens LM216SP 911052 ⓢ	Same blade for mulching. Easy to U-turn, maneuver, attach and empty bag, adjust handle height. Primer bulb for starting. Front wheels swivel. Deadman stops engine. Many clippings dropped after mulching. No throttle control. Remove front wheels to change cutting height. Mulching kit, and chute included. Infinitely variable drive speed (1.0-3.8 mph). **Successor:** LM226SP 911070.
Atlas A2031 ⓓ	Easy to push, U-turn, maneuver. Discharge chute clogged. Hard to attach bag. **Similar:** Wheeler WE20.
Craftsman (Sears) 38271	Same blade for mulching. Narrower than most. Many clippings dropped after mulching. More noisy. Throttle on engine. Hard to adjust handle height. Mulching kit included.
Craftsman (Sears) 38274	Same blade for mulching. Easy to U-turn. Narrower than most. Discharge chute clogged. Throttle on engine. Frame blocks rear cutting-height levers. Hard to adjust handle height. Mulching kit included.
Craftsman (Sears) 38277	Same blade for mulching. Many clippings dropped after mulching. Throttle on engine. Hard to adjust handle height. Mulching kit included.
Cub Cadet 072R	Few clippings dropped after mulching. Easy to push, maneuver. Low emissions, mfr. says. Hard to attach bag, adjust handle height. Mulching kit, $24.
Dynamark 20211X18	Easy to push. Low emissions, mfr. says. Unbolt wheels to change cutting height. **Similar:** Murray 20211, 20213.
Dynamark 21665X18	Bag easy to empty. Mulching kit, $25.
Dynamark 22255X18	Discharge chute clogged. Hard to maneuver. Mulching kit, $15.
Garden Pride 30-9522	Hard to attach bag. Mulching kit, $17.
Honda Harmony HRM215SXA	Easy to attach and empty bag, adjust handle height. Overhead-valve engine. Discharge chute clogged. Hard to maneuver, work deadman control. Mulching kit included. Catcher optional. 2 drive speeds (1.6-2.7 mph).
John Deere 14SB BM18271	Same blade for mulching. Easy to attach bag, adjust handle height. Overhead-valve engine. More noisy. Shift action vague. Throttle lever too close to shift lever. Catcher optional. 5 drive speeds (1.2-3.9 mph). Mulching kit, $26.
Kubota W5021SC	Few clippings dropped after mulching. Less noisy. Easy to attach bag, adjust handle height. Overhead-valve engine. Shift lever poorly located. 2 drive speeds (1.8-2.6 mph). Mulching kit, $40.

Lawn Chief 60 Ⓓ	Same blade for mulching. Easy to push, attach bag, adjust handle height. Many clippings dropped after mulching. Mulching kit, $10.
Lawn Chief 63 Ⓓ	Same blade for mulching. Easy to attach bag, adjust handle height. Many clippings dropped after mulching. Mulching kit, $10.
Lawn Chief 81 Ⓓ	Same blade for mulching. Hard to attach bag. Mulching kit included.
Lawn-Boy Silver Series 10201	Same blade for mulching. Easy to U-turn, adjust handle height. Narrower than most. Hard to pull starter cord. Two-stroke engine may emit more pollution than four-stroke. Discharge chute clogged. Bagging chute blocks cutting-height lever. Mulching kit included.
Lawn-Boy Silver Series 10202	Same blade for mulching. Easy to U-turn, adjust handle height. Narrower than most. Discharge chute clogged. Bagging chute blocks cutting-height lever. Mulching kit included.
MTD Yard Machine 031A 115-031A000	Easy to push, maneuver. No throttle control. Hard to attach bag. Unbolt wheels to change cutting height.
MTD Yard Machine 072A 115-072A000	Few clippings after mulching. Easy to push, maneuver. Hard to attach bag, adjust handle height. Mulching kit, $40.
MTD Yard Machine 081B 115-081B000	Hard to attach bag, adjust handle height. Mulching kit, $40.
MTD Yard Machine 410A 410A000	Easy to maneuver. Many clippings dropped after mulching. Discharge chute clogged. Hard to attach bag, adjust handle height. Mulching kit, $40.
Murray 20221X92	Easy to push. No throttle control. Unbolt wheels to change cutting height. **Similar:** Murray 20211, 20213.
Murray 21665	Bag easy to empty. Mulching kit, $25. **Similar:** Murray 21667.
Murray 22265	Discharge chute clogged. Hard to maneuver. Mulching kit, $15.
Murray Convertible Mulcher 22276	Same blade for mulching. Discharge chute clogged. Hard to maneuver. Mulching kit included.
Murray Mark IV 2nOne 21678X92	Same blade for mulching. Easy to empty bag. Mulching kit included.
Poulan Pro PP722SKA	Many clippings dropped after mulching. Hard to attach bag, adjust handle height. Mulching kit, $36.
Poulan Pro PP835SKA	Few clippings dropped after mulching. Easy to maneuver. Hard to adjust handle height. Mulching kit, $36.
Rally 1B101	Easy to push, U-turn. Narrower than most. No throttle control. Hard to attach bag. Unbolt wheels to change cutting height. **Similar:** Rally 1N101.
Rally 2P379	Few clippings dropped after mulching. Easy to maneuver. More noisy. Hard to adjust handle height. Mulching kit included.
Rally 3P209	Many clippings after mulching. Hard to attach bag, assemble. Mulching kit, $30.
Signature 2000 37086	Low emissions, mfr. says. More noisy. Hard to attach bag, adjust handle height. Mulching kit, $30.
Snapper XP21500 Ⓓ	Few clippings dropped after mulching. Easy to attach and empty bag, adjust handle height. Low emissions, mfr. says. Deadman stops engine. More noisy. 6 drive speeds (1.5-3.9 mph). Mulching kit, $40.

Ratings continued ▶

Ratings continued

Toro 20465	Same blade for mulching. Easy to: empty bag, adjust handle height. Overhead-valve engine. Hard to maneuver, U-turn. Deadman/clutch lever inconvenient. Shift action vague. Catcher optional. 3 drive speeds (1.8-3.6 mph). Mulching kit included.
Vulcan 90-9520	Easy to push, U-turn, maneuver. Discharge chute clogged. Hard to attach bag. Unbolt wheels to change cutting height.
Wheeler WB20 Ⓓ	Easy to push, U-turn, maneuver. Discharge chute clogged. Hard to attach bag. Unbolt wheels to change cutting height.
White SD050 115-050A190 Ⓓ	Easy to push, maneuver. Many clippings dropped after mulching. No throttle control. Hard to attach bag. Unbolt wheels to change cutting height. Mulching kit, $26.
White SD074 115-074A190 Ⓓ	Easy to push, maneuver. Hard to attach bag, adjust handle height. Mulching kit, $26.
Yard-Man 106C 115-106C401 Ⓓ	Same blade for mulching. Easy to push, maneuver. Narrower than most. Hard to adjust handle height. Mulching kit included.

RATINGS MANUAL REEL MOWERS

See report, page 198. Last time rated in Consumer Reports: June 1995.

Brand-name recommendations: Consider the top-rated Agri-Fab, $185, especially if your lawn is level. The mower is fairly heavy, but its no-contact blades make it very smooth and quiet. Its cutting height can be set, without tools, as high as 2½ inches, which should reduce the need to water your lawn. Half the price and nearly as good is the Great States Deluxe Light 815-18.

For most manual mowers, expect: ■ Effective cutting only when grass is 3 in. or less. ■ Max. cutting height of 1½ in. ■ Inability to cut closer than 3 in. from obstacles. ■ Grass-catcher to be impractical. ■ Plastic wheels and gearing. ■ Handle that rests at an uncomfortably low position.

Notes on the table: Price is the estimated average, based on a national survey. A catcher costs $15 to $50 extra. **Score** is based mainly on mowing performance but includes handling and convenience as well. **Swath** is the width of the path cut by the mower. **Even** is an estimate of how close the mower came to producing a smooth, carpetlike cut. **Push** is the relative effort needed to push the mower on level ground. **Model availability:** Ⓓ means discontinued.

Within type, listed in order of performance and convenience

E ⊜ VG ⊖ G ○ F ◒ P ●

Brand and model	Price	Score (P F G VG E)	Swath	Even.	Push	Comments
Agri-Fab Silent Reel 45-0193	$185		18 in.	○	◒	Quiet. Handle-rest positions stable and convenient. Bedknife and cutting height easy to adjust. Metal reel gears. Hard to push in tough grass. Catcher slipped off mower during sharp turns.
Great States Deluxe Light 815-18 [1]	90		18	○	○	Comfortable handle. Pulling backward makes chassis rear up when catcher clips are on.
Craftsman (Sears) 3764 [D]	90		18	○	○	Comfortable handle. Pulling backward makes chassis rear up when catcher clips are on.
Great States Full Feature Standard 414-16 [1]	83		16	○	○	Comfortable handle. Cast-iron drive wheels and metal gears. Cutting height inconvenient to adjust.
Great States Full Feature Light 415-16 [1]	85		16	○	○	Comfortable handle. Pulling backward makes chassis rear up when catcher clips are on. Cutting height inconvenient to adjust.
Great States Promotional 204-14 [1]	66		14	◒	⊖	Pulling backward makes chassis rear up. Cutting height inconvenient to adjust. Reel axle lacks ball bearings.
Great States Economy 304-14 [1]	70		14	◒	⊖	Pulling backward makes chassis rear up. Cutting height inconvenient to adjust.
Great States Standard Light 404-16 [1]	75		16	◒	○	Pulling backward makes chassis rear up when catcher clips are on. Cutting height inconvenient to adjust.
Husqvarna 5400	100		16	○	◒	Bedknife and cutting height easy to adjust. Metal reel gears. Bedknife must be tight against reel blades for best cut. Catcher slips off mower.
GMF 380 SL	68		16	◒	●	In tough grass, hard to push, and cuts unevenly. Bedknife must be tight against reel blades for best cut, but tends to loosen.
GMF 480 SE	76		16	◒	●	Handle-rest positions stable and convenient. In tough grass, hard to push and cuts unevenly. Bedknife must be tight against reel blades for best cut, but tends to loosen.

[1] *All Great States models are also available as American brand; model numbers are similar but start with 1.*

RECREATION

Cameras & lenses

Microchip-driven cameras have taken the guesswork out of photography. Even novices who don't know an f-stop from a bus stop can take sharp, professional-looking pictures.

You don't need to spend a king's ransom anymore on a fancy single-lens-reflex (SLR) model to take first-rate pictures. Today's compact 35mm cameras can be almost as versatile as SLRs—with automatic exposure, film handling, and flash control, plus a built-in zoom lens—but in a lightweight package costing hundreds less. An SLR, though, remains the choice for those who want unrestricted lens options and total control over picture taking. Even those high-tech machines are simpler to master, thanks to automated focus and exposure programs.

The move toward simplicity is evident in the popularity of low-priced, single-use 35mm cameras, the fastest growing segment of the industry. These handy pocket-sized cameras come preloaded with film. After you shoot the roll, you return the camera with film for processing.

The marketplace

Few people pay list price for camera equipment. The discount you get depends mainly on local competition, but also on the customer service and convenience a store provides. For the best prices, especially on expensive gear, check mail-order ads in newspapers and photography magazines. Mail-order houses in large cities sometimes charge as little as half of list for some brands.

Cutthroat competition, though, leads to some questionable selling tactics. Here's what to watch out for:

The classic bait-and-switch. "We're all out of that, but we have something better." Don't accept substitutes.

The "outfit" angle. An unusually low advertised price for a brand-name SLR camera might include a cheap, off-brand lens.

The tie-in. You can buy an item at its advertised price only if you buy something else—a camera case, say.

Stripping. The store removes standard equipment and then sells it back to you. Ask the dealer whether the price includes all manufacturer-supplied accessories—lens cap, case, strap, and so forth. You can call the manufacturer's customer-relations department for confirmation of what's standard and what's extra.

'Gray market' goods. These products may be identical to regular ones, but they're intended for sale in foreign markets. Since they're imported to this country by an unofficial agent of the manufacturer, you may not get the manufacturer's U.S. warranty. An "international" warranty or a camera-store warranty may require you to send the camera abroad or deal with the retailer for repairs. If a store says your sales slip is your warranty, the store, not the manufacturer, assumes responsibility for the warranty. Make sure the warranty arrangement is practical for you.

Shipping fees and returns. Goods sold by mail are often priced seductively. But a company may try to offset a good deal on equipment with outrageous shipping fees. Ask about such fees before ordering. Note, too, that mail-order companies may impose a 5- to 15-percent "restocking" fee for returned merchandise.

Extended warranties. Dealers may try to sell you an extended service contract. We don't recommend it. See page 14.

The choices

The 35mm camera has been around for more than 70 years, but its enduring popularity has more to do with practical considerations than with tradition. The 35mm format's relatively large negative—about 1x1½ inches—yields sharper enlargements than do the smaller negatives from disc and 110 cameras. And a variety of film is available in black and white and in color.

Most 35mm cameras fall into two groups: compacts, which have a built-in lens, and single-lens reflex (SLR) models, which have interchangeable lenses and special accessories that can adapt them to all photo situations. An intermediate type has a built-in zoom lens but still has an SLR viewfinder.

Compacts are by far the most popular. SLRs account for just 5 percent of sales, and the number of brands available is half what it was a decade ago. Manufacturers such as Canon, Minolta, Nikon, Olympus Pentax, and Yashica are among the leading makers of high-end compacts and SLRs. Kodak and Vivitar are the biggest-selling inexpensive compacts.

Compact 35s

▶ **Ratings on page 232.**

Their forté is convenience rather than photographic control, and prices range from about $5 to more than $400. The most basic are about the size of a bar of soap; others, with protruding zoom lenses, weigh about a pound and would strain a coat pocket.

Single-use. These inexpensive cameras have fixed focus and exposure. They come preloaded with print film, usually ISO 400 speed in 12- to 27-exposure rolls. After you shoot the roll, you send both the camera and film for processing. The camera parts are re-used or recycled, according to manufacturers.

The first of these cameras were simple box cameras with no flash. Newer versions are more compact and aim to meet various photographic needs with a flash, a panoramic or telephoto lens, or even underwater capability. All work similarly: You just point and shoot and advance the film. No exposure settings or focusing to fiddle with. Because they lack exposure meters, they're only suited for bright daylights, except for ones with flash. Prices range from $5 to $15.

Although dozens of brands of disposables are available, most carry names familiar from film boxes: Kodak, Fuji, or Konica. The cameras themselves are made overseas by independent manufacturers.

Fixed-focus. Sometimes euphemistically called "focus free," these cameras shoot through a small lens opening, which keeps anything more than a few feet away reasonably sharp. Most of these models have a moderately wide-angle 35mm field of view. Such cameras are adequate for general picture taking in bright daylight, but they may not yield proper exposure in dim light, or they may require a flash when other cameras don't. Prices range from about $25 to $60.

Auto-focus. Most compacts focus automatically. When you aim at your subject and press the shutter release partway, the camera bounces an infrared beam off the subject and tracks the angle it returns, accordingly setting the lens for one of several distance zones.

The most basic ones have a fixed focal-length lens, commonly with a focal length of 35 mm, that covers a wide enough angle of view for convenient indoor snap shooting. Many sell for less than $100.

Zoom. Some compacts have a zoom lens. Models with a medium-range zoom may cover 35 to 70 mm, useful for general photography and portraits. Price: $125 to more than $300. Zoom models extending to about 115 mm at the telephoto end allow greater magnification of distant objects.

INSTANT CAMERAS

A camera that delivers a color print moments after you snap the picture has obvious appeal. But in these days of simple and inexpensive 35mm cameras and one-hour photofinishing, there are fewer and fewer reasons to purchase an instant camera.

Polaroid, the inventor of instant cameras, sells the *Captiva* and the *Spectra*, both priced about $120. Both are basically point-and-shoot cameras that automatically adjust the lens opening, shutter speed, and flash intensity for each picture (the *Captiva's* flash always fires; the *Spectra's* can be turned off). The *Captiva* has a single-lens-reflex viewing system; the image you see in the viewfinder is pretty much what you see on the print. After you shoot the picture, the camera expels a blank that automatically develops into a color print in a few minutes.

Apart from the instant results, there's little to recommend these cameras. Both are bigger and heavier than a typical point-and-shoot camera. A 10-pack of *Captiva* film costs about $12, or $1.20 per shot. We've seen from our tests that the picture quality is inferior to what a 35mm model can do. In addition, the *Polaroid's* prints faded more rapidly than regular color prints in bright light.

Models with a long-range zoom sell for about $175 to nearly $400.

Panoramic. Some models let you take panoramic format pictures by blocking off the top and bottom part of the image. With some, you can only switch format when you load the film. Others let you switch format anytime during a roll.

Features and conveniences

Exposure. Exposure control is automatic on most compacts. A built-in light meter gauges the lighting and adjusts the aperture and shutter speed accordingly. Such a system strikes a balance between fast shutter speed (to prevent blurring of moving objects) and a small aperture (to enhance overall sharpness). Some compacts have a backlight switch or compensation control to offset a bright background, which would otherwise cause the camera to leave the main subject underexposed.

Flash. All but the cheapest compacts have a built-in electronic flash. The maximum flash range with ISO 100 film may be as little as 4 feet, but 10 to 15 feet is more common. Most compacts fire the flash automatically when the exposure system senses insufficient light. You can also use some flash units on demand—in daylight, say, for "fill" flash to lighten deep shadows on faces. Only a few warn you if you're beyond the range of the flash.

Most cameras also have some sort of way to reduce "red eye," which is caused by light reflecting off people's retinas. The various methods—moving the flash farther from the lens, pre-flashing to narrow the pupils—help but don't always totally prevent red eye.

Batteries. Most compacts use one or two lithium cells for power, particularly zoom models. Low-priced compacts usually use alkaline batteries. A few can take either. Lithium cells last longer, but cost more and are not as widely available as alkaline.

Film handling. Most compact 35s have automatic film-handling: You insert the film, extend the leader to a mark inside the camera, shut the back of the camera, and the motor automatically threads the film to the starting position. The motor also advances the film after each shot and rewinds at the end of the roll.

Most models also automatically set the appropriate film speed. Contacts in the camera read the speed from DX-code markings on the film cartridge.

Some cameras can read only the most popular speeds for color-print film, ISO 100 and 400; others read a range of speeds, from as slow as 25 up to 3200. Higher ISO numbers denote faster films, those able to work in dimmer light without flash. Make sure your camera covers the ISO speeds you want to use.

Focusing. With a fixed-focus model, a small lens aperture keeps all objects more than a few feet away reasonably sharp. But the small aperture rules out shooting in dim light unless you use flash. Auto-focus models set the lens for one of several distance zones. One zone might cover subjects 8 to 10 feet away; another, 10 to 14 feet, and so on. Some models use only two crude distance zones (near and far); others, dozens of zones. As a rule, the more zones, the better.

Models with an infinity control—to set the focus to the farthest zone—are useful for shooting through glass or past an object in the foreground that might otherwise confuse the auto-focus.

Viewfinder. Some compacts have a bright-frame viewfinder; others have a sharp edge that frames the entire image. Both kinds are easy to use, even with eyeglasses. The most basic cameras have a simple viewfinder that is less accurate and harder to use correctly. While viewfinders vary in how they deliver a view of the captured image, most we've tested have been fairly accurate.

The tests

We judge image quality with tests for sharpness and for lens shortcomings such as flare, distortion, and chromatic aberration. Tests of exposure accuracy tell how well a camera adjusts its shutter and aperture for a given scene and film. Other tests assess framing accuracy and the range and uniformity of a camera's built-in flash. We also check for light leakage.

Buying advice

Compact cameras are easy to use, and they can take sharp, well-exposed pictures.

When selecting a compact, consider the camera's size and weight. The lighter the camera, the better. Models with a zoom tend to be bulkier, but they offer flexibility impossible with a fixed focal-length lens.

Single-lens reflex cameras

SLRs give you flexibility and control. Because you see exactly what the camera sees through the picture-taking lens, you can interchange lenses to change viewpoints. Attach a super-wide-angle lens and you gain appreciable, peripheral vision, useful for panoramas or capturing groups in tight spaces. Switch to a telephoto lens and you're looking through a telescope, useful for candid shots and bringing in distant objects without having to move in closer. Or you can use a zoom lens for a range of views. Autofocus lenses can be used on such cameras and focused manually.

The choices

SLRs. The characteristic hump atop an SLR camera houses a prism mounted over a mirror, an arrangement that lets you see what the lens sees when you look through the eyepiece behind the hump. A built-in light meter evaluates what the lens takes in.

Accessories—extra lenses, filters, remote shutter release, focusing screens, and other paraphernalia—transform an interchangeable-lens SLR into a total "system." Lenses range from 180-degree-view fisheyes to 1000mm telephotos, providing perspective and magnification not possible with any compact.

So much of the camera's operation has been automated that SLRs can be as easy to use as a compact 35mm camera. Auto-focus SLR camera bodies start at about $230 but can cost well over $1200. Expect to add another $100 to $150 for a moderate-range zoom lens.

Manual-focus SLRs are still available. All the major manufacturers make a few for students and purists. Some command a premium price since they are used by professional photographers who prefer to handle focusing and exposure settings themselves. Camera bodies sell for $200 to more than $2000. General-purpose manual zooms are priced similarly to autofocus ones, but the selection may be more limited.

SLRs with non-interchangeable lenses offer less creative control than an SLR but more versatility than a compact. These cameras, promoted mainly by Olympus, have an SLR viewfinder, but they don't accept interchangeable lenses. The built-in zoom lens has a range of from 28 to 35 mm at the wide angle end to 110 to 180 mm at the tele end. Automation simplifies focusing and many other tasks.

Features and conveniences

Lenses. The lens is the key component of any camera; no amount of creativity will make up for a lens that's not sharp. The zoom has become the lens of choice: About 85 percent of SLR buyers fit their new camera body with a zoom lens, rather than the old standard 50mm lens. A moderate zoom—35 to 105 mm or so—should cover most situations.

SLR zoom lenses have improved markedly in recent years. Although image quality is still apt to drop off slightly at either extreme of the zoom range, imperfections other than distortion aren't likely to be noticeable except under high magnification.

Most SLR bodies can accept either a lens of the same brand or of an independent brand supplied to fit the same lens mount, such as Tamron, Sigma, or Vivitar. Independent brands sell for considerably less than the camera brand models. If you're considering such a lens, check whether it can do everything the camera maker's lens can in the way of automatic operation, and buy it with the proper mount for your camera.

The noninterchangeable zoom lens covers a wider range than the one on a compact camera. You see what the camera sees, just as with an interchangeable-lens SLR, but the framing may be slightly less accurate than typical of interchangeable-lens SLRs. Our tests have shown that framing errors of more than 15 percent in areas. Typically, the lenses themselves are about as good as a middling SLR zoom—very good, but not exceptional.

Exposure controls. Automated SLRs typically offer as many as four ways to control exposure—program, aperture priority, shutter priority, and manual.

Most models have a program mode, which selects both the size of the lens opening (the aperture or f-stop) and shutter speed (how long the shutter remains open to expose the film to light).

Aperture-priority exposure mode lets you manipulate the f-stop while the camera automatically chooses a compatible shutter speed. In shutter-priority mode, the opposite happens. Most exposure controls can also be operated by hand. Typically, an LED indicator in the viewfinder confirms when you've set a suitable f-stop/shutter-speed combination for a given lighting situation and film speed.

Manual exposure control is useful for special effects—when you want to silhouette a model, say, or blur a moving object.

A built-in light meter determines the proper exposure. Some allow you to choose from several metering modes. Center-weighted metering monitors the entire frame but emphasizes the center. Spot metering reads only the light near the center of the frame. Multipattern metering divides the frame into several segments, and selects an exposure setting based on an evaluation of the readings.

Automatic film-handling. Like compact cameras, most SLRs use a tiny motor to load, advance, and rewind the film. Cameras with an auto-winder generally let you fire off two, three, even four shots per second. That's handy for following fast-paced action, but you can go through a roll of film in no time. Automatic DX-code readers set the film speed.

Focusing. With manual-focus SLRs, you turn a lens collar to align halves of a split image in the viewfinder—or to sharpen a shimmering microprism image in a ring around the split-image circle in the viewfinder's center.

Some people, particularly those with poor eyesight, may find manual focusing difficult. Fortunately, technology has solved the focusing problem. At the press of a button, computer chips and a miniature motor focus the lens in a split second, generally with pinpoint precision.

But auto-focusing isn't foolproof, especially in scenes with repetitive graphic patterns or low contrast, or in very dim light.

In some versions, a red beam shines on the subject to help the auto-focus work in low light. Autofocus SLR viewfinders usually lack the microprism and split-image rangefinder focusing aids. So if you must focus by hand, you have to judge when the image on the ground-glass screen looks sharpest, not an easy trick, particularly in dim light.

Flash. Because they're closer to the lens, the built-in electronic flashes found on many current SLR cameras, like those on compacts, are more prone to red eye than the separate flash units that were formerly used. As a result, they have red-eye reduction aids like those on compacts.

Most built-in flashes aren't as powerful as the typical separate flash unit. Add-on flash units provide more power and versatility but are, of course, less convenient. They range from small models with limited features that sell for about $50 to high-powered "potato mashers"—side-mounted, handheld units popular among wedding photographers—that are loaded with features and sell for more than $400.

Your camera's "dedicated" flash capability tends to limit the choices. In general, one camera maker's flash units won't work with another makers camera. Independent manufacturers produce "dedicated" units whose metal contact points match those on the camera's "hot shoe," but such flashes may or may not be as versatile as the camera maker's flash. Check carefully before you buy.

The more expensive flash units are generally more powerful and have special capabilities. They calculate exposure automatically with your camera's metering system or let you override the setting manually. They can rotate or tilt toward the ceiling for "bounce" flash, a more pleasing effect than head-on flash. Other accessories let you diffuse light to soften shadows about faces. Because they're offset farther from the camera lens, flash units that mount atop a camera are much less prone to red eye than built-in flashes.

Buying advice

If your interest in photography is casual, you'll probably be satisfied with an inexpensive compact camera. But if you have the time and interest to invest in photography as a hobby, consider an SLR. The wide selection of lenses and the freedom to handle various exposure situations can enhance your enjoyment of the hobby.

A manual-focus camera takes a little practice to master and it's a little less convenient for routine picture-taking, but it's the traditional way to learn photography. While there are few such models left to choose from, a few bargains still exist, like the venerable *Pentax K-1000*.

Fully automated models are easy to operate in their basic mode, but automation entails complication. Cameras with lots of buttons for various functions can be hard to use. Keep the manual handy for quick reference. Automated models are totally dependent on batteries, so it's important to keep a spare set on hand.

Consider the weight of the camera and the lens—lugging extra ounces around your neck or in your camera bag quickly takes a toll.

If you buy a zoom lens, find out how close an object it can focus on. Some zooms let you come to within a foot; others make you stand well back. Stay away from power zooms that automatically select the focal length. If you consider one, at least make sure it can be turned off.

Whatever camera you're interested in, hold it to your eye and check its viewfinder, controls, grip, and balance. That's the only way to tell whether you'll be comfortable taking pictures with it. Some camera stores rent cameras. If you're not sure which model you prefer, consider renting one or more.

Exercise equipment

You can start an indoor fitness program by buying an expensive machine. But simple equipment like free weights, steps, slide boards, jump ropes, and exercise videos can also help you strengthen muscles and get the pulse going. More expensive equipment may be easier to use, but in weighing price against benefits, remember: A machine you don't enjoy is likely to turn into an expensive coat rack.

Indoor workouts have many advantages. You can exercise when bad weather might otherwise encourage sloth. You can do it at any hour. There's no risk of injury from potholes, dogs, muggers, or cars. Terrain doesn't determine the effort you must expend. You can stop anytime without being miles from home. And you may be able to get a better workout, since a good machine makes it easy to maintain your aerobic target heart rate (220 minus your age; then 60 to 85 percent of that number).

Exercise machines vary in the kind of workout they give. Some machines work just the lower body. Others can improve the tone of the whole body. But if your reason for exercising is to achieve cardiovascular fitness, the kind of exercise matters less than the effort you put into it. Choose a machine that suits your personal preference and your pocketbook.

Before settling on any machine, ask your doctor whether you're making the right choice. A rowing machine, for example, might aggravate some back problems; a stair climber, some knee problems. The obese should probably avoid running on a treadmill, although walking is okay.

Home gyms

Home gyms are essentially scaled down versions of the multistation gyms in health clubs. The price may be as low as $200 or as high as $1500, compared with the $3000 that health-club models start at.

A typical home gym consists of a metal frame, one or more padded seats or benches, and various levers, handles, or straps attached to a device that resists your pushing and pulling. Standard exercises include butterfly, triceps extension, pull-down, shoulder press, leg extension, leg curl, chest press, and biceps curl.

Most models offer various pushing, pulling, and lifting exercises that work your muscles. Add resistance, and you build muscle; add repetitions, and you tone the muscle without bulking up.

You can also use a home gym to get the heart-strengthening benefits of mild aerobic exercise by "circuit training"—performing different strengthening exercises in rapid succession continuously for 20 minutes or more. (On some gyms, though, you have to pause so long between exercises to reconfigure the equipment that the aerobic value is diminished.)

Some of the major manufacturers of home gyms are big names in home exercise or sports equipment—DP, BMI, Nordic Track, ProForm, and Schwinn. Others concentrate mainly in bodybuilding gear—Soloflex, Trimax, and Weider.

The choices

We tested home gyms with a variety of mechanisms for providing resistance and found that all were capable of giving an effective workout. No type of machine was inherently better than the others, but each had a distinctive feel that may or may not appeal to you.

Gyms use one of the following methods to apply resistance:

Weights. You lift a stack of heavy metal plates via a cable-and-pulley system. The more plates you engage with a pin, the higher the resistance—which remains essentially constant throughout the range of your motion.

Rubber bands. Thick rubber bands are attached at one end to the lever you push or pull and at the other end to the gym's frame. You vary resistance, which increases as the bands stretch, by using bands of different thickness or by using more or fewer bands.

Flexible rods. You pull a cable that's attached to one or more springy plastic rods, mounted to the gym's frame. As with bands, you vary resistance by the number and thickness of rods. Resistance increases as the rods bend.

Shock absorbers. Hydraulic or pneumatic cylinders that look and work like a car's shock absorbers resist your pushing or pulling. Changing the point at which the shocks are attached to the lever you push and pull changes the resistance.

Centrifugal brakes. Brake shoes mounted on a spring-loaded pulley in a case lined with friction pads generate friction when you move a lever connected to the pulley. You can increase the amount of resistance by pulling harder on the lever and by rerouting the cable that connects the lever to the pulley.

Features and conveniences

A gym with plenty of padding keeps hard plastic and metal parts from hurting you while you exercise. A minimum of setup and changing makes it easier to do circuit training. A wide range of resistance settings keeps you from outgrowing the gym before you've attained the body you want. We've found that changing resistance is easiest on gyms with weight stacks, flexible rods, and elastic bands.

CHEAP WAYS TO GET AN AEROBIC WORKOUT

Steps. These are sturdy plastic platforms whose height is sometimes adjustable. To exercise, you step on and off, over the top, and across the sides of the platform. Workout videos add music and low-impact aerobic exercise routines. Price: $20 to $75.

Slide board. This is, essentially, a slippery floor mat, about 5x2 feet, with a bumper on each side. Smooth-fabric booties slip over your athletic shoes for easy sliding. You push off from bumper to bumper in a side-to-side skating motion—an excellent aerobic exercise and a low-impact workout that tones the thigh muscles. Check with your doctor, though, if you have back or knee problems. Price: $20 to $75.

Buying advice

Spending more buys a better gym: heavier-gauge metal, more durable moving parts, finer adjustment of resistance, and a wider range of resistance settings. More expensive gyms are also likely to offer more stations so more than one person can work out simultaneously.

If possible, try out a gym before you buy. Look for a design that lets you get in to and out of the stations easily and that feels comfortable while you're there. Watch out for models with potential pinch points or with stations that can't be adjusted to suit your height.

Also, make sure the machine will fit into

the space available—some are quite bulky.

Finally, consider assembly and moving. Home gyms tend to be harder to assemble than other exercise machines. One of the gyms we tested took us five hours to assemble. Also, gyms can be very heavy, which complicates getting one home and moving it once it's set up.

Treadmills

Using a treadmill is as easy as taking a walk, minus the fresh air and scenery. Most home models let you adjust the incline to increase the strenuousness of the workout. Some go fast enough to let you run. A monitor may tell you the speed, distance covered, time elapsed, and such things as heart rate and calories burned.

Walking at a brisk pace, jogging, and running are excellent aerobic conditioners and improve lower-body muscle tone. Increasing the incline can boost the exertion level of even a 3-mph walk to an aerobic level for a fit athlete. Some treadmills come with arms that let you get an upper-body workout at the same time. Perhaps the strongest advantage of treadmills, though, is that people use them: Research has shown that of all types of exercise equipment, treadmills are the most likely to be used by all household members.

A moderate-priced treadmill costs from about $400 to $800. You can also buy a bare-bones machine for as little as $300 or a high-end one for $2200. Health-club models range from $3500 to $8900. DP, Proform, Vitamaster, and Sears (made by Proform) are some of the brands with a selection of inexpensive models. Precor, Lifestride, and Trotter make expensive versions. For more money, you get a more substantial machine with a wider and longer walking surface and the capacity to go faster.

The choices

Motorized. Treadmills with higher horsepower generally have a higher maximum speed and are better able to handle heavy users. But you can't rely on manufacturers' horsepower ratings; many use different standards of measurement. Plus, treadmills with large walking belt areas or higher friction components need more horsepower. Any unit can handle walking, but jogging requires a treadmill that goes at least 5 mph. Most motors are DC-powered, which allows for smooth starts and stops.

Manual. The belt is driven by the user's walking motion. These machines tend to be less expensive and less fancy, with a walking surface that is too short to accommodate a running stride.

Features and conveniences

A long, wide belt and partial handrails make for comfortable, safe use. Handlebars are nice if you want to exercise your upper body while you walk, but they're less practical for a jogger.

Some motorized treadmills have pre-programmed workouts that automatically change the incline to simulate running or walking on hills and in valleys. Inclines are typically more convenient to adjust on motorized machines.

Buying advice

Check that the treadmill's walking surface is large enough to accommodate your full stride. If possible, try a model out in the store. See that the controls are easy to reach and use, and the monitor has the functions you want. Take special note of warranty details—motorized treadmills are more likely to break down than other types of exercise machines.

Ski machines

▶ Ratings on page 230.

To simulate the scissoring stride of cross-country skiing, ski machines have long, narrow boards or sliding foot pads that glide back and forth over rollers. In place of ski poles, the machines use either a rope-and-pulley arrangement, poles mounted on a swivel, or telescoping poles. Since you move both arms and legs, a ski machine gives you something many other exercise machines can't—a workout for the upper as well as lower body. And it doesn't subject the joints to jarring impacts, so the risk of injury is low.

Besides market leader Nordic Track, which was the first to sell ski machines in the mid-1970s, manufacturers include such names as Fitness Quest, Precor, Tunturi, DP, Vitamaster, and CSA—all companies that make other home exercise equipment as well.

Basic ski machines start at $200, but some go as high as $2000. Health-club versions are priced from $2100 to $3500.

The choices

Independent leg-motion. This approach uses unlinked skis or foot platforms, which are hard to master initially. But once you learn the technique, an independent model can give you a more vigorous workout than a dependent model. It also lets you use a more natural leg motion, more akin to cross-country skiing. Typically, independent models are more expensive than those with dependent leg-motion.

Dependent leg-motion. With the linked foot platforms on a dependent model, when the right leg slides forward, the left leg slides backward and vice versa. That keeps a beginner's legs from sliding too far, but it also forces the user into a stiff shuffle. Friction pads or straps in some dependent models provide resistance but don't mimic the feel of snow; other dependent models provide no leg resistance.

Features and conveniences

A machine with variable incline increases the workout for the front thigh muscles. A monitor with a liquid-crystal display (LCD) may show one function—distance, say, or time or speed—or scan through the displays. A readout of your heart rate helps you maintain an effective level of exertion. Some machines have indexed resistance settings so you can repeat the difficulty level from one workout to the next. That's especially helpful if others will be using the machine at a different level. Most machines fold up compactly for storage in a closet. Wheels make them easy to move.

The tests

We put the machines through miles of simulated skiing, judging each machine's range of exercise intensity, comfort for people of different sizes, rigidity and stability, and usefulness of the electronic monitor. A robot testing device gives the machines a year's worth of regular workouts in less than 100 hours. We also check safety and convenience.

Buying advice

Try a ski machine a couple of times at a health club before you buy one. If you decide to buy, you should probably choose a model with independent "skis." They take a bit longer to master, but they offer a smoother, more skilike gait and let even very fit people work out at heart-strengthening intensity. Consider a dependent model if your level of fitness is low or if you find independent leg-motion intimidating.

Exercise bikes

Cycling on a stationary bicycle can be an excellent, low-impact aerobic conditioner. To avoid knee strain, choose a bike you can adjust so your leg extends almost completely when the pedal is down. For a fuller workout, you can buy a "dual action" bike whose handlebars you push and pull while you pedal.

Exercise bikes are made by bicycle companies such as Schwinn and Roadmaster, as well as companies known in the exercise-equipment field, like DP, Vitamaster, Tunturi, and Proform. Lifecycle and Precor make high-end home models and health-club models.

Home-exercise bikes cost between $200 and $800. The models in health clubs cost $2000 to $7500. You can also make your own stationary bike by attaching a regular bike to a stand, which typically costs less than $200.

The choices

Upright models. This type resembles a regular bicycle. Some models have computerized controls that store preset programs of varying resistance. Many offer "dual action"—moving handlebars as well as pedals.

Recumbent models. With this type, you sit back in a chairlike seat and stretch your legs out in front of you. This position works the hamstring muscles more than an upright bike and is helpful for people who find a bicycle seat uncomfortable.

Features and conveniences

Most exercise bikes work against resistance provided by a flywheel or fan system. A few bikes provide electromagnetic resistance. On flywheel models, you can increase resistance without increasing speed. On fan-only models, the primary way to intensify the workout is to pedal faster.

Typically, controls—mechanical or electronic—keep track of speed, "distance," and elapsed time. Many models come with preprogrammed courses and effort levels. Pedal straps let your legs work on the upstroke as well as the downstroke.

Buying advice

Make sure the bike isn't too small or too large for you. The flywheel or fan should turn smoothly. The seat should be well padded and comfortably shaped. Seat height and resistance level should be easy to adjust. The bike should feel solid, and pedaling should be smooth.

Expect to spend at least $200. Bikes that cost less than that are likely to be flimsy.

Stair climbers

A stair climber gives you the aerobic workout of climbing an endless flight of stairs. The machines are fairly easy on the joints, though they may not be a good choice for people with knee problems. Basically, most stair climbers are levers attached to a resistance device. Your legs pump the levers, and a monitor displays steps-per-minute, elapsed time, and calories burned.

DP, Sears, Tunturi, Precor, Proform, and CSA are popular brands of home models. Prices range from about $200 to $2000.

The choices

Step mechanism. Many stair climbers have steps that move independently of each other. Others have steps that are linked—as one goes down, the other goes up. Independent steps are harder to use than dependent ones, but they give you a better workout and allow a more natural movement. Some high-end models have a switch that lets you use either mode.

Style. Steppers mimic the action of climbing stairs. Dual-action steppers exercise the arms as well as the legs. Ladders have steps for the feet and rungs for the hands and mimic the action of climbing a ladder.

Features and conveniences

On some machines, programming changes resistance automatically at preset intervals. Also helpful is an indexed resistance knob you can adjust while exercising.

Some high-end machines come with heart-rate monitors. Some measure your aerobic capacity: You step for a few minutes and take your pulse, then punch in the reading, your age, weight, and sex, and the machine tells you how fit you are.

Buying advice

Try out a machine. It should be stable and provide a smooth pedal motion. Look for comfortable pedals and handles positioned for good posture. Monitors should be clear and versatile but not complicated, and resistance should be easy to adjust.

Bicycles

In simpler times, you chose a two-wheeler based on how many speeds it had. Today, advances in design have greatly increased and complicated the choices. About half of all bicycles sold now are "mountain bikes," designed to handle rugged terrain but more often seen around town. The other hot bike category is the "hybrid," a relative newcomer designed for both on- and off-road riding.

You can spend $300 to $400 on high-end bicycles with names like Schwinn, Trek, Cannondale, and Specialized at specialty bike stores or chains. Bicycles for $200 and less, by Huffy, Murray, and Roadmaster, are available at discount stores, warehouse clubs, and mass merchandisers like Walmart, Kmart, and Toys 'R' Us. General sporting goods stores like Sports Authority and outdoor equipment stores like REI also sell bikes.

The choices

Mountain bike. This is the most popular type sold in the U.S.—partly, no doubt, because of the comfortable ride its cushiony tires and wide saddle provide. Still, with its fat, knobby tires, 26-inch-diameter wheels, upright handlebars, sturdy frame, and perhaps shock-absorbing suspension, a mountain bike may competently handle dirt, but can feel a bit ungainly on pavement. Mountain bikes sell for $150 to $1000 or more, but our tests show that light-duty bikes that are safe and satisfying to ride on pavement and tame dirt paths start at $200. Models better suited for rougher terrain start at $450. Cheaper bikes may be unsafe; those with steel wheel rims have braked poorly in wet conditions in our wet-braking tests.

Road bike. This lightweight bike, designed for racing or touring, comes with thin tires and "drop" handlebars. It's fast and efficient, but casual riders may find it's not particularly comfortable and drop bars are not suited to riding on rough surfaces. Although road bikes are the best choice if you ride fast or far, they continue to decline in popularity. Price: about $400 to $3000.

Hybrid bike. Introduced in the late 1980s, the hybrid marked the return of the casual recreational bike. This type typically uses a lightweight frame, upright handlebars, and moderately knobby tires, marrying a mountain bike's strength and comfort with a road bike's efficiency. A hybrid is a good choice for commuters or for those who occasionally travel a rough dirt road. Low-end hybrids tend to be pricier (and better quality) than low-end mountain or road bikes. Price: about $250 to $700.

Features and conveniences

Frame. The diamond-shaped chassis determines whether a bike will fit you, and how it'll perform. Frames are made from a variety of materials: heavy steel on the cheapest bikes; lightweight aluminum, carbon fiber, or exotic metals like titanium or super-high-strength steel on the most expensive. Lower-priced steel mountain and hybrid bikes weigh 30 pounds or more; an aluminum, titanium, or carbon-fiber road bike can weigh less than 18 pounds.

Handlebars. Their size and shape influence riding efficiency and comfort. The bent-over posture required by the drop handlebars on road bikes and some performance-oriented mountain bikes reduces wind resistance and shocks from bumps and improves handling. That posture also lets muscles work efficiently. For casual rides on pavement, however, an upright position may be more comfortable.

Gears. Most mountain bikes and hybrids have 18 to 24 speeds to let you pedal comfortably despite changes in road slope. Off-road, we consider 18 speeds the minimum needed. On pavement, 12 or 14 may be enough. More important than the number of gears are a bike's highest and lowest gear numbers. These sum up the interaction between the front and rear gears and the wheel size. The lowest should be 22 or less for challenging off-road use, 40 or less for a general-use road bike. High gears around 100 help speed you downhill.

Shifters. Old-fashioned "friction" shifters discouraged would-be riders because they were difficult to master until you developed a feel for them. "Indexed" shifters make changing gears far easier. There are at least three types: a grip shift, which is a collar encircling each handlebar; a lever underneath each handlebar; and a thumb shifter, which is a lever above each handlebar. Some above-the-bar levers offer indexing with a friction mode in case the derailleurs are thrown out of alignment by a fall.

Brakes. Road bikes typically use caliper brakes. Most mountain and hybrid bikes have cantilever brakes mounted directly on the front wheel fork and the seat stay. According to our tests, both types can stop a bike quickly and controllably. If you ride in wet weather, avoid wheels with steel rims. In wet-brake tests, they required a greater distance to stop than did wheels with aluminum rims.

Tires. The tires are a major factor in how the bike handles. They can easily be changed to suit the terrain. For rough trails, a mountain bike's tires should have widely spaced knobs for traction. Such tires produce a "buzzy" ride on pavement, though. Hybrid-bike tires have smaller and closer-spaced knobs and sometimes a ridge down the middle. That reduces off-road traction but also reduces rolling resistance on pavement. Road-bike tires are smooth or have a fine tread.

Saddle. Look for one that's comfortable, but remember that saddles are easy to change—don't let a poor one stop you from buying an otherwise good bike. Some manufacturers claim that seats filled with gel reduce shock and vibration. But testers of both sexes found that the shape of the seat is the most important criteria for comfortable riding.

Buying advice

Bicycle models and components change every fall, but the basics of a good bike remain the same. In September, the previous year's model may prove a good buy, with no compromise in performance or features. Concentrate on the frame and wheels; many other bike parts can easily be changed by the dealer free or for a small service charge and the difference in the price of the components.

Narrow the field by selecting among bikes with frames that fit you. To find the right size, straddle the top tube with both feet flat on the floor. Allow three inches of clearance between the top tube and crotch for mountain bikes, two inches for hybrids, and one inch for road bikes. We recommend that women as well as men buy a "man's" bike, with a straight top tube, if they intend to ride more than just casually.

For convenience, consider buying your bike at a store that's close to home and that appears to offer good after-sales service. Such a store is also more likely to fit the bike correctly to your size, or to change a shifter or saddle, possibly at no charge. If the store allows, before you buy: Ride the bike over varying terrain to check its handling, make sure that your posture and the saddle feel comfortable, and that the brakes respond evenly, without grabbing, as you increase pressure.

RATINGS SKI MACHINES

▶ **See report, page 226.** Last time rated in Consumer Reports: September 1994.

Brand-name recommendations: The independent NordicTrack Pro, $600, is our top-rated model: It's sturdy, operates smoothly, has plenty of useful features, and should stand up to heavy use. The NordicTrack Challenger, nearly as good at $340, is A Best Buy. The Challenger lacks an incline adjustment. Among dependent machines, consider the Vitamaster Northern Trails 83, $300. It's a hybrid, letting you switch between dependent and independent leg motion. Used as an independent, it was just so-so; but as a dependent, it was best in the class.

For the typical ski machine, expect: ■ Electronic monitor with various readouts. ■ Skiing motion from skis or foot platforms riding on rollers or wheels. ■ Friction or flywheel/friction system for resistance. ■ Cord and pulley or poles for arm movement. ■ Unit that folds up. **A choice you'll have to make:** ■ Dependent or independent leg motion.

Notes on the table: Price is the estimated average, based on a national survey. For mail-order models, shipping is extra. **Maximum exercise** indicates the intensity of aerobic exercise each machine can provide. **Fit** assesses the ergonomics of each machine—how well it positions users of various sizes. **Life** scores reflect durability after a mechanical exerciser put each model through a year's worth of use. **Rigidity** is how sturdy each machine feels in use. **Model availability:** Ⓓ means model is discontinued.

Within type, listed in order of performance and durability

E = Excellent, VG = Very good, G = Good, F = Fair, P = Poor

Brand and model	Price	Overall score (P F G VG E)	Max. exercise	Fit	Life	Rigidity
INDEPENDENT LEG-MOTION						
NordicTrack Pro [1]	$600		E	E	E	G
Precor 515E [D]	649		E	E	VG	VG
NordicTrack Challenger, **A BEST BUY** [1]	340		E	E	E	G
NordicSport World Class Ski [1] [D]	770		VG	E	VG	G
Tunturi XC560 SkiFit [D]	649		VG	VG	G	E
Vitamaster Northern Trails 83 (convertible to dependent)	300		VG	VG	F	G
DEPENDENT LEG-MOTION						
Fitness Master FM340 [D]	400		G	G	VG	VG
CSA Alpine XC E382	193		F	F	VG	G
CSA Alpine XC E272	100		F	F	G	F

[1] *Sold mainly by mail order; phone no.: 800 328-5888.*

MODEL DETAILS

Want to know more about a rated model? They're listed here alphabetically.

CSA Alpine XC E272	Independent arm-motion with poles. Quiet. No leg resistance; very low arm resistance. Foot pads make user's feet unsteady. Difficult assembly.
CSA Alpine XC E382	Dependent arm-motion with ropes. No leg resistance. Abdominal pad forces user into awkward position. Foot pads scrape track for heavy users. Difficult assembly. Doesn't fold up.
Fitness Master FM340 [D]	Independent arm-motion with poles. Friction leg resistance. Wheels for moving.
NordicTrack Challenger, **A BEST BUY**	Dependent arm-motion with ropes. Indexed leg resistance. Abdominal pad hard to adjust. Friction/flywheel leg resistance. Feet can bump resistance unit. Detachable skis can hit or trip passerby. Noisy.
NordicTrack Pro	Dependent arm-motion with ropes. Indexed arm and leg resistance. Adjustable incline. Adjustable abdominal pad. Friction/flywheel leg resistance. Wheels for moving. Monitor shows heart rate. Feet can bump resistance unit. Detachable skis can hit or trip passerby. Noisy.
NordicSport World Class Ski [D]	Dependent arm-motion with ropes. Indexed arm and leg resistance. Adjustable incline. Adjustable abdominal pad. Electromagnetic flywheel leg resistance. Monitors show heart rate. Max. leg resistance too low for strong users (but varied among samples). Settings to simulate skiing on different snow. Feet can bump resistance unit. Detachable skis can hit or trip passerby. Noisy.
Precor 515E [D]	Dependent arm-motion with ropes. Indexed leg resistance. Adjustable incline. Adjustable abdominal pad. Friction/flywheeel leg resistance. Base can fall off incline mount during intense workout. Movement rougher after durability tests. Doesn't fold up.

Ratings continued ▶

Ratings continued

Tunturi XC560 SkiFit [D]	Independent arm-motion with poles. Adjustable abdominal pad. Electromagnetic flywheel resistance. Wheels for moving. Max. leg resistance too low for strong users. Movement rougher after durability tests.
Vitamaster Northern Trails 83 (convertible to dependent)	Independent arm-motion with poles. Indexed arm and leg resistance. Adjustable incline. Adjustable abdominal pad (but doesn't stay put). Friction/flywheel leg resistance. Wheels for moving. Max. leg resistance too low for strong users. Movement rougher after durability tests. Noisy.

RATINGS COMPACT 35MM CAMERAS

▶ **See report, page 217.** Last time rated in Consumer Reports: December 1994.

Brand-name recommendations: The Canon Sure Shot Z115 ($320) and the Fuji Discovery 1000 Zoom ($155) lead their respective groups of zoom-lens cameras. (The Nikon is no longer available.) The Canon's longer lens gives you greater flexibility to compose photos. Both offer autofocus, autoexposure, good film handling, and a decent range for their flash. Among nonzoom cameras, consider the Yashica T4 ($170). It's truly compact, with autoexposure and multibeam autofocus. It delivered high image quality, and takes respectable close-ups. The Kodak Star 835AF (successor Star AutoFocus), $60, is a good, no-frills basic camera with autofocus but no automatic exposure system.

For the typical compact 35mm camera, expect: ■ Automatic film loading, advancing, and rewinding. ■ DX film-speed sensing, to set exposure system automatically. ■ Ability to take a range of film speeds, including at least ISO 100 and 400 films. ■ Built-in electronic flash. ■ Some provision to reduce "red eye" in flash pictures. ■ Neck or wrist strap, built-in lens cover, and self-timer.

Notes on the table: Price is the estimated national average, based on a 1994 survey. If camera is available without a date/time imprinter, we give price without that feature. * means price paid. **Overall score** is based largely on factors affecting picture quality. Differences of less than 20 points on the 0 to 100 scale aren't very significant. **Small field** gives the width of the smallest subject that fills the frame at near focus, for the tightest possible close-up with regular focusing. **Image quality** covers sharpness, flare, distortion, and chromatic aberration. **Low light** shows the cameras' ability to cope in dim light without flash or a tripod. **Flash** range gives the farthest distance at which the flash is effective for ISO 100 print film at wide-angle setting; range decreases at telephoto setting. **Framing** gives the percent of the printed image area in a photo that shows in the viewfinder. **Model availability:** [D] means model is discontinued. [S] means model is replaced, according to the manufacturer; successor model is noted in Details. New model was not tested; it may or may not perform similarly. Features may vary.

Within type, listed in order of performance and features

Key: E = Excellent (⊜), VG = Very good (⊖), G = Good (○), F = Fair (◒), P = Poor (●)

Brand and model	Price	Overall score (P F G VG E)	Weight	Small field	Image quality	Low light	Flash range	Framing
LONG ZOOM RANGE, AUTO EXPOSURE (ZOOM RANGE APPROX. 38 TO 110 mm)								
Nikon Zoom-Touch 800 [D]	$360		20 oz.	7 in.	VG	VG	22ft.	92
Canon Sure Shot Z115	320		13	4	E	VG	17	83
Olympus Infinity SuperZoom 3000 [S]	265		13	4	VG	VG	18	73
Pentax IQ Zoom 115-S	280		11	7	VG	VG	14	83
Minolta Freedom Zoom 105EX [S]	255		11	5	VG	VG	15	88
Samsung Maxima Zoom 105	185		15	10	VG	VG	17	71
Ricoh Shotmaster Zoom 105 Plus [D]	290		16	5	G	VG	17	73
MEDIUM ZOOM RANGE, AUTO EXPOSURE (ZOOM RANGE APPROX. 35 TO 70 mm)								
Fuji Discovery 1000 Zoom	155		14	8	E	VG	17	82
Vivitar 500PZ Series 1	135		9	9	E	VG	14	71
Leica Mini Zoom 18005	*340		10	9	E	VG	15	78
Canon Sure Shot Z85 [D]	210		12	7	VG	VG	12	81
Rollei Prego Zoom AF	*300		9	10	VG	VG	13	85
Canon Sure Shot Zoom Max [S]	170		11	8	VG	VG	12	88
Minolta Freedom Zoom 70EX	*190		10	9	VG	VG	14	89
Samsung Maxima AF Slim Zoom	180		9	10	VG	VG	13	85
Ricoh RZ-800	165		14	7	VG	VG	13	77
Konica Big Mini Zoom BM-510Z	*160		10	13	VG	VG	14	84
Pentax IQ Zoom 735 [S]	160		9	9	VG	VG	13	74
Nikon Lite Touch Zoom	190		8	9	VG	G	12	91
Yashica EZ Zoom 70	180		14	7	G	VG	15	84
Olympus Infinity Stylus Zoom	185		9	9	G	VG	12	77
SINGLE-FOCAL-LENGTH LENS, AUTO EXPOSURE (FOCAL LENGTH APPROX. 35 mm)								
Yashica T4	170		7	11	E	VG	10	80
Nikon Lite-Touch	135		6	14	VG	VG	10	79
Olympus Infinity Mini	105		9	16	VG	E	10	84
Konica Big Mini BM-300	*130		7	11	E	VG	10	80
Pentax PC-500	75		9	43	E	G	9	75
Kodak Cameo Motordrive [1] [S]	60		7	45	E	G	9	85 [2]
Nikon One-Touch 300	90		9	17	VG	VG	12	87

[1] *Fixed-focus.* [2] *Optically simple viewfinder makes it hard to frame shots accurately.*

Ratings continued ▶

Ratings continued

Brand and model	Price	Overall score	Weight	Small field	Image quality	Low light	Flash range	Framing
		P F G VG E						
SINGLE-FOCAL-LENGTH LENS, AUTO EXPOSURE *continued*								
Canon Sure Shot M [D]	$100		7	16	⊖	⊖	11	81
Yashica Imagination Micro AF	75		7	45	⊖	○	8	79
Pentax PC-700	85		8	43	⊜	○	8	80
Canon Snappy LX [1]	60		10	55	⊖	○	10	83
Samsung Maxima 40R [D]	*80		8	36	⊖	○	8	71
Ricoh AF-77	85		10	37	○	⊖	7	79
SINGLE-FOCAL-LENGTH LENS, FIXED EXPOSURE (FOCAL LENGTH APPROX. 35 mm)								
Kodak Star 835AF [S]	60		11	45	⊖	◒	11	82
Olympus Trip AF S-2 [S]	65		9	45	⊖	◒	12	83
Pentax PC-100 [1]	45		9	55	⊜	◒	11	99 [2]
Fuji Discovery 80 Plus [S]	55		11	47	○	◒	10	69
Ansco Vision Mini FF [1] [D]	*25		7	45	○	◒	5	90 [2]
Polaroid Focus Free [1]	25		7	43	○	○	9	96 [2]
Polaroid Autofocus	35		7	43	○	◒	9	90 [2]
Vivitar Vista Tele Motor [1]	30		9	32	○	◒	4	73 [2]
Fuji DL-25 Plus [1] [S]	55		10	55	○	◒	11	77 [2]
Nikon Nice-Touch 2 [1]	45		9	18	○	◒	9	96 [2]
Vivitar C35R [D]	45		10	55	◒	○	4	59
Ricoh YF-20 Super [1]	45		9	36	○	◒	9	74 [2]
Olympus Trip 100 [1] [S]	45		9	47	○	◒	10	97 [2]
Keystone Easy Shot 590PD AF	25		8	43	○	◒	9	73 [2]

[1] *Fixed-focus.* [2] *Optically simple viewfinder makes it hard to frame shots accurately.*

MODEL DETAILS

Want to know more about a rated model? They're listed here alphabetically.

Ansco Vision Mini FF [D]	Will take pictures whether flash is ready or not.
Canon Snappy LX	—
Canon Sure Shot M [D]	Autofocus warns when subject is too close. Multibeam autofocus—convenient for subjects off-center. More compact than most.
Canon Sure Shot Z115	Autofocus warns when subject is too close. Multibeam autofocus—convenient for subjects off-center. Autofocus system failed more than most in tricky situations.
Canon Sure Shot Z85 [D]	Autofocus warns when subject is too close. Multibeam autofocus—convenient for subjects off-center. Camera better suited than most for slides.

Model	Comments
Canon Sure Shot Zoom Max Ⓢ	Autofocus warns when subject is too close. Multibeam autofocus—convenient for subjects off-center. Camera better suited than most for slides. **Successor:** Sure Shot 70 Zoom.
Fuji Discovery 80 Plus Ⓢ	Will take pictures whether flash is ready or not. **Successor:** Discovery 90.
Fuji Discovery 1000 Zoom	Accepts panoramic insert. Autofocus warns when subject is too close or is too far for flash. Multibeam autofocus—convenient for subjects off-center. Camera better suited than most for slides.
Fuji DL-25 Plus Ⓢ	Will take pictures whether flash is ready or not. Film-handling fairly cumbersome. **Successor:** Smart Shot Supreme.
Keystone Easy Shot 590PD AF	May leak light, if left in very bright light. Will take pictures whether flash is ready or not. Film-handling fairly cumbersome. Camera does not turn itself off automatically, if idle.
Kodak Cameo Motordrive Ⓢ	More compact than most. **Successor:** Cameo Motor EX.
Kodak Star 835AF Ⓢ	Lacks red-eye reduction capability. Will take pictures whether flash is ready or not. **Successor:** Star Auto-Focus (has red-eye reduction).
Konica Big Mini BM-300	Autofocus warns when subject is too close. Camera better suited than most for slides. May leak light, if left in very bright light. More compact than most. Camera does not turn itself off automatically, if idle.
Konica Big Mini Zoom BM-510Z	Autofocus warns when subject is too close. May leak light, if left in very bright light.
Leica Mini Zoom 18005	Accepts panoramic insert. Autofocus warns when subject is too close. Camera better suited than most for slides. Easy to take multiple shots unintentionally, if shutter is pressed too long.
Minolta Freedom Zoom 70EX	Autofocus warns when subject is too close. Autofocus system failed more than most in tricky situations. Camera better suited than most for slides.
Minolta Freedom Zoom 105EX Ⓢ	Autofocus warns when subject is too close. **Successor:** Freedom Zoom Supreme.
Nikon Lite Touch Zoom	Has a Panorama switch; can mix regular shots and panoramas on the same roll. More compact than most.
Nikon Lite-Touch	Focal length 28 mm. Has a Panorama switch; can mix regular shots and panoramas on the same roll. Camera better suited than most for slides. More compact than most.
Nikon Nice-Touch 2	Lacks red-eye reduction capability. Manual flash. Will take pictures whether flash is ready or not.
Nikon One-Touch 300	—
Nikon Zoom-Touch 800 Ⓓ	Autofocus warns when subject is too close or is too far for flash. Camera better suited than most for slides.
Olympus Infinity Mini	Autofocus warns when subject is too close. More compact than most. Sealed against rain, moisture.
Olympus Infinity Stylus Zoom	Autofocus warns when subject is too close. Autofocus system failed more than most in tricky situations. More compact than most. Sealed against rain, moisture.
Olympus Infinity SuperZoom 3000 Ⓢ	Autofocus warns when subject is too close. Multibeam autofocus—convenient for subjects off-center. May leak light, if left in very bright light. Sealed against rain, moisture. **Successor:** 3500.
Olympus Trip 100 Ⓢ	Lacks red-eye reduction capability. Manual flash. Will take pictures whether flash is ready or not. **Successor:** Trip 200 (has red-eye reduction).

Ratings continued ▶

Ratings continued

Olympus Trip 100 [S]	Lacks red-eye reduction capability. Manual flash. Will take pictures whether flash is ready or not. **Successor:** Trip 200 (has red-eye reduction).
Olympus Trip AF S-2 [S]	Lacks red-eye reduction capability. Will take pictures whether flash is ready or not. Camera does not turn itself off automatically, if idle. **Successor:** Trip AF-21.
Pentax IQ Zoom 115-S	Has a Panorama switch; can mix regular shots and panoramas on the same roll. Autofocus warns when subject is too close. Autofocus system failed more than most in tricky situations. Camera better suited than most for slides.
Pentax IQ Zoom 735 [S]	Autofocus warns when subject is too close. Camera better suited than most for slides. **Successor:** IQ Zoom EZEY.
Pentax PC-100	May leak light, if left in very bright light. Lacks red-eye reduction capability. Manual flash. Will take pictures whether flash is ready or not. Film-handling fairly cumbersome.
Pentax PC-500	May leak light, if left in very bright light.
Pentax PC-700	May leak light, if left in very bright light. Sealed against rain, moisture.
Polaroid Autofocus	Will take pictures whether flash is ready or not.
Polaroid Focus Free	Will take pictures whether flash is ready or not.
Ricoh AF-77	Has a Panorama switch; can mix regular shots and panoramas on the same roll.
Ricoh RZ-800	Autofocus warns when subject is too close. Multibeam autofocus—convenient for subjects off-center. Camera better suited than most for slides.
Ricoh Shotmaster Zoom 105 Plus [D]	Accepts panoramic insert. Autofocus warns when subject is too close. Camera better suited than most for slides.
Ricoh YF-20 Super	Lacks red-eye reduction capability. Manual flash. Will take pictures whether flash is ready or not.
Rollei Prego Zoom AF	Autofocus warns when subject is too close. Camera better suited than most for slides. More compact than most.
Samsung Maxima 40R [D]	Accepts panoramic insert. Will take pictures whether flash is ready or not.
Samsung Maxima AF Slim Zoom	Autofocus warns when subject is too close. Camera better suited than most for slides.
Samsung Maxima Zoom 105	Autofocus warns when subject is too close. Camera better suited than most for slides.
Vivitar 500PZ Series 1	Accepts panoramic insert. Autofocus warns when subject is too close. Camera better suited than most for slides.
Vivitar C35R [D]	Autofocus system failed more than most in tricky situations. Will take pictures whether flash is ready or not. Camera does not turn itself off automatically, if idle.
Vivitar Vista Tele Motor	Focal lengths 35, 70 mm. Accepts panoramic insert. Will take pictures whether flash is ready or not.
Yashica EZ Zoom 70	Autofocus warns when subject is too close. Autofocus system failed more than most in tricky situations. Camera better suited than most for slides.
Yashica Imagination Micro AF	—
Yashica T4	Autofocus warns when subject is too close. Multibeam autofocus—convenient for subjects off-center. Camera better suited than most for slides. May

FAMILY & HEALTH

Condoms

Condoms, say public-health doctors, offer the best protection against AIDS and other sexually transmitted diseases, barring abstinence or confining your relations to one uninfected partner.

The condom shields the wearer's penis from vaginal, cervical, oral, or rectal secretions. At the same time, it protects his partner from potentially infectious semen and lesions on the penis. The U.S. Food and Drug Administration considers the evidence that latex condoms stop germs so solid, it allows condom boxes to list the diseases condoms can avert: syphilis, gonorrhea, chlamydia, herpes, and AIDS.

As a contraceptive, the condom's failure rate is about 12 percent, somewhat worse than birth-control pills but better than the diaphragm. If couples used condoms consistently and correctly, however, the condom's failure rate can be as low as 2 or 3 percent, or less. If used consistently, condoms combined with vaginal spermicide may further reduce the failure rate.

Condoms are now widely available. They're sold in supermarkets and advertised on cable TV and in magazines. The biggest manufacturers—Carter-Wallace (Trojans) and Schmid Laboratories (Ramses, Sheik)—offer a variety of textures, colors, shapes, lubricants, and sizes.

How well a condom works depends in large part on the users—inexperienced users are more likely than others to break

USING CONDOMS WISELY

Breakage can result from misuse, so it's important to learn how to use condoms properly. The key points:

■ Open a packet only when you're ready to use the condom—and open it gently, to avoid tearing the contents.

■ Don the condom when the penis is erect, before sexual contact. If there is a reservoir tip, squeeze out the air (if there's no tip, leave a half-inch space at the end for semen, and squeeze out the air).

■ Unroll the condom down the length of the penis (uncircumcised men should first pull back the foreskin).

■ Right after ejaculation, grasp the condom firmly at the ring and withdraw the penis before losing the erection, to prevent spillage.

■ Use a new condom for each act of intercourse—never reuse condoms.

■ If you want more lubrication, use only water-based lubricants, like surgical jelly. Oil-based lubricants rapidly weaken latex.

■ If a condom fails, both partners should wash genitals with soap and water. Urinating may also help to avoid infections. If breakage is discovered after ejaculation, having a separate spermicide handy to apply quickly may help.

condoms through misuse. But some breakage may be due to real differences among the brands and varieties.

The choices

Latex. Most condoms are made of latex. Nonlatex condoms—skin or plastic—are available for people who find that latex irritates their skin. (Skin reactions, however, can also stem from lubricants, spermicides, and processing chemicals, so try switching brands before considering nonlatex condoms.)

Skin condoms. These are made from a natural pouch in lambs' intestines, a strong membrane that may also enhance sensitivity. While they are effective for contraception, they may not curb disease. They contain microscopic pores that are big enough to pass syphilis and gonorrhea bacteria and the AIDS and herpes viruses, but small enough to block sperm cells (which are giants on the microscopic scale). "Skins" are expensive—several times the cost of latex condoms.

Plastic condoms. These clear polyurethane condoms are intended only for people sensitized to latex condoms. Although polyurethane is said to be stronger than latex, early research indicates there may be a higher breakage rate than latex condoms. The polyurethane condom is very thin and costs somewhat more than a conventional condom.

Features and conveniences

Strength. Products that did especially well in our air-burst test were *Excita Extra Ultra Ribbed*, the domestic version of *Sheik Elite*, and *Ramses Extra Ribbed*. But label claims for extra strength didn't always correlate with our test findings. Products like *Lifestyle Extra Strength* or *Trojan Extra Strength* did not do as well.

Sensitivity. Some brands claim to enhance sensitivity, but it's not clear how—whether through a snug fit, a loose fit, thinness, or texture. As a group, condoms that promise sensitivity aren't especially thin, by our measurements. Very thin products, however, had some of the lowest scores (least safe) in our air-burst tests.

Whether sensitivity is an issue for you or not, try the top-rated *Excita Extra Ultra Ribbed,* which did well in our air-burst test, before trying thinner ones.

Size. Width and length vary. A condom

that's too tight can be uncomfortable, and it may be more likely to break; one that's too loose can slip off. The two condoms tested that claim to be larger than average—*Trojan-Enz Large* and *Trojan Magnum*—were, in fact, longer and wider.

Lubricant. Many condoms come coated with various preparations that feel like oil, glycerine, or surgical jelly. Using a lubricated condom is largely a matter of preference. If couples wish to add their own lubricant, they should be certain not to use petroleum- or mineral-oil-based products, which rapidly weaken latex.

Spermicide. Many condoms' lubricants include a small amount of nonoxynol-9, a spermicide that promises extra protection. In the quantity used, it's a promise without much proof behind it.

Age. Rubber weakens with age, so avoid condoms that are more than a few years old. Unfortunately, different brands date their products differently.

Buying advice

Strength is what our tests gauged and what really counts. As our tests show, claims on packages aren't a reliable guide. Products that did especially well in our airburst tests were *Excita Extra Ultra Ribbed*, the domestic version of *Sheik Elite*, and *Ramses Extra Ribbed*.

Avoid older, and possibly weaker, products by checking the date codes on boxes or shopping at a store with lots of turnover.

Beyond that, choosing a condom is largely a matter of preference—for shape, texture, lubrication, even color.

Blood-pressure monitors

▶ **Ratings on page 247.**

For people diagnosed with hypertension, a home blood-pressure monitor can show whether drugs or alternatives to drug therapy—diet and exercise—are working. For those taking medication, home monitoring can help the doctor determine the lowest effective dose. A home monitor also allows patients to chart their progress, a strong incentive to stay with a treatment regimen.

For those reasons, the National High Blood Pressure Education Program, a Government-sponsored effort, endorses home blood-pressure monitoring for people with hypertension, provided the monitoring is done in collaboration with a physician and not used for self-diagnosis.

Most monitors still rely on a cuff wrapped around the upper arm. A few, aiming at more convenience, take measurements from the wrist or even a finger. Prices start at $15 for a simple mechanical gauge to $200 for an electronic model with digital readout. Major brands: Omron, Sunbeam, Sunmark, Lumiscope, and Marshall.

Drugstores used to be the main source of medical products such as monitors. Now you buy them from mass-merchandisers like Kmart and Walmart.

The choices

Blood pressure, the force exerted by blood against the arteries, is expressed as a measure of height: the number of millimeters of mercury that arterial pressure can push up a vertical tube ("mmHg").

Traditionally, a nurse or doctor wraps an inflatable cuff around the upper arm and inflates the cuff by pumping a rubber bulb. The cuff acts as a tourniquet, cutting off blood flow below the elbow. While gradually deflating the cuff, the nurse listens with a stethoscope to the arm's main artery.

As blood returns to the lower arm, sounds just audible in the artery mark "systolic" pressure (the heart's pumping pressure) and "diastolic" pressure (the lower pressure occurring between heartbeats). Blood pressure is given as the systolic figure over the diastolic—120/80 mmHg, for example, is more or less "normal."

To take your own pressure at home with a mechanical aneroid monitor, you do all the things the doctor or nurse does. Other monitors use electronic circuitry to simplify matters.

Mechanical aneroid models. These are simple mechanical monitors that use a round-dial pressure gauge. This type of monitor is the least expensive, and it can be quite accurate—if it's properly used. But therein lies the drawback: You must don the cuff, pump it up, and listen carefully to the artery as you turn a valve to slowly deflate the cuff while keeping an eye on the gauge's needle.

The procedure for this kind of monitor takes practice. It also demands good eyesight and hearing and the dexterity to do things with one hand.

Electronic models. These are easier to use and more popular than the mechanical type. Typically, an electronic model senses pressure changes in the cuff—no stethoscope is needed—and passes data to a microchip in its console, which calculates the systolic and diastolic pressures and flashes on a digital display. The circuitry sometimes errs, but an error code or an outlandish reading clearly flags mistakes. Some models have a reading-error indicator.

The lowest-priced electronic monitors (about $20) require you to pump up the cuff, but deflation is automatic. More expensive models ($50 to $200) inflate and deflate the cuff automatically.

Finger- and the relatively new wrist-cuff models, which also use automatic circuitry, are still on the pricy side. Electronic finger monitors, for instance, cost from $70 to $180; wrist models, $100 to $160.

Features and conveniences

Cuffs. Most arm models have a D-ring that makes them easier to don with only one hand. The ends of some cuffs, however, can easily slip out of a D-ring unless they have a retaining device sewn in. Also, cuffs made of limp material are hard to handle. With a mechanical gauge, look for a stethoscope sensor sewn into the cuff, rather than a separate sensor that you must hold in place.

With any arm model, you need the right-sized cuff to get accurate readings. People whose upper arms are larger than 13 inches around may have to special order a larger one.

Valves. A sturdy metal deflation valve that works smoothly is easier to control than a plastic valve.

Fuzzy logic. Models with this pricy feature claim to improve accuracy by controlling the cuff inflation.

Displays. Electronic models vary in the clarity of their displays. Look for big, clear numbers that you can read easily.

The tests

We test products like these with a panel of staffers. A nurse takes a simultaneous reading with a professional type mercury gauge and stethoscope. By taking multiple readings at each sitting and comparing the nurse's figures with each monitor's, we're able to assess each model's variability from one reading to another. We also judge ease of use. In the lab, we measure the accuracy of the readout.

Buying advice

Mechanical blood-pressure monitors offer the best value if you're comfortable with them. They cost as little as $15 and, if correctly used, generally proved more accurate in our tests than electronic arm models. With practice, most people should have little trouble using them.

The best electronic arm models approach the accuracy of the better mechanical units. Models that inflate automatically are easier to use but also the more expensive. Semi-automatic models—those that must be inflated manually but that deflate automatically—cost about half what a fully automatic monitor costs.

We do not recommend electronic finger models. All the models we tested in 1992 demonstrated great variability in their readings. The reason is anatomical: Fingers are farther from the heart than arms, and there's a greater likelihood of false readings. Wrist monitors may or may not have the same problem. We haven't tested them.

Eyeglasses

There are more sources for glasses than ever before—including optical "superstores" and general warehouse stores. There is also a wide range of frames from which to choose—including retro-looking plastic, space-age titanium, and a bevy of designers and celebrities willing to put their name on your spectacles. And there are more choices of the lenses themselves—special-purpose materials, lens coatings, and optical designs.

Superstores are eyeglass emporiums where you can have your eyes tested, choose from thousands of frames and, perhaps, have glasses made within an hour. Warehouse stores take the no-frills, mass-merchandising approach—a limited frame selection, perhaps no optometrist on duty, and no in-store lab. In between are various chains and private practitioners—optometrists and ophthalmologists—who examine eyes and sell glasses.

A few years ago, a survey of CONSUMER REPORTS subscribers who had recently bought spectacles found that those whose glasses came from a private practitioner tended to be the most satisfied. Some optical chains earned marks nearly as high. Readers had slightly fewer problems with glasses bought from doctors than with those from the typical chain, however. And more readers felt they got a more thorough exam from private eye-doctors than from those associated with the chains.

The choices

Besides selecting a frame, you'll need to decide about the lens material, special coatings, and optical design.

Lens materials. Glass resists scratching better than some plastic, but it's heavier and more likely to shatter.

Regular plastic (a resin called CR-39) is the most widely used lens material; it is half the weight of glass and more impact-resistant. High-index plastic lenses are about 30 percent thinner than CR-39—a boon for the very nearsighted, whose lenses can be thick at the edges. But they can cost twice the price of regular plastic, or more. Polycarbonate lenses are about as thin as high-index lenses, but very impact-resistant—a plus for people who play sports. They cost about a third more than regular plastic lenses.

Lens treatments. Scratch protection is for anyone who handles glasses roughly. Polycarbonate lenses are inherently soft and so typically come with this coating; you shouldn't pay extra for it. UV protection comes from a gray dye that shields wearers' eyes from ultraviolet rays associated with the formation of cataracts. UV protection is most important for those who spend lots of time in strong sunlight. It's built into high-index and polycarbonate lenses, so don't pay extra. (An appropriate tint for a good pair of sunglasses shields eyes from invisible UV rays and strong visible light.) Antireflection coating cuts some internal reflections in glasses, a benefit for night drivers and computer users alike.

Lens designs. Bifocals come in two traditional styles: flat-top, which has a small field at the bottom for close-up work, and Franklin style, where the entire bottom half of the lens is for near vision, giving good wide-field vision for close work.

Progressive lenses ("no line bifocals") gradually change lens power to give a continuous range of clear vision as eyes move from the top of the lens (distance vision) to the bottom (close); the middle of the lens covers an arm's-length range, especially good for computer users. Progressive lenses take some getting used to, however, and the lenses cost about twice as much as regular bifocals.

Fitting frames

Good eyeglass-fit is crucial to good vision. Here are some guidelines:

- Lenses must be positioned properly in frames—with optical centers directly over pupils—to prevent eyestrain and headaches.
- Avoid oversized frames. They can add weight, distort vision, catch glare, and cost more than regular-sized lenses.
- Temple pieces should not pinch or touch the head until they reach the tops of the ears. The sides should be long enough to wrap behind the ears, and positioned at a level above or below the pupils to avoid blocking peripheral vision. Spring hinges can prevent a frame's sides from bowing outward over time.
- The bridge should not be too tight or too wobbly for the nose. Soft silicon pads are comfortable and less likely than hard plastic to let glasses slip as you perspire.
- If you or your children play sports, get special sports frames, which resemble goggles. They're stronger and have no hinges or bridge that can snap and injure the eyes. Make sure the lenses are polycarbonate.

Buying advice

Doctors not connected with a store have little incentive to prescribe new glasses—they're more likely to be objective. More important, with a prescription in hand, you can shop around. The markup on eyeglasses—sometimes threefold or more—leaves lots of room for price-cutting and bargains. You might save half or even more.

The readers surveyed were generally happiest with the places that charged the least. Some chains offer prices for complete eyeglasses; others charge à la carte for frames, lenses, and lens options, including surcharges for stronger prescriptions, oversized lenses, and coatings.

Strollers

▶ Ratings on page 249.

Stroller styles change, but what new moms and dads seek does not: a compact, comfortable stroller that is convenient and safe. Strollers sell anywhere from $20 to $400, but the typical stroller retails for about $80.

Some three dozen brands are on the market. The largest brands are Century, Graco, Kolcraft, and Peg Perego.

The choices

Carriage/stroller. This type is the most versatile, since you can use it for a newborn and again when the child gets older. The seatback reclines enough to let the baby sleep. Raising the seatback and flipping the handle converts the lie-down carriage into a sitting-position stroller.

Lightweight umbrella strollers, usually the cheapest type, fold into a neat package that you can carry over your arm like an umbrella.

Two-seater. This type holds two stroller-age children. A tandem, which seats one child behind the other, is easier to maneuver than wide side-by-side models but not a easy to fold.

Jogger style. Instead of four sets of small wheels, these models sport three bicycle-type wheels. The design lets a jogger push the stroller relatively easily over rough terrain.

Car-seat combination. This newest type lets you move between sidewalk and car without lifting the baby from the seat.

Safety

Considering that 14,000 children are injured annually in strollers (usually from falls), safety is paramount. Federal regulations bar sharp edges and points, and small parts that a child could swallow or inhale. (A voluntary industry standard that most makers follow supplements Government rules. Strollers that meet the supplementary standards carry a sticker or tag stating "compliance with ASTM F-833.")

Important safety issues include:

Stability. A wide stroller with a long wheelbase and low-mounted seat set deep within the stroller frame is least likely to tip over. With the baby seated, the stroller should resist tipping as you press down lightly on the handle.

Frame. Frames should be checked for hazards like sharp edges and protrusions, gaps between metal parts, uncovered coil springs, small holes, X-joints (where the frame tubes come together, scissors-style), and loose plastic caps on frame ends.

Restraints. The safety belt should wrap snugly and completely around the baby's waist, and there should be a crotch strap. We favor a T-shaped buckle attached to the strap, and waist belts that snap easily into the buckle. (Note that belts that thread through a buckle can slip, if they're improperly threaded.)

Brakes. Most models have a foot-operated lock or bar to lock the rear wheels. A sprocket lock for both rear wheels is more effective than a bar pressing against the tires, we've found in our tests. Carriage/strollers should have two sets of brakes, so you can conveniently engage the brakes regardless of the position of the handle.

Latches. Some latches that lock the stroller in the open position and hold handles in place are safer than others. Avoid models with metal slip rings (mostly on older strollers) that slide over the frame's tubing that can slip, allowing the stroller to collapse. Spring-loaded latches to hold the stroller open have largely replaced slip rings. Safest are strollers that have a lock plus a safety catch, which requires two distinct actions to fold it.

Leg openings. Infants seven months or younger may creep backward while sleeping, slipping through the leg openings and trapping their head. Some carriage/strollers let you close off the leg opening between the hand-rest bar and the front edge of the seat, blocking that danger zone.

Features and conveniences

Heavy, large carriage/strollers tend to offer more creature comforts than do lightweight models. Look for the following on any stroller:

Support. Adequate padding over metal parts; shock absorption to cushion the bumps; and a seat wide and deep enough for large babies. The backrest should have a rigid insert for good back support.

Cleaning. Padding that's removable and machine-washable.

Open/close. The stroller should be easy to open and fold—ideally, with one hand. It should be easy to steer and push, whether you're short or tall.

Maneuverability. Test-drive the stroller: Be sure it can go straight without veering when you use one hand.

Handle. It should be at or slightly below your waist level. An adjustable handle is convenient but uncommon. The plastic or rubbery covering on the handle grip should be securely attached.

Wheels. The larger the wheels, the more easily the stroller will handle curbs and uneven terrain. Strollers with swivel wheels and locks to stop the front wheels from veering on soft ground make maneuvering easier.

The tests

Our tests address convenience, durability, and safety. We check for movable and removable parts capable of injuring children. We also examine brakes, safety belts, and the stroller's stability and sturdiness.

Buying advice

Look for sturdy models that meet the voluntary industry safety standards (those with the ASTM F-833 sticker or tag). Carriage/strollers typically offer more versatility and comforts than do umbrella models. If you have two stroller-age children, choose a tandem; it's easier to maneuver than the side-by-side design.

Child safety seats

▶ **Ratings on page 251.**

The right safety seat goes a long way toward making your child safe. Despite Government standards, though, not all safety seats may provide adequate protection in a crash, as our tests have shown. When we crash-tested 25 safety seats, three failed: two infant seats, the *Century 590* and the *Evenflo On My Way 206,* and one convertible seat, the *Kolcraft Traveler 700.* We rated those three Not Acceptable. The *Evenflo* and *Kolcraft* have been recalled, see page 339.

Those companies make other models that passed our tests without problem. Indeed, Century and Evenflo are the two biggest-selling brands, followed by Kolcraft, Gerry, and Cosco.

The choices

Infant seats. These seats for babies consist of a carrier and a V-shaped harness. A few come with a base that is installed with the vehicle's safety belt and remains in the car. The carrier snaps into and out of the base. Infant seats are installed in a semireclined position that faces rear to help support the baby's head, neck, and back. Two of the Not Acceptable models, the *Century 590* and the *Evenflo On My Way 206,* are infant models. The *Century* failed when used with the base, the *Evenflo* when used without the base.

Infant seats made through the end of 1995 are labeled for use with babies up to 20 pounds. Seats manufactured after that may be labeled for use with babies up to 22 pounds, the weight of a typical 1-year old. In judging fit, it's important to remember that the baby's head must be completely contained within the carrier.

Convertible seats. These are designed for use with both babies and small children. For babies up to 1-year old, convertible seats are installed in the rear-facing position (many babies outgrow an infant seat before they reach age 1, but they still require the extra support and protection of the rear-facing installation). For children up to about 40 pounds, the seat can be installed facing forward. The Not Acceptable *Kolcraft Traveler 700* passed the crash tests in the rear-facing position but failed in the forward position.

Booster seats. These are for children who are too big for a convertible seat but too small to safely use a vehicle's safety belts. There are two basic designs: high-back and no-back. Both come with a removable shield. High-back boosters used with the harness or shield are best for younger children who may not remain seated unless confined. Older children, who understand the importance of buckling up, do best when boosted by either design, without the shield, so they fit the vehicle's safety belts.

Built-in seats. Some GM, Ford, Chrysler, and Volvo models offer an optional safety seat built into the vehicle's seat. Built-ins are suitable for children over 1 year and 20 pounds. Built-ins avoid the problems associated with safety-seat installation and provide added security, because they can't dislodge in a crash and they place the child farther away from the front seat, reducing the risk of head injury.

OWNERS OF CENTURY 590, EVENFLO 206, OR KOLCRAFT 700 SEATS

With *Evenflo On My Way 206* infant seats made between May 7, 1994, and May 31, 1995, install the base in the car and leave it there: With this model, crash protection is inadequate when the carrier is installed without its base. Call 800 225-3056 for information about the seat's recall.

It's safe to use the *Kolcraft Traveler 700* as an infant seat in the rear-facing position. When it's time to put it in the forward-facing position for a small child, the seat should be replaced with a different model. Call 800 453-7673 for information about the recall. Seats affected by the recall were made after November 1, 1994.

If you have the *Century 590* infant seat, throw the base away and install just the carrier in the vehicle. The seat is safe used that way. As we were going to press, NHTSA was investigating the safety of this model.

Features and conveniences

Harness. Convertible seats offer three types of harnesses. The *five-point harness,* consisting of two shoulder straps, two leg straps, and a crotch strap, provides the best upper torso protection for all children and the best fit for infants. It's easy to buckle and unbuckle, but the straps can get in the way when seating the child.

The *T-shield* harness consists of a plastic yoke that draws the shoulder straps over the child and buckles to the seat at the crotch. It provides good protection and is easy to use. But it's not suitable for an infant if the child's head doesn't clear the shield.

An *overhead-shield* harness has a padded, traylike shield that swings down over the child's head. It's generally easy to use, but the shield may block your view of the buckle. The design doesn't protect against head injury as well as the other types and, like the T-shield, it isn't suitable for a baby if the child's head doesn't clear the shield.

Installation. Problems can be caused by the design of the vehicle and its safety belts or by the design of the safety seat itself. Deeply contoured seats or bucket seats tend to make safety seats hard to install. If the car's rear seat is elevated in the center, which is usually the safest place to install a safety seat, a safety seat can wobble and slide.

Safety-belts can sometimes create a problem for installing a safety seat. In many vehicles, the center rear seat has a lap belt that may be too short to encompass a sizable safety seat. In some cars, the distance between the belt anchors may be too narrow to fit a safety seat.

According to new Federal regulations, all cars built since September 1995 must secure a child safety seat without any locking clips. Many lap-and-shoulder belts in older cars, however, need a locking clip. Some vehicles require a supplemental buckle or a replacement belt to secure a safety seat.

Never put an infant seat in the front-passenger seat if the seat is equipped with an air bag. For installation instructions specific to the seat you bought, refer to the section on installation in the car's owner's manual as well as the instructions that come with the safety seat. If the information in either manual isn't clear, call the automaker, the safety-seat manufacturer, or both.

The tests

We use "sled tests" that simulate a 30-mph head-on crash into a fixed barrier. Following manufacturers' instructions, we install each safety seat securely on an automobile seat attached to a test sled, then harness a crash-test dummy snugly into the seat. High-speed cameras track the movement of the dummy and safety seat. After the crash, we examine the seat's structural integrity.

At the time of our most recent tests in mid 1995, infant seats that passed Government-certification tests using a 17-pound crash-test dummy were labeled for use with babies up to 20 pounds. Because of that labeling, we tested the infant seats with a 20-pound test dummy, the weight and size of a typical 9-month-old. For convertible seats used with small children in the forward-facing position, we tested with a 33-pound dummy—the size of a typical 3-year old—the same size used for Government tests. To test their effectiveness with infants, we used the "9-month-old" dummy in the rear-facing position.

Through 1995, Government certification for booster seats required testing with only the "3-year-old" dummy. Because boosters should be used for a number of years, we also tested the seats with a 47-pound dummy, representing a typical 6-year old.

New Government certification tests, effective January 1966 for add-on seats, September 1996 for built-ins, are similar to the tests we used. Among other things, the 20-pound test dummy will be used with infant seats and convertibles in the rear-facing position, and the "3-year" and "6-year" dummies will be used in booster-seat tests.

Buying advice

A seat designed specifically for infants is the best choice for a newborn or small baby. When the baby outgrows the infant seat, we recommend a convertible seat with a five-point harness because that type protects a child's upper torso the best. Any booster seat can safely be used without its shield or harness to position a child to wear a vehicle's safety belts. For younger children who resist staying put, we recommend a high-backed model with its harness or shield.

To find out about recalls on any safety seat, call the National Highway Traffic Safety Administration's Auto Safety Hot Line (800 424-9393) with the seat's make, model, and manufacturing date.

We don't recommend buying or using a used seat. It may have been in a crash and, most likely, won't come with instructions.

RATINGS BLOOD-PRESSURE MONITORS

▶ **See report, page 239.** Last time rated in Consumer Reports: May 1992.

Brand-name recommendations: Look first to the mechanical monitors for the best value. They are the least expensive type and, if used correctly, are generally more accurate than electronic models. Anyone with poor eyesight, hearing, or dexterity, however, should consider the easier-to-use electronic models.

For the typical blood-pressure monitor, expect: ■ A cuff you inflate with a bulb or one that's self-inflating. ■ Metal D-ring on cuff for 1-handed use. ■ Stethoscope for mechanical models. ■ Storage case or pouch. ■ Rapid cuff deflation in emergency. **A choice you'll have to make:** ■ Mechanical model, with dial-type gauge, or electronic arm model, either manual- or auto-inflating type, with digital display.

Notes on the table: Except where separated by a bold rule, closely ranked models differed little in quality. **Price** is the mfr.'s suggested or approx. retail. **Consistency** is for systolic and diastolic pressure readings. **Model availability:** Ⓓ means model is discontinued.

Within type, listed in order of performance, mainly consistency in use

Better ←→ Worse: ⊜ ⊖ ○ ◒ ●

Brand and model	Price	Consistency S / D	Ease of use	Instructions	Comments
MECHANICAL MODELS					
Marshall 104	$25	⊜/⊜	◒	⊖	Stethoscope sounds are easy to hear. Deflation valve must be closed manually. Cuff hard to apply.
Omron HEM-18	22	⊜/⊜	◒	○	Stethoscope sounds are easy to hear. Deflation valve must be closed manually. Cuff hard to apply.
Walgreens 2001	20	⊜/⊜	◒	⊖	Deflation valve must be closed manually. Cuff hard to apply because of tubing.
Lumiscope 100-021	30	⊜/⊜	●	◒	Deflation valve flimsy and hard to adjust; must be closed manually. Uncomfortable stethoscope yoke. Cuff hard to apply.
Sunmark 10	22	⊜/⊜	◒	○	Deflation valve flimsy and hard to adjust; must be closed manually. Uncomfortable stethoscope yoke. Cuff hard to apply.
Sunbeam 7627-10 Ⓓ	20	○/⊜	●	○	Deflation valve flimsy and hard to adjust; must be closed manually. 1-person operation inconvenient. Uncomfortable stethoscope yoke.

Ratings continued ▶

Ratings continued

Brand and model	Price	Consistency S / D	Ease of use	Instructions	Comments
ELECTRONIC ARM MODELS					
Omron HEM-704C	$85	⊜/⊖	⊜	⊜	Self-inflating. Cuff easy to don. Very large, clear digital readout.
Sunbeam 7621 [D]	40	⊜/⊜	○	◒	Cuff may be hard to inflate.
Sunbeam 7650 [D]	80	⊜/⊖	⊖	◒	Self-inflating. Very large, clear digital readout. End of cuff may slip out of D-ring.
Lumiscope 1081 [D]	80	⊖/⊖	⊖	◒	Self-inflating. Very large, clear digital readout. End of cuff may slip out of D-ring.
Marshall 91 [D]	80	⊖/⊖	⊖	⊜	Self-inflating.
AND UA-701 [D]	52	⊖/⊜	○	◒	End of cuff may slip out of D-ring. Cuff may be hard to inflate.
Omron HEM-713C [D]	90	⊖/○	⊖	⊖	Self-inflating.
Sunmark 144	48	⊖/⊖	○	⊖	—
Omron HEM-413C [D]	55	⊖/○	○	⊖	—
Walgreens 80WA	38	⊖/○	○	⊖	—
Marshall 80 [D]	55	⊖/○	○	⊖	—
AND UA-731 [D]	90	◒/⊖	⊖	◒	Self-inflating. Very large, clear digital readout. End of cuff may slip out of D-ring.
ELECTRONIC FINGER MODELS					
The following models were judged Not Acceptable because of the great variability in the readings they gave. Listed alphabetically.					
Lumiscope 1083	99	●/●	⊖	⊖	Self-inflating. Finger cuff difficult to adjust. Systolic and diastolic readings not separated.
Marshall F-89	138	●/●	⊜	⊖	Self-inflating. Inaccurate.
Omron HEM-815F	160	●/●	⊜	◒	Self-inflating. Inaccurate.
Sunbeam 7655-10	60	●/●	⊖	⊖	Self-inflating. Finger cuff difficult to adjust. Systolic and diastolic readings not separated.

RATINGS STROLLERS

▶ **See report, page 242.** Last time rated in Consumer Reports: July 1994.

Brand-name recommendations: Status-laden brand names don't necessarily denote the best strollers. Among the convertible models we tested, for example, the cheaper Graco Brougham LXI-7520 (now replaced by SL2) slightly outranked the two Peg Perego models. But the Graco—at $110—costs much less than the Peg Peregos, which run $189 to $249. A lightweight stroller, the Combi Savvy EX 243 (now replaced by Savvy Z), $225, stood out—though expensive, it's safe and simple to operate. Two tandems—the Graco Duo Ltd., $142, and the Kolcraft Caravan, $119—performed well.

For the typical stroller, expect: ■ Above average overall safety—stability, braking, child-restraint, backup accidental folding protection. ■ At least above average cleanability. ■ Handle that can't be adjusted for height. ■ Wheels 4 to 6 in. in diameter. ■ Swiveling front wheels that can be locked. ■ Brakes on rear wheels only. ■ Canopy. ■ Pocket, basket, or bin to store light items. For a carriage/stroller: ■ Reversing handle. ■ Backrest that reclines to nearly flat position. ■ Ability to stand up when folded.

Notes on the table: Price is the manufacturer's suggested retail price. * means paid price. **Convenience** scores reflect the ease with which a stroller can be opened, closed, steered, and parked, as judged by a panel of parent testers. **Life** scores show each model's durability in normal heavy use. **Model availability:** D means model is discontinued. S means model is replaced, according to the manufacturer; successor model is noted in Comments. New model was not tested; it may or may not perform similarly. Features may vary.

Within type, listed in order of safety, convenience, durability, and cleanability

Better ⟵⟶ Worse: ⊜ ⊖ ○ ◒ ●

Brand and model	Price	Overall score (P F G VG E)	Convenience	Life	Comments
CARRIAGE/STROLLERS					
Graco Brougham LXI-7520 S	$110		⊜	⊜	23 lbs. Designed to keep sleeping infant from creeping out. No backup mechanism to prevent accidental folding. **Successor:** SL2.
Peg Perego PL-50 Domani S	189		⊖	⊜	19 lbs. Designed to keep sleeping infant from creeping out. 4-wheel brakes. All wheels swivel and can be locked in straight-ahead position. **Successor:** CL-41 Domani.
Peg Perego Olympic Shopper D	249		⊖	⊜	21 lbs. Designed to keep sleeping infant from creeping out. 4-wheel brakes. All wheels swivel and can be locked in straight-ahead position.
Kolcraft Royale XT36134	79		⊜	⊜	20 lbs.

Ratings continued ▶

Ratings continued

Brand and model	Price	Overall score P	F	G	VG	E	Conven-ience	Life	Comments
CARRIAGE/STROLLERS *continued*									
Combi Debut-Lite 661 [D]	*$262	■	■	■	■		⊖	⊖	17 lbs. 4-wheel brakes. Backrest adjustment mechanism broke in durability test. Handle height adjustable.
Graco Stroll-a-Bed 7200 Series	*60	■	■	■	■		⊖	○	19 lbs. No backup mechanism to prevent accidental folding. Safety belt broke early in durability test.
STROLLERS									
Combi Savvy EX 243 [S]	225	■	■	■	■		⊖	⊖	8 lbs. Stands up when folded. Multiple backrest positions. **Successor:** Savvy Z.
Aprica Citimini [D]	220	■	■	■	■		⊖	○	9 lbs. Frame parts broke in durability test. Stands up when folded. Multiple backrest positions.
Maclaren Sprint X63	169	■	■	■	■		⊖	⊖	10 lbs. Average cleanability. Nonremovable seat and backrest. 2 backrest positions. No storage pocket.
Spectrum 446 LM	64	■	■	■	■		○	⊖	17 lbs. Backrest reclines to nearly flat position. Rivet securing frame broke late in durability test.
Century E-Z Go Premium [S]	50	■	■	■			○	◒	13 lbs. No backup mechanism to prevent accidental folding. Front wheels swivel but can't be locked straight ahead. 2 backrest positions. Lacks storage pocket. Rivet securing frame broke and latch to keep stroller open bent in durability test. **Successor:** 11-083.
Emmaljunga Kimi [D]	215	■	■	■			○	⊖	25 lbs. Backrest reclines nearly flat. 10-in. wheels that don't swivel. Safety-belt harness harder to latch than most.
TANDEM STROLLERS									
Graco Duo Ltd [S]	142	■	■	■	■		⊖	○	28 lbs. No backup mechanism to prevent accidental folding. Backrests recline nearly flat. Stands up when folded. Rivet securing frame parts broke late in durability test. **Successor:** Duo Ltd. LXI.
Kolcraft Caravan	114	■	■	■	■		⊖	⊖	26 lbs. Backrests recline nearly flat. Stands up when folded.
STROLLER FOR RUNNERS									
Gerry Rollerbaby	179	■	■	■	■		⊖	⊖	22 lbs. Look for unit made after May 1993; wheels can break off earlier ones. Inconvenient brake. Has 3 bicycle-style wheels. Backrest does not recline.

RATINGS CHILD SAFETY SEATS

See report, page 244. Last time rated in Consumer Reports: September 1995.

Brand-name recommendations: Except for the three Not Acceptable seats, any model we tested would be a good choice, provided it fits your vehicle. The clear choices are the top-rated Century 565 infant seat, A Best Buy at $35 and the Century 1000 STE Classic convertible seat, A Best Buy at $53 (or one of the higher-rated models that use a five-point harness). Any tested booster seat can safely be used without its shield or harness to position a child to wear vehicle safety belts. For younger children in a booster who may not stay put: the Century Breverra 4880 (with harness or shield), $60. If you own the Not Acceptable Century 590, use it without the base. The Not Acceptable Evenflo On My Way 206 and Kolcraft Traveler 700 have been recalled (see page 245 and 339). The Evenflo can be safely used with its base, the Kolcraft, only in the rear-facing position.

For the typical safety seat, expect: ■ Adequate protection in a 30-mph head-on crash. ■ Fully assembled product, with adequate instructions. ■ Locking clip for use with vehicle safety belts, if needed. ■ Mail-in registration card in case of a recall. ■ Rear-facing convertibles require more space between safety belts than front-facing ones.

Notes on the table: Price is the estimated average, based on a national survey. * means price paid. Safety scores are based on the seats' performance in our tests simulating a 30-mph head-on crash. Column headings list the "age" of the dummies we used, the seats' orientation (front- or rear-facing), and (for boosters) whether we used the seats' harness or shield or lap-and-shoulder belts like those found in real vehicles. Models similar to those we tested are noted in Comments; features may vary. **Model availability:** [D] means model is discontinued.

Listed by types; within types, listed primarily in order of performance in safety tests

E	VG	G	F	P
⊜	⊖	○	◒	●

Brand and model	Price	Safety	Ease of use	Installation	Comments
INFANT SEATS		9-MO.			
Century 565, **A BEST BUY**	$35*	⊖	⊖	○	V-shaped harness. Requires installation with each use.
Kolcraft Rock'n Ride 13100	30	⊖	⊖	⊖	V-shaped harness. Requires installation with each use. **Similar:** 13102, 13802.
Gerry Guard With Glide 627	56	⊖	⊖	○	V-shaped harness. Requires installation with each use. May not fit with short safety belts. Vehicle belts can be difficult to weave through the safety seat. Hard-to-adjust harness straps. **Similar:** 628.
■ **NOT ACCEPTABLE WHEN USED WITH THE BASE**					
Century 590	62	— [1]	⊖	○	V-shaped harness. Carrier released from base in our safety tests. Without base, requires installation with each use. **Similar:** 590.

[1] *Without base, score is* ⊖.

Ratings continued ▶

Ratings continued

Brand and model	Price	Safety		Ease of use	Install-ation	Comments
INFANT SEATS *continued*			9-MO.			
■ **NOT ACCEPTABLE WHEN USED WITHOUT THE BASE**						
Evenflo On My Way 206 [2]	$65		— [3]	⊖	○	V-shaped harness. Carrier released from sled in our safety tests, when tested without its base.
CONVERTIBLE SEATS		3-YR. FRONT FACING	9-MO. REAR FACING			
■ *The following models are judged suitable for small infants as well as larger infants and small children.*						
Century 1000 STE Classic, **A BEST BUY**	53	⊖	[4]	⊖	○	5-point harness. Rear-facing, requires installation with each use and may not fit with short safety belts. **Similar:** 1500 STE Prestige.
Century SmartMove 4710	128	⊖	⊖	○	○	5-point harness. Wide base may not fit some vehicles. Hard-to-operate reclining mechanism.
Evenflo Trooper 229	77	⊖	[5]	⊖	○	5-point harness. Vehicle safety belt may interfere with buckle on safety seat in rear-facing position.
Cosco Touriva 02514	68	⊖	[6]	⊖	⊖	5-point harness. **Similar:** 02545, 02564, 02584.
Kolcraft Auto-Mate 13225	58	○	⊖	⊖	○	5-point harness. Harness-adjustment dials let straps slip somewhat. Rear-facing, requires installation with each use and may not fit with short safety belts. **Similar:** 13204, 13205, 13224.
Safeline Sit'n'Stroll 3240X	140	○	⊖	○	●	5-point harness. Requires installation with each use. Wide base may not fit some vehicles. When rear-facing, may not fit with short safety belts. Safety-belt pathway may restrict child's movement. Belts could be dislodged by child if not tight. Hard-to-adjust harness straps. **Similar:** 3240S.
■ *The following are judged less suitable for small infants, but suitable for large infants & small children.*						
Century 2000 STE	65	⊖	[4]	⊖	○	T-shield. Rear-facing, requires installation with each use and may not fit vehicles short safety belts. **Similar:** 2500 STE Prestige.
Evenflo Scout 225	63	⊖	[5]	⊖	○	T-shield. Vehicle safety belt may interfere with buckle on safety seat in rear-facing position.
Evenflo Champion 224	64	⊖	⊖	⊖	○	Overhead shield. Vehicle safety belt may interfere with buckle on safety seat in rear-facing position.
Century 5500 STE Prestige	90	○	⊖	⊖	○	Overhead shield. Rear-facing, requires installation with each use and may not fit vehicles with short safety belts.

Brand and model	Price	Safety		Ease of use	Installation	Comments
Gerry Guard SecureLock 691	*$97	○	⊖	⊖	⊖	Overhead shield. Hard-to-operate reclining mechanism. Automatic harness straps.
Century 3000 STE	77	○	⊖	⊖	○	Overhead shield. Rear-facing, requires installation with each use and may not fit with short safety belts. **Similar:** 3500 STE Prestige.
Cosco Touriva 02045	*90	○	[6]	⊖	⊖	Overhead shield. **Similar:** 02044, 02054, 02065, 02244, 02344.
Cosco Touriva 02014	*60	○	○	⊖	⊖	Overhead shield. **Similar:** 02034.
Evenflo Ultara I 235	90	○	⊖	⊖	◒	Overhead shield. Wide base may not fit some vehicles. Vehicle belt may interfere with buckle on safety seat in rear-facing position. Overhead shield may not adjust tightly for small child. **Similar:** Premier 235.
■ NOT ACCEPTABLE IN THE FORWARD-FACING POSITION						
Kolcraft Traveler 700 13405 [7]	60	—	— [8]	○	○	Overhead shield. Buckle failure released harness and dummy. Instructions error may lead to incorrect harness usage for infants. Rear-facing, requires installation with each use and may not fit with short safety belts. **Similar:** 13404, 13424, 13425.

BOOSTER SEATS	Price	3-YR.+ SHIELD	3-YR.+ BELTS	6-YR.+ SHIELD	6-YR.+ BELTS	Ease of use	Installation	Comments
Century Breverra Premiere 4885	58	⊖	⊖	[9]	⊖	○	◒	5-point harness. Vehicles belts may be hard to weave through safety seat. High-back. **Similar:** Sport 4890.
Century Breverra 4880 [D]	60	⊖	⊖	[9]	⊖	⊖	◒	T-shield. Vehicles belts can be hard to weave through the safety seat.
Fisher Price T-Shield A09196	42	○ [10]	⊖	◒	⊖	⊖	○	T-shield. Requires installation with each use when shield is used and then may not fit with short safety belts. No back.
Gerry Double Guard 675	60	○	⊖	●	⊖	◒	◒	Swing-out shield. Shield could pinch child or installer when being lowered. No back. **Similar:** 676.

[1] *Without base, score is ⊖.*
[2] *Mfr. has initiated a recall. Call 800 225-3056.*
[3] *With base, score is ○.*
[4] *Not tested rear-facing. Should perform similarly to Century 3000 STE.*
[5] *Not tested rear-facing. Should perform similarly to Evenflo Champion 224.*
[6] *Not tested rear-facing. Should perform similarly to Cosco Touriva 02014.*
[7] *Mfr. has initiated a recall. Call 800 453-7673.*
[8] *Rear-facing score is ⊖.*
[9] *Mfr. advises against using shield with children over 45 lb.*
[10] *Mfr. advises against using shield with children under 40 lb.*

AUTOS

Each year car manufacturers introduce dozens of new models. CONSUMER REPORTS tests and rates 40-odd cars each year. And we are able to provide test information on many more models, for a couple of reasons:

■ Automakers often sell the same car under different nameplates. Many *Ford* and *Mercury* models and some *Dodges*, *Chryslers*, and *Plymouths* are essentially the same in all the important components. General Motors builds *Buicks*, *Chevrolets*, *Oldsmobiles*, and *Pontiacs* that differ in details, but are basically the same. In addition, different automakers may partner a design: The *Ford Probe*, for example, is similar to the *Mazda MX-6*.

■ Many new models aren't really new. Automakers typically redesign a car every three to five years, with minimal changes in between.

To help you in your research, CONSUMER REPORTS provides information on both new and used cars.

New cars. Ratings of recently tested models start on page 269. Profiles of the 1995 models start on page 256. They include our prediction of reliability for each model. For more details, consult the issue of CONSUMER REPORTS in which the full report appeared (as noted). For some models, you can also order a report by fax (see opposite).

Used cars. Your odds of getting a dependable used car are better if you choose a model with a good track record. The Buying Guide presents reliability records, based on extensive surveys of readers, in two ways:

The Frequency-of-Repair records for 248 models start on page 284 and note exactly which part of the car had problems.

If you don't have a specific model of used

car in mind, start with our list of Reliable Used Cars, on page 279, and our Used Cars to Avoid, on page 282, both based on reliability information.

Prices. A new car's sticker price usually represents an asking, not a selling, price. A car typically costs the dealer 85 to 95 percent of the sticker price. If you're good at negotiating, you may be able to buy the car for close to cost or get a good deal on a lease. The report on page 274 takes you through the negotiating process for buying a new car; the report on page 276 discusses the leasing process.

A used car is a bit riskier than a new one, but it can also be a much better value, since someone else has taken the loss of the first year's sharp depreciation in value. The report on page 277 gives advice on how to buy a used car.

Car prices, particularly for used cars, are too volatile for us to update in the Buying Guide. Each spring, we list general price ranges for current models in the April issue of CONSUMER REPORTS. Each fall, we update those prices and preview the next year's models in the New Car Yearbook, available on newsstands in mid-November. We also offer up-to-date, customized price information by telephone or mail for new and used cars (see below).

In addition, we now offer comprehensive auto information on CD-ROM. This interactive CD-ROM for Windows covers more than 2000 models of new and used cars, minivans, pickups, and sport-utility vehicles from 1987 through 1996 and includes many other features. See below.

AUTO INFORMATION FROM CONSUMER REPORTS

Consumer Reports Cars: The Essential Guide on CD-ROM

This interactive CD-ROM for Windows presents comprehensive information in a fun, easy-to-use format. It covers more than 2000 new and used cars, minivans, pickups, and sport-utility vehicles from 1987 through 1996. It includes tools like financial calculators and auto record keepers for maintenance and fuel. It also explains how we test cars and gives the history of the Consumers Union. It includes 30 minutes of video.

To order, see page 359.

Consumer Reports New Car Price Service

This service provides the latest price information for cars, minivans, sport-utility vehicles, and light trucks. Each Price Report covers:

- Sticker prices and dealer invoice costs for the vehicle and factory options.
- Information on rebates.
- Options recommended by CONSUMER REPORTS auto experts.
- Advice on getting the best price.

To order, see page 358.

Consumer Reports Used Car Price Service

With a touch-tone phone, you can get purchase and trade-in prices for cars, minivans, sport-utility vehicles, and light trucks, 1987 to 1995 models. Prices for used 1995 models are available as of January 1996.

The price information takes into account the vehicle's age, mileage, major options, and condition. Our service also takes the caller's region into account.

A Trouble Index, based on CONSUMER REPORTS' Frequency-of-Repair data, is available for many models.

To order, see page 357.

Profiles of the 1995 cars

Here, listed alphabetically by make and model, you'll find descriptions of nearly all the 1995 models of cars, minivans, sport-utility vehicles, and pickups. For most of these models, our comments are based on a recent test, if not of the '95 model itself, then of its very similar '94 or '93 predecessor (most models don't change significantly from year to year).

At the end of each entry, you'll find the date of the last full road test published in CONSUMER REPORTS. These detailed reports are available at libraries or by fax or mail from our Facts by Fax 24-hour service. To use the service, note the four-digit fax number at the end of the model's entry and call 800 896-7788 from a touch-tone phone. The cost is $7.75 per report.

Predicted reliability is a judgment based on our Frequency-of-Repair data for past models (see page 284). If a vehicle has been recently redesigned, only data for models relevant to the 1995 models are considered. **Depreciation** predicts how well a new model will keep its value, based on the difference between a model's original sticker price and its resale value over the past three years. The average depreciation for all cars was 33 percent. As a group, sport-utility vehicles had the best rate (22 percent). Minivans and sports/sporty cars also tend to hold their value. Large cars have a relatively high depreciation (42 percent, on average).

Throughout, ✔ indicates a model recommended by CONSUMER REPORTS; **NA** means data not available; **New** means there's no data because the car is new or has been redesigned.

◉ ◓ ○ ◒ ●

Much better than average ⟷ Much worse than average

Model	Predicted reliability	Depreciation	Comments
✓ **Acura Integra**	◉	◓	This reliable, fun-to-drive little car accelerates well and handles nimbly. The cabin is a little cramped and noisy. **Last report/fax: November 94/9923**
✓ **Acura Integra Coupe**	◉	◓	The Coupe version of the Integra is a well-rounded package, with zesty acceleration and nimble handling, especially in the GS-R trimline. The ride is stiff and noisy. **Last report/fax: June 94/9742**
✓ **Acura Legend**	◉	○	This luxury sedan (due for replacement in early 1996) is comfortable only for four. It delivers spirited acceleration and a quiet, well-controlled ride. Handling is predictable but not nimble. **Last report/fax: August 92/7746**
Audi 90	◓	◒	The Quattro all-wheel-drive option delivers grippy traction. Handling is safe though not crisp. Numb steering and an unremarkable ride blunt this car's edge. Due for replacement by the A4 in 1996. **Last report/fax: May 93/7914**
Audi A6	◓	◒	Audi claims to have fixed several shortcomings—including a mediocre ride and sluggish acceleration—that plagued this car's predecessor, the Audi 100. We haven't tested the A6 yet. **Last report/fax: —/—**
✓ **BMW 3-Series**	◓	○	Precise sports-car handling and tire grip make the driver feel in control. A firm, comfortable ride that's quiet. **Last report/fax: August 94/9792**

Model	Predicted reliability	Depre-ciation	Comments
BMW 318Ti	New	NA	The newest addition to BMW's 3-Series cars. This hatchback coupe is similar to the regular 318 but shorter. Expect precise sports-car handling and tenacious tire grip, plus a firm but comfortable ride. **Last report/fax: —/—**
✓ BMW 5-Series	⊖	○	The 5-Series offers pure, functional precision. It handles nimbly and gives good feel of the road. The ride is firm but comfortable. **Last report/fax: May 94/7732**
BMW 740i	NA	○	This luxury V8 competes with the world's finest and costliest cars. It delivers exceptional power, smoothness, quietness, and comfort, and comes loaded with accessories. **Last report/fax: —/—**
Buick Century	⊖	◒	The Century is dated and badly outclassed. It's big on the outside but cramped inside. But it is reliable. **Last report/fax: January 95/9981**
✓ Buick Le Sabre	○	○	A quiet, softly sprung freeway cruiser. Expect it to handle sloppily and its body to lean sharply in turns. An optional, firmer suspension helps a lot. **Last report/fax: January 92/7307**
Buick Park Avenue	⊖	○	This longer, more luxurious version of the Buick Le Sabre offers a soft ride and every electronic accessory. **Last report/fax: —/—**
✓ Buick Regal	⊖	○	This mainstream sedan delivers a comfortable, quiet ride on good roads, but rather sloppy handling. Moderately priced, decent reliability. Last report/fax: **February 94/7771**
Buick Riviera	New	NA	Redesigned for 1995, the Riviera serves up an ultraquiet highway ride, but the driving position, controls, and rear access need improvement. Handling is clumsy. **Last report/fax: July 95/9423**
Buick Roadmaster	◒	○	This clumsy, old-fashioned freeway cruiser has a big V8, full-frame construction, and rear-wheel drive. But there's plenty of room inside. **Last report/fax: January 92/7307**
Buick Skylark	○	◒	This unimpressive car responds slowly to its steering, and the body leans sharply in turns. A second air bag was finally added for 1996. Choose the V6. **Last report/fax: June 92/7704**
Cadillac Concours/ De Ville	○	●	The De Ville is a big, plush, roomy land yacht. The upscale Concours version comes with GM's sophisticated aluminum V8. **Last report/fax: —/—**
Cadillac Eldorado	●	○	It's a plush coupe with a powerful aluminum V8 and smooth-shifting automatic transmission. The handling is cumbersome in sharp turns, and the ride isn't very smooth. **Last report/fax: July 93/9325**
Cadillac Fleetwood	●	●	This big, plush freeway cruiser delivers a soft, quiet ride. Its powerful V8 and rear-wheel drive tow a heavy tailer with ease. **Last report/fax: —/—**
Cadillac Seville	○	◒	A sophisticated aluminum V8 helps this luxury sedan accelerate very quickly. The ride is smooth except on poor roads. The rear seat is not comfortable for a luxury car. **Last report/fax: November 93/7361**
Chevrolet Astro	●	○	Though the Astro has a cavernous cargo area, its design is dated. Clumsy handling, uncomfortable ride. All-wheel drive is available. Similar: GMC Safari. **Last report/fax: October 92/7766**

Profiles continued ▶

Profiles continued

Model	Predicted reliability	Depreciation	Comments
Chevrolet Beretta	○	●	This is a sportier Chevy Corsica. The steering feels vague, and the ride is busy on most roads. Low seats make it hard to see over the hood. The back seat is cramped as well. **Last report/fax: —/—**
Chevrolet Blazer	New	⊖	A 1995 redesign improved the Blazer considerably, but the ride remains unimpressive, the brakes mediocre, and rear seat uncomfortable. Similar: GMC Jimmy. **Last report/fax: August 95/9421**
Chevrolet Camaro	●	○	One of the last of the rear-wheel-drive muscle cars. Seating is decent for two, but the driver can't see out well. The optional V8 is the engine of choice. The Pontiac Firebird is similar. **Last report/fax: October 93/7341**
Chevrolet Caprice	●	◒	Expect a smooth ride and, with the optional 5.7-liter V8, powerful drivetrain. Opt for the firmer suspension. **Last report/fax: March 94/9714**
Chevrolet Cavalier	New	◒	This basic economy car, new for 1995, is pleasant to drive. Besides good seating for four, it offers up-to-date controls, modern safety features, and many minor conveniences. **Last report/fax: June 95/9416**
Chevrolet Corsica	○	●	An uninspired economy car. The steering feels vague, and the ride is busy on all but the smoothest roads. Low seats make it hard to see over the hood. Cramped rear seat. **Last report/fax: June 92/7704**
Chevrolet Corvette	◒	○	Sophisticated electronics blend with brute muscle-car power in this legendary sports car. The steering is precise, but the car feels bulky, and the body flexes on rough roads. **Last report/fax: September 92/7758**
✓ Chevrolet Lumina	○	○	The 1995 redesign offers good ergonomics, a quiet cabin, and a smooth drivetrain. The seats are padded thinly. Handling is unexceptional. **Last report/fax: January 95/9981**
Chevrolet Lumina Van	○	○	Expect uninspired overall performance from this and GM's other minivans. Blind spots vex the driver, and the ride and handling are below par. **Last report/fax: July 94/7789**
Chevrolet Monte Carlo	New	NA	A coupe version of the Lumina sedan. The Lumina is a nicer car. The Monte Carlo is neither sporty nor comfortable; both handling and ride are unimpressive. **Last report/fax: July 95/9423**
Chevrolet S Pickup	●	NA	Equipped with a V6, this truck accelerates well and has a quiet cabin. But ride, handling, and comfort are a notch below the Ford Ranger's. Similar: GMC Sonoma. **Last report/fax: —/—**
Chevrolet Suburban	◒	⊖	This huge truck-based station wagon emphasizes utility. It can carry nine people and tow a heavy trailer. Poor reliability. Similar: GMC Suburban. **Last report/fax: —/—**
Chevrolet Tahoe	◒	⊖	The Tahoe is sized between GMC's huge Suburban and compact Blazer. Well suited to hauling cargo or a heavy trailer. Similar: GMC Yukon. **Last report/fax: —/—**
Chrysler Cirrus	New	NA	A roomy compact with spirited acceleration, the Cirrus handles well and has a well-controlled ride. Comfortable seating; sensible interior design. **Last report/fax: March 95/9995**

Model	Predicted reliability	Depre-ciation	Comments
Chrysler Concorde	◒	NA	This large sedan handles as nimbly as a much smaller car, yet it seats five adults comfortably. Reliability problems cloud the fine overall performance. **Last report/fax: March 93/7948**
Chrysler LHS	◒	NA	This is a stretched version of the Chrysler Concorde, Dodge Intrepid, and Eagle Vision. It handles well and boasts about the best rear seat of any car. **Last report/fax: March 94/9714**
Chrysler Sebring	New	NA	New for '95, this sporty coupe has a smooth powertrain, well-controlled ride, and good handling. But it's noisy at speed, and not very quick. Reliability remains a question mark. Similar: Dodge Avenger. **Last report/fax: July 95/9423**
Chrysler Town & Country	◒	⊖	A loaded version of the newly redesigned Dodge and Plymouth minivans. Decent handling, a smooth, quiet ride, comfortable seats, and copious cargo room add to its appeal. **Last report/fax: October 92/7766**
Dodge Avenger	New	NA	New for '95, this sporty coupe has a smooth powertrain, well-controlled ride, and good handling. But it's noisy at speed, not very quick. Reliability is unknown. Similar: Chrysler Sebring. **Last report/fax: July 95/9423**
Dodge Caravan (1996)	New	◒	The Caravan rides and handles well, and converts easily from people carrier to cargo hauler. The 1996 redesign makes it even better. Similar: Plymouth Voyager. **Last report/fax: July 94/7789**
Dodge Dakota	●	NA	A big cargo box and roomy interior don't make up for anemic acceleration and below-par handling, comfort, and maneuverability. **Last report/fax: November 95/9434**
Dodge Grand Caravan (1996)	New	○	A longer-bodied version of the Dodge Caravan. It's a well-designed package, with a smooth, quiet ride, but Chrysler's shorter minivans have been more reliable. Similar: Plymouth Grand Voyager. **Last report/fax: October 95/9431**
Dodge Intrepid	◒	NA	This large sedan handles as nimbly as a much smaller car, yet seats five adults comfortably. Reliability problems cloud the fine overall performance. **Last report/fax: January 95/9981**
Dodge Neon	New	NA	This small car has a roomy interior and a powerful but noisy engine. The ride is choppy. Handling is predictable and safe. Similar: Plymouth Neon. **Last report/fax: October 94/9921**
Dodge Stealth	◒	○	With optional all-wheel drive and twin turbochargers, it's fast and furious, but pricey and not as much fun to drive as, say, a Mazda Miata. Plainer versions are short on ability. Similar: Mitsubishi 3000 GT. **Last report/fax: April 92/9377**
Dodge Stratus	New	NA	A roomy new compact that handles and rides well. The V6 accelerates with verve; the Four is just adequate. **Last report/fax: December 95/9433**
Eagle Summit	○	●	This entry-level subcompact rides uncomfortably and, without the optional antilock brakes, stops poorly. The one saving grace is a zesty powertrain. Similar: Mitsubishi Mirage. **Last report/fax: August 93/7302**
Eagle Summit Wagon	◒	◒	This cross between a small station wagon and an even smaller van delivers peppy acceleration, a quiet ride, and lots of cargo space. **Last report/fax: September 93/7331**

Profiles continued ▶

Profiles continued

Model	Predicted reliability	Depre- ciation	Comments
Eagle Talon	New	○	The redesigned Talon, made by a Chrysler/Mitsibishi partnership, comes in several permutations. Turbocharging and all-wheel drive are available for performance and traction. Similar: Mitsubishi Eclipse. **Last report/fax: January 93/7936**
Eagle Vision	◒	NA	This large sedan handles as nimbly as a much smaller car, yet seats five adults comfortably. Reliability problems cloud the fine overall performance. **Last report/fax: March 93/7948**
Ford Aerostar	○	○	This old-fashioned rear-wheel-drive minivan remains a sound choice for heavy-duty trailer pulling. All-wheel-drive is available, and preferable. **Last report/fax: October 92/7766**
Ford Aspire	NA	NA	This little commuter car is a chore to drive. Good fuel efficiency, plenty of head room, and a large luggage area don't make up for slow acceleration, clumsy handling, and sluggish steering. **Last report/fax: October 94/9921**
Ford Bronco	●	⊖	A big, utilitarian truck to the core, but with various levels of convenience appointments. It carries a long history of worse-than average reliability. **Last report/fax: —/—**
Ford Contour	New	NA	A new model, and a good, solid family sedan. Expect nimble handling but a cramped rear seat. Choose the V6 over the noisy Four. **Last report/fax: March 95/9995**
✓ **Ford Crown Victoria**	○	◒	An old-fashioned V8 freeway cruiser, it handles decently, especially with the upgraded handling package, and it offers a serene ride and a huge trunk. Similar: Mercury Grand Marquis. **Last report/fax: March 94/9714**
Ford Escort	⊖	◒	An unimpressive little econobox except in the top trim-line GT version. The standard 1.9-liter engine is anemic; the steering, slow and sloppy; and the handling, clumsy. **Last report/fax: September 93/7331**
✓ **Ford Explorer**	○	⊖	A roomy, versatile interior, nice controls, decent ride and handling, and optional full-time four-wheel drive give the Explorer an edge. The V6 is just adequate. **Last report/fax: August 95/9421**
Ford Mustang	NA	○	A recent redesign gave this old-fashioned muscle car a stiffer body and new appearance, but the Mustang doesn't feel sporty to drive. The V6 version falls particularly short. **Last report/fax: June 94/9742**
Ford Probe	◒	○	A nicely balanced sporty hatchback made jointly by Ford and Mazda. In GT trim, it accelerates powerfully and handles well, though its ride is stiff and jittery. The Mazda MX-6 is the coupe version. **Last report/fax: January 93/7936**
Ford Ranger	○	NA	Our top-rated compact pickup. It rides and handles well. The interior is quiet, comfortable, and well-laid-out. Similar: Mazda B-series. **Last report/fax: November 95/9434**
✓ **Ford Taurus**	○	●	A well-rounded family sedan. Handling is decent and the seats are comfortable, but the ride is so-so. A redesigned and improved Taurus comes out for 1996. Similar: Mercury Sable. **Last report/fax: January 95/9981**
Ford Taurus SHO	●	◒	A hot-rod version of the Taurus, with a powerful Yamaha V6 that gives quick acceleration. Handling and ride are nothing special. Reliability is poor. **Last report/fax: May 93/7914**

Model	Predicted reliability	Depre-ciation	Comments
Ford Thunderbird	○	◒	Expect a very quiet interior, sensible controls, soft front seats, and a rear seat that's decent for a coupe. Handling is sloppy. **Last report/fax: July 95/9423**
✓ Ford Windstar	○	NA	Among the front ranks of minivans. The ride is exceptional, and the interior is very roomy and quiet. Like many minivans, it feels clumsy in hard turns. **Last report/fax: December 94/9927**
Geo Metro	New	●	A sedan version of the Suzuki Swift, the tiny Metro is under-powered with either of its two engines, and neither nimble nor fun to drive. Long trips become a chore. **Last report/fax: September 95/9429**
✓ Geo Prizm	⊜	○	A very good, reliable small car. Ride and handling are satisfactory, and the interior layout is close to ideal. The rear seat is cramped. **Last report/fax: August 93/7302**
Geo Tracker	○	○	This agile little runabout is better suited to running local errands than cruising long distances. Four-wheel drive is optional. Similar: Suzuki Sidekick. **Last report/fax: —/—**
GMC Jimmy	New	⊖	A 1995 redesign improved the Jimmy but the ride remains unimpressive, and the rear seat is uncomfortable. Similar: Chevrolet Blazer. **Last report/fax: August 95/9421**
GMC Safari	●	○	The Safari has an enormous cargo area, but the design is dated. Handling is clumsy and the ride, uncomfortable. Similar: Chevrolet Astro. **Last report/fax: October 92/7766**
GMC Sonoma	●	NA	Equipped with a V6, this truck accelerates well and has a quiet cabin. But ride, handling, and comfort are a notch below the Ford Ranger's. Similar: Chevrolet S pickup. **Last report/fax: November 95/9434**
GMC Suburban	◒	⊜	This huge truck-based station wagon emphasizes utility. It can carry nine people and tow a heavy trailer. Poor reliability. Similar: Chevrolet Suburban. **Last report/fax: —/—**
GMC Yukon	◒	⊖	The trucklike Yukon nestles between the GMC's huge Suburban and the compact Jimmy. It lends itself well to hauling cargo or a heavy trailer. Similar: Chevrolet Tahoe. **Last report/fax: —/—**
✓ Honda Accord	⊜	○	One of the best family sedans. Expect peppy acceleration, decent handling, a good ride, and comfortable seats. The EX version handles better than the DX or LX. **Last report/fax: March 95/9995**
✓ Honda Civic	⊜	○	A very good small car with peppy acceleration. The interior is well designed. Expect a firm and fairly noisy ride. A redesign is due in 1996. **Last report/fax: May 92/7397**
Honda Civic del Sol	○	NA	Instead of a sports car, it feels like a small sedan, with a busy ride and a body that flexes too much. Think of it as a Civic with a big sun roof. **Last report/fax: October 93/7341**
✓ Honda Odyssey	⊜	NA	Honda's first-ever minivan has four doors like a wagon. Ride and handling are civilized, like the Accord's. Visibility and maneuverability are both good, too. **Last report/fax: October 95/9431**
Honda Passport	NA	NA	It's really an Isuzu Rodeo with a Honda badge. It leans sharply in turns, steers slowly, and delivers a mediocre ride. The Rodeo's reliability has been shaky. **Last report/fax: July 94/7789**

Profiles continued ▶

Profiles continued

Model	Predicted reliability	Depre-ciation	Comments
✓ Honda Prelude	⊜	⊖	This well-rounded coupe blends lively acceleration with nimble handling. It's easy and fun to drive, but the cabin is cramped. **Last report/fax: January 93/7936**
Hyundai Accent	New	NA	A basic runabout with a modern interior and decent levels of standard equipment. It's fairly roomy and quiet, and adequately powerful. Reliability is unknown. **Last report/fax: September 95/9429**
Hyundai Elantra	NA	◒	The Elantra performs decently but rides uncomfortably. Properly equipped, it costs as much as its better Japanese competitors. Reliability is unknown; previous models have been troublesome. New model in 1996. **Last report/fax: May 92/7397**
Hyundai Scoupe	NA	○	A sporty car should be fun to drive—and the Scoupe isn't. It's a basic car, with trendy styling and a crude suspension. Reliability is unknown—but caution is advised. **Last report/fax: —/—**
Hyundai Sonata	New	○	The Sonata tries to imitate the Japanese compacts, but with limited success. Decently equipped, it's not competitive in price. Reliability is unknown—but previous Hyundais have been very troublesome. **Last report/fax: February 95/9992**
✓ Infiniti G20	⊜	○	An overlooked gem. It feels like a good European sports sedan, with nimble handling, a good ride, comfortable seats, plus a good balance of acceleration and fuel economy. **Last report/fax: November 94/9923**
Infiniti I30	New	NA	An upscale version of the Nissan Maxima, and a competent car all around. **Last report/fax: —/—**
✓ Infiniti J30	⊜	NA	This pleasant model emphasizes near-absolute road isolation over sporty handling. A small back seat and trunk make it feel like a luxury coupe, despite its four doors. **Last report/fax: May 93/7914**
✓ Infiniti Q45a	⊖	◒	A fine but expensive luxury car. The latest generation has sacrificed cutting-edge acceleration to create a quieter, more refined ride. Cramped rear seat. **Last report/fax: November 93/7351**
Isuzu Rodeo	◒	⊜	A compact sport-utility vehicle that accelerates modestly and leans heavily during cornering. It offers little more cargo space than does a standard station wagon. **Last report/fax: July 94/7789**
✓ Isuzu Trooper	⊖	⊖	A big box, so heavy that even its powerful engine feels quite slow. Comfortable front seats, but a bouncy ride. It handles sloppily, and its body leans sharply in turns. **Last report/fax: November 92/—**
Jaguar XJ6	NA	◒	This refined sedan has powerful acceleration and a well-mannered ride. The control layout was recently improved. The cockpit is a little cramped. **Last report/fax: November 93/7351**
Jeep Cherokee	◒	⊖	More a tall wagon than a real sport-utility vehicle. Lots of cargo room but a noisy, harsh ride. The narrow seats are comfortable only for slender people. **Last report/fax: September 91/7976**
Jeep Grand Cherokee	●	⊖	A refined sport-utility vehicle, with an almost carlike ride and a sophisticated driveline. All-wheel drive is available. Poor reliability. **Last report/fax: August 95/9421**

Model	Predicted reliability	Depre-ciation	Comments
Jeep Wrangler	●	⊜	The smallest, least expensive, and crudest Jeep. The ride is hard and noisy; the handling, primitive. Popular with off-roaders despite a poor reliability record. **Last report/fax: —/—**
Land Rover Discovery	New	NA	The Discovery is sized and priced between the small, crude Defender and the big, chic Range Rover. Acceleration is slow; handling is mediocre; fuel economy, poor. **Last report/fax: August 95/9421**
✓ **Lexus ES300**	⊜	⊖	It does everything well—but the Toyota Camry does nearly as well for less money. Expect sound handling and strong and quiet performance. **Last report/fax: May 95/9401**
✓ **Lexus GS300**	⊜	NA	Emphasizes the luxury end of the luxury/sports spectrum. Exceptionally quiet ride, but the steering feels too light. Displays and controls are exceptional. **Last report/fax: May 94/7732**
✓ **Lexus LS400**	⊜	○	A 1995 redesign made Toyota's flagship luxury car a tad roomier. Expect an extremely quiet, comfortable ride and plush accommodations. **Last report/fax: November 93/7351**
✓ **Lexus SC400/SC300**	⊜	⊖	This two-door luxury coupe gets fine performance from its aluminum V8 in SC400 trim, but the much-cheaper SC300's Six accelerates well too. Quality and refinement are top-notch. **Last report/fax: July 93/9325**
Lincoln Continental	New	●	Redesigned for '95, the well-equipped Continental picked up a fine-performing aluminum V8. Expect a roomy interior and a quiet ride. **Last report/fax: —/—**
✓ **Lincoln Mark VIII**	○	NA	A sophisticated, rear-wheel drive luxury two-door with a spirited aluminum V8. Handling is agile for such a large car. The cockpit is modern; the front seats, comfortable. **Last report/fax: July 93/9325**
Lincoln Town Car	⊖	●	A big, old-fashioned, rear-wheel-drive highway cruiser with a modern V8 and lots of luxury appointments. Expect a quiet, soft ride and seating for six. **Last report/fax: —/—**
✓ **Mazda 626**	○	○	A well-rounded and high-rated family sedan. The pricey V6 runs particularly smoothly and powerfully, but the Four is a better value. **Last report/fax: January 94/9392**
✓ **Mazda 929**	○	○	Mazda's large luxury sedan, with rear-wheel drive. It doesn't handle as well as it might, but it's quick off the line, and it rides quietly and comfortably. **Last report/fax: August 92/7746**
Mazda B-series Pickup	○	NA	This is our top-rated pickup. It rides and handles well. The interior is quiet, comfortable, and well-laid-out. Similar: Ford Ranger. **Last report/fax: —/—**
✓ **Mazda Millenia**	⊖	NA	A new luxury sedan that's quiet and comfortable, pleasant to drive, and well put together. The high-line S version offers both power and relatively good fuel economy. **Last report/fax: May 95/9401**
Mazda MPV	○	⊖	This minivan has below-par braking, a harsh ride, and limited cargo space. Consider competing vehicles from Ford, Honda, and Chrysler. **Last report/fax: October 92/7766**
Mazda MX-3	◒	⊖	A small coupe. Too bad Mazda has eliminated the smooth V6, leaving only the much-less-able Four. Expect good handling but a stiff, noisy ride. **Last report/fax: July 92/7734**

Profiles continued ▶

Profiles continued

Model	Predicted reliability	Depre-ciation	Comments
✓ **Mazda MX-5 Miata**	⊜	○	A rear-wheel-drive two-seater that's as fun to drive as any sports car, despite a noisy, stiff ride and small trunk. Excellent handling, steering, and brakes and a smooth-running engine add to the fun. **Last report/fax: October 93/7341**
✓ **Mazda MX-6**	○	○	We prefer the V6 to the Four. This coupe's handling is smooth and predictable, and the ride is adequate. Similar: Ford Probe. **Last report/fax: January 93/7936**
✓ **Mazda Protegé**	⊜	○	Redesigned for '95, the Protege is a practical, well-rounded little car with roomy accomodations for a car in this class. **Last report/fax: June 95/9416**
Mazda RX-7	◒	NA	Comfort and practicality take a back seat to pure, uncompromising performance. Handling is top-notch, but the ride is very stiff. Too small for tall people. **Last report/fax: September 92/7758**
✓ **Mercedes-Benz C-Class**	⊜	NA	An expensive car for its size. A strong engine, responsive handling, a supple ride, and quiet interior are strong points. The seats may be too firm for some. **Last report/fax: August 94/9792**
✓ **Mercedes-Benz E-Class**	⊜	○	One of the world's finest production cars, and a joy to drive. A fine balance of spirited acceleration, precise handling, and luxurious ride. **Last report/fax: May 94/7732**
Mercury Cougar	○	◒	A slightly up-market version of the Ford Thunderbird. Good points include a very quiet interior, sensible controls, soft front seats, and a rear seat that's comfortable for a coupe. Handling is a little sloppy. **Last report/fax: —/—**
✓ **Mercury Grand Marquis**	○	◒	A big, old-fashioned V8 freeway cruiser with a serene ride, a huge trunk, and good towing capability. The Handling Package is worthwhile. Similar: Ford Crown Victoria. **Last report/fax: —/—**
Mercury Mystique	New	NA	This mid-sized model handles exceptionally well and is sensibly appointed, but the rear seat is cramped. The V6 is a better choice than the noisy Four. **Last report/fax: March 95/9995**
✓ **Mercury Sable**	○	○	A well-rounded family sedan, but merely middling by modern standards. Handling is decent and the seats are comfortable, but the ride is so-so. The Ford Taurus is similar. A redesign is due for 1996. **Last report/fax: March 93/7948**
Mercury Tracer	⊜	◒	In top-level LTS trim, this is a peppy little car. Lower trim lines are disappointing. The annoying motorized shoulder belts are intrusive in any trim line. **Last report/fax: October 94/9921**
✓ **Mercury Villager**	○	NA	The Villager and its twin, the Nissan Quest, are among the best minivans, very carlike and pleasant to drive. Annoying motorized shoulder belts remain their worst drawback. **Last report/fax: February 93/7943**
Mitsubishi 3000 GT	◒	○	With all-wheel drive and twin turbochargers, this technological showpiece is fast and furious. But it's pricey—and not as much fun to drive as a Mazda Miata. The more basic versions are nothing special. Similar: Dodge Stealth. **Last report/fax: —/—**
✓ **Mitsubishi Diamante**	⊜	◒	Mitsubishi's flagship luxury car is competent in all respects, but it doesn't stand out in the fast company it competes with. The front seats are comfortable, but the rear is cramped. **Last report/fax: February 92/7345**

Model	Predicted reliability	Depre-ciation	Comments
Mitsubishi Eclipse	New	○	This sporty coupe, a sibling of the Eagle Talon, got a slightly longer wheelbase in 1995. The turbocharged versions are the ones to choose. **Last report/fax: —/—**
Mitsubishi Galant	◒	○	A competent, good-performing family sedan. The Four delivers lively acceleration. Reliability has been so-so. **Last report/fax: January 94/9392**
Mitsubishi Mirage	○	○	A small econobox with poor brakes and a rather uncomfortable ride. A zesty powertrain is its sole good point. Similar: Eagle Summit. **Last report/fax: August 93/7302**
Mitsubishi Montero	NA	⊖	The best thing about the high, boxy Montero is its sophisticated all-wheel-drive system. The worst is its unpredictable emergency handling. We'd pass it up. **Last report/fax: November 92/—**
Nissan 200SX	New	NA	A nice little car with a sensible layout, this sporty coupe version of the Nissan Sentra was new for 1995. It's relatively inexpensive in base and SE versions. The SE-R trimline has a guttsier engine. **Last report/fax: —/—**
Nissan 240SX	New	○	A rear-wheel-drive sporty coupe, new in 1995. Expect competent handling and a fairly comfortable ride. As in others of this ilk, the rear seat is best left uninhabited. **Last report/fax: —/—**
✓ Nissan 300ZX	○	○	A two-seater that's everything a sports car should be—fast and fun, and remarkably smooth and easy to drive. One of the best sports cars, but pricey. **Last report/fax: September 92/7758**
✓ Nissan Altima	⊖	NA	This model performs quite decently overall. The sports-oriented SE version handles better than the top-line GLE, but the best value is the mid-level GXE. **Last report/fax: November 94/9923**
✓ Nissan Maxima	⊜	○	We score the Maxima just a notch below the Toyota Camry. The powertrain is first-rate. The ride, seat comfort, and handling are good, not great. **Last report/fax: February 95/9992**
Nissan Pathfinder	⊜	⊜	It rides and handles fairly well, but that's offset by primitive four-wheel drive, no air bags or antilock brakes, and poor crash-test performance. Due for replacement for 1996. **Last report/fax: —/—**
✓ Nissan Quest	○	NA	The Quest and its twin, the Mercury Villager, are among the best minivans, very carlike and pleasant to drive. Annoying motorized shoulder belts remain their worst drawback. **Last report/fax: February 93/7943**
✓ Nissan Sentra	⊖	○	The Sentra broke no new ground with its 1995 redesign. It performs well overall. It has a fairly comfortable, quiet ride, and good fuel economy. The cockpit is a little cramped. **Last report/fax: June 95/9416**
Oldsmobile Achieva	○	○	An uninspired design. The steering is slow and vague, and handling is mediocre. The Four performs weakly; the V6 is peppier and smoother. The seats are comfortable but too low. **Last report/fax: June 92/7704**
Oldsmobile Aurora	New	NA	This new model is very highly styled. The V8 powertrain is top-notch, but heavy steering, poor visibility, lack of room, and middling ride put it behind the luxury competition. **Last report/fax: May 95/9401**
Oldsmobile Ciera	○	◒	Never an inspired design, the Ciera is dated and badly outclassed. It's big on the outside but cramped inside. Reliability is its one strong point. **Last report/fax: January 95/9981**

Profiles continued ▶

Profiles continued

Model	Predicted reliability	Depre-ciation	Comments
Oldsmobile Cutlass Supreme	○	◒	Perhaps the least appealing of GM's family sedans. Expect sloppy handling, a poor ride, and uncomfortable seats. **Last report/fax: February 94/7771**
✓ Oldsmobile Eighty Eight	○	○	A big, quiet, softly sprung freeway cruiser with a responsive V6. The optional touring suspension markedly improves handling. **Last report/fax: January 92/7307**
Oldsmobile Ninety Eight	⊖	●	A big freeway cruiser. Cars like this emphasize a soft ride and a wealth of power accessories. Handling is sloppy, though the optional Touring Suspension package helps. **Last report/fax: —/—**
Oldsmobile Silhouette	◒	○	Expect uninspired overall performance from this and GM's other minivans. Blind spots vex the driver, and the ride and handling are just adequate. **Last report/fax: July 94/7789**
Plymouth Grand Voyager (1996)	◒	○	The Grand Voyager is a longer-bodied Voyager. Overall, it's a well-designed package—but Chrysler's shorter minivans hold up better. **Last report/fax: October 92/7766**
Plymouth Neon	New	NA	This small car has a roomy interior and a powerful though noisy engine. The ride is choppy. Handling is predictable and safe, not sporty. Similar: Dodge Neon. **Last report/fax: October 94/9921**
✓ Plymouth Voyager (1996)	○	○	The Voyager rides and handles well, and converts easily from people carrier to cargo hauler. The 1996 redesign makes this van even better. Similar: Dodge Caravan. **Last report/fax: July 94/7789**
✓ Pontiac Bonneville	○	○	Properly equipped, the Bonneville is one of the best large sedans. The optional firm suspension and touring tires markedly improve handling. The supercharged V6 is very powerful, but the standard V6 does just fine. **Last report/fax: March 94/9714**
Pontiac Firebird	●	○	An old-fashioned rear-wheel-drive muscle car, like its cousin, the Chevrolet Camaro. The optional V8 provides effortless acceleration and makes the standard V6, which is adequate, seem sluggish by comparison. **Last report/fax: October 93/7341**
Pontiac Grand Am	○	○	An uninspired design with a veneer of sportiness. The front end bobs incessantly, handling is second-rate, there's no passenger air bag, and the door-mounted safety belts are annoying. **Last report/fax: June 93/9317**
✓ Pontiac Grand Prix	○	○	This mid-sized sedan is a decent though unexceptional design. Moderate price is the major appeal. The optional 3.4-liter V6 delivers little more punch than the standard 3.1, and it gets worse mileage. **Last report/fax: February 94/7771**
Pontiac Sunfire	New	NA	The Sunfire, a cousin of the Chevrolet Cavalier, is new for 1995. It rides and handles pleasantly and comes with quite a lot of equipment for the money. Reliability is unknown. **Last report/fax: —/—**
Pontiac Trans Sport	●	○	Expect uninspired overall performance from this and GM's other minivans. Blind spots vex the driver, and the ride and handling are below par. **Last report/fax: July 94/7789**
Saab 900	NA	◒	An able but quirky sports sedan. Handling, performance, and accommodations are all good. Several controls are oddly placed on the floor between the front seats. **Last report/fax: August 94/9792**

Model	Predicted reliability	Depreciation	Comments
✓ Saab 9000	○	◒	A well-designed and pleasant-to-drive European-style sports sedan. The controls are a little inconvenient. **Last report/fax: May 94/7732**
Saturn	⊖	⊜	The Saturn is growing long in the tooth, though reliability has been good. The powerful engine is rough and noisy, the interior is cramped, and the seats could be more comfortable. New for '96. **Last report/fax: June 95/9416**
✓ Saturn SC	⊖	⊖	Among the coupe versions of the Saturn, the SC2 is the one to choose. It provides quick acceleration and nimble, precise handling. The ride is stiff, even jarring at times. **Last report/fax: July 92/7734**
✓ Subaru Impreza	⊜	NA	Properly equipped, the Impreza is a very nice small car with good handling and comfortable seats. Choose the L over the base version. Antilock brakes are available only in all-wheel-drive models. **Last report/fax: August 93/7302**
✓ Subaru Legacy	⊜	○	A competent, well-rounded sedan, and one of the few that offer all-wheel drive. Much improved in 1995, and one of our top-rated cars. The station wagon versions are a good bet too. **Last report/fax: February 95/9992**
✓ Subaru SVX	⊖	○	Think of the SVX as more of a touring coupe than a true sports car. It rides comfortably and quietly. Handling is good but not great. All-wheel drive is available. **Last report/fax: September 92/7758**
Suzuki Sidekick	○	⊖	A small Jeeplike runabout similar to the Geo Tracker. The two-door version is very small. The four-door is a foot longer and a measure more practical. **Last report/fax: —/—**
Suzuki Swift	New	○	A hatchback version of the Geo Metro. Redesigned in 1995, it remains a very small, cramped car—okay for zipping around town, but underpowered on the highway. **Last report/fax: September 95/9429**
Toyota 4Runner	⊜	⊜	It feels more like a truck than a car, and the ride is punishing. But it's reliable for a sport-utility vehicle, and it holds its resale value well. **Last report/fax: —/—**
✓ Toyota Avalon	⊜	NA	Think of this as an extended-length Camry—comfortable, quiet, refined, and easy to drive, though not sporty. **Last report/fax: May 95/9401**
✓ Toyota Camry	⊜	○	One of the best sedans on the market—quiet, refined, and easy to drive, with comfortable seating. It feels like a luxury car, and it's been exceptionally reliable. **Last report/fax: January 94/9392**
✓ Toyota Celica	⊖	○	A well-rounded sporty coupe, though not as powerful as competitors like the Ford Probe. It rides and handles well, gives good fuel economy, and has been very reliable. As in most coupes, the rear seat is very cramped. **Last report/fax: June 94/9742**
✓ Toyota Corolla	⊜	○	An able overall performer with good reliability. The car handles predictably, though not nimbly. Front seating is fine, but the rear is cramped. **Last report/fax: August 93/7302**
✓ Toyota Land Cruiser	⊖	⊜	The big, imposing Land Cruiser accelerates just adequately and uses lots of fuel. Expect a high, commanding view and a quiet if stiff ride. **Last report/fax: July 94/7789**

Profiles continued ▶

Profiles continued

Model	Predicted reliability	Depre-ciation	Comments
✓ Toyota MR2	NA	○	A rear-wheel drive two-seater with a mid-mounted engine—the only moderately priced mid-engined sports car still on the market. Expect nimble, ultraresponsive handling, and very little trunk space. **Last report/fax: —/—**
Toyota Paseo	⊜	⊖	A sporty version of the old Tercel, not the newly redesigned Tercel. Acceleration is peppy, but the handling is not nimble. A soft suspension and numb steering rob it of true sportiness. **Last report/fax: July 92/7734**
✓ Toyota Previa	⊜	⊖	A fine though expensive minivan, with responsive steering and a good, quiet ride. Minus the optional supercharger, the engine, is weak. The Previa has been the most reliable of any minivan. **Last report/fax: October 92/7766**
✓ Toyota Supra	⊖	○	In its highest trim, the Supra is a muscular speedster with a bone-jarring ride. The Nissan 300ZX and Mazda RX-7 are more fun to drive. **Last report/fax: June 94/9742**
Toyota Tacoma	New	NA	A peppy and refined power train is Tacoma's main virtue. Ride, handling, and comfort are sub-standard, and the cargo box is flimsy. **Last report/fax: November 95/9434**
Toyota Tercel	⊜	○	First and foremost a Spartan economy car. Redesigned in 1995, it is quite peppy, but noisy and very cramped in the rear. **Last report/fax: September 95/9429**
Volkswagen Golf III	NA	○	A sporty, zippy little hatchback that's fun to drive. Expect a fairly quiet ride. Handling is nimble, although the body leans a lot in turns. **Last report/fax: October 94/9921**
Volkswagen Jetta III	NA	○	Think of the Jetta as a Golf with a very large trunk. **Last report/fax: November 94/9923**
Volkswagen Passat	New	◒	VW's costliest model rides and handles very well. It has a roomy rear seat and big trunk. We recommend the manual transmission. **Last report/fax: February 95/9992**
✓ Volvo 850	⊖	NA	Volvo's only front-wheel-drive car. It's nimble for a Volvo, and turbo-charged versions are fast. Large, comfortable front seats. Stiff ride. **Last report/fax: August 94/9792**
✓ Volvo 940	⊖	○	A boxy, practical, functional car. It features comfortable seats, lots of trunk space, and a welter of safety features. The standard nonturbo Four is weak. Its wagon form is exceptionally roomy. **Last report/fax: September 94/9915**
✓ Volvo 960	⊖	○	The most expensive model in Volvo's 900 Series. Expect good seating for four and a huge trunk. The car rides and handles well, and the Six accelerates enthusiastically. **Last report/fax: August 92/7746**

RATINGS 1995 CARS

The following cars include only those for which we have recent test data. To earn our recommendation—marked by a ✔—a model has to perform well in our tests and must have been at least average in reliability. In some cases, our tests apply to more than one model. These models, called "siblings," are essentially similar models that are sold under different nameplates. They're grouped and marked with bullets in the charts below. **Fuel usage** is overall mpg and is based on our own tests on and off the track. **Tested model** notes the trim line, engine, drivetrain, and braking system of the model tested—items that can affect specific test results.

Model	Overall score (P F G VG E)	Fuel usage	Tested model
SMALL CARS WITH MANUAL TRANSMISSIONS			
Volkswagen Jetta III		23 mpg	GLX 2.8 V6; man 5
✓ Acura Integra		30	LS 1.8 Four; man 5
Volkswagen Golf III		30	GL 2.0 Four; man 5
Dodge/Plymouth Neon		31	Sport 2.0 Four; man 5
✓ Geo Prizm		33	LSi 1.8 Four; man 5
Mercury Tracer		28	LTS 1.8 Four; man 5
✓ Subaru Impreza		29	L 1.8 Four; man 5
Hyundai Accent		35	L 1.5 Four; man 5
Eagle Summit		34	ES 1.8 Four; man 5
Toyota Tercel		39	1.5 Four; man 4
Ford Aspire		36	1.3 Four; man 5
Geo Metro		35	LSi 1.0 Three; man 5
SMALL CARS WITH AUTOMATIC TRANSMISSIONS			
✓ Mazda Protegé		26	ES 1.8 Four; auto 4
Chevrolet Cavalier		26	LS 2.2 Four; auto 3
✓ Honda Civic		29	EX 1.6 Four; auto 4
✓ Toyota Corolla		30	LE 1.8 Four; auto 4
Dodge/Plymouth Neon		31	Highline 2.0 Four; auto 3
✓ Nissan Sentra		28	GXE 1.6 Four; auto 4
Toyota Tercel		29	DX 1.5 Four; auto 4
Saturn		27	SL2 1.9 Four; auto 4
Hyundai Accent		28	1.5 Four; auto 4
Geo Metro		29	LSi 1.3 Four; auto 3

Ratings continued ▶

Ratings continued

Model	Overall score (P F G VG E)	Fuel usage	Tested model
SPORTS/SPORTY CARS UNDER $25,000			
✓ Acura Integra Coupe		30 mpg	GS-R 1.8 Four; man 5
Ford Probe		24	GT 2.5 V6; man 5
Pontiac Firebird		17	Trans Am 5.7 V8; auto 4
✓ Toyota Celica		28	GT 2.2 Four; man 5
✓ Mazda MX-5 Miata		29	1.6 Four; man 5
✓ Mazda MX-6		24	LS 2.5 V6; auto 4
✓ Saturn SC		29	1.9 Four; man 5
✓ Honda Prelude		26	Si 2.3 Four; man 5
Ford Mustang		18	GT 5.0 V8; auto 4
Chevrolet Camaro		19	Base 3.4 V6; auto 4
Toyota Paseo		34	1.5 Four; man 5
Honda Civic del Sol		32	Si 1.6 Four; man 5
SPORTS/SPORTY CARS OVER $25,000			
✓ Toyota Supra		22	3.0 twin-turbo 6; man 6
▪ Dodge Stealth		20	R/T Turbo 3.0 V6; man 5
▪ Mitsubishi 300 GT		20	Dodge Stealth R/T Turbo 3.0 V6; man 5
✓ Nissan 300ZX		21	3.0 twin-turbo V6; man 5
Chevrolet Corvette		17	LT1 5.7 V8; man 6
Mazda RX-7		19	Touring 1.3 twin-turbo; man 5
✓ Subaru SVX		19	LSi 3.3 Six; auto 4
MEDIUM CARS UNDER $25,000			
✓ Toyota Camry		24	LE 2.2 Four; auto 4
✓ Subaru Legacy		23	LS AWD 2.2 Four; auto 4
✓ Infiniti G20		29	2.0 Four; man 5
✓ Nissan Maxima		24	GXE 3.0 V6; auto 4
Chrysler Cirrus		22	LXi 2.5 V6; auto 4
Volkswagen Passat		20	GLX 2.8 V6; auto 4
Mercury Mystique		23	LS 2.5 V6; auto 4
✓ Honda Accord		26	LX 2.2 Four; auto
✓ Mazda 626		25	LX 2.0 Four; auto 4
Saab 900		22	SE 2.5 V6; auto 4
Mitsubishi Galant		24	LS 2.4 Four; auto 4
✓ Buick Regal		20	Gran Sport 3.8 V6; auto 4
✓ Pontiac Grand Prix		19	GT 3.4 V6; auto 4

Model	Overall score (P F G VG E)	Fuel usage	Tested model
Ford Contour		26 mpg	GL 2.0 Four; auto 4
✓ Ford Taurus		22	GL 3.0 V6; auto 4
✓ Mercury Sable		20	LS 3.8 V6; auto 4
✓ Nissan Altima		27	SE 2.4 Four; man 5
✓ Chevrolet Lumina		21	LS 3.1 V6; auto 4
Hyundai Sonata		21	GLS 3.0 V6; auto 4
Dodge Avenger		22	ES 2.5 V6; auto 4
Dodge Stratus		20	2.4 Four; auto 4
✓ ▪ Ford Thunderbird		20	LX 3.8 V6; auto 4
✓ ▪ Mercury Cougar		20	LX 3.8 V6; auto 4
Buick Skylark		21	Gran Sport 3.3 V6; auto 4
Oldsmobile Cutlass Supreme		20	SL Special Edition 3.1 V6; auto 4
Chevrolet Monte Carlo		18	Z34 3.4 V6; auto 4
Pontiac Grand Am		20	GT 3.3 V6; auto 3
Chevrolet Corsica		25	2.2 Four; auto 3
Oldsmobile Achieva		24	S 2.3 Four; auto 3
▪ Buick Century		22	3.1 V6; auto 4
▪ Oldsmobile Ciera		22	Buick Special 3.1 V6; auto 4
MEDIUM CARS OVER $25,000			
✓ Volvo 850		22	Turbo 2.3 Five; auto 4
✓ Toyota Avalon		22	XLS 3.0 V6; auto 4
✓ BMW 3-Series		24	325i 2.5 Six: auto 4
✓ Mazda Millenia		22	S 2.3 V6; auto 4
✓ Volvo 960		20	2.9 Six; auto 4
✓ Saab 9000		21	CSE 2.3 turbo Four; auto 4
✓ Lexus ES300		22	3.0 V6; auto 4
✓ Infiniti J30		20	3.0 V6; auto 4
✓ Mazda 929		20	3.0 V6; auto 4
✓ Mercedes-Benz C-Class		20	C280 2.8 Six; auto 4
✓ Acura Legend		20	L 3.2 V6; auto 4
Ford Taurus SHO		21	3.2 V6; auto 4
✓ Mitsubishi Diamante		20	LS 3.0 V6; auto 4
Audi 90		22	CS Quattro Sport 2.8 V6; man 5
Oldsmobile Aurora		17	4.0 V8; auto 4
Buick Riviera		17	3.8 V6; auto 4

Ratings continued ▶

Ratings continued

Model	Overall score (P F G VG E)	Fuel usage	Tested model
LARGE CARS UNDER $25,000			
▪ Chrysler Concorde		20 mpg	Dodge Intrepid ES 3.5 V6; auto 4
▪ Dodge Intrepid		20	3.3 V6; auto 4
▪ Eagle Vision		20	Dodge Intrepid ES 3.5 V6; auto 4
✓ Pontiac Bonneville		18	SSEi 3.8 supercharged V6; auto 4
✓ ▪ Ford Crown Victoria		19	LX 4.6 V8; auto 4
✓ ▪ Mercury Grand Marquis		19	Ford Crown Victoria LX 4.6 V8; auto 4
Chevrolet Caprice		17	LS Classic 5.7 V8; auto 4
✓ ▪ Buick Le Sabre		19	Olds Eighty Eight 3.8 V6; auto 4
✓ ▪ Oldsmobile Eighty-Eight		19	3.8 V6; auto 4
LARGE CARS OVER $25,000			
Chrysler LHS/New Yorker		20	LHS 3.5 V6; auto 4
Buick Roadmaster		17	Base 5.7 V8; auto 4
LUXURY CARS			
✓ Mercedes-Benz E-Class		21	E320 3.2 Six; auto 4
✓ BMW 5-Series		19	530i 3.0 V8; auto 5
✓ Lexus GS300		21	3.0 Six; auto 4
✓ Infiniti Q45		17	Q45a4.5 liter V8; auto 4
✓ Lexus SC400		19	4.0 V8; auto 4
✓ Lincoln Mark VIII		19	4.6 V8; auto 4
Cadillac Seville		17	STS 4.6 V8; auto 4
Cadillac Eldorado		15	Touring Coupe 4.6 V8; auto 4
MINIVANS			
▪ Dodge Grand Caravan (1996)		18	SE 3.3 V6; auto 4
▪ Chrysler Town & Country		18	Dodge Grand Caravan SE 3.3 V6; auto 4
▪ Plymouth Grand Voyager		18	Dodge Grand Caravan SE 3.3 V6; auto 4
▪ Dodge Caravan (1996)		20	SE 3.3 V6; auto 4
▪ Chrysler Town & Country LX		20	Dodge Caravan LX 3.3 V6; auto 4
▪ Plymouth Voyager		20	Dodge Caravan SE 3.3 V6; auto 4
✓ Ford Windstar		20	LX 3.8 V6; auto 4
✓ Honda Odyssey		21	EX 2.2 Four; auto 4
✓ ▪ Mercury Villager		20	GS 3.0 V6; auto 4
✓ ▪ Nissan Quest		19	GXE 3.0 V6; auto 4
✓ Toyota Previa		18	LE All-Trac 2.4 Four; auto 4

Model	Overall score (P F G VG E)	Fuel usage	Tested model
▪ Pontiac Trans Sport		18 mpg	SE 3.8 V6; auto 4
▪ Chevrolet Lumina		18	Pontiac Trans Sport SE 3.8 V6; auto 4
▪ Oldsmobile Silhouette		18	Pontiac Trans Sport SE 3.8 V6; auto 4
Ford Aerostar		16	Extended AWD 4.0 V6; auto 4
Mazda MPV		16	4WD 3.0 V6; auto 4
▪ Chevrolet Astro		15	Extended LT 4.3 V6; auto 4
▪ GMC Safari		15	Chevrolet Astro Extended LT 4.3 V6; auto 4
SPORT-UTILITY VEHICLES			
✓ Ford Explorer		17	Limited 4.0 V6; auto 4
✓ Toyota Land Cruiser		14	4.5 Six; auto 4
Jeep Grand Cherokee		15	Limited 5.2 V8; auto 4
▪ Chevrolet Blazer		17	LT 4.3 Six; auto 4
▪ GMC Jimmy		17	SLE 4.3 Six; auto 4
✓ Isuzu Trooper		15	LS 3.2 V6; auto 4
Jeep Cherokee		17	4.0 Six; auto 4
Mitsubishi Montero		15	LS 3.0 V6; auto 4
▪ Honda Passport		16	EX 3.2 V6; auto 4
▪ Isuzu Rodeo		16	Honda Passport EX 3.2 V6; auto 4
Land Rover Discovery		13	3.9 V8; auto 4
COMPACT PICKUPS (EXTENDED CABS)			
✓ ▪ Ford Ranger		18	XLT 4.0 V6; auto 4
✓ ▪ Mazda B4000		18	LE 4.0 V6; auto 4
▪ Chevrolet S-10		17	LS 4.3 V6; auto 4
▪ GMC Sonoma		17	SLE 4.3 V6; auto 4
Dodge Dakota		17	SLT 3.9 V6; auto 4
Toyota Tacoma		21	LX 3.4 V6; auto 4

How to buy a new car

First, decide on the type of vehicle—a large luxury car or a small economy model, a practical family sedan or a sporty coupe, a versatile minivan or a trendy sport-utility vehicle.

Then narrow the field to makes and models in your price range. The new-car profiles on page 256 will help you select a few models that meet your criteria. Savings are sometimes possible by considering siblings—essentially similar models sold under different nameplates. The car ratings (page 269) indicate which models have kin.

At this point you're ready for your first trip to a dealership—but only for a test drive and to gather brochures. When you drive the cars, note the comfort of the driving position, the view out in all directions, the convenience of the safety belts and the various controls, and the roominess and accessibility of the cargo area. Drive the car over good roads and bad to get a feel for the overall quality of the ride and noise inside the car.

Ask for a brochure to study. You're not ready to talk seriously with a salesperson. With brochures, you can compare the standard equipment available on the various models. Most models are sold in two or more trim lines (Base, GL, LX, etc.), with different levels of equipment and different base prices.

In some cases, a more expensive trim line may cost less than a basic model with lots of options. Sometimes, too, desirable options are unavailable in the base model.

Options packages often bundle useful and frivolous equipment. But if you want all or most of the extras, it's usually cheaper to buy the package.

How much does it cost?

Traditionally, the seller and the buyer negotiate the ultimate selling price of a new car. Another approach is the one-price policy, pioneered by General Motors' Saturn dealerships, whereby dealers set a non-negotiable, take-it-or-leave-it price. People who hate to haggle may be glad to spend a little more to avoid the process. But a hard-bargaining buyer, armed with the right information—namely, the dealer's cost— can usually get a lower price at a dealership where bargaining is the norm.

The dealer's cost for the average model is about 90 percent of the "sticker price," also known as the "manufacturer's suggested retail price," or MSRP. Pricier vehicles—luxury cars, sport-utility vehicles, sports cars—tend to have higher markups than budget models.

The Consumer Reports New Car Price Service (see the box on page 255) provides a New Car Price Report that notes the latest list prices and dealer-invoice prices for the make, model, and trim line you specify. The printout also itemizes factory options, with their list price and invoice price, and notes the options we recommend. It provides other information hard to find elsewhere, about any special financing deals or factory-to-dealer or factory-to-customer rebates. Finally, it gives you the total list and dealer-invoice prices for the car equipped as you want it.

If you're using another price guide (various guides are available at book stores, newsstands, and public libraries), here's how you can make the most of it: Start with the basic price for each make, model, and trim line you're considering. Add in each option and package you want, by name and manufacturer's code number. In separate columns, total the list prices and invoice prices of each car and its options. To both columns, add the destination charge. If a rebate is in effect, deduct it from the invoice-price column. The difference between the totals of the two columns is your bargaining room.

For a domestic mid-sized car in good supply, $300 to $500 over invoice price may be a good deal. But even $1000 or more over invoice may be reasonable on some imports and desirable domestic models, depending on supply and demand.

Bargaining

Visit at least two or three dealers. Ask the dealership for its lowest figure, and say you're shopping around and are prepared to buy from the dealer who gives the lowest quote. Don't leave a deposit, even if it's refundable, until you're prepared to sign.

Bargain up from the dealer's cost (the dealer-invoice price), not down from the sticker price. Resist add-ons, which are designed to improve dealer profits. "Packs" are dealer-applied extras like rustproofing and undercoating, which are of little or no value. Another costly extra is an extended-service contract. Given the common three- to seven-year warranty, a service contract is not worthwhile, especially for a model with a decent reliability record.

Some dealers charge a "conveyance" or "document" fee for the paperwork involved in registering the car. You have to pay the state's registration fee, but the "conveyance" part may be negotiable.

Many dealers add an advertising surcharge—often more than $400 per car. Ask to see proof that the fee is legitimate.

A salesperson may point out that your figures don't include dealer preparation. In most cases, they shouldn't. That fee is usually included in the base price.

All too often, dealers will mention packs and fees only at the end of the bargaining, when it's time to sign the sales contract. Then, when the dealers cut the price of a pack or waive a fee, buyers think they're getting a break. They're not.

Take time to read the sales contract—including the fine print. If you see something you don't like—or if you think something should be included—ask for changes.

If you turn in your old car on delivery of the new one several weeks later, the sales contract may allow the dealer to reappraise your car at that time. That's only fair. Much can happen to your car that may affect its value in the intervening weeks.

Make sure the sales contract states that you have the option to void it and get your deposit back if, say, there's no delivery by a specified date. And make sure an officer of the dealership signs the agreement. The salesperson's signature may not be binding.

Keep the deal simple

Trade-in. Salespeople usually ask early in the negotiations whether you have a trade-in. Your answer should be "no." You'll have plenty of time to reconsider later. If you talk trade-in too soon, the numbers become so confusing that you don't know how much you're paying for the new car or getting for your old one.

Selling your old car privately can be troublesome, but you'll probably get more for it than if you trade it in. You can learn what your car is worth by consulting price guides at the public library. Or, you can call the Consumer Reports Used Car Price Service (see page 255).

Financing. When sales are sluggish, automakers often offer below-market-rate loans. Compared with typical bank rates, promotional rates can save hundreds of dollars over the life of a loan. In many cases, however, low-rate financing applies only to certain models or short-term loans.

If low-interest financing isn't available on the car you want, don't accept the dealer's financing until you shop around. Credit unions, banks, and even auto-insurance companies may offer better terms.

How to lease a new car

The least expensive way to buy a car is to pay cash. Financing is more costly because of the interest you pay. Leasing, whether a new or used car, is often costlier still, but in certain circumstances, it can make sense.

Leasing requires little or no cash up front. And monthly payments are lower than those for a car loan because, in essence, you're borrowing to cover only the car's depreciation while you have it. But extra charges at lease end can turn a good deal bad.

Sizing up a lease can be difficult because the figures you need may be hard to get.

Sizing up a lease

■ First, find out whether the leasing company is offering open- or closed-end leases. Consider only closed-ended leases, which do not obligate you to buy the car at the end of the lease or to make up any shortfall in its residual value.

■ Read the entire contract. Insist on taking home a copy to study.

■ Look for any setup fees, document charges, and security-deposit requirements. These can be negotiated. Is the yearly mileage limit adequate for your needs? What is the charge for additional miles?

■ Ask about the residual value of the car, its expected value, at lease end. Cars that hold their value—such as sport-utility vehicles—often make the best lease deals. Cars that depreciate steeply may require high monthly payments to offset depreciation.

■ Next, negotiate a price for the car exactly as if you were buying it. (See page 274.) Ask for monthly lease payments based on that price.

■ Ask for the rate or "money factor" of the lease—similar to the annual percentage rate on a car loan.

■ Be especially careful about end-of-lease charges: Does the contract define "excess wear and tear"—damage you'll have to pay for at the end of lease? Ask who's responsible for preparing the car for resale, and for wear on items like brakes and tires.

■ Find out what happens if you want to end the lease before it expires. You may have to make up the difference between the car's depreciation and what's paid. Some leases require you to make all the remaining payments if you terminate early.

■ Make sure "gap insurance" is included. If the car is destroyed or stolen, gap insurance pays the difference between what you owe and what the car is worth. It shouldn't cost more than $100 or $200. Some lease companies toss it in free.

■ Make sure the manufacturer's warranty will cover the car for the entire term of the lease and the number of miles you're likely to drive.

■ If there's an option to purchase at lease end, ask how the price will be determined.

■ If you're leasing a used car, have a mechanic check the vehicle's "wear" parts such as brakes and tires.

Sizing up a lease should get easier at year's end when rules from the Federal Reserve Board are expected to be approved. As they stand now, the rules would require auto companies to provide the car's gross cost, which is basically the car's total cost and the key piece of information needed to negotiate a deal. Consumers would also get a statement about liability for excessive wear and tear, an example of an early termination charge, an itemized account of the money due when the lease is signed, and what the car is estimated to be worth at lease end.

How to buy a used car

The best car values are used cars, not new ones. A new car depreciates about 20 to 30 percent the minute you drive it off the dealer's lot. If you have only $10,000 or so to spend, your new-car choices are few and modest. For the same money, your choices in the used-car market are much broader.

The used-car marketplace, however, can be tricky. Prices vary according to the desirability of the car and its condition. But paint and polish can go a long way toward hiding wear and tear or, worse, the effects of an accident. Odometers can be rolled back to hide the true mileage. Warranties are skimpy, if they're available at all.

What to consider

You can minimize the risk of buying a used car if you stick with a model that has held up well in the past. Our Frequency-of-Repair records, based on readers' experiences with more than 580,000 cars, trucks, sport-utility vehicles, and vans, describe the reliability history of 1987 through 1994 models. From those records, we have derived a list of reliable used cars (see page 279) and another list of models to avoid (page 282). However, the older the car, the less important our records and the more important the condition of the individual car.

To find out how much a model sells for in your area, you can use the Consumer Reports Used Car Price Service (see page 357). Various printed guides, available in public libraries, provide information, too.

Where to buy

New-car dealers, used-car dealers, service stations, auto-rental companies, banks and other lenders, and private owners are sources for used cars. New car dealers are usually the most trustworthy sources, but their prices tend to be high. They will be the best sources of cars coming off a two- or three-year lease—potentially good buys and often with a warranty. Independent used-car dealers may obtain their cars from new-car dealers, auctions, police forces, taxi fleets, so their history is often in doubt. The Federal Trade Commission requires every used car sold by a dealer to display a Buyer's Guide sticker containing warranty information. In most states, "as is" on the sticker constitutes a denial of warranty coverage.

Service stations may sell used cars as a sideline. If the station has serviced the car they're selling, you may be able to learn a lot about its history.

Auto-rental agencies such as Hertz, Avis, and National offer some cars to the public. While these cars may have been driven long and hard, most have been serviced regularly. And some companies provide a limited warranty. You can call the agencies' toll-free numbers to learn the locations of their used-car lots.

Private sellers tend to charge the lowest prices. But, of course, there's no guarantee. If you shop through a newspaper ad, ask about the car's condition and mileage, whether it's been in a wreck, and why it's being sold.

Looking for trouble

Check service and repair bills or the warranty booklet for evidence that it's been treated well and serviced regularly.

Inspecting a car is easier if you bring along a friend to help. Here's what to look for:

Fluids. When the engine is cold, open the radiator cap and inspect the coolant; it shouldn't be rusty. Greenish stains on the radiator suggest leaks. To check an automatic transmission, warm up the engine and remove the dipstick. The fluid should be pinkish; it shouldn't smell burned or contain metal particles. There should be no puddles or stains under the car or excessive residue of lubricants on the engine, transmission or hoses.

Body integrity. Rust isn't a problem with newer cars, but it has ruined older ones. Check the wheel wells and rocker panels (under the doors), the door bottoms, and the floor of the trunk, under the mat. Paint blisters suggest rust. Look for signs of an accident—fresh welds, fresh undercoating on an older car, rippled body work, and panels with mismatched color.

Tires and suspension. A car with fewer than 25,000 miles should have its original tires, still with some useful tread. Bald or new tires could mean that the odometer has been turned back. Uneven tread wear may indicate poor alignment—or it may indicate serious accident damage. Grab the top of each front tire and shake it. Any play or a clunking sound could mean loose or worn wheel bearings or suspension joints. Bounce the car a few times by pushing down on each corner. If it keeps bouncing, the struts or shock absorbers need replacing. Look at the car from the rear and the side: A lopsided stance could mean sagging springs.

Interior. A saggy driver's seat means heavy use (or a heavy user). Excessively worn or new pedals might signal high mileage. Check under carpets in the car and trunk for mildew or moisture. Musty odors suggest a water leak.

The road test

Take a half-hour drive on a variety of roads and at various speeds.

Steering. With the engine off, there should be no more than two inches of play when you jiggle the steering wheel. When you drive, the steering should feel smooth and precise, with minimal vibration. As your assistant watches the car from behind, check for a sideways drift as the car moves forward.

Engine. The car should start easily, pick up smoothly, and maintain power over hills and when passing. Pinging or knocking is a sign of an out-of-tune engine or bad gasoline. And blue smoke from the tailpipe could indicate oil guzzling. A brief bit of white smoke on a cold day is okay, but heavy white smoke is a sign of a serious engine problem. Black smoke may signal the need for a minor fuel adjustment.

Transmission. An automatic transmission shouldn't slam into gear or slip as you drive. With a manual transmission, the clutch shouldn't grab suddenly and make the car buck.

Brakes. On a flat stretch of traffic-free road, try stopping from about 45 mph. Apply the brakes firmly. The car should stop quickly, evenly, and in a straight line. Repeat the exercise several times. To check for leaks in the brake system, press the pedal firmly for 30 seconds. It shouldn't sink to the floor.

Comfort and quiet. Suspension work may be in order if the car bounces or rattles over rough roads. Sputtering sounds from beneath the chassis indicate a leak in the exhaust system.

Closing the deal

A car that passes your inspection is ready for checking by a reliable mechanic or an auto diagnostic center. That may cost from $60 to $100, but it's money well spent. Make sure the mechanic performs a compression test on all cyclinders and checks out anything you may have noticed during your test drive. Get a written estimate of needed repairs to use in price negotiations.

The National Highway Traffic Safety Administration (800 424-9393) can tell you whether a model has been recalled. Also, check page 331 of the Product Recalls chapter for the auto recalls published in CONSUMER REPORTS in the last year.

Used cars—good & bad

The list of reliable used cars includes 1987 to 1993 models whose overall reliability has been better than average for their model year, according to our Frequency-of-Repair data (see page 284).

The reliable cars are grouped by price, as reported in the April issue of CONSUMER REPORTS. Most are likely to have dropped to a lower price by 1996. Prices are averages in the Midwest for cars with average mileage (10,000 to 15,000 miles a year) and with air-conditioning, AM/FM cassette stereo, and automatic transmission. (Prices for sporty cars are with manual transmission.) Luxury cars are priced with leather seats, sun roof, and CD player.

The list of used cars to avoid—see page 282—includes models whose overall records have been considerably worse than their model-year average.

In both lists, problems with the engine, engine cooling, transmission, clutch, and body rust—troubles likely to be serious and costly to repair—have been weighted more heavily than other problems.

Within groups, models are listed alphabetically. Except as noted, a listing covers all body styles, engines, and drive types. Throughout, 2WD is two-wheel drive, 4WD is front-wheel drive.

Reliable used cars

$2000-$4000

DODGE
Ram 50 Pickup 4, '87-89
FORD
Festiva, '88-90
LTD Crown Victoria, '87
HONDA
CRX, '87
Civic 2WD, '87
MAZDA
323, '87-'88
626 4, '87
Pickup 2WD, '87-'88
MERCURY
Grand Marquis, '87
MITSUBISHI
Pickup 4, '87
NISSAN
Pickup 4 2WD, '87-'88;
Pickup V6 2WD, '87
Stanza, '87
TOYOTA
Corolla, '87 [2]
MR2, '87
Pickup 4 2WD, '87-'88
Tercel, '87

$4000-$5000

ACURA
Integra, '87 [2]
EAGLE
Summit Coupe, '91
HONDA
Accord, '87
CRX, '88, '89
Prelude, '87
MAZDA
323, '90
MX-6 4, '88 [1]
Pickup 2WD, '89
MITSUBISHI
Pickup 4, '88
NISSAN
Maxima, '87 [2]
Pickup 4 2WD, '89;
Pickup V6 2WD, '88
Stanza, '88
PLYMOUTH
Colt, Colt Wagon, '91
TOYOTA
Camry 4, '87 [2]
Corolla, '88
Pickup 4 2WD, '89
Tercel, '89
VOLVO
240 Sedan and Wagon, '87

$5000-$6000

ACURA
Legend, '87 [2]
AUDI 80
'88
DODGE
Colt, Colt Wagon, '91
EAGLE
Summit Hatchback, '91
Summit Coupe, '92
HONDA
Accord, '88
CRX, '90
Civic 2WD, '89
LINCOLN
Town Car, '87

[1] *Manual transmission only.* [2] *Automatic transmission only.*

Continued ▶

Continued

MAZDA
323, '91
MX-6 4, '89 [1]
Pickup 2WD, '90
Protege, '90
NISSAN
Maxima, '88 [2]
Pickup 4 2WD, '90;
Pickup V6 2WD, '89, '90
Stanza, '89
TOYOTA
Camry 4, V6, '88
Celica, '88
Corolla, '89
Pickup 4 2WD, '90
VOLVO
740 Sedan & Wagon, '87
740 Turbo Sedan & Wagon, '87

$6000-$7000

DODGE
Colt, Colt Wagon, '92
EAGLE
Summit Hatchback, '92
HONDA
Civic 2WD, '90
Prelude, '89
MAZDA
323, '92
626 4, '89 [1]
929, '88
MX-6 4 Turbo, '89 [1]
Pickup 2WD, '91
MITSUBISHI
Mirage, '91
NISSAN
240SX, '89 [2]
Pickup 4 2WD, '91
Sentra, '91
OLDSMOBILE
Eighty Eight, '89
PLYMOUTH
Colt, Colt Wagon, '92
SATURN
SL Sedan, Wagon, '91
TOYOTA
Camry 4, V6, '89
Celica, '89
Corolla, '90
Cressida, '88
Pickup 4 2WD, '91
Pickup V6 2WD, '90
Tercel, '91
VOLVO
240 Sedan, Wagon, '88
740 Sedan, Wagon, '88

$7000-$8000

BMW
525i, '87
CADILLAC
Seville, '88
GEO
Prizm, '91
HONDA
Accord, '89
CRX, '91
MAZDA
626 4, '90
929, '89
Pickup 2WD, '92
Protegé, '91
MITSUBISHI
Mirage, '92
NISSAN
Maxima, '89 [2]
Pathfinder, '87
Pickup 4 2WD, '92 & 4WD, '90
Pickup V6 2WD, '91
Stanza, '90 [2]
TOYOTA
Camry 4, V6, '90
Corolla, '91
Pickup 4 2WD, '92 & 4WD, '89
Pickup V6 4WD, '89
Supra, Supra Turbo, '88
Tercel, '92
VOLVO
240 Sedan & Wagon, '89
740 Turbo Sedan & Wagon, '88

$8000-$9000

ACURA
Integra, '90
Legend, '88 [2]
AUDI
90 Quattro, '88
CADILLAC
Brougham, '89
Fleetwood, '89
HONDA
Accord, '90
Civic 2WD, '91
Prelude, '90
MAZDA
Protegé, '92
MERCURY
Tracer, '93
NISSAN
Maxima, '90 [2]
Pathfinder, '88
Pickup 4 4WD, '91
Pickup V6 2WD, '92
Pickup V6 4WD, '90
Sentra, '92
Stanza, '91
OLDSMOBILE
Cutlass Ciera, '92
SATURN
SL Sedan & Wagon, '92, '93
SUBARU
Legacy 4WD, '90
TOYOTA
Celica, '90
Corolla, '92
Cressida, '89
Pickup 4 & V6 4WD, '90
VOLVO
240 Sedan & Wagon, '90
760 Sedan & Wagon, '88

$9000-$10,000

ACURA
Integra, '91
BUICK
Century 4 & V6, '92
CADILLAC
De Ville, '89
Seville, '89
GEO
Prizm, '92
HONDA
Civic 2WD, '92
MAZDA
MX-5 Miata, '90
MITSUBISHI
Galant 4, '91
Montero V6, '89
NISSAN
Pickup 4 4WD, '92
Sentra, '93

SUBARU
Legacy 2WD, '91
TOYOTA
4Runner 4 & V6 4WD, '88
Camry 4 & V6, '91
Celica, '91
Paseo, '92
Pickup 4 2WD, '93
Pickup 4 4WD, '91
Pickup V6 2WD, '91
Tercel, '93
VOLVO
740 Sedan & Wagon, '90
760 Turbo Sedan & Wagon, '88

$10,000-$12,000

ACURA
Integra, '92
Legend, '89 [2]
AUDI
100, '90
BMW
5-Series, '88
CADILLAC
De Ville, '90
Fleetwood, Sixty Special, '89
GEO
Prizm, '93
HONDA
Accord, '91, '92
Civic, '93
Prelude, '91
INFINITI
G20, '91
MAZDA
MX-5 Miata, '91, '92
Protegé, '93
MITSUBISHI
Galant 4, '92
Montero V6, '90
NISSAN
240SX, '91
Maxima, '91
Pathfinder, '89
Pickup V6 4WD, '91
Stanza, '92
SATURN
SC Coupe, '93
SUBARU
Impreza, '93
Legacy 2WD & 4WD, '92; 4WD, '91
TOYOTA
4Runner 4 4WD, '89
Corolla, '93
Cressida, '90
MR2 & MR2 Turbo, '91
Pickup 4 4WD, '92
Pickup V6 2WD '92 & V6 4WD, '91, '92
T100 Pickup, '93
VOLVO
760 Sedan & Wagon, '89
760 Turbo Sedan & Wagon, '89

$12,000-$15,000

ACURA
Integra, '93
Legend, '90 [2]
BUICK
Regal, '93
CADILLAC
Fleetwood, Sixty Special, '90
FORD
Crown Victoria, '93
HONDA
Accord, '93
Prelude, '92
INFINITI
G20, '92
LEXUS
ES250, '90, '91
MAZDA
MX-5 Miata, '93
MERCURY
Grand Marquis, '93
NISSAN
240SX, '92, '93
Maxima, '92
Pathfinder, '90, '91
Pickup V6 4WD, '92
SUBARU
Legacy 2WD & 4WD, '93
TOYOTA
4Runner 4 2WD,'90, '91 & 4WD, '90
4Runner V6 2WD, '90, '91 & 4WD, '89, '90
Camry 4 & V6, '92, '93
Celica, '92
Cressida, '91
Pickup 4 4WD, '91, '93
Pickup V6 2WD & 4WD, '93
Previa 2WD & 4WD, '91
VOLVO
740 & 760 Turbo Sedan & Wagon, '90
760 Sedan & Wagon, '90
940 Sedan & Wagon, '91

$15,000-$20,000

ACURA
Legend, '91 [2]
Vigor, '92, '93
AUDI
100, '92
HONDA
Prelude, '93
INFINITI
G20, '93
Q45, '90
MERCEDES-BENZ
300D 2WD, '90
300E 2WD, '90
MITSUBISHI
Diamante, '92
NISSAN
Altima, '93
Maxima, '93
Pathfinder, '92, '93
OLDSMOBILE
Ninety Eight, '93
TOYOTA
4Runner 4 4WD, '91-93
4Runner V6 2WD, '92,'93; 4WD, '91-93
Pickup V6 4WD, '91
Previa 2WD, '92, '93 & 4WD, '92
VOLVO
740 Sedan & Wagon, '92
940 Turbo Sedan & Wagon, '91

$20,000-$25,000

ACURA
Legend, '92, '93
INFINITI
J30, '93
ISUZU
Trooper V6, '93

[1] *Manual transmission only.* [2] *Automatic transmission only.*

Continued ▶

LEXUS
ES300, '92, '93
LS400, '90
LINCOLN
Town Car, '93
MERCEDES-BENZ
300D 2WD, '91
300E 2WD, '91
TOYOTA
Land Cruiser, '91
Previa 4WD, '93

VOLVO
850 GLT, '93
940 Sedan & Wagon & Turbo Sedan & Wagon, '93

$25,000-$30,000

AUDI
90 Quattro, '93
INFINITI
Q45, '92
LEXUS
GS300, '93
LS400, '91
SC300, '92
TOYOTA
Land Cruiser, '93

$30,000 AND UP

BMW
5-Series, '93
LEXUS
LS400, '92, '93
SC300, '93
SC400, '92, '93

Used cars to avoid

ACURA

Integra,'87 [1]
Legend, '87-91 [1]

BMW

3-Series, '91

BUICK

Roadmaster, '92
Somerset, Skylark, '87
Skylark, '88, '90

CADILLAC

Fleetwood RWD, '93
Eldorado, '93

CHEVROLET

Astro Van 2WD & 4WD, '92-93
Blazer, '87-93
Camaro, '87-93
Caprice V8, '90
Cavalier, '87-93
Corsica, Beretta, '88
Corvette, '90-93
K1500-2500 Pickup, '88, '91-92
Lumina APV Van, '90
S-10 Blazer V6 4WD, '88-93
S-10 Pickup 2WD, '93, 4WD, '89, '91
Sportvan, '89-93
Suburban 2WD & 4WD, '87-93

CHRYSLER

Le Baron Coupe/Convertible, '88, '90, '91, '93
New Yorker, '92
Town & Country 2WD, '90, '92-93 & 4WD, '92-93

DODGE

Dakota Pickup 2WD, '92 & 4WD, '92-93
Daytona, '88-90
Dynasty, '92-93
Grand Caravan V6 2WD, '88-93 & 4WD, '91-93
Monaco, '90-91
Omni, '87, '89
Ram Van B150-250, '89-90, '92-93
Shadow, '93

EAGLE

Prémier V6, '88-91
Talon 2WD, '92; Turbo 4WD, '90-92

FORD

Aerostar 2WD, '87-91 & 4WD, '90-92
Bronco, '87-93
Bronco II, '87-90
Club Wagon V8, '88-93
Escort, '88-90
Explorer 2WD, '91-92 & 4WD, '91
F150-250 Pickup 2WD & 4WD, '87-93
Mustang 4, '87-89; V8, '88, '92-93
Probe 4, '91-92; V6, '93
Ranger Pickup V6 4WD, '90-91
Taurus 4, '87-89; V6, '87-88; SHO, '89-93
Tempo, '87-93
Thunderbird V6, '93

GMC

Jimmy, Yukon, '87-93
S-15 Jimmy V6 4WD, '88-93
S-15 Sonoma Pickup 2WD, '93 & 4WD, '89, '91
Safari 2WD & 4WD, '92-93
Sierra K1500-2500 Pickup, '88, '91-92
Suburban 2WD & 4WD, '87-93

HYUNDAI

Excel, '87-93
Sonata, '89-93

ISUZU

Rodeo V6, '91-92
Trooper II 4, '87; V6, '90-91

JEEP

Cherokee/Wagoneer 6, '90
Grand Cherokee 6 & V8, '93
Wrangler, '87-93

LINCOLN

Continental, '88-90
Town Car, '91

MAZDA

323, '89 [2]
626 4, '88-89 [2]
MPV V6 4WD, '90
MX-6 4, '88-89 [2] & V6, '93
Navajo 2WD, '92 & 4WD, '91

MERCURY

Cougar V6, '93
Sable, '87-88
Topaz, '87-93

MITSUBISHI

Eclipse 2WD, '92; Turbo 4WD, '90-92

NISSAN

240SX, '89-90 [1]
Maxima, '87-90 [1]
Stanza, '90 [1]

OLDSMOBILE

Cutlass Calais, '88-90
Cutlass Supreme V6, '93

PLYMOUTH

Grand Voyager V6 2WD, '88-93 & 4WD, '91-93
Horizon, '87, '89
Laser 2WD & Turbo 4WD, '92
Sundance, '93

PONTIAC

Bonneville, '87
Firebird, '87-93
Grand Am, '88-91
Grand Prix V6, '89, '91
Sunbird, '87, '91-93
Trans Sport, '90, '93

SAAB

900 Series 4, '90, '93

SUBARU

Coupe, Sedan, Wagon 4WD, '88-89

TOYOTA

Camry 4, '87 [1]
Corolla, '87 [1]

VOLKSWAGEN

Golf, GTI, '88-89
Jetta, '88-92
Passat, '90-93

[1] *Manual transmission only.* [2] *Automatic transmission only.*

BATTERY BASICS

There are two main types:

- **Low-maintenance** batteries have caps or covers over their cells to permit periodic checking and refilling.
- **Maintenance-free** batteries are the type most new cars come with. They're designed to reduce water loss further; indeed, some have no refill caps. They may not endure a deep discharge as well as low-maintenance batteries.

Size. Manufacturers categorize batteries by group size—24, 26, 34, and so forth—which denotes the size of the case (but has no direct bearing on the power output). You can find the group-size on the case of the old battery or in the battery dealer's handbook.

Cold-cranking amps. Manufacturers rate the cold-cranking amperage (CCA) of their models. The CCA is the amount of current a battery should be able to deliver at 0°F without dropping below a certain cutoff voltage for 30 seconds. That translates into the battery's ability to supply power long enough to start a car in below-freezing weather.

Reserve capacity. This describes the battery's ability to continue supplying power to the engine and headlights if the charging system fails.

Auto reliability

Frequency-of-repair records, 1988-1994

With the help of its readers, CONSUMER REPORTS has been reporting on automobile reliability for some 40 years. Each year, we ask readers to report on a year's worth of car troubles by answering our Annual Questionnaire. This year, we report on cars going back eight years, instead of six.

From all the reports—on more than 580,000 cars, minivans, pickups, and sport-utility vehicles this year—we develop:

■ The Frequency-of-Repair charts, which detail the reliability history of 248 models.

■ The lists of reliable used cars and used cars to avoid on page 279.

■ The predicted reliability of new models in the auto profiles (page 256).

■ Trends and patterns. Cars continue to get more reliable. In 1991 we undertook a major analysis of our data over the previous decade. It demonstrated what we knew intuitively: Automobiles are more reliable than they used to be. Looking at the six major American and Japanese automakers, we saw that American models had improved a lot—in 1990, they had attained a level of reliability that Japanese automakers had attained a decade earlier. But the Japanese products had improved, too, and thus had remained ahead. Judging by the data this year, the trend continues.

How to read the charts

The symbols in the charts show the proportion of owners who have reported serious problems for each trouble spot. The data we used to create the charts are standardized to minimize differences due to varied mileage, and the symbols are on an absolute scale, so a ⊜ means the same for any trouble spot, any year, and any car. A ⊜ means that 2 percent or fewer of our readers' cars of that make, model, and year reported problems during the 120 month survey period. A ● in one or more trouble spots should raise doubt in your mind about the car and point to areas that merit careful inspection.

When our readers were filling out questionnaires, the 1994 models were less than six months old, with an average of 3000 miles. Such cars should score ⊜ in all trouble spots. On a 1994 car, regard any score of ○ or worse as a warning sign.

Of course, as cars grow older, they become more trouble-prone. While some older models still earn a ⊜ in many areas, scores of ⊖ or ○ are not uncommon—and are generally not cause for concern. For most trouble spots, scores of ◒ or ● reflect too many problems, we believe—especially if those low scores are in areas like transmission and body rust, which are costly and difficult to repair. 2WD = 2-wheel drive; 4WD = 4-wheel drive; — = model not made that year; 4, 6,V6 or V8 = 4-, 6-, or 8-cylinder engine.

KEY TO PROBLEM RATES

⊜ .... 2.0% or less

⊖ .... 2.0% - 5.0%

○ .... 5.0% - 9.3%

◒ .... 9.3% - 14.8%

● .... More than 14.8%

★ .... Insufficient data

☐ .... Not applicable

TROUBLE SPOTS EXPLAINED

Compare your car's trouble spots with the average This chart below shows how a hypothetical "average car" for each model year would have scored. Use the chart to assess the Frequency-of-Repair information of the car you're interested in. First, locate the model and year of your car in the charts on the following pages.

The Average Model 87	88	89	90	91	92	93	94	TROUBLE SPOTS	WHAT THEY INCLUDE
◒	◒	○	○	⊖	⊖	⊜	⊜	Engine	Pistons, rings, valves, block, heads, bearings, camshafts, gaskets, turbocharger, cam belts & chains, oil pump, leaks, overhaul.
◒	◒	○	○	⊖	⊖	⊜	⊜	Cooling	Radiator, heater core, water pump, thermostat, hoses, intercooler & plumbing, overheating.
◒	○	○	⊖	⊖	⊖	⊜	⊜	Fuel	Choke, fuel injection, computer & sensors, fuel pump, tank, emissions controls, carburetion setting, leaks, stalling.
○	○	⊖	⊖	⊖	⊜	⊜	⊜	Ignition	Spark or glow plugs, coil, distributor, electronic ignition, sensors & modules, timing, too-frequent tune-ups, knock or ping.
○	○	○	○	⊖	⊖	⊖	⊜	Auto. trans.	Transaxle, gear selector, linkage, coolers & lines, leaks, malfunction or failure.
⊖	⊖	⊖	⊖	⊖	⊖	⊜	⊜	Man. trans.	Gearbox, transaxle, shifter, linkage, leaks, malfunction or failure.
◒	◒	○	○	⊖	⊖	⊖	⊜	Clutch	Lining, pressure plate, release bearing, linkage & hydraulics.
●	●	●	◒	◒	◒	○	⊖	Electrical	Starter, alternator, battery, horn, switches, controls, instruments, lights, radio & sound system, accessory motors, electronics, wiring.
●	◒	◒	○	○	⊖	⊖	⊜	A/C	Compressor, condenser, evaporator, expansion valves, hoses, dryer, fans, electronics, leakage.
◒	◒	○	○	⊖	⊖	⊖	⊜	Suspension	Linkage, power-steering gear, pump, coolers & lines, alignment & balance, springs & torsion bars, ball joints, bushings, shocks & struts, electronic or air suspension.
●	●	●	◒	◒	○	⊖	⊜	Brakes	Hydraulic system, linings, discs & drums, power boost, antilock system; parking brake & linkage, malfunction.
●	◒	◒	○	⊖	⊜	⊜	⊜	Exhaust	Manifold, muffler, catalytic converter, pipes, leaks.
◒	○	⊖	⊖	⊜	⊜	⊜	⊜	Body rust	Corrosion, pitting, perforation.
◒	◒	◒	○	○	○	⊖	⊖	Paint/trim	Fading, discoloring, chalking, peeling, cracking; loose trim, moldings, outside mirrors.
◒	◒	○	○	○	○	○	○	Integrity	Seals, weather stripping, air & water leaks, wind noise, rattles & squeaks.
◒	◒	◒	◒	◒	◒	○	⊖	Hardware	Window, door, seat mechanisms; locks, safety belts, sun roof, glass, wipers.

Then compare your car's reliability scores with the average for that year in the chart above. You expect problems as a car ages. Problems with brakes, electrical system or body hardware are common on a car three or four years old. But a car whose trouble spots are much worse than the average chart could be a headache.

Acura Integra

Trouble spots	87	88	89	90	91	92	93	94
Engine	○	⊖	⊖	⊜	⊜	⊜	⊜	⊜
Cooling	○	⊖	⊖	⊜	⊜	⊜	⊜	⊜
Fuel	○	⊖	⊖	⊜	⊜	⊜	⊜	⊜
Ignition	⊖	◒	◒	⊜	⊜	⊜	⊜	⊜
Auto. trans.	◒	⊖	⊖	⊖	⊖	⊜	⊜	⊜
Man. trans.	⊜	⊜	⊜	⊜	⊜	⊜	⊜	⊜
Clutch	●	◒	○	⊖	⊜	⊜	⊜	⊜
Electrical	◒	◒	◒	○	⊖	⊖	⊜	⊖
A/C	●	◒	◒	⊖	⊖	⊖	⊜	⊜
Suspension	⊖	⊖	⊖	⊖	⊜	⊜	⊜	⊜
Brakes	●	●	◒	○	⊖	⊖	⊜	⊜
Exhaust	●	●	●	○	⊜	⊜	⊜	⊜
Body rust	○	◒	⊖	⊜	⊜	⊜	⊜	⊜
Paint/trim	○	◒	○	⊖	⊖	⊖	⊖	⊜
Integrity	○	○	○	○	○	○	○	⊖
Hardware	○	○	○	⊖	⊖	⊖	⊖	⊖

Acura Legend

Trouble spots	87	88	89	90	91	92	93	94
Engine	○	⊖	⊖	⊜	⊜	⊖	⊜	⊜
Cooling	⊖	⊖	⊜	⊜	○	⊖	⊜	⊜
Fuel	○	⊖	⊖	⊜	⊖	⊜	⊜	⊜
Ignition	⊖	⊜	⊖	○	⊜	⊜	⊜	⊜
Auto. trans.	○	○	⊖	⊜	⊖	⊜	⊜	⊜
Man. trans.	⊜	⊖	⊖	⊜	*	*	*	*
Clutch	●	●	●	◒	*	*	*	*
Electrical	◒	◒	○	◒	◒	○	⊖	⊖
A/C	⊖	⊖	⊖	⊖	⊖	⊖	⊜	⊜
Suspension	◒	◒	⊖	⊖	⊖	⊖	⊜	⊜
Brakes	◒	●	◒	◒	○	⊖	⊜	⊜
Exhaust	○	⊖	⊖	⊜	⊜	⊜	⊜	⊜
Body rust	⊖	⊖	⊖	⊜	⊜	⊜	⊜	⊜
Paint/trim	⊖	⊖	⊖	⊖	⊖	⊖	⊜	⊜
Integrity	○	○	○	⊖	○	⊖	○	⊜
Hardware	◒	○	○	○	○	○	○	⊖

Acura Vigor

Trouble spots	87	88	89	90	91	92	93	94 (Insufficient data)
Engine						⊜	⊜	
Cooling						⊜	⊜	
Fuel						⊜	⊜	
Ignition						○	⊜	
Auto. trans.						⊜	⊜	
Man. trans.						*	*	
Clutch						*	*	
Electrical						○	⊜	
A/C						⊖	⊜	
Suspension						⊖	⊜	
Brakes						⊖	⊜	
Exhaust						⊜	⊜	
Body rust						⊜	⊜	
Paint/trim						⊖	⊜	
Integrity						◒	○	
Hardware						⊖	⊖	

Audi 4000, 80, 90 Quattro

Trouble spots	87	88	89 (Insufficient data)	90 (Insufficient data)	91 (Insufficient data)	92 (Insufficient data)	93	94 (Insufficient data)
Engine	◒	○					⊖	
Cooling	●	◒					⊜	
Fuel	○	○					⊖	
Ignition	○	⊖					⊜	
Auto. trans.	*	*					*	
Man. trans.	*	*					*	
Clutch	*	*					*	
Electrical	●	●					○	
A/C	◒	◒					⊖	
Suspension	○	○					⊖	
Brakes	◒	●					⊜	
Exhaust	●	○					⊜	
Body rust	○	⊜					⊜	
Paint/trim	○	○					⊜	
Integrity	○	⊖					⊜	
Hardware	●	◒					⊖	

Audi 5000, 100, 200, Quattro

Trouble spots	87	88 (Insufficient data)	89	90	91	92	93	94 (Insufficient data)
Engine	◒		⊖	⊖	⊜	⊖	⊖	
Cooling	●		◒	⊜	⊖	○	⊖	
Fuel	◒		◒	●	◒	⊜	⊖	
Ignition	⊖		⊖	⊖	⊖	⊜	⊜	
Auto. trans.	◒		*	*	*	⊖	*	
Man. trans.	*		*	*	*	*	*	
Clutch	*		*	*	*	*	*	
Electrical	●		●	●	●	○	○	
A/C	●		⊖	⊖	⊖	⊜	⊖	
Suspension	●		◒	⊖	○	⊜	⊖	
Brakes	●		●	◒	◒	⊖	⊜	
Exhaust	○		⊜	⊜	⊜	⊜	⊜	
Body rust	⊜		⊜	⊜	⊖	⊜	⊜	
Paint/trim	⊖		⊜	⊖	⊜	⊜	⊜	
Integrity	○		⊖	○	○	⊖	⊖	
Hardware	●		●	◒	○	⊖	◒	

BMW 3-Series

Trouble spots	87	88	89	90	91	92	93	94
Engine	○	○	○	⊖	◒	⊜	⊜	⊜
Cooling	●	◒	○	◒	◒	○	⊜	⊜
Fuel	⊖	⊖	○	◒	◒	○	⊜	⊜
Ignition	⊖	⊖	⊖	⊖	⊖	⊖	⊜	⊜
Auto. trans.	○	*	*	*	*	⊖	⊜	*
Man. trans.	⊜	*	⊜	*	⊜	⊜	⊜	*
Clutch	○	*	⊖	*	⊜	⊖	⊖	*
Electrical	●	●	●	●	◒	●	◒	⊖
A/C	●	◒	◒	○	○	○	⊖	⊜
Suspension	⊖	⊖	⊖	○	⊖	⊖	⊜	⊜
Brakes	●	◒	○	○	◒	○	⊖	⊖
Exhaust	○	○	⊖	⊖	⊖	⊜	⊜	⊜
Body rust	⊖	⊖	⊜	⊜	⊜	⊜	⊜	⊜
Paint/trim	○	⊖	⊖	○	⊖	⊖	⊜	⊜
Integrity	⊖	○	⊖	⊖	○	○	○	○
Hardware	●	●	◒	◒	◒	●	○	⊖

BMW 5-Series

Trouble spots	87	88	89	90	91	92	93	94
Engine	○	⊜	○	○	○	⊜	⊖	⊜
Cooling	○	○	●	◒	⊖	⊖	⊜	⊖
Fuel	◒	⊖	◒	○	⊖	⊖	⊖	⊜
Ignition	⊖	⊜	⊜	⊜	○	⊜	⊜	⊜
Auto. trans.	*	*	*	⊜	*	○	*	⊜
Man. trans.	*	*	*	*	*	*	*	*
Clutch	*	*	*	*	*	*	*	*
Electrical	●	●	●	●	◒	◒	○	○
A/C	◒	◒	○	○	○	⊖	*	⊜
Suspension	○	○	○	⊖	⊖	⊖	⊜	⊜
Brakes	●	●	◒	◒	○	○	⊜	⊜
Exhaust	○	○	○	○	⊜	⊜	⊜	⊜
Body rust	⊖	⊖	⊜	⊜	⊜	⊜	⊜	⊜
Paint/trim	○	⊖	⊖	⊖	⊖	⊖	⊜	⊖
Integrity	○	○	⊖	⊖	⊖	⊖	⊖	⊜
Hardware	◒	○	○	○	○	◒	○	⊖

Buick Century

Trouble spots	87	88	89	90	91	92	93	94
Engine	◒	○	⊖	⊖	⊖	⊜	⊜	⊜
Cooling	◒	◒	○	○	○	⊖	⊜	⊜
Fuel	◒	◒	○	⊖	○	⊖	⊜	⊖
Ignition	○	○	○	⊖	⊜	⊜	⊜	⊜
Auto. trans.	○	⊖	⊖	⊖	⊖	⊖	⊜	⊜
Man. trans.								
Clutch								
Electrical	●	●	◒	◒	○	○	○	⊖
A/C	◒	○	○	⊖	⊖	⊖	⊖	⊖
Suspension	●	◒	○	○	⊖	⊖	⊖	⊜
Brakes	●	●	●	●	●	◒	○	⊜
Exhaust	●	◒	◒	○	⊖	○	⊖	⊜
Body rust	●	○	⊖	⊖	⊖	⊜	⊜	⊜
Paint/trim	●	●	◒	○	⊖	⊖	⊖	⊜
Integrity	◒	○	○	○	○	○	◒	⊖
Hardware	●	◒	○	○	○	⊖	○	⊖

⊜ ⊖ ○ ◒ ●
Few ← **Problems** → Many

* Insufficient data

Buick Electra, Park Avenue & Ultra

TROUBLE SPOTS	87	88	89	90	91	92	93	94
Engine	◒	⊖	⊖	⊜	⊜	⊜	⊜	⊜
Cooling	◒	◒	○	○	⊖	⊖	⊜	⊜
Fuel	●	○	○	⊖	⊖	⊖	⊖	⊜
Ignition	◒	○	○	⊖	○	⊖	⊜	⊜
Auto. trans.	●	○	⊖	⊖	⊖	⊜	⊜	⊜
Man. trans.								
Clutch								
Electrical	●	●	●	●	●	◒	◒	⊖
A/C	◒	○	○	⊖	◒	○	⊖	⊜
Suspension	●	◒	○	⊖	⊖	⊖	⊖	⊖
Brakes	●	●	●	●	◒	○	⊖	⊜
Exhaust	○	⊖	⊜	⊜	⊜	⊜	⊜	⊜
Body rust	⊖	⊜	⊜	⊜	⊜	⊜	⊜	⊜
Paint/trim	●	◒	○	○	○	⊖	⊜	⊜
Integrity	◒	○	○	○	●	◒	○	○
Hardware	◒	◒	◒	◒	●	◒	○	⊖

Buick Estate Wagon

TROUBLE SPOTS	87	88	89	90	91	92	93	94
Engine	◒	◒	◒	⊖				
Cooling	●	◒	◒	⊖				
Fuel	◒	◒	○	⊖				
Ignition	⊖	○	⊖	⊜				
Auto. trans.	○	○	⊖	⊖				
Man. trans.								
Clutch								
Electrical	●	●	●	●				
A/C	○	○	○	○				
Suspension	◒	●	○	○				
Brakes	◒	●	◒	◒				
Exhaust	●	●	◒	⊖				
Body rust	◒	○	○	◒				
Paint/trim	●	◒	○	◒				
Integrity	◒	○	○	◒				
Hardware	◒	●	◒	●				

Buick Le Sabre

TROUBLE SPOTS	87	88	89	90	91	92	93	94
Engine	○	⊖	⊖	⊜	⊜	⊜	⊜	⊜
Cooling	●	◒	○	○	⊖	⊖	⊜	⊜
Fuel	◒	◒	○	○	○	⊜	⊜	⊜
Ignition	○	○	○	○	○	⊜	⊜	⊜
Auto. trans.	●	○	○	⊖	⊖	⊖	⊖	⊜
Man. trans.								
Clutch								
Electrical	●	●	◒	◒	◒	◒	○	⊖
A/C	◒	○	○	○	○	⊖	⊜	⊜
Suspension	●	●	⊖	⊖	⊖	⊖	⊖	⊜
Brakes	●	●	●	●	●	◒	⊖	⊜
Exhaust	⊖	⊖	⊜	⊜	⊜	⊖	⊜	⊜
Body rust	○	○	⊜	⊖	⊖	⊜	⊜	⊜
Paint/trim	◒	○	○	○	○	○	⊜	⊜
Integrity	◒	○	⊖	⊖	○	◒	○	○
Hardware	●	◒	○	○	○	○	○	⊖

Buick Regal

TROUBLE SPOTS	87	88	89	90	91	92	93	94
Engine		○	○	⊖	⊖	⊜	⊜	⊜
Cooling		◒	◒	⊜	⊖	⊜	⊜	⊜
Fuel		◒	◒	⊖	⊖	⊜	⊜	⊜
Ignition		○	◒	⊖	⊜	⊜	⊜	⊜
Auto. trans.		○	○	⊖	⊖	⊖	⊖	⊜
Man. trans.								
Clutch								
Electrical		●	●	◒	◒	◒	○	○
A/C		◒	◒	⊖	○	⊖	⊖	⊜
Suspension		◒	◒	⊖	○	⊖	⊜	⊜
Brakes		●	●	●	●	◒	⊖	⊜
Exhaust		⊖	⊖	⊖	⊜	⊜	⊜	⊜
Body rust		⊜	⊜	⊖	⊜	⊜	⊜	⊜
Paint/trim		⊖	◒	◒	⊖	⊖	⊖	⊖
Integrity		○	◒	○	○	○	○	⊖
Hardware		◒	◒	●	○	○	○	○

Buick Riviera

TROUBLE SPOTS	87 (Insufficient data)	88 (Insufficient data)	89	90	91	92 (Insufficient data)	93 (Insufficient data)	94
Engine			⊖	⊜	⊖			
Cooling			⊜	○	○			
Fuel			○	○	⊖			
Ignition			◒	⊜	⊜			
Auto. trans.			○	○	⊖			
Man. trans.								
Clutch								
Electrical			●	●	◒			
A/C			○	◒	◒			
Suspension			⊖	○	⊖			
Brakes			●	●	●			
Exhaust			⊜	⊜	⊖			
Body rust			⊜	⊜	⊜			
Paint/trim			⊖	⊖	⊖			
Integrity			⊖	⊖	○			
Hardware			◒	◒	●			

Buick Roadmaster

TROUBLE SPOTS	87	88	89	90	91 (Insufficient data)	92	93	94
Engine						⊖	⊜	⊜
Cooling						⊜	⊜	⊜
Fuel						⊜	⊜	⊜
Ignition						⊖	⊖	⊜
Auto. trans.						◒	⊖	⊖
Man. trans.								
Clutch								
Electrical						●	◒	⊖
A/C						◒	⊜	⊜
Suspension						○	○	⊜
Brakes						○	⊜	⊖
Exhaust						⊜	⊜	⊜
Body rust						⊜	⊜	⊜
Paint/trim						○	○	⊜
Integrity						◒	◒	◒
Hardware						◒	○	○

Buick Somerset, Skylark

TROUBLE SPOTS	87	88	89	90	91	92	93	94 (Insufficient data)
Engine	●	●	○	○	⊖	⊜	⊜	
Cooling	●	○	○	○	⊜	⊖	⊖	
Fuel	◒	◒	○	○	⊖	⊜	⊜	
Ignition	◒	●	○	○	⊜	⊜	⊜	
Auto. trans.	◒	◒	⊖	⊖	⊜	○	⊜	
Man. trans.								
Clutch								
Electrical	●	●	●	●	●	◒	○	
A/C	◒	◒	○	○	⊖	⊖	⊖	
Suspension	●	◒	⊖	○	○	○	⊖	
Brakes	●	●	◒	●	◒	●	◒	
Exhaust	◒	●	●	●	◒	⊖	⊜	
Body rust	●	●	●	●	○	⊜	⊜	
Paint/trim	●	●	◒	●	◒	○	⊜	
Integrity	◒	◒	○	◒	○	◒	◒	
Hardware	○	◒	⊖	○	○	●	○	

Cadillac Brougham, Fleetwood (RWD)

TROUBLE SPOTS	87	88	89	90	91	92 (Insufficient data)	93	94 (Insufficient data)
Engine	⊖	◒	○	⊖	○		⊖	
Cooling	◒	◒	⊖	⊜	⊖		⊜	
Fuel	○	⊖	○	⊖	⊖		⊖	
Ignition	○	○	⊖	⊖	⊜		⊖	
Auto. trans.	○	○	⊖	◒	⊜		○	
Man. trans.								
Clutch								
Electrical	●	●	●	◒	◒		●	
A/C	●	◒	○	⊖	⊖		○	
Suspension	◒	○	○	○	○		◒	
Brakes	●	●	◒	◒	⊖		⊖	
Exhaust	◒	●	⊖	⊜	⊖		⊜	
Body rust	◒	◒	⊜	○	⊜		⊜	
Paint/trim	●	●	◒	○	⊖		◒	
Integrity	○	○	○	◒	○		●	
Hardware	○	◒	○	◒	●		●	

Cadillac De Ville, Fleetwood (FWD)

TROUBLE SPOTS	87	88	89	90	91	92	93	94
Engine	●	○	⊖	⊖	○	○	⊖	⊜
Cooling	●	◒	⊖	⊖	⊜	⊜	⊜	⊜
Fuel	○	⊖	⊖	○	○	⊖	⊖	⊜
Ignition	○	⊖	⊜	⊖	⊖	⊜	⊜	⊜
Auto. trans.	○	⊖	⊖	⊖	⊖	⊖	⊖	⊜
Man. trans.								
Clutch								
Electrical	●	●	●	●	◒	○	○	○
A/C	●	●	◒	○	◒	○	⊖	⊖
Suspension	●	◒	⊖	⊖	⊖	⊖	○	⊖
Brakes	●	●	●	●	◒	○	⊖	⊖
Exhaust	⊖	⊜	⊜	⊜	⊜	⊖	⊜	⊜
Body rust	⊖	⊖	⊜	⊜	⊜	⊜	⊜	⊜
Paint/trim	◒	○	⊖	⊖	⊖	⊖	⊖	⊜
Integrity	⊖	○	⊖	○	○	○	◒	⊖
Hardware	◒	●	○	◒	○	⊖	○	⊖

Cadillac Eldorado

TROUBLE SPOTS	87	88	89	90	91	92	93	94
Engine	Insufficient data	◒	○	○	Insufficient data	⊖	⊜	Insufficient data
Cooling		●	○	⊖		⊖	⊖	
Fuel		⊜	⊖	○		⊖	○	
Ignition		⊖	⊖	⊜		⊜	⊖	
Auto. trans.		○	○	⊜		⊖	⊖	
Man. trans.								
Clutch								
Electrical		●	●	●		◒	○	
A/C		◒	●	◒		○	○	
Suspension		○	⊖	⊖		⊖	○	
Brakes		●	●	◒		○	⊖	
Exhaust		⊖	⊜	⊖		⊖	⊜	
Body rust		⊜	⊜	⊜		⊜	⊜	
Paint/trim		⊖	○	○		⊖	○	
Integrity		○	⊖	⊖		●	●	
Hardware		◒	○	○		●	◒	

Cadillac Seville

TROUBLE SPOTS	87	88	89	90	91	92	93	94
Engine	●	◒	⊖	⊖	○	⊖	⊖	⊜
Cooling	●	○	⊖	⊖	⊖	⊜	⊜	⊜
Fuel	○	⊖	⊜	○	○	⊖	⊖	⊜
Ignition	◒	⊖	⊜	⊖	⊜	⊜	⊜	⊜
Auto. trans.	●	⊖	○	⊖	⊖	⊜	⊖	⊜
Man. trans.								
Clutch								
Electrical	●	●	●	●	◒	◒	◒	○
A/C	●	●	◒	◒	○	○	⊖	⊖
Suspension	○	○	○	⊖	⊖	○	⊖	⊖
Brakes	●	●	●	●	◒	⊖	⊜	⊜
Exhaust	○	⊜	⊖	⊖	⊜	⊜	⊜	⊜
Body rust	⊖	⊜	⊜	⊜	⊜	⊜	⊜	⊜
Paint/trim	◒	⊖	○	⊖	⊖	⊖	⊖	⊜
Integrity	●	○	○	○	○	○	◒	○
Hardware	◒	⊖	○	◒	○	◒	◒	○

Chevrolet Astro Van (2WD)

TROUBLE SPOTS	87	88	89	90	91	92	93	94
Engine	◒	◒	◒	⊖	⊖	○	⊖	⊜
Cooling	◒	○	○	⊖	⊜	⊖	⊜	⊜
Fuel	○	⊖	⊖	⊖	⊖	⊖	⊖	⊜
Ignition	⊖	○	⊖	⊖	⊜	⊖	⊜	⊜
Auto. trans.	○	○	⊖	⊖	⊜	○	⊖	⊖
Man. trans.	*	*	*					
Clutch	*	*	*					
Electrical	●	●	●	●	◒	◒	◒	○
A/C	◒	◒	◒	○	○	○	⊖	○
Suspension	●	●	◒	◒	○	⊖	⊖	⊖
Brakes	●	◒	●	●	●	●	○	⊜
Exhaust	◒	◒	○	○	⊖	⊜	⊜	⊜
Body rust	⊖	⊖	⊜	⊜	⊜	⊜	⊜	⊜
Paint/trim	●	●	◒	◒	◒	◒	○	⊜
Integrity	◒	◒	◒	●	●	●	●	◒
Hardware	●	●	●	●	●	●	●	○

Chevrolet Astro Van (4WD)

TROUBLE SPOTS	87	88	89	90	91	92	93	94
Engine				Insufficient data	⊖	⊜	⊖	Insufficient data
Cooling					⊖	⊜	⊖	
Fuel					⊜	○	⊖	
Ignition					⊜	⊖	⊜	
Auto. trans.					⊖	○	⊖	
Man. trans.								
Clutch								
Electrical					●	◒	◒	
A/C					○	⊜	⊖	
Suspension					○	⊜	⊖	
Brakes					●	●	○	
Exhaust					⊖	⊜	⊖	
Body rust					⊜	⊜	⊜	
Paint/trim					◒	◒	○	
Integrity					●	●	◒	
Hardware					●	●	●	

Chevrolet Blazer

TROUBLE SPOTS	87	88	89	90	91	92	93	94
Engine	●	◒	○	⊖	⊖	⊖	⊖	⊜
Cooling	●	◒	○	○	⊜	⊖	⊜	⊜
Fuel	◒	◒	○	⊖	⊖	⊖	⊖	⊜
Ignition	◒	○	⊖	○	○	⊖	⊜	⊜
Auto. trans.	●	◒	⊖	⊖	⊜	○	⊖	⊖
Man. trans.	*	*	*	*	*	*	*	*
Clutch	*	*	*	*	*	*	*	*
Electrical	●	●	●	◒	●	●	○	⊖
A/C	●	○	○	○	⊖	○	⊖	⊜
Suspension	◒	◒	○	⊖	○	○	⊖	⊜
Brakes	●	●	●	◒	●	●	○	⊜
Exhaust	◒	◒	◒	⊖	○	⊖	⊜	⊜
Body rust	●	●	◒	○	○	⊖	⊖	⊜
Paint/trim	●	●	●	●	●	◒	⊖	⊜
Integrity	●	●	●	●	◒	◒	◒	⊖
Hardware	●	●	●	●	●	●	◒	⊖

Chevrolet C1500-2500 Pickup

TROUBLE SPOTS	87	88	89	90	91	92	93	94
Engine	◒	◒	○	⊖	⊖	⊖	⊖	⊜
Cooling	●	●	○	⊖	⊖	⊜	⊜	⊜
Fuel	◒	○	⊖	○	⊖	⊖	⊜	⊜
Ignition	○	○	○	○	○	⊜	⊖	⊜
Auto. trans.	○	○	○	○	◒	○	⊖	⊜
Man. trans.	*	○	⊖	⊖	⊖	○	⊖	*
Clutch	*	●	○	○	◒	◒	○	*
Electrical	●	●	●	●	●	◒	○	⊖
A/C	○	○	○	○	○	○	⊖	⊖
Suspension	⊖	◒	◒	○	○	⊖	⊖	⊖
Brakes	◒	●	◒	◒	○	⊖	⊜	⊖
Exhaust	◒	●	◒	◒	○	⊜	⊜	⊜
Body rust	●	⊖	⊜	⊜	⊜	⊜	⊜	⊜
Paint/trim	●	◒	◒	◒	○	○	○	⊜
Integrity	◒	◒	○	○	○	○	○	○
Hardware	◒	◒	◒	○	○	○	○	○

Chevrolet K1500-2500 Pickup

TROUBLE SPOTS	87	88	89	90	91	92	93	94
Engine	◒	◒	○	○	⊖	⊖	⊖	⊜
Cooling	●	●	○	⊖	⊖	⊖	⊜	⊜
Fuel	●	○	⊖	⊖	⊖	⊖	⊜	⊜
Ignition	◒	○	○	○	⊜	⊖	⊜	⊜
Auto. trans.	●	◒	◒	○	◒	◒	⊖	⊜
Man. trans.	*	○	○	○	*	⊖	⊖	*
Clutch	*	●	◒	◒	*	○	⊖	*
Electrical	●	●	●	●	◒	◒	○	⊖
A/C	○	○	○	○	○	⊖	⊜	⊜
Suspension	◒	●	◒	○	○	○	⊖	⊖
Brakes	●	●	●	◒	◒	○	⊜	⊖
Exhaust	◒	●	●	○	○	⊖	⊜	⊜
Body rust	●	○	⊜	⊜	⊜	⊜	⊜	⊜
Paint/trim	●	◒	●	◒	◒	○	○	⊖
Integrity	◒	◒	◒	○	○	○	◒	○
Hardware	◒	●	◒	○	○	○	○	⊖

⊜ ⊖ ○ ◒ ●
Few ← Problems → Many

* Insufficient data

Chevrolet Camaro

Trouble spots	87	88	89	90	91	92	93	94
Engine	●	Insufficient data	○	Insufficient data	○	⊖	⊖	⊖
Cooling	●		●		○	⊜	⊜	⊜
Fuel	●		◒		⊖	⊖	◒	⊜
Ignition	◒		○		○	⊖	⊖	⊜
Auto. trans.	◒		○		⊖	○	○	⊜
Man. trans.	*		*		*	*	*	*
Clutch	*		*		*	*	*	*
Electrical	●		●		●	●	◒	⊖
A/C	◒		○		○	⊖	○	⊖
Suspension	◒		○		⊖	○	○	⊜
Brakes	●		◒		○	○	○	⊜
Exhaust	●		◒		⊖	⊖	⊜	⊜
Body rust	◒		○		⊖	⊖	⊜	⊜
Paint/trim	●		●		●	◒	○	⊖
Integrity	●		●		●	●	●	◒
Hardware	●		●		◒	●	◒	○

Chevrolet Caprice V8

Trouble spots	87	88	89	90	91	92	93	94
Engine	◒	○	⊖	○	⊖	○	⊜	⊖
Cooling	●	●	◒	◒	⊖	⊜	⊜	⊖
Fuel	◒	○	○	⊖	⊖	⊜	⊖	⊖
Ignition	○	○	○	○	○	⊖	⊜	⊖
Auto. trans.	○	○	○	⊖	⊖	⊖	⊖	◒
Man. trans.								
Clutch								
Electrical	●	◒	●	●	●	◒	○	○
A/C	○	⊖	○	⊖	◒	○	⊖	⊖
Suspension	○	○	○	○	○	○	○	⊖
Brakes	◒	◒	◒	◒	◒	○	⊖	⊖
Exhaust	●	●	●	◒	◒	⊜	⊜	⊜
Body rust	◒	◒	◒	◒	⊜	⊜	⊜	⊜
Paint/trim	●	●	●	◒	○	⊖	⊖	⊖
Integrity	◒	◒	◒	◒	◒	○	○	⊖
Hardware	◒	◒	◒	◒	●	○	○	○

Chevrolet Cavalier

Trouble spots	87	88	89	90	91	92	93	94
Engine	◒	◒	○	○	○	◒	○	⊜
Cooling	●	◒	○	◒	⊖	○	⊖	⊜
Fuel	◒	●	○	○	⊖	○	⊖	⊜
Ignition	○	◒	◒	○	○	⊖	⊖	⊜
Auto. trans.	⊖	○	⊖	⊖	⊖	⊖	⊖	⊖
Man. trans.	*	*	*	*	*	*	*	*
Clutch	*	*	*	*	*	*	*	*
Electrical	●	●	●	●	●	●	○	○
A/C	◒	○	○	○	⊖	○	⊜	⊜
Suspension	◒	◒	○	○	○	⊖	⊖	⊜
Brakes	●	●	◒	●	●	●	○	⊖
Exhaust	●	●	●	⊖	⊖	○	⊖	⊜
Body rust	●	●	◒	○	⊖	⊖	⊜	⊜
Paint/trim	●	●	●	◒	◒	○	⊖	⊜
Integrity	◒	◒	◒	◒	◒	◒	◒	⊖
Hardware	●	○	○	○	◒	●	◒	◒

Chevrolet Celebrity

Trouble spots	87	88	89	90	91	92	93	94
Engine	◒	○	⊖	⊖				
Cooling	◒	○	○	◒				
Fuel	◒	◒	◒	⊖				
Ignition	○	○	○	⊖				
Auto. trans.	○	○	⊖	⊖				
Man. trans.	*	*						
Clutch	*	*						
Electrical	●	●	●	○				
A/C	◒	○	○	⊖				
Suspension	●	◒	⊖	⊖				
Brakes	●	●	●	●				
Exhaust	●	●	●	◒				
Body rust	●	●	○	⊖				
Paint/trim	●	●	◒	○				
Integrity	◒	◒	⊖	○				
Hardware	●	◒	○	○				

Chevrolet Corsica, Beretta

Trouble spots	87	88	89	90	91	92	93	94
Engine	Insufficient data	○	○	⊖	○	○	⊖	Insufficient data
Cooling		◒	○	○	⊖	⊖	⊜	
Fuel		●	●	○	⊖	⊖	⊜	
Ignition		◒	◒	○	⊖	⊜	⊜	
Auto. trans.		○	⊖	⊖	⊖	⊜	⊜	
Man. trans.		○	⊖	*	*	*	*	
Clutch		●	○	*	*	*	*	
Electrical		●	●	●	●	◒	○	
A/C		◒	○	○	⊖	○	⊖	
Suspension		◒	○	○	○	○	⊖	
Brakes		●	●	●	●	●	○	
Exhaust		●	●	◒	⊜	⊜	⊜	
Body rust		○	⊖	⊖	⊖	⊜	⊜	
Paint/trim		●	●	●	◒	⊖	⊖	
Integrity		●	◒	●	●	◒	◒	
Hardware		●	●	●	○	○	◒	

Chevrolet Corvette

Trouble spots	87	88	89	90	91	92	93	94
Engine	Insufficient data	Insufficient data	Insufficient data	Insufficient data	Insufficient data	⊖	⊜	Insufficient data
Cooling						⊖	⊜	
Fuel						⊖	⊜	
Ignition						⊖	⊜	
Auto. trans.						*	*	
Man. trans.						*	*	
Clutch						*	*	
Electrical						●	○	
A/C						○	⊜	
Suspension						⊜	○	
Brakes						⊖	⊖	
Exhaust						⊜	⊜	
Body rust						⊜	⊜	
Paint/trim						○	⊖	
Integrity						●	●	
Hardware						◒	●	

Chevrolet Lumina

Trouble spots	87	88	89	90	91	92	93	94
Engine				○	○	⊖	⊜	⊜
Cooling				⊖	⊖	⊜	⊜	⊜
Fuel				○	⊖	⊖	⊜	⊜
Ignition				○	⊖	⊖	⊖	⊜
Auto. trans.				○	⊖	⊖	⊖	⊜
Man. trans.					*	*	*	
Clutch					*	*	*	
Electrical				◒	○	◒	◒	⊖
A/C				⊖	⊖	⊜	⊜	⊜
Suspension				○	○	⊖	⊖	⊜
Brakes				●	●	●	○	⊖
Exhaust				⊖	⊜	⊖	⊜	⊜
Body rust				⊜	⊜	⊜	⊜	⊜
Paint/trim				◒	○	○	⊖	⊖
Integrity				●	◒	◒	◒	○
Hardware				●	◒	◒	○	○

Chevrolet Lumina APV Van

Trouble spots	87	88	89	90	91	92	93	94
Engine				○	⊜	⊜	⊜	⊜
Cooling				◒	⊖	○	⊜	⊜
Fuel				⊖	⊖	⊖	⊖	⊜
Ignition				⊜	⊜	⊜	⊜	⊜
Auto. trans.				⊖	⊖	⊖	⊜	⊜
Man. trans.								
Clutch								
Electrical				●	◒	◒	◒	⊖
A/C				○	○	○	⊖	⊜
Suspension				⊖	⊖	⊖	⊖	⊜
Brakes				●	●	◒	○	⊖
Exhaust				○	⊜	⊜	⊜	⊜
Body rust				⊜	⊜	⊜	⊜	⊜
Paint/trim				●	◒	⊖	⊖	⊜
Integrity				◒	◒	◒	○	○
Hardware				●	●	●	●	◒

Chevrolet S-10 Blazer V6 (2WD)	87	88	89	90	91	92	93	94
Engine	◒	○	○		⊖	⊖	⊖	
Cooling	◒	●	◒		⊜	⊜	⊜	
Fuel	◒	◒	⊖		⊖	⊖	⊜	
Ignition	○	○	⊖		⊖	⊜	⊜	
Auto. trans.	◒	○	⊜		⊖	*	⊖	
Man. trans.	*	*	*		*	*	*	
Clutch	*	*	*	Insufficient data	*	*	*	Insufficient data
Electrical	●	●	●		◒	◒	○	
A/C	◒	○	○		○	⊖	⊖	
Suspension	⊖	○	○		⊖	⊖	⊖	
Brakes	●	◒	●		◒	●	⊖	
Exhaust	○	○	⊖		⊜	⊜	⊜	
Body rust	○	⊖	○		○	⊖	⊜	
Paint/trim	●	●	●		●	◒	○	
Integrity	◒	●	●		◒	●	●	
Hardware	●	◒	●		●	◒	◒	

Chevrolet S-10 Blazer V6 (4WD)	87	88	89	90	91	92	93	94
Engine	◒	◒	○	○	⊖	○	⊖	⊜
Cooling	◒	◒	○	⊖	⊜	⊖	⊜	⊜
Fuel	○	○	○	⊖	⊖	⊖	⊖	⊖
Ignition	⊖	○	⊖	◒	⊖	⊜	⊜	⊜
Auto. trans.	◒	○	○	○	⊖	⊖	⊖	⊜
Man. trans.	*	*	*	*	*	*	*	*
Clutch	*	*	*	*	*	*	*	*
Electrical	●	●	●	●	●	◒	◒	○
A/C	○	○	⊖	⊖	⊖	⊖	⊖	⊜
Suspension	○	◒	◒	◒	○	⊖	⊖	⊜
Brakes	●	●	●	●	●	●	○	⊜
Exhaust	◒	◒	○	◒	⊖	⊖	⊜	⊜
Body rust	●	◒	●	●	◒	⊖	⊖	⊜
Paint/trim	◒	●	●	●	●	○	○	⊖
Integrity	●	●	●	●	●	◒	●	○
Hardware	●	●	◒	●	●	◒	◒	⊖

Chevrolet S-10 Pickup (2WD)	87	88	89	90	91	92	93	94
Engine	◒	◒	○	○	⊖	⊜	⊖	⊜
Cooling	◒	◒	○	⊖	⊖	⊖	⊜	⊜
Fuel	○	○	○	○	⊖	⊖	⊖	○
Ignition	○	○	○	○	○	⊖	⊜	⊜
Auto. trans.	○	⊖	⊖	⊜	⊜	⊖	⊖	⊜
Man. trans.	⊖	○	⊖	*	⊖	⊖	○	⊖
Clutch	◒	◒	○	*	○	○	○	⊖
Electrical	◒	●	●	●	◒	○	○	○
A/C	○	○	○	⊜	⊖	⊖	⊖	⊜
Suspension	⊖	⊖	⊖	⊖	⊖	⊜	⊖	⊖
Brakes	◒	◒	◒	◒	○	○	⊖	⊖
Exhaust	●	●	◒	◒	○	⊖	⊜	⊜
Body rust	◒	◒	◒	⊖	○	⊖	⊜	⊜
Paint/trim	◒	●	●	●	●	◒	○	⊖
Integrity	◒	◒	◒	◒	○	○	○	○
Hardware	◒	◒	◒	◒	◒	○	○	⊖

Chevrolet S-10 Pickup (4WD)	87	88	89	90	91	92	93	94
Engine	●	○	○		⊜	⊖		⊖
Cooling	◒	◒	◒		⊖	⊜		⊜
Fuel	○	○	⊖		⊖	⊖		○
Ignition	⊜	○	◒		○	○		⊜
Auto. trans.	*	○	○		○	⊖		⊖
Man. trans.	*	*	*		*	*		*
Clutch	*	*	*	Insufficient data	*	*	Insufficient data	*
Electrical	◒	◒	●		●	○		○
A/C	*	○	⊖		⊖	⊖		⊜
Suspension	○	●	◒		○	⊖		⊜
Brakes	◒	◒	◒		◒	◒		⊖
Exhaust	●	●	○		⊖	⊖		⊜
Body rust	●	○	●		○	⊖		⊜
Paint/trim	●	●	●		●	◒		⊜
Integrity	◒	●	◒		●	○		○
Hardware	●	◒	◒		◒	○		⊖

Chevrolet Sportvan	87	88	89	90	91	92	93	94
Engine	◒	○	○	⊖	⊖	⊖	⊖	
Cooling	◒	◒	◒	◒	○	⊖	⊖	
Fuel	○	⊖	⊖	⊜	⊜	⊖	⊖	
Ignition	○	⊖	⊖	⊜	⊜	⊖	⊖	
Auto. trans.	○	○	○	⊖	○	◒	⊖	
Man. trans.	*	*	*					
Clutch	*	*	*					Insufficient data
Electrical	●	●	●	◒	●	●	●	
A/C	●	◒	◒	◒	◒	○	○	
Suspension	◒	●	◒	○	◒	○	○	
Brakes	●	●	●	◒	◒	●	◒	
Exhaust	●	◒	◒	○	⊜	⊜	⊜	
Body rust	◒	◒	◒	◒	⊖	○	⊜	
Paint/trim	●	●	●	●	◒	◒	○	
Integrity	●	●	◒	●	●	●	●	
Hardware	●	●	◒	●	◒	●	●	

Chevrolet Suburban (2WD)	87	88	89	90	91	92	93	94
Engine	◒	○	○	○	⊖	⊖	⊖	⊜
Cooling	●	●	●	○	○	⊖	⊜	⊜
Fuel	●	○	○	⊖	○	⊖	⊖	⊜
Ignition	⊖	⊖	○	⊖	○	⊖	⊜	⊜
Auto. trans.	◒	○	◒	○	○	○	⊖	⊜
Man. trans.	*	*	*	*				
Clutch	*	*	*	*				
Electrical	●	◒	●	●	◒	◒	○	⊖
A/C	●	◒	◒	○	○	◒	⊖	⊜
Suspension	◒	◒	◒	⊖	○	⊖	⊖	⊜
Brakes	◒	●	●	◒	●	◒	○	⊖
Exhaust	●	◒	◒	○	⊖	⊜	⊜	⊜
Body rust	●	●	○	⊖	⊖	⊜	⊖	⊜
Paint/trim	●	●	●	◒	◒	○	○	⊜
Integrity	●	●	●	●	●	◒	◒	⊖
Hardware	●	●	●	●	◒	◒	●	○

Chevrolet Suburban (4WD)	87	88	89	90	91	92	93	94
Engine	●	◒	◒	⊖	⊖	⊖	⊖	⊜
Cooling	●	●	◒	⊖	○	⊜	⊜	⊜
Fuel	●	○	○	○	○	⊜	⊖	⊜
Ignition	○	⊖	○	⊖	○	⊜	⊜	⊜
Auto. trans.	◒	○	◒	○	●	○	⊖	⊜
Man. trans.	*	*	*	*				
Clutch	*	*	*	*				
Electrical	●	◒	●	●	●	◒	◒	⊖
A/C	●	◒	○	○	⊖	○	⊖	⊜
Suspension	◒	○	○	○	◒	⊖	⊖	⊖
Brakes	●	●	●	●	●	◒	○	⊖
Exhaust	◒	◒	◒	⊖	⊜	⊖	⊜	⊜
Body rust	●	●	◒	○	○	⊜	⊖	⊜
Paint/trim	●	●	●	●	●	○	○	⊜
Integrity	●	●	●	●	●	◒	●	○
Hardware	●	●	●	●	◒	◒	●	⊖

Chrysler Concorde	87	88	89	90	91	92	93	94
Engine							⊖	⊜
Cooling							⊜	⊜
Fuel							⊖	⊜
Ignition							⊜	⊜
Auto. trans.							⊖	⊖
Man. trans.								
Clutch								
Electrical							○	○
A/C							⊖	⊖
Suspension							⊜	⊜
Brakes							○	⊖
Exhaust							⊜	⊜
Body rust							⊜	⊜
Paint/trim							⊖	⊖
Integrity							◒	○
Hardware							◒	⊖

⊜ ⊖ ○ ◒ ●
Few ← **Problems** → Many

* Insufficient data

Chrysler Le Baron Sedan 4

Insufficient data / Insufficient data (87–90)

TROUBLE SPOTS	87	88	89	90	91	92	93	94
Engine					○	○	⊖	
Cooling					⊖	⊖	⊜	
Fuel					⊖	⊜	⊖	
Ignition					⊖	⊖	⊜	
Auto. trans.					⊖	⊖	⊜	
Man. trans.								
Clutch								
Electrical					○	○	⊖	
A/C					○	⊖	⊖	
Suspension					⊖	⊖	⊖	
Brakes					○	⊖	⊖	
Exhaust					◒	⊖	⊜	
Body rust					⊜	⊜	⊜	
Paint/trim					○	⊖	⊖	
Integrity					○	○	◒	
Hardware					○	⊖	○	

Chrysler Le Baron Sedan V6

TROUBLE SPOTS	87	88	89	90	91	92	93	94
Engine				○	⊖	⊖	⊜	⊜
Cooling				⊖	⊖	⊜	⊜	⊜
Fuel				○	⊖	⊜	⊖	⊜
Ignition				⊖	⊖	⊜	⊜	⊜
Auto. trans.				●	◒	⊖	○	○
Man. trans.								
Clutch								
Electrical				◒	◒	◒	○	○
A/C				○	○	○	⊖	⊜
Suspension				⊖	⊖	⊖	⊖	⊜
Brakes				◒	○	⊖	⊜	⊜
Exhaust				⊜	○	⊖	⊜	⊜
Body rust				⊜	⊜	⊜	⊜	⊜
Paint/trim				○	○	⊖	⊖	⊖
Integrity				⊖	○	○	○	○
Hardware				⊖	○	○	○	⊖

Chrysler Le Baron Coupe & Conv.

TROUBLE SPOTS	87	88	89	90	91	92	93	94
Engine	●	●	◒	⊖	○	⊖	⊜	Insufficient data
Cooling	●	●	◒	○	⊖	⊖	⊜	
Fuel	◒	○	○	○	⊖	⊖	⊖	
Ignition	◒	○	⊖	⊖	⊖	⊜	⊜	
Auto. trans.	○	○	○	◒	◒	○	○	
Man. trans.	*	*	*	*	*	*	*	
Clutch	*	*	*	*	*	*	*	
Electrical	●	●	●	●	●	◒	○	
A/C	●	●	●	○	○	⊖	⊜	
Suspension	●	●	◒	○	⊖	○	⊖	
Brakes	●	●	●	●	◒	○	⊖	
Exhaust	○	○	⊜	⊜	○	⊜	⊖	
Body rust	○	⊖	⊖	⊜	⊜	⊜	⊜	
Paint/trim	●	◒	○	○	○	○	○	
Integrity	●	●	◒	●	●	●	●	
Hardware	◒	◒	◒	●	●	◒	◒	

Chrysler New Yorker, LHS

TROUBLE SPOTS	87	88	89	90	91	92	93	94
Engine	◒	●	◒	○	⊖	◒	⊖	⊜
Cooling	●	◒	◒	⊖	⊖	⊖	⊜	⊜
Fuel	●	●	○	○	⊖	⊖	⊜	⊜
Ignition	◒	○	⊖	○	⊜	⊖	⊜	⊜
Auto. trans.	○	○	●	●	○	○	⊖	⊖
Man. trans.								
Clutch								
Electrical	●	●	●	●	●	●	○	○
A/C	●	●	◒	○	○	○	○	⊖
Suspension	○	◒	◒	◒	○	○	⊖	⊜
Brakes	●	●	●	●	○	⊖	⊖	⊖
Exhaust	⊜	⊖	⊜	⊜	⊖	⊖	⊜	⊜
Body rust	◒	⊖	⊖	⊜	⊜	⊜	⊜	⊜
Paint/trim	●	◒	○	⊜	⊜	⊖	⊜	⊜
Integrity	○	◒	○	⊖	○	○	○	○
Hardware	○	◒	◒	○	○	○	⊖	○

Chrysler Town & Country Van (2WD)

TROUBLE SPOTS	87	88	89	90	91	92	93	94
Engine				○	⊖	○	⊖	⊜
Cooling				○	⊖	⊖	⊖	⊜
Fuel				○	⊖	⊖	⊜	⊜
Ignition				⊖	⊖	⊜	⊜	⊜
Auto. trans.				●	◒	○	○	⊖
Man. trans.								
Clutch								
Electrical				●	●	●	○	⊖
A/C				○	⊖	⊖	⊖	⊜
Suspension				○	○	○	⊖	⊜
Brakes				●	◒	○	⊖	⊜
Exhaust				⊜	◒	⊜	⊜	⊜
Body rust				⊖	⊜	⊜	⊜	⊜
Paint/trim				○	⊖	⊖	⊖	⊖
Integrity				◒	◒	◒	◒	◒
Hardware				●	◒	◒	◒	○

Chrysler Town & Country Van (4WD)

TROUBLE SPOTS	87	88	89	90	91	92	93	94
Engine						○	⊜	⊜
Cooling						○	⊖	⊜
Fuel						○	⊖	⊜
Ignition						⊜	⊜	⊜
Auto. trans.						◒	○	⊖
Man. trans.								
Clutch								
Electrical						●	○	⊖
A/C						⊖	⊖	⊜
Suspension						○	⊖	⊜
Brakes						◒	○	⊜
Exhaust						◒	⊜	⊜
Body rust						⊜	⊜	⊜
Paint/trim						⊜	⊖	⊖
Integrity						◒	○	○
Hardware						◒	◒	⊖

Dodge Aries

TROUBLE SPOTS	87	88	89	90	91	92	93	94
Engine	◒	◒	◒					
Cooling	●	●	◒					
Fuel	●	◒	○					
Ignition	◒	○	○					
Auto. trans.	⊖	⊖	⊖					
Man. trans.	*	*	*					
Clutch	*	*	*					
Electrical	●	◒	●					
A/C	●	●	●					
Suspension	◒	◒	◒					
Brakes	●	●	●					
Exhaust	○	⊖	⊜					
Body rust	◒	◒	○					
Paint/trim	◒	◒	●					
Integrity	●	◒	●					
Hardware	◒	◒	◒					

Dodge Caravan 4

TROUBLE SPOTS	87	88	89	90	91	92	93	94
Engine	●	●	◒	⊖	○	○	⊖	⊜
Cooling	●	●	○	⊖	⊖	⊖	⊜	⊜
Fuel	●	◒	○	⊖	⊖	⊖	⊖	⊜
Ignition	○	○	⊖	⊖	⊜	⊖	⊜	⊜
Auto. trans.	◒	○	⊖	○	⊖	⊖	⊖	⊜
Man. trans.	○	*	*	*		*	*	
Clutch	●	*	*	*		*	*	
Electrical	●	◒	◒	○	◒	◒	○	⊖
A/C	●	●	●	○	○	⊖	⊖	⊜
Suspension	◒	○	○	○	⊜	⊖	⊖	⊜
Brakes	●	●	●	◒	◒	○	⊖	⊜
Exhaust	○	⊖	⊜	⊖	○	⊖	⊜	⊜
Body rust	○	⊖	⊖	⊖	⊜	⊜	⊜	⊜
Paint/trim	○	○	⊖	○	⊖	⊖	⊜	⊜
Integrity	◒	◒	○	◒	◒	◒	○	○
Hardware	●	◒	◒	●	◒	◒	◒	⊖

TROUBLE SPOTS	Dodge Caravan V6 (2WD) 87	88	89	90	91	92	93	94	Dodge Grand Caravan V6 (2WD) 87	88	89	90	91	92	93	94
Engine	●	●	●	○	○	⊖	⊖	⊜	●	●	●	○	⊖	○	⊖	⊜
Cooling	●	●	◒	○	⊖	⊜	⊜	⊜	◒	●	◒	○	⊖	⊖	⊖	⊜
Fuel	◒	●	○	○	⊖	⊖	⊜	⊜	◒	●	○	○	⊖	⊖	⊜	⊜
Ignition	⊖	○	⊖	⊖	⊖	⊜	⊜	⊜	⊖	○	⊖	⊖	⊖	⊜	⊜	⊜
Auto. trans.	◒	○	◒	◒	○	○	⊖	⊜	◒	◒	●	●	◒	○	○	⊖
Man. trans.																
Clutch																
Electrical	●	●	◒	◒	◒	◒	○	⊖	◒	●	◒	●	●	●	○	⊖
A/C	●	●	◒	○	⊖	⊖	⊖	⊜	●	●	◒	○	⊖	⊖	⊖	⊜
Suspension	◒	◒	○	⊖	⊖	⊖	⊜	⊜	◒	◒	○	○	○	○	⊖	⊜
Brakes	●	●	●	◒	◒	○	⊖	⊜	●	●	●	●	◒	○	⊖	⊜
Exhaust	⊖	⊖	⊜	⊜	◒	⊜	⊜	⊜	⊜	⊜	⊜	⊜	◒	⊜	⊜	⊜
Body rust	○	⊖	⊖	⊖	⊜	⊜	⊜	⊜	○	⊖	⊖	⊖	⊜	⊜	⊜	⊜
Paint/trim	○	○	○	⊖	⊖	⊖	⊖	⊜	●	◒	○	○	⊖	⊖	⊖	⊖
Integrity	◒	○	○	◒	◒	◒	○	⊖	◒	◒	◒	◒	◒	◒	◒	◒
Hardware	●	●	●	●	◒	◒	◒	⊖	●	●	●	●	◒	◒	◒	○

TROUBLE SPOTS	Dodge Grand Caravan V6 (4WD) 87	88	89	90	91	92	93	94	Dodge Colt, Colt Wagon 87	88	89	90	91	92	93	94
Engine					⊖	○	⊜	⊜	●	●	◒	○	⊖	⊜	⊜	Insufficient data
Cooling					⊖	○	⊖	⊜	○	○	⊖	⊜	⊜	⊜	⊜	
Fuel					○	○	⊖	⊜	○	⊖	⊖	⊖	⊜	⊜	⊜	
Ignition					○	⊜	⊜	⊜	⊖	○	⊖	⊜	⊜	⊜	⊜	
Auto. trans.					●	◒	○	⊖	○	○	⊖	⊖	○	⊖	◒	
Man. trans.									⊖	⊖	⊖	⊖	⊖	⊜	*	
Clutch									●	○	⊖	⊖	⊜	⊜	*	
Electrical					◒	●	○	⊖	◒	◒	◒	○	⊖	⊖	⊖	
A/C					⊖	⊖	⊖	⊜	◒	◒	◒	⊖	⊖	⊖	⊖	
Suspension					○	○	⊖	⊜	○	⊖	○	⊖	⊖	⊖	⊜	
Brakes					●	◒	○	⊜	●	●	◒	◒	○	○	⊖	
Exhaust					●	◒	⊜	⊜	●	⊖	⊜	⊜	⊜	⊜	⊜	
Body rust					⊜	⊜	⊜	⊜	◒	○	⊜	⊜	⊖	⊜	⊜	
Paint/trim					○	⊜	⊖	⊖	◒	○	○	◒	○	⊖	⊖	
Integrity					○	◒	○	○	◒	○	◒	●	◒	◒	⊖	
Hardware					◒	◒	◒	⊖	◒	○	○	◒	○	○	⊖	

TROUBLE SPOTS	Dodge Colt Vista Wagon 87	88	89	90	91	92	93	94	Dodge Dakota Pickup (2WD) 87	88	89	90	91	92	93	94
Engine	●	●	◒	Insufficient data	⊜				◒	○	○	⊖	⊖	○	⊜	⊖
Cooling	○	◒	⊖		⊜				◒	○	○	⊖	○	⊖	⊜	⊜
Fuel	●	○	⊖		⊜				◒	◒	○	⊖	⊖	○	⊖	⊖
Ignition	○	⊜	⊖		⊜				◒	●	○	⊜	○	⊖	⊜	⊜
Auto. trans.	*	*	*		*				○	◒	●	●	○	◒	○	○
Man. trans.	●	*	*		*				*	*	*	*	*	*	⊜	*
Clutch	●	*	*		*				*	*	*	*	*	*	○	*
Electrical	◒	◒	●		●				●	●	◒	○	●	◒	⊖	⊖
A/C	◒	○	*		*				●	◒	◒	○	⊖	⊜	⊖	⊜
Suspension	○	◒	○		◒				○	○	○	⊖	⊖	○	⊖	⊖
Brakes	◒	◒	◒		⊖				●	◒	●	◒	◒	◒	⊖	⊖
Exhaust	●	⊖	○		⊖				○	⊜	○	⊜	○	○	⊜	⊜
Body rust	⊖	⊖	⊜		⊜				⊖	⊖	⊖	⊖	⊜	⊖	⊜	⊖
Paint/trim	○	⊖	○		⊖				○	○	○	○	⊖	⊖	⊖	⊖
Integrity	○	○	○		◒				○	○	○	○	○	○	○	○
Hardware	◒	◒	◒		○				○	○	○	○	⊖	⊖	○	○

TROUBLE SPOTS	Dodge Dakota Pickup (4WD) 87	88	89	90	91	92	93	94	Dodge Daytona 87	88	89	90	91	92	93	94
Engine	Insufficient data	Insufficient data	Insufficient data	Insufficient data	⊜	○	⊖	Insufficient data	Insufficient data	●	◒	⊖	Insufficient data	Insufficient data	Insufficient data	
Cooling					⊖	⊖	⊜			●	○	○				
Fuel					⊖	○	⊖			◒	○	○				
Ignition					○	○	⊖			◒	○	⊖				
Auto. trans.					*	◒	◒			○	*	*				
Man. trans.					*	*	*			*	*	*				
Clutch					*	*	*			*	*	*				
Electrical					●	○	⊖			●	●	◒				
A/C					*	⊖	⊖			●	●	*				
Suspension					○	⊖	⊖			●	●	◒				
Brakes					◒	◒	⊖			●	●	●				
Exhaust					○	⊖	⊜			⊖	⊜	⊖				
Body rust					⊖	⊜	⊜			○	⊖	⊖				
Paint/trim					○	○	○			●	●	◒				
Integrity					⊖	○	○			●	●	◒				
Hardware					⊖	⊖	○			●	●	◒				

⊜ ⊖ ○ ◒ ●
Few ← Problems → Many

*
Insufficient data

Trouble spots	Dodge Dynasty 87	88	89	90	91	92	93	94
Engine		◒	◒	⊖	⊖	◒	○	
Cooling		◒	○	⊖	⊜	⊖	⊜	
Fuel		●	○	○	⊖	⊖	⊜	
Ignition		○	⊖	⊖	⊖	⊜	⊜	
Auto. trans.		○	●	●	◒	◒	○	
Man. trans.								
Clutch								
Electrical		●	◒	●	◒	◒	⊖	
A/C		●	○	○	⊖	⊖	⊖	
Suspension		○	○	○	⊖	⊖	⊜	
Brakes		●	●	◒	○	○	⊜	
Exhaust		⊜	⊜	⊜	◒	⊖	⊜	
Body rust		⊖	⊖	⊖	⊜	⊜	⊜	
Paint/trim		○	○	○	⊖	○	⊖	
Integrity		◒	○	○	○	◒	○	
Hardware		●	◒	○	○	○	○	

Trouble spots	Dodge Intrepid 87	88	89	90	91	92	93	94
Engine							⊖	⊜
Cooling							⊜	⊜
Fuel							⊖	⊜
Ignition							⊜	⊜
Auto. trans.							⊖	⊖
Man. trans.								
Clutch								
Electrical							○	○
A/C							⊖	⊖
Suspension							⊜	⊜
Brakes							○	⊖
Exhaust							⊜	⊜
Body rust							⊜	⊜
Paint/trim							⊖	⊖
Integrity							◒	○
Hardware							◒	⊖

Trouble spots	Dodge Monaco 87	88	89	90	91	92	93	94
Engine				○	○			
Cooling				◒	○			
Fuel				⊖	○			
Ignition				○	○			
Auto. trans.				◒	◒			
Man. trans.						Insufficient data		
Clutch								
Electrical				●	●			
A/C				●	◒			
Suspension				○	◒			
Brakes				●	●			
Exhaust				⊜	◒			
Body rust				⊜	⊜			
Paint/trim				○	⊖			
Integrity				◒	◒			
Hardware				◒	●			

Trouble spots	Dodge Omni, Charger 87	88	89	90	91	92	93	94
Engine	◒	○	◒	○				
Cooling	◒	◒	○	○				
Fuel	●	○	◒	○				
Ignition	●	○	○	⊖				
Auto. trans.	○	○	⊖	*				
Man. trans.	○	⊖	*	*				
Clutch	●	○	*	*				
Electrical	●	◒	●	●				
A/C	●	●	●	*				
Suspension	●	○	○	⊖				
Brakes	●	●	●	●				
Exhaust	●	⊖	⊖	⊖				
Body rust	●	●	◒	⊖				
Paint/trim	◒	●	●	○				
Integrity	●	●	●	●				
Hardware	●	◒	○	◒				

Trouble spots	Dodge Ram Pickup 87	88	89	90	91	92	93	94
Engine	◒	○	⊖	⊜				⊜
Cooling	◒	◒	○	○				⊜
Fuel	◒	◒	○	○				⊜
Ignition	◒	○	○	⊖				⊜
Auto. trans.	○	*	◒	●				⊖
Man. trans.	*	*	*	*	Insufficient data	Insufficient data	Insufficient data	*
Clutch	*	*	*	*				*
Electrical	●	◒	◒	○				⊖
A/C	●	*	◒	○				⊜
Suspension	◒	○	○	◒				⊖
Brakes	●	●	●	◒				⊖
Exhaust	○	⊖	○	⊜				⊜
Body rust	○	○	⊖	⊖				⊖
Paint/trim	◒	◒	◒	◒				⊖
Integrity	◒	●	◒	◒				○
Hardware	◒	○	◒	○				○

Trouble spots	Dodge Ram 50 Pickup 4 87	88	89	90	91	92	93	94
Engine	◒	○	○					
Cooling	○	○	○					
Fuel	○	○	⊜					
Ignition	⊖	⊖	⊜					
Auto. trans.	*	*	*					
Man. trans.	○	○	*	Insufficient data	Insufficient data	Insufficient data	Insufficient data	
Clutch	◒	○	*					
Electrical	○	⊖	⊖					
A/C	*	*	*					
Suspension	○	○	○					
Brakes	○	◒	⊖					
Exhaust	●	⊖	⊖					
Body rust	○	⊖	⊜					
Paint/trim	○	⊖	⊖					
Integrity	⊖	⊖	⊖					
Hardware	⊜	⊖	○					

Trouble spots	Dodge Ram Van B150-250 87	88	89	90	91	92	93	94
Engine	◒	○	○	⊖	⊜	⊖	⊜	⊜
Cooling	◒	○	◒	⊖	⊖	⊖	⊜	⊜
Fuel	◒	◒	○	○	○	○	⊖	⊖
Ignition	○	◒	○	⊖	⊖	⊖	⊜	⊜
Auto. trans.	◒	◒	●	◒	○	◒	○	⊖
Man. trans.	*	*	*	*	*	*	*	
Clutch	*	*	*	*	*	*	*	
Electrical	●	●	●	◒	●	◒	◒	⊖
A/C	●	●	●	●	○	○	○	⊖
Suspension	◒	●	◒	○	⊖	○	○	○
Brakes	◒	◒	◒	●	●	○	⊜	⊖
Exhaust	⊖	⊖	⊖	⊖	⊖	⊜	⊜	⊜
Body rust	◒	○	◒	⊖	○	⊖	⊖	⊖
Paint/trim	●	●	●	◒	○	○	⊖	○
Integrity	●	◒	●	◒	○	◒	◒	●
Hardware	●	○	◒	◒	○	◒	○	○

Trouble spots	Dodge Shadow 87	88	89	90	91	92	93	94
Engine	●	●	◒	○	○	○	⊖	⊜
Cooling	●	●	◒	○	○	⊖	⊜	⊜
Fuel	◒	◒	○	○	⊖	⊖	⊖	⊖
Ignition	◒	○	○	○	⊖	⊖	⊖	⊜
Auto. trans.	⊖	○	⊖	⊖	⊜	⊖	⊖	⊜
Man. trans.	⊖	*	*	*	*	⊖	⊖	*
Clutch	●	*	*	*	*	⊜	⊖	*
Electrical	●	◒	●	●	●	◒	○	⊜
A/C	●	●	●	◒	◒	⊜	⊖	⊜
Suspension	◒	◒	◒	○	⊖	⊖	⊜	⊜
Brakes	●	●	●	●	○	⊜	⊜	⊜
Exhaust	○	⊖	⊖	⊖	◒	⊜	⊜	⊜
Body rust	○	○	⊖	⊖	⊖	⊜	⊜	⊜
Paint/trim	◒	●	◒	○	○	○	○	⊖
Integrity	●	◒	○	○	◒	◒	◒	◒
Hardware	●	●	◒	○	○	○	◒	○

Dodge Spirit 4

TROUBLE SPOTS	87	88	89	90	91	92	93	94
Engine			◒	○	○	○	⊖	⊜
Cooling			◒	○	⊖	⊖	⊜	⊜
Fuel			○	⊖	⊖	⊜	⊖	⊜
Ignition			⊖	⊖	⊖	⊖	⊜	⊜
Auto. trans.			⊖	⊖	⊖	⊖	⊜	⊖
Man. trans.			*	*	*	*	*	
Clutch			*	*	*	*	*	
Electrical			◒	◒	○	○	⊖	⊖
A/C			●	○	○	⊖	⊖	⊜
Suspension			○	○	⊖	⊖	⊖	⊜
Brakes			●	●	○	⊖	⊖	⊜
Exhaust			⊜	⊜	◒	⊖	⊜	⊜
Body rust			⊖	⊖	⊜	⊜	⊜	⊜
Paint/trim			○	○	○	⊖	⊖	⊜
Integrity			⊖	⊖	○	○	◒	⊖
Hardware			⊖	○	○	⊖	○	○

Dodge Spirit V6

TROUBLE SPOTS	87	88	89	90	91	92	93	94
Engine			◒	○	⊖	⊖	⊜	⊜
Cooling			◒	⊖	⊖	⊜	⊜	⊜
Fuel			○	○	⊖	⊜	⊖	⊜
Ignition			⊜	⊖	⊖	⊜	⊜	⊜
Auto. trans.			●	●	◒	⊖	○	○
Man. trans.								
Clutch								
Electrical			●	◒	◒	◒	○	○
A/C			●	○	○	○	⊖	⊜
Suspension			○	⊖	⊖	⊖	⊖	⊜
Brakes			●	◒	○	⊖	⊜	⊜
Exhaust			⊖	⊜	○	⊖	⊜	⊜
Body rust			○	⊜	⊜	⊜	⊜	⊜
Paint/trim			◒	○	○	⊖	⊖	⊖
Integrity			○	⊖	○	○	○	○
Hardware			○	⊖	○	○	○	⊖

Dodge Stealth (2WD)

TROUBLE SPOTS	87	88	89	90	91	92	93	94
Engine					⊖	⊖	⊜	Insufficient data
Cooling					⊜	⊜	⊜	
Fuel					⊖	⊜	⊜	
Ignition					⊜	⊜	⊜	
Auto. trans.					*	*	*	
Man. trans.					*	○	⊖	
Clutch					*	⊖	⊖	
Electrical					◒	◒	○	
A/C					⊜	⊖	⊜	
Suspension					○	⊖	⊜	
Brakes					○	⊖	⊖	
Exhaust					⊜	⊜	⊜	
Body rust					⊜	⊜	⊜	
Paint/trim					◒	○	⊖	
Integrity					○	◒	◒	
Hardware					◒	◒	○	

Eagle Premier V6

TROUBLE SPOTS	87	88	89	90	91	92	93	94
Engine		◒	◒	○	○	Insufficient data		
Cooling		●	●	◒	○			
Fuel		◒	○	⊖	○			
Ignition		◒	◒	○	○			
Auto. trans.		◒	◒	◒	◒			
Man. trans.								
Clutch								
Electrical		●	●	●	●			
A/C		●	●	●	◒			
Suspension		◒	◒	○	◒			
Brakes		●	●	●	●			
Exhaust		●	◒	⊜	◒			
Body rust		⊖	⊖	⊜	⊜			
Paint/trim		○	◒	○	⊖			
Integrity		○	◒	◒	◒			
Hardware		●	●	◒	●			

Eagle Summit (except Wagon)

TROUBLE SPOTS	87	88	89	90	91	92	93	94
Engine			◒	○	⊖	⊜	⊜	Insufficient data
Cooling			⊖	⊜	⊜	⊜	⊜	
Fuel			⊖	⊖	⊜	⊜	⊜	
Ignition			⊖	⊜	⊜	⊜	⊜	
Auto. trans.			⊖	⊖	○	⊖	◒	
Man. trans.			⊖	⊖	⊖	⊜	*	
Clutch			⊖	⊖	⊜	⊜	*	
Electrical			◒	○	⊖	⊖	⊖	
A/C			◒	⊖	⊖	⊖	⊖	
Suspension			○	⊖	⊖	⊖	⊜	
Brakes			◒	◒	○	○	⊖	
Exhaust			⊜	⊜	⊜	⊜	⊜	
Body rust			⊜	⊜	⊖	⊜	⊜	
Paint/trim			○	◒	○	⊖	⊖	
Integrity			◒	●	◒	◒	⊖	
Hardware			○	◒	○	○	⊖	

Eagle Summit Wagon

TROUBLE SPOTS	87	88	89	90	91	92	93	94
Engine						⊜	⊜	Insufficient data
Cooling						⊖	⊖	
Fuel						⊖	⊜	
Ignition						⊜	⊜	
Auto. trans.						⊜	⊖	
Man. trans.						*	*	
Clutch						*	*	
Electrical						○	○	
A/C						⊖	⊜	
Suspension						⊖	⊖	
Brakes						⊜	⊜	
Exhaust						○	⊖	
Body rust						⊜	⊜	
Paint/trim						⊖	⊖	
Integrity						◒	◒	
Hardware						◒	○	

Eagle Talon (2WD)

TROUBLE SPOTS	87	88	89	90	91	92	93	94
Engine				●	◒	◒	⊜	Insufficient data
Cooling				⊖	⊖	⊜	⊖	
Fuel				⊖	⊖	⊜	⊜	
Ignition				⊖	⊜	⊜	⊜	
Auto. trans.				○	⊖	⊖	*	
Man. trans.				○	○	⊖	⊖	
Clutch				⊖	⊖	⊖	⊜	
Electrical				◒	◒	◒	⊖	
A/C				⊜	⊖	⊜	⊜	
Suspension				⊖	⊖	⊖	⊖	
Brakes				◒	○	○	⊖	
Exhaust				⊖	○	◒	⊜	
Body rust				⊜	⊜	⊜	⊜	
Paint/trim				○	○	○	⊖	
Integrity				○	○	◒	○	
Hardware				◒	◒	●	○	

Eagle Talon Turbo (4WD)

TROUBLE SPOTS	87	88	89	90	91	92	93	94
Engine				●	●	⊖	Insufficient data	Insufficient data
Cooling				⊜	○	⊖		
Fuel				⊖	○	⊖		
Ignition				⊖	⊖	⊜		
Auto. trans.					*	*		
Man. trans.				●	◒	○		
Clutch				◒	○	○		
Electrical				◒	●	◒		
A/C				○	⊖	⊖		
Suspension				⊖	⊖	⊖		
Brakes				◒	◒	○		
Exhaust				⊖	⊜	⊜		
Body rust				⊜	⊜	⊜		
Paint/trim				○	○	○		
Integrity				○	◒	○		
Hardware				◒	○	●		

⊜ ⊖ ○ ◒ ●
Few ← Problems → Many

*
Insufficient data

Eagle Vision

TROUBLE SPOTS	87	88	89	90	91	92	93	94
Engine							⊖	⊜
Cooling							⊜	⊜
Fuel							⊖	⊜
Ignition							⊜	⊜
Auto. trans.							⊖	⊖
Man. trans.								
Clutch								
Electrical							○	○
A/C							⊖	⊖
Suspension							⊜	⊜
Brakes							○	⊖
Exhaust							⊜	⊜
Body rust							⊜	⊜
Paint/trim							⊖	⊖
Integrity							◒	○
Hardware							◒	⊖

Ford Aerostar Van (2WD)

TROUBLE SPOTS	87	88	89	90	91	92	93	94
Engine	●	◒	○	○	○	○	⊜	⊜
Cooling	●	●	●	○	○	⊖	⊜	⊜
Fuel	◒	◒	○	⊖	⊖	⊖	⊜	⊜
Ignition	○	○	⊖	⊖	⊖	⊜	⊜	⊜
Auto. trans.	●	●	○	○	○	⊖	⊖	⊜
Man. trans.	*	*	*	*	*	*	*	*
Clutch	*	*	*	*	*	*	*	*
Electrical	●	●	●	●	◒	◒	○	⊖
A/C	●	●	●	●	●	◒	⊖	⊖
Suspension	●	●	◒	○	○	○	⊖	⊜
Brakes	●	●	●	●	●	●	○	⊖
Exhaust	◒	●	◒	◒	◒	⊖	⊜	⊜
Body rust	◒	◒	◒	⊖	⊜	⊜	⊜	⊜
Paint/trim	◒	●	○	⊖	⊖	⊖	⊜	⊜
Integrity	●	●	◒	○	○	○	○	○
Hardware	●	●	●	○	◒	◒	○	⊖

Ford Aerostar Van (4WD)

TROUBLE SPOTS	87	88	89	90	91	92	93	94
Engine				◒	●	○	⊖	Insufficient data
Cooling				◒	○	⊖	⊜	
Fuel				⊖	⊖	⊖	⊜	
Ignition				⊖	⊖	⊖	⊜	
Auto. trans.				○	○	⊖	⊖	
Man. trans.								
Clutch								
Electrical				●	●	◒	⊖	
A/C				●	●	○	⊖	
Suspension				○	○	○	⊖	
Brakes				●	●	●	○	
Exhaust				●	◒	⊖	⊜	
Body rust				⊖	⊜	⊜	⊜	
Paint/trim				○	⊜	⊖	⊖	
Integrity				○	⊖	○	○	
Hardware				●	○	○	○	

Ford Bronco

TROUBLE SPOTS	87	88	89	90	91	92	93	94
Engine	◒	◒	◒	◒	○	⊖	⊖	Insufficient data
Cooling	◒	●	○	○	⊖	⊖	⊜	
Fuel	●	●	◒	◒	◒	◒	⊖	
Ignition	◒	◒	○	⊖	⊖	⊖	⊜	
Auto. trans.	○	◒	○	◒	○	*	⊖	
Man. trans.	*	*	*	*	*	*	*	
Clutch	*	*	*	*	*	*	*	
Electrical	●	●	●	◒	◒	◒	◒	
A/C	●	●	◒	○	⊖	◒	○	
Suspension	●	◒	◒	○	⊖	⊖	○	
Brakes	●	●	●	●	●	●	●	
Exhaust	●	●	●	◒	⊖	⊜	⊜	
Body rust	●	●	●	◒	○	○	⊜	
Paint/trim	●	●	●	●	●	○	◒	
Integrity	◒	◒	◒	◒	◒	◒	●	
Hardware	●	◒	●	◒	●	●	◒	

Ford Bronco II

TROUBLE SPOTS	87	88	89	90	91	92	93	94
Engine	◒	◒	◒	◒				
Cooling	●	●	◒	◒				
Fuel	○	○	⊖	⊖				
Ignition	○	⊖	⊖	⊖				
Auto. trans.	●	◒	◒	*				
Man. trans.	○	⊖	⊖	*				
Clutch	○	◒	○	*				
Electrical	●	●	◒	◒				
A/C	●	●	●	●				
Suspension	◒	○	○	⊖				
Brakes	◒	◒	◒	◒				
Exhaust	●	●	●	●				
Body rust	●	◒	○	○				
Paint/trim	●	●	◒	○				
Integrity	●	◒	⊖	○				
Hardware	◒	◒	◒	○				

Ford Club Wagon, Van V8

TROUBLE SPOTS	87	88	89	90	91	92	93	94
Engine	◒	◒	◒	○	○	⊖	⊖	Insufficient data
Cooling	◒	◒	◒	○	○	○	⊖	
Fuel	●	◒	◒	○	○	○	⊖	
Ignition	○	○	○	⊖	⊖	⊖	⊖	
Auto. trans.	⊖	○	○	○	○	⊖	⊜	
Man. trans.	*							
Clutch	*							
Electrical	●	●	●	◒	◒	◒	○	
A/C	●	●	●	●	●	◒	○	
Suspension	◒	◒	○	○	○	◒	○	
Brakes	●	●	●	●	○	◒	○	
Exhaust	●	●	◒	○	○	⊖	⊜	
Body rust	●	●	◒	○	⊖	⊖	⊜	
Paint/trim	◒	◒	◒	○	○	○	○	
Integrity	●	●	◒	●	●	◒	○	
Hardware	●	●	●	◒	◒	◒	◒	

Ford & LTD Crown Victoria

TROUBLE SPOTS	87	88	89	90	91	92	93	94
Engine	○	○	⊖	⊖	⊜	⊖	⊜	⊜
Cooling	○	◒	○	○	⊖	⊜	⊜	⊜
Fuel	◒	○	○	○	⊖	⊜	⊜	⊜
Ignition	○	⊖	⊖	⊖	⊖	⊖	⊜	⊜
Auto. trans.	○	○	○	⊖	⊖	⊖	⊖	⊜
Man. trans.								
Clutch								
Electrical	●	◒	◒	●	◒	◒	⊖	⊖
A/C	●	●	●	◒	○	○	⊖	⊜
Suspension	○	○	○	○	○	⊖	⊖	⊖
Brakes	◒	●	◒	●	●	●	○	⊖
Exhaust	●	●	◒	○	⊖	●	⊜	⊜
Body rust	○	○	⊖	⊜	⊖	⊜	⊜	⊜
Paint/trim	◒	○	⊖	⊖	⊖	⊖	⊖	⊖
Integrity	○	⊖	○	⊖	⊖	○	○	○
Hardware	◒	◒	○	◒	◒	○	⊖	⊖

Ford Escort

TROUBLE SPOTS	87	88	89	90	91	92	93	94
Engine	●	◒	◒	○	⊖	⊖	⊜	⊜
Cooling	●	●	◒	○	⊖	⊖	⊖	⊜
Fuel	●	◒	●	◒	⊖	⊖	⊖	⊜
Ignition	◒	◒	○	○	⊖	⊜	⊜	⊜
Auto. trans.	○	◒	◒	○	○	⊜	⊜	⊜
Man. trans.	⊜	⊜	⊖	⊖	⊖	⊜	⊜	⊜
Clutch	○	◒	○	◒	⊖	⊜	⊜	⊜
Electrical	●	●	●	●	◒	○	○	⊖
A/C	●	●	●	◒	●	⊖	⊖	⊜
Suspension	◒	●	◒	◒	⊖	⊖	⊜	⊜
Brakes	●	●	●	◒	●	○	⊖	⊜
Exhaust	○	◒	○	⊖	⊜	⊜	⊜	⊜
Body rust	●	◒	○	⊖	⊖	⊜	⊜	⊜
Paint/trim	◒	◒	○	○	○	⊖	⊖	⊜
Integrity	●	●	●	◒	◒	○	○	⊖
Hardware	◒	●	◒	○	◒	○	○	⊖

TROUBLE SPOTS	Ford Explorer (2WD) 87	88	89	90	91	92	93	94
Engine					◒	○	⊖	⊜
Cooling					○	⊖	⊜	⊜
Fuel					⊖	⊜	⊜	⊜
Ignition					⊖	⊜	⊜	⊜
Auto. trans.					○	⊖	⊜	⊜
Man. trans.					◒	○	⊜	*
Clutch					○	⊜	⊖	*
Electrical					●	●	⊖	⊖
A/C					●	◒	⊖	⊜
Suspension					◒	◒	○	⊜
Brakes					●	○	○	⊖
Exhaust					○	⊜	⊜	⊜
Body rust					⊜	⊜	⊜	⊜
Paint/trim					○	○	⊜	⊜
Integrity					○	○	○	⊖
Hardware					○	○	○	⊜

TROUBLE SPOTS	Ford Explorer (4WD) 87	88	89	90	91	92	93	94
Engine					◒	○	⊖	⊜
Cooling					○	⊖	⊜	⊜
Fuel					⊖	⊜	⊜	⊜
Ignition					⊜	⊜	⊜	⊜
Auto. trans.					⊖	⊖	⊜	⊜
Man. trans.					○	◒	⊜	⊜
Clutch					⊖	⊖	⊜	⊜
Electrical					◒	◒	⊖	⊖
A/C					◒	○	⊜	⊜
Suspension					○	○	○	⊖
Brakes					◒	◒	○	⊖
Exhaust					◒	⊖	⊜	⊜
Body rust					⊜	⊜	⊜	⊜
Paint/trim					○	⊖	⊜	⊜
Integrity					○	○	⊜	⊖
Hardware					○	○	⊖	⊖

TROUBLE SPOTS	Ford F150-250 Pickup (2WD) 87	88	89	90	91	92	93	94
Engine	◒	◒	○	○	○	⊖	⊖	⊜
Cooling	◒	◒	◒	○	⊖	⊖	⊜	⊜
Fuel	●	◒	◒	●	◒	◒	○	⊜
Ignition	○	○	○	⊖	⊖	⊜	⊖	⊜
Auto. trans.	○	○	○	◒	◒	○	⊖	⊜
Man. trans.	○	○	⊖	⊖	⊜	⊖	⊖	*
Clutch	●	◒	○	○	⊖	⊖	⊖	*
Electrical	●	●	◒	◒	○	◒	○	⊖
A/C	●	●	◒	⊖	⊖	○	⊖	⊖
Suspension	◒	●	◒	◒	○	⊖	○	⊖
Brakes	●	●	◒	●	◒	◒	○	⊖
Exhaust	●	●	●	◒	○	⊜	⊜	⊜
Body rust	◒	◒	○	○	⊖	⊜	⊜	⊜
Paint/trim	●	●	●	●	●	○	○	⊖
Integrity	◒	◒	○	○	○	◒	◒	○
Hardware	○	◒	○	○	○	◒	○	○

TROUBLE SPOTS	Ford F150-250 Pickup (4WD) 87	88	89	90	91	92	93	94
Engine	◒	●	◒	○	○	⊖	⊖	⊜
Cooling	◒	◒	◒	○	○	⊖	⊖	⊖
Fuel	●	◒	◒	◒	◒	◒	○	⊜
Ignition	◒	○	○	○	○	⊖	⊜	⊜
Auto. trans.	◒	○	◒	●	●	○	⊖	⊖
Man. trans.	⊖	○	⊖	○	⊖	⊖	○	*
Clutch	●	●	◒	○	○	⊜	○	*
Electrical	●	●	●	●	◒	◒	○	⊖
A/C	◒	◒	○	⊖	⊖	○	⊖	⊜
Suspension	●	●	●	○	○	○	○	⊖
Brakes	●	●	●	●	●	●	◒	⊖
Exhaust	●	●	●	●	◒	⊜	⊜	⊜
Body rust	●	●	○	○	⊖	⊜	⊖	⊜
Paint/trim	●	●	●	●	●	○	○	⊖
Integrity	◒	◒	○	○	○	◒	◒	○
Hardware	○	◒	◒	○	◒	●	◒	○

TROUBLE SPOTS	Ford Festiva 87	88	89	90	91	92	93	94
Engine		○	⊖	⊜	⊖	Insufficient data	⊜	
Cooling		⊜	⊖	⊜	⊖		⊜	
Fuel		○	⊜	⊜	⊖		⊜	
Ignition		⊖	⊖	⊜	⊜		⊜	
Auto. trans.			*	*	*		*	
Man. trans.		⊜	⊜	⊜	⊜		⊜	
Clutch		⊖	⊜	⊖	⊖		⊜	
Electrical		◒	○	○	○		○	
A/C		◒	○	*	*		*	
Suspension		⊖	○	⊖	⊖		⊜	
Brakes		●	●	●	●		○	
Exhaust		●	●	●	◒		⊜	
Body rust		○	⊜	⊖	⊜		⊜	
Paint/trim		○	⊜	○	⊜		⊖	
Integrity		○	○	○	◒		◒	
Hardware		◒	○	○	◒		◒	

TROUBLE SPOTS	Ford Mustang 4 87	88	89	90	91	92	93	94
Engine	◒	○	○	Insufficient data	Insufficient data	Insufficient data	Insufficient data	
Cooling	●	●	◒					
Fuel	●	◒	○					
Ignition	○	○	⊖					
Auto. trans.	●	●	◒					
Man. trans.	*	*	*					
Clutch	*	*	*					
Electrical	●	●	●					
A/C	●	●	○					
Suspension	○	○	⊖					
Brakes	◒	◒	◒					
Exhaust	●	●	●					
Body rust	●	◒	◒					
Paint/trim	●	●	●					
Integrity	◒	◒	◒					
Hardware	●	●	●					

TROUBLE SPOTS	Ford Mustang V8 87	88	89	90	91	92	93	94
Engine	⊖	◒	○	⊖	⊖	⊜	⊖	⊜
Cooling	●	●	⊖	○	○	⊜	⊜	⊜
Fuel	◒	◒	○	○	⊖	⊖	⊜	⊜
Ignition	○	⊖	⊖	⊖	⊜	⊖	⊜	⊜
Auto. trans.	*	*	◒	*	*	*	*	*
Man. trans.	⊖	○	○	⊖	*	*	*	*
Clutch	◒	◒	○	◒	*	*	*	*
Electrical	●	●	●	●	●	◒	○	⊜
A/C	●	●	●	◒	⊖	⊖	○	⊜
Suspension	⊖	○	○	⊖	○	○	⊖	⊜
Brakes	○	○	○	○	○	●	◒	⊖
Exhaust	●	●	○	⊜	⊜	⊜	⊜	⊜
Body rust	●	○	○	⊖	⊖	⊖	⊜	⊜
Paint/trim	●	●	●	●	●	●	●	⊖
Integrity	●	●	◒	◒	○	●	●	⊖
Hardware	●	◒	●	◒	○	●	●	⊖

TROUBLE SPOTS	Ford Probe 4 87	88	89	90	91	92	93	94
Engine			⊖	⊜	⊖	⊜	⊜	Insufficient data
Cooling			◒	◒	◒	⊖	⊜	
Fuel			⊜	⊖	⊖	⊜	⊜	
Ignition			⊜	⊜	⊜	⊜	⊖	
Auto. trans.			◒	○	⊖	*	⊜	
Man. trans.			⊜	⊜	*	*	⊖	
Clutch			⊖	⊖	*	*	⊖	
Electrical			●	●	●	●	○	
A/C			●	●	◒	*	⊖	
Suspension			⊖	○	○	◒	⊜	
Brakes			◒	◒	◒	○	⊖	
Exhaust			●	◒	⊖	⊜	⊜	
Body rust			⊜	⊖	⊖	⊜	⊜	
Paint/trim			○	○	◒	◒	○	
Integrity			◒	●	●	●	●	
Hardware			◒	●	◒	◒	◒	

⊜ ⊖ ○ ◒ ●
Few ← Problems → Many

*
Insufficient data

Trouble spots	Ford Probe V6 87	88	89	90	91	92	93	94	Ford Ranger Pickup 4 (2WD) 87	88	89	90	91	92	93	94
Engine				○	⊜	⊖	○	⊜	●	◒	○	○	○	○	⊖	⊜
Cooling				○	⊖	⊜	⊜	⊖	◒	○	⊖	○	⊖	⊜	⊜	⊜
Fuel				○	⊖	◒	⊖	⊖	◒	○	◒	○	○	⊖	⊜	⊖
Ignition				⊖	⊜	⊖	⊜	⊜	○	○	○	⊖	⊖	⊖	⊜	⊜
Auto. trans.				○	⊖	*	⊜	*	*	*	*	*	*	*	*	*
Man. trans.				⊜	*	*	⊖	*	◒	⊖	⊖	⊜	⊖	⊖	⊜	⊜
Clutch				⊜	*	*	⊜	*	○	○	○	○	○	○	⊜	⊜
Electrical				●	●	◒	◒	○	◒	◒	●	◒	○	○	○	⊖
A/C				◒	◒	⊖	⊜	⊜	●	●	●	●	◒	⊖	⊖	⊜
Suspension				○	⊖	⊖	⊜	⊜	◒	⊖	⊖	○	⊜	⊜	⊖	⊖
Brakes				◒	◒	○	⊖	⊜	◒	○	○	○	⊖	⊖	○	⊖
Exhaust				◒	⊜	⊖	○	⊜	●	●	●	⊖	⊖	⊜	⊜	⊜
Body rust				⊜	⊖	⊜	⊜	⊜	●	○	⊖	⊖	⊖	⊜	⊜	⊜
Paint/trim				⊖	○	◒	○	⊖	●	◒	◒	◒	○	⊖	⊖	⊜
Integrity				◒	●	●	●	◒	◒	○	⊖	⊖	○	○	⊖	⊖
Hardware				◒	◒	○	◒	⊖	○	○	◒	⊖	⊖	○	⊖	⊜

Trouble spots	Ford Ranger Pickup V6 (2WD) 87	88	89	90	91	92	93	94	Ford Ranger Pickup V6 (4WD) 87	88	89	90	91	92	93	94
Engine	○	◒	◒	◒	⊖	⊖	⊖	⊜	◒	◒	●	◒	◒	⊖	⊜	⊜
Cooling	●	●	○	○	⊖	⊖	⊜	⊜	●	●	◒	◒	⊖	⊜	⊜	⊜
Fuel	○	○	⊖	⊖	⊖	⊖	⊖	⊜	○	○	⊖	⊖	⊖	⊜	⊖	⊖
Ignition	○	⊖	⊖	⊜	⊖	⊖	⊜	⊜	○	⊖	⊜	⊖	⊖	⊜	⊜	⊜
Auto. trans.	◒	◒	○	○	○	⊖	⊜	⊜	*	*	*	○	*	*	⊖	*
Man. trans.	◒	⊖	○	⊖	⊖	○	⊜	⊜	◒	○	⊖	*	*	*	⊜	*
Clutch	◒	◒	○	⊖	⊖	⊖	⊜	⊜	◒	◒	○	*	*	*	⊖	*
Electrical	◒	◒	◒	◒	○	○	⊖	⊖	◒	◒	◒	◒	⊖	○	⊖	○
A/C	●	●	●	●	◒	○	⊜	⊜	●	●	◒	●	●	○	⊜	⊜
Suspension	◒	○	○	○	⊖	⊖	⊖	⊜	◒	◒	○	○	⊖	⊖	⊜	⊖
Brakes	◒	◒	◒	○	○	○	⊖	⊖	●	●	◒	◒	◒	○	⊖	⊖
Exhaust	●	●	●	◒	○	⊜	⊜	⊜	●	●	◒	◒	○	⊖	⊜	⊜
Body rust	◒	○	⊖	⊜	⊖	⊜	⊜	⊜	●	◒	⊖	⊜	⊖	⊜	⊜	⊜
Paint/trim	●	●	◒	◒	○	○	⊖	⊖	●	●	◒	◒	◒	⊜	○	⊜
Integrity	○	○	⊖	○	○	○	⊖	⊖	○	○	○	○	○	○	⊖	⊖
Hardware	◒	○	◒	○	⊜	○	⊜	⊜	○	○	⊖	○	○	○	⊖	⊖

Trouble spots	Ford Taurus 4 87	88	89	90	91	92	93	94	Ford Taurus V6 87	88	89	90	91	92	93	94
Engine	●	●	●	⊖					◒	◒	○	⊖	⊖	⊜	⊜	⊜
Cooling	●	●	○	⊖					●	●	◒	○	⊖	⊖	⊜	⊜
Fuel	●	●	●	⊖					◒	◒	○	○	⊖	⊖	⊖	⊜
Ignition	◒	●	○	○					○	○	⊖	⊖	⊖	⊜	⊜	⊜
Auto. trans.	●	●	●	*					◒	◒	◒	○	◒	⊖	⊖	⊜
Man. trans.	○	*														
Clutch	●	*														
Electrical	●	●	●	●					●	●	●	●	◒	◒	○	⊖
A/C	●	●	●	*					●	●	●	◒	○	⊖	⊖	⊜
Suspension	●	●	◒	◒					●	●	●	◒	◒	○	⊖	⊜
Brakes	●	●	●	●					●	●	●	●	●	◒	○	⊖
Exhaust	●	●	●	⊖					⊖	⊜	⊜	⊜	⊜	⊜	⊜	⊜
Body rust	●	◒	◒	⊖					●	◒	○	⊖	⊖	⊜	⊜	⊜
Paint/trim	●	◒	◒	⊖					●	◒	○	⊜	⊖	⊖	⊖	⊜
Integrity	●	◒	◒	○					◒	◒	○	○	○	◒	◒	○
Hardware	◒	◒	◒	◒					●	◒	◒	◒	◒	◒	○	⊖

Trouble spots	Ford Taurus SHO 87	88	89	90	91	92	93	94	Ford Tempo 87	88	89	90	91	92	93	94
Engine			⊜	⊖	⊖	⊜	⊜	Insufficient data	◒	◒	◒	◒	○	⊖	⊖	⊜
Cooling			○	○	⊜	◒	○		●	●	◒	○	⊖	⊖	⊜	⊖
Fuel			⊖	⊖	⊜	⊖	⊖		●	●	●	●	●	○	○	⊜
Ignition			⊖	⊖	⊖	⊜	⊜		◒	◒	○	○	○	⊖	⊜	⊜
Auto. trans.							○		●	◒	○	⊖	⊖	○	⊖	⊜
Man. trans.			⊖	○	⊜	⊖	*		⊜	⊜	⊖	*	*	*	*	*
Clutch			●	●	●	◒	*		●	◒	◒	*	*	*	*	*
Electrical			◒	●	●	◒	◒		●	●	●	●	●	○	○	○
A/C			●	●	◒	⊖	⊖		●	●	●	●	○	⊖	⊖	⊜
Suspension			◒	◒	◒	○	○		●	●	●	●	○	⊖	⊖	⊜
Brakes			◒	●	●	◒	●		●	●	●	●	●	○	○	⊖
Exhaust			⊜	⊜	⊖	⊜	⊜		●	●	●	●	●	⊖	⊜	⊜
Body rust			○	⊖	⊖	⊜	⊜		●	○	○	⊖	⊖	⊖	⊜	⊜
Paint/trim			○	○	○	○	○		●	◒	◒	◒	○	○	⊖	⊜
Integrity			○	○	○	●	◒		●	●	◒	◒	○	◒	◒	⊖
Hardware			○	◒	◒	◒	○		◒	◒	◒	◒	○	○	○	⊜

Ford Thunderbird V6 87	88	89	90	91	92	93	94	Ford Thunderbird V8 87	88	89	90	91	92	93	94	TROUBLE SPOTS
○	◒	○	⊖	⊜	⊖	⊜	⊜	○	⊖			⊜	⊜	⊜	⊜	Engine
●	◒	○	⊖	⊖	⊖	⊖	⊜	◒	○			○	⊖	○	⊜	Cooling
◒	○	○	⊖	⊖	⊖	⊜	⊜	◒	◒			⊖	⊖	⊜	⊖	Fuel
◒	○	⊖	⊖	⊖	⊜	⊖	⊜	○	⊖			⊜	⊜	⊜	⊜	Ignition
○	○	○	⊖	⊜	⊖	⊖	⊜	◒	○			○	⊖	⊖	⊜	Auto. trans.
		*	*	*	*	*	*									Man. trans.
		*	*	*	*	*	*									Clutch
●	●	●	●	◒	◒	○	⊖	●	●			●	◒	○	⊖	Electrical
●	●	●	●	●	○	○	○	●	●			●	○	○	⊜	A/C
◒	◒	○	○	○	○	⊖	⊜	●	◒			⊖	⊖	⊖	⊜	Suspension
●	●	●	●	●	◒	○	⊖	●	●			●	●	○	⊖	Brakes
●	●	⊜	⊖	⊜	⊜	⊜	⊜	◒	●			⊜	⊜	⊜	⊜	Exhaust
○	○	⊖	⊜	⊖	⊜	⊜	⊜	○	○			⊜	⊜	⊜	⊜	Body rust
◒	◒	◒	◒	◒	◒	○	○	◒	◒			○	○	○	⊖	Paint/trim
○	◒	◒	○	○	○	◒	⊖	◒	○			○	○	◒	⊖	Integrity
◒	◒	●	◒	◒	◒	◒	⊖	◒	○			○	◒	◒	⊖	Hardware

TROUBLE SPOTS	Geo Metro 87	88	89	90	91	92	93	94	Geo Prizm 87	88	89	90	91	92	93	94
Engine			○	⊖	⊖	⊜	⊖	⊜				⊜	⊜	⊜	⊜	⊜
Cooling			⊖	⊜	⊖	⊜	⊜	⊜				⊖	⊜	⊜	⊜	⊜
Fuel			○	○	⊖	⊖	⊖	⊖				⊜	⊜	⊜	⊜	⊜
Ignition			○	⊖	⊖	⊜	⊖	⊖				⊜	⊜	⊜	⊜	⊜
Auto. trans.			*	*	*	*	*	*				⊜	⊖	⊖	⊜	⊜
Man. trans.			*	⊖	⊖	⊜	⊜	*				⊜	⊜	*	⊜	⊜
Clutch			*	○	○	⊜	⊜	*				⊜	⊖	*	⊜	⊜
Electrical			◒	○	◒	◒	○	⊖				○	◒	○	⊖	⊖
A/C			*	●	⊖	⊖	⊖	*				⊜	⊜	⊜	⊜	⊜
Suspension			◒	○	⊖	⊖	⊖	⊜				⊖	⊖	⊖	⊖	⊜
Brakes			◒	○	○	⊖	⊜	⊜				◒	○	⊜	⊜	⊜
Exhaust			●	●	●	⊜	⊜	⊜				●	◒	⊜	⊜	⊜
Body rust			⊖	⊖	⊜	⊜	⊜	⊜				⊖	⊖	⊜	⊜	⊜
Paint/trim			○	○	○	○	⊖	⊜				○	○	⊖	⊖	⊖
Integrity			●	◒	◒	◒	○	⊖				●	○	⊖	⊖	⊖
Hardware			●	●	●	●	◒	○				●	◒	○	○	⊖

Geo Storm 87	88	89	90	91	92	93	94	Geo Tracker 87	88	89	90	91	92	93	94	TROUBLE SPOTS
			○	⊜	⊖	Insufficient data				○	⊖	○	⊖	⊜	⊜	Engine
			⊖	⊖	⊖					⊖	⊖	⊜	⊖	⊖	⊜	Cooling
			⊖	⊖	⊜					○	⊖	⊖	⊜	⊜	⊜	Fuel
			○	⊖	⊜					⊖	⊜	⊖	⊜	⊜	⊜	Ignition
			*	*	*					*	*	*	*	⊖	*	Auto. trans.
			⊜	*	*					*	*	⊜	⊖	⊜	*	Man. trans.
			○	*	*					*	*	○	⊖	⊜	*	Clutch
			●	○	⊖					◒	○	○	○	⊖	⊖	Electrical
			○	⊜	*					*	*	*	*	⊖	*	A/C
			○	◒	○					⊖	⊜	⊖	⊜	⊜	⊜	Suspension
			◒	◒	◒					●	◒	◒	○	⊖	⊖	Brakes
			●	●	○					●	●	◒	⊜	⊜	⊜	Exhaust
			⊖	⊖	⊜					◒	⊖	⊖	⊜	⊜	⊜	Body rust
			◒	○	○					○	⊖	○	⊖	⊖	⊖	Paint/trim
			○	○	○					◒	○	○	○	○	○	Integrity
			●	⊖	◒					◒	◒	○	◒	◒	○	Hardware

TROUBLE SPOTS	GMC Jimmy, Yukon 87	88	89	90	91	92	93	94	GMC S-15 Jimmy, Typhoon V6 (2WD) 87	88	89	90	91	92	93	94
Engine	●	◒	○	⊖	⊖	⊖	⊖	⊜	◒	○	○	Insufficient data	⊖	⊖	⊖	Insufficient data
Cooling	●	◒	○	○	⊜	⊖	⊜	⊜	◒	●	◒		⊜	⊜	⊜	
Fuel	◒	◒	○	⊖	⊖	⊖	⊖	⊜	◒	◒	⊖		⊖	⊖	⊜	
Ignition	◒	○	⊖	○	○	⊖	⊜	⊜	○	○	⊖		⊖	⊜	⊜	
Auto. trans.	●	◒	⊖	⊖	⊜	○	⊖	⊖	◒	○	⊜		⊖	*	⊖	
Man. trans.	*	*	*	*	*	*	*	*	*	*	*		*	*	*	
Clutch	*	*	*	*	*	*	*	*	*	*	*		*	*	*	
Electrical	●	●	●	◒	●	●	○	⊖	●	●	●		◒	◒	○	
A/C	●	○	○	○	⊖	○	⊖	⊜	◒	○	○		○	⊖	⊖	
Suspension	◒	◒	○	⊖	○	○	⊖	⊜	⊖	○	○		⊖	⊖	⊖	
Brakes	●	●	●	◒	●	●	○	⊜	●	◒	●		◒	●	⊖	
Exhaust	◒	◒	◒	⊖	○	⊖	⊜	⊜	○	○	⊖		⊜	⊜	⊜	
Body rust	●	●	◒	○	○	⊖	⊖	⊜	○	⊖	○		○	⊖	⊜	
Paint/trim	●	●	●	●	●	◒	⊖	⊜	●	●	●		●	◒	○	
Integrity	●	●	●	●	◒	◒	◒	⊖	◒	●	●		◒	●	●	
Hardware	●	●	●	●	●	●	◒	⊖	●	◒	●		●	◒	◒	

⊜ ⊖ ○ ◒ ●

Few ← **Problems** → Many

* Insufficient data

GMC S-15 Jimmy, Typhoon V6 (4WD)

Trouble spots	87	88	89	90	91	92	93	94
Engine	◒	◒	○	○	⊜	○	⊖	⊜
Cooling	◒	◒	○	⊖	⊜	⊖	⊜	⊜
Fuel	○	○	○	⊖	⊖	⊖	⊖	⊖
Ignition	⊖	○	⊖	◒	⊖	⊜	⊜	⊜
Auto. trans.	◒	○	○	○	⊖	⊖	⊖	⊜
Man. trans.	*	*	*	*	*	*	*	*
Clutch	*	*	*	*	*	*	*	*
Electrical	●	●	●	●	●	◒	◒	○
A/C	○	○	⊖	⊖	⊖	⊖	⊖	⊜
Suspension	○	◒	◒	◒	○	⊜	⊖	⊜
Brakes	●	●	●	●	●	●	○	⊜
Exhaust	◒	◒	○	◒	⊜	⊖	⊜	⊜
Body rust	●	◒	●	●	◒	⊜	⊖	⊜
Paint/trim	◒	●	●	●	●	○	○	⊜
Integrity	●	●	●	●	●	◒	●	○
Hardware	●	●	◒	●	●	◒	◒	⊜

GMC S-15 Sonoma Pickup (2WD)

Trouble spots	87	88	89	90	91	92	93	94
Engine	◒	◒	○	○	⊖	⊖	⊖	⊜
Cooling	◒	◒	○	⊖	⊖	⊖	⊜	⊜
Fuel	○	○	○	○	⊖	⊖	⊖	○
Ignition	○	○	○	○	○	⊖	⊜	⊜
Auto. trans.	○	⊖	⊖	⊜	⊜	⊖	⊖	⊜
Man. trans.	⊖	○	⊖	*	⊖	⊖	○	⊖
Clutch	◒	◒	○	*	○	○	○	⊖
Electrical	◒	●	●	●	◒	○	○	○
A/C	○	○	○	⊜	⊖	⊖	⊖	⊜
Suspension	⊖	⊖	⊖	⊖	⊖	⊜	⊖	⊖
Brakes	◒	◒	◒	◒	○	○	⊖	⊖
Exhaust	●	●	◒	◒	○	⊖	⊜	⊜
Body rust	◒	◒	◒	⊖	○	⊖	⊜	⊜
Paint/trim	◒	●	●	●	●	◒	○	⊖
Integrity	◒	◒	◒	◒	○	○	○	○
Hardware	◒	◒	◒	◒	◒	○	○	⊖

GMC S-15 Sonoma Pickup (4WD)

Trouble spots	87	88	89	90	91	92	93	94
Engine	●	○	○	Insufficient data	⊜	⊖	Insufficient data	⊖
Cooling	◒	◒	◒		⊖	⊜		⊜
Fuel	○	○	⊖		⊖	⊖		○
Ignition	⊜	○	◒		○	○		⊜
Auto. trans.	*	○	○		○	⊖		⊖
Man. trans.	*	*	*		*	*		*
Clutch	*	*	*		*	*		*
Electrical	◒	◒	●		●	○		○
A/C	*	○	⊖		⊖	⊖		⊜
Suspension	○	●	◒		○	⊖		⊜
Brakes	◒	◒	◒		◒	◒		⊖
Exhaust	●	●	○		⊖	⊖		⊜
Body rust	●	○	●		○	⊖		⊜
Paint/trim	●	●	●		●	◒		⊜
Integrity	◒	●	◒		●	○		○
Hardware	●	◒	◒		◒	○		⊖

GMC Safari Van (2WD)

Trouble spots	87	88	89	90	91	92	93	94
Engine	◒	◒	◒	⊖	⊖	○	⊖	⊜
Cooling	◒	○	○	⊖	⊜	⊖	⊜	⊜
Fuel	○	⊖	⊖	⊖	⊖	⊖	⊖	⊜
Ignition	⊖	○	⊖	⊖	⊜	⊖	⊜	⊜
Auto. trans.	○	○	⊖	⊖	⊜	○	⊖	⊖
Man. trans.	*	*	*					
Clutch	*	*	*					
Electrical	●	●	●	●	◒	◒	◒	○
A/C	◒	◒	◒	○	○	○	⊖	○
Suspension	●	●	◒	◒	○	⊖	⊖	⊖
Brakes	●	◒	●	●	●	●	○	⊜
Exhaust	◒	◒	○	○	⊖	⊜	⊜	⊜
Body rust	⊖	⊖	⊜	⊜	⊜	⊜	⊜	⊜
Paint/trim	●	●	◒	◒	◒	◒	○	⊜
Integrity	◒	◒	◒	●	●	●	●	◒
Hardware	●	●	●	●	●	●	●	○

GMC Safari Van (4WD)

Trouble spots	87	88	89	90	91	92	93	94
Engine				Insufficient data	⊖	⊖	⊖	Insufficient data
Cooling					⊖	⊜	⊖	
Fuel					⊜	○	⊜	
Ignition					⊜	⊖	⊜	
Auto. trans.					⊖	○	⊖	
Man. trans.								
Clutch								
Electrical					●	◒	◒	
A/C					○	⊖	⊖	
Suspension					○	⊜	⊖	
Brakes					●	●	○	
Exhaust					⊖	⊜	⊖	
Body rust					⊜	⊜	⊜	
Paint/trim					◒	◒	○	
Integrity					●	●	◒	
Hardware					●	●	●	

GMC Sierra C1500-2500 Pickup

Trouble spots	87	88	89	90	91	92	93	94
Engine	◒	◒	○	⊖	⊖	⊖	⊖	⊜
Cooling	●	●	○	⊖	⊖	⊜	⊜	⊜
Fuel	◒	○	⊖	○	⊖	⊖	⊜	⊜
Ignition	○	○	○	○	○	⊖	⊖	⊜
Auto. trans.	○	○	○	○	◒	○	⊖	⊜
Man. trans.	*	○	⊖	⊖	⊖	○	⊖	*
Clutch	*	●	○	○	◒	◒	○	*
Electrical	●	●	●	●	●	◒	○	⊖
A/C	○	○	○	○	○	○	⊖	⊖
Suspension	⊖	◒	◒	○	○	⊖	⊖	⊖
Brakes	◒	●	◒	◒	○	⊖	⊜	⊖
Exhaust	◒	●	◒	◒	○	⊜	⊜	⊜
Body rust	●	⊖	⊜	⊜	⊜	⊜	⊜	⊜
Paint/trim	●	◒	◒	◒	○	○	○	⊜
Integrity	◒	◒	○	○	○	○	○	○
Hardware	◒	◒	◒	○	○	○	○	○

GMC Sierra K1500-2500 Pickup

Trouble spots	87	88	89	90	91	92	93	94
Engine	◒	◒	○	○	⊜	⊖	⊖	⊜
Cooling	●	●	○	⊖	⊖	⊖	⊜	⊜
Fuel	●	○	⊖	⊖	⊖	⊖	⊜	⊜
Ignition	◒	○	○	○	⊜	⊖	⊜	⊜
Auto. trans.	●	◒	◒	○	◒	◒	⊖	⊜
Man. trans.	*	○	○	○	*	⊖	⊖	*
Clutch	*	●	◒	◒	*	○	⊖	*
Electrical	●	●	●	●	◒	◒	○	⊖
A/C	○	○	○	○	○	⊖	⊜	⊜
Suspension	◒	●	◒	○	○	○	⊜	⊖
Brakes	●	●	●	◒	◒	○	⊜	⊖
Exhaust	◒	●	●	○	○	⊖	⊜	⊜
Body rust	●	○	⊜	⊜	⊜	⊜	⊜	⊜
Paint/trim	●	◒	●	◒	◒	○	○	⊖
Integrity	◒	◒	◒	○	○	○	◒	○
Hardware	◒	●	◒	○	○	○	○	⊖

GMC Suburban (2WD)

Trouble spots	87	88	89	90	91	92	93	94
Engine	◒	○	○	○	⊖	⊖	⊖	⊜
Cooling	●	●	●	○	○	⊖	⊜	⊜
Fuel	●	○	○	⊖	○	⊖	⊖	⊜
Ignition	⊖	⊖	○	⊖	○	⊖	⊜	⊜
Auto. trans.	◒	○	◒	○	○	○	⊖	⊜
Man. trans.	*	*	*	*				
Clutch	*	*	*	*				
Electrical	●	◒	●	●	◒	◒	○	⊖
A/C	●	◒	◒	○	○	◒	⊖	⊜
Suspension	◒	◒	◒	⊖	○	⊖	⊖	⊜
Brakes	◒	●	●	◒	●	◒	○	⊖
Exhaust	●	◒	◒	○	⊖	⊜	⊜	⊜
Body rust	●	●	○	⊖	⊖	⊜	⊖	⊜
Paint/trim	●	●	●	◒	◒	○	○	⊜
Integrity	●	●	●	●	●	◒	◒	⊖
Hardware	●	●	●	●	◒	◒	●	○

GMC Suburban (4WD)

TROUBLE SPOTS	87	88	89	90	91	92	93	94
Engine	●	◒	◒	⊖	⊖	⊜	⊖	⊜
Cooling	●	●	◒	⊖	○	⊜	⊜	⊜
Fuel	●	○	○	○	○	⊜	⊖	⊜
Ignition	○	⊖	○	⊖	○	⊜	⊜	⊜
Auto. trans.	◒	○	◒	○	●	○	⊖	⊜
Man. trans.	*	*	*	*				
Clutch	*	*	*	*				
Electrical	●	◒	●	●	●	◒	◒	⊖
A/C	●	◒	○	○	⊖	○	⊖	⊜
Suspension	◒	○	○	○	◒	⊖	⊖	⊖
Brakes	●	●	●	●	●	◒	○	⊖
Exhaust	◒	◒	◒	⊖	⊜	⊖	⊜	⊜
Body rust	●	●	◒	○	○	⊜	⊖	⊜
Paint/trim	●	●	●	●	●	○	○	⊜
Integrity	●	●	●	●	●	◒	●	○
Hardware	●	●	●	●	◒	◒	●	⊖

Honda Accord

TROUBLE SPOTS	87	88	89	90	91	92	93	94
Engine	⊖	⊖	⊜	⊜	⊜	⊜	⊜	⊜
Cooling	○	⊖	⊖	⊜	⊜	⊜	⊜	⊜
Fuel	○	⊖	⊜	⊜	⊜	⊜	⊜	⊜
Ignition	⊜	⊖	⊖	◒	⊖	⊜	⊜	⊜
Auto. trans.	⊖	⊖	⊜	⊖	⊖	⊜	⊜	⊜
Man. trans.	⊜	⊜	⊜	⊜	⊜	⊜	⊜	⊜
Clutch	◒	◒	⊖	⊖	⊖	⊖	⊜	⊜
Electrical	◒	○	○	◒	○	⊖	⊖	⊜
A/C	◒	◒	○	⊖	⊖	⊖	⊜	⊜
Suspension	○	⊖	⊖	⊖	⊖	⊜	⊜	⊜
Brakes	●	●	●	○	⊖	⊖	⊜	⊜
Exhaust	◒	○	⊖	⊖	⊜	⊜	⊜	⊜
Body rust	⊖	⊖	⊜	⊜	⊜	⊜	⊜	⊜
Paint/trim	⊖	⊖	⊖	⊖	⊖	⊖	⊜	⊜
Integrity	○	⊖	⊖	○	○	○	○	⊖
Hardware	○	○	○	○	○	○	⊖	⊖

Honda Civic (2WD)

TROUBLE SPOTS	87	88	89	90	91	92	93	94
Engine	○	⊖	⊖	⊖	⊜	⊜	⊜	⊜
Cooling	⊖	⊖	⊖	⊜	⊜	⊜	⊜	⊜
Fuel	⊖	⊖	⊖	⊖	⊜	⊜	⊜	⊜
Ignition	⊜	●	◒	◒	○	⊜	⊜	⊜
Auto. trans.	⊜	⊖	⊖	⊖	⊖	⊜	⊖	⊜
Man. trans.	⊜	⊜	⊜	⊜	⊜	⊜	⊜	⊜
Clutch	◒	◒	○	⊖	⊖	⊜	⊜	⊜
Electrical	◒	●	◒	◒	○	⊖	⊖	⊜
A/C	◒	◒	○	○	⊜	⊖	⊜	⊜
Suspension	○	⊖	⊖	⊖	⊖	⊜	⊖	⊜
Brakes	●	●	●	●	◒	⊖	⊜	⊜
Exhaust	◒	●	●	◒	⊖	⊜	⊜	⊜
Body rust	○	○	⊖	⊜	⊜	⊜	⊜	⊜
Paint/trim	⊖	⊖	⊖	⊖	⊖	⊖	⊖	⊜
Integrity	○	○	○	○	○	○	⊖	⊖
Hardware	⊖	○	○	⊖	○	○	⊖	⊜

Honda Civic del Sol

TROUBLE SPOTS	87	88	89	90	91	92	93	94
Engine							⊜	Insufficient data
Cooling							⊜	
Fuel							⊜	
Ignition							⊜	
Auto. trans.							⊖	
Man. trans.							⊜	
Clutch							⊜	
Electrical							⊖	
A/C							⊜	
Suspension							⊜	
Brakes							⊜	
Exhaust							⊜	
Body rust							⊜	
Paint/trim							⊖	
Integrity							●	
Hardware							◒	

Honda CRX

TROUBLE SPOTS	87	88	89	90	91	92	93	94
Engine	⊖	⊖	⊖	⊖	⊜			
Cooling	⊖	⊖	⊖	⊖	⊜			
Fuel	⊖	⊖	⊜	⊖	⊜			
Ignition	⊖	◒	○	◒	⊖			
Auto. trans.	*	*	*	*	*			
Man. trans.	⊖	⊜	⊜	⊜	⊖			
Clutch	◒	◒	○	⊖	⊖			
Electrical	◒	○	○	○	○			
A/C	◒	◒	○	⊖	⊖			
Suspension	⊖	⊖	⊖	⊜	⊖			
Brakes	●	◒	◒	○	○			
Exhaust	●	●	●	●	⊖			
Body rust	○	○	⊖	⊜	⊜			
Paint/trim	○	○	⊜	⊖	⊖			
Integrity	○	◒	○	○	○			
Hardware	○	○	○	○	○			

Honda Prelude

TROUBLE SPOTS	87	88	89	90	91	92	93	94
Engine	⊖	⊖	⊖	⊜	⊜	⊜	⊜	Insufficient data
Cooling	○	⊖	⊜	⊜	⊖	⊜	⊜	
Fuel	○	⊖	⊜	⊜	⊜	⊜	⊜	
Ignition	⊖	⊜	⊜	⊜	⊜	⊜	⊜	
Auto. trans.	○	⊖	⊖	*	⊜	⊖	*	
Man. trans.	⊜	⊜	⊜	⊜	⊜	⊜	⊜	
Clutch	◒	◒	○	⊖	○	⊜	⊜	
Electrical	◒	◒	◒	○	○	⊜	⊖	
A/C	◒	◒	○	⊖	⊖	⊜	⊜	
Suspension	○	◒	○	⊜	⊖	⊜	⊜	
Brakes	●	●	●	○	○	⊖	⊖	
Exhaust	◒	◒	○	⊜	⊖	⊜	⊜	
Body rust	◒	◒	⊖	⊜	⊜	⊜	⊜	
Paint/trim	○	○	⊖	⊖	⊖	⊖	⊖	
Integrity	○	○	⊖	⊖	⊖	◒	⊖	
Hardware	⊖	○	○	⊖	○	⊖	⊜	

Hyundai Excel

TROUBLE SPOTS	87	88	89	90	91	92	93	94
Engine	●	●	●	○	⊖	Insufficient data	Insufficient data	Insufficient data
Cooling	●	●	●	◒	○			
Fuel	●	◒	○	●	○			
Ignition	○	◒	◒	○	○			
Auto. trans.	*	●	◒	*	*			
Man. trans.	◒	◒	●	*	*			
Clutch	●	●	●	*	*			
Electrical	●	●	●	●	●			
A/C	◒	◒	●	●	*			
Suspension	●	●	○	○	○			
Brakes	◒	●	●	◒	◒			
Exhaust	●	●	●	●	●			
Body rust	●	◒	◒	⊖	⊖			
Paint/trim	●	●	●	○	○			
Integrity	●	●	●	●	●			
Hardware	●	●	●	◒	◒			

Hyundai Sonata

TROUBLE SPOTS	87	88	89	90	91	92	93	94
Engine			●	◒	Insufficient data	Insufficient data	Insufficient data	Insufficient data
Cooling			●	◒				
Fuel			○	◒				
Ignition			○	⊖				
Auto. trans.			●	*				
Man. trans.			*	*				
Clutch			*	*				
Electrical			●	●				
A/C			●	●				
Suspension			◒	○				
Brakes			●	●				
Exhaust			●	●				
Body rust			○	⊖				
Paint/trim			●	◒				
Integrity			◒	◒				
Hardware			●	●				

⊜ ⊖ ○ ◒ ●
Few ← Problems → Many

* Insufficient data

Infiniti G20

TROUBLE SPOTS	87	88	89	90	91	92	93	94 (Insufficient data)
Engine					⊜	⊜	⊜	
Cooling					⊜	⊜	⊜	
Fuel					⊖	⊜	⊜	
Ignition					⊜	⊜	⊜	
Auto. trans.					⊜	⊜	⊜	
Man. trans.					*	*	⊜	
Clutch					*	*	⊜	
Electrical					○	⊖	⊖	
A/C					⊖	⊜	⊜	
Suspension					⊜	⊜	⊜	
Brakes					⊖	⊜	⊜	
Exhaust					⊜	⊜	⊜	
Body rust					⊜	⊜	⊜	
Paint/trim					⊖	⊖	⊜	
Integrity					⊖	⊜	⊖	
Hardware					◒	○	⊖	

Infinity J30

TROUBLE SPOTS	87	88	89	90	91	92	93	94 (Insufficient data)
Engine							⊜	
Cooling							⊜	
Fuel							⊜	
Ignition							⊜	
Auto. trans.							⊜	
Man. trans.								
Clutch								
Electrical							⊖	
A/C							⊜	
Suspension							⊜	
Brakes							⊜	
Exhaust							⊜	
Body rust							⊜	
Paint/trim							⊖	
Integrity							⊜	
Hardware							○	

Infiniti Q45

TROUBLE SPOTS	87	88	89	90	91	92	93 (Insufficient data)	94
Engine				○	⊖	⊜		⊜
Cooling				⊜	⊜	⊜		⊜
Fuel				○	○	⊖		⊜
Ignition				⊜	⊖	⊖		⊜
Auto. trans.				⊖	○	⊖		⊜
Man. trans.								
Clutch								
Electrical				○	○	◒		⊖
A/C				◒	⊖	⊜		⊖
Suspension				⊖	⊖	⊖		⊜
Brakes				●	●	◒		⊖
Exhaust				⊜	⊜	⊜		⊜
Body rust				⊜	⊜	⊜		⊜
Paint/trim				⊜	⊖	⊜		○
Integrity				⊖	⊖	⊖		⊜
Hardware				◒	●	○		⊖

Isuzu Pickup 4

TROUBLE SPOTS	87	88	89	90	91 (Insufficient data)	92 (Insufficient data)	93 (Insufficient data)	94 (Insufficient data)
Engine	◒	○	○	⊖				
Cooling	●	○	⊖	⊖				
Fuel	○	◒	◒	⊖				
Ignition	⊜	⊖	⊖	⊖				
Auto. trans.	*	*	*	*				
Man. trans.	⊜	*	⊜	⊜				
Clutch	◒	*	⊖	⊖				
Electrical	○	◒	◒	○				
A/C	*	*	*	*				
Suspension	⊖	○	⊜	○				
Brakes	●	◒	●	●				
Exhaust	●	◒	●	⊖				
Body rust	●	○	○	⊖				
Paint/trim	◒	○	⊖	○				
Integrity	◒	○	⊖	○				
Hardware	○	○	○	○				

Isuzu Rodeo V6

TROUBLE SPOTS	87	88	89	90	91	92	93	94 (Insufficient data)
Engine					⊖	○	⊜	
Cooling					◒	◒	⊜	
Fuel					⊖	⊜	⊜	
Ignition					⊖	⊖	⊜	
Auto. trans.					*	*	⊖	
Man. trans.					*	*	*	
Clutch					*	*	*	
Electrical					◒	○	○	
A/C					○	◒	○	
Suspension					○	⊖	○	
Brakes					◒	◒	⊜	
Exhaust					⊖	⊖	⊜	
Body rust					⊖	⊖	⊜	
Paint/trim					●	○	◒	
Integrity					●	⊖	◒	
Hardware					●	○	◒	

Isuzu Trooper II, Trooper 4

TROUBLE SPOTS	87	88	89	90	91 (Insufficient data)	92	93	94
Engine	●	●	○	⊖				
Cooling	●	●	⊖	⊖				
Fuel	○	○	○	⊜				
Ignition	○	⊜	⊖	⊜				
Auto. trans.		⊖	*	*				
Man. trans.	○	⊖	⊖	⊜				
Clutch	◒	◒	◒	○				
Electrical	◒	◒	○	◒				
A/C	◒	○	○	*				
Suspension	○	⊖	⊜	⊖				
Brakes	●	●	●	◒				
Exhaust	●	●	◒	◒				
Body rust	●	◒	○	○				
Paint/trim	◒	○	○	○				
Integrity	●	○	◒	○				
Hardware	○	○	○	⊖				

Isuzu Trooper II, Trooper V6

TROUBLE SPOTS	87	88	89 (Insufficient data)	90	91	92	93	94 (Insufficient data)
Engine				○	○	⊖	⊜	
Cooling				○	○	⊜	⊜	
Fuel				⊖	⊖	○	⊖	
Ignition				⊜	⊜	⊖	⊜	
Auto. trans.				*	*	⊖	⊖	
Man. trans.				*	*	*	*	
Clutch				*	*	*	*	
Electrical				○	◒	●	⊖	
A/C				⊖	⊖	⊜	⊜	
Suspension				⊖	○	⊖	⊜	
Brakes				●	●	⊖	⊜	
Exhaust				○	⊖	⊜	⊜	
Body rust				○	◒	⊜	⊜	
Paint/trim				○	○	⊖	○	
Integrity				⊖	◒	○	◒	
Hardware				◒	◒	○	⊖	

Jeep Cherokee,/ Wagoneer 6

TROUBLE SPOTS	87	88	89	90	91	92	93	94
Engine	○	○	○	○	⊖	⊖	⊜	⊖
Cooling	●	●	◒	○	⊖	⊜	⊜	⊜
Fuel	◒	◒	◒	◒	⊖	⊖	⊜	⊜
Ignition	○	○	○	○	⊖	⊜	⊜	⊜
Auto. trans.	○	○	⊖	⊖	⊖	⊖	⊖	⊜
Man. trans.	⊖	○	⊖	*	*	*	*	*
Clutch	●	●	○	*	*	*	*	*
Electrical	●	●	●	●	●	○	○	○
A/C	◒	○	○	○	⊖	⊖	⊜	⊖
Suspension	○	◒	○	○	⊖	⊖	⊖	⊜
Brakes	●	●	●	●	●	○	⊖	⊖
Exhaust	●	●	●	●	◒	○	⊜	⊜
Body rust	○	⊖	⊖	⊖	⊜	⊜	⊜	⊜
Paint/trim	◒	●	◒	○	○	○	⊖	⊜
Integrity	◒	◒	●	◒	◒	●	●	◒
Hardware	●	◒	●	◒	◒	◒	◒	○

Jeep Grand Cherokee 6

TROUBLE SPOTS	87	88	89	90	91	92	93	94
Engine							⊖	⊜
Cooling							⊜	⊜
Fuel							⊜	⊜
Ignition							○	⊜
Auto. trans.							○	⊖
Man. trans.							*	*
Clutch							*	*
Electrical							◒	⊖
A/C							⊖	⊜
Suspension							●	⊖
Brakes							○	⊖
Exhaust							⊜	⊜
Body rust							⊜	⊜
Paint/trim							○	⊖
Integrity							◒	○
Hardware							◒	⊖

Jeep Grand Cherokee V8

TROUBLE SPOTS	87	88	89	90	91	92	93	94
Engine							⊖	⊜
Cooling							⊜	⊜
Fuel							⊖	⊜
Ignition							⊜	⊜
Auto. trans.							○	⊖
Man. trans.								
Clutch								
Electrical							◒	⊖
A/C							⊖	⊜
Suspension							◒	⊜
Brakes							⊖	⊜
Exhaust							⊜	⊜
Body rust							⊜	⊜
Paint/trim							○	⊜
Integrity							◒	○
Hardware							◒	⊖

Jeep Wrangler

TROUBLE SPOTS	87 (Insufficient data)	88 (Insufficient data)	89	90	91	92	93	94
Engine			○	◒	⊜	⊜	⊖	⊜
Cooling			○	○	⊜	⊖	⊜	⊖
Fuel			●	●	○	⊜	⊖	⊜
Ignition			○	◒	⊖	⊜	⊜	⊜
Auto. trans.			*	*	*	*	*	*
Man. trans.			*	*	*	*	⊖	*
Clutch			*	*	*	*	○	*
Electrical			●	●	●	◒	◒	⊖
A/C			*	*	*	*	*	*
Suspension			○	⊖	⊖	⊜	⊜	⊜
Brakes			◒	◒	⊖	○	⊖	⊜
Exhaust			●	●	○	⊜	⊖	⊜
Body rust			◒	◒	○	◒	⊖	⊖
Paint/trim			○	◒	◒	○	◒	⊖
Integrity			●	●	●	○	●	◒
Hardware			●	●	●	○	●	○

Lexus ES 250

TROUBLE SPOTS	87	88	89	90	91	92	93	94
Engine				⊖	⊜			
Cooling				⊖	⊜			
Fuel				⊜	⊜			
Ignition				⊜	⊜			
Auto. trans.				⊖	⊜			
Man. trans.				*	*			
Clutch				*	*			
Electrical				◒	○			
A/C				⊖	⊖			
Suspension				⊖	⊖			
Brakes				○	⊖			
Exhaust				⊜	⊜			
Body rust				⊜	⊜			
Paint/trim				⊖	⊖			
Integrity				○	○			
Hardware				○	○			

Lexus ES 300

TROUBLE SPOTS	87	88	89	90	91	92	93	94
Engine						⊜	⊜	⊜
Cooling						⊜	⊜	⊜
Fuel						⊜	⊜	⊜
Ignition						⊜	⊜	⊜
Auto. trans.						⊜	⊜	⊜
Man. trans.						*	*	
Clutch						*	*	
Electrical						⊖	⊜	⊜
A/C						○	⊜	⊜
Suspension						⊖	⊖	⊜
Brakes						⊖	⊜	⊜
Exhaust						⊜	⊜	⊜
Body rust						⊜	⊜	⊜
Paint/trim						⊖	⊖	⊜
Integrity						⊖	⊖	⊖
Hardware						⊖	⊖	⊜

Lexus GS 300

TROUBLE SPOTS	87	88	89	90	91	92	93	94 (Insufficient data)
Engine							⊜	
Cooling							⊖	
Fuel							⊜	
Ignition							⊜	
Auto. trans.							⊜	
Man. trans.								
Clutch								
Electrical							⊜	
A/C							⊜	
Suspension							⊖	
Brakes							⊜	
Exhaust							⊜	
Body rust							⊜	
Paint/trim							⊜	
Integrity							⊜	
Hardware							⊜	

Lexus LS 400

TROUBLE SPOTS	87	88	89	90	91	92	93	94 (Insufficient data)
Engine				⊜	⊜	⊜	⊜	
Cooling				⊜	⊜	⊜	⊜	
Fuel				⊜	⊜	⊜	⊜	
Ignition				⊜	⊜	⊜	⊜	
Auto. trans.				⊜	⊜	⊜	⊜	
Man. trans.								
Clutch								
Electrical				○	⊖	⊖	⊖	
A/C				⊖	⊖	⊜	⊜	
Suspension				⊖	⊖	⊜	⊜	
Brakes				○	⊖	⊖	○	
Exhaust				⊜	⊜	⊜	⊜	
Body rust				⊜	⊜	⊜	⊜	
Paint/trim				⊜	⊜	⊜	⊜	
Integrity				⊜	⊖	⊖	⊖	
Hardware				⊖	⊖	⊖	⊜	

Lexus SC 300/400

TROUBLE SPOTS	87	88	89	90	91	92	93	94 (Insufficient data)
Engine						⊜	⊜	
Cooling						⊜	⊜	
Fuel						⊜	⊜	
Ignition						⊜	⊜	
Auto. trans.						⊖	⊜	
Man. trans.						*	*	
Clutch						*	*	
Electrical						○	⊜	
A/C						⊜	⊜	
Suspension						⊖	⊖	
Brakes						⊜	⊜	
Exhaust						⊜	⊜	
Body rust						⊜	⊜	
Paint/trim						⊜	⊖	
Integrity						⊖	⊖	
Hardware						○	⊖	

⊜ ⊖ ○ ◒ ●
Few ← Problems → Many

*
Insufficient data

Lincoln Continental

Trouble spots	87	88	89	90	91	92	93	94
Engine		●	●	○	⊖	⊜	⊜	⊜
Cooling		◒	◒	⊖	⊜	⊜	⊜	⊜
Fuel		◒	◒	○	⊖	⊖	⊜	⊜
Ignition		○	○	⊖	⊖	⊖	⊜	⊜
Auto. trans.		●	◒	○	◒	⊖	⊜	⊜
Man. trans.								
Clutch								
Electrical		●	●	●	●	◒	○	⊜
A/C		●	●	●	◒	○	⊖	⊜
Suspension		●	●	●	◒	○	⊖	⊜
Brakes		●	●	●	●	●	○	⊜
Exhaust		○	⊜	⊖	⊜	⊜	⊜	⊜
Body rust		⊖	⊜	⊜	⊜	⊜	⊜	⊜
Paint/trim		◒	○	⊖	○	⊖	⊖	⊖
Integrity		◒	○	○	○	◒	○	○
Hardware		●	●	●	◒	◒	○	⊜

Lincoln Mark VII

Trouble spots	87	88	89	90	91	92	93	94
Engine	⊖	⊜	⊖	⊜	Insufficient data	Insufficient data		
Cooling	◒	○	⊜	○				
Fuel	●	○	○	⊖				
Ignition	○	⊖	⊖	⊖				
Auto. trans.	○	○	○	○				
Man. trans.								
Clutch								
Electrical	●	●	●	●				
A/C	●	●	●	●				
Suspension	●	◒	◒	○				
Brakes	●	●	●	●				
Exhaust	◒	●	○	⊖				
Body rust	○	○	⊜	⊖				
Paint/trim	⊖	○	○	○				
Integrity	◒	○	○	⊖				
Hardware	●	◒	◒	◒				

Lincoln Mark VIII

Trouble spots	87	88	89	90	91	92	93	94
Engine							⊜	⊜
Cooling							⊜	⊜
Fuel							⊖	⊖
Ignition							⊜	⊜
Auto. trans.							⊖	⊜
Man. trans.								
Clutch								
Electrical							◒	○
A/C							⊖	⊜
Suspension							○	⊖
Brakes							⊖	⊜
Exhaust							⊜	⊜
Body rust							⊜	⊜
Paint/trim							⊖	⊜
Integrity							○	⊖
Hardware							○	⊖

Lincoln Town Car

Trouble spots	87	88	89	90	91	92	93	94
Engine	⊖	○	⊖	⊖	⊖	⊜	⊜	⊜
Cooling	◒	○	◒	⊖	⊜	⊜	⊜	⊜
Fuel	○	○	○	⊖	⊖	⊖	⊜	⊜
Ignition	○	○	⊖	⊖	○	⊜	⊜	⊜
Auto. trans.	⊖	○	○	⊖	⊖	○	⊖	⊜
Man. trans.								
Clutch								
Electrical	●	●	●	●	●	◒	⊖	⊜
A/C	●	●	◒	○	◒	○	⊖	⊜
Suspension	○	◒	◒	○	⊖	⊖	⊜	⊖
Brakes	◒	◒	●	●	●	●	○	⊜
Exhaust	●	◒	◒	●	●	⊜	⊜	⊜
Body rust	⊖	⊖	⊜	⊜	⊜	⊜	⊜	⊜
Paint/trim	○	○	○	○	○	⊖	⊜	⊜
Integrity	○	○	○	○	○	○	○	⊖
Hardware	●	◒	◒	●	●	◒	○	⊖

Mazda 323

Trouble spots	87	88	89	90	91	92	93	94
Engine	◒	○	○	○	⊖	⊜	Insufficient data	Insufficient data
Cooling	○	○	⊖	⊖	⊜	⊜		
Fuel	⊖	⊖	⊜	⊜	⊜	⊜		
Ignition	⊖	⊖	⊖	⊜	⊜	⊜		
Auto. trans.	○	◒	◒	⊖	○	*		
Man. trans.	⊖	⊜	⊜	⊜	⊜	*		
Clutch	◒	⊖	⊖	⊜	⊖	*		
Electrical	○	◒	◒	○	○	○		
A/C	◒	○	○	○	⊖	⊜		
Suspension	○	⊖	⊖	⊖	⊖	⊜		
Brakes	●	●	●	○	○	⊜		
Exhaust	●	●	●	○	⊖	⊜		
Body rust	⊖	⊜	⊖	⊜	⊜	⊜		
Paint/trim	⊖	⊖	○	⊜	⊖	○		
Integrity	○	○	○	○	◒	○		
Hardware	○	⊖	○	○	◒	○		

Mazda 626 4

Trouble spots	87	88	89	90	91	92	93	94
Engine	○	○	⊖	⊖	⊜	⊜	⊜	⊜
Cooling	○	○	⊖	⊖	⊖	⊖	⊜	⊜
Fuel	⊜	⊜	⊜	⊜	⊖	⊜	⊜	⊜
Ignition	⊖	⊜	⊜	⊜	⊜	⊜	⊜	⊜
Auto. trans.	◒	●	●	⊖	⊖	○	⊖	○
Man. trans.	⊜	⊜	⊜	⊜	⊜	⊜	⊜	⊜
Clutch	⊖	⊖	⊜	⊜	⊜	⊜	⊜	⊜
Electrical	●	◒	○	○	○	⊖	○	⊜
A/C	◒	○	○	⊖	⊜	⊖	⊜	⊜
Suspension	○	⊖	⊖	⊖	⊖	○	⊖	⊜
Brakes	●	●	◒	◒	◒	○	⊖	⊜
Exhaust	●	●	●	○	⊖	⊜	⊜	⊜
Body rust	⊖	⊜	⊜	⊜	⊜	⊜	⊜	⊜
Paint/trim	○	⊖	⊖	⊖	○	⊖	⊖	⊜
Integrity	○	◒	○	◒	◒	◒	◒	○
Hardware	◒	●	◒	◒	◒	◒	○	○

Mazda 626 V6

Trouble spots	87	88	89	90	91	92	93	94
Engine							⊖	⊜
Cooling							⊜	⊜
Fuel							⊖	⊜
Ignition							⊜	⊜
Auto. trans.							⊖	⊖
Man. trans.							⊜	*
Clutch							⊜	*
Electrical							○	⊖
A/C							⊜	⊜
Suspension							⊖	⊜
Brakes							○	⊜
Exhaust							⊜	⊜
Body rust							⊜	⊜
Paint/trim							⊖	○
Integrity							◒	◒
Hardware							◒	○

Mazda 929

Trouble spots	87	88	89	90	91	92	93	94
Engine		◒	○	⊖	○	◒	⊜	Insufficient data
Cooling		⊖	⊜	⊖	⊜	⊜	⊜	
Fuel		○	⊜	⊖	⊖	⊖	⊜	
Ignition		⊖	⊜	⊜	⊜	⊖	⊜	
Auto. trans.		○	○	○	◒	⊖	⊜	
Man. trans.		*						
Clutch		*						
Electrical		●	◒	○	◒	◒	⊖	
A/C		⊖	⊖	⊜	○	⊜	⊖	
Suspension		○	○	⊖	⊖	⊖	⊜	
Brakes		●	●	●	●	◒	●	
Exhaust		●	◒	◒	○	⊜	⊜	
Body rust		⊜	⊜	⊜	⊜	⊜	⊜	
Paint/trim		⊖	⊖	⊖	⊖	◒	⊖	
Integrity		⊖	⊖	○	○	○	○	
Hardware		●	◒	○	◒	●	○	

Mazda MPV V6 (2WD)

TROUBLE SPOTS	87	88	89	90	91	92	93	94
Engine			◒	○	○	○	⊜	Insufficient data
Cooling			⊖	⊜	⊜	⊜	⊜	
Fuel			⊜	⊜	⊖	⊖	⊜	
Ignition			⊖	⊜	⊖	⊖	⊜	
Auto. trans.			○	⊖	○	⊖	⊜	
Man. trans.			*					
Clutch			*					
Electrical			◒	○	◒	○	○	
A/C			◒	◒	○	⊖	⊖	
Suspension			○	⊖	⊖	⊖	⊖	
Brakes			●	●	●	○	⊖	
Exhaust			◒	○	⊖	⊜	⊜	
Body rust			⊜	⊜	⊜	⊜	⊜	
Paint/trim			⊖	○	○	○	⊖	
Integrity			⊖	⊖	⊖	○	○	
Hardware			◒	○	○	○	⊖	

Mazda MPV V6 (4WD)

TROUBLE SPOTS	87	88	89	90	91	92	93	94
Engine			Insufficient data	◒	⊖	◒	Insufficient data	Insufficient data
Cooling				⊖	⊜	⊜		
Fuel				⊜	⊖	○		
Ignition				⊜	⊜	⊖		
Auto. trans.				●	◒	⊜		
Man. trans.				*				
Clutch				*				
Electrical				◒	◒	⊖		
A/C				◒	⊖	*		
Suspension				◒	○	◒		
Brakes				●	●	⊖		
Exhaust				○	⊖	⊜		
Body rust				⊜	⊜	⊜		
Paint/trim				⊖	⊖	○		
Integrity				⊖	○	⊖		
Hardware				◒	◒	⊖		

Mazda MX-3

TROUBLE SPOTS	87	88	89	90	91	92	93	94
Engine						⊜	Insufficient data	Insufficient data
Cooling						⊖		
Fuel						⊜		
Ignition						⊜		
Auto. trans.						*		
Man. trans.						⊖		
Clutch						⊖		
Electrical						○		
A/C						⊜		
Suspension						⊜		
Brakes						⊜		
Exhaust						⊜		
Body rust						⊖		
Paint/trim						◒		
Integrity						◒		
Hardware						○		

Mazda MX-5 Miata

TROUBLE SPOTS	87	88	89	90	91	92	93	94
Engine				⊖	⊖	⊜	⊜	Insufficient data
Cooling				⊜	⊜	⊜	⊜	
Fuel				⊜	⊜	⊜	⊜	
Ignition				⊖	⊖	⊜	⊜	
Auto. trans.					*	*	*	
Man. trans.				⊖	⊜	⊜	⊜	
Clutch				○	⊜	⊜	⊜	
Electrical				◒	○	○	⊖	
A/C				⊖	⊖	⊜	⊜	
Suspension				⊜	⊜	⊜	⊜	
Brakes				⊖	⊖	⊜	⊜	
Exhaust				⊖	⊜	⊜	⊜	
Body rust				⊜	⊜	⊜	⊜	
Paint/trim				○	⊖	⊜	⊖	
Integrity				○	○	○	○	
Hardware				◒	○	⊜	⊖	

Mazda MX-6 4

TROUBLE SPOTS	87	88	89	90	91	92	93	94
Engine		○	⊖	⊖	⊖	Insufficient data	⊖	Insufficient data
Cooling		○	⊖	⊖	⊖		⊜	
Fuel		⊖	⊖	⊜	⊖		⊜	
Ignition		⊜	⊜	⊖	⊜		⊜	
Auto. trans.		*	◒	⊖	⊖		*	
Man. trans.		⊖	⊜	⊖	⊜		⊖	
Clutch		⊖	⊜	⊖	⊜		⊖	
Electrical		◒	◒	○	○		○	
A/C		○	○	○	⊜		⊜	
Suspension		○	⊖	○	○		⊖	
Brakes		◒	◒	◒	◒		⊖	
Exhaust		●	●	◒	⊜		⊜	
Body rust		⊖	⊜	⊜	⊜		⊜	
Paint/trim		○	○	○	◒		○	
Integrity		○	○	●	●		●	
Hardware		◒	●	●	●		●	

Mazda MX-6 V6

TROUBLE SPOTS	87	88	89	90	91	92	93	94
Engine							⊖	Insufficient data
Cooling							⊜	
Fuel							⊖	
Ignition							⊜	
Auto. trans.							⊖	
Man. trans.							⊜	
Clutch							⊜	
Electrical							◒	
A/C							⊖	
Suspension							⊜	
Brakes							○	
Exhaust							⊖	
Body rust							⊜	
Paint/trim							○	
Integrity							●	
Hardware							●	

Mazda Navajo (2WD)

TROUBLE SPOTS	87	88	89	90	91	92	93	94
Engine						○	⊖	⊜
Cooling						⊖	⊜	⊜
Fuel						⊜	⊜	⊜
Ignition						⊜	⊜	⊜
Auto. trans.						⊖	⊜	⊜
Man. trans.						○	⊜	*
Clutch						⊖	⊖	*
Electrical						●	⊖	⊖
A/C						◒	⊖	⊜
Suspension						◒	○	⊜
Brakes						○	○	⊖
Exhaust						⊜	⊜	⊜
Body rust						⊜	⊜	⊜
Paint/trim						○	⊖	⊜
Integrity						○	○	⊖
Hardware						○	○	⊜

Mazda Navajo (4WD)

TROUBLE SPOTS	87	88	89	90	91	92	93	94
Engine					◒	○	⊖	⊜
Cooling					○	⊖	⊜	⊜
Fuel					⊖	⊜	⊜	⊜
Ignition					⊜	⊜	⊜	⊜
Auto. trans.					⊖	⊖	⊜	⊜
Man. trans.					○	◒	⊜	⊜
Clutch					⊖	⊖	⊜	⊜
Electrical					◒	◒	⊖	⊖
A/C					◒	○	⊜	⊜
Suspension					○	○	○	⊖
Brakes					◒	◒	○	⊖
Exhaust					◒	⊖	⊜	⊜
Body rust					⊜	⊜	⊜	⊜
Paint/trim					○	⊖	⊖	⊜
Integrity					○	○	⊖	⊖
Hardware					○	○	⊖	⊖

⊜ ⊖ ○ ◒ ●
Few ◄— **Problems** —► Many

* Insufficient data

Mazda Pickup (2WD)

TROUBLE SPOTS	87	88	89	90	91	92	93	94
Engine	◒	○	○	⊖	⊖	⊜	⊖	⊜
Cooling	○	⊖	⊖	⊖	⊜	⊜	⊜	⊜
Fuel	○	○	○	⊖	⊜	⊖	○	⊖
Ignition	⊜	⊖	⊖	⊜	⊖	⊜	⊖	⊜
Auto. trans.	*	*	⊜	⊖	⊜	*	*	⊖
Man. trans.	⊜	⊜	⊜	⊜	⊜	⊜	⊜	⊜
Clutch	○	⊖	⊜	⊜	⊜	⊖	⊜	⊜
Electrical	○	○	⊖	⊖	⊖	⊜	⊖	○
A/C	●	◒	○	⊖	⊖	⊖	⊖	⊜
Suspension	⊜	⊖	⊖	⊖	⊖	⊖	⊖	⊜
Brakes	◒	●	◒	◒	○	⊖	⊖	⊖
Exhaust	◒	●	◒	○	⊖	⊜	⊜	⊜
Body rust	○	○	⊖	⊖	⊜	⊜	⊜	⊜
Paint/trim	○	○	⊜	⊜	⊖	⊖	⊖	⊖
Integrity	⊖	⊖	⊖	⊖	⊖	⊖	⊖	⊖
Hardware	○	⊖	⊜	⊖	⊖	⊖	⊖	⊖

Mazda Protege

TROUBLE SPOTS	87	88	89	90	91	92	93	94
Engine				⊖	⊖	⊜	⊜	⊜
Cooling				⊖	⊖	⊖	⊜	⊜
Fuel				⊖	⊜	⊜	⊜	⊜
Ignition				⊖	⊖	⊜	⊜	⊜
Auto. trans.				⊖	⊖	⊜	⊜	*
Man. trans.				⊜	⊜	⊜	⊜	*
Clutch				⊖	⊖	⊜	⊜	*
Electrical				○	○	○	⊖	⊖
A/C				⊖	⊖	⊜	⊜	⊖
Suspension				○	⊖	⊖	⊜	⊜
Brakes				◒	○	⊖	⊖	⊖
Exhaust				○	⊖	⊜	⊜	⊜
Body rust				⊜	⊜	⊜	⊜	⊜
Paint/trim				○	○	○	⊖	⊜
Integrity				○	⊖	○	⊖	⊖
Hardware				◒	◒	◒	○	⊜

Mazda RX-7

TROUBLE SPOTS	87	88	89	90	91	92	93	94
Engine	⊖	⊖						
Cooling	⊖	⊖						
Fuel	◒	○						
Ignition	⊖	○						
Auto. trans.	*	*						
Man. trans.	⊖	⊖						
Clutch	●	●						
Electrical	●	●	Insufficient data	Insufficient data	Insufficient data		Insufficient data	Insufficient data
A/C	◒	○						
Suspension	⊖	⊖						
Brakes	◒	◒						
Exhaust	◒	◒						
Body rust	⊖	⊜						
Paint/trim	○	○						
Integrity	○	○						
Hardware	●	◒						

Mercedes-Benz 190

TROUBLE SPOTS	87	88	89	90	91	92	93	94
Engine	◒				○		⊖	
Cooling	●				○		⊜	
Fuel	⊖				⊖		⊜	
Ignition	⊖				⊖		⊖	
Auto. trans.	○				*		⊜	
Man. trans.	*				*		*	
Clutch	*				*		*	
Electrical	●	Insufficient data	Insufficient data	Insufficient data	◒	Insufficient data	◒	
A/C	●				*		○	
Suspension	⊖				⊜		⊖	
Brakes	●				◒		○	
Exhaust	◒				⊜		⊜	
Body rust	⊖				⊜		⊜	
Paint/trim	⊖				⊜		⊜	
Integrity	⊖				⊜		⊜	
Hardware	●				○		○	

Mercedes-Benz E-Class

TROUBLE SPOTS	87	88	89	90	91	92	93	94
Engine	○	●	○	○	○	⊖	⊜	
Cooling	●	◒	◒	○	○	⊖	⊖	
Fuel	⊖	○	○	⊖	⊜	⊖	○	
Ignition	⊜	⊜	⊜	⊖	⊜	⊜	⊖	
Auto. trans.	○	⊖	⊜	⊖	⊜	⊖	⊖	
Man. trans.	*	*						
Clutch	*	*						
Electrical	●	●	◒	◒	◒	○	◒	Insufficient data
A/C	●	●	○	○	⊜	⊖	⊖	
Suspension	○	⊖	⊖	○	⊖	○	⊖	
Brakes	○	◒	○	◒	○	○	⊖	
Exhaust	○	⊜	⊜	⊜	⊜	⊜	⊜	
Body rust	⊜	⊜	⊜	⊜	⊜	⊜	⊜	
Paint/trim	⊖	⊜	⊜	⊜	⊜	⊜	⊜	
Integrity	⊖	⊜	⊜	⊜	⊜	⊖	⊖	
Hardware	◒	●	○	○	○	○	○	

Mercedes-Benz C-Class

TROUBLE SPOTS	87	88	89	90	91	92	93	94
Engine								⊜
Cooling								⊜
Fuel								⊖
Ignition								⊜
Auto. trans.								⊜
Man. trans.								
Clutch								
Electrical								○
A/C								⊜
Suspension								⊖
Brakes								⊜
Exhaust								⊜
Body rust								⊜
Paint/trim								⊜
Integrity								⊖
Hardware								○

Mercury Cougar V6

TROUBLE SPOTS	87	88	89	90	91	92	93	94
Engine	○	◒	○	⊖	⊜	⊖	⊜	⊜
Cooling	●	◒	○	⊖	⊖	⊖	⊖	⊜
Fuel	◒	○	○	⊖	⊖	⊖	⊜	⊜
Ignition	◒	○	⊖	⊖	⊖	⊜	⊖	⊜
Auto. trans.	○	○	○	⊖	⊜	⊖	⊖	⊜
Man. trans.			*	*				
Clutch			*	*				
Electrical	●	●	●	●	◒	◒	○	⊖
A/C	●	●	●	●	●	○	○	○
Suspension	◒	◒	○	○	○	○	⊖	⊜
Brakes	●	●	●	●	●	◒	○	⊖
Exhaust	●	●	⊜	⊖	⊜	⊜	⊜	⊜
Body rust	○	○	⊖	⊜	⊖	⊜	⊜	⊜
Paint/trim	◒	◒	◒	◒	◒	◒	○	○
Integrity	○	◒	◒	○	○	○	◒	⊖
Hardware	◒	◒	●	◒	◒	◒	◒	⊖

Mercury Cougar V8

TROUBLE SPOTS	87	88	89	90	91	92	93	94
Engine	○	⊖			⊜	⊜	⊜	⊖
Cooling	◒	○			○	⊖	○	⊜
Fuel	◒	◒			⊖	⊖	⊜	⊖
Ignition	○	⊖			⊜	⊜	⊜	⊜
Auto. trans.	◒	○			○	⊖	⊖	⊜
Man. trans.								
Clutch								
Electrical	●	●			●	◒	○	⊖
A/C	●	●			●	○	○	⊜
Suspension	●	◒			⊖	⊖	⊖	⊜
Brakes	●	●			●	●	○	⊖
Exhaust	◒	●			⊜	⊜	⊜	⊜
Body rust	○	○			⊜	⊜	⊜	⊜
Paint/trim	◒	◒			○	○	○	⊖
Integrity	◒	○			○	○	◒	⊖
Hardware	◒	○			○	◒	◒	⊖

Mercury Grand Marquis

TROUBLE SPOTS	87	88	89	90	91	92	93	94
Engine	○	○	⊖	⊖	⊜	⊖	⊜	⊜
Cooling	○	◒	○	○	⊖	⊜	⊜	⊜
Fuel	◒	○	○	○	⊖	⊖	⊜	⊜
Ignition	○	⊖	⊖	⊖	⊖	⊖	⊜	⊜
Auto. trans.	○	○	○	⊖	⊖	⊖	⊖	⊜
Man. trans.								
Clutch								
Electrical	●	◒	◒	●	◒	◒	⊖	⊖
A/C	●	●	●	◒	○	○	⊖	⊜
Suspension	○	○	○	○	○	⊖	⊖	⊖
Brakes	◒	●	◒	●	●	●	○	⊖
Exhaust	●	●	◒	○	⊖	●	⊜	⊜
Body rust	○	○	⊖	⊜	⊖	⊜	⊜	⊜
Paint/trim	◒	○	⊖	⊖	⊖	⊖	⊖	⊖
Integrity	○	⊖	○	⊖	⊖	○	○	○
Hardware	◒	◒	○	◒	◒	○	⊖	⊖

Mercury Sable

TROUBLE SPOTS	87	88	89	90	91	92	93	94
Engine	◒	◒	○	⊖	⊖	⊜	⊜	⊜
Cooling	●	●	◒	○	⊖	⊖	⊜	⊜
Fuel	◒	◒	○	○	⊖	⊖	⊖	⊜
Ignition	○	○	⊖	⊖	⊖	⊜	⊜	⊜
Auto. trans.	◒	◒	◒	○	◒	⊖	⊖	⊜
Man. trans.								
Clutch								
Electrical	●	●	●	●	◒	◒	○	⊖
A/C	●	●	●	◒	○	⊖	⊖	⊜
Suspension	●	●	●	◒	◒	○	⊖	⊜
Brakes	●	●	●	●	●	◒	○	⊖
Exhaust	⊖	⊜	⊜	⊜	⊜	⊜	⊜	⊜
Body rust	●	◒	○	⊖	⊖	⊜	⊜	⊜
Paint/trim	●	◒	○	⊖	⊖	⊜	⊖	⊜
Integrity	◒	◒	○	○	○	◒	◒	○
Hardware	●	◒	◒	◒	◒	◒	○	⊖

Mercury Topaz

TROUBLE SPOTS	87	88	89	90	91	92	93	94
Engine	◒	◒	◒	◒	○	⊖	⊖	⊜
Cooling	●	●	◒	○	⊖	⊖	⊜	⊖
Fuel	●	●	●	●	●	○	○	⊜
Ignition	◒	◒	○	○	○	⊖	⊜	⊜
Auto. trans.	●	◒	○	⊖	⊖	○	⊖	⊜
Man. trans.	⊜	⊜	⊖	*	*	*	*	*
Clutch	●	◒	◒	*	*	*	*	*
Electrical	●	●	●	●	●	○	○	○
A/C	●	●	●	●	○	⊖	⊖	⊜
Suspension	●	●	●	●	○	⊖	⊖	⊜
Brakes	●	●	●	●	●	○	○	⊖
Exhaust	●	●	●	●	●	⊖	⊜	⊜
Body rust	●	○	○	⊖	⊖	⊖	⊜	⊜
Paint/trim	●	◒	◒	◒	○	○	⊜	⊜
Integrity	●	●	◒	◒	○	◒	◒	⊖
Hardware	◒	◒	◒	◒	○	○	○	⊜

Mercury Tracer

TROUBLE SPOTS	87	88	89	90	91	92	93	94
Engine		◒	◒		⊖	○	⊖	Insufficient data
Cooling		◒	◒		⊖	⊜	⊜	
Fuel		⊖	⊖		○	⊖	⊜	
Ignition		⊖	⊖		⊖	⊜	⊜	
Auto. trans.		○	⊖		⊖	⊖	⊜	
Man. trans.		⊜	⊜		⊖	*	*	
Clutch		○	⊖		⊖	*	*	
Electrical		◒	○		●	◒	⊖	
A/C		●	◒		●	⊖	⊖	
Suspension		○	○		○	⊖	⊜	
Brakes		●	●		○	○	⊖	
Exhaust		●	●		⊜	⊜	⊜	
Body rust		⊖	⊜		⊜	⊜	⊜	
Paint/trim		○	⊖		○	⊜	⊜	
Integrity		○	⊖		○	○	○	
Hardware		◒	○		◒	◒	○	

Mercury Villager Van

TROUBLE SPOTS	87	88	89	90	91	92	93	94
Engine							⊜	⊜
Cooling							⊜	○
Fuel							⊜	⊜
Ignition							⊜	⊜
Auto. trans.							⊜	⊜
Man. trans.								
Clutch								
Electrical							○	⊖
A/C							⊖	⊜
Suspension							⊖	⊜
Brakes							⊖	⊜
Exhaust							⊜	⊜
Body rust							⊜	⊜
Paint/trim							⊖	⊜
Integrity							◒	○
Hardware							◒	⊖

Mitsubishi 3000GT (2WD)

TROUBLE SPOTS	87	88	89	90	91	92	93	94
Engine					⊖	⊖	⊜	Insufficient data
Cooling					⊜	⊜	⊜	
Fuel					⊖	⊜	⊜	
Ignition					⊜	⊜	⊜	
Auto. trans.					*	*	*	
Man. trans.					*	○	⊖	
Clutch					*	⊖	⊖	
Electrical					◒	◒	○	
A/C					⊜	⊖	⊜	
Suspension					○	⊖	⊜	
Brakes					○	⊖	⊖	
Exhaust					⊜	⊜	⊜	
Body rust					⊜	⊜	⊜	
Paint/trim					◒	○	⊖	
Integrity					○	◒	◒	
Hardware					◒	◒	○	

Mitsubishi Diamante

TROUBLE SPOTS	87	88	89	90	91	92	93	94
Engine						⊜	⊖	Insufficient data
Cooling						⊜	⊖	
Fuel						⊜	⊜	
Ignition						⊜	⊜	
Auto. trans.						⊖	⊖	
Man. trans.								
Clutch								
Electrical						○	○	
A/C						⊖	⊖	
Suspension						⊖	⊖	
Brakes						○	⊖	
Exhaust						⊖	⊜	
Body rust						⊜	⊜	
Paint/trim						⊖	⊖	
Integrity						⊖	○	
Hardware						○	○	

Mitsubishi Eclipse (2WD)

TROUBLE SPOTS	87	88	89	90	91	92	93	94
Engine				●	◒	◒	⊜	Insufficient data
Cooling				⊖	⊖	⊜	⊖	
Fuel				⊖	⊖	⊜	⊜	
Ignition				⊖	⊜	⊜	⊜	
Auto. trans.				○	⊖	⊖	*	
Man. trans.				○	○	⊖	⊖	
Clutch				⊖	⊖	⊖	⊜	
Electrical				◒	◒	◒	⊖	
A/C				⊜	⊖	⊜	⊜	
Suspension				⊖	⊖	⊖	⊖	
Brakes				◒	○	○	⊖	
Exhaust				⊖	○	◒	⊜	
Body rust				⊜	⊜	⊜	⊜	
Paint/trim				○	○	○	⊖	
Integrity				○	○	◒	○	
Hardware				◒	◒	●	○	

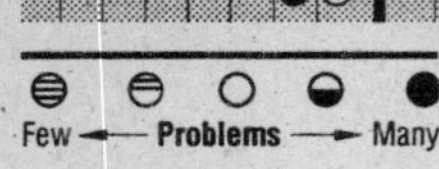

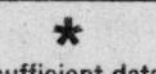

Mitsubishi Eclipse Turbo (4WD)	87	88	89	90	91	92	93	94
Engine				●	●	⊖		
Cooling				⊜	○	⊜		
Fuel				⊖	○	⊜		
Ignition				⊖	⊖	⊜		
Auto. trans.					*	*		
Man. trans.				●	◒	○		
Clutch				◒	○	○	Insufficient data	Insufficient data
Electrical				◒	●	◒		
A/C				○	⊖	⊖		
Suspension				⊖	⊖	⊖		
Brakes				◒	◒	○		
Exhaust				⊖	⊜	⊜		
Body rust				⊜	⊜	⊜		
Paint/trim				○	○	○		
Integrity				○	◒	○		
Hardware				◒	○	●		

Mitsubishi Expo	87	88	89	90	91	92	93	94
Engine						⊖		
Cooling						⊜		
Fuel						⊜		
Ignition						⊜		
Auto. trans.						*		
Man. trans.						*		
Clutch						*	Insufficient data	Insufficient data
Electrical						○		
A/C						⊜		
Suspension						⊖		
Brakes						⊖		
Exhaust						⊖		
Body rust						⊜		
Paint/trim						○		
Integrity						○		
Hardware						○		

Mitsubishi Expo LRV	87	88	89	90	91	92	93	94
Engine						⊜	⊜	
Cooling						⊖	⊖	
Fuel						⊖	⊜	
Ignition						⊜	⊜	
Auto. trans.						⊜	⊖	
Man. trans.						*	*	
Clutch						*	*	Insufficient data
Electrical						○	○	
A/C						⊖	⊜	
Suspension						⊖	⊖	
Brakes						⊜	⊜	
Exhaust						○	⊖	
Body rust						⊜	⊜	
Paint/trim						⊖	⊖	
Integrity						◒	◒	
Hardware						◒	○	

Mitsubishi Galant 4	87	88	89	90	91	92	93	94
Engine	○		◒	◒	⊖	⊖		⊜
Cooling	○		⊜	⊖	⊜	⊜		⊜
Fuel	○		⊜	⊜	⊜	⊜		⊜
Ignition	⊖		⊖	⊖	⊜	⊜		⊜
Auto. trans.	●		○	⊖	⊜	⊜		⊖
Man. trans.	*		⊖	○	⊜	*		*
Clutch	*		◒	◒	⊖	*	Insufficient data	*
Electrical	●		○	○	○	○		○
A/C	○		◒	⊜	⊖	⊖		⊜
Suspension	●		⊖	⊖	⊖	⊖		⊖
Brakes	◒		◒	○	○	○		⊖
Exhaust	●		⊜	⊜	⊜	⊜		⊜
Body rust	○		⊜	⊜	⊜	⊜		⊜
Paint/trim	○		○	⊖	⊖	⊖		⊜
Integrity	◒		⊖	⊖	⊖	◒		○
Hardware	◒		⊖	⊖	⊖	○		○

Mitsubishi Mirage	87	88	89	90	91	92	93	94
Engine	●	●	◒	○	⊖	⊜	⊜	
Cooling	○	○	⊖	⊜	⊜	⊜	⊜	
Fuel	○	⊖	⊖	⊖	⊜	⊜	⊜	
Ignition	⊖	○	⊖	⊜	⊜	⊜	⊜	
Auto. trans.	○	○	⊖	⊖	○	⊖	◒	
Man. trans.	⊖	⊖	⊖	⊖	⊖	⊜	*	
Clutch	●	○	⊖	⊖	⊜	⊜	*	Insufficient data
Electrical	◒	◒	◒	○	⊖	⊖	⊖	
A/C	◒	◒	◒	⊖	⊖	⊖	⊖	
Suspension	○	⊖	○	⊖	⊖	⊖	⊜	
Brakes	●	●	◒	◒	○	○	⊖	
Exhaust	●	⊖	⊜	⊜	⊜	⊜	⊜	
Body rust	◒	○	⊜	⊜	⊖	⊜	⊜	
Paint/trim	◒	○	○	◒	○	⊖	⊖	
Integrity	◒	○	◒	●	◒	◒	⊖	
Hardware	◒	○	○	◒	○	○	⊖	

Mitsubishi Montero V6	87	88	89	90	91	92	93	94
Engine			○	⊖	○			
Cooling			⊜	⊖	⊜			
Fuel			⊖	⊖	⊖			
Ignition			⊖	⊖	⊜			
Auto. trans.			*	⊜	*			
Man. trans.			*	*	*			
Clutch			*	*	*	Insufficient data	Insufficient data	Insufficient data
Electrical			◒	○	○			
A/C			⊜	⊜	*			
Suspension			○	⊖	○			
Brakes			◒	○	●			
Exhaust			⊜	⊜	⊜			
Body rust			⊜	⊜	⊜			
Paint/trim			⊖	⊖	○			
Integrity			⊖	○	◒			
Hardware			○	○	○			

Mitsubishi Pickup 4	87	88	89	90	91	92	93	94
Engine	◒	◒						
Cooling	◒	⊖						
Fuel	○	○						
Ignition	⊖	⊖						
Auto. trans.	*	*						
Man. trans.	○	○						
Clutch	◒	○	Insufficient data	Insufficient data	Insufficient data	Insufficient data	Insufficient data	Insufficient data
Electrical	○	○						
A/C	*	*						
Suspension	⊖	⊖						
Brakes	○	⊜						
Exhaust	●	⊖						
Body rust	⊖	⊜						
Paint/trim	○	○						
Integrity	⊖	⊖						
Hardware	⊖	⊖						

Nissan 240SX	87	88	89	90	91	92	93	94
Engine			⊖	⊖	⊜	⊜	⊖	
Cooling			⊜	⊜	⊜	⊜	⊜	
Fuel			⊜	⊖	○	⊜	⊜	
Ignition			⊜	⊖	⊜	⊜	⊜	
Auto. trans.			⊜	⊖	*	*	*	
Man. trans.			⊖	⊜	⊜	*	*	
Clutch			●	◒	⊖	*	*	Insufficient data
Electrical			○	◒	◒	⊖	⊖	
A/C			○	○	⊜	⊖	⊖	
Suspension			⊜	⊜	⊜	⊖	⊖	
Brakes			◒	◒	○	○	⊖	
Exhaust			●	○	⊜	⊜	⊜	
Body rust			⊜	⊜	⊜	⊜	⊜	
Paint/trim			⊖	⊖	⊖	○	⊖	
Integrity			○	○	○	○	○	
Hardware			◒	◒	○	⊖	⊖	

Nissan 300ZX

TROUBLE SPOTS	87	88	89	90	91	92	93	94
Engine	⊖	⊖	Insufficient data	⊖	⊜	Insufficient data	⊜	Insufficient data
Cooling	⊖	⊜		⊜	⊜		⊜	
Fuel	◒	⊖		⊖	⊖		⊜	
Ignition	⊖	⊖		⊖	⊜		⊖	
Auto. trans.	*	*		○	*		*	
Man. trans.	⊖	*		⊖	⊜		*	
Clutch	●	*		●	◒		*	
Electrical	●	●		◒	○		⊖	
A/C	○	⊜		⊖	⊖		⊜	
Suspension	◒	⊖		⊖	⊖		⊖	
Brakes	●	◒		●	●		○	
Exhaust	◒	◒		⊖	⊖		⊜	
Body rust	○	⊜		⊜	⊜		⊜	
Paint/trim	○	⊖		⊖	⊖		⊖	
Integrity	○	○		○	○		○	
Hardware	⊖	◒		⊖	⊜		○	

Nissan Altima

TROUBLE SPOTS	87	88	89	90	91	92	93	94
Engine							⊜	⊜
Cooling							⊜	⊜
Fuel							○	⊖
Ignition							⊜	⊜
Auto. trans.							⊜	⊜
Man. trans.							⊜	⊜
Clutch							⊖	⊖
Electrical							○	⊖
A/C							⊖	⊜
Suspension							⊜	⊜
Brakes							⊖	⊜
Exhaust							⊜	⊜
Body rust							⊜	⊜
Paint/trim							⊖	⊜
Integrity							⊖	⊖
Hardware							○	⊜

Nissan Maxima

TROUBLE SPOTS	87	88	89	90	91	92	93	94
Engine	○	⊖	⊖	⊜	⊜	⊜	⊜	⊜
Cooling	⊖	⊖	⊖	⊜	⊜	⊜	⊜	⊜
Fuel	○	○	⊖	⊖	⊜	⊜	⊜	⊜
Ignition	⊖	⊖	⊜	⊜	⊜	⊜	⊜	⊜
Auto. trans.	○	⊖	⊖	⊖	⊜	⊜	⊜	⊜
Man. trans.	○	*	○	⊖	⊜	⊜	⊜	*
Clutch	●	*	●	◒	⊖	⊜	⊜	*
Electrical	●	●	◒	○	○	○	⊖	⊖
A/C	◒	○	⊖	⊖	⊜	⊜	⊖	⊜
Suspension	◒	○	⊖	⊖	⊜	⊜	⊜	⊜
Brakes	◒	●	●	◒	●	○	⊖	⊜
Exhaust	●	●	○	⊖	⊜	⊜	⊜	⊜
Body rust	⊖	⊖	⊜	⊜	⊜	⊜	⊜	⊜
Paint/trim	○	⊜	⊖	○	⊖	⊖	⊖	⊜
Integrity	○	○	⊖	⊖	⊜	⊖	⊖	⊜
Hardware	○	○	◒	○	○	○	⊖	⊜

Nissan Pathfinder V6

TROUBLE SPOTS	87	88	89	90	91	92	93	94
Engine	⊖	⊖	⊖	⊜	⊜	⊜	⊜	⊜
Cooling	○	⊖	⊜	⊜	⊜	⊜	⊜	⊜
Fuel	⊖	○	⊖	⊜	⊖	⊖	⊜	⊜
Ignition	⊖	⊖	⊜	⊜	⊜	⊜	⊜	⊜
Auto. trans.	⊖	⊖	*	○	⊖	⊜	⊖	⊖
Man. trans.	⊖	⊜	*	*	⊖	⊜	⊜	*
Clutch	○	◒	*	*	⊜	⊜	⊜	*
Electrical	◒	◒	○	○	◒	○	○	⊖
A/C	○	⊖	⊜	⊖	⊜	⊜	⊜	⊜
Suspension	⊖	⊖	○	⊖	○	○	○	⊜
Brakes	◒	○	○	⊖	⊖	⊖	⊜	⊜
Exhaust	●	●	●	◒	⊖	⊜	⊜	⊜
Body rust	○	○	⊖	⊖	⊜	⊜	⊜	⊜
Paint/trim	○	○	○	⊖	⊜	⊖	⊜	⊜
Integrity	⊖	○	○	○	○	○	○	⊖
Hardware	○	●	◒	○	○	○	○	⊖

Nissan Pickup (2WD)

TROUBLE SPOTS	87	88	89	90	91	92	93	94
Engine	⊖	⊖	⊜	⊜	⊜	⊜	⊜	⊖
Cooling	⊖	⊖	⊜	⊜	⊜	⊜	⊜	⊜
Fuel	○	⊖	⊖	⊖	⊖	⊜	⊖	⊜
Ignition	○	⊖	⊜	⊜	⊜	⊜	⊜	⊜
Auto. trans.	⊖	*	⊖	⊖	⊜	⊖	⊖	*
Man. trans.	⊜	⊜	⊜	⊖	⊖	⊜	⊜	*
Clutch	○	○	○	○	⊖	⊖	⊖	*
Electrical	◒	○	○	○	⊜	○	⊖	⊖
A/C	○	○	○	⊖	⊖	⊖	⊖	⊖
Suspension	○	⊖	⊖	⊖	⊖	⊖	⊖	⊖
Brakes	○	○	○	⊜	⊖	⊜	⊜	⊜
Exhaust	◒	◒	○	◒	⊖	⊜	⊜	⊜
Body rust	◒	◒	○	○	⊖	⊜	⊜	⊜
Paint/trim	◒	◒	◒	○	⊖	⊖	⊖	⊜
Integrity	⊖	○	⊖	⊖	⊖	○	○	○
Hardware	○	○	◒	○	○	⊖	○	⊖

Nissan Pickup (4WD)

TROUBLE SPOTS	87	88	89	90	91	92	93	94
Engine	⊜	○	⊖	⊜	⊜	⊜	⊜	Insufficient data
Cooling	⊖	⊖	⊖	⊜	⊜	⊜	⊜	
Fuel	○	⊖	⊖	⊖	⊖	⊖	⊜	
Ignition	○	⊜	⊜	⊖	⊜	⊜	⊜	
Auto. trans.	*	*	*	*	*	*	*	
Man. trans.	○	*	⊜	*	⊖	*	⊖	
Clutch	◒	*	⊖	*	⊖	*	⊜	
Electrical	◒	○	○	⊖	○	○	⊖	
A/C	◒	*	*	*	*	*	⊜	
Suspension	○	⊖	⊖	⊖	◒	○	◒	
Brakes	◒	⊖	◒	⊖	⊖	⊜	⊖	
Exhaust	●	◒	●	●	○	⊖	⊜	
Body rust	●	●	●	⊖	⊖	⊖	⊖	
Paint/trim	●	◒	●	○	⊖	⊜	⊖	
Integrity	○	⊖	⊖	⊖	○	○	⊖	
Hardware	○	○	◒	◒	○	⊖	⊖	

Nissan Pulsar NX, NX 1600/2000

TROUBLE SPOTS	87	88	89	90	91	92	93	94
Engine	◒	◒	Insufficient data	Insufficient data	Insufficient data	Insufficient data	Insufficient data	
Cooling	⊖	○						
Fuel	◒	○						
Ignition	⊖	○						
Auto. trans.	*	*						
Man. trans.	○	*						
Clutch	○	*						
Electrical	●	●						
A/C	○	*						
Suspension	○	◒						
Brakes	●	◒						
Exhaust	●	●						
Body rust	○	⊜						
Paint/trim	◒	○						
Integrity	◒	●						
Hardware	◒	○						

Nissan Quest Van

TROUBLE SPOTS	87	88	89	90	91	92	93	94
Engine							⊜	⊜
Cooling							⊜	○
Fuel							⊜	⊜
Ignition							⊜	⊜
Auto. trans.							⊜	⊜
Man. trans.								
Clutch								
Electrical							○	⊖
A/C							⊖	⊜
Suspension							⊖	⊜
Brakes							⊖	⊜
Exhaust							⊜	⊜
Body rust							⊜	⊜
Paint/trim							⊖	⊜
Integrity							◒	○
Hardware							◒	⊖

⊜ ⊖ ○ ◒ ●
Few ◄— Problems —► Many

*
Insufficient data

Nissan Sentra

TROUBLE SPOTS	87	88	89	90	91	92	93	94
Engine	◒	○	○	○	⊜	⊜	⊜	⊜
Cooling	◒	○	⊖	⊖	⊜	⊜	⊜	⊜
Fuel	◒	⊖	⊖	⊖	◒	◒	⊖	⊖
Ignition	○	⊖	⊖	⊖	⊜	⊜	⊜	⊜
Auto. trans.	◒	◒	○	◒	○	⊖	⊜	⊜
Man. trans.	⊖	⊜	⊖	⊜	⊜	⊜	⊜	⊜
Clutch	◒	○	○	⊖	⊖	⊖	⊜	⊜
Electrical	◒	◒	○	○	○	○	⊖	⊜
A/C	◒	○	⊖	⊖	⊖	⊜	⊖	⊜
Suspension	○	◒	○	⊖	⊖	⊖	⊜	⊜
Brakes	◒	◒	◒	◒	◒	○	⊖	⊜
Exhaust	●	●	◒	○	○	⊜	⊜	⊜
Body rust	◒	○	○	○	⊜	⊜	⊜	⊜
Paint/trim	◒	○	○	○	○	⊖	⊖	⊖
Integrity	◒	○	○	○	○	○	○	⊖
Hardware	◒	○	○	◒	○	○	○	⊖

Nissan Stanza

TROUBLE SPOTS	87	88	89	90	91	92	93	94
Engine	⊖	⊖	⊖	⊜	⊜	⊜		
Cooling	⊖	○	⊜	⊜	⊜	⊜		
Fuel	○	○	⊖	⊖	⊖	⊜		
Ignition	○	⊖	⊖	⊜	⊖	⊜		
Auto. trans.	○	⊖	⊖	⊖	⊜	⊜		
Man. trans.	⊖	⊖	*	⊜	⊖	⊖		
Clutch	◒	○	*	◒	○	⊖		
Electrical	◒	◒	◒	○	○	○		
A/C	○	○	⊜	○	⊖	⊜		
Suspension	◒	○	○	⊖	⊜	⊜		
Brakes	◒	◒	◒	◒	○	⊖		
Exhaust	●	●	●	⊜	⊜	⊜		
Body rust	○	⊖	○	⊜	⊜	⊜		
Paint/trim	○	○	○	○	○	⊖		
Integrity	◒	○	○	○	○	⊖		
Hardware	◒	◒	○	⊖	○	○		

Oldsmobile 88

TROUBLE SPOTS	87	88	89	90	91	92	93	94
Engine	○	⊖	⊖	⊜	⊖	⊖	⊜	⊜
Cooling	◒	◒	○	○	⊖	⊖	⊜	⊜
Fuel	●	◒	○	○	◒	⊖	⊜	⊜
Ignition	○	○	○	◒	○	⊖	⊜	⊜
Auto. trans.	●	○	⊖	⊖	⊖	⊖	⊖	⊜
Man. trans.								
Clutch								
Electrical	●	●	●	●	●	◒	○	⊖
A/C	◒	○	○	○	○	○	⊖	⊜
Suspension	●	◒	○	⊖	⊖	⊖	⊖	⊜
Brakes	●	●	●	●	●	◒	⊖	⊜
Exhaust	○	⊖	⊜	⊜	⊜	⊖	⊜	⊜
Body rust	◒	○	⊜	⊖	⊜	⊜	⊜	⊜
Paint/trim	●	◒	○	○	⊖	○	⊖	⊜
Integrity	◒	○	⊖	⊖	○	◒	○	○
Hardware	●	●	○	○	○	◒	○	○

Oldsmobile 98

TROUBLE SPOTS	87	88	89	90	91	92	93	94
Engine	◒	⊖	⊖	⊜	⊜	⊜	⊜	⊜
Cooling	◒	○	○	○	⊖	⊜	⊜	⊜
Fuel	●	⊖	○	⊖	⊜	⊖	⊜	⊜
Ignition	◒	◒	◒	○	⊖	⊜	⊜	⊜
Auto. trans.	●	○	⊖	⊖	⊖	⊜	⊖	⊜
Man. trans.								
Clutch								
Electrical	●	●	●	●	●	◒	⊖	○
A/C	◒	○	◒	○	◒	○	⊖	⊜
Suspension	●	◒	⊖	⊖	⊖	⊖	⊜	⊜
Brakes	●	●	●	●	◒	◒	⊖	⊜
Exhaust	○	⊜	⊖	⊜	⊜	⊜	⊖	⊜
Body rust	⊖	⊜	⊜	⊜	⊜	⊜	⊜	⊜
Paint/trim	◒	○	◒	⊖	○	○	⊖	⊜
Integrity	◒	○	○	○	○	◒	○	○
Hardware	◒	◒	◒	◒	◒	◒	○	⊖

Oldsmobile Achieva

TROUBLE SPOTS	87	88	89	90	91	92	93	94
Engine						⊖	⊜	
Cooling						⊜	⊜	
Fuel						⊜	⊜	
Ignition						⊜	⊜	
Auto. trans.						⊖	⊜	
Man. trans.						*	*	
Clutch						*	*	
Electrical						○	○	
A/C						⊖	⊜	
Suspension						○	⊖	
Brakes						◒	○	
Exhaust						⊜	⊜	
Body rust						⊜	⊜	
Paint/trim						◒	⊖	
Integrity						●	○	
Hardware						●	○	

94: Insufficient data

Oldsmobile Custom Cruiser Wagon

TROUBLE SPOTS	87	88	89	90	91	92	93	94
Engine	◒	◒	◒	⊖				
Cooling	●	◒	◒	⊖				
Fuel	◒	◒	○	⊖				
Ignition	⊖	○	⊖	⊜				
Auto. trans.	○	○	⊖	⊖				
Man. trans.								
Clutch								
Electrical	●	●	●	●				
A/C	○	○	○	○				
Suspension	◒	●	○	○				
Brakes	◒	●	◒	◒				
Exhaust	●	●	◒	⊖				
Body rust	◒	○	○	◒				
Paint/trim	●	◒	○	◒				
Integrity	◒	○	○	◒				
Hardware	◒	●	◒	●				

91: Insufficient data
92: Insufficient data

Oldsmobile Cutlass Calais

TROUBLE SPOTS	87	88	89	90	91	92	93	94
Engine	◒	●	●	○	⊖			
Cooling	◒	◒	◒	⊖	⊖			
Fuel	◒	◒	◒	○	⊖			
Ignition	◒	◒	◒	○	⊖			
Auto. trans.	○	○	⊖	⊖	⊖			
Man. trans.	*	*	*	*	*			
Clutch	*	*	*	*	*			
Electrical	●	●	●	●	●			
A/C	◒	○	○	⊖	⊖			
Suspension	◒	○	○	○	⊖			
Brakes	●	●	◒	●	●			
Exhaust	●	●	●	●	●			
Body rust	●	◒	◒	●	○			
Paint/trim	●	●	●	●	◒			
Integrity	◒	◒	◒	◒	◒			
Hardware	●	◒	◒	○	○			

Oldsmobile Cutlass Ciera

TROUBLE SPOTS	87	88	89	90	91	92	93	94
Engine	◒	○	⊖	⊖	⊖	⊜	⊜	⊜
Cooling	◒	●	◒	○	○	⊜	⊜	⊜
Fuel	◒	◒	○	⊖	⊖	⊖	⊜	⊖
Ignition	◒	◒	○	⊖	⊖	⊜	⊜	⊜
Auto. trans.	○	⊖	⊖	⊖	⊖	⊖	⊖	⊜
Man. trans.								
Clutch								
Electrical	●	●	●	◒	◒	⊖	○	○
A/C	◒	○	⊖	⊖	⊖	⊖	⊜	⊖
Suspension	●	◒	⊖	○	⊖	⊖	⊖	⊜
Brakes	●	●	●	●	●	◒	⊖	⊖
Exhaust	●	◒	◒	○	⊖	○	⊖	⊜
Body rust	●	◒	◒	⊖	⊖	⊜	⊜	⊜
Paint/trim	●	◒	○	○	⊖	⊖	⊖	⊖
Integrity	○	○	○	○	⊖	○	○	⊖
Hardware	●	◒	○	○	○	○	⊖	⊖

Oldsmobile Cutlass Supreme

Trouble spots	87	88	89	90	91	92	93	94
Engine		○	⊖	⊖	⊖	⊜	⊖	⊜
Cooling		○	◒	⊖	⊖	⊜	⊜	⊜
Fuel		◒	◒	○	○	⊖	⊖	⊜
Ignition		○	○	⊖	⊖	⊖	⊜	⊜
Auto. trans.		○	○	○	⊜	⊜	⊖	⊜
Man. trans.		*	*		*	*		
Clutch		*	*		*	*		
Electrical		●	●	●	●	●	◒	⊖
A/C		○	◒	○	⊖	⊖	⊜	⊖
Suspension		○	○	○	○	⊖	⊖	⊜
Brakes		●	●	●	●	◒	○	⊜
Exhaust		○	⊖	⊜	⊜	⊜	⊜	⊜
Body rust		○	⊜	⊜	⊜	⊜	⊜	⊜
Paint/trim		●	●	●	◒	○	○	⊖
Integrity		◒	◒	◒	◒	○	●	○
Hardware		●	●	◒	◒	◒	◒	○

Oldsmobile Silhouette Van

Trouble spots	87	88	89	90	91	92	93	94 (Insufficient data)
Engine				⊖	⊜	⊜	⊖	
Cooling				◒	⊖	⊖	⊜	
Fuel				⊜	⊜	⊜	⊜	
Ignition				⊜	⊜	⊜	⊜	
Auto. trans.				⊜	⊜	⊖	⊖	
Man. trans.								
Clutch								
Electrical				●	●	◒	◒	
A/C				○	⊖	⊖	○	
Suspension				⊖	⊖	⊜	⊜	
Brakes				◒	◒	○	⊖	
Exhaust				⊖	⊜	⊜	⊜	
Body rust				⊜	⊜	⊜	⊜	
Paint/trim				●	◒	⊖	○	
Integrity				◒	○	○	○	
Hardware				●	●	●	●	

Plymouth Acclaim 4

Trouble spots	87	88	89	90	91	92	93	94
Engine			◒	○	○	○	⊖	⊜
Cooling			◒	○	⊖	⊖	⊜	⊜
Fuel			○	⊖	⊖	⊜	⊖	⊜
Ignition			⊖	⊖	⊖	⊖	⊜	⊜
Auto. trans.			⊖	⊖	⊖	⊖	⊜	⊖
Man. trans.			*	*	*	*	*	
Clutch			*	*	*	*	*	
Electrical			◒	◒	○	○	⊖	⊖
A/C			●	○	○	⊖	⊖	⊜
Suspension			○	○	⊖	⊖	⊖	⊜
Brakes			●	●	○	⊖	⊖	⊜
Exhaust			⊜	⊜	◒	⊖	⊜	⊜
Body rust			⊖	⊖	⊜	⊜	⊜	⊜
Paint/trim			○	○	○	⊖	⊖	⊜
Integrity			⊖	⊖	○	○	◒	⊖
Hardware			⊖	○	○	⊖	○	○

Plymouth Acclaim V6

Trouble spots	87	88	89	90	91	92	93	94
Engine			◒	○	⊖	⊖	⊜	⊜
Cooling			◒	⊖	⊖	⊜	⊜	⊜
Fuel			○	○	⊖	⊜	⊖	⊜
Ignition			⊜	⊖	⊖	⊜	⊜	⊜
Auto. trans.			●	●	◒	⊖	○	○
Man. trans.								
Clutch								
Electrical			●	◒	◒	◒	○	○
A/C			●	○	○	○	⊖	⊜
Suspension			○	⊖	⊖	⊖	⊖	⊜
Brakes			●	◒	○	⊖	⊜	⊜
Exhaust			⊖	⊜	○	⊖	⊜	⊜
Body rust			○	⊜	⊜	⊜	⊜	⊜
Paint/trim			◒	○	○	⊖	⊖	⊖
Integrity			○	⊖	○	○	○	○
Hardware			○	⊖	○	○	○	⊖

Plymouth Colt, Colt Wagon

Trouble spots	87	88	89	90	91	92	93	94 (Insufficient data)
Engine	●	●	◒	○	⊖	⊜	⊜	
Cooling	○	○	⊖	⊜	⊜	⊜	⊜	
Fuel	○	⊖	⊖	⊖	⊜	⊜	⊜	
Ignition	⊖	○	⊖	⊜	⊜	⊜	⊜	
Auto. trans.	○	○	⊖	⊖	○	⊖	◒	
Man. trans.	⊖	⊖	⊖	⊖	⊖	⊜	*	
Clutch	●	○	⊖	⊖	⊜	⊜	*	
Electrical	◒	◒	◒	○	⊖	⊖	⊖	
A/C	◒	◒	◒	⊖	⊖	⊖	⊖	
Suspension	○	⊖	○	⊖	⊖	⊖	⊜	
Brakes	●	●	◒	◒	○	○	⊖	
Exhaust	●	⊖	⊜	⊜	⊜	⊜	⊜	
Body rust	◒	○	⊜	⊜	⊖	⊜	⊜	
Paint/trim	◒	○	○	◒	○	⊜	⊖	
Integrity	◒	○	◒	●	◒	◒	⊖	
Hardware	◒	○	○	◒	○	○	⊖	

Plymouth Colt Vista Wagon

Trouble spots	87	88	89	90 (Insufficient data)	91	92	93	94 (Insufficient data)
Engine	●	●	◒		⊜	⊜	⊜	
Cooling	○	◒	⊖		⊜	⊖	⊖	
Fuel	●	○	⊖		⊜	⊖	⊜	
Ignition	○	⊜	⊖		⊜	⊜	⊜	
Auto. trans.	*	*	*		*	⊜	⊖	
Man. trans.	●	*	*		*	*	*	
Clutch	●	*	*		*	*	*	
Electrical	◒	◒	●		●	○	○	
A/C	◒	○	*		*	⊖	⊜	
Suspension	○	◒	○		◒	⊖	⊖	
Brakes	◒	◒	◒		⊖	⊜	⊜	
Exhaust	●	⊖	○		⊖	○	⊖	
Body rust	⊖	⊖	⊜		⊜	⊜	⊜	
Paint/trim	○	⊖	○		⊖	⊖	⊖	
Integrity	○	○	○		◒	◒	◒	
Hardware	◒	◒	◒		○	◒	○	

Plymouth Horizon, Turismo

Trouble spots	87	88	89	90	91	92	93	94
Engine	◒	○	◒	○				
Cooling	◒	◒	○	○				
Fuel	●	○	◒	○				
Ignition	●	○	○	⊖				
Auto. trans.	○	○	⊖	*				
Man. trans.	○	⊖	*	*				
Clutch	●	○	*	*				
Electrical	●	◒	●	●				
A/C	●	●	●	*				
Suspension	●	○	○	⊖				
Brakes	●	●	●	●				
Exhaust	●	⊖	⊖	⊖				
Body rust	●	●	◒	⊖				
Paint/trim	◒	●	●	○				
Integrity	●	●	●	●				
Hardware	●	◒	○	◒				

Plymouth Laser 2WD

Trouble spots	87	88	89	90	91	92	93	94 (Insufficient data)
Engine				●	◒	◒	⊜	
Cooling				⊖	⊖	⊜	⊖	
Fuel				⊖	⊖	⊜	⊜	
Ignition				⊖	⊜	⊜	⊜	
Auto. trans.				○	⊖	⊖	*	
Man. trans.				○	○	⊖	⊖	
Clutch				⊖	⊖	⊖	⊜	
Electrical				◒	◒	◒	⊖	
A/C				⊜	⊖	⊜	⊜	
Suspension				⊜	⊜	⊖	⊖	
Brakes				◒	○	○	⊖	
Exhaust				⊖	○	◒	⊜	
Body rust				⊜	⊜	⊜	⊜	
Paint/trim				○	○	○	⊖	
Integrity				○	○	◒	○	
Hardware				◒	◒	●	○	

⊜ ⊖ ○ ◒ ●
Few ← Problems → Many

* Insufficient data

Trouble spots	Plymouth Reliant 87	88	89	90	91	92	93	94
Engine	◒	◒	◒					
Cooling	●	●	◒					
Fuel	●	◒	○					
Ignition	◒	○	○					
Auto. trans.	⊖	⊖	⊖					
Man. trans.	*	*	*					
Clutch	*	*	*					
Electrical	●	◒	●					
A/C	●	●	●					
Suspension	◒	◒	◒					
Brakes	●	●	●					
Exhaust	○	⊜	⊜					
Body rust	◒	◒	○					
Paint/trim	◒	◒	●					
Integrity	●	◒	●					
Hardware	◒	◒	◒					

Trouble spots	Plymouth Sundance 87	88	89	90	91	92	93	94
Engine	●	●	◒	○	○	○	⊜	⊜
Cooling	●	●	◒	○	○	⊖	⊜	⊜
Fuel	◒	◒	○	○	⊜	⊜	⊖	⊖
Ignition	◒	○	○	○	⊜	⊜	⊖	⊜
Auto. trans.	⊖	○	⊖	⊖	⊜	⊖	⊖	⊜
Man. trans.	⊖	*	*	*	*	⊖	⊖	*
Clutch	●	*	*	*	*	⊜	⊖	*
Electrical	●	◒	●	●	●	◒	○	⊜
A/C	●	●	●	◒	◒	⊜	⊖	⊜
Suspension	◒	◒	◒	○	⊖	⊖	⊜	⊜
Brakes	●	●	●	●	○	⊜	⊜	⊜
Exhaust	○	⊖	⊖	⊖	◒	⊜	⊜	⊜
Body rust	○	○	⊖	⊖	⊖	⊜	⊜	⊜
Paint/trim	◒	●	◒	○	○	○	○	⊖
Integrity	●	◒	○	○	◒	◒	◒	◒
Hardware	●	●	◒	○	○	○	◒	○

Trouble spots	Plymouth Voyager 4 87	88	89	90	91	92	93	94
Engine	●	●	◒	⊖	○	○	⊖	⊜
Cooling	●	●	○	⊖	⊖	⊖	⊜	⊜
Fuel	●	◒	○	⊖	⊖	⊖	⊖	⊜
Ignition	○	○	⊖	⊖	⊜	⊖	⊜	⊜
Auto. trans.	◒	○	⊖	○	⊖	⊖	⊖	⊜
Man. trans.	○	*	*	*		*	*	
Clutch	●	*	*	*		*	*	
Electrical	●	◒	◒	○	◒	◒	○	⊖
A/C	●	●	●	○	○	⊖	⊖	⊜
Suspension	◒	○	○	○	⊖	⊖	⊖	⊜
Brakes	●	●	●	◒	◒	○	⊖	⊜
Exhaust	○	⊖	⊜	⊖	○	⊖	⊜	⊜
Body rust	○	⊖	⊖	⊖	⊜	⊜	⊜	⊜
Paint/trim	○	○	⊖	○	⊜	⊖	⊜	⊜
Integrity	◒	◒	○	◒	◒	◒	○	○
Hardware	●	◒	◒	●	◒	◒	◒	⊖

Trouble spots	Plymouth Voyager V6 (2WD) 87	88	89	90	91	92	93	94
Engine	●	●	●	○	○	⊖	⊖	⊜
Cooling	●	●	◒	○	⊖	⊜	⊜	⊜
Fuel	◒	●	○	○	⊖	⊖	⊜	⊜
Ignition	⊖	○	⊖	⊖	⊜	⊜	⊜	⊜
Auto. trans.	◒	○	◒	◒	○	○	⊖	⊜
Man. trans.								
Clutch								
Electrical	●	●	◒	◒	◒	◒	○	⊖
A/C	●	●	◒	○	⊖	⊖	⊜	⊜
Suspension	◒	◒	○	⊖	⊖	⊖	⊜	⊜
Brakes	●	●	●	◒	◒	○	⊖	⊜
Exhaust	⊖	⊖	⊜	⊜	◒	⊜	⊜	⊜
Body rust	○	⊖	⊖	⊖	⊜	⊜	⊜	⊜
Paint/trim	○	○	○	⊖	⊜	⊜	⊜	⊜
Integrity	◒	○	○	◒	◒	◒	○	⊖
Hardware	●	●	●	●	◒	◒	◒	⊖

Trouble spots	Plymouth Grand Voyager V6 (2WD) 87	88	89	90	91	92	93	94
Engine	●	●	●	○	⊖	○	⊖	⊜
Cooling	◒	●	◒	○	⊖	⊖	⊖	⊜
Fuel	◒	●	○	○	⊖	⊖	⊜	⊜
Ignition	⊖	○	⊖	⊖	⊖	⊜	⊜	⊜
Auto. trans.	◒	◒	●	●	◒	○	○	⊖
Man. trans.								
Clutch								
Electrical	◒	●	◒	●	●	●	○	⊖
A/C	●	●	◒	○	⊖	⊖	⊖	⊜
Suspension	◒	◒	○	○	○	○	⊖	⊜
Brakes	●	●	●	●	◒	○	⊖	⊜
Exhaust	⊜	⊜	⊜	⊜	◒	⊜	⊜	⊜
Body rust	○	⊖	⊖	⊖	⊜	⊜	⊜	⊜
Paint/trim	●	◒	○	○	⊖	⊖	⊖	⊖
Integrity	◒	◒	◒	◒	◒	◒	◒	◒
Hardware	●	●	●	●	◒	◒	◒	○

Trouble spots	Plymouth Grand Voyager V6 (4WD) 87	88	89	90	91	92	93	94
Engine					⊖	○	⊜	⊜
Cooling					⊖	○	⊖	⊜
Fuel					○	○	⊖	⊜
Ignition					○	⊜	⊜	⊜
Auto. trans.					●	◒	○	⊖
Man. trans.								
Clutch								
Electrical					◒	●	○	⊖
A/C					⊖	⊖	⊖	⊜
Suspension					○	○	⊖	⊜
Brakes					●	◒	○	⊜
Exhaust					●	◒	⊜	⊜
Body rust					⊜	⊜	⊜	⊜
Paint/trim					○	⊜	⊖	⊖
Integrity					○	◒	○	○
Hardware					◒	◒	◒	⊖

Trouble spots	Pontiac 6000 87	88	89	90	91	92	93	94
Engine	◒	○	⊖	⊖	Insufficient data			
Cooling	◒	◒	○	⊖				
Fuel	◒	◒	◒	○				
Ignition	◒	◒	◒	⊖				
Auto. trans.	○	○	○	⊖				
Man. trans.	*	*						
Clutch	*	*						
Electrical	●	●	●	○				
A/C	◒	○	○	⊖				
Suspension	●	◒	○	○				
Brakes	●	●	●	●				
Exhaust	●	●	●	○				
Body rust	●	◒	◒	⊜				
Paint/trim	●	●	●	○				
Integrity	◒	○	○	○				
Hardware	●	◒	○	○				

Trouble spots	Pontiac Bonneville 87	88	89	90	91	92	93	94
Engine	○	○	⊖	⊖	⊖	⊖	⊜	⊜
Cooling	●	◒	○	○	⊖	⊖	⊜	⊜
Fuel	◒	◒	○	◒	○	⊜	⊜	⊜
Ignition	◒	○	◒	○	○	⊖	⊜	⊜
Auto. trans.	●	○	⊖	⊖	⊖	⊖	⊖	⊜
Man. trans.								
Clutch								
Electrical	●	●	●	●	●	●	◒	⊖
A/C	◒	○	○	○	○	⊖	⊜	⊜
Suspension	●	◒	⊖	⊖	⊜	⊖	⊜	⊜
Brakes	●	●	●	●	◒	◒	⊖	⊜
Exhaust	○	⊖	⊜	⊜	⊜	⊖	⊜	⊜
Body rust	●	◒	○	⊖	⊜	⊜	⊜	⊜
Paint/trim	●	●	◒	○	⊖	○	⊖	⊜
Integrity	●	○	○	⊖	○	◒	○	○
Hardware	●	●	○	○	○	◒	○	⊖

Pontiac Firebird

Trouble spots	87	88 (Insufficient data)	89	90 (Insufficient data)	91 (Insufficient data)	92 (Insufficient data)	93 (Insufficient data)	94
Engine	◒		⊖					⊜
Cooling	●		○					⊜
Fuel	●		◒					○
Ignition	◒		○					⊜
Auto. trans.	○		*					⊖
Man. trans.	*		*					*
Clutch	*		*					*
Electrical	●		●					○
A/C	◒		◒					⊜
Suspension	◒		⊖					⊜
Brakes	◒		○					⊜
Exhaust	●		◒					⊜
Body rust	◒		○					⊜
Paint/trim	●		●					⊜
Integrity	●		●					○
Hardware	●		●					⊖

Pontiac Grand Am

Trouble spots	87	88	89	90	91	92	93	94
Engine	◒	●	●	◒	○	⊖	⊜	⊜
Cooling	●	◒	◒	○	○	⊖	⊜	⊜
Fuel	◒	○	◒	⊖	○	⊖	⊖	⊜
Ignition	◒	◒	○	⊖	⊖	⊖	⊜	⊜
Auto. trans.	○	○	○	⊖	⊖	⊜	⊖	⊜
Man. trans.	*	*	*	*	*	*	*	*
Clutch	*	*	*	*	*	*	*	*
Electrical	●	●	●	◒	◒	●	○	○
A/C	○	○	⊖	⊖	⊖	⊖	⊖	⊜
Suspension	◒	◒	○	○	○	○	⊖	⊜
Brakes	◒	●	●	◒	●	◒	○	⊜
Exhaust	●	●	●	●	●	⊜	⊜	⊜
Body rust	●	●	●	◒	○	⊜	⊜	⊜
Paint/trim	●	●	●	●	◒	○	○	⊜
Integrity	◒	◒	◒	◒	◒	◒	◒	○
Hardware	◒	○	○	○	◒	◒	○	○

Pontiac Grand Prix V6

Trouble spots	87	88	89	90	91	92	93	94
Engine		⊖	⊖	○	⊖	⊜	⊜	⊜
Cooling		◒	◒	○	○	⊜	⊜	⊜
Fuel		○	◒	○	○	⊖	⊖	⊜
Ignition		○	◒	○	⊖	⊖	⊜	⊜
Auto. trans.		◒	◒	○	○	⊖	⊖	⊜
Man. trans.		*	*	*	*	*	*	
Clutch		*	*	*	*	*	*	
Electrical		●	●	●	●	●	◒	◒
A/C		○	○	○	○	⊖	⊖	⊜
Suspension		◒	◒	○	○	⊖	⊖	⊜
Brakes		●	●	●	●	◒	○	⊜
Exhaust		⊜	⊜	⊜	⊜	⊜	⊜	⊜
Body rust		⊖	⊜	⊖	⊜	⊜	⊜	⊜
Paint/trim		●	●	◒	○	○	○	⊖
Integrity		○	◒	○	○	◒	◒	○
Hardware		◒	◒	●	●	○	◒	○

Pontiac Sunbird

Trouble spots	87	88	89	90	91	92	93	94 (Insufficient data)
Engine	●	○	◒	○	◒	○	⊖	
Cooling	●	◒	◒	○	○	○	⊖	
Fuel	◒	◒	○	⊖	○	○	⊖	
Ignition	◒	○	⊖	⊖	○	⊖	⊖	
Auto. trans.	⊖	⊖	⊖	⊜	⊜	⊖	⊖	
Man. trans.	*	*	*	*	*	*	*	
Clutch	*	*	*	*	*	*	*	
Electrical	●	●	●	●	●	●	●	
A/C	●	○	⊖	○	⊖	⊖	⊜	
Suspension	◒	◒	⊖	⊖	○	○	⊖	
Brakes	◒	◒	●	●	●	●	○	
Exhaust	●	●	●	◒	⊖	⊜	⊜	
Body rust	●	●	◒	○	○	⊖	⊜	
Paint/trim	●	◒	○	○	○	◒	◒	
Integrity	◒	◒	◒	◒	◒	◒	●	
Hardware	◒	◒	○	○	◒	◒	◒	

Pontiac Trans Sport Van

Trouble spots	87	88	89	90	91	92	93	94
Engine				○	⊖	⊜	⊜	⊜
Cooling				◒	⊖	○	⊖	⊖
Fuel				⊜	⊜	⊜	⊜	⊜
Ignition				⊜	⊜	⊜	⊖	⊜
Auto. trans.				⊖	⊖	⊖	○	⊖
Man. trans.								
Clutch								
Electrical				●	◒	◒	○	○
A/C				○	⊜	⊖	○	⊜
Suspension				⊖	⊜	⊖	⊜	⊜
Brakes				●	◒	○	○	⊖
Exhaust				⊖	⊜	⊜	⊜	⊜
Body rust				⊜	⊜	⊜	⊜	⊜
Paint/trim				●	●	⊖	⊖	⊖
Integrity				●	◒	◒	◒	○
Hardware				●	●	●	●	⊖

Saab 900

Trouble spots	87	88	89	90	91	92	93	94 (Insufficient data)
Engine	○	○	○	○	○	⊜	⊖	
Cooling	◒	●	◒	○	⊖	⊖	⊖	
Fuel	⊖	○	○	○	⊖	⊜	⊜	
Ignition	⊜	⊖	○	⊖	⊜	⊖	⊜	
Auto. trans.	*	*	*	*	*	*	*	
Man. trans.	◒	◒	⊖	*	*	*	*	
Clutch	○	○	⊖	*	*	*	*	
Electrical	◒	●	●	●	●	●	◒	
A/C	◒	◒	◒	○	○	⊖	⊜	
Suspension	◒	○	○	⊖	⊖	⊖	⊜	
Brakes	●	●	◒	○	○	⊖	⊖	
Exhaust	●	●	◒	○	⊖	⊖	⊜	
Body rust	⊜	⊜	⊖	⊖	⊖	⊜	⊜	
Paint/trim	○	○	○	⊖	⊖	⊖	⊖	
Integrity	○	◒	◒	◒	◒	◒	●	
Hardware	◒	●	●	◒	◒	◒	●	

Saab 9000

Trouble spots	87	88	89	90 (Insufficient data)	91	92	93	94 (Insufficient data)
Engine	○	⊖	○		○	⊖	⊖	
Cooling	○	◒	●		○	⊜	⊜	
Fuel	○	⊖	⊖		⊖	⊜	⊖	
Ignition	⊖	⊖	⊜		⊖	⊜	⊜	
Auto. trans.	*	*	*		*	*	*	
Man. trans.	*	*	*		*	*	*	
Clutch	*	*	*		*	*	*	
Electrical	●	●	●		●	◒	○	
A/C	◒	○	◒		⊖	○	⊖	
Suspension	⊖	○	○		⊜	⊖	⊜	
Brakes	◒	◒	●		○	○	⊖	
Exhaust	●	◒	◒		⊖	⊜	⊖	
Body rust	⊖	○	⊖		⊜	⊜	⊜	
Paint/trim	⊖	⊖	○		⊖	⊜	⊖	
Integrity	○	◒	○		○	○	○	
Hardware	●	◒	●		○	○	○	

Saturn SL Sedan, Wagon

Trouble spots	87	88	89	90	91	92	93	94
Engine					⊖	⊖	⊜	⊜
Cooling					⊜	⊜	⊜	⊜
Fuel					⊖	⊖	⊜	⊜
Ignition					⊜	⊜	⊜	⊜
Auto. trans.					○	⊖	⊜	⊜
Man. trans.					⊜	⊜	⊜	⊜
Clutch					⊖	⊜	⊖	⊜
Electrical					◒	○	⊖	⊖
A/C					⊖	⊜	⊜	⊜
Suspension					⊜	⊜	⊜	⊜
Brakes					⊖	○	⊖	⊜
Exhaust					⊜	⊜	⊜	⊜
Body rust					⊜	⊜	⊜	⊜
Paint/trim					⊖	⊜	⊜	⊜
Integrity					○	○	○	⊖
Hardware					◒	◒	⊖	⊖

⊜ ⊖ ○ ◒ ●
Few ← Problems → Many

* Insufficient data

Saturn SC Coupe

TROUBLE SPOTS	87	88	89	90	91	92	93	94
Engine	Insufficient data					○	⊜	⊜
Cooling						⊜	⊜	⊜
Fuel						⊖	⊜	⊜
Ignition						⊜	⊜	⊜
Auto. trans.						⊖	⊜	⊜
Man. trans.						⊜	⊜	⊜
Clutch						⊜	⊖	⊜
Electrical						◒	⊖	⊜
A/C						⊖	⊜	⊜
Suspension						⊜	⊜	⊜
Brakes						⊖	⊖	⊜
Exhaust						⊜	⊜	⊜
Body rust						⊜	⊜	⊜
Paint/trim						⊖	⊖	⊜
Integrity						◒	◒	⊖
Hardware						◒	○	⊖

Subaru Impreza

TROUBLE SPOTS	87	88	89	90	91	92	93	94
Engine							⊜	Insufficient data
Cooling							⊜	
Fuel							⊜	
Ignition							⊜	
Auto. trans.							⊜	
Man. trans.							⊜	
Clutch							⊜	
Electrical							⊜	
A/C							⊖	
Suspension							⊜	
Brakes							⊜	
Exhaust							⊜	
Body rust							⊜	
Paint/trim							⊜	
Integrity							⊖	
Hardware							○	

Subaru Legacy (2WD)

TROUBLE SPOTS	87	88	89	90	91	92	93	94
Engine				⊖	⊜	⊜	⊜	Insufficient data
Cooling				⊖	⊜	⊜	⊜	
Fuel				⊖	⊜	⊖	⊜	
Ignition				⊖	⊜	⊖	⊜	
Auto. trans.				○	⊖	⊖	⊜	
Man. trans.				⊜	*	*	*	
Clutch				⊖	*	*	*	
Electrical				○	⊖	⊖	⊖	
A/C				○	○	⊖	⊖	
Suspension				○	○	⊜	⊜	
Brakes				●	◒	⊖	⊜	
Exhaust				⊜	⊜	⊜	⊜	
Body rust				⊜	⊜	⊜	⊜	
Paint/trim				○	○	○	○	
Integrity				○	⊖	○	○	
Hardware				●	○	○	○	

Subaru Legacy (4WD)

TROUBLE SPOTS	87	88	89	90	91	92	93	94
Engine				⊖	⊜	⊜	⊜	⊜
Cooling				⊖	⊜	⊜	⊜	⊜
Fuel				⊖	⊜	⊖	⊜	⊜
Ignition				⊜	⊜	⊖	⊜	⊜
Auto. trans.				○	○	⊜	⊜	⊜
Man. trans.				⊜	⊜	⊜	⊖	*
Clutch				○	⊖	⊜	⊜	*
Electrical				○	⊖	⊖	⊖	⊖
A/C				⊖	⊖	⊖	⊜	⊜
Suspension				○	⊖	⊖	⊜	⊜
Brakes				●	◒	⊖	⊜	⊜
Exhaust				⊜	⊜	⊜	⊜	⊜
Body rust				⊖	⊜	⊜	⊜	⊜
Paint/trim				○	◒	○	⊖	⊜
Integrity				○	○	○	○	⊖
Hardware				◒	○	○	⊖	⊖

Subaru & Subaru Loyale (2WD)

TROUBLE SPOTS	87	88	89	90	91	92	93	94
Engine	●	●	●	●	○	○	Insufficient data	Insufficient data
Cooling	●	●	◒	○	○	⊜		
Fuel	○	⊖	⊖	⊖	⊜	⊖		
Ignition	○	⊖	⊖	○	⊖	⊖		
Auto. trans.	○	⊖	○	*	*	*		
Man. trans.	⊖	⊜	*	*	*	*		
Clutch	●	●	*	*	*	*		
Electrical	◒	◒	◒	◒	○	○		
A/C	◒	◒	◒	*	⊜	⊖		
Suspension	⊖	⊖	⊖	○	○	⊖		
Brakes	◒	○	○	○	○	⊖		
Exhaust	●	◒	◒	○	⊜	⊜		
Body rust	●	●	◒	◒	⊖	⊜		
Paint/trim	○	○	⊖	⊖	○	○		
Integrity	○	○	○	◒	○	○		
Hardware	○	⊖	○	⊖	○	○		

Subaru & Subaru Loyale (4WD)

TROUBLE SPOTS	87	88	89	90	91	92	93	94
Engine	●	●	●	●	◒	⊖	Insufficient data	Insufficient data
Cooling	●	●	●	○	⊖	⊖		
Fuel	○	○	⊖	⊜	⊖	⊖		
Ignition	⊖	⊖	○	⊖	⊜	⊜		
Auto. trans.	○	⊖	*	*	*	*		
Man. trans.	⊖	○	⊜	⊜	⊜	⊜		
Clutch	●	◒	○	○	○	⊜		
Electrical	◒	◒	◒	○	○	○		
A/C	○	○	○	○	⊜	⊖		
Suspension	○	○	⊜	⊖	⊖	⊜		
Brakes	◒	◒	◒	⊖	⊖	⊜		
Exhaust	●	●	●	○	⊜	⊜		
Body rust	●	●	◒	○	⊜	⊜		
Paint/trim	○	○	○	○	⊖	⊖		
Integrity	○	○	◒	○	⊖	◒		
Hardware	○	○	○	○	○	○		

Suzuki Sidekick

TROUBLE SPOTS	87	88	89	90	91	92	93	94
Engine			○	⊖	○	⊖	⊜	⊜
Cooling			⊖	⊖	⊜	⊖	⊖	⊜
Fuel			○	⊜	⊜	⊜	⊜	⊜
Ignition			⊖	⊜	⊖	⊜	⊜	⊜
Auto. trans.				*	*	*	⊖	*
Man. trans.			*	*	⊜	⊖	⊜	*
Clutch			*	*	○	⊜	⊜	*
Electrical			◒	○	○	○	⊖	⊖
A/C			*	*	*	*	⊖	*
Suspension			⊖	⊜	⊖	⊜	⊜	⊜
Brakes			●	◒	◒	○	⊜	⊖
Exhaust			●	●	◒	⊖	⊜	⊜
Body rust			◒	⊜	⊜	⊜	⊜	⊜
Paint/trim			○	⊜	○	⊖	⊜	⊖
Integrity			◒	○	○	○	○	○
Hardware			◒	◒	○	◒	◒	○

Toyota 4Runner

TROUBLE SPOTS	87	88	89	90	91	92	93	94
Engine	○	⊖	○	⊖	⊜	⊜	⊜	⊜
Cooling	◒	○	⊖	⊖	⊖	⊜	⊜	⊜
Fuel	⊜	⊖	⊖	⊖	⊜	⊜	⊜	⊜
Ignition	⊖	⊜	⊜	⊜	⊜	⊜	⊜	⊜
Auto. trans.	*	*	*	⊖	⊜	⊖	⊜	⊜
Man. trans.	○	⊖	⊜	⊖	⊖	⊜	⊜	*
Clutch	●	◒	○	⊖	○	⊖	⊜	*
Electrical	○	○	⊖	○	○	⊖	⊖	⊜
A/C	⊖	⊖	⊖	◒	○	⊖	⊜	⊜
Suspension	⊖	⊖	⊜	⊖	⊖	⊖	⊜	⊜
Brakes	○	◒	◒	◒	○	○	⊖	⊜
Exhaust	◒	○	○	⊖	⊖	⊜	⊜	⊜
Body rust	○	○	⊖	⊖	⊜	⊜	⊜	⊜
Paint/trim	◒	○	○	⊖	⊜	⊖	⊜	⊜
Integrity	○	⊖	⊖	⊖	⊜	⊖	○	⊜
Hardware	◒	⊖	○	○	⊖	⊖	⊖	⊜

TROUBLE SPOTS	Toyota Camry 4 87	88	89	90	91	92	93	94	Toyota Camry V6 87	88	89	90	91	92	93	94
Engine	○	○	⊖	⊜	⊜	⊜	⊜	⊜		○	⊖	⊖	⊖	⊜	⊜	⊜
Cooling	⊖	⊖	⊜	⊜	⊜	⊜	⊜	⊜		⊖	⊖	⊖	⊖	⊜	⊜	⊜
Fuel	⊖	⊖	⊖	⊖	⊜	⊜	⊜	⊜		⊖	⊖	⊜	⊜	⊜	⊜	⊜
Ignition	○	⊖	⊖	⊜	⊜	⊜	⊜	⊜		⊖	⊖	⊜	⊜	⊜	⊜	⊜
Auto. trans.	⊖	⊖	⊜	⊜	⊜	⊜	⊜	⊜		◒	⊖	⊖	⊜	⊜	⊜	⊜
Man. trans.	⊖	⊖	⊖	⊖	⊜	⊜	⊜	*		*	*	*	*	*	⊜	
Clutch	●	⊖	⊖	⊖	⊖	⊖	⊜	*		*	*	*	*	*	⊖	
Electrical	●	◒	○	○	◒	⊖	⊖	⊜		●	◒	◒	◒	⊖	⊖	⊖
A/C	○	⊖	⊖	⊜	⊜	○	⊜	⊜		○	⊖	⊜	⊖	○	⊜	⊜
Suspension	○	⊖	⊖	⊖	⊖	○	⊖	⊜		○	○	○	⊖	⊖	⊖	⊖
Brakes	●	◒	◒	◒	◒	⊖	⊖	⊜		◒	◒	◒	◒	⊖	⊖	⊜
Exhaust	●	●	●	◒	⊜	⊖	⊜	⊜		●	◒	○	⊜	⊜	⊖	⊜
Body rust	○	○	○	⊖	⊜	⊜	⊜	⊜		○	⊖	⊜	⊜	⊜	⊜	⊜
Paint/trim	○	○	○	⊖	⊖	⊖	⊖	⊜		⊖	○	⊖	⊖	⊖	⊖	⊜
Integrity	○	○	○	⊖	⊖	⊖	⊖	⊖		○	⊖	⊖	⊖	○	⊖	⊖
Hardware	○	○	○	○	⊖	⊖	⊖	⊖		○	○	○	○	⊖	⊖	⊖

TROUBLE SPOTS	Toyota Celica 87	88	89	90	91	92	93	94	Toyota Corolla 87	88	89	90	91	92	93	94
Engine	◒	○	⊖	⊜	⊜	⊜	⊜	⊜	○	⊖	⊖	⊜	⊜	⊜	⊜	⊜
Cooling	○	⊖	⊖	⊖	⊜	⊜	⊜	⊜	○	○	○	⊖	⊜	⊜	⊜	⊜
Fuel	○	⊖	⊖	⊖	⊜	⊜	⊜	⊜	○	⊖	⊜	⊜	⊜	⊜	⊜	⊜
Ignition	○	⊖	⊜	⊜	⊜	⊜	⊜	⊜	⊖	○	⊖	⊜	⊜	⊜	⊜	⊜
Auto. trans.	○	⊖	⊖	⊖	⊜	⊜	⊖	*	⊖	⊖	⊖	⊜	⊜	⊜	⊜	⊜
Man. trans.	⊖	⊖	⊜	⊜	⊜	⊜	⊖	*	⊜	⊜	⊜	⊜	⊜	⊜	⊜	⊜
Clutch	○	⊖	⊖	⊖	⊜	⊜	⊜	*	●	◒	⊖	⊖	⊖	⊜	⊜	⊜
Electrical	●	◒	◒	◒	○	○	⊖	⊖	○	◒	○	○	◒	○	⊖	⊖
A/C	○	○	⊖	◒	○	○	○	⊜	○	⊖	⊖	⊜	⊖	⊜	⊜	⊜
Suspension	○	○	⊖	⊖	⊜	⊜	⊖	⊖	○	⊖	⊖	⊖	⊖	⊖	⊜	⊜
Brakes	●	◒	◒	○	⊖	⊜	⊜	⊜	●	◒	◒	○	○	⊖	⊜	⊜
Exhaust	●	●	●	⊜	⊜	⊜	⊜	⊜	●	●	●	◒	◒	⊜	⊜	⊜
Body rust	◒	⊖	○	⊜	⊜	⊜	⊜	⊜	⊖	⊖	⊖	⊜	⊜	⊜	⊜	⊜
Paint/trim	◒	○	○	⊖	⊜	⊖	⊖	⊜	○	⊖	⊖	⊖	⊖	⊜	⊖	⊜
Integrity	○	○	⊖	⊖	○	○	○	○	○	⊖	⊖	○	⊖	⊖	○	⊖
Hardware	○	○	○	○	○	○	○	⊖	⊖	○	○	○	○	○	○	⊖

TROUBLE SPOTS	Toyota Cressida 87	88	89	90	91	92	93	94	Toyota Land Cruiser 87	88	89	90	91	92	93	94
Engine	◒	○	○	⊖	⊜	Insufficient data			Insufficient data	Insufficient data	⊖	Insufficient data	⊖	Insufficient data	⊜	Insufficient data
Cooling	●	◒	○	○	⊖						○		⊜		⊜	
Fuel	○	⊖	⊜	⊖	⊖						⊖		⊜		⊜	
Ignition	○	⊖	⊜	⊖	⊖						⊜		⊜		⊜	
Auto. trans.	⊖	⊜	⊜	⊖	⊖						⊖		⊖		*	
Man. trans.	*															
Clutch	*															
Electrical	●	●	○	○	○						⊜		○		○	
A/C	●	○	◒	○	○						⊖		○		⊖	
Suspension	○	⊖	⊜	⊜	⊜						⊜		⊜		⊖	
Brakes	◒	●	◒	◒	◒						◒		●		○	
Exhaust	○	○	⊖	⊜	⊜						◒		⊖		⊜	
Body rust	○	⊖	⊖	⊜	⊜						◒		⊜		⊜	
Paint/trim	○	○	⊖	⊖	⊜						○		⊖		⊖	
Integrity	⊖	⊖	⊖	⊖	⊜						⊖		○		○	
Hardware	○	◒	⊖	⊜	⊖						⊖		○		⊖	

TROUBLE SPOTS	Toyota MR2 87	88	89	90	91	92	93	94	Toyota Paseo 87	88	89	90	91	92	93	94
Engine	⊖	Insufficient data	Insufficient data		⊖	Insufficient data	Insufficient data	Insufficient data						⊜	Insufficient data	Insufficient data
Cooling	○				⊜									⊜		
Fuel	⊜				⊜									⊜		
Ignition	⊜				⊜									⊜		
Auto. trans.	*				*									⊜		
Man. trans.	⊖				○									⊜		
Clutch	⊖				⊜									⊜		
Electrical	⊖				◒									⊖		
A/C	○				○									⊖		
Suspension	⊖				⊖									⊜		
Brakes	○				○									⊜		
Exhaust	○				⊖									⊜		
Body rust	○				⊜									⊜		
Paint/trim	◒				○									○		
Integrity	◒				○									⊖		
Hardware	⊖				○									⊖		

⊜ ⊖ ○ ◒ ●
Few ← **Problems** → Many

*
Insufficient data

Toyota Pickup (2WD)

TROUBLE SPOTS	87	88	89	90	91	92	93	94
Engine	○	⊖	⊖	⊜	⊜	⊜	⊜	⊜
Cooling	○	○	○	⊖	⊖	⊜	⊜	⊜
Fuel	⊖	⊖	⊖	⊜	⊜	⊖	⊜	⊜
Ignition	⊜	⊜	⊜	⊜	⊜	⊜	⊜	⊜
Auto. trans.	⊖	⊖	⊖	⊖	⊜	⊖	⊜	*
Man. trans.	⊜	⊜	⊜	⊜	⊜	⊜	⊜	⊜
Clutch	◒	○	⊖	⊖	⊜	⊖	⊜	⊜
Electrical	○	○	⊜	⊖	⊖	⊖	⊜	⊜
A/C	⊖	○	⊖	⊜	⊜	⊖	⊖	⊜
Suspension	⊜	⊖	⊖	⊖	⊖	⊖	⊜	⊜
Brakes	○	◒	◒	○	⊖	⊖	⊜	⊜
Exhaust	◒	◒	○	⊖	⊜	⊜	⊜	⊜
Body rust	◒	◒	⊜	⊜	⊜	⊜	⊜	⊜
Paint/trim	○	⊖	⊖	⊖	⊜	⊜	⊜	⊜
Integrity	⊖	⊖	⊖	⊖	⊜	⊖	⊖	⊖
Hardware	⊖	⊜	⊖	⊖	⊖	⊖	⊖	⊜

Toyota Pickup (4WD)

TROUBLE SPOTS	87	88	89	90	91	92	93	94
Engine	○	⊖	⊖	⊜	⊖	⊜	⊜	⊜
Cooling	○	○	○	⊖	⊖	⊜	⊜	⊜
Fuel	⊖	⊖	⊖	⊖	⊜	⊜	⊜	⊜
Ignition	⊜	⊜	⊜	⊜	⊜	⊜	⊜	⊜
Auto. trans.	*	*	*	*	*	*	*	*
Man. trans.	⊖	⊖	⊜	⊜	⊜	⊜	⊜	⊜
Clutch	●	◒	○	⊖	○	⊖	⊜	⊖
Electrical	○	⊖	⊖	⊖	⊖	⊖	⊖	⊖
A/C	○	○	⊖	⊜	⊜	⊖	⊜	⊜
Suspension	⊖	⊖	⊖	⊖	⊖	⊖	⊜	⊜
Brakes	◒	○	○	○	○	⊖	⊜	⊜
Exhaust	◒	●	◒	⊖	⊖	⊜	⊜	⊜
Body rust	●	●	⊖	⊜	⊖	⊜	⊖	⊜
Paint/trim	◒	○	⊖	⊖	⊖	⊜	⊜	⊜
Integrity	○	⊖	⊖	⊜	○	⊖	⊖	⊖
Hardware	⊖	⊖	○	⊖	⊖	⊖	⊖	⊖

Toyota Previa Van

TROUBLE SPOTS	87	88	89	90	91	92	93	94
Engine					⊜	⊜	⊜	Insufficient data
Cooling					⊜	⊜	⊜	
Fuel					⊜	⊜	⊜	
Ignition					⊜	⊜	⊜	
Auto. trans.					⊜	⊜	⊜	
Man. trans.					*	*	*	
Clutch					*	*	*	
Electrical					◒	○	⊖	
A/C					●	◒	⊖	
Suspension					⊖	⊜	⊜	
Brakes					○	⊖	⊜	
Exhaust					⊜	⊜	⊜	
Body rust					⊜	⊜	⊜	
Paint/trim					⊜	⊜	⊜	
Integrity					○	⊖	⊖	
Hardware					◒	○	⊖	

Toyota Supra

TROUBLE SPOTS	87	88	89	90	91	92	93	94
Engine	◒	◒	○	Insufficient data	Insufficient data	Insufficient data		Insufficient data
Cooling	●	◒	◒					
Fuel	⊖	⊖	⊜					
Ignition	⊖	⊜	⊜					
Auto. trans.	○	*	*					
Man. trans.	⊖	*	⊖					
Clutch	●	*	○					
Electrical	●	●	◒					
A/C	●	◒	●					
Suspension	⊖	○	⊖					
Brakes	◒	○	⊖					
Exhaust	◒	○	○					
Body rust	⊖	⊜	⊜					
Paint/trim	◒	○	○					
Integrity	◒	○	◒					
Hardware	○	○	◒					

Toyota T100 Pickup

TROUBLE SPOTS	87	88	89	90	91	92	93	94
Engine							⊜	Insufficient data
Cooling							⊜	
Fuel							⊜	
Ignition							⊜	
Auto. trans.							⊜	
Man. trans.							⊖	
Clutch							⊖	
Electrical							⊜	
A/C							⊜	
Suspension							⊖	
Brakes							⊜	
Exhaust							⊜	
Body rust							⊜	
Paint/trim							⊖	
Integrity							⊖	
Hardware							○	

Toyota Tercel

TROUBLE SPOTS	87	88	89	90	91	92	93	94
Engine	◒	◒	○	○	⊜	⊜	⊜	⊜
Cooling	○	◒	⊖	⊖	⊖	⊜	⊜	⊜
Fuel	○	◒	◒	◒	⊜	⊜	⊜	⊜
Ignition	⊖	○	⊖	⊖	⊜	⊜	⊜	⊜
Auto. trans.	⊖	⊜	⊜	○	⊜	⊜	⊜	*
Man. trans.	⊖	⊜	⊜	⊜	⊜	⊜	⊜	*
Clutch	◒	○	⊖	⊜	⊜	⊜	⊜	*
Electrical	◒	◒	○	○	⊖	⊖	⊜	⊜
A/C	◒	◒	⊖	⊜	⊖	⊖	⊜	*
Suspension	⊖	⊖	⊖	⊖	⊜	⊜	⊜	⊜
Brakes	◒	●	◒	○	⊖	⊜	⊜	⊜
Exhaust	●	●	●	●	⊜	⊜	⊜	⊜
Body rust	○	⊖	⊖	⊖	⊜	⊜	⊜	⊜
Paint/trim	○	○	○	⊖	⊖	⊖	⊖	⊜
Integrity	○	○	⊖	○	⊖	○	⊖	⊜
Hardware	○	○	○	⊖	⊖	⊖	⊖	⊜

Volkswagen Fox

TROUBLE SPOTS	87	88	89	90	91	92	93	94
Engine	Insufficient data	○	○	Insufficient data	Insufficient data	Insufficient data	Insufficient data	
Cooling		●	◒					
Fuel		○	⊖					
Ignition		⊖	○					
Auto. trans.								
Man. trans.		⊖	⊖					
Clutch		◒	○					
Electrical		●	●					
A/C		◒	*					
Suspension		◒	○					
Brakes		●	●					
Exhaust		●	◒					
Body rust		○	⊖					
Paint/trim		●	○					
Integrity		◒	◒					
Hardware		◒	●					

Volkswagen Golf, GTI, Golf III 4

TROUBLE SPOTS	87	88	89	90	91	92	93	94
Engine	○	◒	○	Insufficient data	Insufficient data	Insufficient data	Insufficient data	Insufficient data
Cooling	●	●	●					
Fuel	○	◒	◒					
Ignition	⊖	○	○					
Auto. trans.	*	*	*					
Man. trans.	⊖	⊖	⊜					
Clutch	○	○	○					
Electrical	●	●	●					
A/C	◒	●	○					
Suspension	◒	◒	◒					
Brakes	◒	●	●					
Exhaust	●	●	●					
Body rust	⊖	○	○					
Paint/trim	○	○	○					
Integrity	●	●	●					
Hardware	●	●	●					

Volkswagen Jetta, Jetta III 4

Trouble spots	87	88	89	90	91	92	93	94
Engine	○	○	⊖	○	○	○	Insufficient data	⊜
Cooling	●	●	●	●	○	◒	Insufficient data	⊜
Fuel	◒	◒	◒	◒	◒	◒	Insufficient data	⊜
Ignition	⊖	○	⊖	○	○	⊖	Insufficient data	⊜
Auto. trans.	⊖	◒	*	*	*	*	Insufficient data	*
Man. trans.	○	⊖	⊖	⊖	⊖	*	Insufficient data	*
Clutch	◒	◒	○	⊖	⊖	*	Insufficient data	*
Electrical	●	●	●	●	●	●	Insufficient data	⊖
A/C	●	◒	○	○	○	⊖	Insufficient data	⊜
Suspension	◒	○	○	◒	○	⊖	Insufficient data	⊜
Brakes	◒	◒	◒	◒	○	○	Insufficient data	⊜
Exhaust	●	●	◒	○	⊖	⊜	Insufficient data	⊜
Body rust	○	○	⊖	⊖	○	⊜	Insufficient data	⊜
Paint/trim	○	○	○	○	◒	◒	Insufficient data	⊜
Integrity	●	●	◒	◒	●	◒	Insufficient data	⊖
Hardware	●	●	●	●	●	●	Insufficient data	◒

Volkswagen Passat

Trouble spots	87	88	89	90	91	92	93	94
Engine				◒	⊖	Insufficient data	⊜	Insufficient data
Cooling				○	◒	Insufficient data	⊜	Insufficient data
Fuel				○	○	Insufficient data	⊖	Insufficient data
Ignition				○	⊖	Insufficient data	⊖	Insufficient data
Auto. trans.				●	*	Insufficient data	*	Insufficient data
Man. trans.				*	*	Insufficient data	*	Insufficient data
Clutch				*	*	Insufficient data	*	Insufficient data
Electrical				●	●	Insufficient data	●	Insufficient data
A/C				◒	⊖	Insufficient data	⊖	Insufficient data
Suspension				◒	○	Insufficient data	○	Insufficient data
Brakes				◒	◒	Insufficient data	⊜	Insufficient data
Exhaust				○	⊖	Insufficient data	⊜	Insufficient data
Body rust				⊖	⊜	Insufficient data	⊜	Insufficient data
Paint/trim				⊖	⊖	Insufficient data	○	Insufficient data
Integrity				◒	○	Insufficient data	◒	Insufficient data
Hardware				●	●	Insufficient data	●	Insufficient data

Volvo 240 Series

Trouble spots	87	88	89	90	91	92	93	94
Engine	○	⊖	⊖	⊜	⊜	⊜	⊜	
Cooling	◒	◒	○	⊜	○	○	⊜	
Fuel	○	⊖	○	○	○	⊖	⊖	
Ignition	⊖	⊖	⊖	⊖	⊖	⊜	⊜	
Auto. trans.	⊖	⊖	⊖	⊖	⊜	⊜	⊜	
Man. trans.	⊖	*	*	*	*	*	*	
Clutch	◒	*	*	*	*	*	*	
Electrical	◒	●	●	◒	◒	◒	●	
A/C	●	●	◒	⊖	⊖	⊖	⊖	
Suspension	○	⊖	⊖	⊜	⊖	○	⊜	
Brakes	●	●	●	●	●	●	⊖	
Exhaust	◒	◒	○	⊖	○	⊖	⊜	
Body rust	⊖	⊖	⊜	⊜	⊜	⊜	⊜	
Paint/trim	○	⊖	⊜	⊖	○	⊖	⊜	
Integrity	○	○	⊖	⊖	⊖	○	⊖	
Hardware	○	○	○	○	○	◒	○	

Volvo 740 Series

Trouble spots	87	88	89	90	91	92	93	94
Engine	○	○	○	⊖	⊜	⊜		
Cooling	◒	○	○	⊖	○	○		
Fuel	⊖	⊖	○	○	⊖	⊜		
Ignition	⊖	⊖	⊖	⊖	⊖	⊜		
Auto. trans.	⊖	⊖	⊖	⊖	⊜	⊜		
Man. trans.	*	*	*	*	*			
Clutch	*	*	*	*	*			
Electrical	◒	●	●	◒	◒	◒		
A/C	◒	●	●	⊖	⊖	⊖		
Suspension	⊖	○	○	⊖	⊖	⊜		
Brakes	●	●	●	●	◒	⊖		
Exhaust	◒	○	◒	○	⊖	⊖		
Body rust	⊜	⊖	⊜	⊜	⊜	⊜		
Paint/trim	⊖	⊖	⊖	⊖	⊖	⊖		
Integrity	○	◒	○	○	⊖	⊜		
Hardware	◒	●	●	◒	◒	○		

Volvo 760 Series

Trouble spots	87	88	89	90	91	92	93	94
Engine	◒	○	○	○				
Cooling	●	◒	○	⊖				
Fuel	○	⊜	⊖	⊜				
Ignition	⊖	⊜	⊜	⊖				
Auto. trans.	⊜	⊜	⊜	⊜				
Man. trans.								
Clutch								
Electrical	●	◒	●	◒				
A/C	●	●	◒	⊖				
Suspension	◒	○	○	⊖				
Brakes	●	●	●	●				
Exhaust	◒	○	○	⊖				
Body rust	⊜	⊖	⊜	⊜				
Paint/trim	⊖	○	⊜	⊜				
Integrity	◒	◒	⊖	⊖				
Hardware	●	●	●	●				

Volvo 850 Series

Trouble spots	87	88	89	90	91	92	93	94
Engine							⊜	⊜
Cooling							⊜	⊜
Fuel							⊜	⊜
Ignition							⊜	⊜
Auto. trans.							⊜	⊜
Man. trans.							⊜	*
Clutch							⊖	*
Electrical							○	⊖
A/C							⊖	⊖
Suspension							⊖	⊜
Brakes							⊜	⊜
Exhaust							⊜	⊜
Body rust							⊜	⊜
Paint/trim							⊜	⊖
Integrity							⊖	⊖
Hardware							○	⊖

Volvo 940 Series

Trouble spots	87	88	89	90	91	92	93	94
Engine					⊜	⊜	⊜	⊜
Cooling					○	○	⊜	⊜
Fuel					⊜	⊖	⊖	⊜
Ignition					⊜	⊜	⊖	⊜
Auto. trans.					⊜	⊜	⊖	⊜
Man. trans.								
Clutch								
Electrical					○	○	○	⊖
A/C					○	⊖	⊖	⊜
Suspension					⊖	⊖	⊜	⊜
Brakes					⊖	○	⊖	⊜
Exhaust					⊜	⊜	⊜	⊜
Body rust					⊜	⊜	⊜	⊜
Paint/trim					⊜	⊖	⊖	⊜
Integrity					○	⊖	○	⊖
Hardware					◒	○	⊖	⊖

Volvo 960 Series

Trouble spots	87	88	89	90	91	92	93	94
Engine						Insufficient data	⊜	Insufficient data
Cooling						Insufficient data	⊜	Insufficient data
Fuel						Insufficient data	⊖	Insufficient data
Ignition						Insufficient data	⊜	Insufficient data
Auto. trans.						Insufficient data	⊜	Insufficient data
Man. trans.						Insufficient data		Insufficient data
Clutch						Insufficient data		Insufficient data
Electrical						Insufficient data	○	Insufficient data
A/C						Insufficient data	⊜	Insufficient data
Suspension						Insufficient data	⊖	Insufficient data
Brakes						Insufficient data	⊖	Insufficient data
Exhaust						Insufficient data	⊜	Insufficient data
Body rust						Insufficient data	⊜	Insufficient data
Paint/trim						Insufficient data	⊜	Insufficient data
Integrity						Insufficient data	⊖	Insufficient data
Hardware						Insufficient data	○	Insufficient data

⊜ ⊖ ○ ◒ ●
Few ← **Problems** → Many

* Insufficient data

Auto insurance

The cost of insurance is one of the biggest expenses of owning a car.

The choices

An auto policy consists of several types of insurance. Some are mandatory and some are optional, depending on state laws.

Liability (bodily injury and property damage). Most states require liability coverage, which is commonly split into two parts: bodily injury and property damage.

Bodily-injury liability compensates victims of accidents caused by you or someone who drives your car. It can be "single limit" or "split limit." Single-limit coverage pays a specified amount per accident, no matter how many people are involved. CONSUMER REPORTS recommends split-limit coverage, which pays up to a certain amount to each person injured in an accident. Property-damage liability covers damage to another person's property.

The minimum coverage limits require by most states are inadequate for individuals with assets to protect. CONSUMER REPORTS recommends buying bodily-injury coverage of at least $100,000 per person and $300,000 per accident, and property-damage coverage of at least $50,000.

Uninsured motorist coverage, mandatory in some states, insures you, your family, and your passengers for accidents caused by uninsured or hit-and-run drivers. Most policies cover only bodily injury; some pay for damage to your car as well. It's a good idea to buy amounts equal to your bodily-injury and property-damage coverage.

Underinsured motorist coverage pays accident-related expenses that exceed the other driver's coverage.

Medical-payments insurance. This coverage is what pays your medical bills and those of your passengers who are injured. It can be purchased without a deductible, unlike typical health insurance. If you have good health coverage, however, you probably don't need it. In addition to covering medical expenses and some funeral bills, this coverage reimburses for lost wages and incidental expenses.

Collision coverage pays for damage to your car. The law doesn't require it, but you'll probably have to buy it if you have a car loan or lease. Collision coverage usually has a deductible of at least $100 per accident. CONSUMER REPORTS recommends choosing the highest deductible you can afford.

Comprehensive coverage is usually required by lenders, too. It covers damage to your car from events other than crashes—fire, vandalism, theft, and falling trees, for example.

Car-rental and towing coverage. Insurance that pays for a rental car while yours is laid up or that covers towing after an accident doesn't cost much. But you may not need it if your repair shop gives loaners, or if you have towing through an auto club.

Keeping costs down

You can keep insurance costs under control by choosing an appropriate car, one that insurers consider less risky. An insurance agent can tell you which cars are more or less expensive to insure. Insurers maintain that your age, sex, and where you live are factors that determine the likelihood of your being involved in an accident and use them to determine your auto premium. You can do a number of things to reduce the cost of your auto insurance.

- Drive safely. Accidents can drive up

your premium. Typically, you will pay an accident surcharge for three years after the incident.

■ Increase the deductible. Choosing a $500 or even $1000 deductible can substantially lower collision and comprehensive premiums.

■ Drop collision coverage after four or five years, or as soon as the collision premium adds up to 10 percent of the car's market value.

■ Take a defensive-driving course for an insurance discount.

■ Buy auto and homeowners insurance from the same company to get a multi-policy discount.

■ Insure more than one car on the same policy for a multi-car discount.

■ Buy a car with air bags, built-in antitheft devices, and antilock brakes for applicable discounts.

■ Insure teen-agers on the family policy. It's cheaper than getting separate policies under their own names.

■ Pay your premium in full, instead of by installments.

Buying advice

In most states, you can save substantial money by price-shopping. Be sure to ask each company to quote rates for comparable coverage.

Tires

Many brands of tires crowd the market, but most are made by a few corporate giants—Bridgestone, Continental, Goodyear, Michelin, Pirelli, and Sumitomo—and the companies they control. Each brand offers a wide range of price lines, so there may be little resemblance among various tires bearing the same name.

The choices

Virtually all tires sold these days are radials, which are far better than the old-fashioned bias-ply tires. They fall into three loosely defined and overlapping groups. The three most important groups are:

All-season tires. They're standard tires on most family sedans. This type tends to perform reasonably well under a variety of driving conditions—dry, wet, and snow—without excelling in any one. Price: $30 and up.

Performance tires. They're wider than all-season tires and their shallower tread puts more rubber on the road. They provide better traction than other types of tires on wet and dry roads. Those with an all-weather design provide good traction in snow, too. Unlike previous generations of performance tires, current models do not exact a significant penalty in ride, noise, or fuel-economy. Prices start about $70.

Touring tires. An in-between designation, touring tires are usually premium all-season tires with some characteristics of performance tires.

Tire information

The U.S. Department of Transportation requires tire makers to provide information on the sidewall of every tire. Here's how to decipher the codes:

Tire size and aspect ratio. Width, height of the sidewall, and wheel diameter are indicated on the tire by a number such as: P205/60R15 90H. The "P" (if present) indicates a passenger-car tire. The "205" is the nominal width of the tire's cross-section in millimeters. The "60" indicates the height of the sidewall—actually, the ratio of the sidewall's height to the tire's cross-section width. The "R" stands for radial. The "15" is the diameter, in inches, of the metal wheel rim the tire fits.

Load index and speed rating. The load index is a code—the "90" noted in the example above—indicating the maximum weight the tire can carry at its maximum rated speed. The speed symbol is typically a letter code. That indicates the maximum speed that the tire can safely sustain. S stands for 112 mph; T, for 118; U, for 124; H, for 130; V, for 149; Z, for 149+. Performance tires have a speed rating of H or higher.

Tread-wear rating. Under conditions specified by the Government tire makers must test and rate the tread life of their tires. The index won't tell you how long the tire will last on your car—driving conditions vary too much. But a tire with an index of 200 should wear out about twice as quickly as one with an index of 400. (The tread wear tests are run by the manufacturers without outside verification, so there's some question about accuracy. Still, it's the only available guide to tread wear.)

Traction and temperature. Tires are also graded for their ability to stop on wet pavement and to resist heat build-up under Government-specified conditions. Grades range from A (highest) to C (lowest). The tests aren't too demanding; most tires score A or B.

Date of manufacture. Every passenger tire also carries a DOT number—for example, DOT B9PA B55X 104. The last three digits indicate the date of manufacture. Here, "104" means the 10th week of 1994. Even while sitting on a shelf, tires deteriorate with age. Look for a tire made within the past year when you shop.

Buying advice

Among the performance tires in our last test, the *Dunlop D60 A2* came out on top. It scored at or near the top in every braking and cornering test without compromising the ride or noise level. We also deemed its handling the best of the lot. In size 205/60R15, it lists for $153, but in the stores we surveyed sold for $81, on average. We've seen it for as little as $59 by mail order.

To determine the size tire you need, check the car owner's manual. No matter what type of tires came with your car, we recommend all-weather performance tires as a replacement. They give even an ordinary family sedan better braking and cornering performance with only a small penalty in noise and fuel-economy.

Save ultrahigh performance tires for sports cars. They grip the road better than standard high performance tires, but they have poor traction in snow, provide a relatively harsh ride, and wear more quickly.

A tire's list price means little. Many dealers offer sizable discounts, and special promotions may further reduce the price. Discounted tires are also available by mail.

PRODUCT RECALLS

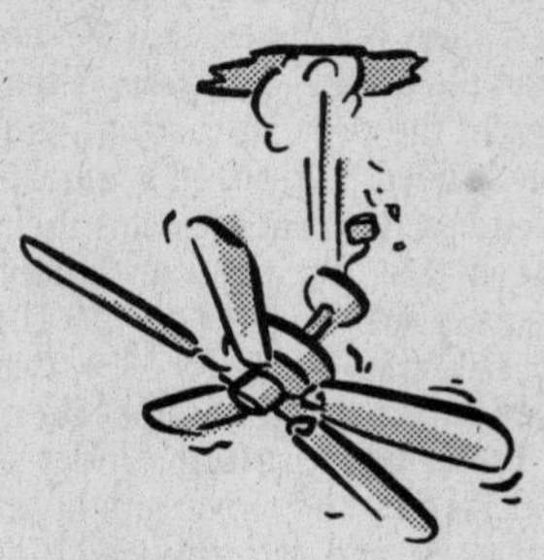

Products ranging from child safety seats to chain saws are recalled when there are safety defects. Various Federal agencies—the Consumer Product Safety Commission, the National Highway Traffic Safety Administration, the U.S. Coast Guard, and the Food and Drug administration—monitor consumer complaints and injuries and, when there's a problem, issue a recall.

However, the odds of your hearing about an unsafe product are slim. Manufacturers are reluctant to issue a recall in the first place because they can be costly. And getting the word out to consumers can be haphazard.

A selection of the most far-reaching recalls are published monthly in CONSUMER REPORTS. The following pages gather together a year's worth of recalls published in the November 1994 through October 1995 issues of CONSUMER REPORTS. For the latest information, see the current issue of the magazine.

If you wish to report an unsafe product or get recall information, call the CPSC's hotline, 800 638-2772.

Recall notices about your automobile can be obtained from a new-car dealer or by calling the NHTSA hotline at 800 424-9393. The FDA runs a seafood hotline: 800 332-4010; other questions about food and drugs are handled by the FDA's Office of Consumer Affairs, 301 443-3170.

You can better assure yourself of getting a recall notice by returning warranty cards that come with many products. That way, the manufacturer will know where to contact you. If you're concerned about privacy, give just your name and address. You're not obligated to answer questions asked for marketing purposes.

Children's products

Dakin Big Top Playmates soft fabric toys

Pom-poms could come off and choke child.

Products: 66,500 animal toys, sold 2/94-4/95, including bear, bunny, and elephant soft fabric dolls (item no. 40319); finger puppets (item 40320); bottle-hugging dolls (item 40321); dolls attached to musical mobile (item 40324); ring-shaped rattles with soft plush animal head and feet (item 40325); and crib attachments (item 40335). Toys have pink, yellow, and blue trim and ½-inch pom-poms. Tag includes item no., product name, and "THE FRASER COLLECTION, DAKIN, INC. San Francisco, CA, Product of China." Mobile sold for $50; other toys, $5-$15.

What to do: Cut off and discard pom-poms.

Disney Play 'N Pop activity toy

Small parts could come off and choke child.

Products: 200,000 toys, model no. 66004, sold in '94 for $13. Toy, intended for children ages 9 to 36 months, has 5 brightly colored Disney pop-up figures—Baby Mickey Mouse, Donald Duck, Goofy, Minnie Mouse, and Pluto—that are activated by manipulating panel controls. One control, a purple key shaped like Mickey Mouse's head, can break off, posing small-parts hazard. Only Play 'N Pop toys made in China are subject to recall. Country of origin is molded onto bottom of toy.

What to do: Return toy to manufacturer for refund. Mail to Arcotoys, Attention: Nancy Nelson, 15930 East Valley Blvd., City of Industry, Calif. 91744. Consumers will also receive postage reimbursement and discount coupon toward purchase of another Arcotoys product.

Dolphin Baby Float child flotation device

If water leaks into hollow center of float's inner tube, device could tip and drown child.

Products: 18,000 dolphin-shaped flotation devices, made by Torpedo, Inc., and sold 2/93-12/94 for $70-$90. White plastic dolphin measures 37 inches long, 28 inches wide, and 9 inches high. Device has detachable red umbrella and blue nylon seat, adjustable for babies from six months to two years. Products made since 1/95 have reinforced walls and are not recalled.

What to do: Call 800 639-0361 for replacement float.

El Rancho/Seffi wooden bunk beds

Space between mattress frame and guard rail could trap child's head and strangle child.

Products: 10,000 to 14,000 pine bunk beds, with twin-sized upper and lower births, sold 5/90-10/12/94 for $200. Label on inside frame of bottom bunk identifies El Rancho or Seffi as manufacturer.

What to do: Call 800 622-7171 for replacement guard rail that should eliminate risk of head entrapment by closing up gap.

Fisher-Price Baseball Training Center

Batteries could overheat and explode.

Products: 100,000 toys, model 2875, sold 2/15/95-7/95 for $35. Baseball Training Center has blue plastic base and white mesh net attached to large semicircle by yellow fabric. Toy measures 3 feet high, 3 feet wide, and 15 inches deep, and comes with brown plastic bat and five white plastic baseballs. Toy is intended for children three and older; child hits or throws baseballs into large net, and machine in base returns balls. Toys with round, baseball-sized fluorescent-orange sticker on end panel have been modified and aren't affected.

What to do: Call 800 355-8882 for repair kit.

Gerber infant and toddler sandals sold at Kmart stores

Buckle could come off strap and choke child.

Products: 170,000 pairs of sandals, made by Angeletts of California, licensed under Gerber name and sold in '95. Infant sandals are white (model 55101) or brown (model 55103) and sold for $5. Toddler sandals are white (model 59006), brown (model 59401), or blue denim (model 59682), and sold for $9. "Gerber" appears on insole, and model no. is on inside of strap.

What to do: Return sandals to Kmart for refund.

Gerber NUK othodontic pacifier

Could come apart and choke child.

Products: 10 million pacifiers sold singly or in multipacks for $1.29 to $4.99. "NUK" is on mouth shield. Date code on back of package ranges from 070193 (7/1/93) to 063094 (6/30/94). Package reads, in part: "Nipple made in Germany. Plastic parts molded and unit assembled in USA. Printed in USA. Distributed by Gerber Products Company." Pacifiers with "NEW" on front of packaging are not being recalled. Nor are pacifiers distributed by hospitals.

What to do: Call 800 443-7237 for replacement pacifier. Gerber will also replace any NUK pacifier that lacks packaging.

"Hey Diddle Diddle" nursery-rhyme book published by Farrar, Straus, and Giroux

Triangular-shaped rattle that comes with book could separate into small parts that pose choking hazard to children.

Products: 52,000 books, by James Marshall, sold 8-12/94 for $6. Book consists of 10 heavy cardboard pages and measures 6 inches by 5¼ inches. Rattle is built into spine of book. Cover includes title, author, and depicts cow jumping over crescent moon. Back of book reads: "*** A RATTLE BOARD BOOK Farrar Straus Giroux New York."

What to do: Return book to store for refund. Consumers who received book from Book of the Month Club will be notified directly about refund.

Home and Roam and Baby Express portable crib/playpens

If top rails are not fully locked in place, product may appear to be properly set up, but crib could collapse and strangle child.

Products: 100,000 crib/playpens sold '92-94 for $60 to $130. Product came in variety of colors and fabrics and in three sizes: 40x40 inches, 40x28 inches, and 41x31 inches. "Home and Roam" or "Baby Express" and "Baby Trend" appear on 2 of 4 top rails. The recall affects all Home and Roam and Baby Express crib playpens, regardless of purchase date.

What to do: Call 800 234-1879 for free redesigned top-rail lock and installation instructions.

Jaguar bicycle helmet

Failed manufacturer's head-impact test, and may not prevent injuries from a fall.

Products: 25,000 helmets, model 3060, made by Protective Technologies International and sold at Toys 'R' Us and Target stores 9/94-1/95 for $23-$25. White plastic helmet has 20 vent holes on front, top, and sides, white front visor, and black head and chin straps. Helmet is decorated with bright orange and yellow decals. Square blue "PTI" label appears on back. PTI helmets bearing '95 date code and "QC" sticker inside aren't being recalled.

What to do: Call 800 515-0074 for free replacement.

Kaleidoscope Art sets sold at Toys R Us stores

Although marked "non-toxic," crayons contain high lead levels. Chewing on crayons could poison children.

Products: 14,000 art sets, item no. 820, sold 1-8/94. Each set contains box of 8 crayons, 6 sheets of geometric shapes, and 6-inch kaleidoscope. Children are supposed to color geometric shapes and view them through kaleidoscope. Set is labeled for "Ages 4 & up."

What to do: Return set to Toys R Us store for refund.

Kenner Colorblaster 3-D spray art design toy

Toy uses pump to pressurize plastic cylinder. If toy is overpumped, pump handle and cap could fly off and injure user.

Products: 176,000 toys, model 14290.11, sold 8/94-1/95 for $27. Recall affects only toys with orange handle and purple cap.

What to do: Return toy to store for refund, or call 800 327-8264 for prepaid mailing label to return handle and cap to company.

Littlest Pet Shop toy tea set

Small, removable plastic animals on teapot and sugar bowl could choke child.

Products: 42,000 sets sold 7-11/94 for $10. Set, made of pink, blue, purple, and red plastic, is about 2/3 normal size and includes teapot with lid, serving tray, sugar bowl with lid, creamer, 4 cups, 4 saucers, and 4 spoons. Plastic animals on cups and creamer are permanently attached. Toy package is labelled, in part: "Littlest Pet Shop Tea Set featuring adorable Hangimal characters, No. 27310, 1994 Kid Dimension Inc., a subsidiary of Hasbro, Inc., Pawtucket, RI." Newer set without hazardous small parts has starburst label on package that reads: "Contains No Small Parts."

What to do: If child is less than 3 years old, return set to store for refund.

My Alphabet toy truck (sold door-to-door)

Small parts could come off and choke child.

Products: 82,000 trucks, style SHYE-AT-002, sold 8/93-6/94 for $5. Laquered wooden truck is 12 in. long, has red wheels and one or two nonremovable wooden peg men in front cab; 30 wooden blocks with picture on one side and corresponding letter on other side are on truck bed. "MADE IN CHINA" sticker appears on underside of toy.

What to do: Call 800 775-1975 for postage-paid envelope in which to return truck for $5 refund.

Okla Homer Smith cribs

Missing or loose siderail slats could allow child's head to become entrapped. That poses strangulation hazard.

Products: 278,000 cribs made 4/92-12/93 and sold for $100. Recalled models include nos. 30562, 80005, 80007, 80010, 80012, 80023, 80029, 80035, 80038, 80054, 80056, 80057, 80068, and 80090. Model no. and date of manufacture appear on bottom of headboard below mattress.

What to do: Check drop siderail to see if slats are in place and secure. If not, discontinue use and call 800 261-3440 for repair kit and installation instructions.

Paci-Faces pacifiers

Nipple could come off and choke child.

Products: 35,000 pacifiers sold 1/94-6/94 for $3. Pacifier comes in 3 styles: Mustache pacifier, model 00001, resembles black handlebar mustache with red lip below; Lip pacifier, model 00002, and Smile pacifier, model 00003, have two large lips and two rows of teeth. Pacifiers are 2½ inches wide, 1½ inches long, and have small air hole on either side of beige rubber nipple. Label on back of shield reads, in part: "MADE IN CHINA © 1986 Paci-Face, Inc. Patent pending." Pacifiers whose packaging bears date code of 5/1/95 or later are not being recalled.

What to do: Return pacifier to store for refund.

Playskool 1-2-3 Swing

In infant mode, restraint shield on front of swing may not lock securely. Child could fall out.

Products: 123,000 swings sold 3/95-5/95 for $25. Plastic swing has blue seat, yellow chair back, red T-shaped restraint, green trim, and yellow ropes.

What to do: Return swing to store for refund.

"Professor Wacko's Exothermic Exuberance" chemistry set

Kits lack adequate warnings and directions for safe use.

Products: 5100 chemistry sets, made by Wild Goose Co. of Salt Lake City, Utah, and distributed by Carson-Dellosa Publishing of Greensboro, N.C., sold 9/93-2/94 for $6. Chemistry set, intended for children ages 10 and older, was sold at school supply stores and Natural Wonders stores. Each set contains two 2-oz. bottles of glycerine and potassium permanganate. Bottles are identical, except for labels and contents. If bottle caps are switched, allowing even small amounts of chemicals to mix, fire may result.

What to do: For refund, return chemistry set to store or contact manufacturer at 800 373-1498.

Quick N' Easy Micro-Bake Cake Set for Kids

May pose fire hazard.

Products: 168,000 covered baking chambers, designed to be inserted in microwave oven, sold 8/94-11/6/94 for $20. Cake-baking set, marketed to children ages 8 and older, includes white plastic baking chamber that holds small metal cake pan. Recall affects all models made before 11/7/94.

What to do: Call 800 514-8697 for help in identifying recalled product and for free replacement.

Rolling Ball Rattle Teether

Handle poses choking hazard.

Products: 21,200 rattle-teethers, models 520-Z and 520-E, sold 4-12/94 for $2. Flower-shaped rattle has blue turning petals and round, rotating pink center. Base and handle are yellow. Turquoise rubber teething ring at base of handle also moves. Rubber ring is flexible enough to allow rattle handle to fit into child's throat. Rattle is 6½ in. long and comes in cardboard blister package. Label on package reads, in part: "NURSERY NEEDS Rolling Ball Rattle-Teether, No. 520-Z [No. 520-E]...SANITOY ®, INC...Made in China."

What to do: Return product to store for refund. For information, call Sanitoy Inc. at 800 786-8595.

Rubbermaid Li'l Roughneck Humphrey the Dinosaur and Bubbles the Whale clothes hampers

If child crawls inside hamper, head could get lodged in whale's tail or dinosaur's head.

Products: 150,000 hampers sold in '93 for $30. Colored-plastic hampers measure 30 inches long and 19 inches high and have removable lid.

What to do: Call Rubbermaid at 800 786-5588 for shipping carton to return hamper to company for refund.

6-inch Barney dinosaur doll with red and white scarf and red Santa hat

Pom-pom could come off hat and choke child.

Products: 594,000 dolls sold during '93 holiday season as part of Barney Holiday Gift Pack, which also included videotape.

What to do: Remove pom-pom before letting child play with doll.

Stuffed toy bears distributed as premiums or prizes by traveling carnivals

Bears' eyes and nose could come off and choke child.

Products: 4000 stuffed toys distributed 6-8/94 throughout the U.S. by Brass Show and Hildebrand Show, both based in Fla., and Crabtree Show, based in Tex. Three different toys, all with sewn-on "MADE IN CHINA" labels, are being recalled: white bear; black and white panda; and white bear with 2 red ears, 2 blue paws, and 2 neon-yellow paws. White bear and panda have red sweater with raised lettering that says "I ♥ You." All bears measure 11 inches tall from permanent sitting position and have black plastic nose and black/brown eyes.

What to do: Call 800 528-8259 for postage-paid envelope to exchange bear for similar item.

The First Years 3-in-1 booster seat

May not attach securely to full-sized chair. Seat could fall off and injure child.

Products: 41,000 booster seats, model 4200, sold 3/95-5/95. Plastic seats are 14 inches high and 12 inches deep. Seat and seatback are teal; arms and removable tray are white. White mesh belts can be attached to bottom of seat to restrain child and to secure seat to adult chair. Device folds for carrying; handle is molded into seatback. Belts may have improperly threaded buckles, or one of the two belts may be missing.

What to do: Call 800 533-6708 for information on how to repair belts. Not affected: newer 3-in-1 booster seats, which have 4-piece belt sets with properly threaded buckles; model number 4200C appears on box.

Tornado and Power tricycles made by Radio Flyer

Front fork may break and allow child to fall.

Products: 24,975 tricycles. Tornado tricycles were sold through warehouse clubs in Western U.S. 8/1/94-12/31/95 for $30; frame is blue with light-blue trim. Power tricycles were sold nationwide 8/1/94-6/95 for $40; frame is green with red trim, purple with pink trim, or blue with light-blue trim. Power tricycles have Radio Flyer decal on frame. On both models, front wheel measures about 12 inches in diameter.

What to do: If 1½-inch washer between front fork and tricycle frame is same color as frame, return tricycle to store for exchange or refund, or call manufacturer at 800 621-7613 for replacement piece. Tricycles with black 1½-inch washer are not being recalled.

TQ8+ Professional Tire Formula for model racing cars

Contains methyl salicylate, a toxin, but lacks child-resistant packaging required by Federal law.

Products: 25,000 4- and 8-fluid-ounce cans sold at hobby supply stores 11/90-6/95 for approximately $6.75. Product is used on tires of model racing cars to provide traction.

What to do: Return unused portion of product to manufacturer for replacement and gift of Pro Diff Lube, also for model cars. Mail to: R.C. Products Inc., 6N258 Acacia Lane, P.O. Box 405, Medinah, Ill. 60157. For information call 708 980-4863 or fax company at 708 980-5420.

Vinyl squeeze toys in various shapes

Small button-shaped squeak mechanism can come off toy and choke child.

Products: 57,000 toys sold 4/92-4/94 for $2. Toys come in numerous shapes including balls, Santa Claus, shoe, foot, and 15 animals. Each toy has "Malaysia" or "Made in Malaysia" embossed near white-plastic squeaker. Clear-plastic package has large yellow label with red lettering that reads, in part: "STA VINYL TOY *** SQUEEZE TOYS *** MADE IN MALAYSIA." Label also has girl's face on one side and crawling baby on other.

What to do: Return toy to store for refund. For information, call distributor, The Bazaar Inc., at 708 583-1800.

Welsh Juvenile Products' Jenny Lind cribs

Missing or loose siderail spindles could allow child's head to become entrapped.

Products: 5000-7000 Jenny Lind cribs, model 6982, bearing lot nos. 8021, 8024, 8025, 8052, 8053, 8055, 8056, 8070; and model 6983, bearing lot nos. 8022, 8023, 8026, 8027, 8031, and 8032. Model and lot information appear on headboard. Cribs were sold 7/94-1/95 for $100 in Kmart stores.

What to do: Return crib to Kmart for refund. Or call manufacturer at 800 648-4505 for replacement siderail.

Wooden bunk beds (various brands)

Openings in top bunk can entrap child's head, posing risk of strangulation.

Products: 320,000 beds distributed by numerous companies since early '80s and sold through furniture and specialty stores. Affected models may not meet voluntary industry standard requiring that spaces be less than 3½ inches wide between guardrail and bed frame, and in headboard and footboard of top bunk. Danger is greatest for children under age 6. Beds were manufactured or imported by:

- Backwoods Design, models GII and GIIC, sold 10/94-11/94 in Ore. and Wash. Company logo is burned into guardrail. Company is out of business.

• Brill Furniture, models 648 (sold '94), 880 (sold '91-94), and 2048 (sold '90-94). All were sold in Central and Eastern U.S. Manufacturer's name is stamped on inside rail on top, head end of bed. (Call 616 843-2430.)
• Dover Furniture, models 501 and 550, sold nationwide '92-94. (Call 800 433-3485.)
• Fine Pine, models 1010, 1020, 1060, 1100, 1130, sold nationwide '90-94. (Call 205 734-7588.)
• H&H Furniture, 5000 Series, sold '81-94 in Conn., Fla., Kan., Me., Md., Mass., Mich., Neb., N.H., N.J., N.M., N.Y., N.C., Ohio, Okla., Pa., Tenn., Tex., Va., and W. Va. Recalled beds are from Casual Crates Collection. Bed ends are 3½-inch pine boards. Permanently attached ladder and steps are made of 1½ x 1½-inch. pine fastened with hex-head lag bolts. (Call 800 789-3132.)
• Houston Wood, Stackable model, only with nonadjustable guard rail, sold '88-92. (Call 205 221-0584.)
• Lexington Furniture, models 194-187c, 224-187c, 730-187c, and 950-187c, sold nationwide early '80s-'93. Beds were part of larger furniture arrangement. (Call 800 461-8895.)
• Mafco Inc., models T/18, T/19, and T/28, distributed 1/94-11/94 out of Tex. "Hecho en Mexico" is stamped on inside of wood rails or under headboard. (Call 713 643-7676.).
• Sumter Cabinet Co., model 1880, sold nationwide '92-94. Beds are solid oak in light brown finish. (Call 803 778-5444.)
• Tech Designs, model 200 Loft, sold early '80s-88. (Call 203 336-2801.)
• Woodcrest Sales, various models sold nationwide '83-94. Model 2602 converts to twin beds; WW2000 is shaped like wagon wheel with spindle spokes; PB300 and PB400 are poster beds with 3-inch spindles on arched frame; BK1000 has built-in 8-inch bookcase; BK2000 has hourglass-shaped vertical boards on scalloped frame and 10-inch built-in bookcase (Call 800 878 4948).
All models have attached ladder.

What to do: Call company or store for instructions. For help in identifying maker, ask retailer or call U.S. Consumer Product Safety Commission at 800 638-2772.

Wooden Fudge Pop and Lolly Pop rattles

Child could choke on handle.

Products: 1993 wooden rattles, in varying shades from dark brown to near white, sold for $14 at arts and crafts galleries, museums, and gift shops, including the Smithsonian Museum Shop and An American Craftsman. Fudge Pop resembles chocolate-coated vanilla ice-cream bar. Bite indentation near top of pop reveals "vanilla ice cream" inside. Rattle is 7¾ inches long and 2 inches wide, and is glued to 3½-inch handle. Lolly Pop, 3 inches in diameter, is glued to 4-inch handle. Both types have 1¼-inch wooden ball glued to end of handle.

What to do: Return rattle to store for refund.

Household products

Adult-sized bean-bag chairs

If zipper is undone, child could inhale small foam pellets and suffocate.

Products: 2.5 million chairs sold '90-94 for $20 at Wal-Mart, Kmart, Target, Lillian Vernon, and other outlets. Chairs came in various colors, patterns, and fabrics. "Base Line Design" appears on label.

What to do: Call 800 649-8558 to have chair modified.

Amana and Sears Kenmore side-by-side refrigerators

Screw on light cover could contact hidden electrical wire and, if touched, cause electric shock.

Products: 5000 refrigerators, including various models, made 4/93-9/8/94 for $1200 to $2200. Affected units bear serial no. 9304000000 to 9409156208. Nos. run sequentially and are located on plate in fresh-food compartment.

What to do: Call 800 262-6226 for kit with replacement screw.

Beacon Hill children's wooden lamps sold at Hills department stores

Defect in socket could cause electrical short, resulting in fire or shock hazard.

Products: 6500 lamps, with base in shape of dinosaur, frog, airplane, or rocking horse, sold '93-94 for less than $15. Lamp is 16 inches high with white and red striped shade, and has green, red, and yellow painted wooden base. Lamp carton is marked SKU #8000 (for dinosaur) or SKU #8001 (for frog, airplane, and rocking horse).

What to do: Return lamp to store for refund.

Bemis Waterwick whole-house humidifiers

Electrical switches could overheat and cause fire.

Products: 400,000 whole-house humidifiers, with 10- to 12-gallon capacity, sold at hardware stores and home centers in U.S. and Canada since '90. Humidifiers come in various colors and styles. Control panel in upper right corner of grill has two knobs and is labelled, in part: "BEMIS WATERWICK." Two 2.6-gallon or larger white water bottles fit inside humidifier's cabinet. Recalled units bear one of following model nos. on large white Underwriters Laboratories (UL) sticker on back of humidifier: 4261, 4261CN, 4262, 4273, 4362, 4363, 4363CN, 4371, 4963, 4971, 4973, 6964, 6964CN, 6974. Hazard exists if cleaning, descaling, or disinfecting solution is applied to electrical controls.

What to do: Phone 800 765-1122 for free pickup and repair. Company will include free two-stage Bemis Air-Care air filter with each repaired unit. Also, company will extend warranty for 12 months.

Black & Decker 10-inch miter saw

Defective cord poses shock hazard.

Products: 7500 saws, model no. 1710, type 1, sold 2/95 to mid-4/95. Recalled models have date codes 9501-9516 on underside of handle.

What to do: Check entire cord for nicks or cuts. If cord is damaged, return saw to store for replacement saw, or to Black & Decker service center for cord replacement.

Bonde TV cabinets sold at IKEA stores

Shelf could collapse under weight of 31- or 35-inch TV set.

Products: 1700 cabinets, model nos. 27371276, 17371205, and 57371208, sold 7/93-11/94 for about $360. Unit was sold unassembled in brown cardboard box labeled with Bonde name and model no. Cabinet measures 57 inches high, 42 inches wide, and 21 inches deep, and came in red-brown, ash, and beech finishes.

What to do: Call 800 455-8800 for in-home repair, exchange, replacement, or refund.

Brinkmann and COOK'N CA'JUN charcoal water smokers

Pose fire hazard if used over wooden deck or other flammable surface. Also, sharp edges on metal brackets holding water pan or grills could cause cuts.

Products: More than 1 million smokers sold before 1993. Exposed charcoal pan has hole that could allow coals to fall out. "Brinkmann" or "COOK'N CA'JUN" appears on top or body of smoker. (Later models, without exposed pan, aren't affected. Nor are Brinkmann Gourmet and COOK'N CA'JUN S-80 models.)

What to do: Call Brinkmann at 800 675-5301 for kit to close hole in pan and replace sharp brackets. Don't operate smoker on or near flammable surfaces even after hole is closed.

Dayton electric ceiling heater

Poses electric-shock and fire hazard.

Products: 661 heaters made by Fasco Consumer Products and sold at Grainger wholesale branch stores 1/93-8/94 for $55. Metal heater, which attaches to ceiling, is 10 in. in diameter, with wire mesh grill over heating element. Round metal nameplate in center of cover bears model no. 4E154. To see whether unit is involved, turn off power at circuit breaker and check data plate on upper inside of heater housing; recall applies to units with following date codes: A93, B93, C93, D93, E93, F93, G93, H93, J93, K93, L93, M93, A94, B94, C94, and D94.

What to do: Contact nearest Grainger store for replacement heater and have electrician install it. Return recalled heater to Fasco Consumer Products for refund of labor and freight charges. For information, call 800 915-9590.

Dualit-Plus 2- and 4-slice electronic toasters

Toaster could turn on by itself after interruption in electrical power, creating fire hazard.

Products: 2700 toasters, made in England by Dualit Ltd. and imported by Waring Products, sold mostly through Williams-Sonoma retail stores and catalogs from 10/93-9/94. Some were also sold at Waring Products' retail outlet in New Hartford, Conn. Two-slice toasters ($215) have model no. CTS2E/DOM and code no. 11EA36 on baseplate on bottom of unit. Four-slice machine ($299) has model no. CTS4E/DOM and code no. 11EA42. Recalled models also have serial nos. between 310 and 408 on baseplate. Dualit toasters without the letter "E" as fifth character of model no. aren't involved.

What to do: Call 800 831-3960 for instructions. Company will send package for return of toaster free of charge. Owner can have toaster repaired or get refund. Those who opt for repair will receive $25 Williams-Sonoma gift certificate.

Empire Style Metaline 600 Series porcelain door-knob set

Could break and cut hand.

Products: 8000 door-knob sets made by Gainsborough Hardware Ind. and sold 1/91-5/93 for $10. Knobs, in sets of 2, are white or ivory and have gold-colored oval backplate with rope design around edge. Number 178 is on underside of backplate.

What to do: Return knobs to store for refund or replacement.

Fab liquid Color-Plus laundry detergent in 50-ounce container

Contains high level of sodium hydroxide, which can irritate skin.

Products: 25,000 containers sold since 8/94 in Ark., Del., Ind., Ia., Kan., Ky., Md., Mo., Neb., N.J., N.Y., Ohio, Pa., Tenn., and W. Va., and possibly in Wash., D.C., Richmond, Va., Detroit, and Chicago. Recalled detergent has 8-digit date code beginning with 4213 in rectangular box at bottom center of back panel.

What to do: Return detergent to store for refund or exchange.

Fake-fur cardigan and pullover sweaters

Fabric is dangerously flammable.

Products: 907 sweaters sold 7/93-10/94 for $175-$200 at major retailers like Nordstrom, Bloomingdale's, Lord & Taylor, and Loehmann's. Sweaters were sold in four styles: # 7348 Spot cardigan in black and white; #7384X Puppy cardigan in black; #9047 Fur cardigan; and # 9048 Fur Popover pullover in black, ivory, steel blue, or pink. Sweaters came in sizes 1 (small to medium) and 2 (medium to large)Sewn-in neck label says "MICHAEL SIMON NEW YORK." Second neck label reads, in part: "88% Rayon/Rayonne 12% Nylon/Nylon Made in HONG KONG...." or "Made in CHINA... RN 73106."

What to do: Return sweater to store for refund.

Game Tracker Deluxe Safety Belt & Climbing Harness and Lifeline Safety Harness

Belt could break and allow hunter to fall from tree or tree stand.

Products: 92,500 Safety Belts & Climbing Harnesses, models GTDSB and 3020, and Lifeline Safety Harnesses, model 3040, sold '90-95 for $19-$21 in sporting-goods and archery stores. Belt-and-harness set consists of black 2-inch-wide nylon webbing, 5/16-inch-thick nylon cord, metal D-ring, and metal adjustment clasp. Model 3040 also has leg harness made of black nylon webbing.

What to do: For replacement harness and $3 for postage, send harness to Game Tracker, Attn: Product Safety Coordinator, 3476 Eastman Dr., Flushing, Mich. 48433. Include address and phone number.

Hewlitt-Packard Officejet combination printer/fax machine/copier

May pose electric-shock hazard.

Products: 10,000 products, model C2890A, made 11-12/94. Recalled units have 10-digit serial no. that begins with following code: US4B1-US4B9; US4BA-US4BU; US4C1-US4C9; and US4CA-US4CK. Serial no. is on rear label above power cord.

What to do: Call Hewlitt-Packard at 800 233-8999 for next-day replacement.

IBM Thinkpad laptop computer

AC adapter may pose electric-shock hazard.

Products: 32,000 adapters, supplied with Thinkpad models 360CS, 755C, 755CE, and 755CD, sold after 10/1/94. Recall involves adapters bearing "Model AA19210" on black part of label on bottom of unit and date code 9452 or lower (such as 9451, 9450, etc.), which appears on white strip of label.

What to do: Consumers with questions or those who need help in identifying faulty adapter can call IBM at 800 238-1967. Company will immediately ship free replacement.

Imported tankless electric water heaters

Defective pressure switch could cause explosion and fire.

Products: More than 100 heaters, models CTH-10 and CTH-40, made in Brazil by Productos Electricos Corona Ltd. Heaters are designed to be attached to cold-water pipes and to heat water immediately before use. Heaters were imported in late '80s by Pecbras of Dania, Fla., and in '89-90 by Host Prods. of Laguna Hills, Calif. Heaters were then sold to GAR Services of St. Croix, Virgin Islands, G.C. Enterprises of Belmont, N.H., and directly to the public. Most people who bought heaters from Pecbras or Host lived in Southeastern U.S. or Virgin Islands.

What to do: Both importers are out of business, and heater can't be repaired. Stop using heater immediately and have it replaced.

Juice Master Chef's Choice electric juicer

Plastic cover and wire-mesh basket could shatter and injure anyone nearby.

Products: 61,000 juicers, model XTIV, sold 10/91-5/94 through TV shopping channels, catalogs, and discount stores for $20-$30.

What to do: Return juicer to place of purchase or mail it to HSN Marketing, 85 Fulton St., Boonton, N.J. 07005, for refund. (Company will reimburse shipping costs.)

Krups blenders

Blades could break apart, get into food, and cause serious injury.

Products: 62,000 blenders, models 238 Power X and 239 Power X Plus, sold 9/93-10/94 for $40 and $60.

What to do: Call 800 526-5377 for redesigned blades and $5 rebate toward purchase of any Krups product.

Krups model 963 espresso/ cappuccino machine

Excessive pressure could make filter holder fly out, strike glass carafe, and spray surrounding area with hot coffee and pieces of glass and metal.

Products: 1,472,000 coffee machines sold since '85. Note that *min* marking on filter holder's locking mechanism doesn't refer to strength of coffee, but rather to position of filter holder. Hazard exists if holder is set far to left of *min* position. Later machines, marked Lock rather than *min*, are not subject to corrective action.

What to do: Rotate filter holder to "max" position and call 800 526-5377 for sticker to cover *min/max* wording and for revised instructions. You will also receive $5 rebate toward any other Krups product.

Krups VitaMini vegetable- and fruit-juice extractor

Strainer-basket could break, allowing lid to fly off or shatter and injure anyone nearby.

Products: 150,000 extractors, model 290, sold 6/90-5/94 for $40 to $75. Models with redesigned basket, shipped from factory beginning 6/1/94, have label on box that reads "NEW! IMPROVED STRAINER AND LID," and strainer basket has "ABS" and numerals embossed in basket.

What to do: Call 800 526-5377 for redesigned strainer basket and lid.

LockTop fireplace damper and cap set

If soot builds up and causes chimney fire, vent dampers could close, allowing deadly carbon monoxide gas and smoke to back up into house.

Products: 36,000 devices sold by chimney sweeps and wood-fuel appliance contractors since 12/89. Box-shaped damper/cap assembly is 8 in. high and has hollow, square, cast-aluminum base ranging from 8x8 to 17x17 in. Collapsible sides are connected to solid cast-aluminum lid. Unit can be permanently mounted to top of chimney and serves as both damper and chimney cap. Damper/cap sets bought after 5/15/95 are not involved in recall.

What to do: Call chimnery sweep who installed device or 800 737-1067 for free installation of kit to prevent vent from closing during chimney fire.

M-1 Deck & Roof Cleaner

Liquid contains high levels of of sodium hydroxide, which can cause severe burns, but package lacks required warnings and first-aid guidelines.

Products: 25,000 containers sold 3/94-3/95 at Home Depot stores and paint stores. Quart plastic bottle sold for $5; gallon can, for $21. Label reads, in part: "M-1 Deck & Roof 'CLEANER'... Concentrate... Cleans and restores... DANGER Eye & Skin Irritant... See additional cautions on back panel." Captioned photos of cedar-shake shingles, treated pine deck, and asphalt-shingle roof appear on front of label.

What to do: Return cleaner to store for refund. Products currently sold have proper labels, according to Consumer Product Safety Commission.

Meco charcoal water smokers

Pose fire hazard if used over wooden deck or other flammable surface.

Products: 253,000 smokers sold since '83 for $75 to $180. Hole in charcoal pan could allow coals to fall out. Model 5022-3 is red or black painted steel. Model 5024-2 has stainless-steel body and black hood. Model 5025-2 has stainless-steel body and hood.

What to do: Call 800 251-7558 for kit to close hole in pan. Don't operate smoker on or near flammable surface even after hole is closed.

Makita random-orbital finishing sander

Metal fan can break in use and eject pieces through motor cover, possibly injuring user.

Products: 130,000 5-inch sanders, model B05000, sold 4/92-6/94 for $125. Model no. appears on sticker on housing. Sanders repaired by company prior to sale—and hence not subject to corrective action—have letter "N" stamped on top left of sticker (printed before serial no.).

What to do: Return sander to nearest Makita factory or authorized service center, listed in phone book.

Melitta Aroma Brew automatic-drip coffee maker

Filter holder could swing open during brewing and spill hot water or coffee.

Products: 175,000 coffee makers sold 4/93-1/94 for $30 to $35. Coffee makers are black, white, teal, or plum, with "Melitta" printed on filter holder and "MODEL ACM-10S" on bottom of unit. Coffee makers sold as of 2/94 are not affected.

What to do: Call 800 451-1694 for replacement filter holder and installation instructions.

Monarch and Red Lion well pumps

Pose electrocution hazard.

Products: 250 pumps sold 12/93-4/94 to: Mills Fleet Farm in Minn. and Wisc.; D&B Supply in Idaho; Saginaw Plumbing and Heating in Saginaw, Mich.; and Weber Industries, St. Louis. Check serial and model nos. on nameplate on pump casing. Affected units bear serial numbers 0194, 0294, 0394, 0494, 0594, 0694, 0794, 0894, 0994, 1094, 1194, 1294, 1394, 5093, 5193, and 5293,. Also, model numbers JKC-1, JKC-20, JKC-S2, JKC-S2/JR44HS, JKC-S3, JKC-S4, JKC1/JR-15S, JKCS2/JR-15S, JKS-1, JKS-20, JKS-30, JKS-40, JKS-S2, JKS-S3, JKS-S4, JKS1/JR15S, JKSS2/JR-15S, RLC-1, RLC-2, RLC-2/RLI14H, RLC-2MM, RLC-3, RLCI-RL4H, RLC2/RL4H, RLS-2.

What to do: Don't touch pump. If feasible, turn off power, and call 800 667-1457 for repair, replacement, or refund.

Morrone Co. charcoal smoker and grill
Poses fire hazard if used over wooden deck or other flammable surface.

Products: 35,000 smoker grills, model SG-1, sold since 11/92 for $30. Exposed charcoal pan has hole that could allow coals to fall out.

What to do: Call Morrone Co. at 800 826-8863 for kit to close hole in pan. To further reduce risk of fire, don't operate smoker on or near flammable surfaces even after hole is closed.

New Creative Enterprises electric potpourri cookers
Poses shock hazard.

Products: 100,000 white ceramic potpourri cookers, item numbers 32872, 32881, 32882, 32883, and 92891, sold 1/89-4/95 for $13. Item number appears on outside of box. Cookers are used as warming or serving dish or as decorative novelty. All have white lid and power cord and come with one of three designs painted on side—flowers, humming birds, or sun and stars. Each cooker holds about 1 1/2 cups of water. Sticker on bottom reads: "NEW CREATIVE ENTERPRISES INC Made in Taiwan."

What to do: Return cooker to store for refund.

Neon art prints
Faulty wiring poses fire hazard.

Products: 510 prints sold at Spencer Gifts/DAPY stores 11/94-12/94 for $130. The prints, titled "Hollywood Diner," "Night Hawks," or "Fab Four Neon," measure 25 x 36 in., are framed in plastic, and have manufacturer's name, "FALLON," printed on back. Prints with wooden frames are not subject to recall.

What to do: Return print to store for refund.

Oxygen Krypton KR in-line roller skates made by Atomic Ski USA.
Rear wheel could come off and make skater lose control and fall.

Products: 18,000 skates sold 1-4/94 including following models: KR01, KR03, KR03L, KR05, and KR05L.

What to do: Return skates to store for replacement of all wheel axles (which should take about 10 minutes), or phone 800 258-5020 to arrange for factory repairs.

Parliament cigarettes key chain
If child puts key fob in mouth, petroleum inside could leak out and cause serious illness.

Products: 500,000 key chains, distributed free with purchase of two packs of Parliament cigarettes in Northeast and at promotional events in Panama City, Fla., 8/93-9/94. Disk-shaped fob is almost 2 in. across and 1/2-in. thick. Plastic sailboat with "Parliament" on sail floats in liquid on one side of disk. Other side says, "PARLIAMENT Out-Of-This-World GETAWAY II."

What to do: Call Philip Morris at 800 230-1101 for postpaid mailer to return key chain for $5 refund.

Rival indoor electric-crock grills
Heating element may not have been sealed during production, exposing user to electric-shock hazard.

Products: 1.1 million grills, models 5740 and 5750, sold 1/90-12/93 for $20. Product consists of chrome-plated 11-inch steel grill, heating element, and support bar. Model 5740 has steel base; model 5750 has stoneware base. Heating element stamped with letter "E" before part no. are not subject to corrective action.

What to do: Call Rival at 800 577-4825 to find out how to identify faulty grill and obtain new heating element.

Rotating desk chair sold at Kmart stores
Seat post could break away from pedestal base.

Products: 148,990 chairs, with gray upholstery, sold 7/93-3/95 for $30. Chair came unassembled and has nontilting seat and fixed back. Seat is attached to 5-prong metal pedestal base by 1-in.-wide steel rod. Each prong of base has 2 wheel casters.

What to do: Return chair to Kmart for refund.

Singer Sewing Co.'s Juice Giant electric juicer
Strainer basket could break apart in use and spew components about, possibly injuring anyone nearby.

Products: 767,000 juices, models 774 and 774B, sold 10/91-12/93 for $60. Model no. appears on bottom on unit.

What to do: Call Singer at 800 877-7391 for free replacement basket.

Stihl chain saws

Ignition ground wire could wear prematurely and create fire hazard.

Products: 50,000 series 1127 chain saws, models 029 and 039, made 3/7/93-8/12/94 and sold for $400 to $450. Recalled model 029 saws bear serial no. 226585676 or higher. Recalled model 039 saws bear serial no. 227236569 or higher. Model no. is on top of engine; serial no. is stamped into housing next to exhaust opening.

What to do: Return saw to authorized Stihl dealer for repair of ground wire.

Sub-Zero built-in refrigerator/freezers, models 501 and 550

With improper installation, refrigerator could tip and injure anyone nearby.

Products: 61,000 refrigerators installed 6/89-12/92. Affected units are 36 in. wide and have "Sub-Zero" on ventilating grille. Model no. is on sticker inside door. Both models have single door. Model 501 has motor on bottom. Model 550 has drawer at bottom, motor on top. Failure to secure refrigerator properly to wall studs or solidly attached surrounding cabinets could allow unit to tip.

What to do: Call Sub-Zero at 800 222-7820 for free inspection and, if necessary, corrected installation.

Tefal Hi-Speed toaster

Heating element may not turn off, posing fire hazard.

Products: 6775 toasters sold 6/94-12/94 for $30. White plastic toaster is 14 inches long, 6 inches high, and 4½ inches wide. "TEFAL Hi-Speed Thick 'n' Thin" appears on side. Dial with six control settings is on bottom right corner of toaster. Model no. is on metal plate underneath; units with model no. 8781 are affected.

What to do: Disconnect toaster and call 800 395-8325 for replacement or refund.

Various zippered bean-bag chairs

Child could unzip cover, crawl inside, and suffocate from inhaling foam pellets.

Products: 10 million chairs made by various companies including the following: Ace Bayou Corp., New Orleans (tel. no. 800 782-2770), distributed '92-94; Ace Novelty, Bellvue, Wash. (800 325-7888), distributed '90-94; American Bean Bag Co., Corona, Calif. (800 338-8667), distributed '90-94; American Home Furnishings Corp., Ft. Wayne, Ind. (800 860-2432), distributed '92-94; Colortex USA, Ft. Smith, Ark. (800 681-1308), distributed '93-94; Gold Medal, Richmond, Va. (800 986-1010), distributed '86-94; Jordan Manufacturing Co., Monticello, Ind. (800 328-6522), distributed '89-93; Mr. Bean Bag, Garland, Tex. (800 525-7077), distributed '71-94; and Now Products, Chicago (800 669-5520), distributed '87-94.

What to do: Check chair for label identifying manufacturer and call company's toll-free number listed above to find out how to make necessary repairs so bag won't open. Consumers who are unsure whether their chair is affected can call U.S. Consumer Product Safety Commission hotline at 800 638-2772 for assistance.

Various-brand garments made of polyester and cotton fleece

Material is dangerously flammable.

Products: 160,000 garments, with raised fiber surface that resembles inside-out sweatshirt, sold since 5/1/94. Seventy percent of garments are sweatshirts, hooded pullovers, casual shirts, and other types of tops. Other garments include pants, shorts, vests, dresses, robes, and skirts. About 12 percent of items are children's clothes, excluding sleepwear. Garments were sold at thousands of stores including Macy's, Express Inc., Capezio, Kohl's, Marianne, Jeanne Nicole, and Stewarts, as well as boutiques, surf shops, and hotel gift shops. Recalled items were sold under more than 40 brand names including: 26 Red—label no. RN 87162, Autins, Black Parrot, Cannondale, Carushka Body Wear, Dalandz of Colorado, dtw-Durango Colorado, Firethorn —RN 88645, Gold's Gym—RN 56814, IN Charge—RN 59628, Klondike Dry Goods—RN 65063, Limited—RN 54003, Native "O" Apparel, Oarsman 913, Orvis—RN 90860, Pes Menz Pes, ETNIKO—RN 79686, Spyder—RN 64902, Stryke—RN 64902, Surf Style—RN87965, Suzy Phillips—RN 59628, T. Hayes, Turnberry, A Month of Sundays, Back Country Clothing, California Dynasty—RN 64211, Capezio—RN 88647, Christina—RN 59628, Danielle Allen, Express Tricot—RN 54003, Fresh Produce, Gordon & Smith (G&S), Joe's—RN 71693, Limit Line, Limelight by Jan-R, North Shore Trading, Ojai, PA Company Boston, BLOOZ—RN 12345, Sea Isle Sportswear—RN 60300, Straight Down Clothing Company, STE (Surf the Earth), Susan Barry Seattle, Swept Away Santa Barbara, CA, The North Face—RN 61661.

What to do: Return garment to store to find out if it is subject to recall and, if so, obtain refund. For information, call U.S. Consumer Product Safety Commission's toll-free hotline at 800 638-2772 or 800 638-8270 (if hearing or speech impaired).

Various whirlpool baths

Bather's hair could be drawn into high-pressure suction openings, creating drowning hazard.

Products: 40,000 whirlpool baths. Baths typically have 1 or 2 suction openings to draw in and circulate water. Each opening should have cover to protect against entrapment of hair and body parts. Round covers made by HydraBaths and sold to manufacturers and plumbing distributors before 1985 don't offer such protection. Affected covers have slotted or square holes larger than ⅛-inch and bear no model information. Covers sold after 1985 are not being recalled; they bear markings HB-8, SC-1, or SC-4 and have round holes ⅛-inch in diameter or smaller.

What to do: For replacement suction covers, call 714 708-0652 or write to Hydrabaths, Recall Dept., 2100 S. Fairview, Santa Ana, Calif. 92704. If writing, enclose photo of cover.

Various zippered bean-bag chairs

Child could unzip cover, crawl inside, inhale or ingest foam pellets, and suffocate.

Products: 142,000 chairs made by following companies: B.A.T., Irving, Tex. (214 986-4413), sold '91-1/95 and bearing no. TX 004408 on label; Golden Needle Co., Ft. Worth, Tex. (800 569-0801), sold '91-3/95; Holbrook-Patterson Inc., Angola, Ind. (800 822-8121), sold '89-3/95; Lazy Bean, San Francisco (415 957-9502), sold '93-3/95; and Lewco Corp., Stamford, Conn. (800 867-8857), sold since 4/93 at Toys 'R' Us stores.

What to do: Call manufacturer to learn how to modify chair so children can't unzip it easily. If you're unsure whether your chair is affected, call U. S. Consumer Product Safety Commission at 800 638-2772.

West Bend automatic bread and dough makers (all models)

Could overheat and catch fire.

Products: 425,000 appliances made 6/1/94-4/9/95 and sold for up to $300. Box-shaped breadmakers mix, knead, and bake bread. Products are made of white or black metal with matching plastic lid. Part of lid that contains control panel is labeled, in part: "Automatic Bread & Dough Maker... West Bend...." Check 5- or 6-digit manufacture-date stamp (listing month, date, and year) on back of unit.

What to do: Call 800 367-0111 for free pickup and repair. Company will extend warranty for 1 yr. and will include 6 free bread mixes with repaired appliance.

Marine products

'94-95 EZ Loader boat trailers

Suspension springs could fall out and cause accident.

Models: 5200 bunk and roller boat trailers made 8/93-7/94, including '94-95 models EZ1525, EZ1650, EZ2000, EZN1400, EZN1550, and EZN2000, and '94 models EZW1650 and EZW2100.

What to do: Have dealer replace spring hanger/step assembly.

Cars

'94-95 BMW 525i, 525iA, and 525iTA

Double-locking feature could prevent occupants from opening windows and doors and exiting car, and would prevent engine from starting.

Models: 2180 cars made 1-8/94.

What to do: Have dealer replace general control module.

'95 BMW 318iC and 318iCA

Label in door jamb overstates car's vehicle load and seating capacity. Overloading could damage tires or mechanical components and cause accident.

Models: 5200 sedans and convertibles made 1/94-3/95.

What to do: If you don't get revised label by mail, contact dealer.

'88-90 Buick, Chevrolet, Oldsmobile, and Pontiac (various models)

Wheels could separate from vehicle and cause crash.

Models: 22,361 cars with Kelsey Hayes steel wheels, models RPO PB9 (14 inch) and PG1 (15 inch), made 4/88-3/90, including: '88-90 Buick Regal, Oldsmobile Cutlass, and Pontiac Grand Prix; and '90 Chevrolet Lumina.

What to do: Have dealer check manufacturing-date codes stamped on each wheel and replace as necessary.

'90-93 Buick Riviera, '90-91 Cadillac Eldorado, and '90-92 Oldsmobile Toronado

Front shoulder belts could jam in retractor and be difficult to pull out.

Models: 113,343 cars made 3/89-7/92.

What to do: Have dealer install webbing-stop button.

'94 Buick Century and Oldsmobile Ciera
Right front wheel could come off.

Models: 206 cars made 1/94.

What to do: Have dealer check right front spindle nut. If it's not tight enough, dealer will replace wheel-bearing assembly and nut.

'94 Buick Century and Oldsmobile Ciera
Water could seep into and short out power door-lock assembly, creating fire hazard.

Models: 139,542 cars made 11/93-5/94.

What to do: Have dealer replace door-lock relay and any corroded terminals, and reposition new relay where water is less likely to enter it.

'94 Buick Roadmaster, Cadillac Fleetwood, and Chevrolet Caprice
Fuel tank could sag and strike pavement, creating fire hazard.

Models: 130,581 cars made 3/93-6/94.

What to do: Have dealer tighten fuel-tank strap.

'94 Buick Skylark, Oldsmobile Achieva, and Pontiac Grand Am
Too much fuel could leak from tank if car is struck from behind, posing fire hazard.

Models: 1681 cars made 2-3/94.

What to do: Have dealer install rivets to reinforce tank's welds.

'94-95 Buick Regal and '94 Oldsmobile Cutlass
Brake hoses could wear through and leak, causing loss of stopping ability.

Models: 199,572 cars made 6/93-10/94.

What to do: Have dealer inspect and, if necessary, replace rear brake hoses.

'94-95 Buick Roadmaster, Cadillac Fleetwood, and Chevrolet Caprice
At low temperatures, engine might not return to idle speed when accelerator is released.

Models: 87,039 cars made 4/94-12/94.

What to do: Have dealer replace accelerator-pedal assembly.

'95 Buick Regal
Front turn-signal lights aren't bright enough to be seen by other motorists.

Models: 1022 cars made 9/94.

What to do: Have dealer replace bulbs.

'95 Buick Regal cars and Chevrolet Lumina minivans
Steering could fail.

Models: 420 vehicles made 10/94.

What to do: Have dealer tighten bolts on steering-column support bracket.

'91-93 Cadillac DeVille
Oil could leak from transaxle cooler hose, creating fire hazard.

Models: 403,273 cars made 1/90-7/93.

What to do: Have dealer replace upper oil-cooler hose to transaxle.

'93-94 Cadillac Eldorado and Seville and '93 Allante
Auxiliary engine oil-cooler hose could abrade and leak creating fire hazard.

Models: 56,269 cars, with 4.6-liter V8, made 3/92-7/94.

What to do: Have dealer install tie strap to keep hose away from clutch assembly of air-conditioning compressor.

'94-95 Chevrolet Beretta
Right-side panel may not be reinforced properly. That subjects occupants to increased injury in side crash.

Models: 1604 cars made 8/94.

What to do: Contact dealer. Chevrolet will replace car.

'95 Chevrolet Cavalier and Pontiac Sunfire
Front suspension components could separate, resulting in loss of vehicle control.

Models: 21,340 cars made 2/94-1/95.

What to do: Have dealer inspect lower-control-arm assemblies and, if necessary, replace.

'95 Chevrolet Lumina and Monte Carlo
Steering could fail.

Models: 221 cars made 8/94.

What to do: Have dealer replace right lower control arm and ball-joint stud.

'95 Eagle Talon and Mitsubishi Eclipse
Hydraulic unit for antilock brake system could break loose, disabling brakes.

Models: 2025 cars made 2-7/94.

What to do: Have dealer reattach and reinforce hydraulic unit.

'92-94 Ferrari 512TR
Fuel hoses could leak, creating fire hazard.

Models: 408 cars made 4/91-1/94.

What to do: Have dealer install redesigned fuel hoses.

'94 Ford Aspire
Fuel hoses could abrade and leak, creating fire hazard.

Models: 26,700 cars made 9/93-5/94.

What to do: Have dealer reposition and, if necessary, replace hoses.

'94 Ford Aspire
Certification label lacks date of vehicle manufacture, required by law.

Models: 599 cars made 2-3/94.

What to do: Have dealer affix proper label.

'94 Ford Crown Victoria, Lincoln Town Car, and Mercury Grand Marquis
Service brakes and parking brake could fail.

Models: 214,000 cars made 11/93-7/94.

What to do: Have dealer check and, if necessary, repair rear brake system.

'94 Ford Mustang GT
Front seat-cushion supports could abrade wiring harness, posing fire hazard.

Models: 54,000 cars, made 5/93-6/94, with power lumbar adjustment.

What to do: Have dealer reposition wiring harness.

'94-95 Ford Escort and Mercury Tracer
Driver's-side air bag might not deploy properly in crash, and hot gasses could cause burns.

Models: 240 cars made 9-10/94.

What to do: Have dealer replace air-bag module.

'95 Ford Contour and Mercury Mystique
Metal shield on fuel-filler pipe could develop static electrical charge during refueling, creating fire hazard.

Models: 8000 cars made 7-9/94.

What to do: Have dealer inspect filler-pipe shield and, if necessary, install ground strap from shield to car's body panel.

'95 Ford Contour and Mercury Mystique
If rear passenger-side door windows break, glass could shatter into large fragments, a violation of Federal safety standard.

Models: 2512 cars made 11/94.

What to do: Have dealer replace windows.

'95 Ford Crown Victoria, Lincoln Town Car, and Mercury Grand Marquis
Fuel could leak from tank and pose fire hazard.

Models: 100,000 cars made 6/94-12/94.

What to do: Have dealer replace seal at fuel-filler pipe.

'95 Ford Escort
Bolts securing passenger-side air-bag module may be missing. If so, air bag might not provide adequate protection in crash.

Models: 29,000 cars made 8-9/94.

What to do: Have dealer install bolts, if necessary.

'95 Ford, Lincoln, and Mercury cars, vans, and sport-utility vehicles
Passenger-side air bag might not deploy properly in crash. Also, air-bag ignitor could spew hot gases, possibly resulting in fire and burn injuries to anyone nearby.

Models: 8600 vehicles made 1-2/95 including Ford Contour, Crown Victoria, Explorer, Mustang, Probe, and Windstar; Lincoln Town Car; and Mercury Grand Marquis and Mystique.

What to do: Have dealer replace air-bag module.

'95 Ford Mustang
Suspension components could fracture, causing vehicle to shake and wheels to tuck inward or outward. That could result in crash.

Models: 1300 cars made 2/95.

What to do: Have dealer inspect outer tie-rod ends and, if necessary, replace incorrectly tapered ball studs.

'95 Ford Taurus and Mercury Sable
Brakes could fail.

Models: 1500 cars made 9/94.

What to do: Have dealer check brake linkage and, if necessary, install retainer clip that links master cyclinder to brake pedal.

'94 Geo Prizm
Front safety belts could fail.

Models: 38,502 cars made 11/93-6/94.

What to do: Have dealer inspect buckle-assembly anchor straps and replace those with suspect date codes 52733D 032and 52733D 042.

'94-95 Hyundai Elantra
Air bag could fail.

Models: 14,651 cars made 6/94-10/94.

What to do: Have dealer inspect air-bag assembly wiring-harness connector; if terminal holder is missing, dealer will install one.

'95 Hyundai Accent

Depressing clutch could abrade insulation on engine control module wiring harness. That could result in sudden engine stall.

Models: 5306 cars, with manual transmission, made 8/94-2/95.

What to do: Have dealer inspect wiring harness for damage and reposition harness to avoid contact with clutch-pedal lever.

'95 Hyundai Sonata

Label on left rear door overstates car's weight capacity. Label should read 860 pounds, not 1100 pounds. Overloading could damage tires or mechanical components and cause accident.

Models: 4842 cars made 11/93-3/94.

What to do: If you don't get correct label by mail, contact dealer.

'94 Kia Sephia

Electronic speedometer sensor could seize, disabling speedometer and cruise control.

Models: 6945 cars made 11/93-3/94.

What to do: Have dealer replace speedometer drive gear, electronic sensor, and flexible-shaft assembly.

'95 Kia Sportage

Rear brakes could fail or rear wheel and axle shaft could come off.

Models: 1319 sport/utility vehicles made 10/94-1/95.

What to do: Have dealer inspect and tighten rear-axle bearing oil-seal retainers and brake backing plates.

'90-91 Lincoln Town Car

Hood could pop open and block driver's view.

Models: 142,800 cars made 7/89-3/91 and sold or registered in Ala., Conn., Del., Fla., Ga., Ill., Ind., La., Me., Md., Mass., Mich., Miss., N.H., N.J., N.Y., N.C., Ohio, Pa., R.I., S.C., Tex., Vt., Va., Wash., D.C., and Wisc. Road salt could corrode component.

What to do: Have dealer install new hood inner-panel reinforcement and galvanized hood-latch striker plate.

'94 Lincoln Continental and Town Car

Brakes could fail.

Models: 2500 cars made 6/94.

What to do: Have dealer check and, if necessary, replace hairpin clip on brake pedal push rod.

'93-94 Lexus GS300

Front suspension could fail and cause accident.

Models: 27,604 cars made 9/92-5/94.

What to do: Have dealer inspect and, if necessary, replace lower ball joints.

'93-94 Mazda RX-7

Engine heat could make fuel hoses deteriorate and leak prematurely, posing fire hazard.

Models: 13,400 cars made 12/91-9/94.

What to do: Have dealer modify electric engine-cooling fan so it goes on after engine is turned off if coolant gets too hot. Also, have dealer replace fuel hoses.

'95 Mazda Protegé

Engine valve springs could break, damaging pistons and causing engine to stall.

Models: 5760 cars, with 1.5-liter engine, made 10-11/94.

What to do: Have dealer replace all 16 valve springs in engine.

'92-95 Mercedes-Benz 300-Series and E-Class

Front passenger's footrest could abrade wiring harness underneath. Short circuit could stall engine or deploy air bag.

Models: Models: 50,000 cars made 2/92-10/94.

What to do: What to do: Have dealer cover sharp edges of footrest and install additional cable ties to secure harness.

'88-89 Mitsubishi Precis

Hot fluid could leak from heater and burn front passenger's legs.

Models: 1906 cars, made 4/88-4/89, whose heater valve stem was replaced in a 1994 recall. Wrong valve stem may have been installed.

What to do: Have dealer inspect and, if necessary, replace valve stem.

'93-94 Nissan Maxima with aluminum wheels

Protective coating applied to wheels may prevent adequate tightening of lug nuts. Nuts could loosen over time, allowing wheel to come off.

Models: 97,000 cars made 11/92-2/93.

What to do: Have dealer remove coating where back of wheel mates with brake rotor and front mates with lug nuts. If necessary, dealer will replace wheels, hub bolts, and lug nuts.

'95 Nissan Altima

Transmission can suddenly shift from Park to Drive or Neutral, making car move unexpectedly.

Models: 1000 cars, with automatic transmission, made 7-8/94.

What to do: Have dealer install bracket to prevent breakage of shift-lever lock plate.

'95 Nissan 240SX
Warning light on dash may not go on if brake-fluid level is low. Low fluid level could be caused by leak, which could result in brake failure.

Models: 7500 cars made 2-7/94.
What to do: Have dealer repair warning-light circuit.

'93-94 Oldsmobile Cutlass
Brake hoses could abrade and leak, causing partial loss of stopping ability.

Models: 70,676 cars made 5/93-3/94.
What to do: Have dealer inspect and, if necessary, reroute or replace brake hoses.

'94-95 Oldsmobile 88 and 98
Headlights could go out unexpectedly.

Models: 1487 cars made 6/94.
What to do: Have dealer inspect and, if necessary, replace light switch.

'95 Oldsmobile Ninety Eight and Pontiac Bonneville
Headlights and parking lights could go out suddenly. Also, headlights could go on by themselves after being switched off, draining battery.

Models: 1997 cars, with Twilight Sentinel lights, made 6-7/94.
What to do: Have dealer replace headlight module.

'90-93 Pontiac Lemans
Shoulder-belt assembly may not travel properly along track. That could discourage belt use.

Models: 91,275 cars made 1/90-7/93.
What to do: Have dealer lubricate guide-track system.

'92-94 Saab 9000
Even in low-speed frontal collision, oil-cooler hose assembly could break and leak oil, creating fire hazard.

Models: 12,040 cars with engine-oil coolers made 6/91-5/94.
What to do: Have dealer install protective cover over oil cooler.

'92-94 Saab 9000
Antilock brakes could malfunction and decrease stopping ability.

Models: 12,091 cars made 6/91-5/94, including '92 models with MK II antilock brakes, '93 Turbo models with manual transmission, and '94 Aero models.
What to do: Have dealer inspect and, if necessary, replace electrical connections, and install shrink hose to keep out moisture.

'94 Saab 900
Improperly welded side beams in rear doors could subject passengers to increased injury in side crash.

Models: 9814 cars made 9/93-7/94.
What to do: Have dealer install extra brackets in doors.

'94 Saab 900 S
Front seat could move on tracks during hard braking or in crash, increasing risk of injury.

Models: 1015 cars, with nonpower front seat, made 3-6/94.
What to do: Have dealer replace springs on seat-adjustment lever.

'94-95 Saab 900
Transmission may be in Neutral when shifter is in Reverse. Car could roll away if it's parked with parking brake disengaged.

Models: 8993 cars with manual transmission made 8/93-9/94.
What to do: Have dealer repair transmission linkage.

'94-95 Saab 900
Missing welds on front-seat recliners could allow seatback to fall backwards suddenly.

Models: 10,584 cars made 3/94-10/94.
What to do: Have dealer inspect seats and, if necessary, replace frames and recliners.

'95 Saab 900
Engine speed could fluctuate dramatically for up to half a minute after engine is started, possibly causing unexpected movement if transmission is in gear.

Models: 5383 nonturbocharged cars made 7/94-12/94.
What to do: Have dealer replace engine-control module.

'95 Saturn SL
Driver could completely lose steering control.

Models: 931 cars, with nonpower steering, made 8/94.
What to do: Have dealer replace steering assembly.

'95 Saturn models with automatic transmission
Shifter could be moved out of Park with ignition key removed, or key could be removed with shifter in position other than Park, allowing vehicle to move unexpectedly.

Models: 20,518 cars made 7-8/94.
What to do: If either condition exists in your car, have dealer adjust Park-lock cable.

'93-94 Toyota Corolla without power windows, door locks, and sun roof
In winter, water or road salt from driver's shoes could short out harness connector for power accessories, creating fire hazard.

Models: 16,497 cars, registered in Conn., Ill., Ind, Me., Mass., Mich., N.H., N.J., N.Y., Ohio, Pa., R.I., Vt., and Wisc., made 9/92-7/94.

What to do: Have dealer remove unused harness connector.

'94 Toyota Corolla and Geo Prism
Front safety belts could fail.

Models: 107,227 cars made 11/93-1/94.

What to do: Have dealer replace safety-belt anchor straps.

'87-93 Volkswagen Fox
Hot coolant could leak under dash and burn passenger's feet.

Models: 164,000 cars made 10/86-7/93.

What to do: Have dealer install bypass-valve kit and plastic cover under dash.

'93-95 Volkswagen Golf and Jetta
Jack could collapse in use.

Models: 104,000 cars made 4/93-10/94.

What to do: Have dealer replace jack.

'90-93 Volvo 200, 700, and 900 series
Owner's manual lacks important warning: If instructions aren't followed, air bag could deploy.

Models: 269,000 cars made 6/89-6/93.

What to do: Have dealer supply cautionary information to add to manual. (Warning says that if car was flooded and has soaked carpeting or water on flooring, you shouldn't try to start engine; have car towed to dealer.)

'92-93 Volvo 745, 944, 945, 964, and 965
Front safety belts might not provide adequate protection in accident.

Models: 11,562 sedans and station wagons made 5/92-8/92.

What to do: Have dealer reinforce metal plates that are part of D-ring webbing guides for shoulder belts.

'94 Volvo 850 with turbocharged engine
In very cold and humid weather, throttle could ice up and keep engine racing when accelerator is released.

Models: 14,000 cars made 8/93-7/94 and bearing following vehicle-identification nos. Wagons: Last 8 characters run sequentially from R2011800 to R2073165. Sedans: Last 8 characters are R1150126 to R1172469 or R2100400 to R2169367.

What to do: Have dealer reroute crankcase ventilation tube and intercooler piping and replace throttle-housing assembly and throttle cable.

'95 Volvo 850, 854, and 855
Jack may lack sufficient load capacity. If so, device could collapse in use.

Models: 31,315 cars made 6/94-1/95.

What to do: Have dealer make sure jack is sufficient to support vehicle load and, if not, replace.

'95 Volvo 854 and 855
Front safety belts might not provide adequte protection in severe crash.

Models: 475 sedans and stations wagons, with one or two power seats, made 2/95.

What to do: Have dealer replace threaded insert that connects safety-belt catch to front seat.

'95 Volvo 964 and 965
Spare tire could fail if inflated according to incorrect labeling. Also, label lists wrong tire size.

Models: 5199 sedans and station wagons made 6/94-11/94.

What to do: Have dealer supply label noting correct size (T125/90R15) and pressure (60 psi).

Sport-utility vehicles, trucks & vans

'92-94 Chevrolet and Dodge vans converted by Sherry Designs
Front seatbacks are too low to provide proper whiplash protection.

Models: 381 Chevrolet Astro and G20 and Dodge B250 conversion vans made 9/91-1/94.

What to do: Have dealer install head restraints to raise height of seatbacks.

'94 Chevrolet S10 and GMC S15 pickup trucks

Vacuum hose could come off check valve on power-brake booster, causing loss of power-brake assist and faster engine idle. Loss of assist would require driver to step much harder on brake pedal to stop car.

Models: 30,263 trucks, with four-cylinder engine, made 6/93-12/93.

What to do: Have dealer install clamp on power-brake booster assist.

'95 Chevrolet Asto and GMC Safari

Hoses from fuel tank could leak, creating fire hazard.

Models: 3037 minivans made 9/94.

What to do: Have dealer tighten hoses to fuel tank.

'95 Chevrolet Blazer and GMC Jimmy

Brakes could fail.

Models: 262 vehicles made 11/94.

What to do: Have dealer inspect break pedal pivot bolt in weld nut and tighten adequately.

'95 Chevrolet Lumina APV, Oldsmobile Silhouette, and Pontiac Transport

Brake-pedal arm could fracture in use, resulting in diminished stopping ability.

Models: 6523 minivans made 11/94-2/95.

What to do: Have dealer replace all suspect brake-pedal assemblies.

'95 Chevrolet Tahoe and GMC Yukon

Center-rear safety belt might not provide adequate protection in crash.

Models: Models: 8323 sport-utility vehicles with 2 doors and 4-wheel drive made 4/94-12/94.

What to do: Owners will receive instructions on rerouting belt—or have dealer reroute it.

'95 Chevrolet and GMC pickup trucks and vans

Transmission fluid could leak onto hot exhaust manifold and cause possible fire.

Models: 13,853 vehicles, with 4L80-E automatic transmission, made 12/94-1/95 including Chevrolet C20, C30, G30, K20, K30, P, Sportvan, Suburban, and GMC C25, C35, G35, K25, K35, P, Rally, Sierra, and Suburban.

What to do: Have dealer inspect transmission-case assembly to determine if casting is too thin and, if necessary, replace transmission.

'95 Chevrolet and GMC light trucks

When shifter is placed in Park, indicator light may not go on.

Models: 36,641 sport-utility vehicles and pickup trucks with M30/MT1 automatic transmission made 3/94-10/94, including Chevrolet and GMC C3500HD and Suburban; Chevrolet Tahoe; and GMC Sierra and Yukon.

What to do: Have dealer adjust transmission shift cable and install lock clip.

'93-94 Chrysler, Ford, and GM vans converted by Mark III Ind.

Transformer that powers neon center light fixture could overheat, creating fire hazard.

Models: 6088 long-wheelbase conversion vans made 11/93-5/94, including '93-94 Chevrolet G20; '94 Dodge Ram; '93-94 Ford E150 and Econoline; and '93-94 GMC G25.

What to do: Have Mark III dealer replace neon fixture with incandescent lights that run directly on van's 12-volt battery.

'91 Dodge Dakota and Ram

Steering wheel could break off.

Models: Models: 78,000 light-duty trucks and vans, with upgraded steering wheel in upscale trim package, made 7/90-4/91.

What to do: Have dealer reinforce or replace wheel.

'94 Dodge Ram pickup truck

Passenger-side safety belt could fail.

Models: 185,000 pickups made 7/93-7/94.

What to do: Have dealer replace cinch bar inside buckle assembly.

'94-95 Dodge Dakota and '95 Dodge Ram pickup trucks

In a turn, extra keys on ring could get stuck in screw-access holes on back cover of steering wheel, impairing steering ability or shutting off engine ignition.

Models: 285,000 pickups made 7/93-7/94.

What to do: Have dealer plug holes.

'94 Dodge Dakota and '94-95 Dodge Ram

Extra keys on ring could jam in screw-access holes in back cover of steering wheel and impair steering or turn off ignition.

Models: Models: 293,043 light and club-cab trucks made 7/93-7/94.

What to do: Have dealer replace back cover of steering wheel.

'94-95 Dodge Ram pickup truck
Secondary hood latch might not engage properly. That could cause hood to fly up suddenly and unexpectedly.

Models: 175,000 pickups made 1-12/94.
What to do: Have dealer replace secondary hood-latch bracket.

'92-94 Ford light-duty pickup trucks and sport-utility vehicles
Parking brake could fail, allowing vehicle to roll.

Models: 884,400 vehicles made 7/91-5/94, including '92-94 Bronco, F150, F250, and F350, and '93-94 Explorer and Ranger.
What to do: Have dealer modify parking-brake mechanism.

'95 Ford Aerostar
Spare tire could rub against rear-axle brake hoses, damaging hose and resulting in reduced stopping ability.

Models: 9400 light-duty vans, with spare mounted in underbody tire carrier, made 10-11/94.
What to do: Have dealer install "low profile" mini-spare tire on existing mini-spare wheel.

'95 Ford Explorer
Steering components could break and cause vehicle to shake or shimmy at low speeds. That increases likelihood of accident.

Models: 49,300 sport-utility vehicles made 11/94-2/95.
What to do: Have dealer inspect and, if necessary, replace inner tie rods.

'95 Ford Windstar
Loose alternator output wire could overheat, creating fire hazard.

Models: 112,000 light-duty minivans made 1-9/94.
What to do: Have dealer inspect and, if necessary, tighten connection. Also, if plastic housing for power-distribution box is damaged, dealer will replace box and underhood wiring harness.

'95 Ford Windstar
Wiring harness could short out, creating fire hazard.

Models: 72,000 light-duty minivans made 1-6/94.
What to do: Have dealer insulate wiring harnesses to prevent abrasion.

Honda and Isuzu sport-utility vehicles
Oil could leak from camshaft onto hot exhaust system, creating fire hazard. Also, engine could be damaged by loss of oil.

Models: 122,297 vehicles with Isuzu 6VDI engine made 11/91-4/94, including '94 Honda Passport, '93-94 Isuzu Rodeo, and '92-94 Isuzu Trooper.
What to do: Have dealer install retainer plates for camshaft end-seal plugs.

'95 Jeep Cherokee
Driver-side air bag might not deploy in crash.

Models: 70,000 sport-utility vehicles made 6/94-2/95.
What to do: Have dealer inspect air-bag module for presence of arming lever and replace module if lever is missing.

'93 Tiara conversion vans
Driver's safety belt isn't long enough to fit large people when seat is adjusted fully forward.

Models: 2419 Chevrolet Astro, GMC Safari, and Tiara Elite vans made 9/92-9/93.
What to do: Have dealer install longer safety belt.

Child safety seats

All Our Kids Travel Vest portable child safety seats
Padding is too flammable, a violation of Federal safety standard.

Products: 25,482 safety seats, model 600, made 4/93-3/94, and model 602, made 3/94-9/94. Date of manufacture appears on label on seat. Seats, designed for use in vehicles or airplanes by children weighing 25-40 pounds, include: model 600 BK (black fabric, black webbing); 600 HP (green and purple fabric, pink webbing); 600 PR (blue/ red); 600 SI (silver/silver); 602 BK (black/black), 602 CW (black and white cow-print fabric, black webbing), 602 PF (purple/pink); 602 PR (blue/red).
What to do: Mail seat to All Our Kids, 1540 Beach St., Montebello, Calif. 90640. Company will treat fabric with flame-retardant agents.

Cosco convertible T-shield and soft-shield child safety seats
Might not provide adequate protection in crash.

Products: 1397 seats, models 02-084 and 02-404, made 5/6/94-8/10/94. Model no. and date of manufacture appear on label on seat shell.
What to do: Call 800 221-6736 for replacement buckle housing and installation instructions.

Evenflo On My Way infant safety seat
May not adequately protect infant in crash when used without detachable base.

Products: 193,332 safety seats, bearing model nos. beginning with digits 206, made 5/94-5/95. Model no. and manufacturing date appear on label on seat shell.

What to do: Call 800 225-3056 for retrofit kit containing a set of plastic inserts that when installed will make seat safer, according to company. Until then, attach seat by threading vehicle's safety belt through detachable base.

Fisher-Price model 9173 infant safety seat
Warning label on seat may be improperly located. Improper use of seat could injure child in crash.

Products: 11,020 seats, made 9-11/94. Label warns that no safety seat should be installed in rear-facing position in front seat of vehicle equipped with airbag.

What to do: Call 800 432-5437 for new label and instructions on proper placement.

Kolcraft Traveler 700 convertible child safety seat
Might not provide adequate protection in crash.

Products: 100,000 seats made after 11/1/94. Date of manufacture appears on label on seat shell.

What to do: Call 800 453-7673 for replacement buckle and installation instructions.

Motorcycles & bicycles

'94-95 BMW RL1100 RS motorcycle
Handlebars could break. Also, nut that secures front-suspension components could loosen. Either problem could cause loss of control.

Models: 2000 motorcycles made 2/93-11/94.

What to do: Have dealer replace right and left handlebars. Also replace front-fork lower-bridge ball joint and secure it with adhesive.

Cannondale, Gary Fisher, and Specialized bicycles
Seat could break off.

Products: 42,753 Cannondale bikes, including '94 C6, F4, F5, H3, H4, M3, M4, R6, and T7 models; '94-1/2 F4 and F5 models; and '95 E7, E9, F2, F5, F6, H3, H4, H6, H7, K5, M3, M4, M5, MT1, and T7 models. Also, 14,000 Gary Fisher bikes, including Advance and Rangitoto models, distributed 8/93-12/93. Also, 130,000 Specialized bikes, including '94 Hard Rock and Rock Hopper Future Shock and '95 Stump Jumper and Stump Jumper Future Shock models, distributed 8/93-11/94.

What to do: Return bike to store for replacement of seat-post clamp assembly (free for Cannondale and Gary Fisher bikes, $5 labor for Specialized bikes). For further information, call Cannondale at 800-245-3872; Gary Fisher at 800 879-8735; Specialized at 800 214-1468.

'95 GT Aggressor bicycle
Suspension fork could break and cause loss of control.

Products: 4000 bright-blue or candy-red bicycles in adult sizes from 14½ to 22 inches, sold 10/94-3/95 for $400. "Aggressor" appears on frame.

What to do: Have authorized dealer inspect and, if necessary, repair bicycle.

'88-93 Honda motorcycles
Engine could shut off suddenly during abrupt turns or on bumpy surfaces.

Models: 54,388 motorcycles made 7/87-4/93, including '91-93 Aspencade, Interstate, and ST1100; '88-90 GL 1500; '90-93 GL 1500SE; and '92-93 ST1100A. Recall affects models with bank-angle sensor.

What to do: Have dealer replace bank-angle sensor.

'93-94 Kawasaki ZX 600 motorcycle
Welds on rear suspension components could break and cause loss of control.

Models: 5530 motorcycles made 1/93-3/94.

What to do: Have dealer replace rear swing arm.

Specialized Bicycle Components "Future Shock" suspension fork installed on '92 Stumpjumper FS mountain bike and '92 S-Works M2 frameset
Fork, which connects front wheel to main frame of mountain bike, could come apart.

Products: 12,500 suspension forks, sold 9/91-11/93 for $315 by Specialized bicycle retailers and accessory dealers and by mail order from Bike Nashbar. In recalled suspension forks, stanchion tubes (upper fork legs) don't pass through fork crown. In later models, they do.

What to do: Return bike with recalled fork to Specialized dealer for repair. For further information, call 800 214-1468 and ask for Reed Pike.

Motor homes

'90 Chevrolet and GMC P300 motor-home chassis

"Auto Apply" parking brake may not release, or may engage automatically.

Models: 3762 vehicles made 8/89-7/90.

What to do: Have dealer replace brake-system components, bleed hydraulic power system, and adjust parking brake.

'93-94 Coachmen Santara motor home

TV set could fall out of overhead cabinet onto driver.

Models: 1286 class-A motor homes made 4/92-6/94.

What to do: Have dealer remount TV set with longer screws.

'93-95 Cobra Cardinal, Sandpiper, Sierra, and Wildwood trailers

Rear lights aren't bright enough to following drivers.

Models: 819 travel and fifth-wheel trailers made 11/92-7/94.

What to do: Have dealer install bezels to improve visibility of lights.

'94 Dodge B350 and Maxivan and Home and Park Roadtrek motor homes

Brakes could fail partially.

Models: 271 class B motor homes made 2-8/94.

What to do: Have dealer reroute parking-brake cable away from steel brake hose and, if necessary, replace hose.

'94 Fleetwood Jamboree Rallye and Tioga Arrow motor homes

Front cabover window could break while vehicle is moving and shower occupants with glass.

Models: 934 motor homes made 10/93-8/94.

What to do: Have dealer replace tempered-glass window with one made of laminated safety glass.

'94-95 Fleetwood park trailers

Trailer's brakes may not engage automatically, as they should, if trailer disconnects from towing vehicle.

Models: 365 trailers, models 35C, 39D, and 39F, made 11/93-3/95, including '95 Prowler and Wilderness and '94-95 Terry.

What to do: Have dealer rewire breakaway switch on A-frame.

'95 Fleetwood Southwind Storm and '94 Fleetwood Coronado motor homes

Spare tire and wheel assembly could contact road, fall off, and cause accident.

Models: 159 motor homes made 7/93-6/94.

What to do: Have dealer relocate spare to rear wall above bumper.

'93-94 Holiday Rambler Endeavor motor homes

Protective cover may not have been installed over electrical components. That make them susceptible to short circuit,or fire.

Models: 138 motor homes, on Oshkosh diesel-powered chasis, made 3/93-6/94.

What to do: Have dealer install protective shield over 12-volt buss bar and terminal connector lug post.

'93-94 Holiday Rambler Imperial class-A motor home and fifth-Wheel travel trailer

Solar-panel circuit could short out, creating fire hazard.

Models: 99 motor homes and travel trailers made 9/92-6/94.

What to do: Have dealer install in-line 2-amp fuse within 18 inches of vehicle's battery.

'94-95 Jayco Eagle and Jay 10-foot fold-down travel trailers

Rear-axle mounting bolt could break, making trailer sway wildly and, possibly, allowing axle to come off.

Models: 1045 travel trailers made 3-7/94, including '94 Eagle and Jay models BG, BM, and FJ, and '95 Jay FJ.

What to do: Have dealer replace rear-axle mounting bolt and, if necessary, entire axle.

'95 Jayco Designer and Eagle motor homes

Step box could collapse under person's weight.

Models: 676 class "C" mini-motor homes made 8/94-3/95.

What to do: Have dealer reinforce step box.

'95 Jayco Sportster slide-in truck camper

When furnace and cooktop are operating simultaneously, furnace fan could draw flame into aluminum burner, melting burner and causing fire.

Models: 154 campers, models 8 PG, 8D PH, 9½ PK, and 9½ D PL with Wedgewood high-output cooktop model C36, made 6-12/94.

What to do: Have dealer install enclosure under cooktop to correct air-flow problem.

'93-95 Monaco Executive motor home

Windshield wipers could fail.

Models: 189 motor homes made 1/93-1/95.

What to do: Have dealer replace windshield-wiper motor assembly.

Vehicle accessories

'93 Acura, Honda, Mazda, Subaru and Toyota models with Bridgestone Tracompa-3 emergency spare tire

Tire could fail prematurely.

Products: 14,000 tires, sizes T115/70D14 and T125/70D15, made 7/92-8/92. Tire came as standard equipment on Acura Integra; Honda Accord and Prelude; Mazda Familia; Subaru Justy; and Toyota Corolla, Paseo, and Tercel. Recalled size T115/7OD14 tires bear DOT identification no s. ENTABEE272, ENTABEE282, ENTABEE292, and ENTABEE302. Size T125/7OD15 tires bear DOT no. EHMNBEB302.

What to do: Have Bridgestone dealer replace tire.

Alliedsignal and Fram motorcycle oil filters

Could blow off and spew oil onto motorcycle and road, possibly causing accident.

Products: 25,115 Alliedsignal and Fram (model PH6017) oil filters made 1/95-3/95. Recalled filters and packaging say "MADE IN KOREA."

What to do: Return filter to dealer for credit. Dealer-installed filters will be replaced free.

Cooper Discoverer Radial LT light-truck tires

Could fail prematurely, if inflated as per incorrect markings on sidewall.

Models: 6603 tires, size LT235/75R15 load-range C, made 5/94-11/94, bearing DOT nos. UTHKCLK204 008L-UTHKCLK314 008L, UTHKCLK344 P08L-UTHKCLK374 P08L, and UTCHCLK424 OOR -UTHK-CLK474 OOR.

What to do: Have dealer replace tires.

'93 Honda Civic

Goodyear temporary spare tire could fail.

Products: 1790 tires, size T105/80D13, made 8/92, bearing DOT identification no. PCF76H94P432.

What to do: Have Goodyear dealer replace tire.

Monroe replacement shock absorbers for '86-94 Ford Taurus and Mercury Sable

Could fail and puncture tire or damage wheel.

Models: 98,000 shock absorbers, part nos. 71780 and 81780, made 1/94-11/94.

What to do: Have Monroe dealer replace shock absorbers.

Replacement fuel filters for '82-85 Cadillacs

Filter could leak and create fire hazard.

Products: 1724 fuel filters sold 10/94-11/94, including Big A, model 95093; Carquest, model 86093; Napa, model 3093; and Wix, model 33093. Filters have "FL" stamped on outlet end, and are intended for Cadillac Deville, Eldorado, Fleetwood, and Seville.

What to do: Return to store for replacement filter.

Turtle Wax automotive protective-sealtant sprays

May be contaminated with bacteria that could cause skin rash.

Products: 37,400 containers of Turtle Wax Protectant in 10-oz. finger-pump spray bearing codes E20410, E20411, E21410, or E 21411. Also, 2000 containers of Turtle Wax Formula 2001 Super Protectant in 16-oz. trigger spray pump bearing code G054601. Products were distributed 5-8/94 and sold for $7. Code appears on container.

What to do: Return product to store for refund. For information call company at 800 805-7695.

Various tires made by Kelly Springfield

Could fail.

Products: 76,699 tires made 9/94, including Arizonian (sizes 185/70R14, 195/70R14, P195/75R14); Big O (185/70R14, 195/70R14, P185/75R14, P195/75R14); Concorde (P185/75R14, P195/75R14); Cordovan (195/70R14); Doral (P195/75R14); Douglas (185/70R14, 195/70R14, P185/75R14, P195/75R14); Jetzon (P185/75R14); Kelly (185/70R14, 195/70R14, P185/75R14, P195/75R14); Laramie (P185/75R14, P195/75R14); Lee (P195/75R14); Mohave (P195/75R14); Monarch (P185/75R14); Motomaster (P185/75R14, P195/75R14); Multi-Mile (185/70R14, P185/75R14, P195/75R14); Reliant (195/70R14, P185/75R14, P195/75R14); Republic (P195/75R14); Rocky Mountain (P185/75R14, P195/75R14); Sears (185/70R14, 195/70R14); Shell (P185/75R14); Sigma (195/70R14, P185/75R14, P195/75R14); Star (P185/75R14, P195/75R14); Summit (185/70R14, 195/70R14, P185/75R14, P195/75R14); Super Ride (P185/75R14, P195/75R14); Telstar (P195/75R14); and Vanderbilt (P195/75R14). Recalled tires bear DOT identification nos. beginning with "PL" and ending in "374."

What to do: Have dealer replace tires.

Manufacturers' telephone numbers

Below is an alphabetical list of brand names in this year's Buying Guide and the telephone numbers of their manufacturers. Use it to track down a specific model that you want to buy or for getting more information from the manufacturer about a product.

Ace	800 223-8663
Admiral	
Washing machines, clothes dryers	800 688-9920
Refrigerators, microwave ovens	515 791-8911
Advent	800 323-0707
Agri-Fab	217 728-8388
Air Chek (mail-order only)	800 247-2435
Aiwa	800 424-2492
All Our Kids	800 545-3265
Allison	606 236-8298
Altec Lansing	800 258-3288
Amana	800 843-0304
America's Finest	800 553-3199
American LaFrance	800 446-3857
American Sensors	800 387-4219
American Standard	800 524-9797
AND	800 726-3364
Ansco	708 593-7404
Ansul Sentry	800 862-6785
Apple	800 538-9696
Aprilaire	608 257-8801
Aqua-Dri	800 950-3226
Argus	708 513-1600
Ariens	800 678-5443
Asko	800 367-2444
AST	800 876-4278
AT&T	
Phones, answering machines	800 222-3111
Cellular telephones	800 232-5179
Atlas	800 325-3800
Audiovox	516 233-3300
Autoflo	800 423-4270
Behr	800 854-0133
BellSouth	800 338-1694
Bemis	800 547-3888
Benjamin Moore	contact local store
Betty Crocker	800 688-8782
Beverly Hills	800 826-6192
BF Goodrich	800 521-9796
Bianchi	510 264-1001
Bionaire	800 253-2764
Black & Decker	800 231-9786
BMI	
Home gyms	714 771-3963
Stair climbers	800 321-9838
Bolens	800 345-4454
Bose	800 444-2673
Boston Acoustics	617 592-9000
Braun	800 272-8611
Bridgestone	800 367-3872
Briggs	800 888-4458
BRK	800 323-9005
Brother	
Computer printers	800 276-7746
California	714 859-9700, ext. 329
Fax machines	908 356-8880
Bunn	800 352-2866
Caloric	800 843-0304
Cambridge Soundworks	
U.S.	800 367-4434
Canada	800 525-4434
Cannondale	800 245-3872
Canon	800 652-2666
Carrier	800 227-7437
Casablanca	800 759-3267
Celestion	508 429-6706
Century	800 837-4044
Cerwin-Vega	805 584-9332
Challenger	Check phone directory
Chamberlain	800 528-9131
Citizen	800 477-4683
Cobra	800 262-7222
Code One 2000	708 963-2850
Compaq	800 345-1518
Conairphone	800 366-0937
Cosco	800 544-1108
COsensor II	800 387-4219
Craftsman (Sears)	Contact local store
Crane	800 877-6678
CSA	800 272-9568
Cub Cadet	216 273-4550
Cuisinart	800 726-0190
Daewoo	201 935-8700
DCM	800 878-8463
Dell (mail-order only)	800 879-3355
Denon	201 575-7810
Designer Series (Wards)	800 695-3553
DeVilbiss/Hankscraft	800 394-2326
Devoe	800 654-2616
Diamond Back	800 776-7641
DiamondTel	706 654-3011 ext. 560
Dicon	800 387-4219
Dimango	800 346-2646
DP	800 633-5730
Dunlop	800 548-4714
Duracraft	800 554-4558
Dutch Boy	800 828-5669

Dynamark 800 247-7464

Echo 800 432-3246
Electrolux 800 243-9078
Eljer 214 407-2600
Emerson
TVs, VCRs, camcorders, TV/VCR combos, microwave ovens 201 884-5800
Ceiling fans, humidifiers 314 595-1300
Emerson Quiet Kool, Fedders 800 333-4125
Encon 800 433-5542
Enzone....................................800 448-0535
Epson 800 289-3776
Eureka 800 282-2886
Evenflo 800 233-5921

Family Gard, First Alert...............800 323-9005
Fantom 800 276-0912
Farberware 718 863-8000
Fasco 800 334-4126
Firestone....................................800 367-3872
Firex 708 963-1550
First Alert....................................800 323-9005
Fisher 818 998-7322
Fisher Price 800 432-5437
Fitness Master 800 328-8995
Fox 800 229-7892
Franzus ....203 723-6664, ext. 22
Friedrich.........................210 225-2000, ext. 230
Frigidaire
Washing machines, clothes dryers, air-conditioners, dehumidifiers, electric ranges, refrigerators.....800 451-7007
Dishwashers 800 944-9044
Fuji...........................800 659-3854, ext. 33
Fujitsu....................................800 424-1500
Fuller O'Brien....................................800 368-2068
Fyr Fyter 800 654-9677

Galaxy....................................800 394-3267
Garden Pride, Vulcan....................334 874-7405
Gateway (mail-order only)............800 846-2000
GE 800 227-3663
Gemini....................................800 342-7436
General
Tires 800 847-3349
Fire extinguishers 708 272-7500
General Electric, Hotpoint
Dishwashers 800 626-2000
Telephones 800 447-1700
Genesis....................................317 849-4045
Genie 800 654-3643
Gerber 708 675-6570
Gerry 800 626-2996
Giant....................................800 874-4268
Gibson....................................800 458-1445
Giro 800 969-4476
Glidden 800 221-4100
GMF....................................404 889-9299
Goldstar....................................800 222-6457
Goodyear....................................800 321-2136
GPX 314 585-2255
Great States 800 633-1501
GT 714 513-7100

Hamilton Beach 800 851-8900
Hampton Bay .....Contact local Home Depot store
Hewlett-Packard 800 752-0900
Hitachi 800 448-2244
Holmes Air....................................800 546-5637
Home Diagnostics 607 565-3500
Homelite....................................704 588-3200
Homestead 800 229-1326
Honda....................................800 426-7701
Hoover....................................800 944-9200
Hotpoint 800 626-2000
Huffy....................................800 872-2453
Hunter 901 745-9222
Husqvarna 800 438-7297

IBM 800 426-2968
IDC 800 345-8746
Impex 800 999-8899
Infinity 818 407-0228
ITT/Cortelco....................................800 288-3132

J.C. Penney ....Contact local store
Jameson....................................800 779-1719
JBL....................................800 336-4525
Jenn-Air....................................800 536-6247
John Deere 800 537-8233
JVC....................................800 252-5722

Kmart...............................Contact local store
Kaz 800 477-0457
Kenmore ....Call local Sears store
Kenwood 800 536-9663
Key-Rad-Kit, Key-Trac-Kit.............800 523-4964
Keystone....................................908 499-8280
Kidde 800 654-9677
Kirby....................................800 437-7170
KitchenAid 800 422-1230
Kitchenmate 800 344-4563
Kodak 800 242-2424
Kohler....................................414 457-4441
Kolcraft....................................800 453-7673
Konica 800 695-6642
Koss 800 726-3801
Krups....................................800 526-5377
Kubota....................................310 370-3370

Lakewood....................................312 722-4300
Lawn Boy (Lawn-Boy) 800 348-2424
Lawn Chief....................................800 800-7310
Leica....................................800 222-0118
Lexmark 800 358-5835
Lifesaver....................................800 654-7665
Lift-Master....................................800 528-9131
Lucite 800 441-9695
Lumiscope....................................800 221-5746

Macurco....................................303 781-4062
Magic Chef 800 688-1120

Magnavox....................................800 531-0039
Mansfield....................................419 938-5211
Marantz 708 307-3100
Marcy 800 426-1421
Marshall 800 634-4350
Master Mechanic..........................800 528-9131
Maxim 800 233-9054
Maytag 800 688-9900
McCulloch
  Power blowers,
  string trimmers........................800 423-6302
  String trimmers in Arizona........800 221-6507
Melitta 800 451-1694
Memorex.....................................408 982-5098
Michelin.......................................800 997-8810
Miller & Kreisel............................310 204-2854
Minolta 201 825-4000
Mister Loaf 800 858-3277
Mister Miser 217 228-6900
Mitsubishi
  TV sets, VCRs, camcorders 800 937-0000
Mongoose.........................check phone directory
Moore-O-Matic.............................800 826-1313
Motorola......................................800 331-6456
Mr. Coffee 800 672-6333
MTD
  Lawn mowers & tractors 800 228-9683
  Cellular telephones 800 347-3393
Muratec 800 543-4636
Murray...800 528-5087

NEC
Printers, notebook computers.......800 632-4636
Cellular telephones.......................800 421-2141
NHT 800 648-9993
Nighthawk 800 880-6788
Nikon...800 645-6687
Nishiki 206 395-1100
Nokia 800 666-5553
Nordic Track 800 445-2360
Norelco..800 243-7884
Novatel 800 231-5100

Oki..800 342-5654
Okidata 800 654-3282
Olympus......................................800 645-8100
Omron...800 323-1482
One for All 3 ....800 394-3000
Onkyo 201 825-7950
Optimus ....Contact local Radio Shack store
Oreck...800 989-4200
Oster..800 597-5978
Overhead 800 543-2269

Pama 516 766-5997
Panafax.......................................201 348-9090
Panasonic
  Phones, answering machines.....800 922-0028
  Breadmakers,
  microwave ovens......................800 871-5279
  All other products 201 348-9090
Paradigm.....................................905 632-0180
Patton..800 333-1930
Peerless Pottery 800 457-5785
Pentax 800 877-0155
Performance Tough ......714 442-5000, ext. 5500
Phase Technology........................904 777-0700
Philips 800 851-8885
Philips (Norelco) 800 243-7884
PhoneMate 310 618-9910
Pioneer..800 421-1404
Pirelli 800 243-0167
Pittsburgh....................................800 441-9695
Polaroid.......................................800 343-5000
Polk Audio...................................800 377-7655
Poulan 318 687-0100
Poulan Pro...................................800 554-6723
Pratt & Lambert...........................800 289-7728
Precor..800 477-3267
Presto..715 839-2209
Procter-Silex................................800 851-8900
Proform.......................................800 727-9777
Pro–Tec 800 338-6068

Quantum
Carbon-monoxide detectors 800 432-5599
Quasar
  TV sets, VCRs, camcorders 708 468-5600
  Air-conditioners,
  microwave ovens......................201 348-9090
Quinton..800 426-0337

Radio Shack
Blood-pressure monitors 817 390-3011
Other products ....Contact local store
Radon Zone 800 448-0535
Radtrak..708 755-7911
Raleigh 206 395-1100
Rally 800 849-9273
Raynor...800 472-9667
RCA 800 336-1900
RDL 800 227-0390
Realistic ....Contact local Radio Shack store
Regal 414 626-2121
Regina 800 847-8336
Remington...................................800 736-4648
Rexair 810 643-7222
Ricoh...800 225-1899
Rival 816 826-6600
Roadmaster.................................618 393-2991
Roper 800 447-6737
Rowenta.........................617 396-0600, ext. 400
Royal 800 321-1134
RTCA 800 457-2366
Ryan..800 345-8746
Ryobi...800 525-2579

S-Tech..800 643-5377
Safe House ....Contact local Radio Shack store
Safeline..800 829-1625
Safety's Sake 800 877-1250
Salton 800 233-9054
Samsung
  35mm cameras.........................800 762-7746

Other products..........800 767-4675
Sanyo..........800 421-5013
Schwinn..........303 939-0100
Sears
Clothes dryers, toasters, gas ranges, washing machines....Contact local Sears store
Interior latex paints..........800 972-4687
Lawn tractors, blenders, string trimmers, stair climbers..........800 366-3000
Sears Craftsman..........Contact local Sears store
Sears Kenmore..........Contact local Sears store
Sharp
Fax machines..........800 447-4700
TV sets, VCRs, camcorders, air-conditioners, microwave ovens, notebook computers, CD boom boxes, TV/VCR combos..........800 237-4277
Sherwin Williams..........Contact local store
Sherwood..........800 962-3203, ext. 310
Shop-Vac..........717 326-0502
Signature 2000 (Wards)
Dehumidifiers..........Call local store
Lawn mowers..........800 228-9683
Signet..........216 963-5959
Simplicity..........414 284-8669
Singer
Blenders..........800 877-1329
Steam irons..........800 877-7762
Vacuum cleaners..........800 845-5020
Snapper..........770 954-2500
Sole Control..........800 962-3986
Soloflex (mail-order only)..........800 547-8802
Sony..........800 222-7669
Southwestern Bell..........800 255-8480
Specialized..........408 779-6229
Spectra-phone..........312 463-1030
Speed Queen..........800 843-0304
Spirit..........800 258-4555
Stairmaster..........800 635-2936
Stamina..........800 375-7520
Stanley..........800 521-5262
Stihl..........800 467-8445
Sunbeam..........800 597-5978
Sunmark..........415 983-8471
Symphonic..........800 242-7158, ext. 232

Tanaka..........206 395-3900
Tappan
Electric ranges, dishwashers, microwave ovens..........800 537-5530
Gas ranges..........800 451-7007
Teac..........213 726-0303
Technics..........201 348-9090
Technophone..........800 666-5553
Tefal..........800 395-8325
Teledyne..........800 666-0222
Texas Instruments..........800 848-3927
Toastmaster
Fans..........314 445-8666
Humidifiers, toasters, breadmakers..........800 947-3744
Toro..........800 348-2424
Toshiba..........800 631-3811
Toto Kiki..........714 282-8686
Trek..........800 369-8735
Trillium..........800 800-8455
Trimax (mail-order only)..........800 866-5676
Tropez (V Tech)..........800 624-5688
Troy-Bilt..........800 345-4454
Tru-Test..........Contact local True Value hardware store
Tunturi..........800 827-8717

Uniden
Cellular telephones..........800 364-1944
Phones/answering machines..........800 297-1023
Unisonic..........212 255-5400
Univega..........310 426-0474
Universal Rundle..........800 955-0316

Valspar..........800 845-9061
Versaclimber..........800 237-2271
Vitamaster..........800 626-2811
Vivitar..........800 421-2385 ext. 440
Vornado..........800 234-0604

Walmart..........Contact local store
Walgreens..........Contact local store
Walker..........800 426-3738
Wards Signature 2000..........800 695-3553
Waring..........203 379-0731
Weed Eater..........800 554-6723
Weider..........800 423-5713
Welbilt..........800 807-7772
West Bend..........414 334-2311
Wheeler..........800 892-6121
Whirlpool..........800 253-1301
White..........800 949-4483
White-Westinghouse
Dishwashers..........800 944-9044
Refrigerators, washing machines, clothes dryers, air-conditioners, dehumidifiers, electric ranges...800 245-0600
Vacuum cleaners..........309 823-5778
Winbook..........800 468-7502
Windmere..........610 644-4077
Wynmor..........800 633-5730

Yamaha..........800 292-2982
Yard-Man..........800 927-3626
Yashica..........800 526-0266
Yokohama
Central..........800 231-9987
North/South..........800 678-3279
elsewhere..........800 722-9888

Zenith
TV sets, VCRs, camcorders, remote controls, TV/VCR combos..........708 391-8100
Notebook computers..........800 533-0331
Remote controls..........TDD No., 800 448-8129
Zeos (mail-order only)..........800 423-5891
Zojirushi..........800 733-6270

8-year index to the last full report in CONSUMER REPORTS

This index indicates when the last full report on a given subject was published in CONSUMER REPORTS. It goes back as far as 1988. Bold type indicates Ratings reports or brand-name discussions; italic type indicates corrections or followups. **Facts by Fax:** Some reports are available by fax or mail from our Facts by Fax 24-hour service. To order a report, note the fax number at the left of the entry and call 800 896-7788 from a touch-tone phone. (No code or * means a report is not available by fax.) You can use MasterCard or Visa. Each report is $7.75.

Buying Guide index

This index covers all the reports, brand-name Ratings' charts, and Repair Histories in this year's Buying Guide. To find the last full report published in CONSUMER REPORTS, see the eight-year guide that starts on page 346.